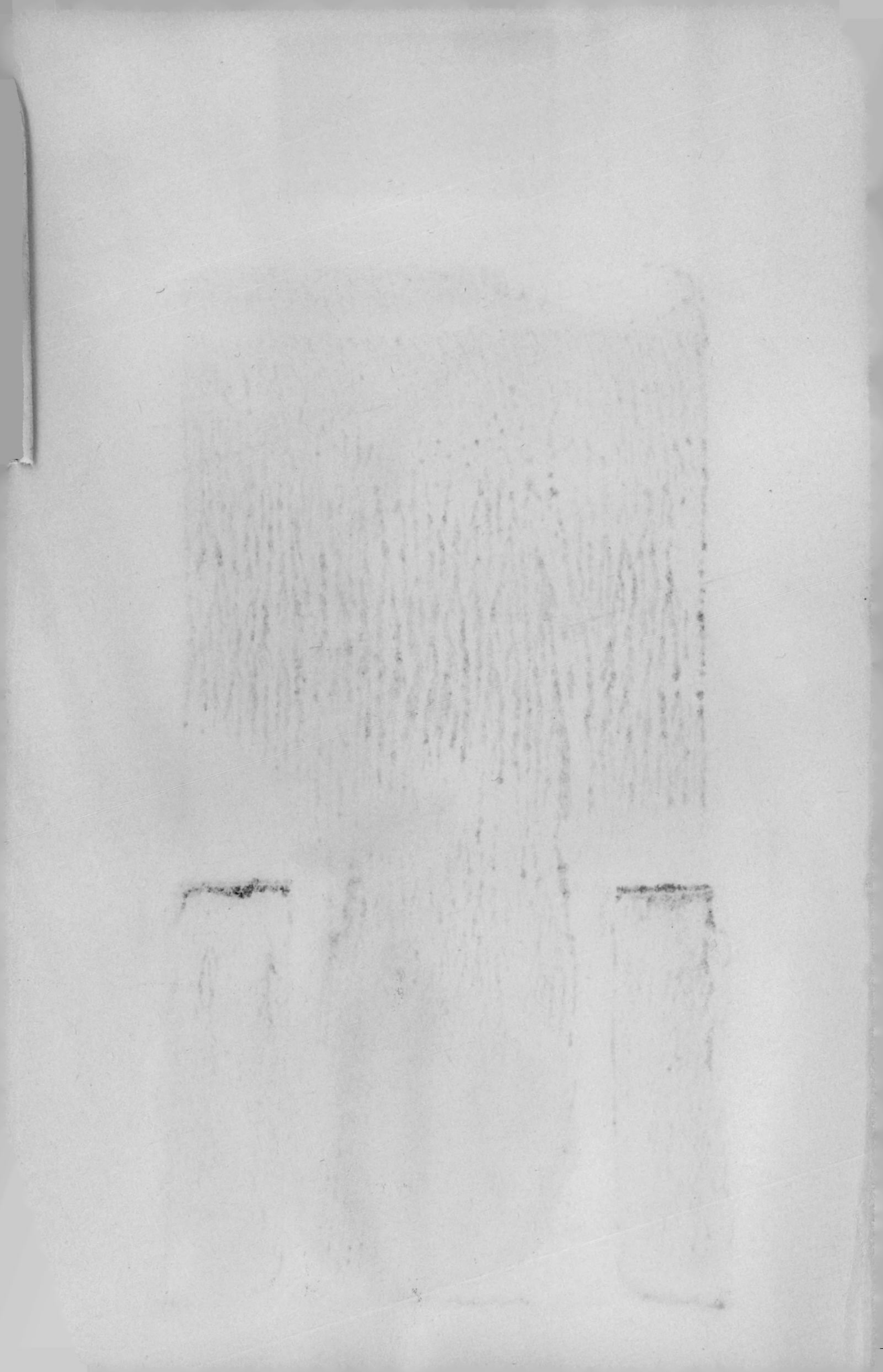

AMERICAN THOUGHT AND WRITING

VOLUME ONE

The Colonial Period

RIVERSIDE EDITIONS

RIVERSIDE EDITIONS

UNDER THE GENERAL EDITORSHIP OF

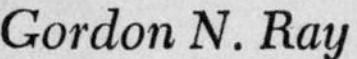

Gordon N. Ray

American Thought and Writing

VOLUME ONE

The Colonial Period

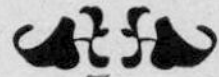

EDITED BY

RUSSEL B. NYE, *Michigan State University*

AND

NORMAN S. GRABO, *University of California, Berkeley*

HOUGHTON MIFFLIN COMPANY • BOSTON

The Riverside Press Cambridge

Acknowledgment is made to the following for permission to reprint material from their publications and to modernize texts as to spelling and capitalization in accordance with the textual policy of this anthology.

American Antiquarian Society — Thomas Tillam's "First Sight of New England," from Harold S. Jantz, "The First Century of New England Verse," in *Proceedings of the American Antiquarian Society*, October, 1943.
Harper & Row, Publishers — Urian Oakes' "Elegy," from *The Puritans*, ed. Perry Miller and Thomas H. Johnson (New York: American Book Company, 1938; Harper Torchbooks edition, 1963).
Harvard University Press — Selection from "New England's First Fruits," from Samuel E. Morison, *The Founding of Harvard College* (Cambridge, Mass.: Harvard University Press, 1935); copyright 1935 by the President and Fellows of Harvard College and 1962 by Samuel Eliot Morison. Selection from Wigglesworth's "Of Eloquence," from Samuel E. Morison, *Harvard College in the Seventeenth Century*, Vol. I (Cambridge, Mass.: Harvard University Press, 1936); copyright 1936 by the President and Fellows of Harvard College. Anagram by John Wilson from Kenneth B. Murdock, *Handkerchiefs from Paul* (Cambridge, Mass.: Harvard University Press, 1927); copyright 1927 by the President and Fellows of Harvard College.
Houghton Mifflin Company — Selections from *Benjamin Tompson His Poems*, ed. Howard Judson Hall (Boston: Houghton Mifflin Company, 1924).
Thomas H. Johnson and the *New England Quarterly* — Edward Taylor's "Meditation 40," from "Some Edward Taylor Gleanings," by Thomas H. Johnson, in *New England Quarterly*, XVI (1943), copyright 1943 by the New England Quarterly.
Massachusetts Historical Society — Selection from John Winthrop's "Model of Christian Charity," from *Winthrop Papers*, Vol. II (Massachusetts Historical Society, 1931). Selections from William Bradford, *History of Plymouth Plantation, 1620–1647*, ed. Worthington Chauncey Ford, 2 vols. (Boston: Published for the Massachusetts Historical Society by Houghton Mifflin Company, 1912), copyright 1912 by the Massachusetts Historical Society.
Kenneth B. Murdock — Selections from his edition of Michael Wigglesworth, *The Day of Doom* (New York: The Spiral Press, 1929).
The Philadelphia Yearly Meeting of the Society of Friends — Selections from *The Journal and Essays of John Woolman*, ed. Amelia Gummere (New York: The Macmillan Company, 1922).
Princeton University Press — "Meditation 8," "Meditation 12," "The Experience," and "Huswifery," reprinted from *The Poetical Works of Edward Taylor*, ed. Thomas H. Johnson, by permission of Princeton University Press; copyright 1943 by Princeton University Press.
University of Minnesota Press — Selection from Father Louis Hennepin's *Description of Louisiana*, trans. Marion E. Cross (Minneapolis: University of Minnesota Press, 1938); copyright 1938 by the University of Minnesota.
University of North Carolina Press — Selection from Robert Beverley, *The History and Present State of Virginia*, ed. Louis B. Wright (Chapel Hill: University of North Carolina Press, 1947).
Yale University Press — "Meditation 138," from *The Poems of Edward Taylor*, ed. Donald E. Stanford, © 1960 by Yale University Press, Inc. Selections from: Jonathan Edwards, *Freedom of the Will*, ed. Paul Ramsey, © 1957 by Yale University Press, Inc.; Jonathan Edwards, *Religious Affections*, ed. John E. Smith, © 1959 by Yale University Press, Inc.; *Edward Taylor's Christographia*, ed. Norman S. Grabo, © 1962 by Yale University.

PRINTED IN THE U.S.A.

CONTENTS

Brave New World

The Flesh and the Spirit

Parsley Wreaths and Bays

Redskins, Rebels, and Witches

Redskins

Rebels

Witches

Man and Nature: The Critical View

INTRODUCTION

The Quest for Order

> And freely men confess that this world's spent,
> When in the planets, and the firmament
> They seek so many new; they see that this
> Is crumbled out again to his atomies.
> 'Tis all in pieces, all coherence gone!

Thus lamented John Donne in 1611. Copernicus and Galileo, Brahe and Kepler had indeed called the Ptolemaic cosmos in doubt. The sixteenth century had done much to throw off the traditions and restraints of medieval learning; in the opening decades of the seventeenth century, the growth of a skeptical attitude toward the world, accompanied by new tools for analysis, fractured many traditional concepts and with them much of the era's assurance about the nature of God, man, and the universe.

But while insecurity bred uneasiness, it also generated a more profitable kind of restlessness. Men were encouraged to explore their world within and without, to look inside themselves and across immense uncharted seas. The great, hazy, relatively unknown continent of America, already penetrated at its edges by European adventurers, possessed a particular attraction. But the circumstances and motives that thrust Englishmen toward this New World were both varied and confused.

High among these was the assertion of British national pride and honor, especially against the Spanish, Dutch, and French. English sea dogs had plundered galleons returning from South and Central America, where Spaniards and Portuguese had exploited natural riches since the 1490's; and by the end of the sixteenth century, an American base for operations against the Spanish seemed not only a tactical necessity but a patriotic duty. Also, the English attitude towards business finance, especially the lending of money at a profitable rate of interest (long condemned as "usury") and the substitution of credit for goods and services, underwent considerable change in the first half of the sixteenth century, concentrating financial power in the hands of the large joint-stock trading companies chartered by the Crown. The first of these, the Muscovy Company, chartered in 1553 to find a Northeast passage to the Orient, established the pattern for the larger Levant and East India companies, and they in turn provided models for the companies formed to settle and exploit America. Until the late sixteenth century, North America was viewed primarily as an obstacle barring the way to the riches of the Indies. Only very slowly did its natural resources of fish, fur, and timber come to be looked upon as sufficiently valuable to justify merchant adventurers in risking plantations there.

Poverty and want in England, especially in the cities, created virtually insoluble social problems. The infant factory system could not hope to accommodate the hosts of unskilled farm workers who streamed city-ward, displaced by agricultural reforms. Vagabonds and tramps, thieves and beggars plagued the land; the British government seemed unable to provide for the needy. The colonization of America therefore appeared to furnish an attractive possibility for alleviating England's social problems. As early as 1515, Thomas More's *Utopia* had held out the promise of a New World free of social ills; later writers, both English and American, continued to exploit the Utopian potential as one of the strongest attractions for colonization.

Tying the patriotic, economic, and social motives together was the religious tenor of sixteenth-century England. Henry VIII had made the all-decisive break with the Roman Catholic Church in 1531. As supreme head of the Church of England, he forced the English clergy to render him not only spiritual support but also the financial support that formerly had gone to Rome. Rome thereupon made it clear that any support of the English crown constituted serious religious disobedience. English monarchs consequently made the frustration of the Roman Catholic hierarchy both a patriotic and a religious duty, with every blow against Catholic Spain an assertion of British honor and of true Protestant religion. Moreover, as Richard Hakluyt reasoned in 1584, "it remaineth to be considered by what means and by whom this most godly and Christian work may be performed of enlarging the glorious gospel of Christ." That Spaniards should corrupt nations of Indians by introducing them to Roman Catholicism was intolerable to loyal Englishmen.

Thus out of the intellectual, social, economic, and religious unrest and confusion grew seventeenth-century England's dream of a better and more profitable world overseas. Writers like Hakluyt did their best to present America as the cure-all of England's problems and the end-all of her ambitions. But his ardent hope that "God, which doth all things in his due time, and hath in his hand the hearts of all princes, [might] stir up the mind of her majesty at length to assist her most willing and forward subjects to the performance of this most

godly and profitable action" was to be frustrated for some years. True, Sir Humphrey Gilbert made a futile attempt to colonize Newfoundland in 1583, and the following year Sir Walter Raleigh undertook the first of several short-lived ventures to colonize what are now North Carolina and Virginia. But with the tragic disappearance of the Roanoke colonists by 1589, the project seemed abandoned.

Shortly after the turn of the century the formation of two new trading companies—the Virginia Company of London and the Virginia Company of Plymouth—again fanned interest in establishing plantations across the ocean. By May of 1607, Captain Christopher Newport's three ships dropped anchor, supplies, and colonists at the mouth of the James River, where the settlers built a stockade and erected the tents and huts they regally named Jamestown. In spite of their expectations of gold and precious stones, their unwillingness to blister gentlemanly hands with hoe and axe, the squabbles that had erupted among them even before they landed, and the selection of swampy, mosquito-ridden Jamestown "island" as a roosting place, the little band of settlers hung on to become England's first permanent settlement in America. Unfortunately for London stockholders, the Jamestown colony proved to be "such stuff / As dreams are made on" rather than a profitable investment.

Poets, playwrights, preachers, and travelers found ways not only to take advantage of popular interest in America, but to sustain it. Edmund Spenser, for example, hinted strongly in 1590 that if America was not actually the setting for his famous *Faerie Queene*, it was no less implausible. Five years later, after the failure of his friend Raleigh's Roanoke expedition, he berated England for not exploiting the new land:

> And shame on you, O men, which boast your strong
> And valiant hearts, in thoughts less hard and bold,
> Yet quail in conquest of that land of gold!
> But this to you, O Britons, most pertains,
> To whom the right hereof itself hath sold;
> The which, for sparing little cost or pains,
> Lose so immortal glory, and so endless gains.

Michael Drayton gave the Jamestown settlers a royal send-off in 1606 with his ode "To the Virginia Company," still ringing the old tune of hoped-for riches, but also looking forward to a time when English literature would flourish under the impulse of the American experience. Three years later another expedition left England, nine ships Virginia-bound and carrying the new governor, Sir Thomas Gates. Off Bermuda the convoy met a tremendous storm, losing two ships before it staggered into Jamestown in August 1609. One of the two lost ships — the *Sea-Adventure* — was actually driven upon the reefs of Bermuda, then rumored to be dreadfully enchanted. The following summer in the *Deliverance* and *Patience,* two pinnaces constructed on the island, the party made its way to Jamestown; and by September 1610, several members were back in London with the exciting story of their marvelous adventures. A crewman of the *Sea-Adventure,* Sylvester Jourdain, immediately published *A Discovery of the Bermudas,* declaring that "my opinion sincerely of this island is, that whereas it hath been, and is still accounted, the most dangerous, infortunate and most forlorne place of the world, it is in truth the richest, healthfullest, and pleasing land . . . as ever man set foot upon." All one had to do for a meal was whistle up a bird and knock it down with a stick, while whales were so accommodating they rolled right up to the shore to be eaten. Needless to say, the tall tale very early became characteristic of American expression. But in London, Jourdain's account and another by William Strachey so teased English imaginations that Shakespeare used the Bermuda episode as the basis for *The Tempest.*

Factious Virginians, however, found their new settlement nothing like Prospero's fairyland. Hard-headed stockholders in London expected a return on their investment; but what little glass, iron, pitch, wood-products (for shipbuilding), and sassafras roots the colonists shipped home was hardly profitable. In 1612 John Rolfe discovered a method of curing Indian tobacco, and the following year, when the home company began making land available to private owners, the settlers cultivated the plant with an energy they had never displayed for company profits alone. Within about a dozen years, Virginia had a marketable commodity. But as the colonists dispersed on their newly-gotten farms, rule from the London office became increasingly inadequate and inconvenient. On July 30, 1619, therefore, under Governor George Yeardley's leadership, Virginia's first representative assembly met in Jamestown's Anglican church. From that meeting dates the South's long experience in self-rule that was to prove so valuable in creating an independent America in the following century. Still Virginia's central concern was wealth, which was so anguishingly slow in coming that in 1624 King James annulled the distressed Virginia Company's charter, making the colony a royal dependent, subject to royal governorship.

Though Captain John Smith once wrote in irritation, "I am not so simple to think that ever any other motive than wealth will ever erect there a commonweal," Mammon alone was not capable of sustaining American colonization. Settlers looking for quick riches were discouraged by brutally hard labor, the threat of Indian attacks, squabbling among the colony's leaders, and complaints from England. The John Donne who cried "all coherence gone!" was also a shareholder

in the Virginia Company, for whom America was a symptom of unrest and dissolution, rather than a symbol of order. If the coherence Donne sought in politics, religion, and the minds of men was to flower in America, it would have to spring from another quarter and other motives.

The Religious Point of View

In August 1609, the very month in which Sir Thomas Gates's *Sea-Adventure* was tempest-driven upon the Bermuda reefs, still another expedition left England. Unprovided with poets' odes, sent on its way with good riddance, and bound for Holland rather than for America, it nevertheless carried with it the seeds of order, the dedication, and the sense of urgency that would soon characterize America. The men making up this expedition belonged to a group of religious radicals, the extreme left-wing of the Puritan reform movement in England, called Separatists then because they denounced and separated from the established Anglican church, but now known as Pilgrims.

The origins of Puritanism are quite complex, springing directly from the reform movements on the Continent in the sixteenth century. Martin Luther's dramatic break with the Church of Rome in 1517 marked the beginning, though one would hardly have expected Puritanism to result from England's immediate reaction to Luther. (King Henry VIII, staunchly Catholic and an excellent scholar, volunteered to write a defense of Roman Catholicism in answer to Luther's protests against the legalism of Rome, its rites and rituals, its over-subtle theology, and its elaborate hierarchical structure. His Latin treatise — "The Assertion of the Seven Sacraments Against Luther" — netted Henry the title "Defender of the Faith," which ironically he converted to defense of his own reformed English faith within a dozen years.) Throughout the 1520's and 1530's, a swelling number of dissatisfied clergymen, scholars, and evangelists joined in the dissent from Rome. Luther's following grew.

Though most Protestants merely protested, offering no full-scale reform for what they believed were the errors and inadequacies of the Roman faith, John Calvin provided a theological and ecclesiastical system to replace it. His *Institutes of the Christian Religion* (1536–59), combined with his own extraordinary intellectual and evangelistic talents, gained him a zealous following, not only in his native France, but in Geneva (to which he was banished) and in Holland. Englishmen came to know and respect Calvin's thought, especially when under Mary Tudor (1553–58) England returned to Catholicism and the queen drove hundreds of learned and dedicated English Protestants into exile. Calvin's revival of the relatively uncomplicated theology of St. Augustine, and the practices of the early apostolic church, appealed to them; and when they returned to England after Elizabeth's accession to the throne, they pushed English church reform in the direction of Calvinism.

Almost at once a deep rift developed between those Church of England men to whom the old traditions were valuable and satisfying and those who, while still content to remain within the established church, believed that its reformation had not gone far enough. Queen Elizabeth's Settlement of 1562, which retained much of the Roman ecclesiastical system, revised the prayerbook and services, and reduced the sacraments from seven to two (baptism and communion), failed to satisfy purists who insisted that the Church still retained too many relics of Catholicism. By 1572 these dissidents were called Puritans, a term applied to any religious group that demonstrated extreme scrupulosity regarding religious behavior. This separation increased between the two church parties — Anglo-Catholic and Puritan — until the Civil War of 1642 settled the issue in the Puritans' favor, at least temporarily.

Although there was wide diversity among them, English Puritans generally demanded a literal interpretation of the Bible and its application to the affairs of everyday life. Following Augustine and Calvin, they emphasized God's complete and unquestionable sovereignty, and man's innate weakness, incapacity for good, and perverse habit of dignifying wilfulness by the term "free will." They held that God not only foresaw but predestined all worldly events, controlling even the most minute circumstances by His unceasing providence; that some men were thereby elected to everlasting glory while others were bound for hell. Man's salvation, the Puritans believed, depended not on good works (for how could an innately depraved creature be capable of *any* good?), nor on the externals of elaborate public services and rituals, but solely on full faith in Christ. The high seriousness and missionary zeal with which the English Puritans held and argued their beliefs made them a sober people, and gave them an unshakable reputation (often unwarranted) as enemies of frivolity, humor, and beauty. Although it was possible for Anglo-Catholics to agree with many Puritan principles without objecting to the form of the established church (even King James was reputed to be strongly Calvinistic), they could not accept the Puritan demand that the church give up its episcopal system and adopt Congregational or Presbyterian forms of church government.

One group went too far even for most purists. Robert Browne, an early spokesman, argued in *A Treatise of Reformation* (1582) that since not all who attended and supported the Church of England were godly, the truly pious should meet and worship separately. Only the

godly should receive the sacraments; only those whose lives gave evidence of God's special grace and favor were entitled to membership in "particular" congregations; and only such a congregation had the God-given authority to elect one of its own members as a teacher or pastor. Each congregation, said Browne, stood apart from the main body of the Anglican establishment and owed it no allegiance. For their complete repudiation of the Anglican Church, the so-called "Separatists," or "Brownists," were subjected to a great deal of harassment and persecution.

It was one such group of persecuted Separatists in Scrooby, Nottinghamshire, that removed in 1609 from England to Amsterdam and thence to Leyden. They found tolerance in Holland, but not peace. Aliens in a foreign land, their means of livelihood restricted, their young people restive, these English expatriates by 1619 felt it imperative to seek a new land where, under more favorable conditions, they might establish their commonwealth of believers. Their destiny might lie, some thought, even in "those vast and unpeopled countries of America, which are fruitful and fit for habitation, being devoid of all civil inhabitants, where there are only savage and brutish men which range up and down little otherwise than the wild beasts."

The ten-year exile in Holland, difficult as it had been, was yet valuable to the Separatists. First, it confirmed their confidence in themselves, cemented the group together, and helped to winnow the strong from the weak. Second, it taught them the intolerableness of toleration; their highly respected pastor John Robinson strongly criticized the Dutch for the very latitude of religious opinion that made it possible for his people to be there. Third, and most important, their last years in Holland saw the celebrated Synod of Dort (1618–19), where Calvinists from all over Europe gathered to codify their understanding of Calvin's teachings against the onslaughts of the Socinians and the Dutch theologian Jacobus Arminius (1560–1609).

The result of that Synod was the reduction of Calvin's teachings to Five Points: first, that since the original sin of Adam (which passed by generation or imputation to all his progeny), both mankind and nature were depraved and corrupt, and therefore incapable of any good by their own exertions. Second, that the salvation of a chosen few was completely unconditional, and therefore no amount of good intentions or good works could earn one salvation; no man could thus will to be saved. Third, that Christ died only for this limited "elect" and for no others; the grace derivable from His atonement for Adam's sin went only to them. Fourth, that this grace was irresistible — that is, no man could will himself not to be saved. And fifth, that Christ's saints, blessed with saving grace, must persevere in their salvation; they must be saved, willy-nilly, though they backslide ever so far.

The English Separatists in Holland wholeheartedly accepted the Five Points. When they decided to remove to America, it was this rigid Calvinism of the Synod of Dort which sustained their determination.

Accordingly, they negotiated with the Virginia Company of London, secured a leaky ship called the *Speedwell*, abandoned it in September for the *Mayflower*, and in November 1620 arrived not in Virginia as planned, but at Cape Cod. Knowing they were outside the legal jurisdiction of their patent, and fearing lest the lack of authority completely upset their "plantation," forty-one passengers agreed to create a "civil body politic," just as they had made a covenant to form an independent congregation. This famous Mayflower Compact, or Covenant, has been described as "the fundamental instrument of government for the little democracy which it established without any authority than the wishes of the signers." But it must be remembered that these Pilgrims had not left Europe to found a democracy or to establish a free state. They merely sought a refuge for their own religious society, and while they professed allegiance as "loyal subjects of our dread Sovereign Lord King James, . . . Defender of the Faith," they were equally determined to keep all who differed with them out of their new Jerusalem. Given half a chance, they would willingly have forced their theology, church discipline, and way of life upon all England. In the new continent the Plymouth colony survived the rigors of the wilderness, the ineptitude of its London agents, and the diversions of a few free spirits (such as Thomas Morton of Merrymount) who wandered into it. Under the firm and sagacious leadership of William Bradford and the elders, the Pilgrims sold enough cod, lumber, and furs to find a modest prosperity, maintained their New England foothold, and promised to thrive.

Back in England the Non-Separatist Puritans found themselves involved in increasingly difficult religious and political conflicts. By the time Charles I came to the throne in 1625, after James's death, the Puritans had gained control of Parliament, so that the subsequent struggles between Parliament and King, which later erupted into civil war, became, in part at least, a struggle as well between royal and Puritan power. Even before this, a number of Puritan leaders, discouraged with the state of things both religious and political in England, observed the Pilgrim experiment with growing interest. In 1623 the Dorchester Adventurers was formed to maintain fishing and trading operations in New England; in 1628 and 1629, expeditions were sent to what is now Salem to prepare the way for a second colonial venture; and on March 4, 1629, within a week of Charles's dissolution of Parliament, the Dorchester Adventurers, now called the New England Company for a Plantation in Massachusetts Bay, secured a generous charter. The following year, under the leadership of Governor John Winthrop aboard the *Arbella*, the first four ships of what has come to be called the Great Migration arrived and settled at Massachusetts Bay.

As Winthrop told his people, their purpose in the New World was not to amass wealth, but to worship God in their own fashion — to establish a "true" religious society, "to improve our lives to do more service to the Lord, the comfort and increase of the body of Christ whereof we are members, that ourselves and posterity may be the better preserved from the common corruptions of this evil world, to serve the Lord and work out our salvation under the power and purity of His holy ordinances." The Massachusetts Bay Colony had a concept of order and a singleness of purpose that Virginia had lacked. Winthrop was careful to let his company know their holy experiment was being observed by all Christendom: "For we must consider that we shall be as a city upon a hill, the eyes of all people are upon us." From 1630 until the end of the century, New England did its best to preserve its purity of mission as a society of the godly. For the next ten years in England, as Charles I and Archbishop Laud pursued their political and religious tyrannies, thousands of Puritans fled to Massachusetts Bay, hoping to find safety from the long arm of Court and Church. By 1640 there were nearly twenty-five thousand people scattered in small villages along the Massachusetts coast, among them many of England's finest preachers and theologians. It seemed indeed, in the words of the Anglican poet George Herbert, that "Religion stands on tip-toe in our land, / Ready to pass to the American strand."

Two distinctive qualities soon marked the religious life of Massachusetts Bay. First, in spite of their jealous insistence that they had not separated from the Church of England, the Bay colonists immediately adopted Congregational practices indistinguishable from those of Plymouth. Historians have speculated that Salem's contacts with Plymouth wrought a conversion which the later Bay ministry followed, or that the new settlers left England as Anglicans but arrived in America as Congregationalists, undergoing a "sea change" en route. More likely, perhaps, the Massachusetts Bay leaders had fully intended all along to adopt Congregationalist church discipline. Whatever the reason, they acted like Separatists once they landed in Massachusetts, disturbing and confusing their supporters in England.

The second distinctive quality developed more slowly — a modification of Calvinism known as the "covenant" or "federal" theology. Following the lead of certain English theologians, among them William Perkins, John Preston, and William Ames, the New Englanders assumed that the true Christian church originated in a series of covenants or agreements. God, they pointed out, made the original

Covenant of Works with Adam, by which Adam agreed to do His will and God agreed to provide Adam with everlasting bliss. When Adam broke the contract, since he was the "federal" head or agent of all mankind to follow, the penalty of death and damnation passed down to his descendants. God then made a second covenant with Abraham, a Covenant of Grace, whereby He promised to bring eternal salvation to those who believed fully in Him and His promise. This covenant (also known as the New Covenant) gave certain men, the elect, a special saving grace, earned for them by the sacrifice of Christ. This sacrifice derived from yet a third covenant, the Covenant of Redemption, wherein God agreed to accept Christ's death in payment for Adam's sin, and to extend the redeeming grace of His Son's death to those elect souls who composed the true church. To every man, then, the most important activity in life became the quest in his daily experience, his conscience, and his soul for signs of this grace.

Of course, no one could know infallibly that he belonged among the elect. Since hypocrites might fool themselves as well as others, there were said to be two kinds of church members: "true" saints, whose salvation had been assured from the beginning by God's decree, and "visible" saints, who showed every sign of sanctification and who thought they found special signs of God's saving grace in the recesses of their inward religious experience. These two groups made up the church, partook of the sacraments, and enjoyed full civil rights, including the vote. They also constituted a powerful and envied status group in what soon became a kind of saint-watching society. The New Englanders' covenant to "walk together in mutual helpfulness and love" in no way interfered with their proclivity for criticizing their neighbors and for arguing among themselves; the gathering of churches never proceeded very smoothly.

As time passed, it became increasingly difficult to get unanimity among the various stiffly independent churches on matters social, ecclesiastical, or religious; the device of a "synod" or occasional congress of ministers operated with only partial success in unifying the churches of New England. Still, the unshakable duty implied by the covenants under which these churches were formed provided a sense of distinction, prestige, even self-righteousness, which bound New Englanders into a group somewhat apart from other colonists. From their churches the covenant theology radiated to all other spheres of life, affecting the nature of laws drawn up as the Massachusetts Body of Liberties in 1637, dictating the interests and sometimes the actions of the civil magistracy, and constituting a government by the godly in which, though the church and state were ostensibly separate, their identity of interests really meant that the governor and his deputies served the church rather than the state.

The Puritan found evidences of his progress toward salvation by constant surveillance of the state of his soul. To attain salvation, he believed, a man's soul moved through regular, identifiable stages — an effectual calling, justification (by which a soul knows Christ's sacrifice to be efficacious for itself), sanctification (righteous behavior), and finally, with death, glorification. Self-knowledge, then, was a spiritual necessity; but since God revealed His will through the every-day workings of nature, it became necessary, in order to know one's self, to know the world too. As John Cotton put it, the faithful soul applies its faithfulness to all its worldly activities: "though you may have a godly man busy in his calling from sun rising to sun setting, and may by God's providence fill both his hand and his head with business, yet a living Christian, when he lives a most busy life in this world, yet he lives not a worldly life." Cotton did not mean that the good life was perforce a worldly, materialistic life; yet for many New Englanders, following out Cotton's doctrine often meant substantially that. As a result, New England Puritanism faced two ways. On the one hand, it demanded deep and constant thought about the nature of the universe, about the nature of man and his relation to God, about man's duties to God and his neighbors, and about the high seriousness of life in this world. On the other hand, it hallowed every human activity in the state and in society at large, in government and business, with the sanctity of a religious act. One consequence of this bifurcation was to turn New Englanders into successful business-men, merchants, and traders, as well as into "saints." And thus it became increasingly difficult to maintain the great dream of a holy commonwealth.

The Colonial Way of Life

Virginia and the New England colonies established the basic patterns of life in seventeenth-century America. New settlements, Hartford and Providence, for example, splintered off from Massachu-setts as early as 1635, the former becoming Connecticut and the latter Rhode Island. In 1638 another group left the Bay to establish the colony of New Haven. Expansion was contagious. But the impetus for most new colonization came from abroad. Groups in England and Europe were quick to capitalize on the dreams of land, profit, power, and political and religious refuge that America represented. The newer settlements were made not under the directorship of trade companies but under individual proprietors whose patents gave them virtually royal power in the New World.

Catholic George Calvert, Lord Baltimore, secured a grant north of the Potomac as a refuge for persecuted English Catholics. The colony, tactfully named "Maryland" in honor of King Charles's queen, was settled at St. Mary's City in 1633; careful to offend neither the Massachusetts Puritans nor the Virginia Anglicans, it opened its land to all Christians, excluding only Jews and the forerunners of Unitarianism. Holland, England's most shrewd and powerful economic and colonial rival, moved into the area between Maryland and Connecticut, named it New Netherland, founded the town of New Amsterdam in 1625, and began to penetrate Connecticut territory. Though Swedes settled along the Delaware as early as 1638, neither they nor their Dutch neighbors received substantial support from their homelands. They combined in 1635 to form a population of some ten thousand, but fell easily before English power and were converted into New York in 1664.

By that time, though, the Duke of York was already interested in other holdings. In 1655 he and eight others became Lords Proprietors of land reaching from Virginia to below St. Augustine, Florida. They hoped to oust the Spanish outpost there, develop a tropical economy, and establish a grand aristocracy along lines laid out by the Earl of Shaftesbury, John Locke, and James Harrington's Utopian *Oceana*. But their plan for an American nobility (the "Fundamental Constitutions") proved desperately impractical for Carolina, and was soon abandoned. While unauthorized settlers congregated at Albemarle Sound, forming the colony to be known after 1719 as North Carolina, the Lords Proprietors sent another expedition to settle the southern part of the colony in 1670. Under Governor William Sayle, they settled along the Ashley River, moving near its mouth a few years later to establish Charleston, which by 1680 became the seat of government and in time the most graceful of southern colonial cities.

To the north another proprietary grant was made in 1665 to Sir George and Philip Carteret and Lord John Berkeley for New Jersey. The venture was not profitable, and in 1679 they sold out to William Penn, who three years later also secured the proprietorship of Pennsylvania from the Lords of Trade. Penn thus controlled the last uncommitted coastal lands, which he opened to religious refugees, especially Quakers, though by this time Swedish Lutherans, Dutch, and Finns were firmly planted along the Delaware, and Penn was obliged by the Lords of Trade to permit Anglican churches to develop as the need arose.

By 1700 the American coast from Florida to Maine was in English hands, either as corporate (trade company), proprietary, or royal colonies. Living under governments much like those in England, and enjoying what Raleigh's charter had called "all the privileges of free denizens, and persons native of England," the colonists were yet not quite Englishmen, nor simply Englishmen living away from home.

Nor could they be called Americans, for the alembic of transatlantic life had not yet distilled the type that St. Jean de Crèvecoeur described in 1782. Instead, the colonies were a crazy-quilt of migrants, the rawest of raw materials for the "melting pot." There were even Polish and German laborers and craftsmen as part of the original Jamestown venture, soon joined by Italian glassmakers and French vintners. The Dutch, of course, predominated in early New York, but the area fell increasingly under the influence of French, Germans, Danes, Swedes, Finns, Portuguese, Spanish, Italians, Bohemians, and Poles. Jews in New York enjoyed surprising freedom, built synagogues, and early in the eighteenth century could amaze young Puritans like Jonathan Edwards, who furtively observed one — "the devoutest person that I ever saw in my life" — from his adjoining window. French Huguenots lived along the coast, concentrated in Pennsylvania, Virginia, and the Carolinas. German Pietists, Mennonites, and Baptists, attracted by the *Neu-gefundenes Eden,* as one propaganda tract described it, made all haste to the New World, especially to Pennsylvania, while Scotsmen joined the wave of immigrants early in the eighteenth century, settling largely in the New Jersey area.

The quarter million Europeans in America by the end of the seventeenth century brought with them their national languages, customs, styles of living, foods, dress, trades and diversions, architecture, and ornamental arts. Even though Anglicanism was the official faith of the royal and proprietary colonies, and Congregationalism deeply ingrained in New England, the religious toleration which accompanied Charles II's return to the throne in 1660 drew Quakers, Baptists, Lutherans, Pietists, and even Roman Catholics and Jews to the colonies. After 1684, when Massachusetts Bay lost its charter, even New England had to suffer the encroachments of other faiths or risk political reprisal from England. Indeed, there was much more variety and contrast in American colonial life in the later seventeenth and early eighteenth centuries than the myths of somber Puritan New England and romantic Cavalier South would indicate.

That there should be very real distinctions between northern and southern life, even in the seventeenth century, was inevitable. The control of immense tobacco lands fell into the hands of the most resourceful and influential settlers quite early, so that Virginia's leading class was largely self-made. Theirs was recently acquired wealth, and though they assumed the *noblesse oblige* of traditional English aristocracy in managing their estates, they resembled English country gentry rather than nobility. The large plantation owner was perforce lawyer, doctor, teacher, farmer, judge, surveyor, and engineer. His immediate concerns were practical and numerous, and though he often yielded to the extravagance of sending his children to England for schooling, he could not on the whole afford a very gay or carefree life. That was usually left to the third generation. Carolinians, after surrendering hopes of cultivating tropical fruits, turned to rice, and, using Negro and Indian slaves to work the malarial inland rice fields, escaped whenever they could to the coast. Flocking to Charleston, they soon created a sophisticated miniature of London social life unmatched elsewhere in the colonies.

New England, on the other hand, unsuited for large-scale farming and held tightly together by church as well as social covenants, turned to manufacture and trade in its primarily urban economy. The quick result was a merchant aristocracy that built its own ships, stored them with codfish, wood products, food grains, and salted meats, and sent them to trade along the American coast and to England and Europe. New England grew rich on trade, and as its wealth grew, the bonds of its religious dedication loosened. Whereas the early Puritan assumed that God's favor to a man might be manifested in his life, his grandson, reversing the logic, believed that a man's material success might well be evidence of his saintliness. One could always recognize a saint, some wryly complained, since he dressed better than anyone else. But even in New England early colonists had to be extremely versatile and resourceful; one wrote that "men be generally carpenters, joiners, wheelwrights, coopers, butchers, tanners, shoemakers, tallow-chandlers, watermen, and what not; women soapmakers, starch-makers, dyers, etc. He or she who cannot do all these things . . . over and above all the common occupations of both sexes will have but a bad time of it; for help is not to be had at any rate, everyone having business enough of his own." But the development of urban community life in time relieved the colonist from such jack-of-all-trades responsibilities. In the growing cities and towns, labor soon divided into specialized tasks, and the homespun-to-riches pattern of a town like Boston had ceased to be a novelty long before Benjamin Franklin grew up there. Increasing prosperity revealed itself in the multiplication of worldly comforts — bigger and fancier houses, imported furniture, expensive books for private libraries, and, by the early eighteenth century, private coaches and footmen.

Economic, religious, and political differences drove Virginia and New England further and further apart in the early eighteenth century. But material prosperity allowed both areas to pursue their happiness with increasing comfort and grace. No sooner were streets laid and houses erected than settlers put aside their drab homespun for colorful and elegant fashions from England and France. By the turn of the century, coffee houses, imitative of those in London, vied with taverns from Charleston to Boston as haunts of idleness. And as leisure increased, so did the variety of diversions — traveling shows and exhibits, clowns, mechanical marvels, cockfights, horse-racing, hunting and fishing, waxworks, and gaming. Those who could afford it, both North and South, fell into the extravagant habit of having their portraits painted by amateur limners. Silversmiths and goldsmiths, furniture-makers and jewelers found their works in constant demand, and by 1716 even Boston had its own bold dancing master. In short, by the second quarter of the eighteenth century, the rude and rugged way of the frontier had practically disappeared from America's major towns. In its place stood a charming, sophisticated life undreamed of in the philosophies of John Smith and William Bradford.

Polishing God's Altar

Largely because of their closer social and economic connections, more highly organized political system, and reasonably good network of roads, the New England colonies developed a distinctive intellectual life much more quickly than the southern colonies. Attempts to establish schools at Jamestown as early as 1619, when a university was planned, dissolved before the Indian menace of 1622; the earliest elementary schools did not open until 1635; and it was 1693 before the College of William and Mary could be established at Williamsburg. But in 1635, Boston, only five years old itself, founded a Latin School, an example immediately followed by several nearby towns. Harvard College, founded in 1636, was actually instructing students by 1639. Three years later the Massachusetts General Court made it an offense, punishable by fine, for a town to fail to furnish adequate instruction for its children. In 1647 Massachusetts required every community of fifty householders to hire a schoolmaster, and every town of over one hundred householders to provide a Latin school to train students for Harvard. "Dame schools," often informally taught by neighborhood women, assumed responsibility for the basic education of girls, beginning in the 1650's; and while the emphasis was likely to be largely practical, as in the boys' "Free schools," the attention given to reading and writing gave assurance that New England would not have the problems of illiteracy that were to plague the South.

New England's emphasis on learning was closely connected with its religious commitment. The bedrock of the Reformation was its insistence that the faith upon which the salvation of every individual depended was available through the scriptures. Since to "search the scriptures" one had to be able to read, illiteracy was a tool of Satan. Moreover, saving grace came not through miraculous or supernatural means, but through "hearing the word preached." To hear the word intelligently, church-goers were encouraged to follow the carefully organized delivery of the preacher, to scribble down outlines of his sermons, and to discuss them after meeting with family and neighbors. All this required a high degree of literacy, and much of our knowledge of early American preaching comes from the shorthand notes of avid listeners. Also, New England had from the beginning as great a percentage of university-trained men in proportion to its population as Old England, a fact that encouraged intellectual pursuits. The deep respect in which these Calvinists held learning promoted their desire to maintain a learned ministry and accounts for the promptness with which they established schools and a university, gathered private libraries, and circulated books.

Preaching, of course, forced men to write, but while sermons flowed from their quills, New Englanders turned to other kinds of literary production as well. As early as 1636 plans were under way to turn the Psalms of David into English verse, attending "conscience rather than elegance, fidelity rather than poetry," and early in 1639 Governor John Winthrop noted in his journal that "a printing house was begun at Cambridge by one [Stephen] Day, at the charge of Mr. Glover, who died on sea hitherward. The first thing which was printed was the freeman's oath; the next was an almanac made for New England by Mr. William Pierce, mariner; the next was the Psalms newly turned into meter." This press, even though strictly regulated by the College and by the General Court, immediately groaned under the multitude of informative and edifying works submitted for publication. It was 1681 before a printing press appeared in Virginia, and that was immediately suppressed. In 1683 Virginians were instructed to "allow no person to use a printing press on any occasion whatsoever," and Virginia's lone printing house did not even get started until 1729. There was probably greater need for New Englanders to write: their arguments about theology and church government needed statement and distribution; bothersome differences between the New England Way and English expectations required explanation; and after the revolution of 1642, when victorious English Puritans accused their colonial brethren of deserting the glorious cause by escaping to America, New Englanders wrote to defend their actions. The surprising thing is not that so much was written and printed in the colonies during the seventeenth century, but that out of all the literary activity there grew no great book.

There are probably two reasons for this, neither of which detracts from the intellectual capability or the literary sophistication of colonial writers. In the first place, in keeping with the utilitarian, polemical, and didactic nature of the documents they produced, their style was plain, perspicuous, and (as they liked to say) "spiritual." Its ideals were clarity, logical consistency, general intelligibility, and decorum, and except for the crabbed wit of Nathaniel Ward and the later pomposities of Cotton Mather, early American writing avoided the current fads of Senecan curtness and Ciceronian elaboration. In this the Puritan plain style looked forward to the scientific style idealized by London's Royal Society, described by Bishop Sprat as "a close, naked, natural" style — and admirably adapted to American purposes by Benjamin Franklin. Second, most seventeenth-century colonial writings were occasional, designed to speak to specific problems at particular times. Thus they never display the comprehensive sweep of ideas that marks great books, nor does any single volume synthesize the variety and breadth of colonial thought. Each work stands like a stone in an elaborate building — structurally necessary, sturdy, often interesting in itself, but no real clue to the nature or meaning of the whole structure.

Early New England writing looked two ways simultaneously: outward toward the experience of building a new land, and inward toward the emotional and spiritual life of the individual. Biographies, histories, accounts of exploration, funeral sermons, and elegies expressed the one; autobiographies, diaries, and meditations, the other. William Bradford's consciously constructed *Of Plymouth Plantation* was no simple chronicle of daily events, but a selective and carefully arranged interpretation of the colonial experience coupled with a remarkable awareness of the historical significance of the great new American adventure. To stir emulation and to maintain respect for the worthies of New England, ministers wrote little biographies celebrating the public virtues and private spirituality of eminent divines and magistrates, heedful to point out that godliness often paved the road to public prominence. Sensational accounts of adventures among the Indians, featuring massacres, flights over torturous terrain, horrible torments, and the final joy of returning to civilization, were so popular that they were being issued in anthologies before the end of the seventeenth century. Cotton Mather's ambitious *Magnalia Christi Americana,* so large it had to be sent to London for publication in 1702, incorporated most of the established literary forms, revealing what was implicit in them from the beginning — that this was a literature designed to build saintly heroes and to trace God's support of New England's holy experiment by the favor He showed its individuals. Indeed, from its beginnings, American literature is an individualistic literature, designed to explore the passions and emotions (an aspect of the Puritan character often overlooked) as well as to recount the rigors of life in the wilderness.

When the Puritan turned inward, emphasizing the spiritual, devotional side of his religious experience, his writing tended to become less a part of his distinctly American experience and to partake more fully of the Western, Christian literary tradition. The poetic meditations of Edward Taylor, America's finest seventeenth-century poet, and the prose-poem passages of Jonathan Edwards gain their literary eminence at the same time they cast off their American significance. The amazing thing about colonial literary art as a whole is not, however, that it occasionally achieves real poetic excellence, but that poetry or verse is so dominant.

Theoretically, poetry was to Puritans (as to most contemporary Englishmen and Europeans, no matter how sophisticated) a branch of rhetoric, and a very minor one at that. Like all rhetorical forms, its end was to persuade, and its primary function lay in the decorating or ornamenting of ideas. Similar views of the nature of poetry did not keep English and Continental poets from magnificent literary achievements, and one must not suppose that the Puritans' low view of poetry was peculiar to them or that they held any special animus towards poetry. For poetry — at least verse — is inescapable in colonial writing.

Five main kinds of verse writing predominated. First, those who took the prevailing poetic theory literally were likely to produce "poems" constructed of rhymed statements whose function was merely to assist the reader's memory. An obvious example would be the *New England Primer*'s alphabet for children, running from "In Adam's Fall/ We sinned all" to "Zaccheus he/ Did climb the Tree/ His Lord to see." Such mnemonic verse was frequently included in histories and treatises to sum up at the ends of chapters. A second kind, closely related to the first, was the long didactic poem, more elaborate in thought and structure, such as Michael Wigglesworth's *The Day of Doom* or his reflective *Meat Out of the Eater.* A third favorite was historical verse, intended not merely to teach, but to express an action too magnificent for prose (as in Captain Edward Johnson's *Wonder-Working Providence*), or to recount current events (as in Benjamin Tompson's *New England's Crisis*), or to celebrate the greatness of times past (as in Roger Wolcott's outright epic on the founding of Connecticut). A fourth type was the funeral elegy, commemorating the deaths of prominent and obscure persons alike, and reminding readers of the brevity and purposefulness of life. These were printed broadside for distribution at the funeral service, incorporated into formal histories and biographies, as in Cotton Mather's *Magnalia,* or simply recorded in diaries, letter-books, and family papers. By and large, this commemorative verse is without poetic merit, but it provides some useful insights into Puritan emotional values, and occasionally flowers into excellence, as in Urian Oakes's elegy on Thomas Shepard and Edward Taylor's on Samuel Hooker. Finally, there was the personal, reflective, meditative, and often lyrical poetry developed by Philip Pain, Anne Bradstreet, and Edward Taylor.

There was, then, no prejudice against literary beauty among early New Englanders. Frivolity, however, was another matter. Ministers were often known for their conversational wit and urbane humor, but a favorable attitude towards such social graces did not extend to the production of literary forms like the novel or drama. French and occasionally English romances made their way to America well before 1700; an edition of John Bunyan's *Pilgrim's Progress* was printed in Boston in 1681, and in that same year *Guy of Warwick*, a pious medieval romance, was sold in Boston's bookstores. But for the most part the New Englander satisfied his natural appetite for fiction through a variety of modes not overtly fictional, each of which, however, contributed to the later development of the American novel. The sermon, for example, frequently offered character sketches, anecdotal exempla, and tales of remarkable providences, all designed to excite interest as well as to edify. The formal character sketches practiced in school also found their way to the pulpit and, in extended form, into biographies and histories. Where fact leaves off and fiction starts cannot be clearly seen. William Bradford and Edward Johnson obviously designed parts of their accounts for literary effect, freely feigning speeches and experimenting with character development. Confessions of faith or personal relations of conversion gave form, conflict, change of fortune, and stupendous consequences to the spiritual life; they could not have been heard without excitement and pleasure. The narrative of captivity, marked by a surprising sentimentality, by psychological probing, and, later, by pure sensationalism, duplicated in frontier reality the great struggles waged in the infinite world of spirit between Satan and the captive soul of man. The romance of a soul's rise from poverty to glorious riches enabled colonial writers to experiment with numerous literary devices, and one can easily see in colonial narratives the seeds of the frontier adventure story, the folk tale, the novel of sensibility, the allegorical romance, and the epistolary and Gothic techniques that came to fruition in the fiction of the late eighteenth and early nineteenth century.

When every natural phenomenon, every qualm of conscience, was assumed to be emblematic of the great dramatic struggle between good and evil, no formal dramatic literature seemed necessary to the early colonist. So, except for dialogues and debates worked into treatises and poems, and sometimes into histories, American literary drama did not develop until after the middle of the eighteenth century. In England, Puritans closed the theaters in 1642, partly because of the licentiousness of the plays, but more because of the social problems endemic to playhouses — the effeminate tradition of boys playing the parts of women, the low character of actors (who were lumped with vagabonds and rogues), and the tendency of playgoing to distract men from both business and godliness. This same attitude prevailed in New England. But it is also true, as Louis B. Wright has put it, that "the primary reason that drama did not flourish in seventeenth-century America was the simple fact that no towns were large enough to support theatrical entertainment." Traveling actors occasionally made their ways to the colonies, often to be turned away, and it was approximately 1716 before the first known playhouse was erected in the colonies at Williamsburg, Virginia. Philadelphia, New York, and Charleston all had theaters by the middle of the eighteenth century, though they showed English plays exclusively, and New England college students even presented plays designed to give them practice in Latin and Greek declamation. The first play to be written by a native American was Thomas Godfrey's *The Prince of Parthia,* published in 1765, two years after Godfrey's death; this was a bombastic blank-verse tragedy that strangely and sometimes effectively mingles Elizabethan and Restoration dramatic ideas. But drama did not gain acceptance until after the Revolution, and did not become a distinguished form of American literary art until the twentieth century.

On the whole, while the colonial period provided an excellent apprenticeship for American literature, its products were not of a very high order. The usual explanation — that Puritans were inveterately hostile to beauty and art — is, if not a fiction in itself, at least an oversimplification. The failure of American colonial writing to approach or equal the level of contemporary English or European literature is due rather to other factors. First, the American Puritans represented but one slice of English middle-class society, a class with no very impressive artistic attainments even in England at the time. In the colonies that class was completely removed from contact with the more cultured classes at home. We must remember that the first English settlers in America were born before the golden era of English writing, and that the colonial experience spanned the work of Spenser, Shakespeare, the metaphysical poets, Milton, Dryden, and Pope — a period during which American intellectual life was dominated by one class of people with one overriding concern. Second, the prevailing Calvinism of the American colonists, especially the New England Puritans, contributed to aesthetic barrenness in making art seem impotent if not irrevelant: God's beauty was all-sufficing, and works of nature and of art could be only weak reflections thereof. Moreover, many seventeenth-century Americans believed that the millennium — Christ's second coming — was imminent; with that event all the works of man would pass. This intense conviction of earthly transience further discouraged painstaking artistic creation and concern with form. Emphasis was on ideas and themes rather than on beauty of expression — a fact which may indeed account for the easy acceptance of English literary forms, themselves sometimes inconsistent with

American ideas. And finally, Americans of the seventeenth century were simply too busy establishing themselves in the New World to develop and refine a literary culture.

"God's altar needs not our polishing," wrote John Cotton in his preface to the Bay Psalm Book. But by 1740, a full century later, a more secular America was not so sure.

Order Disordered

At what point the Puritan city upon a hill — and the dominant colonial culture it represented — began to be undermined is not clear. Perhaps the promise of its dissolution lay in the very aims that permitted it originally to bring order out of the English political and religious chaos. But in America, isolated at first from foreign ideologies, its distinctive theology realized more fully in Massachusetts and Connecticut than anywhere else in the world, Puritanism stiffened into orthodoxy, crystallized, cracked, and began to flake away. The strength derived from adversity in England rigidified in New England to become a fatal defect. More than a religious creed, Puritanism was a way of life that organized all of man's activities, reducing all the arts and sciences to "handmaids" of Theology. As Clarence Faust has pointed out, the Puritan's emphasis on God's sovereignty — with its familiar image of God as a king — hardened into legalism and collapsed in the face of political and social change that everywhere weakened men's trust in monarchical principles. The power of God's providence over man, in the Puritan's view, made him a passive tool in an age when men were — in matters of faith, politics, and ethics — asserting their responsibility and independence; so counter did Calvinism run to eighteenth-century thought and sentiment, that it forced men to look elsewhere for their creeds. The Puritan's concept of an eternal, changeless, static God led him toward an ideal, eternal system of absolutes fully explicable by the logical system of Ramus, but incapable of adjustment to the new science and the new logic of Descartes, Locke, and Newton. Adverse to change, Puritanism became oversimplified and exposed to ridicule by its own pious defenders. Then, too, the Puritan's emphasis on reason and his respect for human learning opened the door to skepticism, while his glorification of industry slipped almost imperceptibly down the road to materialism.

But if the eventual disintegration of New England Calvinism was inherent in the system from the beginning, its course was gradual. The first problem arose from dissatisfaction over the relationship of the clergy to the civil magistrates. One of the early enticements to church membership was the power to vote: church membership remained a necessary qualification for the franchise until 1664. All

inhabitants of towns were obliged to attend religious worship, and the obligation was enforced by the civil magistrates. A Massachusetts statute of 1637, forbidding strangers to remain in any community for more than three weeks without permission, gave the magistrates power to judge the orthodoxy of its new members. Religious disorders were prosecuted as social disturbances by the civil courts. Roger Williams in 1635 was the first to attack the civil government's prying into a man's religious opinions, and we must remember that he and Anne Hutchinson shortly thereafter were both banished from Massachusetts Bay by civil authorities, not the church, which had only the right to censure and excommunicate. Though the church and magistracy thus acted together, there were occasional conflicts of jurisdiction, and public irritation arose over both the interest of the clergy in civil matters and the interference of the magistracy in the world of spirit. Moreover, while some forty per cent of the adult male population were "freemen" in 1665, the rapid increase in population after that date made the percentage of voters dwindle. And as the unfranchised group grew larger, its dissatisfaction mounted.

With the passing of the first generation of New Englanders, the era of colonial autonomy was also drawing to a close. Under the early Stuarts and the Commonwealth, the home government had made little attempt to define a colonial policy and exercise any effective control. Operating under its corporate charter, Massachusetts Bay had been free to develop as a Puritan state with a minimum of outside interference. From the mid-seventeenth century on, however, it was in inescapable relationship with an emergent colonial superstructure and with political changes affecting all the colonies. By 1660 Parliament and Crown were agreed that colonial affairs needed closer supervision, for greater ease and efficiency of administration, tighter economic regulation, and unification of the military defenses against France and Spain in the New World. One by one, therefore, the colonies were turned into royal colonies, governed from London under a somewhat unwieldy system of eight agencies, with the major share of responsibility vested in Parliament and the King's Privy Council. New Hampshire became a royal colony in 1679, New York in 1685, Massachusetts in 1691, New Jersey in 1702, the Carolinas in 1719–29, Georgia in 1752. Virginia had been a royal colony since 1624. Pennsylvania, Delaware, and Maryland remained proprietary, but since their governments were restrained from any acts contrary to Parliament and their policies were subject to review, they were to all purposes no differently handled than royal colonies. Connecticut and Rhode Island were allowed to elect their own governors and lesser officials, and therefore maintained somewhat greater political autonomy than the eleven other colonies. The pattern of government of the royal colonies

paralleled that of England itself, with the royal governor representing the King, the Governor's Council the Privy Council, and the elected colonial assembly Parliament.

The official view concerning the status of the colonies held them to be dependencies which existed for the benefit of the empire; what rights and privileges they possessed stemmed from the central imperial government in London. Colonial government functioned through the representatives of various agencies assigned to colonial affairs — naval clerks, military officers, customs officers, tax collectors, judges and legal officers, and so on. The royal governor, even though his jurisdiction did not extend over all other agents in the colonies, served as the focal point of imperial power. He did, however, have virtually complete authority over the colonial assembly — in theory, if not always in practice. He called and reviewed its elections, determined its size and representation, could dissolve or prorogue its meetings, and possessed an absolute veto power over its actions. As Parliament contested with the King in seventeenth-century England, so the American assemblies, as the colonies developed their own interests, contested with their royal governors.

The earliest and most deepseated conflict between the colonies and their royal officials arose over differences of economic interest, involving the subordination of colonial trade, the channeling of all colonial commerce through London, the limitation of the colonial production to raw materials, the manipulation of currency, the collection of duties and taxes, and other points often at issue. Throughout the seventeenth century, colonial assemblies engaged in a constant, determined struggle with Parliament's Boards and the King's representatives. By 1700 they had won two extremely important privileges — the right to assent to laws and taxes, and the right to initiate legislation — which meant that the colonials could make their demands known, and cause trouble if these were not met. In the earlier eighteenth century, as colonial interests solidified and more points of conflict emerged between colonists and home government, the grounds for compromise gradually narrowed. At the close of the French and Indian War, which for once and all removed the "Gallic peril" from the Northwest, Edmund Burke claimed for Parliament "an imperial character in which, as from the throne of Heaven, she superintends all the several inferior legislatures, and guides and controls them. . . ." The heavenly nature of the British imperial system, however, was not fully concurred in by the American colonies.

New Englanders — though never admitting that the road to the throne of Heaven wound through Parliament — could not, of course, escape these powerful political and social forces. And from the outset, any concern for nonreligious matters exposed the entire

Puritan system to several kinds of attack. Anne Hutchinson, Roger Williams, the Quakers, and other seekers after the Spirit accused the ministry of paying too much attention to things of this world. The accusation implied that clergymen depended too much on learning and ignored the direct influence of the Holy Ghost. As a result, in 1636 and 1637 a wave of anti-intellectualism swept Massachusetts, leaving behind a residue of anti-ministerial feeling that was never wholly dissipated.

In 1642 an epidemic of sinfulness gave further evidence that all was not well in New Jerusalem; for not only were townspeople involved, church members and their children were too. Reflecting on the matter, churchmen concluded that the zeal of the first generation was waning. The primary concern of the ministry became to re-ignite the religious affections of young Puritans who had missed the glorious experience of settling the New World. As it became increasingly obvious that youngsters, even though baptized, were decidedly less than saintly, a movement developed to keep baptism from becoming a means of introducing unworthy persons into the church. The controversy over infant baptism in the 1640's marked the first extensive division among the Puritans; even Harvard's president, Henry Dunster, lost his post in 1654 for insisting that children ought not to be baptized.

By 1662 the problem of baptism, itself representative of a far deeper theological conflict, had come to a head. The new generation had proved to be notoriously unmindful of their religious obligations, avoiding the sacrament of the Lord's Supper and resisting the requirement of declaring their conversion in a public confession. And now a third generation of children was ready for baptism, and the ministry's question was what to do about them. The Boston Synod of 1662 decided to compromise. Children would continue to be baptized, and would become church members. But until they were able to declare their conversion in a public speech called a "relation," they would be barred from full membership and could not take the Lord's Supper. Thereby they entered only half-way into the church, and the measure became known derisively as the "Half-Way Covenant." Its purpose was to make entrance into the church somewhat easier, without lowering the barriers to the obviously unworthy, and thereby to encourage New Englanders to keep their church life going. But membership continued to fall, and people continued in increasing numbers to avoid the Lord's Supper. Originally each community had consisted of two parts: the unconverted whose taxes and attendence largely supported the church (called the "town"), and the "church" of visible saints. After the Half-Way Covenant, the division was threefold: the town (which grew larger and larger); the church (those baptized, half-way members who never were converted); and the "saints," whose public relations gave them full church privileges, and whose numbers steadily dwindled.

In 1679 another synod met in Boston to decry the failure of the people to support the church, their growing sinfulness, wanton violations of the sabbath, widespread swearing and sleeping at sermons, tavern-going, dancing, immodest dress, cheating and lying in business, and general immorality. Though in official and intellectual matters the church remained the most influential organization in seventeenth-century America, there was no question that control of society was slipping from its grasp. That the clergy knew it is reflected in the sudden rise of what Perry Miller has called "jeremiads," sermons which pointed out the evils of the time, attributed every conceivable misfortune to God's disfavor, and urged repentance. Histories and biographies of saintly founders held up the proper ideals for the apathetic to emulate; ministers wrote devotional guides to instruct children in the joys of worship and so to attract them to the fold; and the stiff independence of individual congregations broke down as they joined "consociations" — county organizations which sought to maintain orthodoxy and regulate the qualifications of clergymen and church-members.

But nothing availed. Churches disintegrated, and God continued to frown upon the New England Way. Control of England fell from Puritan hands, with the death of Oliver Cromwell in 1658, and into the grip of the Catholic-sympathizer, Charles II, who was restored to the throne in 1660. In 1684, James II revoked the Massachusetts Bay charter; and though the new charter of 1691 retained many of the traditional freedoms, Massachusetts now became a royal province, less autonomous and less parochial henceforth.

The ministry continued to lose ground. Ministerial prestige, damaged by Increase Mather's thankless part in securing the unpopular new charter, suffered further from the Salem witchcraft trials of 1692. The growing distance between the leaders of the church and the moneyed townsmen became obvious as secular interests began to gain control over Harvard College. Popular demand for a bank, credit, and paper money to solve the difficulties of a lack of specie in 1720 again found the ministry opposing the interests of influential citizens; and criticism of the clergy became rabid when Cotton Mather, contrary to all medical and popular opinion, urged that people be inoculated against smallpox. Such oppositions began to draw clergymen away from a central, clear position on social problems; as Perry Miller has put it: "Intellectuals were falling not so much into opposing camps as into splinter fragments, not over theological or abstract issues . . . but because they were identified with diverging interests."

Some of the anti-ministerial feeling followed sectional lines, as churches on the frontier disavowed the authority of Boston and turned to the leadership of Northampton's Solomon Stoddard. Stoddard relaxed the requirements for church membership and began an evangelistic campaign that converted frontier churches to his liberal practices with alarming rapidity. To the Boston ministry, his lowering of standards was reprehensible, and they waged a brisk pamphlet war with him from 1685 to 1710; by 1750, however, well after Stoddard's death, "Stoddardism" had clearly won. But the crucial conflict between the old orthodoxy and popular religion came not so much in Stoddard's time as in that of his grandson, Jonathan Edwards. And it came, ironically, in the same form that first brought order to the New World — separatism. By 1730 most of the older conservatives (Increase Mather, Edward Taylor, Samuel Sewall, Samuel Willard, and Cotton Mather) were gone, and old-fashioned Puritanism was moribund. Between 1740 and 1745 it went through one last spasm called the Great Awakening.

Religious thought had grown more and more liberal in the last years of the seventeenth century, and many orthodox Calvinists learned to distrust the free-thinking ministers turned out by Harvard. By 1701 they were so dissatisfied that they founded a second college, called Yale, at New Haven, for the express purpose of producing orthodox Calvinist ministers. But "Arminianism," as all liberal thought came to be called, continued to increase. It was not so much that the new breed of ministers spoke against Calvinist doctrines; they simply ignored them, preaching more and more as if man's will were free and his actions had something to do with his salvation. Alarmed by such irresponsible talk, Jonathan Edwards turned aside from intellectual argument to preach a demonstration of the absolutely real and meaningful nature of Calvin's tenets. Preaching to the senses of his congregation, he vivified the consequences of election, damnation, and God's sovereign will, and pictured the depraved condition of their own unconverted souls in such graphic detail that his hearers fell — some literally — before the excitement of his preaching. In 1734 and 1735 his intense sermons brought some to God, many to hysteria, still others to madness and even suicide.

By 1736 Edwards began to moderate his preaching, but religious emotionalism surged up once more when the Reverend George Whitefield, a young English evangelist who had been preaching through the South, arrived in New England in 1740. His intense spirituality and brilliant oratory pierced hardened hearts and melted the religious affections of countless souls as he left a trail of evangelical fire from Georgia to Massachusetts, even joining Edwards for one successful tour. Galleries were packed with hysterical listeners, and a grandstand in Boston collapsed, killing five. Whitefield was succeeded by raving James Davenport, who tore off his clothes as he preached; intemperate Gilbert Tennent, who lashed out at the established ministry without mercy; and dozens of other itinerant preachers distinguished only by their wild enthusiasm.

By 1745 the Great Awakening was over, but its effects were permanent. Under the lash of its evangelical emotionalism, thirty to forty thousand converts flooded the churches, most of them either distrustful or actively critical of the orthodox clergy whose over-intellectualism and laxity, they believed, had brought religion to its sorry state. Some congregations, accusing their own ministers of being unconverted, substituted fervent but uneducated exhorters. Congregations split, consociations collapsed, church authority and unity almost disappeared. New England divided into the "New Light" followers of Edwards and Whitefield, and the "Old Light" followers of the Half-Way Covenant, but the range of differences within each group was so great that traditional New England Puritanism was barely recognizable.

The divisions of the Great Awakening drove many people into non-Congregational churches — Anglican, Quaker, Baptist, and Methodist — and also opened the way for the rational religion called "deism," which appeared in America during the latter half of the eighteenth century. Deism received its first clear statement of principle in seventeenth-century England, where the widely traveled, urbane adventurer Edward Herbert of Cherbury attempted to establish those religious principles basic to all societies. He published his conclusions in *De Veritate* (1624), *De Religione Laici* (1645), and *De Religione Gentilium* (1663). Emphasizing man's free will as the Arminians did, Herbert called for a church based on five fundamental religious beliefs: that there is a God; that He is to be worshipped; that the essentials of worship are virtue and piety; that men should repent of their sins; and that man's immortal soul will be punished or rewarded according to its earthly actions in an after-life. Without formally instituting these principles, Englishmen and Americans more and more tended to echo Herbert's ideas. Learned laymen such as Franklin, Paine, and Jefferson, impatient with the arguments and divisions of orthodoxy, found deism highly compatible with the new science of Newton and its concepts of the world. Extending Herbert's eminently rational approach to religion into acceptable eighteenth-century terms, they held that God was the Divine Architect of the world; that He originated and designed the intricate mechanism called the universe, set its natural laws in motion, and then withdrew; that His providence was merely Natural Law working itself out according to the Supreme Being's preconceived plan; and that to know God as fully as man could required the rational study of the nature He created. Thus deists tended to de-personalize God, to ignore or deny the divinity of Christ, to study nature rather than the Bible, and to turn religion into natural philosophy.

Deism served the needs of some of the intellectual, philosophically minded men of the period, but its appeal was limited, and the extremism of a few of its explicators, such as Thomas Paine and Elihu Palmer, alienated many of its followers. Unitarianism, a somewhat less radical form of religious rationalism, attracted more support. Like the early deists, liberal Congregationalists emphasized the trustworthiness of human reason and moral conscience, but relied more heavily on the revelations of the Bible, squaring revelation with reason when they could, certain that virtue and benevolence were natural to man. Moral and rational discipline were their way to salvation. Because they emphasized the "unity" of God, they were sometimes called "Unitarians," though they did not (until 1826) form a separate church. By 1800 this "liberal" theology was endorsed by many Congregationalists, who by 1808 were so entrenched in Harvard that conservatives had to withdraw to form their own seminary. As the "Unitarian" group developed its theology, it came into greater conflict with traditional Calvinism; it denied Christ's divinity and the whole concept of trinitarianism; it emphasized ethical and humanitarian action as the center of religious worship; and it affirmed man's potential for achieving perfection. Unitarianism, in effect, pointed the way to American Transcendentalism.

When in 1832 Ralph Waldo Emerson surrendered his Unitarian ministry to strike his own original relationship with the universe, he did so from the pulpit of Boston's Second Church, the same pulpit that once held Increase and Cotton Mather. As the impulse for order that first gave seventeenth-century America its most elaborate and distinctive culture, and even as a formal movement of serious significance in American life, Puritanism was indeed dead.

A NOTE ON THE TEXTS

The problems of establishing authoritative texts for much of the material in this anthology, and particularly in the first volume, are manifold and complex. Twentieth-century editions from manuscript, as those of William Bradford, Edward Taylor, and John Woolman, are generally trustworthy; but they are few. Modern editions of work originally printed in the seventeenth and eighteenth centuries, as for example the fine Yale edition of Benjamin Franklin's *Papers*, sometimes differ substantially from earlier "standard" editions, but do not record the differences, and force the reader back to original publications to determine correct readings. Widely used and respected editions, rightly termed standard, such as the Original Narratives of Early American History series, generally prove to be excellent reprints of nineteenth-century reprints. And while the student of early American thought and writing cannot review the materials preserved in the *Collections* and the *Proceedings* of the Massachusetts Historical Society without gratitude and admiration, he is still obliged to confirm the accuracy of these printings by recourse to original publications where they exist.

Fortunately, the American Antiquarian Society's project of microfilming all the verifiable titles in Charles Evans' *American Bibliography* has made copies of American publications to 1820 widely available, and must stand as the most authoritative source for many of the selections in this anthology. But given the irregularities of early American printing, the variations among existing copies of these books, the lack of thoroughgoing collations, and the fact that some important works by Americans were printed in England but not in America, the Evans microfilms can only be a first step in securing definitive texts. The problem is complicated further by the fact that books of the same title often appeared in considerably different form when published in England (as in the case of Thomas Hooker's *The Application of Redemption*), that piracies and posthumous editions of questionable authority were common, that works like Robert Beverley's *The History and Present State of Virginia* were sometimes mutilated by the author himself in revised editions, and that when writers like Jonathan Edwards gained sufficient stature to be collected into *Works*, their language was frequently "improved" by their editors. The present efforts of the National Historical Commission and the Center for Editions of American Authors of the Modern Language Association are doing much to solve these problems, but it will be years before any but the major figures of American history and literature will be represented by definitive readings.

The present editors have therefore attempted, on a variety of grounds, to use the best or most representative texts in the selections that follow, giving priority to first editions and modern critical editions, and comparing texts when variant lifetime or other putatively authoritative editions exist. The authorities for the verbal sequence of the selections are cited in the headnotes. Colonial printing practice regarding capitals, abbreviations, italics, and spelling was often whimsical and inconsistent. For this reason, the editors have generally modernized the texts in these respects, retaining unusual spellings, however, when they may be presumed to distinguish colonial pronunciation from modern American English (e.g., *shew* for *show, then* for *than, learnt* for *learned*), and allowing the consequent irregularities to stand; special care has been taken not to impair the pronunciation of the poetry. To maintain the rhythms of early American writing, we have in general retained the punctuation of the source texts, emending only occasionally to remove impediments to understanding.

R. B. N.
N. S. G.

AMERICAN THOUGHT AND WRITING

VOLUME ONE

The Colonial Period

Brave New World

THE FIRST writers of English America — adventurers, explorers, merchants, travelers, settlers, official agents, and promoters — brought their enthusiasm and sometimes their disgust with the New World to an avid English and European audience. Whatever their purposes, their writings join in a common fascination with what they encountered in America: a novel and savage people, virgin and abundant forests, exotic plants and animals, limitless lands, new problems needing new solutions — and everywhere the natural enticement to men of honor, faith, industry, and ambition to make a place for themselves in this ample portion of God's creation. Here was the chance for men of courage to begin again, and curious readers demanded information about climate, geography, and social structures, the dangers and advantages, and in time the course of events. They did not have far to seek, for pamphlets and letters, reports and poems, ranging from the most mundane descriptions to the most idealistic exhortations, from smug assurance to wry cynicism, immediately competed for their attention. And as the great experiment gained dimensions in time, early descriptive writing evolved into history, a history that retained the freshness and excitement of discovery, a history always with a special purpose or case to plead, but a history that promised as much for the future as it recorded of the past.

John Smith (1580–1631)

BORN in Lincolnshire, England, and apprenticed to a merchant, John Smith soon found mercantile life too dull for his taste. At the age of fifteen he ran away to spend ten years as a soldier of fortune in Europe and the Near East, undergoing (if his own stories can be believed) tremendous trials and experiencing marvellous adventures. In 1605 he returned to England and joined the group of colonists bound for Jamestown in 1607, where he played a major role in holding the colony together by strong leadership and uncompromising discipline. In 1609 he returned to England, but in 1614 he joined a voyage of exploration to New England, and would have made another in 1615 had he not been captured by the French. After a brief imprisonment, he lived quietly in England until his death in 1631.

Smith was a tough, professional soldier, and a hard-handed administrator with a zest for adventure. The veracity of his personal exploits, in which he presents himself in heroic proportions, has been questioned, but envisioning the American adventure as a kind of chivalric romance in which sturdy Englishmen could attain honor and glory, Smith not only contributed an enduring and charming legend to American lore, but introduced the narrative of Indian war and captivity, one of the earliest and strongest strains of American literature. His various books, particularly *A True Relation of . . . Virginia* (1608), *A Map of Virginia* (1612), *A Description of New England* (1616), *The General History of Virginia* (1624), and *The True Travels, Adventures, and Observations of Captain John Smith* (1630), form the first substantial body of literary work done in and about America.

TEXTS: John Smith, *A True Relation*, ed. Charles Deane (Boston, 1866); *A Description of New England,* in Peter Force, *Tracts,* II (New York, 1836, 1947).

The Landing at Jamestown

[From *A True Relation,* 1608]

Kind Sir, commendations remembered, etc. You shall understand that after many crosses in The Downs by tempests, we arrived safely upon the Southwest part of the great Canaries: within four or five days after we set sail for Dominica, the 26. of April: the first land we made, we fell with Cape Henry, the very mouth of the Bay of Chissiapiacke, which at that present we little expected, having by a cruel storm been put to the Northward. Anchoring in this Bay twenty or thirty went ashore with the captain, and in coming aboard, they were assaulted with certain Indians, which charged them with pistol shot: in which conflict, Captain Archer and Matthew Morton were shot: whereupon Captain Newport seconding them, made a shot at them, which the Indians little respected, but having spent their arrows retired without harm. And in that place was the box opened, wherein the Council for Virginia was nominated: and arriving at the place where we are now seated, the Council was sworn, and the President elected, which for that year was Master Edm. Maria Wingfield, where was made choice for our situation, a very fit place for the erecting of a great city, about which some contention passed between Captain Wingfield and Captain Gosnold: notwithstanding, all our provision was brought ashore, and with as much speed as might be we went about our fortification.

The two and twenty day of April, Captain Newport and myself with divers others, to the number of twenty-two persons, set forward to discover the river, some fifty or sixty miles, finding it in some places broader, and in some narrower, the country (for the most part) on each side plain high ground, with many fresh springs, the people in all places kindly entreating us, dancing and feasting us with strawberries, mulberries, bread, fish, and other their country provisions whereof we had plenty: for which Captain Newport kindly requited their least favors with bells, pins, needles, beads, or glasses, which so contented them that his liberality made them follow us from place to place, and ever kindly to respect us. In the midway staying to refresh ourselves in a little isle, four or five savages came unto us which described unto us the course of the river, and after in our journey, they often met us, trading with us for such provision as we had, and arriving at Arsatecke, he whom we supposed to be the chief king of all the rest, most kindly entertained us, giving us in a guide to go with us up the river to Powhatan, of which place their great emperor taketh his name, where he that they honored for king used us kindly. But to finish this discovery, we passed on further, where within a mile we were intercepted with great craggy stones in the midst of the river, where the water falleth so rudely, and with such a violence, as not any boat can possibly pass, and so broad disperseth the stream, as there is not past five or six foot at a low water, and to the shore scarce passage with a barge, the water floweth four foot, and the freshes by reason of the rocks have left marks of the inundations eight or nine foot: the south side is plain low ground, and the north side is high mountains, the rocks being of a gravelly nature, interlaced with many veins of glistring spangles.

That night we returned to Powhatan: the next day (being Whitsunday after dinner) we returned to the falls, leaving a mariner in pawn with the Indians for a guide of theirs; he that they honored for king followed us by the river. That afternoon we trifled in looking upon the rocks and river (further he would not go) so there we erected a cross, and that night taking our man at Powhatan, Captain Newport congratulated his kindness with a gown and a hatchet: returning to Arsetecke, and stayed there the next day to observe the height thereof, and so with many signs of love we departed.

The Advantages of the New World

[From *A Description of New England,* 1616]

❰[The first great need of the colonies was population — farmers, tradesmen, skilled workmen, professional men. Smith's description of the opportunities available in the new settlements is typical of dozens of similar promotional writings designed to encourage immigration. Such descriptions exerted tremendous appeal to the adventurous, alert, and ambitious who were at home in England. Smith, who misses few of the multitude of attractions that the New World might offer, rings all the changes on patriotism, piety, self-interest, and sport.]❱

. . . Worthy is that person to starve that here cannot live; if he have sense, strength, and health: for there is no such penury of these blessings in any place, but that a hundred men may, in one hour or two, make their provisions for a day: and he that hath experience to manage well these affairs, with forty or thirty honest industrious men, might well undertake (if they dwell in these parts) to subject the salvages, and feed daily two or three hundred men, with as good corn, fish, and flesh, as the earth hath of those kinds, and yet make that labor but their pleasure: provided that they have engines, that be proper for their purposes.

Who can desire more content, that hath small means; or but only his merit to advance his fortune, then to tread, and plant that ground he hath purchased by the hazard of his life? If he have but the taste of virtue, and magnanimity, what to such a mind can be more pleasant, then planting and building a foundation for his posterity, got from the rude earth, by God's blessing and his own industry, without prejudice to any? If he have any grain of faith or zeal in religion, what can he do less hurtful to any; or more agreeable to God, then to seek to convert those poor salvages to know Christ, and humanity, whose labors with discretion will triple requite thy charge and pains? What so truly suits with honor and honesty, as the discovering things unknown? erecting towns, peopling countries, informing the ignorant, reforming things unjust, teaching virtue; and gain to our native mother-country a kingdom to attend her; find employment for those that are idle, because they know not what to do: so far from wronging any, as to cause posterity to remember thee; and remembring thee, ever honor that remembrance with praise? . . .

Then, who would live at home idly (or think in himself any worth to live) only to eat, drink, and sleep, and so die? Or by consuming that carelessly, his friends got worthily? Or by using that miserably, that maintained virtue honestly? Or, for being descended nobly, pine with the vain vaunt of great kindred, in penury? Or to (maintain a silly show of bravery) toil out thy heart, soul, and time, basely, by shifts, tricks, cards, and dice? Or by relating news of others' actions, shark here or there for a dinner, or supper; deceive thy friends, by fair promises, and dissimulation, in borrowing where thou never intendest to pay; offend the laws, surfeit with excess, burden thy country, abuse thy self, despair in want, and then cozen thy kindred, yea even thine own brother, and with thy parents' death (I will not say damnation) to have their estates? though thou seest what honors, and rewards, the world yet hath for them will seek them and worthily deserve them.

I would be sorry to offend, or that any should mistake my honest meaning: for I wish good to all, hurt to none. But rich men for the most part are grown to that dotage, through their pride in their wealth, as though there were no accident could end it, or their life. And what hellish care do such take to make it their own misery, and their country's spoil, especially when there is most need of their employment? drawing by all manner of inventions, from the Prince and his honest subjects, even the vital spirits of their powers and estates: as if their bags or brags, were so powerful a defense, the malicious could not assault them; when they are the only bait, to cause us not to be only assaulted; but betrayed and murdered in our own security, ere we well perceive it. . . .

And lest any should think the toil might be insupportable, though these things may be had by labor and diligence: I assure myself there are who delight extremely in vain pleasure, that take much more pains in England, to enjoy it, then I should do here to gain wealth sufficient; and yet I think they should not have half such sweet content: for, our pleasure here is still gains, in England charges and loss. Here nature and liberty affords us that freely which in England we want, or it costeth us dearly. What pleasure can be more, then (being tired with any occasion ashore) in planting vines, fruits, or herbs, in contriving their own grounds, to the pleasure of their own minds, their fields, gardens, orchards, buildings, ships, and other works, etc., to recreate themselves before their own doors, in their own boats upon the sea;

where man, woman, and child, with a small hook and line, by angling, may take divers sorts of excellent fish, at their pleasures? And is it not pretty sport, to pull up two pence, six pence, and twelve pence, as fast as you can hale and veer a line? He is a very bad fisher, cannot kill in one day with his hook and line, one, two, or three hundred cods: which dressed and dried, if they be sold there for ten shillings the hundred, though in England they will give more then twenty; may not both the servant, the master, and merchant, be well content with this gain? If a man work but three days in seven, he may get more then he can spend, unless he will be excessive. Now that carpenter, mason, gardener, tailor, smith, sailor, forgers, or what other, may they not make this a pretty recreation though they fish but an hour in a day, to take more then they eat in a week? or if they will not eat it, because there is so much better choice; yet sell it, or change it, with the fishermen, or merchants, for anything they want? And what sport doth yield a more pleasing content, and less hurt or charge then angling with a hook; and crossing the sweet air from isle to isle, over the silent streams of a calm sea? Wherein the most curious may find pleasure, profit, and content. Thus, though all men be not fishers: yet all men, whatsoever, may in other matters do as well. For necessity doth in these cases so rule a commonwealth, and each in their several functions, as their labors in their qualities may be as profitable, because there is a necessary mutual use of all.

For gentlemen, what exercise should more delight them, then ranging daily those unknown parts, using fowling and fishing, for hunting and hawking? and yet you shall see the wild hawks give you some pleasure, in seeing them stoop (six or seven after one another) an hour or two together, at the schools of fish in the fair harbors, as those ashore at a fowl; and never trouble nor torment yourselves with watching, mewing, feeding, and attending them: nor kill horse and man with running and crying, "See you not a hawk?" For hunting also: the woods, lakes, and rivers afford not only chase sufficient, for any that delights in that kind of toil, or pleasure; but such beasts to hunt, that besides the delicacy of their bodies for food, their skins are so rich, as may well recompense thy daily labor, with a captain's pay.

For laborers, if those that sow hemp, rape, turnips, parsnips, carrots, cabbage, and such like give 20, 30, 40, 50 shillings yearly for an acre of ground, and meat, drink, and wages to use it, and yet grow rich; when better, or at least as good ground, may be had, and cost nothing but labor; it seems strange to me, any such should there grow poor.

My purpose is not to persuade children from their parents; men from their wives; nor servants from their masters: only, such as with free consent may be spared: but that each parish, or village, in city or country, that will but apparel their fatherless children, of thirteen or fourteen years of age, or young married people, that have small wealth to live on, here by their labor may live exceeding well: provided always that first there be a sufficient power to command them, houses to receive them, means to defend them, and meet provisions for them; for, any place may be overlain: and it is most necessary to have a fortress (ere this grow to practice) and sufficient masters (as carpenters, masons, fishers, fowlers, gardeners, husbandmen, sawyers, smiths, spinsters, tailors, weavers, and such like) to take ten, twelve, or twenty, or as there is occasion, for apprentices. The masters by this may quickly grow rich; these may learn their trades themselves, to do the like; to a general and an incredible benefit, for king, and country, master, and servant. . . .

Religion, above all things, should move us (especially the clergy) if we were religious, to shew our faith by our works; in converting those poor salvages, to the knowledge of God, seeing what pains the Spaniards take to bring them to their adulterated faith. Honor might move the gentry, the valiant, and industrious; and the hope and assurance of wealth, all; if we were that we would seem, and be accounted. Or be we so far inferior to other nations, or our spirits so far dejected, from our ancient predecessors, or our minds so upon spoil, piracy, and such villainy, as to serve the Portugal, Spaniard, Dutch, French, or Turk (as to the cost of Europe, too many do), rather then our God, our king, our country, and ourselves? excusing our idleness, and our base complaints, by want of employments; when here is such choice of all sorts, and for all degrees, in the planting and discovering these North parts of America.

John Hammond (*fl.* 1635–1656)

John Hammond came to Virginia in 1635, developing a great enthusiasm for the new country in which he was to live for nineteen years. In 1654 he moved for two years to Maryland, and then in 1656 returned to England, where he encountered a badly warped image of Virginia in English minds, and in the English cities themselves poverty and want of the most appalling sort. To bring the English picture of Virginia into proper focus and to contrast the New World's plenty with England's penury, Hammond immediately published *Leah and Rachel; or, The Two Fruitful Sisters, Virginia and Maryland* (London, 1656), which acknowledges the South's tribulations while it at the same time affirms the prosperity Southerners had come to enjoy since the adventures of Captain John Smith.

Text: Peter Force, *Tracts,* III (New York, 1844, 1947).

The Present State of Virginia

[From *Leah and Rachel,* 1656]

The country is very full of sober, modest persons, both men and women, and many that truly fear God and follow that perfect rule of our blessed Saviour, to do as they would be done by; and of such a happy inclination is the country, that many who in England have been lewd and idle, there in emulation or imitation (for example moves more than precept) of the industry of those they find there, not only grow ashamed of their former courses, but abhor to hear of them, and in small time wipe off those stains they have formerly been tainted with; yet I cannot but confess, there are people wicked enough (as what country is free) for we know some natures will never be reformed; . . . there are for each of these, severe and wholesome laws and remedies made, provided and duly put in execution: I can confidently affirm, that since my being in England, which is not yet four moneths, I have been an eye and ear witness of more deceits and villainies (and such as modesty forbids me to utter) than I either ever saw or heard mention made of in Virginia, in my one and twenty years abode in those parts.

And therefore those that shall blemish Virginia any more, do but like the dog bark against the moon, until they be blind and weary; and Virginia is now in that secure growing condition, that like the moon so barked at, she will pass on her course, maugre all detractors, and a few years will bring it to that glorious happiness, that many of her calumniators will intercede to procure admittance thither, when it will be hard to be attained to; for in small time, little land will be to be taken up; and after a while none at all; and as the mulberry trees grow up, which are by everyone planted, tobacco will be laid by, and we shall wholly fall to making of silk (a sample of 400 lbs. hath already been sent for England, and approved of), which will require little labor; and therefore shall have little use of servants; besides, children increase and thrive so well there, that they themselves will sufficiently supply the defect of servants: and in small time become a nation of themselves sufficient to people the country. And this good policy is there used: as the children there born grow to maturity, and capable (as they are generally very capable and apt) they are still preferred and put into authority, and carry themselves therein civilly and discreetly; and few there are but are able to give some portions with their daughters, more or less, according to their abilities; so that many coming out of England have raised themselves good fortunes there merely by matching with maidens born in the country. . . .

The country is not only plentiful but pleasant and profitable, pleasant in regard of the brightness of the weather, the many delightful rivers, on which the inhabitants are settled (every man almost living in sight of a lovely river), the abundance of game, the extraordinary good neighborhood and loving conversation they have one with the other.

Pleasant in their building, which although for most part they are but one story besides the loft, and built of wood, yet contrived so delightful that your ordinary houses in England are not so handsome, for usually the rooms are large, daubed and white-limed, glazed and flowered, and if not glazed windows, shutters which are made very pretty and convenient.

Pleasant in observing their stocks and flocks of cattle, hogs, and poultry, grazing, whisking and skipping in their sights, pleasant in having all things of their own, growing or breeding without drawing the penny to send for this and that, without which, in England they cannot be supplied.

The manner of living and trading there is thus, each man almost lives a freeholder, nothing but the value of 12 d. a year to be paid as rent, for every fifty acres of land; firing costs nothing; every man plants his own corn and need take no care for bread: if anything be bought, it is for commodity, exchanged presently, or for a day, payment is usually made but once a year, and for that bill taken (for accounts are not pleadable).

In summer when fresh meat will not keep (seeing every man kills of his own, and quantities are inconvenient), they lend from one to another, such portions of flesh as they can spare, which is repaid again when the borrower kills his.

If any fall sick, and cannot compass to follow his crop which if not followed, will soon be lost, the adjoining neighbors will either voluntarily or upon a request join together, and work in it by spells, until the honor recovers, and that gratis, so that no man by sickness lose any part of his year's work.

Let any travel, it is without charge, and at every house is entertainment as in a hostery, and with hearty welcome are strangers entertained.

In a word, Virginia wants not good victual, wants not good dispositions, and as God hath freely bestowed it, they as freely impart with it, yet are there as well bad natures as good.

The profit of the country is either by their labor, their stocks, or their trades.

By their labors is produced corn and tobacco, and all other growing provisions, and this tobacco however now low-rated, yet a good maintenance may be had out of it (for they have nothing of necessity but clothing to purchase), nor can this mean price of tobacco long hold, for these reasons, first that in England it is prohibited, next that they have attained of late those sorts equal with the best Spanish, thirdly that the sickness in Holland is decreasing, which hath been a great obstruction to the sale of tobacco.

And lastly, that as the mulberry tree grows up, tobacco will be neglected and silk, flax, two staple commodities generally fallen upon.

Of the increase of cattle and hogs, much advantage is made, by selling beef, pork, and bacon, and butter, etc., either to shipping, or to send to the Barbadoes, and other islands, and he is a very poor man that hath not sometimes provision to put off.

By trading with Indians for skin, beaver, furs, and other commodities oftentimes good profits are raised. The Indians are in absolute subjection to the English, so that they both pay tribute to them and receive all their several kings from them, and as one dies they repair to the English for a successor, so that none need doubt it a place of security.

Several ways of advancement there are and employments both for the learned and laborer, recreation for the gentry, traffic for the adventurer, congregations for the ministry (and oh that God would stir up the hearts of more to go over, such as would teach good doctrine, and not paddle in faction, or state matters; they could not want maintenance, they would find an assisting, an embracing, a conforming people).

It is known (such preferment hath this country rewarded the industrious with) that some from being wool-hoppers and of as mean and meaner employment in England have there grown great merchants, and attained to the most eminent advancements the country afforded. . . .

Now having briefly set down the present state of Virginia not in fiction, but in reality, I wish the judicious reader to consider what dislike can be had of the country, or upon what grounds it is so infamously injured, I only therein covet to stop those black mouthed babblers, that not only have and do abuse so noble a plantation, but abuse God's great blessing in adding to England so flourishing a branch, in persuading many souls, rather to follow desperate and miserable courses in England, then to engage in so honorable an undertaking as to travel and inhabit there; but to those I shall (if admonition will not work on their recreant spirits) only say: Let him that is filthy be filthy still.

A Story of Colonial Ingratitude

[From the same]

Having for nineteen year served Virginia the elder sister, I casting my eye on Maryland the younger, grew enamored on her beauty, resolving like Jacob when he had first served for Leah, to begin a fresh service for Rachel.

Two year and upward have I enjoyed her company with delight and profit, but was enforced by reason of her unnatural disturbances to leave her weeping for her children and would not be comforted, because they were not; yet will I never totally forsake or be beaten off from her. . . .

Maryland is a province not commonly known in England, because the name of Virginia includes or clouds it. It is a country wholly belonging to that honorable gentleman the Lord of Baltimore, granted him by patent under the broad seal of England long since, and at his charge settled, granted for many reasons, and this for one; that Virginia having more land then they could manure or look after in convenient time, first the Dutch came and took from the English much land which they still hold, next the Swede, who entrenched nearer and had not this patent came and prevented it, Dutch, Swede, French, and other strangers had penned up our nation within the bounds of Virginia, whereas now they have now all Maryland, as it were their own, it being only granted for the use of Britons and Irish.

It is (not an island as is reported, but) part of that main adjoining to Virginia, only separated or parted from Virginia, by a river of ten miles broad, called Patomack river, the commodities and manner of living as in Virginia, the soil somewhat more temperate (as being more Northerly), many stately and navigable rivers are contained in it, plentifully stored with wholesome springs, a rich and pleasant soil, and so that its extraordinary goodness hath made it rather desired then envied, which hath been fatal to her (as beauty is oftentimes to those that are endued with it), and that the reader may thoroughly be informed how she hath suffered, I shall in brief relate, and conclude.

It is to be understood that in the time of the late King, Virginia being whole for monarchy, and the last country belonging to England that submitted to obedience of the Commonwealth of England. And there was in Virginia a certain people congregated into a church, calling themselves Independents, which daily increasing, several consultations were had by the state of that colony, how to suppress and extinguish them, which was daily put in execution, as first their pastor was banished, next their other teachers, then many by informations clapt up in prison, then generally disarmed (which was very harsh in such a country where the heathen live round about them) by one Colonel Samuel Mathews then a Counsellor in Virginia and since Agent for Virginia to the then parliament, and lastly in a condition of banishment, so that they knew not in those straits how to dispose of themselves.

Maryland (my present subject) was courted by them as a refuge, the Lord Proprietor and his Governor solicited to, and several addresses and treaties made for their admittance and entertainment into that province, their conditions were pitied, their propositions were hearkened to and agreed on, which was that they should have convenient portions of land assigned them, liberty of conscience and privilege to choose their own officers, and hold courts within themselves, all was granted them. They had a whole county of the richest land in the province assigned them, and such as themselves made choice of, the conditions of plantations (such as were common to all adventurers) were shewed and propounded to them, which they extremely approved of, and nothing was in those conditions exacted from them, but appeals to the provincial court, quit-rents, and an oath of fidelity to the proprietor. An assembly was called throughout the whole country after their coming over (consisting as well of themselves as the rest), and because there were some few Papists that first inhabited these themselves, and others of being different judgments, an act passed that all professing in Jesus Christ should have equal justice, privileges, and benefits in that province, and that none on penalty (mentioned) should disturb each other in their several professions, nor give the urging terms, either of roundheads, sectary, Independent, Jesuit, Papist, etc. Intending an absolute peace and union, the Oath of Fidelity (although none other then such as every lord of a manor requires from his tenant) was overhauled, and this clause added to it (provided it infringe not the liberty of the conscience).

They sat down joyfully, followed their vocations cheerfully, trade increased in their province, and divers others were by this encouraged and invited over from Virginia.

But these people finding themselves in a capacity not only to capitulate, but to oversway, those that had so received and relieved them, began to pick quarrels, first with the Papists, next with the oath, and lastly declared their averseness to all conformality, wholly aiming (as themselves since confessed) to deprive the Lord Proprietor of all his interest in that country, and make it their own. What unworthiness? What ingratitude? What unparalleled inhumanity was in these practices made obvious?

Amongst others that became tenants in this aforesaid distress was one Richard Bennet, merchant, who seated and settled amongst them, and so (not only owed obedience to that government, but) was obliged as a man received in his pretended distress, to be a grateful benefactor; upon the setting forth of a fleet intended for the reducement of Virginia, the said Bennet and one Claiborne, a pestilent enemy to the welfare of that province and the Lord Proprietor, although he had formerly submissively acknowledged he owed his forfeited life to the said proprietor, for dealing so favorably with him for his misdemeanors, as by his treacherous letters under his hand (now in print) is manifest, and many other acts of grace conferred on him, having a commission directed to them and others (who miscarried by sea) to reduce Virginia (not Maryland, for they were in obedience to the Commonwealth of England, and great assistance to the said fleet) although they knew Maryland to be excluded and dasht out of their commission, yet because the commission mentioned the Bay of Chessapeake, in which Maryland was (as well as Virginia) yet they were resolved to wreth and stretch their commission to the prejudice of Maryland and becoming abettors and confederates with those serpents that have been so taken in, presumed to alter the government and take away the governor's commission, putting in others in their place, viz., a Papist in chief, and one more, who misgoverning the country, they were excluded, and the former governor restored with an addition of commissioners of their own creatures, and as taking power from them, until further knowledge from England, driving herein at their own interest.

The Governor (so restored) being truly informed that their proceedings were illegal, held courts and proceeds as if no such alteration had been made, issues out writs (according to order) in the name of the Lord Proprietor, but they require and command them to do it in the name of the Keepers of the Liberties of England, according to act of Parliament; to which answer sufficient was given, that they never were in opposition to the present power, they had taken the engagement, and for the tenure or form of writs, they were not compelled by virtue of that act to make them otherwise then they always had done, for by patent from the late King they had power to issue out in the Proprietor's name, and never had used the King's name at all, therefore that act requiring all writs formerly issuing out in the late King's name, now to revolve to the Keepers of the Liberties of England, was no way binding to them, who had never used the King's name at all.

But it was not religion, it was not punctilios they stood upon, it was that sweet, that rich, that large country they aimed at; and therefore agrees amongst themselves to frame petitions, complaints, and subscriptions from those bandittos to themselves (the said Bennet and Claiborne) to ease them of their pretended sufferings, and then come with arms, and again make the province their own, exalting themselves in all places of trust and command, totally expulsing the Governor, and all the hospitable Proprietor's officers out of their places.

But when his Highness (not acquainted with these machinations) had owned and under his hand and signet acknowledged Capt. Will. Stone (the former governor) Governor for the Lord Baltimore of his Province of Maryland, he again endeavored to reassume the government, and fetched away the records from those usurpers, proclaimed peace to all not obstinate, and favorably received many submissives, who with seeming joy returned, bewailing their unworthy ingratitude and inhumanity, blaming the unbridled ambition and base avarice of those that had misled them. . . .

The Governor desirous to reclaim those opposing, takes a party about one hundred and thirty persons with him, and sails into those parts, one Roger Heamans who had a great ship under him, and who had promised to be instrumental to the Governor, to wind up those differences (being, Judas-like, hired to join with those opposing countries) and having the Governor and his vessels within reach of his ordnance, perfidiously and contrary to his undertaking and engagements, fires at them and enforces them to the first shore to prevent that mischief.

The next morning he sends messengers to those of Anne Arundall to treat, and messengers aboard that shittlecock Heamans, but all were detained; and on the 25th of March last (being the next day and the Lord's day) about one hundred and seventy and odd of Kent and Anne Arundall [counties] came marching against them, Heaman fires apace at them, and a small vessel of New England under the command of one John Cutts comes near the shore and seizes the boats, provision, and ammunition belonging to the Governor and his party, and so in a nick, in a strait were they fallen upon.

The Governor being shot in many places yields on quarter, which was granted; but being in hold, was threatened (notwithstanding that quarter given) to be immediately executed, unless he would write to the rest to take quarter, which upon his request they did. Twenty odd were killed in this skirmish, and all the rest prisoners on quarter, who were disarmed and taken into custody.

But these formerly distressed supplicants for admittance, being now become high and mighty states, and supposing their conquest unquestionable, consult with themselves (notwithstanding their quarter given) to make their conquest more absolute, by cutting off the heads of the Province, viz., the governor, the council and commanders thereof; and so make themselves a council of war, and condemn them to death. Four were presently executed, *scilicet,* Mr. William Eltonhead, one of the Council; Capt. William Lewis, Mr. John Legate, gentleman, and John Pedro; the rest at the importunity of some women, and resolution of some of their soldiers (who would not suffer their design to take thorough effect, as being pricked in conscience for their ingratitudes) were saved, but were amerced, fined, and plundered at their pleasures. And although this was prophetically foreseen by divers eminent merchants of London, who petitioned his Highness for prevention, and that his Highness sent a gracious command to Bennet, and all others, not to disturb the Lord Baltimore's officers, nor people in Maryland, but recalled all power or pretense of power from them; yet they still hold, and possess (in defiance of so sacred a mandate) the said Province of Maryland, and sent an impious agent home to parley whilst they plundered; but he hath long since given up his account to the great avenger of all injuries. Although sticklers (somewhat more powerful, but by many degrees more brazen-faced than his spirit could bare him forth to appear) now labor to justify these inhumanities, disorders, contempts, and rebellions; so that I may say with the prophet Jeremiah: How doth the city sit solitary that was full of people? How is she become as a widow? She that was great amongst the nations, and princess amongst the provinces? How is she become tributary? Thus have they brought to desolation, one of the happiest plantations that ever Englishmen set foot in, and such a country (that if it were again made formal) might harbor in peace and plenty all such as England shall have occasion to disburthen, or desire to forsake England.

George Alsop (1638–?)

Ten years after John Hammond's balanced defense of Virginia and Maryland, George Alsop produced his own answer to the critics of the New World in a jumble of letters, descriptions of the country and its people, and absurd doggerel titled *A Character of the Province of Maryland* (London, 1666). Alsop himself called it "wild and confused," explaining that insofar as it is so, "it is because I am so myself; and the world, as far as I can perceive, is not much out of the same trim." Alsop's acquaintance with Maryland was the result of four years spent there as an indentured servant (1658–62). His humorous view of the American experience finds expression in a grotesque witty style so broadly burlesque that it is often not clear whether he really means to defend Maryland or to undermine her. In drollness, quaintness, and verbal energy, Alsop's *Character* is a worthy Southern match for Nathaniel Ward's *Simple Cobbler*.

TEXT: George Alsop, *A Character of the Province of Maryland*, ed. John G. Shea (Baltimore, 1880).

Emblem of Virtuous Tranquillity

[From *A Character of the Province of Maryland*, 1666]

Here if the lawyer had nothing else to maintain him but his bawling, he might button up his chops, and burn his buckram bag, or else hang it upon a pin until its antiquity had eaten it up with dirt and dust. Then with a spade, like his grandsire Adam, turn up the face of the creation, purchasing his bread by the sweat of his brows, that before was got by the motionated water-works of his jaws. So contrary to the genius of the people, if not to the quiet government of the Province, that the turbulent spirit of continued and vexatious law, with all its quirks and evasions, is openly and most eagerly opposed, that might make matters either dubious, tedious, or troublesome. All other matters that would be ranging in contrary and improper spheres (in short) are here by the power moderated, lowered, and subdued. All villainous outrages that are committed in other states, are not so much as known here. A man may walk in the open woods as secure from being externally dissected, as in his own house or dwelling. So hateful is a robber, that if but once imagined to be so, he's kept at a distance, and shunned as the pestilential noisomeness.

It is generally and very remarkably observed, that those whose lives and conversations have had no other gloss nor glory stampt on them in their own country, but the stigmatization of baseness, were here (by the common civilities and deportments of the inhabitants of this Province) brought to detest and loathe their former actions. . . . Here's no Newgates for pilfering felons, nor Ludgates for debtors, nor any Bridewells to lash the soul of concupiscence into a chaste repentance. For as there is none of these prisons in Maryland, so the merits of the country deserves none, but if any be foully vicious, he is so reserved in it, that he seldom or never becomes popular. Common ale-houses (whose dwellings are the only receptacles of debauchery and baseness, and those schools that trains up youth, as well as age, to ruin), in this Province there are none; neither hath youth his swing or range in such a profuse and unbridled liberty as in other countries; for from an ancient custom at the primitive seating of the place, the son works as well as the servant (an excellent cure for untamed youth), so that before they eat their bread, they are commonly taught how to earn it; which makes them by that time age speaks them capable of receiving that which their parents' indulgency is ready to give them, and which partly is by their own laborious industry purchased, they manage it with such a serious, grave, and watching care, as if they had been masters of families, trained up in that domestic and governing power from their cradles. These Christian natives of the land, especially those of the masculine sex, are generally conveniently confident, reservedly subtle, quick in apprehending, but slow in resolving; and where they spy profit sailing towards them with the wings of a prosperous gale, there they become much familiar. The women differ something in this point, though not much. They are extreme bashful at the first view, but after a continuance of time hath brought them acquainted, there they become discreetly familiar, and are much more talkative than men. All complimental courtships, dressed up in critical rarities, are mere strangers to them, plain wit comes nearest their genius; so that he that intends to court a Maryland girl, must have something more than the tautologies of a long-winded speech to carry on his design, or else he may (for aught I know) fall under the contempt of her frown, and his own windy oration.

One great part of the inhabitants of this Province are desiredly zealous, great pretenders to holiness; and where anything appears that carries on the frontispiece of its effigies the stamp of religion, though fundamentally never so imperfect, they are suddenly taken with it, and out of an eager desire to anything that's new, not weighing the sure matter in the balance of reason, are very apt to be catched. Quakerism is the only opinion that bears the bell away. The Anabaptists have little to say here, as well as in other places, since the ghost of John of Leyden haunts their conventicles. The Adamite, Ranter, and Fifth-Monarchy men, Maryland cannot, nay will not digest within her liberal stomach such corroding morsels: so that this Province is an utter enemy to blasphemous and zealous imprecations, drained from the limbec of hellish and damnable spirits, as well as profuse profaneness, that issues from the prodigality of none but cract-brain sots.

'Tis said the gods lower down that chain above
That ties both prince and subject up in love;
And if this fiction of the gods be true,
Few, Maryland, in this can boast but you:
Live ever blest, and let those clouds that do
Eclipse most states, be always lights to you;
And dwelling so, you may forever be
The only emblem of tranquility.

Robert Beverley (1673?–1722)

BY THE END of the seventeenth century the land and inhabitants of Virginia had been sufficiently mastered to produce for some the fruits of plenty and leisure that Captain John Smith had promised. Men of wealth and land, and of cultivated, aristocratic tastes, were ready to look back proudly upon the accomplishment of the Virginia Colony. But misunderstanding still persisted in England, as Virginia-born, English-educated Robert Beverley discovered in 1703 when he inspected the not-then-published *British Empire in America* by John Oldmixon. Beverley, long familiar with the colony's records, immediately composed *The History and Present State of Virginia* (London, 1705), with the prefatory comment that "I wonder nobody has ever presented the world, with a tolerable account of our *plantations*. Nothing of that kind has yet appeared, except some few general descriptions, that have been calculated more for the benefit of the bookseller, than for the information of mankind." Beverley's judgment was essentially correct, and so his *History* became the first one of the colony by a native. Covering Virginia's remarkable events, natural circumstances, and Indians, the *History*'s most significant portions are those that treat the social activities of his own day and those that discuss — often very harshly — the growing political concern of early eighteenth-century Virginia. The book was translated into French (Paris, Amsterdam, 1707) and revised and enlarged just before Beverley's death.

TEXT: Robert Beverley, *The History and Present State of Virginia,* ed. Louis B. Wright (Chapel Hill, 1947).

Corruptions of a Royal Governor

[From *The History and Present State of Virginia,* 1705]

In November, 1698, Francis Nicholson, Esq., was removed from Maryland, to be Governor of Virginia. But he went not then with that smoothness on his brow, he had carried with him, when he was appointed Lieutenant-Governor. He talked then no more of improving of manufactures, towns, and trade. Neither was he pleased to make the acts of assembly the rule of his judgments, as formerly, but his own all-sufficient will and pleasure. Instead of encouraging the manufactures, he sent over inhuman memorials against them, which were so opposite to all reason, that they refuted themselves. In one of these, he remonstrates, "That the tobacco of that country often bears so low a price, that it will not yield clothes to the people that make it"; and yet presently after, in the same memorial, he recommends it to the parliament, "to pass an act, forbidding the plantations to make their own clothing"; which, in other words, is desiring a charitable law, that the planters shall go naked. In a late memorial concerted between him and his creature, Col. Quarry, 'tis most humbly proposed, "That all the English colonies on the continent of North America, be reduced under one government, and under one Viceroy; and that a standing army be there kept on foot, to subdue the Queen's enemies"; which in plain English, is imploring her majesty, to put the plantations under martial law, and in the consequence, to give the Viceroy a fair opportunity of shaking off his dependence upon England.

He began his government with a pompous shew of zeal for the church; though his practice was not of a piece with his pious pretensions. It must be confessed, that he has bestowed some liberalities upon the clergy, but always upon condition, that they should proclaim his charity, either by signing addresses dictated by himself, in his own commendation, or at least by writing letters of it to the bishops in England. And he would ever be so careful to hinder these representations from miscarrying, that he constantly took copies of them, and sent 'em with his own letters.

He likewise gave himself airs of encouraging the college, but he used this pretext for so many by-ends, that at last the promoters of that good work, grew weary of the mockery. They perceived his view was to gain himself a character, and if he could but raise that, the college might sink. And in truth he has been so far from advancing it, that now after the six years of his government, the scholars are fewer than at his arrival.

Soon after his accession to the government, he caused the assembly and courts of judicature, to be removed from Jamestown, where there were good accommodations for people, to Middle Plantation, where there were none. There he flattered himself with the fond imagination of being the founder of a new city. He marked out the streets in many places, so as that they might represent the figures of a *W*, in memory of his late Majesty King William, after whose name the town was called Williamsburg. There he procured a stately fabric to be erected, which he placed opposite to the college, and graced it with the magnificent name of the "Capitol."

This imaginary city is yet advanced no further, than only to have a few public houses, and a store-house, more than were built upon the place before. And by the frequency of public meetings, and the misfortune of his residence, the students are interrupted in their study, and make less advances than formerly.

To defray the charge of building the Capitol, he suggested the pernicious duty of fifteen shillings for each Christian servant imported, except English, and twenty shillings for each Negro. I call this a pernicious duty, because 'tis a great hindrance to the increase of that young colony, as well as a very unequal tax upon their labor.

It has been the constant maxim of this gentleman to set the people at variance as much as possible amongst themselves. Whether this proceed from his great fondness to the Machiavelian principle, *divide et impera,* or from his exceeding good nature, I won't pretend to determine. But 'tis very certain, that by his management, he has divided the most friendly, and most united people in the world, into very unhappy factions. And, what is still worse, he has been heard to declare publicly to the populace, "That the gentlemen imposed upon them, and that the servants had been all kidnapped, and had a lawful action against their masters."

And that these things may make the more effectual impression, he takes care to vilify the gentlemen of the council in public places, by the grossest and most injurious language. He is frequently pleased to send vexatious commands, to summon people in her Majesty's name, to attend him at some general meeting, and when they come, all the business perhaps he has with them, is to affront them before all the company.

In the General Court, of which he is chief judge, he has often behaved himself in that boisterous manner, that neither the rest of the judges on the bench, nor the lawyers at the bar, could use their just freedom. There 'tis usual with him to fall into excessive passions, and utter the most abusive language against those that presume to oppose his arbitrary proceedings. If the Attorney-General be so scrupulous as to excuse himself from executing his illegal commands, he runs a great risk of being ill used. For in the year 1700, Mr. Fowler, who was then the King's attorney, declining some hard piece of service, as being against law, his Excellency in a fury took him by the collar, and swore, that he knew of no laws they had, and that his commands should be obeyed without hesitation or reserve. He often commits gentlemen to jail, without the least shadow of complaint against them, and that without bail, or mainprise, to the great oppression of the Queen's loyal subjects. Some of those have taken the liberty to tell him, that such proceedings were illegal, and not to be justified in any country, that had the happiness to be governed by the laws of England. To whom he has been heard to reply, "That they had no right at all to the liberties of English subjects, and that he would hang up those that should presume to oppose him, with Magna Charta about their necks."

He often mentions the absolute government of Fez and Morocco with great pleasure, and extols the inhuman cruelties of that prince towards his subjects. And particularly one day at a meeting of the governors of the college; upon some opposition they made against one of his violent proceedings, he vouchsafed to tell them, "That they were dogs, and their wives were bitches; that he knew how to govern the Moors, and would beat them into better manners."

Neither does this gentleman treat the assemblies with more gentleness than particular people; for he has said very publicly, "That he knew how to govern the country without assemblies; and if they should deny him anything, after he had obtained a standing army, he would bring them to reason, with halters about their necks."

But no wonder that he deals so freely with the people there, since neither Her Majesty's instructions, nor the laws of that country can restrain him. Thus he takes upon him to transact matters of the greatest moment, without advice of the Council: as for example, he has appointed several officers, without their advice, which he ought not to do. Sometimes he has brought his orders in his hand, into the Council, and signed them at the board, without so much as acquainting the Council what they were, though at the same time they ought not to pass without their advice; and after he had done this, he ordered the clerk to enter them into the minutes, as if they had been acted by the consent of the Council.

If any of the Council happen to argue, or vote anything contrary to this gentleman's inclinations, he instantly flies out into the most outrageous passions, and treats them with terms very unbecoming his station. By this means he takes away all freedom of debate, and makes the Council of no other use than to palliate his arbitrary practices. Sometimes, when he finds he can't carry matters as he desires, he makes no scruple of entering them in the Council-books by his own authority; he likewise causes many things to be razed out, and others put in, by his own absolute will and pleasure. Nay, sometimes, too, he has caused an abstract of the journals to be sent to England, instead of the journals themselves; by which artifice he leaves out, or puts in, just as much as he thinks fit.

He is very sensible how unwarrantable and unjust these proceedings are, and therefore has been always jealous, lest some of the many that have been injured, should send over their complaints to England. This has put him upon a practice most destructive to all trade and correspondence, which is, the intercepting, and breaking open of letters. His method was, to give directions to some of his creatures, dwelling near the mouths of the rivers, to send on board the several ships, that happened to arrive, and in the Governor's name demand the letters. Thus he used to get them, and open as many as he thought fit, after which sometimes he would cause 'em to be sent where they were directed, and sometimes keep them. By this management many people have not only suffered the loss of their letters, and of their accounts, invoices, etc., but likewise have missed great advantages, for want of timely advice, occasioned by the stopping of their letters.

Another effect of his jealousy was, to set spies upon such people, as he suspected. These were to give him an account of all the words and actions of those which were most likely to complain. Nay, his Excellency has condescended to act the low part of an eves-dropper himself, and to stand under a window to listen for secrets, that would certainly displease him. This practice has made every man afraid of his neighbor, and destroyed the mutual confidence of the dearest friends.

But the most extraordinary method of learning secrets, that ever was used in an English government, was a kind of inquisition, which this gentleman has been pleased to erect frequently in that country. He would call courts at unusual times, to inquire into the life, and conversation of those persons, that had the misfortune to be out of his favor; though there was not the least public accusation against them. To these courts he summoned all the neighbors of the party he intended to expose, especially those that he knew were most intimate with him. Upon their appearance, he administered an oath to them, to answer truly, to all such interrogatories as he should propose. Then he would ask them endless questions, concerning the particular discourse and behavior of the party, in order to find out something that might be the ground of an accusation. . . .

Of Recreations and Pastimes

[From the same]

For their recreation, the plantations, orchards, and gardens constantly afford 'em fragrant and delightful walks. In their woods and fields, they have an unknown variety of vegetables, and other rarities of nature to discover and observe. They have hunting, fishing, and fowling, with which they entertain themselves an hundred ways. Here is the most good nature and hospitality practiced in the world, both towards friends and strangers; but the worst of it is, this generosity is attended now and then, with a little too much intemperance. The neighborhood is at much the same distance, as in the country in England; but with this advantage, that all the better sort of people have been abroad, and seen the world, by which means they are free from that stiffness and formality, which discover more civility, than kindness. And besides, the goodness of the roads, and the fairness of the weather, bring people oftener together.

The Indians . . . had in their hunting, a way of concealing themselves, and coming up to the deer, under the blind of a stalking-head, in imitation of which, many people have taught their horses to stalk it, that is, to walk gently by the huntsman's side, to cover him from the sight of the deer. Others cut down trees for the deer to browse upon, and lie in wait behind them. Others again set stakes, at a certain distance within their fences, where the deer have been used to leap over into a field of peas, which they love extremely; these stakes they so place, as to run into the body of the deer, when he pitches, by which means they impale him.

They hunt their hares (which are very numerous) a-foot, with mongrels or swift dogs, which either catch them quickly, or force them to hole in a hollow tree, whither all their hares generally tend, when they are closely pursued. As soon as they are thus holed, and have crawled up into the body of the tree, the business is to kindle a fire, and smother them with smoke, till they let go their hold, and fall to the bottom stifled; from whence they take them. If they have a mind to spare their lives, upon turning them loose, they will be as fit as ever to hunt at another time; for the mischief done them by the smoke, immediately wears off again.

They have another sort of hunting, which is very diverting, and that they call vermin-hunting; it is performed a-foot, with small dogs in the night, by the light of the moon or stars. Thus in summer time they find abundance of raccoons, opossums, and foxes in the cornfields, and about their plantations; but at other times, they must go into the woods for them. The method is to go out with three or four dogs, and as soon as they come to the place, they bid the dogs seek out, and all the company follow immediately. Wherever a dog barks, you may depend upon finding the game; and this alarm draws both men and dogs that way. If this sport be in the woods, the game by that time you come near it is perhaps mounted to the top of an high tree, and then they detach a nimble fellow up after it, who must have a scuffle with the beast, before he can throw it down to the dogs; and then the sport increases, to see the vermin encounter those little curs. In this sort of hunting, they also carry their great dogs out with them, because wolves, bears, panthers, wild cats, and all other beasts of prey, are abroad in the night.

For wolves they make traps, and set guns baited in the woods, so that, when he offers to seize the bait, he pulls the trigger, and the gun discharges upon him. What Elian and Pliny write, of the horses benumbed in their legs, if they tread in the track of a wolf, does not hold good here; for I myself, and many others, have rid full speed after wolves in the woods, and have seen live ones taken out of a trap, and dragged at a horse's tail; and yet those that followed on horse-back have not perceived any of their horses to falter in their pace. . . .

There is yet another kind of sport, which the young people take great delight in, and that is, the hunting of wild horses; which they pursue sometimes with dogs, and sometimes without. You must know they have many horses foaled in the woods of the uplands, that never were in hand, and are as shy as any savage creature. These having no mark upon them belong to him that first takes them. However, the captor commonly purchases these horses very dear, by spoiling better in the pursuit; in which case he has little to make himself amends, besides the pleasure of the chase. And very often this is all he has for it, for the wild horses are so swift, that 'tis difficult to catch them; and when they are taken, 'tis odds but their grease is melted, or else being old, they are so sullen, that they can't be tamed.

The inhabitants are very courteous to travelers, who need no other recommendation, but the being human creatures. A stranger has no more to do, but to inquire upon the road, where any gentleman or good housekeeper lives, and there he may depend upon being received with hospitality. This good nature is so general among their people, that the gentry when they go abroad, order their principal servant to entertain all visitors, with everything the plantation affords. And the poor planters, who have but one bed, will very often sit up, or lie upon a form or couch all night, to make room for a weary traveler to repose himself after his journey.

If there happen to be a churl, that either out of covetousness, or ill nature, won't comply with this generous custom, he has a mark of infamy set upon him, and is abhorred by all. But I must confess (and am heartily sorry for the occasion), that this good neighborhood has of late been much depraved by the present Governor, who practices the detestable politics of governing by parties; by which, feuds and heart-burnings have been kindled in the minds of the people; and friendship, hospitality, and good-neighborhood have been extremely discouraged.

William Bradford (1588–1657)

William Bradford was born in Yorkshire, England, into a farming family. After his parents' death he was raised by William Brewster, who later became an elder of the Plymouth colony, and was converted to the Separatist sect. A weaver by trade, Bradford educated himself by rigorous study and wide reading. He emigrated to Holland with the Separatists in 1609, and, despite his comparative youth, soon emerged as one of the group's most respected leaders. He was among those who urged removal to America, and was instrumental in planning the *Mayflower's* voyage. When Governor John Carver died a few months after the Plymouth landing, Bradford was chosen to succeed him. For the rest of his life he virtually ran the colony, organizing its fishing and fur trade, supervising its agriculture and finances, negotiating its treaties with the Indians, and handling all its relations with other colonies and with England. He was re-elected Governor thirty times, and for a number of years also served as the colony's judge and treasurer.

Shortly after landing at Plymouth in 1620, Bradford started a journal of daily happenings in the colony, which became the basis for his *Of Plymouth Plantation,* begun about 1630. Though aiming at the "simple truth" in all things, Bradford found that truth implied in the pages of John Foxe's *Actes and Monuments,* seeing the Separatists as the people chosen of God to carry His truth ever westward in what Foxe called an age of "trial and travail." Bradford therefore set out to demonstrate America's manifest destiny through a careful selection of events and the conscious manipulation of a plain, dignified, unpretentious, and often very gripping style. His constant intent to illustrate God's providence supporting the grand venture provides insight into the Puritan mind as well as information about daily life in the Plymouth colony. The manuscript of Bradford's history, which disappeared presumably during the British occupation of Boston in the Revolutionary War, was discovered in the library of the Bishop of London in 1855 and was finally published by the Massachusetts Historical Society in 1856.

Text: William Bradford, *History of Plymouth Plantation,* ed. Worthington C. Ford (Boston, 1912), Vol. I.

The Voyage of the Mayflower

[From *Of Plymouth Plantation*]

Now all being compact together in one ship, they put to sea again with a prosperous wind, which continued divers days together, which was some encouragement unto them; yet, according to the usual manner, many were afflicted with seasickness. And I may not omit here a special work of God's providence. There was a proud and very profane young man, one of the seamen, of a lusty, able body, which made him the more haughty; he would alway be contemning the poor people in their sickness and cursing them daily with grievous execrations, and did not let to tell them that he hoped to help to cast half of them overboard before they came to their journey's end, and to make merry with what they had; and if he were by any gently reproved, he would curse and swear most bitterly. But it pleased God before they came half seas over, to smite this young man with a grievous disease, of which he died in a desperate manner, and so was himself the first that was thrown overboard. Thus his curses light on his own head, and it was an astonishment to all his fellows for they noted it to be the just hand of God upon him.

After they had enjoyed fair winds and weather for a season, they were encountered many times with cross winds and met with fierce storms with which the ship was shroudly shaken, and her upper works made very leaky; and one of the main beams in the midships was bowed and cracked, which put them in some fear that the ship could not be able to perform the voyage. So some of the chief of the company, perceiving the mariners to fear the sufficiency of the ship as appeared by their mutterings, they entered into serious consultation with the master and other officers of the ship, to consider in time of the danger, and rather to return then to cast themselves into a desperate and inevitable peril. And truly there was great distraction and difference of opinion amongst the mariners themselves; fain would they do what could be done for their wages' sake (being now near half the seas over) and on the other hand they were loath to hazard their lives too desperately. But in examining of all opinions, the master and others affirmed they knew the ship to be strong and firm under water; and for the buckling of the main beam, there was a great iron screw the passengers brought out of Holland, which would raise the beam into his place; the which being done, the carpenter and master affirmed that with a post put under it, set firm in the lower deck and otherways bound, he would make it sufficient. And as for the decks and upper works, they would caulk them as well as they could, and though with the working of the ship they would not long keep staunch, yet there would otherwise be no great danger, if they did not overpress her with sails. So they committed themselves to the will of God and resolved to proceed.

In sundry of these storms the winds were so fierce and the seas so high, as they could not bear a knot of sail, but were forced to hull for divers days together. And in one of them, as they thus lay at hull in a mighty storm, a lusty young man called John Howland, coming upon some occasion above the gratings, was, with a seele of the ship, thrown into sea; but it pleased God that he caught hold of the topsail halyards which hung overboard and ran out at length. Yet he held his hold (though he was sundry fathoms under water) till he was hauled up by the same rope to the brim of the water, and then with a boat hook and other means got into the ship again and his life saved. And though he was something ill with it, yet he lived many years after and became a profitable member both in church and commonwealth. In all this voyage there died but one of the passengers, which was William Butten, a youth, servant to Samuel Fuller, when they drew near the coast.

But to omit other things (that I may be brief), after long beating at sea they fell with that land which is called Cape Cod; the which being made and certainly known to be it, they were not a little joyful. After some deliberation had amongst themselves and with the master of the ship, they tacked about and resolved to stand for the southward (the wind and weather being fair) to find some place about Hudson's River for their habitation. But after they had sailed that course about half the day, they fell amongst dangerous shoals and roaring breakers, and they were so far entangled therewith as they conceived themselves in great danger; and the wind shrinking upon them withal, they resolved to bear up again for the Cape and thought themselves happy to get out of those dangers before night overtook them, as by God's good providence they did. And the next day they got into the cape harbor where they rid in safety. . . .

Being thus arrived in a good harbor, and brought safe to land, they fell upon their knees and blessed the God of heaven who had brought them over the vast and furious ocean, and delivered them from all the perils and miseries thereof, again to set their feet on the firm and stable earth, their proper element. And no marvel if they were thus joyful, seeing wise Seneca was so affected with sailing a few miles on the coast of his own Italy, as he affirmed,[1] that he had rather remain twenty years on his way by land then pass by sea to any place in a short time, so tedious and dreadful was the same unto him.

[1] Epistle 53 [*ad Lucilium Epistulæ Morales;* Bradford's note]

But here I cannot but stay and make a pause, and stand half amazed at this poor people's present condition; and so I think will the reader, too, when he well considers the same. Being thus passed the vast ocean, and a sea of troubles before in their preparation (as may be remembered by that which went before), they had now no friends to welcome them nor inns to entertain or refresh their weatherbeaten bodies; no houses or much less towns to repair to, to seek for succor. It is recorded in scripture, as a mercy to the Apostle and his shipwrecked company, that the barbarians shewed them no small kindness in refreshing them, but these savage barbarians, when they met with them (as after will appear), were readier to fill their sides full of arrows then otherwise. And for the season it was winter, and they that know the winters of that country know them to be sharp and violent, and subject to cruel and fierce storms, dangerous to travel to known places, much more to search an unknown coast. Besides, what could they see but a hideous and desolate wilderness, full of wild beasts and wild men — and what multitudes there might be of them they knew not. Neither could they, as it were, go up to the top of Pisgah to view from this wilderness a more goodly country to feed their hopes; for which way soever they turned their eyes (save upward to the heavens) they could have little solace or content in respect of any outward objects. For summer being done, all things stand upon them with a weatherbeaten face, and the whole country, full of woods and thickets, represented a wild and savage hue. If they looked behind them, there was the mighty ocean which they had passed and was now as a main bar and gulf to separate them from all the civil parts of the world. If it be said they had a ship to succor them, it is true; but what heard they daily from the master and company? But that with speed they should look out a place (with their shallop) where they would be, at some near distance; for the season was such as he would not stir from thence till a safe harbor was discovered by them, where they would be, and he might go without danger; and that victuals consumed apace but he must and would keep sufficient for themselves and their return. Yea, it was muttered by some that if they got not a place in time, they would turn them and their goods ashore and leave them. Let it also be considered what weak hopes of supply and succor they left behind them, that might bear up their minds in this sad condition and trials they were under; and they could not but be very small. It is true, indeed, the affections and love of their brethren at Leyden was cordial and entire towards them, but they had little power to help them or themselves; and how the case stood between them and the merchants at their coming away hath already been declared. What could now sustain them but the Spirit of God and His grace? May not and ought not the children of these fathers rightly say: "Our fathers were Englishmen which came over this great ocean, and were ready to perish in this wilderness; but they cried unto the Lord, and He heard their voice and looked on their adversity," etc. "Let them therefore praise the Lord, because He is good: and His mercies endure forever." "Yea, let them which have been redeemed of the Lord, shew how He hath delivered them from the hand of the oppressor. When they wandered in the desert wilderness out of the way, and found no city to dwell in, both hungry and thirsty, their soul was overwhelmed in them. Let them confess before the Lord His lovingkindness and His wonderful works before the sons of men."

The Mayflower Covenant and the First Indian Treaty

[From the same]

[1620] I shall a little return back, and begin with a combination made by them before they came ashore; being the first foundation of their government in this place. Occasioned partly by the discontented and mutinous speeches that some of the strangers amongst them had let fall from them in the ship, that when they came ashore they would use their own liberty, for none had power to command them, the patent they had being for Virginia and not for New England, which belonged to another government, with which the Virginia Company had nothing to do. And partly that such an act by them done, this their condition considered, might be as firm as any patent, and in some respects more sure.

The form was as followeth:

In the name of God, Amen. We whose names are underwritten, the loyal subjects of our dread sovereign lord, King James, by the grace of God of Great Britain, France, and Ireland, king, defender of the faith, etc.

Having undertaken, for the glory of God and advancement of the Christian faith and honor of our king and country, a voyage to plant the first colony in the northern parts of Virginia, do by these presents solemnly and mutually in the presence of God and one of another, covenant and combine ourselves together into a civil body politic, for our better ordering and preservation and furtherance of the ends aforesaid; and by virtue hereof to enact, constitute, and frame such just and equal laws, ordinances, acts, constitutions, and offices, from time to time, as shall be thought most meet and convenient for the general good of the colony, unto which we promise all due submission and obedience. In witness whereof we have hereunder subscribed our names at Cape Cod, the 11th of November, in the year of the reign of our sovereign lord, King James, of England, France and Ireland the eighteenth, and of Scotland the fifty-fourth. *Anno Domini* 1620.

After this they chose, or rather confirmed, Mr. John Carver (a man godly and well approved amongst them) their governor for that year. And after they had provided a place for their goods, or common store (which were long in unlading for want of boats, foulness of the winter weather and sickness of divers), and begun some small cottages for their habitation, as time would admit, they met and consulted of laws and orders, both for their civil and military government as the necessity of their condition did require, still adding thereunto as urgent occasion in several times, and as cases did require.

In these hard and difficult beginnings they found some discontents and murmurings arise amongst some, and mutinous speeches and carriages in other; but they were soon quelled and overcome by the wisdom, patience, and just and equal carriage of things, by the Governor and better part, which clave faithfully together in the main. But that which was most sad and lamentable was, that in two or three months' time half of their company died, especially in January and February, being the depth of winter, and wanting houses and other comforts; being infected with the scurvy and other diseases which this long voyage and their inaccommodate condition had brought upon them. So as there died sometimes two or three of a day in the foresaid time, that of one hundred and odd persons, scarce fifty remained. And of these, in the time of most distress, there was but six or seven sound persons who to their great commendations, be it spoken, spared no pains night nor day, but with abundance of toil and hazard of their own health, fetched them wood, made them fires, dressed them meat, made their beds, washed their loathsome clothes, clothed and unclothed them. In a word, did all the homely and necessary offices for them which dainty and queasy stomachs cannot endure to hear named; and all this willingly and cheerfully, without any grudging in the least, shewing herein their true love unto their friends and brethren; a rare example and worthy to be remembered. Two of these seven were Mr. William Brewster, their reverend elder, and Myles Standish, their captain and military commander, unto whom myself and many others were much beholden in our low and sick condition. And yet the Lord so upheld these persons as in this general calamity they were not at all infected either with sickness or lameness. And what I have said of these I may say of many others who died in this general visitation, and others yet living; that whilst they had health, yea, or any strength continuing, they were not wanting to any that had need of them. And I doubt not but their recompense is with the Lord.

. . . .

All this while the Indians came skulking about them, and would sometimes show themselves aloof off, but when any approached near them, they would run away. And once they stole away their tools where they had been at work and were gone to dinner. But about the 16th of March, a certain Indian came boldly amongst them and spoke to them in broken English, which they could well understand, but marveled at it. At length they understood by discourse with him, that he was not of these parts, but belonged to the eastern parts where some English ships came to fish, with whom he was acquainted and could name sundry of them by their names, amongst whom he had got his language. He became most profitable to them in acquainting them with many things concerning the state of the country in the east parts where he lived, which was afterwards profitable unto them; as also of the people here, of their names, number, and strength, of their situation and distance from this place, and who was chief amongst them. His name was Samoset; he told them also of another Indian whose name was Squanto, a native of this place, who had been in England and could speak better English than himself. Being, after some time of entertainment and gifts dismissed, a while after he came again, and five more with him, and they brought again all the tools that were stolen away before, and made way for the coming of their great Sachem, called Massasoit, who, about four or five days after, came with the chief of his friends and other attendants, with the aforesaid Squanto. With whom, after friendly entertainment and some gifts given him, they made a peace with him (which hath now continued this twenty-four years) in these terms.

1. That neither he nor any of his should injure or do hurt to any of their people.

2. That if any of his did any hurt to any of theirs, he should send the offender, that they might punish him.

3. That if anything were taken away from any of theirs, he should cause it to be restored; and they should do the like to his.

4. That if any did unjustly war against him, they would aid him; if any did war against them, he should aid them.

5. He should send to his neighbors confederates to certify them of this, that they might not wrong them, but might be likewise comprised in the conditions of peace.

6. That when their men came to them, they should leave their bows and arrows behind them.

Edward Johnson (1598–1672)

THE FIRST published history of New England appeared under the title *A History of New England* in London, 1653. Although it was published anonymously, everyone knew that its author was Captain Edward Johnson, founder of Woburn, Massachusetts. Johnson had arrived in New England in 1630, probably in the same ship with Governor John Winthrop. By trade a ship's carpenter, Johnson rose to a position of respect in the colonial militia and government, knew the problems and the development of Massachusetts Bay at first hand, and undertook in 1650 to declare the fruits as well as the trials of the Puritans' holy experiment in America in epic terms. His running-title, *The Wonder-Working Providence of Sion's Saviour in New England,* by which the *History* is better known, betrays Johnson's main purpose. Like Bradford, Johnson sees his people as particularly called of God to conquer the wilderness; but Johnson has a much higher dramatic sense and a greater willingness to express it. Indeed the opening of the book is a long but lively proclamation, supposedly by Christ, literally calling true English Christians to New England: "see that with all diligence you encourage every soldier-like spirit among you, for the Lord Christ intends to achieve greater matters by this little handful than the world is aware of."

The work is divided into three books: the first from the beginnings to 1636; the second from the Pequot War to 1644; and the last from 1645 to 1651. Johnson invents typical scenes and feigns speeches, but does a completely honest job of tracing the spirit of the times he describes. He mingles the sentimental with the heroic, and terse understated description with inflated rhetoric and very awkward verses. The resulting comments on churches and towns, education and Indians, heretics and heroes make one of the most colorful books in colonial history.

TEXT: Edward Johnson, *The Wonder-Working Providence,* ed. William F. Poole (Andover, Mass., 1867).

Leaving England

[From *The Wonder-Working Providence*, 1653]

And now behold the several regiments of these soldiers of Christ, as they are shipped for His service in the western world, part thereof being come to the town and port of Southampton in England, where they were to be shipped, that they might prosecute this design to the full. One ship called the *Eagle,* they wholly purchase, and many more they hire, filling them with the seed of man and beast to sow this yet untilled wilderness withal, making sale of such land as they possess, to the great admiration of their friends and acquaintance, who thus expostulate with them, "What, will not the large income of your yearly revenue content you, which in all reason cannot choose but be more advantageous both to you and yours, then all that rocky wilderness, whither you are going, to run the hazard of your life? Have you not here your tables filled with great variety of food, your coffers filled with coin, your houses beautifully built and filled with all rich furniture? (Or otherwise) have you not such a gainful trade as none the like in the town where you live? Are you not enriched daily? Are not your children very well provided for as they come to years? (Nay) may you not here as pithily practice the two chief duties of a Christian (if Christ give strength), namely mortification and sanctification, as in any place of the world? What helps can you have there that you must not carry from hence?" With bold resolvedness these stout soldiers of Christ reply: "As Death, the king of terror, with all his dreadful attendance, inhuman and barbarous tortures, doubled and trebled by all the infernal furies, have appeared but light and momentary to the soldiers of Christ Jesus, so also the pleasure, profits, and honors of this world, set forth in their most glorious splendor and magnitude by alluring Lady of Delight, proffering pleasant embraces, cannot entice with her syren songs such soldiers of Christ, whose aims are elevated by Him many millions above that brave warrior Ulysses."

Now seeing all can be said will but barely set forth the immovable resolutions that Christ continued in these men, pass on and attend with tears, if thou hast any, the following discourse, while these men, women, and children are taking their last farewell of their native country, kindred, friends, and acquaintance, while the ships attend them. Many make choice of some solitary place to echo out their bowel-breaking affections in bidding their friends farewell. "Dear friends" (says one), "as near as my own soul doth thy love lodge in my breast, with thought of the heart-burning ravishments, that thy heavenly speeches have wrought; my melting soul is poured out at present with these words." Both of them had their farther speech strangled from the depth of their inward dolor, with breast-breaking sobs, till leaning their heads each on other's shoulders, they let fall the salt-dropping dews of vehement affection, striving to exceed one another, much like the departure of David and Jonathan. Having a little eased their hearts with the still streams of tears, they recovered speech again. "Ah! my much honored friend, hath Christ given thee so great a charge as to be leader of His people into that far remote and vast wilderness? Ay, oh, and alas! thou must die there and never shall I see thy face in the flesh again! Wert thou called to so great a task as to pass the precious ocean, and hazard thy person in battle against thousands of malignant enemies there, there were hopes of thy return with triumph; but now after two, three, or four moneths spent with daily expectation of swallowing waves and cruel pirates, you are to be landed among barbarous Indians, famous for nothing but cruelty, where you are like to spend your days in a famishing condition for a long space." Scarce had he uttered this, but presently he locks his friend fast in his arms; holding each other thus for some space of time, they weep again. But, as Paul to his beloved flock, the other replies: "What do you, weeping and breaking my heart? I am now prest for the service of our Lord Christ, to rebuild the most glorious edifice of Mount Sion in a wilderness, and as John Baptist, I must cry, 'prepare ye the way of the Lord, make His paths straight,' for behold He is coming again, He is coming to destroy Antichrist, and give the whore double to drink the very dregs of His wrath. Then my dear friend unfold thy hands, for thou and I have much work to do — aye, and all Christian soldiers the world throughout."

Then hand in hand they lead each other to the sandy banks of the brinish ocean, when clenching their hands fast, they unloose not till enforced to wipe their watery eyes, whose constant streams forced a watery path upon their cheeks, which to hide from the eyes of others they shun society for a time, but being called by Occasion, whose bald back part none can lay hold on, they thrust in among the throng now ready to take ship, where they beheld the like affections with their own among divers relations. Husbands and wives with mutual consent are now purposed to part for a time nine hundred leagues asunder, since some providence at present will not suffer them to go together; they resolve their tender affections shall not hinder this work of Christ. The new married and betrothed man, exempt by the law of God from war, now will not claim their privilege, but being constrained by the love of Christ, lock up their natural affections for a time, till the Lord shall be pleased to give them a meeting in this western world, sweetly mixing it with spiritual love in the meantime. Many fathers now take their young Samuels, and give them to this service of Christ all their lives. Brethren, sisters, uncles, nephews, nieces, together with all kindred of blood that binds the bowels of affection in a true lover's knot, can now take their last farewell, each of other, although natural affection will still claim her right, and manifest herself to be in the body by looking out at the windows in a mournful manner. Among this company, thus disposed, doth many reverend and godly pastors of Christ present themselves, some in a seaman's habit, and their scattered sheep coming as a poor convoy loftily to take their leave of them as followeth: "What doleful days are these, when the best choice our orthodox ministers can make is to take up a perpetual banishment from their native soil, together with their wives and children; we their poor sheep they may not feed, but by stoledred should they abide here. Lord Christ, here they are at thy command, they go; this is the door thou hast opened upon our earnest request, and we hope it shall never be shut; for England's sake they are going from England to pray without ceasing for England, O England! Thou shalt find New England prayers prevailing with their God for thee, but now woe alas, what great hardship must these our endeared pastors endure for a long season!"

With these words they lift up their voices and wept, adding many drops of salt liquor to the ebbing ocean. . . .

Providence in Need

[From the same]

Those honored persons who were now in place of government, having the propagation of the churches of Christ in their eye, labored by all means to make room for inhabitants, knowing well that where the dead carcass is, thither will the eagles resort. But herein they were much opposed by certain persons, whose greedy desire for land much hindered the work for a time, as indeed all such persons do at this very day, and let such take notice how these were cured of this distemper. Some were taken away by death, and then to be sure they had land enough; others fearing poverty and famishment, supposing the present scarcity would never be turned into plenty, removed themselves away, and so never beheld the great good the Lord hath done for His people. But the valiant of the Lord waited with patience, and in the miss of beer supplied themselves with water, even the most honored, as well as others, contentedly rejoicing in a cup of cold water, blessing the Lord that had given them the taste of that living water, and that they had not the water that slacks the thirst of their natural bodies, given them by measure, but might drink to the full; as also in the absence of bread they feasted themselves with fish. The women once a day, as the tide gave way, resorted to the mussels, and clambanks, which are a fish as big as horse-mussels, where they daily gathered their families' food with much heavenly discourse of the provisions Christ had formerly made for many thousands of His followers in the wilderness. Quoth one, "My husband hath traveled as far as Plymouth (which is near forty miles), and hath with great toil brought a little corn home with him, and before that is spent the Lord will assuredly provide." Quoth the other, "Our last peck of meal is now in the oven at home abaking, and many of our godly neighbors have spent all, and we owe one loaf of that little we have." Then spake a third, "My husband hath ventured himself among the Indians for corn, and can get none, as also our honored Governor hath distributed his so far, that a day or two more will put an end to his store, and all the rest, and yet methinks our children are as cheerful, fat, and lusty with feeding upon those mussels, clambanks, and other fish, as they were in England, with their fill of bread, which makes me cheerful in the Lord's providing for us, being further confirmed by the exhortation of our pastor to trust the Lord with providing for us; whose is the earth and the fulness thereof." And as they were encouraging one another in Christ's careful providing for them, they lift up their eyes and saw two ships coming in, and presently this news came to their ears, that they were come from Jacland full of victuals. Now their poor hearts were not so much refreshed in regard of the food they saw they were like to have, as their souls rejoiced in that Christ would now manifest himself to be the Commisary-General of this His army, and that He should honor them so far as to be poor sutlers for His camp. They soon up with their mussels, and hie them home to stay their hungry stomachs. After this manner did Christ many times graciously provide for this His people, even at the last cast.

Thomas Tillam (*fl.* c. 1660–1670)

THOMAS TILLAM was a Puritan seeking an ideal, utopian society, and perhaps came to New England in 1638 in hopes of finding the perfect state. For unknown reasons he returned to England, flourished there as pastor to a number of churches (1661–67), and finally moved with his followers to a German communal society. This verse, recently published from manuscript, reflects the same blending of enthusiastic dedication and sense of hardship that marks Edward Johnson's *Wonder-Working Providence.* Tillam also wrote a hymn to the Lord's Day in his *The Seventh-Day Sabbath Sought Out and Celebrated* (London, 1657).

TEXT: Harold S. Jantz, "The First Century of New England Verse," *Proceedings of the American Antiquarian Society,* LIII:2 (October 1943), 331.

Upon the First Sight of New England

June 29, 1638

Hail, holy-land, wherein our Holy Lord
Hath planted His most true and Holy Word;
Hail, happy people, who have dispossest
Yourselves of friends, and means, to find some rest
For your poor wearied souls, opprest of late
For Jesus' sake, with envy, spite, and hate,
To you that blessed promise truly's given,
Of sure reward, which you'll receive in heaven.
Methinks I hear the Lamb of God thus speak:
"Come, my dear little flock, who for my sake
Have left your country, dearest friends, and goods,
And hazarded your lives o' th' raging floods;
Possess this country, free from all annoy;
Here I'll be with you, here you shall injoy
My sabbaths, sacraments, my ministry,
And ordinances in their purity;
But yet beware of Sathan's wily baits,
He lurks amongst you, cunningly he waits
To catch you from me; live not then secure,
But fight 'gainst sin, and let your lives be pure;
Prepare to hear your sentence thus expressed,
Come ye, my servants, of my Father blessed."

William Penn (1644–1718)

PENN's father, Sir William Penn, was an admiral of the Royal Navy and a friend of the powerful Duke of York. William was educated at Oxford, at a Huguenot academy in France, and in law at Lincoln's Inn, London. While serving as overseer of his father's estates in Ireland, he was converted to the Quaker faith, and on his return to England he was arrested and imprisoned several times for his writings in defense of his faith. In 1670 he inherited his father's estates and a sizable fortune. He bought into the West New Jersey colonization enterprise and in 1681 was granted the province of Pennsylvania by Charles II in payment of a debt owed his father by the Crown — the most valuable single grant ever made to an individual in America. The following year he arrived in America himself to oversee his new acquisition. While there he observed with great interest both the land and its inhabitants, communicating his enthusiasm in the following report (1683), which, especially in its description of Philadelphia, anticipates the writing of Benjamin Franklin and Charles Brockden Brown. Penn went back to England in 1684; accused of treason, he lost the colony from 1692 to 1694; and he returned to Pennsylvania only once more, for two years (1699–1701), before his death.

TEXT: *A Collection of the Works of William Penn* (London, 1726), Vol. I.

A Description of Pennsylvania

[From a letter *To the Committee of the Free Society of Traders,* 1683]

My Kind Friends;

The kindness of yours by the ship *Thomas and Anne,* doth much oblige me; for by it I perceive the interest you take in my health and reputation, and the prosperous beginnings of this Province, which you are so kind as to think may much depend upon them. In return of which, I have sent you a long letter, and yet containing as brief an account of myself, and the affairs of this Province, as I have been able to make.

In the first place, I take notice of the news you sent me, whereby I find some persons have had so little wit, and so much malice, as to report my death, and to mend the matter, dead a Jesuit too. One might have reasonably hoped, that this distance, like death, would have been a protection against spite and envy; and indeed, absence being a kind of death, ought alike to secure the name of the absent as the dead; because they are equally unable, as such, to defend themselves: but they that intend mischief, do not use to follow good rules to effect it. However, to the great sorrow and shame of the inventors, I am still alive, and no Jesuit, and I thank God, very well. And without injustice to the authors of this, I may venture to infer, that they that wilfully and falsely report, would have been glad it had been so. But I perceive many frivolous and idle stories have been invented since my departure from England, which, perhaps, at this time, are no more alive, than I am dead.

But if I have been unkindly used by some I left behind me, I found love and respect enough where I came; an universal kind welcome, every sort in their way. For here are some of several nations, as well as divers judgments: nor were the natives wanting in this, for their kings, queens, and great men, both visited and presented me; to whom I made suitable returns, etc.

For the Province, the general condition of it take as followeth.

I. The country itself in its soil, air, water, seasons, and produce, both natural and artificial, is not to be despised. The land containeth divers sorts of earth, as sand yellow and black, poor and rich: also gravel, both loamy and dusty; and in some places a fast fat earth, like to our best vales in England, especially by inland brooks and rivers, God in His wisdom having ordered it so, that the advantages of the country are divided, the backlands being generally three to one richer, than those that lie by navigable waters. We have much of another soil, and that is a black hazel mould, upon a stony or rocky bottom.

II. The air is sweet and clear, the heavens serene, like the South-parts of France, rarely overcast; and as the woods come by numbers of people to be more cleared, that itself will refine.

III. The waters are generally good, for the rivers and brooks have mostly gravel and stony bottoms, and in number hardly credible. We have also mineral waters, that operate in the same manner with Barnet and North-hall, not two miles from Philadelphia.

IV. For the seasons of the year, having by God's goodness now lived over the coldest and hottest, that the oldest liver in the Province can remember, I can say something to an English understanding.

First, Of the fall, for then I came in: I found it from the 24th of October, to the beginning of December, as we have it usually in England in September, or rather like an English mild spring. From December to the beginning of the month called March, we had sharp frosty weather; not foul, thick, black weather, as our North-East winds bring with them in England; but a sky as clear as in summer, and the air dry, cold, piercing, and hungry; yet I remember not, that I wore more clothes than in England. The reason of this cold is given, from the great lakes that are fed by the fountains of Canada. The winter before was as mild, scarce any ice at all; while this, for a few days, froze up our great River Delaware. From that month to the month called June, we enjoyed a sweet spring, no gusts, but gentle showers, and a fine sky. Yet this I observe, that the winds here, as there, are more inconstant spring and fall, upon that turn of nature, than in summer or winter. From thence to this present month, which endeth the summer (commonly speaking), we have had extraordinary heats, yet mitigated sometimes by cool breezes. The wind that ruleth the summer season, is the South-West; but spring, fall, and winter, 'tis rare to want the wholesome North Wester seven days together: and whatever mists, fogs, or vapors foul the heavens by Easterly or Southerly winds, in two hours' time are blown away; the one is followed by the other: a remedy that seems to have a peculiar providence in it to the inhabitants; the multitude of trees, yet standing, being liable to retain mists and vapors, and yet not one quarter so thick as I expected.

. . . .

XI. The natives I shall consider in their persons, language, manners, religion, and government, with my sense of their original. For their persons, they are generally tall, straight, well-built, and of singular proportion; they tread strong and clever, and mostly walk with a lofty chin. Of complection, black, but by design, as the Gypsies in England; they grease themselves with bear's-fat clarified, and using no defense against sun or weather, their skins must needs be swarthy; their eye is little and black, not unlike a straight-looked Jew. The thick lip and flat nose, so frequent with East-Indians and Blacks, are not common to them; for I have seen as comely European-like faces among them of both, as on your side the sea; and truly an Italian complection hath not much more of the White, and the noses of several of them have as much of the Roman.

XII. Their language is lofty, yet narrow, but like the Hebrew; in signification full, like short-hand in writing; one word serveth in the place of three, and the rest are supplied by the understanding of the hearer: imperfect in their tenses, wanting in their moods, participles, adverbs, conjunctions, interjections: I have made it my business to understand it, that I might not want an interpreter on any occasion: and I must say, that I know not a language spoken in Europe, that hath words of more sweetness or greatness, in accent and emphasis, than theirs; for instance, *Octorockon, Rancocas, Ozicton, Shakamacon, Poquerim,* all of which are names of places, and have grandeur in them. Of words of sweetness, *anna,* is mother; *issimus,* a brother; *netap,* friend; *usque ozet,* very good; *pone,* bread; *metse,* eat; *matta,* no; *hatta,* to have; *payo,* to come; *Sepassen, Passijon,* the names of places; *Tamane, Secane, Menanse, Secatereus,* are the names of persons. If one ask them for anything they have not, they will answer, *mattá ne hattá,* which to translate is, "not I have," instead of "I have not." . . .

XVIII. They are great concealers of their own resentments, brought to it, I believe, by the revenge that hath been practiced among them; in either of these, they are not exceeded by the Italians. A tragical instance fell out since I came into the country; a king's daughter thinking herself slighted by her husband, in suffering another woman to lie down between them, rose up, went out, plucked a root out of the ground, and ate it, upon which she immediately died; and for which, last week, he made an offering to her kindred, for atonement, and liberty of marriage; as two others did to the kindred of their wives, that died a natural death: for till widowers have done so, they must not marry again. Some of the young women are said to take undue liberty before marriage, for a portion; but when married, chaste; when with child, they know their husbands no more, till delivered; and during their month, they touch no meat they eat, but with a stick, lest they should defile it; nor do their husbands frequent them, till that time be expired.

. . . .

XXII. Their government is by kings, which they call *Sachema,* and those by succession, but always of the mother's side; for instance, the children of him that is now king, will not succeed, but his brother by the mother, or the children of his sister, whose sons (and after them the children of her daughters) will reign; for no woman inherits; the reason they render for this way of descent, is, that their issue may not be spurious.

XXIII. Every king hath his council, and that consists of all the old and wise men of his nation, which perhaps is two hundred people: nothing of moment is undertaken, be it war, peace, selling of land, or traffic, without advising with them; and which is more, with the young men too. 'Tis admirable to consider, how powerful the kings are, and yet how they move by the breath of their people. I have had occasion to be in council with them upon treaties for land, and to adjust the terms of trade; their order is thus: the king sits in the middle of an half moon, and hath his council, the old and wise on each hand; behind them, or at a little distance, sit the younger fry, in the same figure. Having consulted and resolved their business, the king ordered one of them to speak to me; he stood up, came to me, and in the name of his king saluted me, then took me by the hand, and told me, he was ordered by his king to speak to me, and that now it was not he, but the king that spoke, because what he should say, was the king's mind. He first prayed me, to excuse them that had not complied with me the last time; he feared, there might be some fault in the interpreter, being neither Indian nor English; besides, it was the Indian custom to deliberate, and take up much time in council, before they resolve; and that if the young people and owners of the land had been as ready as he, I had not met with so much delay. Having thus introduced his matter, he fell to the bounds of the land they had agreed to dispose of, and the price (which now is little and dear, that which would have bought twenty miles, not buying now two). During the time that this person spoke, not a man of them was observed to whisper or smile; the old, grave, the young, reverend in their deportment; they do speak little, but fervently, and with elegancy: I have never seen more natural sagacity, considering them without the help (I was going to say, the spoil) of tradition; and he will deserve the name of wise, that outwits them in any treaty about a thing they understand. When the purchase was agreed, great promises passed between us of kindness and good neighborhood, and that the Indians, and English must live in love, as long as the sun gave light. Which done, another made a speech to the Indians, in the name of all the *Sachamakers* or kings, first to tell them what was done; next, to charge and command them, to love the Christians, and particularly live in peace with me, and the people under my government: that many governors had been in the River, but that no governor had come himself to live and stay here before; and having now such a one that had treated them well, they should never do him or his any wrong. At every sentence of which they shouted, and said, "Amen," in their way.

XXIV. The justice they have is pecuniary: in case of any wrong or evil fact, be it murther itself, they atone by feasts and presents of the *wampum,* which is proportioned to the quality of the offense or person injured, or of the sex they are of: for in case they kill a woman, they pay double, and the reason they render, is, that she breedeth children, which men cannot do. 'Tis rare that they fall out, if sober; and if drunk, they forgive it, saying, it was the drink, and not the man, that abused them.

XXV. We have agreed, that in all differences between us, six of each side shall end the matter: don't abuse them, but let them have justice, and you win them: the worst is, that they are the worse for the Christians, who have propagated their vices, and yielded them tradition for ill, and not for good things. But as low an ebb as these people are at, and as glorious as their own condition looks, the Christians have not out-lived their sight with all their pretensions to an higher manifestation. What good then might not a good people graft, where there is so distinct a knowledge left between good and evil? I beseech God to incline the hearts of all that come into these parts, to out-live the knowledge of the natives, by a fixt obedience to their greater knowledge of the will of God; for it were miserable indeed for us to fall under the just censure of the poor Indian conscience, while we make profession of things so far transcending.

XXVI. For their original, I am ready to believe them of the Jewish race, I mean, of the stock of the Ten Tribes, and that for the following reasons; first, they were to go to a land not planted or known, which to be sure Asia and Africa were, if not Europe; and He that intended that extraordinary judgment upon them, might make the passage not uneasy to them, as it is not impossible in itself, from the Eastermost parts of Asia, to the Westermost of America. In the next place, I find them of like countenance, and their children of so lively resemblance, that a man would think himself in Dukes-place or Berry-street in London, when he seeth them. But this is not all; they agree in rites, they reckon by moons; they offer their first fruits, they have a kind of feast of tabernacles; they are said to lay their altar upon twelve stones; their mourning a year, customs of women, with many things that do not now occur.

. . . .

XXXII. Philadelphia, the expectation of those that are concerned in this Province, is at last laid out, to the great content of those here, that are any ways interested therein; the situation is a neck of land, and lieth between two navigable rivers, Delaware and Schuylkill, whereby it hath two fronts upon the water, each a mile, and two from river to river. Delaware is a glorious river, but the Schuylkill being an hundred miles boatable above the falls, and its course North-East toward the fountain of Susquehannah (that tends to the heart of the Province, and both sides our own) it is like to be a great part of the settlement of this age. I say little of the town itself, because a plat-form will be shewn you by my agent, in which those who are purchasers of me, will find their names and interests. But this I will say for the good providence of God, that of all the many places I have seen in the world, I remember not one better seated; so that it seems to me to have been appointed for a town, whether we regard the rivers, or the conveniency of the coves, docks, springs, the loftiness and soundness of the land and the air, held by the people of these parts to be very good. It is advanced within less than a year to about four score houses and cottages, such as they are, where merchants and handicrafts are following their vocations as fast as they can, while the country-men are close at their farms; some of them got a little winter corn in the ground last season, and the generality have had a handsome summer crop, and are preparing for their winter corn. They reaped their barley this year in the month called May; the wheat in the month following; so that there is time in these parts for another crop of divers things before the winter season. We are daily in hopes of shipping to add to our number; for blessed be God, here is both room and accommodation for them; the stories of our necessity being either the fear of our friends, or the scarecrows of our enemies; for the greatest hardship we have suffered, hath been salt meat, which by fowl in winter, and fish in summer, together with some poultry, lamb, mutton, veal, and plenty of venison the best part of the year, hath been made very passable. I bless God, I am fully satisfied with the country and entertainment I can get in it; for I find that particular content which hath always attended me, where God in His providence hath made it my place and service to reside. You cannot imagine my station can be at present free of more than ordinary business, and as such, I may say, it is a troublesome work; but the method things are putting in will facilitate the charge, and give an easier motion to the administration of affairs. However, as it is some men's duty to plow, some to sow, some to water, and some to reap; so it is the wisdom as well as duty of a man, to yield to the mind of providence, and cheerfully, as well as carefully, embrace and follow the guidance of it.

XXXIII. For your particular concern, I might entirely refer you to the letters of the President of the Society; but this I will venture to say, your provincial settlements both within and without the town, for situation and soil, are without exception; your city lot is an whole street, and one side of a street, from river to river, containing near one hundred acres, not easily valued, which is besides your four hundred acres in the city liberties, part of your twenty thousand acres in the country. Your tannery hath such plenty of bark, the sawmill for timber, and the place of the glass-house are so conveniently posted for water carriage, the city lot for a dock, and the whalery for a sound and fruitful bank, and the town Lewis by it to help your people, that by God's blessing the affairs of the Society will naturally grow in their reputation and profit. I am sure I have not turned my back upon any offer that tended to its prosperity; and though I am ill at projects, I have sometimes put in for a share with her officers, to countenance and advance her interest. You are already informed what is fit for you farther to do; whatsoever tends to the promotion of wine, and to the manufacture of linen in these parts, I cannot but wish you to promote it; and the French people are most likely in both respects to answer that design: to that end, I would advise you to send for some thousands of plants out of France, with some able vinerons, and people of the other vocation. But because I believe you have been entertained with this and some other profitable subjects by your President, I shall add no more, but to assure you, that I am heartily inclined to advance your just interest, and that you will always find me,

Your Kind Cordial Friend,
William Penn

Gabriel Thomas (1661–1714)

THE Pennsylvania colony, established by William Penn in 1681, attracted large numbers of the Society of Friends (or Quakers) and other dissident sects because of Penn's openly enunciated policies of tolerance. Gabriel Thomas, of Welsh farming stock, came early to Pennsylvania and knew every corner of it intimately. His pamphlet *An Historical and Geographical Account of the Province and Country of Pennsylvania* (London, 1698) was one of the most effective "Come to America" tracts printed in the colonial period. Translated into German and widely circulated in Europe, it undoubtedly was instrumental in encouraging large numbers of immigrants from the Palatinate into Pennsylvania.

Thomas was a careful, shrewd observer, with a great curiosity about all aspects of the colony's life. He is less interested in providing religious, patriotic, or recreational incentive for colonization than in enumerating the ways in which the ambitious newcomer may improve his lot. What he has to say about Pennsylvania is calculated to appeal most strongly to the yeoman, the workman, the tradesman, and the shopkeeper. It is not difficult to perceive, in Thomas' hardheaded totting up of opportunities, more than a little of the spirit of Franklin's Philadelphia a generation later.

TEXT: Cyrus Townsend Brady, ed., *An Account of Pennsylvania and West New Jersey by Gabriel Thomas* (Cleveland, 1903).

Opportunities in Pennsylvania

[From *An Historical and Geographical Account,* 1698]

Pennsylvania lies between the latitude of forty and forty-five degrees: West-Jersey on the East, Virginia on the West, Maryland South, and Canada on the North. In length three hundred, and in breadth one hundred and eighty miles.

The natives, or first inhabitants of this country in their original, are supposed by most people to have been of the ten scattered tribes, for they resemble the Jews very much in the make of their persons, and tincture of their complections. . . .

They are very charitable to one another, the lame and the blind (amongst them) living as well as the best; they are also very kind and obliging to the Christians.

The next that came there, were the Dutch (who called the country New Netherland), between fifty and sixty years ago, and were the first planters in those parts; but they made little or no improvement (applying themselves wholly to traffic in skins and furs, which the Indians or natives furnished them with, and which they bartered for rum, strong liquors, and sugar, with others, thereby gaining great profit), till near the time of the wars between England and them, about thirty or forty years ago.

Soon after them came the Swedes and Finns, who applied themselves to husbandry, and were the first Christian people that made any considerable improvement there.

There were some disputes between these two nations some years, the Dutch looking upon the Swedes as intruders upon their purchase and possession, which was absolutely terminated in the surrender made by John Rizeing, the Swedes' governor, to Peter Styreant, governor for the Dutch, in 1655. In the Holland War about the year 1665, Sir Robert Carr took the country from the Dutch for the English, and left his cousin, Captain Carr, governor of that place; but in a short time after, the Dutch re-took the country from the English, and kept it in their possession till the peace was concluded between the English and them, when the Dutch surrendered that country with East and West Jersey, New York (with the whole countries belonging to that government), to the English again. But it remained with very little improvement till the year 1681, in which William Penn, Esq., had the country given him by King Charles the Second, in lieu of money that was due to (and signal service done by) his father, Sir William Penn, and from him bore the name of Pennsylvania.

Since that time, the industrious (nay indefatigable) inhabitants have built a noble and beautiful city, and called it Philadelphia, which contains above two thousand houses, all inhabited; and most of them stately, and of brick, generally three stories high, after the mode in London, and as many several families in each. . . .

It hath in it three fairs every year, and two markets every week. They kill above twenty fat bullocks every week, in the hottest time in summer, for their present spending in that city, besides many sheep, calves, and hogs.

This city is situated between Schuylkill River and the great river Delaware, which derives its name from Captain Delaware, who came there pretty early: ships of two or three hundred tons may come up to this city, by either of these two rivers. Moreover, in this Province are four great market-towns, viz., Chester, the German Town, New Castle, and Lewis Town, which are mightily enlarged in this latter improvement. Between these towns, the watermen constantly ply their wherries; likewise all these towns have fairs kept in them, besides there are several country villages, viz., Dublin, Harford, Merioneth, and Radnor in Cumbry; all which towns, villages, and rivers, took their names from the several countries whence the present inhabitants came.

. . . .

And now for their lots and lands in city and country, in their great advancement since they were first laid out, which was within the compass of about twelve years, that which might have been bought for fifteen or eighteen shillings, is now sold for fourscore pounds in ready silver; and some other lots, that might have been then purchased for three pounds, within the space of two years, were sold for a hundred pounds apiece, and likewise some land that lies near the city, that sixteen years ago might have been purchased for six or eight pounds the hundred acres, cannot now be bought under one hundred and fifty, or two hundred pounds.

Now the true reason why this fruitful country and flourishing city advance so considerably in the purchase of lands both in the one and the other, is their great and extended traffic and commerce both by sea and land, viz., to New York, New England, Virginia, Maryland, Carolina, Jamaica, Barbados, Newfoundland, Maderas, Saltetudeous, and Old England; besides several other places. Their merchandise chiefly consists in horses, pipe staves, pork and beef salted and barreled up, bread, and flour, all sorts of grain, peas, beans, skins, furs, tobacco, or potashes, wax, etc., which are bartered for rum, sugar, molasses, silver, Negroes, salt, wine, linen, household goods, etc.

However, there still remain lots of land both in the aforesaid city and country, that any may purchase almost as cheap as they could at the first laying out or parceling of either city or country; which is (in the judgment of most people) the likeliest to turn to account to those that lay their money out upon it, and in a shorter time than the aforementioned lots and lands that are already improved, and for several reasons. In the first place, the country is now well inhabited by the Christians, who have great stocks of all sorts of cattle, that increase extraordinarily, and upon that account they are obliged to go farther up into the country, because there is the chiefest and best place for their stocks, and for them that go back into the country, they get the richest land, for the best lies thereabouts.

Secondly, farther into the country is the principal place to trade with the Indians for all sorts of pelt, as skins and furs, and also fat venison, of whom people may purchase cheaper by three parts in four than they can at the city of Philadelphia.

Thirdly, backwards in the country lies the mines, where is copper and iron, besides other metals, and minerals, of which there is some improvement made already in order to bring them to greater perfection; and that will be a means to erect more inland market-towns, which exceedingly promote traffic.

Fourthly, and lastly, because the country at the first laying out, was void of inhabitants (except the heathens, or very few Christians not worth naming), and not many people caring to abandon a quiet and easy (at least tolerable) life in their native country (usually the most agreeable to all mankind) to seek out a new, hazardous, and careful one in a foreign wilderness or desert country, wholly destitute of Christian inhabitants, and even to arrive at which they must pass over a vast ocean, exposed to some dangers, and not a few inconveniencies. But now all those cares, fears, and hazards are vanished, for the country is pretty well peopled, and very much improved, and will be more every day, now the dove is returned with the olive branch of peace in her mouth.

I must needs say, even the present encouragements are very great and inviting, for poor people (both men and women) of all kinds, can here get three times the wages for their labor they can in England or Wales.

I shall instance in a few, which may serve; nay, and will hold in all the rest. The first was a blacksmith (my next neighbor) who himself and one Negro man he had, got fifty shillings in one day, by working up a hundred pound weight of iron, which at six pence per pound (and that is the common price in that country) amounts to that sum.

And for carpenters, both house and ship, bricklayers, masons, either of these tradesmen, will get between five and six shillings every day constantly. As to journeymen shoemakers, they have two shillings per pair both for men and women's shoes. And journeymen tailors have twelve shillings per week and their diet. Sawyers get between six and seven shillings the hundred for cutting of pine boards. And for weavers, they have ten or twelve pence the yard for weaving of that which is little more than half a yard in breadth. Wool combers have for combing twelve pence per pound. Potters have sixteen pence for an earthen pot which may be bought in England for four pence. Tanners may buy their hides green for three half pence per pound, and sell their leather for twelve pence per pound. And curriers have three shillings and four pence per hide for dressing it; they buy their oil at twenty pence per gallon. Brick makers have twenty shillings per thousand for their bricks at the kiln. Felt makers will have for their hats seven shillings apiece, such as may be bought in England for two shillings apiece; yet they buy their wool commonly for twelve or fifteen pence per pound. And as to the glaziers, they will have five pence a quarry for their glass. The rule for the coopers I have almost forgot, but this I can affirm of some who went from Bristol (as their neighbors report) that could hardly get their livelihoods there, are now reckoned in Pennsylvania, by a modest computation to be worth some hundreds (if not thousands) of pounds. The bakers make as white bread as any in London, and as for their rule, it is the same in all parts of the world that I have been in. The butchers for killing a beast, have five shillings and their diet; and they may buy a good fat large cow for three pounds, or thereabouts. The brewers sell such beer as is equal in strength to that in London, half ale and half stout for fifteen shillings per barrel; and their beer hath a better name, that is, is in more esteem than English beer in Barbados, and is sold for a higher price there. And for silversmiths, they have between half a crown and three shillings an ounce for working their silver, and for gold equivalent. Plasterers have commonly eighteen pence per yard for plastering. Last-makers have sixteen shillings per dozen for their lasts. And heel makers have two shillings a dozen for their heels. Wheel and mill wrights, joiners, braziers, pewterers, dyers, fullers, comb makers, wire drawers, cage makers, card makers, painters, cutlers, rope makers, carvers, block makers, turners, button makers, hair and wood sieve makers, bodice makers, gunsmiths, locksmiths, nailers, file cutters, skinners, furriers, glovers, patten makers, watch makers, clock makers, saddlers, collar makers, barbers, printers, book binders, and all other tradesmen, their gains and wages are about the same proportion as the forementioned trades in their advancements, as to what they have in England.

Of lawyers and physicians I shall say nothing, because this country is very peaceable and healthy; long may it so continue and never have occasion for the tongue of the one, nor the pen of the other, both equally destructive to men's estates and lives; besides forsooth, they, hangman like, have a license to murder and make mischief. Laboringmen have commonly here, between fourteen and fifteen pounds a year, and their meat, drink, washing, and lodging; and by the day their wages is generally between eighteen pence and half a crown, and diet also; but in harvest they have usually between three and four shillings each day, and diet. The maid servant's wages is commonly betwixt six and ten pounds per annum, with very good accommodation. And for the women who get their livelihood by their own industry, their labor is very dear, for I can buy in London a cheesecake for two pence, bigger than theirs at that price, when at the same time their milk is as cheap as we can buy it in London, and their flour cheaper by one half.

Corn and flesh, and what else serves man for drink, food, and raiment, is much cheaper here than in England, or elsewhere; but the chief reason why wages of servants of all sorts is much higher here than there, arises from the great fertility and produce of the place; besides, if these large stipends were refused them, they would quickly set up for themselves, for they can have provision very cheap, and land for a very small matter, or next to nothing in comparison of the purchase of lands in England; and the farmers there, can better afford to give that great wages than the farmers in England can, for several reasons very obvious.

As first, their land costs them (as I said but just now) little or nothing in comparison, of which the farmers commonly will get twice the increase of corn for every bushel they sow, that the farmers in England can from the richest land they have.

In the second place, they have constantly good price for their corn, by reason of the great and quick vent into Barbados and other islands; through which means silver is become more plentiful than here in England, considering the number of people, and that causes a quick trade for both corn and cattle; and that is the reason that corn differs now from the price formerly, else it would be at half the price it was at then; for a brother of mine (to my own particular knowledge) sold within the compass of one week, about one hundred and twenty fat beasts, most of them good, handsome, large oxen.

Thirdly, they pay no tithes, and their taxes are inconsiderable; the place is free for all persuasions, in a sober and civil way; for the Church of England and the Quakers bear equal share in the government. They live friendly and well together; there is no persecution for religion, nor ever like to be; 'tis this that knocks all commerce on the head, together with high imposts, strict laws, and cramping orders. Before I end this paragraph, I shall add another reason why women's wages are so exorbitant; they are not yet very numerous, which makes them stand upon high terms for their several services, in sempstering, washing, spinning, knitting, sewing, and in all the other parts of their employments; for they have for spinning either worsted or linen, two shillings a pound, and commonly for knitting a very coarse pair of yarn stockings, they have half a crown a pair; moreover they are usually married before they are twenty years of age, and when once in that noose, are for the most part a little uneasy, and make their husbands so too, till they procure them a maid servant to bear the burden of the work, as also in some measure to wait on them too.

Louis Hennepin (1640?–1701)

LOUIS HENNEPIN, a Flemish-born priest, accompanied La Salle on his journey through Lakes Huron and Michigan and down the Illinois River in 1679. A year later he led a small party to the headwaters of the Mississippi, was captured by the Sioux and later released. After his return to Montreal and eventually to Europe, he wrote several accounts of his travels, the first of which was the famous *Description de la Louisiane* (1683). Hennepin was not the most trustworthy of the early French explorer-chroniclers, but he had a great curiosity about what he saw, excellent powers of observation, and a keen sense of wonder at the new and strange lands through which he traveled in mid-continent. Among the fauna of the New World which especially caught the imagination of Europeans, the buffalo probably stood first, and Hennepin's is one of the earliest accurate descriptions of them.

TEXT: Father Louis Hennepin, *Description of Louisiana,* trans. Marion E. Cross (Minneapolis, 1938).

The Great Buffalo

[From *Description de la Louisiane,* 1683]

The Seignelay River, which flows through the Illinois country, rises on this plain in a great swamp where it is almost impossible to walk. This river is only a league and a half from the Miami River. We transported all our equipment and canoes by a path which we marked for those who were to follow us. We had also left at the fork of the Miami River, as well as at the fort we constructed at its mouth, letters of instruction for the twenty-five men who were to join us, coming on the bark.

The Seignelay River is navigable for canoes a hundred paces from its source. It widens so rapidly that within a short distance it is almost as broad as, and deeper than, the Marne. Its course is through vast swamps where, in spite of its fairly strong current, it meanders to such an extent that after paddling an entire day, one has sometimes traveled only two leagues in a straight line. As far as the eye can see, there is only swamp land covered with rushes and alders. We might not have been able to find any place to camp for more than forty leagues of the way if there had not been mounds of frozen earth on which we built fires and lay down. We were short of food and even after passing this swamp, we did not find the game that we had hoped for.

The region we entered was a great open plain on which nothing grows except high grass, which, being dry at that season, had been burned by the Miami in hunting buffaloes. However hard our hunters tried to kill deer, during more than sixty leagues of our voyage they bagged only one lean stag, a little roe deer, some swans, and two geese; and there were thirty-two people to be fed. We saw the flames of the plains set afire by the Indians to facilitate the killing of buffaloes. If our canoemen had found an opportunity, they would certainly have deserted across country and joined these Indians.

That buffaloes are usually very numerous here is apparent from the bones, horns, and skulls to be seen on all sides. The Miami hunt buffaloes at the end of the autumn in the following manner:

When they see a herd the Indians assemble in great numbers. They set fire to the grass all around these animals except for one passage left on purpose. There the Indians station themselves with their bows and arrows. The buffaloes, wanting to avoid the fire, are thus forced to pass by the Indians, who at times kill as many as a hundred and twenty of them in one day. The buffaloes are distributed according to the needs of the families. These Indians, triumphant over the slaughter of so many animals, give notice to their wives, who attend to bringing in the meat. The women sometimes carry three hundred pounds on their backs, throwing their babies on top of their load, which to them does not seem more of a burden than does the sword at his side to a soldier.

Instead of hair buffaloes have very fine wool, which is longer on the female than on the male. Their horns are almost entirely black and are shorter but much thicker than those of the European oxen. They have an enormous head and an extremely short but very thick neck, sometimes six hands wide. They have a hump or small protuberance between their shoulders. Their legs are extremely thick and short and are covered with very long wool. From their heads between their horns, long black hair falls over their eyes, giving them a frightful appearance. Their meat is most succulent; they are very fat in autumn because they have been in grass up to their necks all summer long. This vast prairie region seems to be the natural habitat of the buffalo. Scattered here and there are groves where these animals retire to chew their cud and avoid the heat of the sun.

Buffaloes, or wild oxen, migrate with the changing seasons and temperatures. When they sense the approach of winter in the north, they move southward, sometimes traveling in a single file a league long. They all lie down together; the place where they have lain is often full of wild purslane, which we have sometimes eaten. The paths where they have passed are beaten like our European roads and are bare of grass. They cross streams and rivers. Buffalo cows go to islands to prevent wolves from eating their calves. When the calves are able to run, wolves would not dare to come near because the cows would kill them. In order not to drive these animals out of their country entirely, the Indians make a practice of pursuing only those that they have wounded with arrows. They refrain from further pursuit of the others, permitting them to escape so as not to frighten them unduly.

Although the Indians of this vast continent are habitually inclined to destroy animals, they have never been able to exterminate the buffalo. These animals multiply naturally, in spite of being hunted, and return in season the following years in increasing numbers.

The Indian women spin buffalo wool on a spindle and from the yarn make bags to carry the smoked or dried meat. They sometimes dry their meat in the sun. Frequently they keep meat three or four months; for although they have no salt, they cure the flesh so well that it does not spoil at all. Four months after meat has been prepared in this way, one would say on eating it that the animal was freshly killed. Instead of water, we drank broth with these Indians. This is the usual drink of all Indians of America who have had no contact with Europeans.

The average buffalo hide weighs a hundred to a hundred and twenty pounds. The Indians cut away the back and around the neck where the skin is thickest. Using only the thinnest part of the belly, they dress it very carefully with the brains of all sorts of animals, thereby making it as supple as our chamois skins dressed in oil. They paint it with various colors, trim it with red and white porcupine quills, and make it into ceremonial robes to wear at feasts. In winter, especially at night, they cover themselves with buffalo robes, which feel very comfortable on account of the curly wool.

When buffalo cows have been killed by the Indians, the little calves follow the hunters, licking their hands and fingers. The Indians sometimes take them to their children and after the children have played with them, the calves are killed with a club, and eaten. The Indians keep their hoofs, dry them, and attach them to switches, which shake and rattle to accompany the changing postures and steps of the singers and dancers. This contrivance somewhat resembles a Basque tambourine.

The calves could easily be domesticated and used for tilling the soil.

In all seasons of the year, buffaloes find food as they go. When they are surprised by winter and cannot reach the warm southland before the ground is covered with snow, they are skillful at breaking through the snow and pushing it aside in order to graze on the hidden grass. Their bellowing can be heard but not as commonly as that of European oxen.

The bodies of buffaloes are much larger than those of our European oxen, especially in the fore portion. Their great bulk does not keep them from moving so fast that few Indians are able to overtake them on the run. Buffaloes often kill those who have wounded them. In season, herds of two and even four hundred are to be seen.

The Flesh and the Spirit

As in all religions, the ultimate issue among the American Puritans was the relationship of the individual human soul with God. But God's concern was not solely with individuals. He had chosen a people, and the Puritans were from the beginning sure that they were that chosen people. The unique thing about their experience in the New World was that they here made up a society of "elect" people, a more homogeneous society of God's favored than existed anywhere else in Christendom; and so it was natural that they considered their public and social activities, not as an adjunct to their religious life, but as an intrinsic part of it. Their faith in the providence that sustained them in the howling wilderness manifested itself inwardly in soul-searching prayer and private meditation — which they often called the religion of the closet — and outwardly not only in the formation of churches, but in civil politics, education, and even the everyday affairs of business, turning every act into a sacrament, every deed into a religious duty.

John Winthrop (1588–1649)

JOHN WINTHROP was born in Suffolk, England, of wealthy parents. He was educated at Trinity College, Cambridge, and after first considering the ministry, turned instead to law. An intense Puritan, he was one of the leaders of the group which began the Great Migration to Massachusetts Bay in 1630; in fact, he was elected governor of the new colony a year before the emigrants' departure. He served as governor and deputy governor of Massachusetts for all but seven of his remaining years, while his son became governor of the neighboring colony of Connecticut.

Winthrop was an educated, cultured English gentleman, one of the few lawyers in all the New England settlements. As Bradford, the self-educated weaver, dominated the saintly Separatist society at Plymouth, so Winthrop the lawyer (with John Cotton the theologian) dominated life in much more sophisticated and powerful Massachusetts Bay. The journal which he kept from 1630 to 1649 (titled by a later editor *The History of New England,* which it is not) was published in part in 1790 and in full in 1825–26. Much of it is simply a factual account of daily events, lacking the historical perspective, artistic control, and conscious dignity of Bradford's, but it reveals much about the workings of political and religious policies as they determined the course of colonial government. A strong believer in centralized authority and theological orthodoxy, Winthrop set forth the ideals of the Christian society he envisioned in *A Model of Christian Charity,* a lay-sermon he preached aboard the flagship *Arbella* during the voyage to the new colony.

TEXTS: Allyn B. Forbes, ed., *Winthrop Papers,* Vol. II (Boston, 1931); and James Savage, ed., *The History of New England from 1630 to 1649,* Vol. II (Boston, 1826).

A City upon a Hill

[From *A Model of Christian Charity,* an address of 1630]

God Almighty in His most holy and wise providence hath so disposed of the condition of mankind, as in all times some must be rich, some poor; some high and eminent in power and dignity, others mean and in subjection. . . . All men being thus (by divine providence) ranked into two sorts, rich and poor; under the first, are comprehended all such as are able to live comfortably by their own means duly improved; and all others are poor according to the former distribution.

There are two rules whereby we are to walk one towards another: Justice and Mercy. These are always distinguished in their act and in their object, yet may they both concur in the same subject in each respect; as sometimes there may be an occasion of shewing mercy to a rich man, in some sudden danger of distress, and also doing of mere justice to a poor man in regard of some particular contract, etc. There is likewise a double law by which we are regulated in our conversation one towards another: in both the former respects, the law of nature and the law of grace, or the moral law or the law of the gospel. . . .

The law of grace or the gospel hath some difference from the former, as in these respects: first, the law of nature was given to man in the estate of innocency; this of the gospel in the estate of regeneracy. Secondly, the former propounds one man to another, as the same flesh and image of God; this as a brother in Christ also, and in the communion of the same spirit, and so teacheth us to put a difference between Christians and others. . . . Thirdly, the law of nature could give no rules for dealing with enemies, for all are to be considered as friends in the estate of innocency; but the gospel commands love to an enemy. . . .

It rests now to make some application of this discourse by the present design which gave the occasion of writing of it. Herein are four things to be propounded: first, the persons; secondly, the work; thirdly, the end; fourthly, the means.

First. For the persons, we are a company professing ourselves fellow members of Christ, in which respect only though we were absent from each other many miles, and had our employments as far distant, yet we ought to account ourselves knit together by this bond of love, and live in the exercise of it, if we would have comfort of our being in Christ; this was notorious in the practice of the Christians in former times. . . .

Secondly. For the work we have in hand, it is by a mutual consent through a special overruling providence, and a more then an ordinary approbation of the churches of Christ to seek out a place of cohabitation and consortship under a due form of government both civil and ecclesiastical. In such cases as this the care of the public must oversway all private respects, by which not only conscience, but mere civil policy doth bind us; for it is a true rule that particular estates cannot subsist in the ruin of the public.

Thirdly. The end is to improve our lives to do more service to the Lord, the comfort and increase of the body of Christ whereof we are members, that ourselves and posterity may be the better preserved from the common corruptions of this evil world, to serve the Lord and work out our salvation under the power and purity of His holy ordinances.

Fourthly. For the means whereby this must be effected, they are twofold: a conformity with the work and end we aim at, these we see are extraordinary, therefore we must not content ourselves with usual, ordinary means; whatsoever we did or ought to have done when we lived in England, the same must we do and more also where we go. That which the most in their churches maintain as a truth in profession only, we must bring into familiar and constant practice, as in this duty of love we must love brotherly without dissimulation, we must love one another with a pure heart fervently, we must bear one another's burthens, we must not look only on our own things, but also on the things of our brethren, neither must we think that the Lord will bear with such failings at our hands as He doth from those among whom we have lived. . . .

Thus stands the cause between God and us: we are entered into covenant with Him for this work, we have taken out a commission, the Lord hath given us leave to draw our own articles, we have professed to enterprise these actions upon these and these ends, we have hereupon besought Him of favor and blessing. Now if the Lord shall please to hear us, and bring us in peace to the place we desire, then hath He ratified this covenant and sealed our commission, [and] will expect a strict performance of the articles contained in it, but if we shall neglect the observation of these articles which are the ends we have propounded, and dissembling with our God, shall fall to embrace this present world and prosecute our carnal intentions, seeking great things for ourselves and our posterity, the Lord will surely break out in wrath against us, be revenged of such a perjured people, and make us know the price of the breach of such a covenant.

Now the only way to avoid this shipwrack and to provide for our posterity is to follow the counsel of Micah, to do justly, to love mercy, to walk humbly with our God; for this end, we must be knit together in this work as one man, we must entertain each other in brotherly affection, we must be willing to abridge ourselves of our superfluities, for the supply of others' necessities, we must uphold a familiar commerce together in all meekness, gentleness, patience, and liberality; we must delight in each other, make others' conditions our own, rejoice together, mourn together, labor and suffer together, always having before our eyes our commission and community in the work, our community as members of the same body; so shall we keep the unity of the spirit in the bond of peace, the Lord will be our God and delight to dwell among us, as His own people, and will command a blessing upon us in all our ways, so that we shall see much more of His wisdom, power, goodness, and truth, then formerly we have been acquainted with. We shall find that the God of Israel is among us, when ten of us shall be able to resist a thousand of our enemies, when He shall make us a praise and glory, that men shall say of succeeding plantations: the Lord make it like that of New England; for we must consider that we shall be as a city upon a hill, the eyes of all people are upon us; so that if we shall deal falsely with our God in this work we have undertaken, and so cause Him to withdraw His present help from us, we shall be made a story and a byword through the world, we shall open the mouths of enemies to speak evil of the ways of God and all professors for God's sake; we shall shame the faces of many of God's worthy servants, and cause their prayers to be turned into curses upon us till we be consumed out of the good land whither we are going. And to shut up this discourse with that exhortation of Moses, that faithful servant of the Lord, in his last farewell to Israel (Deut. 30): Beloved, there is now set before us life and good, death and evil, in that we are commanded this day to love the Lord our God, and to love one another, to walk in His ways and to keep His commandments and His ordinance, and His laws, and the articles of our covenant with Him, that we may live and be multiplied, and that the Lord our God may bless us in the land whither we go to possess it. But if our hearts shall turn away so that we will not obey, but shall be seduced and worship other gods, our pleasures and profits, and serve them; it is propounded unto us this day, we shall surely perish out of the good land whither we pass over this vast sea to possess it; therefore let us choose life, that we, and our seed, may live; by obeying His voice, and cleaving to Him, for He is our life, and our prosperity.

Remarks on Liberty

[From *Journal*]

❮[In 1645 the militia company of Hingham, Massachusetts, dismissed its company commander and elected another in his place. The deposed officer appealed to the colonial government at Boston, which remonstrated with the Hingham citizens to no avail. The case was called to trial, and Deputy Governor Winthrop argued that the citizens of Hingham had exceeded their powers; the same accusation was then leveled at Winthrop. After long and bitter debate, the court decided in favor of Winthrop, who concluded with some pertinent remarks on political liberty as the Massachusetts theocracy perceived it.]❯

I suppose something may be expected from me, upon this charge that is befallen me, which moves me to speak now to you; yet I intend not to intermeddle in the proceedings of the court, or with any of the persons concerned therein. Only I bless God, that I see an issue of this troublesome business. I also acknowledge the justice of the court, and, for mine own part, I am well satisfied; I was publicly charged, and I am publicly and legally acquitted, which is all I did expect or desire. And though this be sufficient for my justification before men, yet not so before the God, who hath seen so much amiss in my dispensations (and even in this affair) as calls me to be humble. For to be publicly and criminally charged in this court, is matter of humiliation (and I desire to make a right use of it), notwithstanding I be thus acquitted. If her father had spit in her face (saith the Lord concerning Miriam), should she not have been ashamed seven days? Shame had lien upon her, whatever the occasion had been. I am unwilling to stay you from your urgent affairs, yet give me leave (upon this special occasion) to speak a little more to this assembly. It may be of some good use, to inform and rectify the judgments of some of the people, and may prevent such distempers as have arisen amongst us. The great questions that have troubled the country, are about the authority of the magistrates and the liberty of the people. It is yourselves who have called us to this office, and being called by you, we have our authority from God, in way of an ordinance, such as hath the image of God eminently stamped upon it, the contempt and violation whereof hath been vindicated with examples of divine vengeance. I entreat you to consider, that when you choose magistrates, you take them from among yourselves, men subject to like passions as you are. Therefore when you see infirmities in us, you should reflect upon your own, and that would make you bear the more with us, and not be severe censurers of the failings of your magistrates, when you have continual experience of the like infirmities in yourselves and others. We account him a good servant, who breaks not his covenant. The covenant between you and us is the oath you have taken of us, which is to this purpose, that we shall govern you and judge your causes by the rules of God's laws and our own, according to our best skill. When you agree with a workman to build you a ship or house, etc., he undertakes as well for his skill as for his faithfulness, for it is his profession, and you pay him for both. But when you call one to be a magistrate, he doth not profess nor undertake to have sufficient skill for that office, nor can you furnish him with gifts, etc., therefore you must run the hazard of his skill and ability. But if he fail in faithfulness, which by his oath he is bound unto, that he must answer for. If it fall out that the case be clear to common apprehension, and the rule clear, also, if he transgress here, the error is not in the skill, but in the evil of the will: it must be required of him. But if the cause be doubtful, or the rule doubtful, to men of such understanding and parts as your magistrates are, if your magistrates should err here, yourselves must bear it.

For the other point concerning liberty, I observe a great mistake in the country about that. There is a twofold liberty, natural (I mean as our nature is now corrupt) and civil or federal. The first is common to man with beasts and other creatures. By this, man, as he stands in relation to man simply, hath liberty to do what he lists; it is a liberty to evil as well as to good. This liberty is incompatible and inconsistent with authority, and cannot endure the least restraint of the most just authority. The exercise and maintaining of this liberty makes men grow more evil, and in time to be worse than brute beasts: *omnes sumus licentia deteriores.* This is that great enemy of truth and peace, that wild beast, which all the ordinances of God are bent against, to restrain and subdue it. The other kind of liberty I call civil or federal; it may also be termed moral, in reference to the covenant between God and man, in the moral law, and the politic covenants and constitutions, amongst men themselves. This liberty is the proper end and object of authority, and cannot subsist without it; and it is a liberty to that only which is good, just, and honest. This liberty you are to stand for, with the hazard (not only of your goods, but) of your lives, if need be. Whatsoever crosseth this, is not authority, but a distemper thereof. This liberty is maintained and exercised in a way of subjection to authority; it is of the same kind of liberty wherewith Christ hath made us free. The woman's own choice makes such a man her husband; yet being so chosen, he is her lord, and she is to be subject to him, yet in a way of liberty, not of bondage; and a true wife accounts her subjection her honor and freedom, and would not think her condition safe and free, but in her subjection to her husband's authority. Such is the liberty of the church under the authority of Christ, her king and husband; His yoke is so easy and sweet to her as a bride's ornaments; and if through frowardness or wantonness, etc., she shake it off, at any time, she is at no rest in her spirit, until she take it up again; and whether her lord smiles upon her, and embraceth her in his arms, or whether he frowns, or rebukes, or smites her, she apprehends the sweetness of his love in all, and is refreshed, supported, and instructed by every such dispensation of his authority over her. On the other side, ye know who they are that complain of this yoke and say, let us break their bands, etc., we will not have this man to rule over us. Even so, brethren, it will be between you and your magistrates. If you stand for your natural corrupt liberties, and will do what is good in your own eyes, you will not endure the least weight of authority, but will murmur, and oppose, and be always striving to shake off that yoke; but if you will be satisfied to enjoy such civil and lawful liberties, such as Christ allows you, then will you quietly and cheerfully submit unto that authority which is set over you, in all the administrations of it, for your good. Wherein, if we fail at any time, we hope we shall be willing (by God's assistance) to hearken to good advice from any of you, or in any other way of God; so shall your liberties be preserved, in upholding the honor and power of authority amongst you.

John Cotton (1585–1652)

JOHN COTTON was born in Derbyshire, England, and educated at Trinity College, Cambridge, where he graduated when he was thirteen. He remained at Cambridge, taking his M.A. in 1606, and serving as Fellow and head lecturer of Emmanuel College, the intellectual center of Puritanism. He accepted a pastorate in 1612 at Boston, in Lincolnshire, where he was in constant trouble with the Church of England for his unorthodox opinions, and a favorite preacher of many Dissenters. Indeed it was he who preached the farewell sermon for John Winthrop's group when it left for America; in 1633 Cotton himself was finally ousted by Archbishop Laud and emigrated to Boston. Cotton was, with Thomas Hooker, one of the two most learned men in the colonies; as teacher of Boston's First Church, he became as powerful an influence in New England theology as Winthrop was in its government. New Englanders, Roger Williams once said, "could hardly believe that God would suffer Mr. Cotton to err."

Cotton may have agreed, for though he was neither an illiberal man nor a vengeful one, he saw himself as the great defender of orthodox Calvinism in New England, and spent his life guarding the faith and pursuing heretics, a task he passed on to his grandson, Cotton Mather. He wrote voluminously in defense of New England Congregationalism, gaining wide recognition for *The Keys to the Kingdom of Heaven* (1644), *The Way of the Churches of Christ in New England* (1645), and *The Way of the Congregational Churches Cleared* (1648). Thousands of New England children learned their catechism from his *Milk for Babes* (1646).

TEXTS: John Cotton, *An Exposition upon the Thirteenth Chapter of the Revelation* (London, 1656); *God's Promise to His Plantations* (Boston, 1686).

The Limitations of Power

[From *An Exposition upon . . . Revelation,* 1656]

This may serve to teach us the danger of allowing to any mortal man an inordinate measure of power to speak great things, to allow to any man uncontrollableness of speech, you see the desperate danger of it. Let all the world learn to give mortal men no greater power then they are content they shall use, for use it they will: and unless they be better taught of God, they will use it ever and anon, it may be make it the passage of their proceeding to speak what they will. And they that have liberty to speak great things, you will find it to be true, they will speak great blasphemies. No man would think what desperate deceit and wickedness there is in the hearts of men. And that was the reason why the Beast did speak such great things; he might speak, and nobody might control him: "What," saith the Lord in Jer. 3:5: "Thou hast spoken and done evil things as thou couldst." If a church or head of a church could have done worse, he would have done it. This is one of the strains of nature, it affects boundless liberty, and to run to the utmost extent: whatever power he hath received, he hath a corrupt nature that will improve it in one thing or other; if he have liberty, he will think why may he not use it. Set up the Pope as Lord Paramount over kings and princes, and they shall know that he hath power over them, he will take liberty to depose one, and set up another. Give him power to make laws, and he will approve, and disprove as he list; what he approves is canonical, what he disproves is rejected. Give him that power, and he will so order it at length, he will make such a state of religion, that he that so lives and dies shall never be saved, and all this springs from the vast power that is given to him, and from the deep depravation of nature. He will open his mouth, "His tongue is his own, who is Lord over him," Psal. 12:3, 4. It is therefore most wholesome for magistrates and officers in church and commonwealth, never to affect more liberty and authority then will do them good, and the people good; for whatever transcendent power is given, will certainly overrun those that give it, and those that receive it. There is a strain in a man's heart that will sometime or other run out to excess, unless the Lord restrain it, but it is not good to venture it: it is necessary therefore, that all power that is on earth be limited, church power or other. If there be power given to speak great things, then look for great blasphemies, look for a licentious abuse of it. It is counted a matter of danger to the state to limit prerogatives; but it is a further danger, not to have them limited: they will be like a tempest, if they be not limited. A prince himself cannot tell where he will confine himself, nor can the people tell. But if he have liberty to speak great things, then he will make and unmake, say and unsay, and undertake such things as are neither for his own honor, nor for the safety of the state. It is therefore fit for every man to be studious of the bounds which the Lord hath set: and for the people, in whom fundamentally all power lies, to give as much power as God in His Word gives to men; and it is meet that magistrates in the commonwealth, and so officers in churches should desire to know the utmost bounds of their own power, and it is safe for both. All intrenchment upon the bounds which God hath not given, they are not enlargements, but burdens and snares; they will certainly lead the spirit of a man out of his way sooner or later. It is wholesome and safe to be dealt withal as God deals with the vast sea; "Hitherto shalt thou come, but there shalt thou stay thy proud waves"; and therefore if they be but banks of simple sand, they will be good enough to check the vast roaring sea. And so for imperial monarchies, it is safe to know how far their power extends; and then if it be but banks of sand, which is most slippery, it will serve, as well as any brazen wall. If you pinch the sea of its liberty, though it be walls of stone or brass, it will beat them down. So it is with magistrates, stint them where God hath not stinted them, and if they were walls of brass, they would beat them down, and it is meet they should: but give them the liberty God allows, and if it be but a wall of sand it will keep them: as this liquid air in which we breathe, God hath set it for the waters of the clouds to the earth; it is a firmament, it is the clouds, yet it stands firm enough; because it keeps the climate where they are, it shall stand like walls of brass. So let there be due bounds set, and I may apply it to families; it is good for the wife to acknowledge all power and authority to the husband, and for the husband to acknowledge honor to the wife, but still give them that which God hath given them, and no more nor less. Give them the full latitude that God hath given, else you will find you dig pits, and lay snares, and cumber their spirits, if you give them less: there is never peace where full liberty is not given, nor never stable peace where more then full liberty is granted. Let them be duly observed, and give men no more liberty then God doth, nor women, for they will abuse it. The Devil will draw them, and God's providence lead them thereunto; therefore give them no more then God gives. And so for children, and servants, or any others you are to deal with: give them the liberty and authority you would have them use, and beyond that stretch not the tether; it will not tend to their good nor yours. And also from hence gather, and go home with this meditation: that certainly here is this distemper in our natures, that we cannot tell how to use liberty, but we shall very readily corrupt ourselves: Oh! the bottomless depth of sandy earth! of a corrupt spirit, that breaks over all bounds, and loves inordinate vastness; that is it we ought to be careful of.

God's Promise to His Plantations

[From a sermon of 1630]

The placing of a people in this or that country is from the appointment of the Lord.

This is evident in the text [II Sam. 7:10]; and the Apostle speaks of it as grounded in nature, Acts 17:26: "God hath determined the times before appointed, and the bounds of our habitation," Deut. 2 chapt., 5, 9. God would not have the Israelites meddle with the Edomites, or the Moabites, because He had given them their land for a possession. God assigned out such a land for such a posterity, and for such a time.

Question. Wherein doth this work of God stand in appointing a place for a people?

Answer. First, when God espies or discovers a land for a people, as in Ezek. 20:6, He brought them into a land that He had espied for them: and that is, when either He gives them to discover it themselves, or hear of it discovered by others, and fitting them.

Secondly, after He hath espied it, when He carries them along to it, so that they plainly see a providence of God leading them from one country to another, as in Exod. 19:4: "you have seen how I have borne you as on eagles' wings, and brought you unto myself." So that though they met with many difficulties, yet He carried them high above them all, like an eagle, flying over seas and rocks, and all hinderances.

Thirdly, when He makes room for a people to dwell there, as in Psal. 80:9: "Thou preparedst room for them." When Isaac sojourned among the Philistines, he digged one well, and the Philistines strove for it, and he called it *Esek,* and he digged another well, and for that they strove also, therefore he called it *Sitnah:* and he removed thence, and digged another well, and for that they strove not, and he called it *Rehoboth,* and said, "For now the Lord hath made room for us, and we shall be fruitful in the land." Now no Esek, no Sitnah, no quarrel or contention, but now he sits down in Rehoboth in a peaceable room.

Now God makes room for a people three ways:

First, when He casts out the enemies of a people before them, by lawful war with the inhabitants, which God calls them unto: as in Psal. 44:2: "Thou didst drive out the heathen before them." But this course of warring against others, and driving them out without provocation, depends upon special commission from God; or else it is not imitable.

Secondly, when He gives a foreign people favor in the eyes of any native people to come and sit down with them either by way of purchase, as Abraham did obtain the field of Machpelah; or else when they give it in courtesy, as Pharaoh did the land of Goshen unto the sons of Jacob.

Thirdly, when He makes a country, though not altogether void of inhabitants, yet void in that place where they reside. Where there is a vacant place, there is liberty for the son of Adam or Noah to come and inhabit, though they neither buy it, nor ask their leaves.

Abraham and Isaac, when they sojourned[1] amongst the Philistims, they did not buy that land to feed their cattle, because they said there is room enough. And so did Jacob pitch his tent by Sechem, Gen. 34:21. There was "room enough," as Hamor said, "Let them sit down amongst us." And in this case, if the people who were former inhabitants did disturb them in their possessions, they complained to the king, as of wrong done unto them: as Abraham did because they took away his well, in Gen. 21:25. For his right whereto, he pleaded not his immediate calling from God (for that would seem frivolous amongst the heathen), but his own industry and culture in digging the well, verse 30. Nor doth the king reject his plea, with what had he to do to dig wells in their soil? but admitteth it as a principle in nature, that in a vacant soil, he that taketh possession of it, and bestoweth culture and husbandry upon it, his right it is. And the ground of this is, from the grand charter given to Adam and his posterity in Paradise, Gen. 1:28: "multiply, and replenish the earth, and subdue it." If therefore any son of Adam come, and find a place empty, he hath liberty to come, and fill, and subdue the earth there. This charter was renewed to Noah, Gen. 9:1: "Fulfill the earth and multiply," so that it is free from that common grant for any to take possession of vacant countries. Indeed no nation is to drive out another without special commission from heaven, such as the Israelites had; unless the natives do unjustly wrong them, and will not recompense the wrongs done in peaceable sort, and then they may right themselves by lawful war, and subdue the country unto themselves.

This placing of people in this or that country, is from God's sovereignty over all the earth, and the inhabitants thereof: as in Psal. 24:1, "The earth is the Lord's, and the fulness thereof." And in Jer. 10:7, God is there called "the King of Nations," and in Deut. 10:14. Therefore it is meet He should provide a place for all nations to inhabit, and have all the earth replenished. Only in the text here is meant some more special appointment, because God tells them it by His own mouth; He doth not so with other people; He doth not tell the children of Sier, that He hath appointed a place for them: that is, He gives them the land by promise; others take the land by His providence, but God's people take the land by promise. And therefore the land of Canaan is called a land of promise, which they discern, first, by discerning themselves to be in Christ, in whom all the promises are yea and amen.

[1] This sojourning was a constant residence there, as in a possession of their own; although it be called sojourning or dwelling as strangers; because they neither had the sovereign government of the whole country in their own hand, nor yet did incorporate themselves into the commonwealth of the natives, to submit themselves unto their government. [Cotton's note]

Secondly, by finding His holy presence with them, to wit, when He plants them in the holy mountain of His inheritance, Exod. 15:17. And that is, when He giveth them the liberty, and purity of His ordinances. It is a land of promise, where they have provision for soul as well as for body. Ruth dwelt well for outward respects while she dwelt in Moab; but when she cometh to dwell in Israel, she is said to come under the wings of God, Ruth 2:12. When God wraps us in with His ordinances, and warms us with the life and power of them as with wings, there is a land of promise.

This may teach us all where we do now dwell, or where after we may dwell, be sure you look at every place appointed to you, from the hand of God; we may not rush into any place, and never say to God, by your leave; but we must discern how God appoints us this place. There is poor comfort in sitting down in any place, that you cannot say, this place is appointed me of God. Canst thou say that God spied out this place for thee, and there hath settled thee above all hindrances? didst thou find that God made room for thee, either by lawful descent, or purchase, or gift, or other warrantable right? Why then this is the place God hath appointed thee; here He hath made room for thee, He hath placed thee in Rehoboth, in a peaceable place.

This we must discern, or else we are but intruders upon God. And when we do withal discern, that God giveth us these outward blessings from His love in Christ; and maketh comfortable provision as well for our souls as for our bodies, by the means of grace, then do we enjoy our present possession, as well by gracious promise, as by the common, and just, and bountiful providence of the Lord. Or if a man do remove, He must see that God hath espied out such a country for him.

Secondly, though there be many difficulties, yet He hath given us hearts to overlook them all, as if we were carried upon eagles' wings.

And thirdly, see God making room for us by some lawful means.

Question. But how shall I know whether God hath appointed me such a place? If I be well where I am, what may warrant my removal?

Answer. There be four or five good things, for procurement of any of which, I may remove. Secondly, there be some evil things, for avoiding of any of which, we may transplant ourselves. Thirdly, if withal we find some special providence of God concurring in either of both concerning ourselves, and applying general grounds of removal to our personal estate.

First, we may remove for the gaining of knowledge. Our Saviour commends it in the queen of the South, that she came from the utmost parts of the earth, to hear the wisdom of Solomon, Matt. 12:42. And surely, with him she might have continued for the same end, if her personal calling had not recalled her home.

Secondly, some remove and travel for merchandise, and gainsake; "daily bread may be sought from far," Prov. 31:14. Yea, our Saviour approveth travel for merchants, Matt. 13:45–46, when He compareth a Christian to a merchantman seeking pearls, for He never fetcheth a comparison from any unlawful thing, to illustrate a thing lawful. The comparison from the unjust steward, and from the thief in the night, is not taken from the injustice of the one, or the theft of the other; but from the wisdom of the one, and the suddenness of the other; which in themselves are not unlawful.

Thirdly, to plant a colony, that is, a company that agree together to remove out of their own country, and settle a city or commonwealth elsewhere. Of such a colony we read in Acts 16:12, which God blessed and prospered exceedingly, and made it a glorious church. Nature teacheth bees to do so, when as the hive of the commonwealth is so full, that tradesmen cannot live one by another, but eat up one another, in this case it is lawful to remove.

Fourthly. God alloweth a man to remove, when he may employ his talents and gifts better elsewhere, especially when where he is, he is not bound by any special engagement. Thus God sent Joseph before to preserve the church: Joseph's wisdom and spirit was not fit for a shepherd, but for a counsellor of state, and therefore God sent him into Egypt. "To whom much is given, of him God will require the more," Luke 12:48.

Fifthly, for the liberty of the ordinances. II Chron. 11:13, 14, 15. When Jeroboam made a defection from Judah, and set up golden calves to worship, all that were well affected, both priests and people, sold their possessions, and came to Jerusalem for the ordinances' sake. This case was of seasonable use to our fathers in the days of Queen Mary; who removed to France and Germany in the beginning of her reign, upon proclamation of alteration of religion, before any persecution began.

Secondly, there be evils to be avoided that may warrant removal. First, when some grievous sins overspread a country, that threaten desolation, Mic. 2:6 to 11 verse: when the people say to them that prophesy, "prophesy not"; then verse 10, "Arise then, this is not your rest." Which words, though they be a threatning, not a commandment, yet as in a threatning a wise man forseeth the plague, so in the threatning he seeth a commandment, to hide himself from it. This case might have been of seasonable use unto them of the Palatinate, when they saw their orthodox ministers banished; although themselves might for a while enjoy liberty of conscience.

Secondly, if men be overburdened with debts and miseries, as David's followers were, they may then retire out of the way (as they retired to David for safety) not to defraud their creditors (for God is an avenger of such things, I Thess. 4:6), but to gain further opportunity to discharge their debts, and to satisfy their creditors, I Sam. 22:1–2.

Thirdly, in case of persecution, so did the Apostle in Acts 13:46–47.

Thirdly, as these general cases, where any of them do fall out, do warrant removal in general, so there be some special providences or particular cases, which may give warrant unto such or such a person to transplant himself, and which apply the former general grounds to particular persons.

First, if sovereign authority command and encourage such plantations, by giving way to subjects to transplant themselves, and set up a new commonwealth. This is a lawful and expedient case for such particular persons as be designed and sent, Matt. 8:9, and for such as they who are sent have power to command.

Secondly, when some special providence of God leads a man unto such a course. This may also single out particulars. Psal. 32:8: "I will instruct, and guide thee with mine eye." As the child knows the pleasure of his father in his eye, so doth the child of God see God's pleasure in the eye of his heavenly Father's providence. And this is done three ways:

First, if God give a man an inclination to this or that course, for that is the spirit of man; and "God is the Father of spirits," Rom. 1:11–12; I Cor. 16:12. Paul discerning his calling to go to Rome by his . . . ready inclination to that voyage, and Apollos his loathing to go to Corinth, Paul accepted as a just reason of his refusal of a calling to go thither. And this holdeth, when in a man's inclination to travel, his heart is set on no by-respects, as to see fashions, to deceive his creditors, to fight duels, or to live idly; these are vain inclinations. But if his heart be inclined upon right judgment to advance the gospel, to maintain his family, to use his talents fruitfully, or the like good end; this inclination is from God. As the beams of the moon darting into the sea, leads it to and fro, so doth a secret inclination darted by God into our hearts, lead and bow (as a bias) our whole course.

Secondly, when God gives other men hearts to call us, as the men of Macedon did Paul, "Come to us into Macedonia, and help us." When we are invited by others who have a good calling to reside there, we may go with them; unless we be detained by weightier occasions. One member hath interest in another, to call to it for help, when it is not diverted to greater employment.

Thirdly, there is another providence of God concurring in both these, that is, when a man's calling and person are free; and not tied by parents, or magistrates, or other people that have interest in him. Or when abroad he may do himself and others more good, than he can do at home. Here is then an eye of God that opens a door there, and sets him loose here; inclines his heart that way, and outlooks all difficulties. When God makes room for them, no binding here, and an open way there; in such a case God tells them, He will appoint a place for them.

John Davenport (1597–1670)

JOHN DAVENPORT, born in Coventry, England, was a graduate of Oxford. At the age of nineteen he was appointed pastor of St. Stephen's Church in London, where he soon enjoyed a wide reputation as a pulpit orator. He moved progressively away from the Church of England, however, and in 1633 joined the Puritan group resident in Holland. At John Cotton's invitation, he came to Boston in 1637, and the next year moved to the new colony of New Haven, in Connecticut, to become its first minister. For the next thirty years he was the theological ruler of New Haven. Davenport, who was especially concerned about the relationship of church and state in the new settlement, was a staunch defender of the orthodox theocratic position in numerous controversies. He wrote several pamphlets, of which one of the best examples is *A Discourse about Civil Government in a New Plantation Whose Design is Religion* (1663), an answer to some remarks of John Cotton's. In 1667, feeling that he had satisfactorily established the proper arrangement of civil and ecclesiastical powers in New Haven, he accepted a call to the First Church in Boston, where, he believed, theological discipline had become unduly relaxed. He died there, however, within three years.

TEXT: John Davenport, *A Discourse about Civil Government* (Cambridge, Mass., 1663).

The Necessity of a Theocracy

[From *A Discourse about Civil Government*, 1663]

Query: Whether a new plantation, where all or the most considerable part of free planters profess their purpose and desire of securing to themselves and to their posterity, the pure and peaceable enjoyment of Christ's ordinances; whether, I say, such planters are bound in laying the foundations of church and civil state, to take order, that all the free burgesses be such as are in fellowship of the church or churches which are, or may be gathered according to Christ; and that those free burgesses have the only power of choosing from among themselves civil magistrates, and men to be entrusted with transacting all public affairs of importance, according to the rules and directions of scripture?

I hold the affirmative part of this question upon this ground, that this course will most conduce to the good of both states; and by consequence to the common welfare of all, whereunto all men are bound principally to attend in laying the foundation of a commonwealth, lest posterity rue the first miscarriages, when it will be too late to redress them. They that are skilful in architecture observe, that the breaking or yielding of a stone in the groundwork of a building but the breadth of the back of a knife, will make a cleft of more then half a foot in the fabric aloft. So important (saith mine author) are fundamental errors. The Lord awaken us to look to it in time, and send us His light and truth to lead us into the safest ways in these beginnings.

The question being thus stated, I now proceed with God's help to prove the affirmative part; and thus I argue, to prove that the form of government which is described in the true stating of the question is the best, and by consequence, that men that are free to choose (as in new plantations they are) ought to establish it in a Christian commonwealth.

Theocraty, or to make the Lord God our Governor, is the best form of government in a Christian commonwealth, and which men that are free to choose (as in new plantations they are) ought to establish. The form of government described in the true stating of the question is theocraty, or that wherein we make the Lord God our Governor. Therefore that form of government which is described in the true stating of the question, is the best form of government in a Christian commonwealth, and which men that are free to choose (as in new plantations they are) ought to establish. The proposition is clear of itself. The assumption I prove thus:

That form of government where 1. the people that have the power of choosing their governors are in covenant with God; 2. wherein the men chosen by them are godly men, and fitted with a spirit of government; 3. in which the laws they rule by are the laws of God; 4. wherein laws are executed, inheritances allotted, and civil differences are composed, according to God's appointment; 5. in which men of God are consulted with in all hard cases, and in matters of religion, is the form which was received and established among the people of Israel whilest the Lord God was their Governor, as the places of scripture . . . shew; and this is the very same with that which we plead for, as will appear to him that shall examine the true stating of the question. The conclusion follows necessarily.

That form of government which giveth unto Christ His due preheminence, is the best form of government in a Christian commonwealth, and which men that are free to choose (as in new plantations they are) ought to establish. The form of government described in the true stating of the question, is that which giveth unto Christ His due preheminence. Therefore the form of government which is described in the true stating of the question, is the best form of government in a Christian commonwealth, and which men that are free to choose (as in new plantations they are) ought to establish.

The proposition is proved out of two places of scripture, Col. 1:15 to 19, with Eph. 1:21–22. From which texts it doth appear, that it is a preheminence due to Christ, that all things, and all governments in the world, should serve to Christ's ends, for the welfare of the church whereof He is the head. For 1. in relation to God, He hath this by right of primogeniture, as He is the first-born, and so heir of all things, higher then the kings of the earth; 2. in relation to the world, it is said, all things were made by Him, and for Him, and do consist in Him, and therefore it is a preheminence due to Him, that they all serve Him; 3. in relation to the church, it is said, He hath made all things subject under His feet, and hath given Him over all things to be head of the church, that in all things He might have the preheminence. And indeed that He upholdeth the creatures, and the order that is in them, it is for His churches' sake; when that is once complete, the world shall soon be at an end. And if you read the stories of the great monarchies that have been, and judge of them by scripture-light, you will find they stood or fell, according as God purposed to make use of them about some service to be done about His church. So that the only considerable part for which the world standeth at this day, is the church; and therefore it is a preheminence due to Christ, that His headship over the church should be exalted and acknowledged, and served by all. In which respect also the title of the first-born is given to the members of the church, and they are called the first fruits of His creatures, to shew both their preheminence above others, and that they are fittest to serve to God's ends.

The assumption (that the form of government described in the true stating of the question, doth give unto Christ His due preheminence) will easily be granted by those that shall consider what civil magistrates and rulers in the commonwealth those are, who are fittest to serve to Christ's ends for the good and welfare of His church; which will be evident from two places of scripture: first, in Psal. 2:10, 11, 12, you have a description of those that are fitted to order civil affairs in their magistracy to Christ's ends; they are such as are not only wise and learned in matter of religion, but also do reduce their knowledge into practice: they worship the Lord in fear; and not only so, but kiss the Son, which was a solemn and outward profession of love, and of subjection, and of religious worship, and so fitly serveth to express their joining themselves to the church of Christ. Secondly, in Isa. 49:23, it is promised to the church, that kings and queens shall be their nursing-fathers and nursing-mothers, and therefore it is added, they shall worship "with their faces to the earth, and lick up the dust of thy feet"; which is a proverbial expression of their voluntary humbling of themselves to Christ in His ordinances (taken from the manner of the Persians, in declaring their subjection to their emperor), which the Apostle calls a voluntary submission to the gospel, which is the spirit of the members of the churches of Christ. And for this reason it is, that the Lord, when He moulded a communion among His own people, wherein all civil administrations should serve to holy ends, He described the men to whom that trust should be committed, by certain properties, which also qualified them for fellowship in church ordinances, as men of ability and power over their own affections; secondly, fearing God, truly religious, men of courage, hating covetousness, men of wisdom, men of understanding, and men known or approved of among the people of God, and chosen by the Lord from among their brethren, and not a stranger, which is no brother: the most of which concur to describe church members in a church rightly gathered and ordered, who are also in respect of their union with Christ, and fellowship together, called brethren frequently in the New Testament, wherein the equity of that rule is established to us. Objection: Christ will have His due preheminence, though the civil rulers oppose Him, and persecute the churches, as in Rome: therefore it is not necessary that this course be taken in civil affairs to establish Christ's preheminence. Answer: the question is of a Christian commonwealth that should willingly subject themselves to Christ, not of a heathen state that shall perforce be subdued unto Christ. It is concerning what God's people being free should choose, not what His enemies are compelled unto. . . .

James Noyes (1608–1656)

BORN in England in 1608, James Noyes attended Brasenose College, Oxford, became an assistant schoolmaster to Thomas Parker in Berkshire, was converted, and established a reputation for his piety. Uneasy under the restrictions of Anglican church worship, he married and emigrated to New England in 1634, eventually becoming teacher of the church of Newbury, Massachusetts, under the pastorate of Thomas Parker, who followed him across the ocean. He wrote a catechism for the use of his congregation in Newbury, and a book titled *Moses and Aaron: or, The Rights of Church and State,* both of which were published after his death. But the relationship of magistracy and clergy had interested him for some time before these books, and he had published one treatise on the subject before his death — *The Temple Measured: or, A Brief Survey of the Temple Mystical, which is the Instituted Church of Christ* (London, 1647), from which the following excerpt comes. His position here prompted several retorts from English writers; Noyes never answered them. He died in 1656, after twenty years of dedicated service to Newbury.

TEXT: James Noyes, *The Temple Measured* (London, 1647).

The Power of Magistrates in the Church

[From *The Temple Measured,* 1647]

The acts of magistracy are not only civil laws, precepts, punishments, rewards; but also spiritual laws, precepts, prayers, blessing, instructions, admonitions. These spiritual acts do denominate magistratical power to be spiritual power though not ecclesiastical. Church power is spiritual generically in respect of acts which are spiritual in common, but by way of specialty it is spiritual, as it is ecclesiastical. Magistratical power is both civil and spiritual, yet not ecclesiastical; or civil as it is opposed to ecclesiastical power, not as opposed to spiritual. The next ends of magistratical acts are spiritual, and acts are distinguished by their ends or immediate objects. The spiritual good of men is both intended and acquired in magistratical acts as primarily as the temporal good of men. A magistrate doth instruct, pray, etc., to the end he might confer some spiritual good, and the act itself doth as naturally and immediately produce such an effect as if it were the act of an ecclesiastical person; and such an act is supposed to be the act of a magistrate as he is a magistrate, not only as he is a Christian. And if the magistrate be profane and should not intend any spiritual good (as it was said of one, that he was *bonus rex,* but *malus homo*), it is sufficient that the act itself doth.

The spiritual good of men and the glory of God are primary ends of the constitution of magistracy in nature. A throne of magistracy is erected (and ought to be in the intention of men) as directly for religion as for civil peace. Though a prince hath not all the means to make a good man which a priest hath, yet he hath some, and is to improve them for the making of his subjects good men spiritually as well as civilly; and he that is *integrè bonus civis est bonus vir,* in respect of all virtues in both tables. Else why is it the duty of magistrates to instruct, pray, provide by laws, etc., for the preservation and promotion of religion? Such ends were primary ends of magistracy in Adam, only we must remember that axiom, *finem legis cadere sub legem.*

The priesthood itself is naturally a branch of magistracy; it remained in the patriarchs till God severed one from the other; and God did not give all spiritual power to Aaron when he distinguished the priesthood; much remained still in Moses. The ecumenical power of a master of a family is not ecclesiastical, yet he hath spiritual power to teach, pray, bless, command as he is a *pater-familias.* Else a magistrate as a magistrate, must subordinate the first table to the second, the glory of God to the temporal good of men, God to man, religion to civility. A magistrate when he prays, blesseth, or commandeth all to seek the God of Israel, as he his *custos utriusque tabulae,* is not supposed to use any of these means in the first place for the temporal prosperity of the commonwealth. Must a magistrate as a magistrate pray only for corn, wine, and oil? or may he serve God only for corn, wine, and oil, and bless only with the dew of heaven and fatness of the earth? A physician, indeed, as a physician doth only heal and intend to heal the natural man, because he hath only natural mediums, but a magistrate hath spiritual mediums, as he is a magistrate. A magistrate as a man may make a temporal being his first and last and only end, but as a magistrate he intends both temporals and spirituals. A Christian as a man, may be for the world, but as a Christian he is for the Lord. A magistrate's office is spiritual, though the magistrate's person be profane and heathenish.

Thomas Walley (1616–1678)

BORN in England, Thomas Walley became rector of St. Mary's Whitechapel, Middlesex, where he was occupied from 1648 until 1662, when he was ejected for nonconformity. Moving to New England, he refused an invitation to Boston in order to take a ministry at troubled Barnstable, where he soon earned a high reputation for his conciliatory temper. In 1671 he was on the committee that drafted the body of laws of Plymouth Colony (1672); in 1677 he began to fail, and the following year he died. *Balm in Gilead to Heal Sion's Wounds,* from which the following excerpt comes, was an election sermon preached at Plymouth on June 1, 1669; it was immediately printed in two editions at Cambridge. This sermon is interesting both for Walley's relating the spiritual to the civil disorders of the commonwealth (a favorite strategy of preachers after 1660) and for his use of the metaphor of a diseased body politic (a typical Renaissance concept).

TEXT: Thomas Walley, *Balm in Gilead to Heal Sion's Wounds,* 2d ed. (Cambridge, Mass., 1670).

The Languishing Commonwealth

[From *Balm in Gilead,* 1669]

We have cause to fear that our condition is but sad this day, for our case looks like the case of this people that the prophet speaks of. We have Gilead's balm and Gilead's physicians, and yet we are a sick people; we have the means of healing amongst us, that means that is proper and suitable, and yet we continue a wounded and weak people. What means can a people have more for cure then we have? God is yet in our Sion, we have healing ordinances, the preaching of the gospel, the seals of the covenant of grace, magistrates that would heal the sicknesses of Sion, and ministers that mourn for the hurt of the daughter of Sion.

Surely this day New England is sick, the country is a sickly country; the country is full of healthful bodies, but sick souls.

I shall name two or three of the diseases that reign amongst us and do most mischief.

1. The lethargy, a cold sleepy disease; there seems to be an insensibleness of sin and danger. Faith is dead, and love is cold, and zeal is gone; the wise and foolish virgins seem to be all asleep, in a deep sleep of security. The power of godliness decays, the trumpet sounds, the alarm is given, yet the most sleep on.

Oh ye Christians that are not quite asleep! do not you perceive that the love of the most of the professors of religion is grown cold to Christ, to truth, to ordinances, to one another? And that which renders our case the more sad, is, that neither the Word of God, nor the rod of God awakens us; though we see that Satan is busy, yet we are idle. Indeed when saints do least good, the Devil doth most hurt; while they sleep, he is awake. It is to be feared, that we shall be awakened in some dreadful way, by some sudden and unexpected tempest of divine wrath. A Laodicean frame of spirit is hateful to God, Rev. 3:15, 16.

2. There is a burning fever amongst us, a fire of contention in towns, in churches; fuel is laid upon this fire daily. What town or what church is there that is free from this disease? The work of contention is followed, as though it were the work of our day, as though we had nothing else to do. Many through the pride of their hearts are very unquiet, and cannot be content in the places God hath set them in, but strive for mastery, dominion and rule, forgetting that counsel of the Apostle: "My brethren, be not many masters," James 3:1. This comes from pride and self-love. Proud Nature is discontented with the condition that God hath put man in. The great reason why many are unquiet, is, because they do not think they are high enough either in the church or in the commonwealth. The contentions and divisions that are amongst us are a sign that lust reigns, and that God's destroying judgments are not far off. This fire of contention will consume all, except God prevent.

3. Many are possessed with an evil spirit. It's observed, that when Christ came into the world there were more possessed with evil spirits, than had been in any age; and it is to be wondered at, that in this time, in which the gospel is so clearly preached, and religion so much professed, that so many should be possessed with evil spirits.

Some, with a spirit of oppression, cruelty and covetousness; some, with a spirit of error and delusion; some, with a spirit of envy and jealousy; others are filled with pride in heart and manners. Was it ever worse among the Jews, then it is with us? That which is threatened as a sore judgment to the Jews, is in a great measure fulfilled among us this day, Isa. 3:5: "The people shall be oppressed, every one by another, and every one by his neighbor; the child shall behave himself proudly against the ancient, and the base against the honorable." Many of the children of this generation, if they consider their carriage to their parents, will have little cause to expect much obedience from their children, and are like in their latter years to reap the fruit of their present disobedience to their parents. Oh, how sad is it, that there should be such a spirit of profaneness, looseness, and wilfulness against counsel in our days! Truly, if the means we have do not cure us, what is like to cure us? God will either make us better, or leave us; God would heal us, and we will not be healed. . . .

Let this be matter of admiration, as well as of humiliation to us, that a sick people that have all means to heal them, are not healed; that those who have Gilead's balm and Gilead's physicians, are yet sick; and if we do not wonder at it, strangers will hereafter, that a people that have such proper suitable means are still unrecovered, and dying under them. I speak not to flatter. We have a godly magistracy, that have made it manifest that they are willing, yea earnestly desirous of healing the sicknesses of church and state. We have godly ministers, that I am confident would spend and be spent for the recovery of the health of the daughter of Sion. We have holy ordinances, and we have some mourning and praying saints, that lament the evils that are among us; and God's providences call upon us daily to get our sicknesses healed. And is it not a wonder, that a people that have such means and mercies should still languish of their diseases? Oh that that which is said of Nineveh, might never be said of us: "There is no healing of thy bruises, thy wound is grievous"! Nahum 3:19. It would be sad, if God should threaten us as He doth Egypt, Jer. 46:11: "In vain shalt thou use many medicines, for thou shalt not be cured." Or if God should say as once concerning Babylon, Jer. 51:9: "We would have healed Babylon, but she is not healed; forsake her, and let us go every one into his own country." It was no wonder that these heathen nations could not be healed, but it is matter of astonishment that Sion is not, that New England should have so much means of healing, and yet continue sick; that a people that are lifted up to heaven with mercies, should be so likely to be thrown down to hell.

New England's First Fruits

"THE best thing that ever New England thought upon," in Cotton Mather's learned judgment, was Harvard College. The General Court declared its determination to found a school or college as early as 1636, but was unable to turn attention to the matter (because of the defections of Anne Hutchinson and Roger Williams, and the annoyance of the Pequot War) until the following year, when a house and an acre of land were secured in Cambridge. In 1638 John Harvard died, bequeathing his four hundred books, some money, and his name to the new college, whose first class graduated in 1642. The following year, in London, there appeared a brief account of the new college that ignored its tenuous legal position (as a chartered corporation, the Massachusetts Bay Company could not legally charter another corporation, that of the college), but emphasized the curriculum.

Although the account of 1643, *New England's First Fruits,* clearly confesses that the dread of leaving an illiterate ministry was one of the main motives for founding the college, it must not be supposed that the new school was narrowly parochial, or functioned as a theological seminary. Insofar as abundant religious study was requisite to a liberal education, this occupied a good deal of student time; but the new Cambridge did its best to emulate the English Cambridge and Oxford in teaching the "Arts" — Grammar, Logic, Rhetoric (called the *trivium*), and Arithmetic, Geometry, and Astronomy (omitting only Music from the medieval *quadrivium*); the "Philosophies" — Metaphysics, Ethics, and what we would call Natural Science; and Greek, Hebrew, and Ancient History. The curriculum, extended from three to four years in 1652, was therefore designed to provide a liberal education; and it may have been for just that reason that less than half of Harvard's seventeenth-century graduates entered the ministry, and that Yale College was founded in 1701 to balance the freethinking of Cambridge. The full story of Harvard's early years may be found in Samuel Eliot Morison, *The Founding of Harvard College* (Cambridge, Mass., 1935) and *Harvard College in the Seventeenth Century* (Cambridge, Mass., 1936).

TEXT: Samuel Eliot Morison, *The Founding of Harvard College* (Cambridge, Mass., 1935).

In Respect of the College

[From *New England's First Fruits,* 1643]

1. After God had carried us safe to New England, and we had builded our houses, provided necessaries for our livelihood, reared convenient places for God's worship, and settled the civil government, one of the next things we longed for and looked after was to advance learning and perpetuate it to posterity; dreading to leave an illiterate ministry to the churches, when our present ministers shall lie in the dust. And as we were thinking and consulting how to effect this great work, it pleased God to stir up the heart of one Mr. Harvard (a godly gentleman, and a lover of learning, there living amongst us) to give the one half of his estate (it being in all about £1700) towards the erecting of a college, and all his library: after him, another gave £300, others after them cast in more, and the public hand of the state added the rest. The college was, by common consent, appointed to be at Cambridge (a place very pleasant and accommodate) and is called (according to the name of the first founder) Harvard College.

The edifice is very fair and comely within and without, having in it a spacious hall (where they daily meet at commons, lectures, exercises), and a large library with some books to it, the gifts of divers of our friends, their chambers and studies also fitted for, and possessed by the students, and all other rooms of office necessary and convenient, with all needful offices thereto belonging. And by the side of the College, a fair grammar school, for the training up of young scholars, and fitting of them for academical learning, that still as they are judged ripe, they may be received into the College of this school. Master Corlet is the master, who hath very well approved himself for his abilities, dexterity, and painfulness in teaching and education of the youth under him.

Over the College is Master Dunster placed, as president, a learned, conscionable, and industrious man, who hath so trained up his pupils in the tongues and arts, and so seasoned them with the principles of divinity and Christianity, that we have to our great comfort (and in truth, beyond our hopes) beheld their progress in learning and godliness also; the former of these hath appeared in their public declamations in Latin and Greek, and disputations logical and philosophical, which they have been wonted (besides their ordinary exercises in the College hall), in the audience of the magistrates, ministers, and other scholars, for the probation of their growth in learning, upon set days, constantly once every month, to make and uphold. The latter hath been manifested in sundry of them, by the savory breathings of their spirits in their godly conversation, insomuch that we are confident, if these early blossoms may be cherished and warmed with the influence of the friends of learning, and lovers of this pious work, they will, by the help of God, come to happy maturity in a short time.

Over the College are twelve overseers chosen by the General Court: six of them are of the magistrates, the other six of the ministers, who are to promote the best good of it, and (having a power of influence into all persons in it) are to see that everyone be diligent and proficient in his proper place.

2. *Rules, and Precepts that are Observed in the College.*

1. When any scholar is able to understand Tully or such like classical author *extempore,* and make and speak true Latin in verse and prose, *suo ut aiunt marte,* and decline perfectly the paradigms of nouns and verbs in the Greek tongue: let him then, and not before, be capable of admission into the College.

2. Let every student be plainly instructed and earnestly pressed to consider well, the main end of his life and studies is, "to know God and Jesus Christ which is eternal life," John 17:3, and therefore

to lay Christ in the bottom, as the only foundation of all sound knowledge and learning.

And seeing the Lord only giveth wisdom, let everyone seriously set himself by prayer in secret to seek it of Him, Prov. 2:3.

3. Everyone shall so exercise himself in reading the scriptures twice a day, that he shall be ready to give such an account of his proficiency therein, both in theoretical observations of the language, and logic, and in practical and spiritual truths, as his tutor shall require, according to his ability; seeing "the entrance of the Word giveth light, it giveth understanding to the simple," Psalm 119:130.

4. That they, eschewing all profanation of God's name, attributes, word, ordinances, and times of worship, do study with good conscience, carefully to retain God, and the love of His truth in their minds. Else, let them know, that (notwithstanding their learning) God may give them up "to strong delusions," and in the end "to a reprobate mind," 2 Thes. 2:11, 12, Rom. 1:28.

5. That they studiously redeem the time; observe the general hours appointed for all the students, and the special hours for their own classes; and then diligently attend the lectures, without any disturbance by word or gesture. And if in anything they doubt, they shall inquire, as of their fellows, so (in case of "non-satisfaction"), modestly of their tutors.

6. None shall, under any pretense whatsoever, frequent the company and society of such men as lead an unfit and dissolute life.

Nor shall any without his tutor's leave, or (in his absence) the call of parents or guardians, go abroad to other towns.

7. Every scholar shall be present in his tutor's chamber at the seventh hour in the morning, immediately after the sound of the bell, at his opening the scripture and prayer; so also at the fifth hour at night, and then give account of his own private reading, as aforesaid in particular the third, and constantly attend lectures in the hall at the hours appointed. But if any (without necessary impediment) shall absent himself from prayer or lectures, he shall be liable to admonition, if he offend above once a week.

8. If any scholar shall be found to transgress any of the laws of God, or the school, after twice admonition, he shall be liable, if not *adultus*, to correction; if *adultus*, his name shall be given up to the overseers of the College, that he may be admonished at the public monthly act.

3. *The Times and Order of Their Studies, unless Experience Shall Shew Cause to Alter.*

The second and third day of the week, read lectures, as followeth:

To the first year, at eight of the clock in the morning, logic the first three quarters, physics the last quarter.

To the second year, at the ninth hour, ethics and politics, at convenient distances of time.

To the third year, at the tenth, arithmetic and geometry the first three quarters, astronomy the last.

Afternoon:

The first year disputes at the second hour.

The second year at the third hour.

The third year at the fourth, everyone in his art.

The fourth day, reads Greek:

To the first year, the etymology and syntax at the eighth hour. To the second, at the ninth hour, *prosodia* and *dialects.*

Afternoon:

The first year, at second hour, practice the precepts of grammar in such authors as have variety of words.

The second year, at third hour, practice in poesy. . . .

The third year, perfect their theory before noon, and exercise style, composition, imitation, epitome, both in prose and verse, afternoon.

The fifth day, reads Hebrew and the Eastern tongues:

Grammar to the first year, hour the eighth.

To the second, Chaldee at the ninth hour.

To the third, Syriac at the tenth hour.

Afternoon:

The first year, practice in the Bible at the second hour.

The second, in Ezra and Daniel at the third hour.

The third, at the fourth hour in Trostius' New Testament.

The sixth day, reads rhetoric to all at the eighth hour:

Declamations at the ninth. So ordered that every scholar may declaim once a month. The rest of the day, *vacat rhetoricis studiis.*

The seventh day, reads divinity catechetical at the eighth hour; commonplaces at the ninth hour.

Afternoon:

The first hour, reads history in the winter, the nature of plants in the summer.

The sum of every lecture shall be examined, before the new lecture be read.

Every scholar, that on proof is found able to read the originals of the Old and New Testament into the Latin tongue, and to resolve them logically, withal being of godly life and conversation, and at any public act hath the approbation of the overseers and master of the College, is fit to be dignified with his first degree.

Every scholar that giveth up in writing a *system* or *synopsis*, or sum of logic, natural and moral philosophy, arithmetic, geometry, and astronomy, and is ready to defend his theses or positions, withal skilled in the originals as abovesaid, and of godly life and conversation, and so approved by the overseers and master of the College, at any public act, is fit to be dignified with his second degree.

Samuel Sewall (1652–1730)

ON JUNE 19, 1700, Samuel Sewall, probably reflecting on his court experience with John Saffin's slave Adam (*q.v.*, p. 312), made the following entry in his *Diary:* "Having been long and much dissatisfied with the trade of fetching Negroes from Guinea, at last I had a strong inclination to write something about it, but it wore off. At last reading Bayne, . . . about servants, who mentions Blackamoors, I began to be uneasy that I had so long neglected doing anything. When I was thus thinking, in came Brother Belknap to show me a petition he intended to present to the General Court for the freeing a Negro and his wife who were unjustly held in bondage. And there is a motion by a Boston committee to get a law that all importers of Negroes shall pay 40 s. per head, to discourage the bringing of them. And Mr. C. Mather resolves to publish a sheet to exhort masters to labor their conversion, which makes me hope that I was called of God to write this apology for them; let His blessing accompany the same." This entry, and the apology itself, titled *The Selling of Joseph* (1700), show the private world of Christian morality influencing society in general and the law in particular.

TEXT: Samuel Sewall, *The Selling of Joseph: A Memorial* (Boston, 1700).

The Selling of Joseph: A Memorial

For as much as liberty is in real value next unto life: None ought to part with it themselves, or deprive others of it, but upon most mature consideration.

The numerousness of slaves at this day in the Province, and the uneasiness of them under their slavery, hath put many upon thinking whether the foundation of it be firmly and well laid; so as to sustain the vast weight that is built upon it. It is most certain that all men, as they are the sons of Adam, are coheirs; and have equal right unto liberty, and all other outward comforts of life. "God hath given the earth [with all its commodities] unto the sons of Adam," Psal. 115:16.

"And hath made of one blood, all nations of men, for to dwell on all the face of the earth, and hath determined the times before appointed, and the bounds of their habitation: That they should seek the Lord. Forasmuch then as we are the offspring of God," etc. Acts 17:26, 27, 29. Now although the title given by the last Adam doth infinitely better men's estates, respecting God and themselves; and grants them a most beneficial and inviolable lease under the broad seal of heaven, who were before only tenants at will: yet through the indulgence of God to our first parents after the fall, the outward estate of all and every of their children, remains the same, as to one another. So that originally, and naturally, there is no such thing as slavery. Joseph was rightfully no more a slave to his brethren, than they were to him: and they had no more authority to sell him, than they had to slay him. And if they had nothing to do to sell him, the Ishmaelites bargaining with them, and paying down twenty pieces of silver, could not make a title. Neither could Potiphar have any better interest in him than the Ismaelites had, Gen. 37:20, 27, 28. For he that shall in this case plead alteration of property, seems to have forfeited a great part of his own claim to humanity. There is no proportion between twenty pieces of silver, and liberty. The commodity itself is the claimer. If Arabian gold be imported in any quantities, most are afraid to meddle with it, though they might have it at easy rates; lest if it should have been wrongfully taken from the owners, it should kindle a fire to the consumption of their whole estate. 'Tis pity there should be more caution used in buying a horse, or a little lifeless dust, than there is in purchasing men and women: whenas they are the offspring of God, and their liberty is *auro pretiosior omni.*

And seeing God hath said, "He that stealeth a man and selleth him, or if he be found in his hand, he shall surely be put to death." Exod. 21:16, this law being of everlasting equity, wherein man stealing is ranked among the most atrocious of capital crimes: what louder cry can there be made of that celebrated warning, *caveat emptor!*

And all things considered, it would conduce more to the welfare of the Province, to have white servants for a term of years, than to have slaves for life. Few can endure to hear of a Negro's being made free; and indeed they can seldom use their freedom well; yet their continual aspiring after their forbidden liberty, renders them unwilling servants. And there is such a disparity in their conditions, color and hair, that they can never embody with us, and grow up into orderly families, to the peopling of the land: but still remain in our body politic as a kind of extravasate blood. As many Negro men as there are among us, so many empty places there are in our train bands, and the places taken up of men that might make husbands for our daughters. And the sons and daughters of New England would become more like Jacob, and Rachel, if this slavery were thrust quite out of doors. Moreover, it is too well known what temptations masters are under, to connive at the fornication of their slaves; lest they should be obliged to find them wives, or pay their fines. It seems to be practically pleaded that they might be lawless; 'tis thought much of, that the law should have satisfaction for their thefts, and other immoralities; by which means, holiness to the Lord is more rarely engraven upon this sort of servitude. It is likewise most lamentable to think, how in taking Negroes out of Africa, and selling of them here, that which God has joined together men do boldly rend asunder; men from their country, husbands from their wives, parents from their children. How horrible is the uncleanness, mortality, if not murder, that the ships are guilty of that bring great crowds of these miserable men, and women! Methinks, when we are bemoaning the barbarous usage of our friends and kinsfolk in Africa: it might not be unseasonable to inquire whether we are not culpable in forcing the Africans to become slaves amongst ourselves. And it may be a question whether all the benefit received by Negro slaves, will balance the account of cash laid out upon them; and for the redemption of our own enslaved friends out of Africa; besides all the persons and estates that have perished there.

Objection 1. These blackamoors are of the posterity of Cham, and therefore are under the curse of slavery. Gen. 9:25, 26, 27.

Answer. Of all offices, one would not beg this; viz., uncalled for, to be an executioner of the vindictive wrath of God; the extent and duration of which is to us uncertain. If this ever was a commission, how do we know but that it is long since out of date? Many have found it to their cost, that a prophetical denunciation of judgment against a person or people, would not warrant them to inflict that evil. If it would, Hazael might justify himself in all he did against his master, and the Israelites, from II Kings 8:10, 12.

But it is possible that by cursory reading, this text may have been mistaken. For Canaan is the person cursed three times over, without the mentioning of Cham. Good expositors suppose the curse entailed on him, and that this prophecy was accomplished in the extirpation of the Canaanites, and in the servitude of the Gibeonites. . . . Whereas the blackamoors are not descended of Canaan, but of Cush. Psal. 68:31. "Princes shall come out of Egypt [Mizraim;] Ethiopia [Cush] shall soon stretch out her hands unto God." Under which names, all Africa may be comprehended; and their promised conversion ought to be prayed for. Jer. 13:23. "Can the Ethiopian change his skin?" This shews that black men are the posterity of Cush, who time out of mind have been distinguished by their color. And for want of the true, Ovid assigns a fabulous cause of it. . . .

Objection 2. The *nigers* are brought out of a pagan country, into places where the gospel is preached.

Answer. Evil must not be done, that good may come of it. The extraordinary and comprehensive benefit accruing to the church of God, and to Joseph personally, did not rectify his brethren's sale of him.

Objection 3. The Africans have wars one with another; our ships bring lawful captives taken in those wars.

Answer. For aught is known, their wars are much such as were between Jacob's sons and their brother Joseph. If they be between town and town, provincial or national, every war is upon one side unjust. An unlawful war can't make lawful captives. And by receiving, we are in danger to promote, and partake in their barbarous cruelties. I am sure, if some gentlemen should go down to the Brewsters to take the air, and fish: and a stronger party from Hull should surprise them, and sell them for slaves to a ship outward bound, they would think themselves unjustly dealt with; both by sellers and buyers. And yet 'tis to be feared, we have no other kind of title to our *nigers*. "Therefore all things whatsoever ye would that men should do to you, do ye even so to them: for this is the law and the prophets." Matt. 7:12.

Objection 4. Abraham had servants bought with his money, and born in his house.

Answer. Until the circumstances of Abraham's purchase be recorded, no argument can be drawn from it. In the meantime, charity obliges us to conclude, that he knew it was lawful and good.

It is observable that the Israelites were strictly forbidden the buying, or selling one another for slaves. Levit. 25:39, 46. Jer. 34:8–22. And God gaged His blessing in lieu of any loss they might conceit they suffered thereby. Deut. 15:18. And since the partition wall is broken down, inordinate self love should likewise be demolished. God expects that Christians should be of a more ingenuous and benign frame of spirit. Christians should carry it to all the world, as the Israelites were to carry it one towards another. And for men obstinately to persist in holding their neighbors and brethren under the rigor of perpetual bondage, seems to be no proper way of gaining assurance that God has given them spiritual freedom. Our blessed Saviour has altered the measures of the ancient love-song, and set it to a most excellent new tune, which all ought to be ambitious of learning. Matt. 5:43, 44. John 13:34. These Ethiopians, as black as they are, seeing they are the sons and daughters of the first Adam, the brethren and sisters of the last Adam, and the offspring of God; they ought to be treated with a respect agreeable.

John Norton (1606–1663)

John Norton was born in Hertfordshire, England, graduated from Cambridge, and came to Plymouth in 1635. He moved to Boston and later to Ipswich, where he soon became one of the most powerful ministers in Massachusetts. In 1648 he was active in drawing up the Cambridge Platform, which imposed a measure of unity on the various Calvinist sects, and was also one of the most rigorous persecutors of Quakers in New England and owner of one of the largest libraries in the colony. A learned, hard-minded man, Norton had little of John Cotton's breadth of intellect or the Mathers' depth of learning. A prolific writer, he was author of three important books, *The Orthodox Evangelist* (1654), *The Life of the Reverend John Cotton* (1658), and *The Heart of New England Rent by the Blasphemies of the Present Generation* (1660). The following excerpt is an excellent brief statement of the Calvinist concept of God's absolute sovereignty over man and the creation.

Text: John Norton, *The Orthodox Evangelist* (London, 1654).

God's Relation to Man

[From *The Orthodox Evangelist,* 1654]

The justice of God is considered either in respect of Himself, or in respect of the reasonable creature; in order to Himself (whereby He is a necessary debtor to Himself), it is called essential justice; in order to the reasonable creature (whereby He hath freely made Himself a debtor unto them), it is called relative justice.

In the essential justice of God is contained that which is called the justice of condecency, or comeliness; which necessitates not God to constitute any rule of relative justice between Himself, and the creature; only, in case He be pleased to constitute any, it necessitates Him so to do it, as becometh such an agent, and as serveth best unto His end: and which (being done) continueth inviolable, and infallible. The essential justice, constancy, and truth of God, permitteth not any defect, or alteration concerning the execution of His decree after He had once decreed it; notwithstanding before the decree He was free to have decreed, or not to have decreed that decree.

Relative, or moral justice, is an external work of God, whereby He proceeds with man according to the Law of righteousness freely constituted between Him and them; rendring to everyone what is due unto them thereby, either by way of recompense, in case of obedience; or by way of punishment, in case of disobedience.

For our better understanding of this moral justice of God, in respect of man, consider: 1. That nothing can be due from God to man as of himself. 2. That which is due from God to man, is from the free and mere good pleasure of God. 3. That this good pleasure, or will of God, is the rule of righteousness. 4. That God proceeding to execution, according to this rule of righteousness constituted by His good pleasure, can do no wrong.

Nothing can be due from God to man as of himself; the creature of itself being a mere nothing, and God being all, He cannot become a debtor to the creature, either of good or evil; otherwise then He is pleased to make himself a debtor. Should God be looked at as a necessary debtor unto the creature, it must either be to the creature not yet in being, or to the creature in actual being; but He cannot be a debtor to the creature not yet in being; for to it nothing can be due but creation, and that should be due unto nothing. Thence it would follow, that God were bound to create every creature that were possible to be created, and that also from eternity.

Neither can He be a debtor to the creature in actual being, to which, if He can owe anything, it must either be the continuation of it in its being, or annihilation. If God doth not owe unto the creature its creation, He cannot owe unto it its continuation; continuation being nothing else, but the continuance of creation; He that is not bound to give a creature its being for one instant, which is done in creation, is much less bound to give unto a creature its being for many instants, which is included in continuation. Besides, were God bound to continue the creature in actual being for one year, by the same reason He were bound to continue them forever.

Neither can He owe unto the creature in actual being, annihilation; for then neither could the godly enjoy eternal life, nor the wicked be punished with eternal death. To owe annihilation is to owe nothing. The worth of the creature in order unto God, is not intrinsical; "For who hath first given to him, and it shall be recompensed unto him again?" Rom. 11:35.

Whatsoever is due from God to man, is from the mere will, and good pleasure of God. Moral justice floweth from the good pleasure of God. The manifestation of the glory of God in a way of justice is the end, the permission of sin is the means; that this should be the means, and that should be the end, is wholly of the will of God. The creation of man is an effect of God's good pleasure. That prohibition of Adam to eat of the forbidden fruit, upon the transgression of which followed the death of mankind, was an interdict of God's free will. The moral law itself is an effect of God's good pleasure. What reasonable man but will yield that the being of the moral law hath no necessary connection with the Being of God? That this moral law should be a constant rule of manners, and that all man's actions should fall within the compass of this rule, is from the mere will of God. That the actions of men, not conformable to this law, should be sin; that death should be the punishment of sin; that this punishment should be suffered in our own persons, or in our surety, as should seem good unto the Law-giver — all these are the constitutions of God, proceeding from Him, not by way of necessity of nature, but freely, as effects and products of His eternal good pleasure.

Thomas Shepard (1605–1649)

THOMAS SHEPARD was born at Towcester, England, and, like so many of his Cambridge University contemporaries, absorbed his dissenting ways at college. He took his B.A. in 1624, and his M.A. in 1627. After preaching for a time, he was one of those driven out of the church by Archbishop Laud, and he sailed for America in 1634. Storms at sea, however, forced his ship to return to England, where he hid until the following spring. Arriving in New England in 1635, Shepard accepted a pastorate at Cambridge and became one of the overseers of Harvard College. "A poor, weak, pale-complectioned man," he was nevertheless a tireless writer and a powerful orator. Author of a number of volumes, he wrote *The Sincere Convert* in 1641, after which it went through more than twenty editions. Shepard was especially skillful at the elucidation of Calvinist doctrine, possessed of the ability to combine clear, logical exposition with evangelistic fervor in an unusually effective pulpit manner. A paragon of piety to writers of Edward Taylor's generation, Shepard was also a rich quarry of hard arguments to Jonathan Edwards.

TEXT: Thomas Shepard, *The Sincere Convert,* 2d ed. (London, 1664).

The Strait Gate to Heaven

[From *The Sincere Convert,* 1641]

That those that are saved are very few; and that those that are saved, are saved with very much difficulty.

"Strait is the gate, and narrow is the way that leadeth unto life, and few there be that find it" (Matt. 7:14).

Here are two parts:

1. The paucity of them that shall be saved; few find the way thither.

2. The difficulty of being saved; strait and narrow is the way and gate unto life.

Hence arise two doctrines:

1. That the number of them that shall be saved is very small (Luke 13:24). The Devil hath his drove, and swarms to go to hell, as fast as bees to their hive; Christ hath His flock, and that is but a little flock; hence God's children are called jewels (Mal. 3:17), which commonly are kept secret, in respect of the other lumber in the house; hence they are called strangers and pilgrims, which are very few in respect of the inhabitants of the country through which they pass; hence they are called "sons of God" (I John 3:2), of the blood royal, which are few in respect of common subjects.

But see the truth of this point in these two things:

First, look to all ages and times of the world; secondly, to all places and persons in the world, and we shall see few men were saved.

1. Look to all ages, and we shall find but a handful saved. As soon as ever the Lord began to keep house, and there were but two families in it, there was a bloody Cain living, and a good Abel slain. And as the world increased in number, so in wickedness. (Gen. 6:12) It is said, "All flesh had corrupted their ways," and amongst so many thousand men, not one righteous but Noah and his family; and yet in the ark there crept in a cursed Cham.

Afterwards as Abraham's posterity increased, so we see their sin abounded. When his posterity was in Egypt, where one would think, if ever men were good, now it would appear, being so heavily afflicted by Pharaoh, being by so many miracles miraculously delivered by the hand of Moses, yet most of these God was wroth with (Heb. 3:12), and only two of them, Caleb and Joshua, went into Canaan, a type of heaven. Look into Solomon's time: What glorious, what great profession was there then! Yet after his death ten tribes fell to the odious sin of idolatry, following the command of Jeroboam, their king. Look further into Isaiah's time, when there were multitudes of sacrifices and prayers (Isa. 1.11); yet then there was but a remnant, nay, a very little remnant that should be saved. And look to the time of Christ's coming in the flesh (for I pick out the best time of all), when one would think by such sermons He preached, such miracles He wrought, such a life as He led, all the Jews would have entertained Him; yet it is said, "He came unto His own, and they received Him not." So few, that Christ Himself admires at one good Nathaniel, "Behold an Israelite in whom there is no guile." In the Apostle's time, many indeed were converted, but few comparatively; and amongst the best churches many bad: as that at Philippi

(Philippians 3:18). Many had a name to live, but were dead, and few only kept their garments unspotted. And presently, after the Apostle's time, many grievous wolves came and devoured the sheep, and so in succeeding ages (Rev. 12:9): "All the earth wondered at the whore in scarlet."

And in Luther's time, when the light began to arise again, he saw so many carnal gospellers, that he breaks out in one sermon into these speeches: "God grant I may never live to see those bloody days, that are coming upon an ungodly world." Latimer heard so much profaneness in his time, that he thought verily doomsday was just at hand. And have not our ears heard censuring those in the Palatinate where (as 'tis reported) many have fallen from the glorious Gospel to popery, as fast as leaves fall in autumn? Who would have thought there had lurked such hearts under such a shew of detesting popery, as was among them before? And at Christ's coming, shall He find faith on the earth?

2. Let us look unto all places and persons, and see how few shall be saved. The world is now split into four parts: Europe, Asia, Africa, and America, and the three biggest parts are drowned in a deluge of profaneness and superstition; they do not so much as profess Christ; you may see the sentence of death written on these men's foreheads (Jer. 10:ult.). But let us look upon the best part of the world, and that is Europe; how few shall be saved there? First, the Grecian Church, howsoever now in these days their good Patriarch of Constantinople is about a general reformation among them, and hath done much good; yet are they for the present, and have been for the most part of them, without the saving means of knowledge. They content themselves with their old superstitions, having little or no preaching at all. And for the other part, as Italy, Spain, France, Germany, for the most part they are popish, and see the end of these men (II Thess. 2:9, 10, 11, 12). And now amongst them that carry the badge of honesty, I will not speak what mine ears have heard, and my heart believes concerning other churches: I will come unto our own Church of England, which is the most flourishing church in the world. Never had church such preachers, such means; yet have we not some chapels and churches stand as dark lanthorns without light, where people are led with blind, or idle, or licentious ministers, and so both fall into the ditch?

Nay, even among them that have the means of grace, but few shall be saved. It may be sometimes among ninety-nine in a parish, Christ sends a minister to call some one lost sheep among them (Matt. 13). Three grounds were bad where the seed was sown, and only one ground good. It's a strange speech of Chrysostom in his fourth sermon to the people of Antioch, where he was much beloved, and did much good: "How many do you think" (saith he) "shall be saved in this city? It will be an hard speech to you, but I will speak it; though here be so many thousands of you, yet there cannot be found an hundred that shall be saved; and I doubt of them too. For what villainy is there among youth? What sloth in old men?" and so he goes on. So say I, never tell me we are baptized and are Christians and trust to Christ; let us but separate the goats from the sheep, and exclude none but such as the scriptures doth, and set a cross upon their doors with "Lord, have mercy upon them," and we shall see only few in the city shall be saved.

1. Cast out all the profane people among us, as drunkards, swearers, whores, liars, which the scripture brands for black sheep and condemns them in an hundred places.

2. Set by all civil men that are but wolves chained up, tame devils, swine in a fair meadow, that pay all they owe, and do nobody any harm, yet do none any great good, that plead for themselves and say, "Who can say black is mine eye?" These are righteous men, whom Christ never came to call; for he came not to call the righteous, but sinners to repentance.

3. Cast by all hypocrites, that like stage-players, in the sight of others, act the parts of kings, and honest men; when look upon them in their tiring house, they are but base varlets.

4. Formal professors, and carnal gospellers, that have a thing like faith, and like sorrow, and like true repentance, and like good desires; but yet they be but pictures; they deceive others and themselves too (II Tim. 3:5).

Set by these four sorts, how few then are to be saved, even among them that are hatcht in the bosom of the church?

First, here then is an use of encouragement. Be not discouraged by the name of singularity. What? do you think yourself wiser then others? And shall none be saved but such as are so precise as ministers prate? Are you wiser then others, that you think none shall go to heaven but yourself? I tell you, if you would be saved, you must be singular men, not out of faction, but out of conscience (Acts 24:16).

Secondly, here is matter of terror to all those that be of opinion, that few shall be saved; and therefore, when they are convinced of the danger of sin by the Word, they fly to this shelter: "If I be damned, it will be woe to many more beside me then"; as though most should not be damned. Oh yes, the most of them that live in the church shall perish. And this made an hermit, which Theodoret mentions, to live fifteen years in a cell, in a desolate wilderness, with nothing but bread and water, and yet doubted after all his sorrow, whether he should be saved or no. Oh, God's wrath is heavy, which thou shalt one day bear.

Thirdly, this ministereth exhortation to all confident people, that think they believe, and say, they doubt not but to be saved, and hence do not much fear death. Oh! learn hence to suspect and fear your estates, and fear it so much that thou canst not be quiet until thou hast got some assurance thou shalt be saved. When Christ told His disciples that one of them should betray Him, they all said, "Master, is it I?" But if He had said eleven of them should betray Him, all except one, would they not all conclude, surely it is I? If the Lord had said, only few shall be damned, every man might fear, it may be it is I; but now He says most shall, every man may cry out and say, surely it is I. No humble heart, but is driven to and fro with many stinging fears this way; yet there is a generation of presumptuous, brazen-faced, bold people, that confidently think of themselves, as the Jews of the Pharisees (being so holy and strict) that if God save but two in the world, they shall make one.

The child of God indeed is bold as a lion; but he hath God's spirit and promise, assuring him of his eternal welfare. But I speak of divers that have no sound ground to prove this point (which they pertinaciously defend) that they shall be saved. This confident humour rageth most of all in our old professors at large, who think, that's a jest indeed, that having been of a good belief so long, that they now should be so far behindhand, as to begin the work, and lay the foundation anew. And not only among these, but amongst divers sorts of people whom the Devil never troubles, because he is sure of them already, and therefore cries peace in their ears, whose conscience never troubles them, because that hath shut its eyes. And hence they sleep, and sleeping, dream that God is merciful unto them, and will be so; yet never see they are deceived, until they awake with the flames of hell about their ears. And the world troubles them not, they have their hearts' desire here, because they are friends to it, and so enemies to God. And ministers never trouble them, for they have none such as are fit for that work near them; or if they have, they can sit and sleep in the church and choose whether they will believe him. And their friends never trouble them, because they are afraid to displease them. And God Himself never troubles them, because that time is to come hereafter. This one truth well pondered and thought on, may damp thine heart, and make thy conscience fly in thy face and say, "Thou art the man." It may be there are better in hell then thyself, that art so confident; and therefore tell me, what hast thou to say for thyself, that thou shalt be saved? In what thing hast thou gone beyond them that think they are rich and want nothing, who yet are poor, blind, miserable, and naked?

Thou wilt say haply, first, I have left my sins I once lived in, and am now no drunkard, no swearer, no liar, etc.

I answer: Thou mayest be washed from thy mire (the pollution of the world) and yet be a swine in God's account (II Pet. 2:20); thou mayest live a blameless, innocent, honest, smooth life, and yet be a miserable creature still (Phil. 3:6).

But I pray, and that often.

This thou mayest do, and yet never be saved. (Isa. 1:11) "To what purpose is your multitude of sacrifices?" Nay, thou mayest pray with much affection, with a good heart as thou thinkest, yet a thousand miles off from being saved (Prov. 1:28).

But I fast sometimes, as well as pray.

So did the scribes and Pharisees, even twice a week, which could not be public, but private fasts. And yet this righteousness could never save them.

But I hear the Word of God, and like the best preachers.

This thou mayest do too, and yet never be saved. Nay, thou mayest so hear, as to receive much joy and comfort in hearing — nay, to believe and catch hold on Christ, and so say and think he is thine — and yet not be saved: as the stony ground did (Matt. 13) who heard the Word with joy and for a season believed.

I read the scriptures often.

This you may do too, and yet never be saved; as the Pharisees, who were so perfect in reading the Bible, that Christ needed but only say, "It hath been said of old time," for they knew the text and place well enough without intimation.

But I am grieved and am sorrowful, and repent for my sins past.

Judas did thus; (Matt. 27:3) he repents himself with a legal repentance for fear of hell, and with a natural sorrow for dealing so unkindly with Christ, in betraying not only blood, but innocent blood. True humiliation is ever accompanied with hearty reformation.

Oh, but I love good men, and their company.

So did the five foolish virgins love the company, and (at the time of extremity) the very oil and grace of the wise; yet they were locked out of the gates of mercy.

But God hath given me more knowledge than others, or than I myself had once.

This thou mayest have, and be able to teach others and think so of thyself too, and yet never be saved.

But I keep the Lord's day strictly.

So did the Jews whom yet Christ condemned, and they were never saved.

I have very many good desires and endeavors to get heaven.

These thou and thousands may have, and yet miss of heaven.

Many shall seek to enter in at that narrow gate, and not be able.

True, thou wilt say, many men do many duties, but without any life or zeal; I am zealous.

So thou mayest be, and yet never be saved, as Jehu. Paul was zealous when he was a Pharisee; and if he was so for a false religion, and a bad cause, why, much more mayest thou be for a good cause — so zealous as not only to cry out against profaneness in the wicked, but civil honesty of others, and hypocrisy of others, yea, even of the coldness of the best of God's people. Thou mayest be the fore-horse in the team, and the ring-leader of good exercises amongst the best men (as Joash, a wicked king, was the first that complained of the negligence of his best officers in not repairing the Temple) and so stir them up unto it. Nay, thou mayest be so forward, as to be persecuted, and not yield an inch, nor shrink in the wetting, but mayest manfully and courageously stand it out in time of persecution, as the thorny ground did. So zealous thou mayest be as to like best of, and to flock most unto, the most zealous preachers that search men's consciences best, as the whole country of Judea came flocking to John's ministry, and delighted to hear him for a season. Nay, thou mayest be so zealous as to take sweet delight in doing of all these things — (Isa. 58:2, 3) "They delight in approaching near unto God" — yet come short of heaven.

But thou wilt say, true, many a man rides post that breaks his neck at last; many a man is zealous, but his fire is soon quenched, and his zeal is soon spent; they hold not out; whereas I am constant, and persevere in godly courses.

So did that young man, yet he was a graceless man (Matt. 19:20): "All these things have I done from my youth; what lack I yet?"

It is true, hypocrites may persevere, but they know themselves to be naught all the while, and so deceive others; but I am persuaded that I am in God's favor, and in a safe and happy estate, since I do all with a good heart for God.

This thou mayest verily think of thyself, and yet be deceived, and damned, and go to the devil at last. "There is a way" (saith Solomon) "that seemeth right to a man, but the end thereof is the way of death." For he is an hypocrite, not only that makes a seeming outward shew of what he hath not, but also that hath a true shew of what indeed there is not. The first sort of hypocrites deceive others only; the latter, having some inward yet common work, deceive themselves too. (James 1:26) "If any man seem to be religious," (so many are and so deceive the world) but it is added, "deceiving his soul." Nay, thou mayest go so fairly, and live so honestly, that all the best Christians about thee may think well of thee, and never suspect thee; and so mayest pass through the world, and die with a deluded comfort [that] thou shalt go to heaven, and be canonized for a saint in thy funeral sermon, and never know thou art counterfeit, till the Lord brings thee to thy strict and last examination, and so thou receive that dreadful sentence, "Go, ye cursed!" So it was with the five foolish virgins that were never discovered by the wise, nor by themselves, until the gate of grace was shut upon them. If thou hast therefore no better evidences to shew for thyself that thine estate is good then these, I'll not give a pin's point for all thy flattering false hopes of being saved. But it may be thou hast never yet come so far as to this pitch; and if not, Lord, what will become of thee? Suspect thyself much, and when in this shipwrack of souls thou seest so many thousands sink, cry out and conclude: It's a wonder of wonders, and a thousand and a thousand to one, if ever thou comest safe to shore.

Oh, strive then to be one of them that shall be saved, though it cost thee thy blood, and the loss of all that thou hast; labor to go beyond all those that go so far, and yet perish at the last. Do not say, that seeing so few shall be saved, therefore this discourageth me from seeking because all my labor may be in vain. Consider that Christ here makes another and a better use of it. (Luke 3:24) Seeing that many shall seek and not enter, "therefore," (saith he) "strive to enter in at the strait gate"; venture at least, and try what the Lord will do for thee.

Wherein doth the child of God (and so how may I) go beyond these hypocrites that go so far?

In three things principally.

First, no unregenerate man, though he go never so far, let him do never so much, but he lives in some one sin or other, secret or open, little or great. Judas went far, but he was covetous. Herod went far, but he loved his Herodias. Every dog hath his kennel, every swine hath his swill, and every wicked man his lust. For no unregenerate man hath fruition of God to content him; and there is no man's heart but it must have some good to content it — which good is to be found only in the fountain of all good, and that is God; or in the cistern, that is, in the creatures. Hence a man having lost full content in God, he seeks and feeds upon contentment in the creature, which he makes a God to him; and here lies his lust or sin, which he must needs live in. Hence, ask those men that go very far, [and take their penny for good silver,] and commend themselves for their good desires — I say — ask them if they have no sin. Yes, say they, who can live without sin? And so they give way to sin, and therefore live in sin. Nay, commonly all the duties, prayers, care, and zeal of the best hypocrites are to hide a lust; as the whore in the Proverbs that wipes her mouth, and goes to the Temple, and pays her vows; or to feed a lust, as Jehu his zeal against Baal was to get a kingdom. There remains a root of bitterness in the best hypocrites, which howsoever it be lopt off, sometimes by sickness or horror of conscience, and a man hath purposes never to commit again, yet there it secretly lurks. And though it seemeth to be bound and conquered by the Word, or by prayer, or by outward crosses. or while the hand of God is upon a man, yet the inward strength and power of it remains still. And therefore when temptations, like strong Philistines, are upon this man again, he breaks all vows, promises, bonds of God, and will save the life of his sin.

Secondly, no unregenerate man or woman ever came to be poor in spirit, and so to be carried out of all duties unto Christ. If it were possible for them to forsake and break loose forever from all sin, yet here they stick as the scribes and Pharisees. And so like zealous Paul before his conversion, they fasted and prayed and kept the Sabbath, but they rested in their legal righteousness, and in the performance of these and the like duties. Take the best hypocrite that hath the most strong persuasions of God's love to him, and ask him why he hopes to be saved. He will answer, I pray, read, hear, love good men, cry out of the sins of the time. And tell him again, that an hypocrite may climb these stairs, and go as far. He will reply, True indeed, but they do not what they do with a sound heart but to be seen of men. Mark now, how these men feel a good heart in themselves, and in all things they do, and therefore feel not a want of all good, which is poverty of spirit; and therefore here they fall short (Isa. 66:2). There were divers hypocrites forward for the worship of God in the Temple; but God loathes these, because not poor in spirit, to them only, it is said, the Lord will look. I have seen many professors very forward for all good duties, but as ignorant of Christ, when they are sifted, as blocks. And if a man (as few do) know not Christ, he must rest in his duties, because he knows not Christ, to whom he must go and be carried if ever he be saved. I have heard of a man that, being condemned to die, thought to escape the gallows and to save himself from hanging, by a certain gift he said he had of whistling. So men seek to save themselves by their gift of knowledge, gift of memory, gift of prayer, when they see they must die for their sins. This is the ruin of many a soul, that though he forsake Egypt, and his sins and fleshpots there, and will never be so as he hath been, yet he never cometh into Canaan, but loseth himself and his soul in a wilderness of many duties, and there perisheth.

Thirdly, if any unregenerate man come unto Christ, he never gets into Christ — that is, never takes his eternal rest and lodging in Jesus Christ only (Heb. 4:4). Judas followed Christ for the bag; he would have the bag and Christ too. The young man came unto Christ to be His disciple, but would have Christ and the world too. They will not content themselves with Christ alone, nor with the world alone, but make their markets out of both, like whorish wives, that will please their husbands and others too. Men in distress of conscience, if they have comfort from Christ, they are contented; if they have salvation from hell by Christ, they are contented; but Christ himself contents them not. Thus far an hypocrite goes not. So much for the first doctrine observed out of the text. I come now to the second:

DOCTRINE 2. That those that are saved, are saved with much difficulty; or, it is a wonderful hard thing to be saved.

The gate is strait, and therefore a man must sweat and strive to enter. Both the entrance is difficult, and the progress of salvation too. Jesus Christ is not got with a wet finger. It is not wishing and desiring to be saved will bring men to heaven: hell's mouth is full of good wishes. It is not shedding a tear at a sermon, or blubbering now and then in a corner, and saying over thy prayers, and crying God mercy for thy sins, will save thee. It is not "Lord, have mercy upon us" will do thee good. It is not coming constantly to church. These are easy matters. But it is a tough work, a wonderful hard matter to be saved (I Pet. 4:18). Hence the way to heaven is compared to a race, where a man must put forth all his strength, and stretch every limb, and all to get forward. Hence a Christian's life is compared to wrestling (Ephes. 6:12). All the policy and power of hell buckle together against a Christian; therefore he must look to himself, or else he falls. Hence it is compared to fighting (II Tim. 4:7). A man must fight against the Devil, the world, himself, who shoot poisoned bullets into the soul, where a man must kill or be killed. God hath not lined the way to Christ with velvet, nor strewed it with rushes. He will never feed a slothful humor in man, who will be saved if Christ and heaven will drop into their mouths, and if any would bear their charges thither. If Christ might be bought for a few cold wishes and lazy desires, He would be of small reckoning amongst men, who would say: lightly come; lightly go. Indeed, Christ's yoke is easy in itself; and when a man is got into Christ, nothing is so sweet. But for a carnal, dull heart it is hard to draw in it; for,

There are four strait gates which everyone must pass through before he can enter into heaven.

1. There is the strait gate of humiliation. God saveth none, but first He humbleth them. Now it is hard to pass through the gates and flames of hell; for a heart as stiff as a stake to bow; as hard as a stone, to bleed for the least prick; not to mourn for one sin but all sins; and not for a fit but all a man's life-time. Oh, it is hard for a man to suffer himself to be loaden with sin, and prest to death for sin, so as never to love sin more, but to spit in the face of that which he once loved as dearly as his life. It is easy to drop a tear or two, and be sermon-sick; but to have a heart rent *for* sin, and *from* sin, this is true humiliation, and this is hard.

2. The strait gate of faith (Ephes. 1:19). It's an easy matter to presume, but hard to believe in Christ. It is easy for a man that was never humbled to believe and say, 'Tis but believing; but it is an hard

matter for a man humbled — when he sees all his sins in order before him, the Devil and conscience roaring upon him, and crying out against him, and God frowning upon him — now to call God "Father" is an hard work. Judas had rather be hanged then believe. It is hard to see a Christ as a rock to stand upon, when we are overwhelmed with sorrow of heart for sin. It is hard to prize Christ above ten thousand worlds of pearl. 'Tis hard to desire Christ, and nothing but Christ; hard to follow Christ all the day long, and never to be quit till he is got in thine arms, and then with Simeon to say, "Lord, now lettest thou thy servant depart in peace."

3. The strait gate of repentance. It is an easy matter for a man to confess himself to be a sinner, and to cry God forgiveness until next time; but to have a bitter sorrow, and so to turn from all sin, and to return to God and all the ways of God, which is true repentance indeed — this is hard.

4. The strait gate of opposition of devils, the world, and a man's own self, who knock a man down when he begins to look towards Christ and heaven.

Hence learn, that every easy way to heaven is a false way, although ministers should preach it out of their pulpits, and angels should publish it out of heaven.

Now there are nine easy ways to heaven (as men think) all which lead to hell.

1. The common broad way, wherein a whole parish may all go a-breadth in it. Tell these people they shall be damned; their answer is: then woe to many more besides me.

2. The way of civil education, whereby many wild natures are by little and little tamed, and like wolves are chained up easily while they are young.

3. Balaam's way of good wishes, whereby many people will confess their ignorance, forgetfulness, and that they cannot make such shews as others do; but they thank God, their hearts are as good, and God for His part accepts (say they) the will for the deed. And, my son, give me thy heart; the heart is all in all, and so long they hope to do well enough. Poor deluded creatures think to break through armies of sins, devils, temptations, and to break open the very gates of heaven with a few good wishes. They think to come to their journey's end without legs, because their hearts are good to God.

4. The way of formality, whereby men rest in the performance of most or of all external duties without inward life (Mark 1:14). Every man must have some religion, some fig-leaves to hide their nakedness. Now this religion must be either true religion, or the false one. [If] the true, he must either take up the power of it, but that he will not because it is burdensome; or the form of it, and this being

easy, men embrace it as their God, and will rather lose their lives than their religion thus taken up. This form of religion is the easiest religion in the world; partly, because it easeth men of trouble of conscience, quieting that: Thou hast sinned, saith conscience, and God is offended; take a book and pray, keep thy conscience better, and bring thy Bible with thee. Now conscience is silent, being charmed down with the form of religion, as the Devil is driven away (as they say) with holy water. Partly also, because the form of religion credits a man; partly, because it is easy in itself. It's of a light carriage, being but the shadow and picture of the substance of religion. As now, what an easy matter is it to come to church! They hear (at least outwardly) very attentively an hour and more, and then to turn to a proof, and to turn down a leaf; here's the form. But now to spend Saturday night, and all the whole sabbath day morning, in trimming the lamp, and in getting oil in the heart, to meet the Bridegroom the next day; and so meet Him in the Word, and there to tremble at the voice of God, and suck the breast while it is open; and when the Word is done, to go aside privately, and there to chew upon the Word, there to lament with tears all the vain thoughts in duties, deadness in hearing — this is hard, because this is the power of godliness, and this men will not take up. So for private prayer. What an easy matter is it for a man to say over a few prayers out of some devout book; or to repeat some old prayer got by heart since a child, or to have two or three short-winded wishes for God's mercy in the morning and at night? This form is easy. But now to prepare the heart by serious meditation of God and man's self before he prays, then to come to God with a bleeding hunger-starved heart, not only with a desire, but with a warrant, I must have such or such a mercy, and there to wrestle with God, although it be an hour or two together, for a blessing — this is too hard; men think none do thus, and therefore they will not.

Fifthly, the way of presumption, whereby men, having seen their sins, catch hold easily upon God's mercy, and snatch comforts before they are reached out unto them. There is no word of comfort in the book of God intended for such as regard iniquity in their hearts, though they do not act it in their lives. Their only comfort is, that the sentence of damnation is not yet executed upon them.

Sixthly, the way of sloth, whereby men lie still, and say God must do all. If the Lord would set up a pulpit at the alehouse door, it may be they would hear oftener. If God will always thunder, they will always pray; if strike them now and then with sickness, God shall be paid with good words and promises enough, that they will be better if they live. But as long as peace lasts, they will run to hell as fast as they can; and if God will not catch them, they care not, they will not return.

Seventhly, the way of carelessness, when men, feeling many difficulties, pass through some of them, but not all, and what they cannot get now, they feed themselves with a false hope they shall hereafter. They are content to be called precisians, and fools, and crazy brains; but they want brokenness of heart. And they will pray (it may be) for it, and pass by that difficulty. But to keep the wound always open, this they will not do. To be always sighing for help, and never to give themselves rest till their hearts are humbled; that they will not. These have a name to live, yet are dead.

Eighthly, the way of moderation, or honest discretion (Rev. 3:16), which indeed is nothing but luke-warmness of the soul; and that is, when a man contrives and cuts out such a way to heaven, as he may be hated of none, but please all, and so do anything for a quiet life, and so sleep in a whole skin. The Lord saith, "He that will live godly, must suffer persecution." No, not so, Lord. Surely (think they), if men were discreet and wise, it would prevent a great deal of trouble and opposition in good courses. This man will commend those that are most zealous, if they were but wise. If he meet with a black-mouthed swearer, he will not reprove him, lest he be displeased with him. If he meet with an honest man, he'll yield to all he saith, that so he may commend him. And when he meets them both together, they shall be both alike welcome (whatever he thinks) to his house and table, because he would fain be at peace with all men.

Ninthly, and lastly, the way of self-love, whereby a man, fearing terribly he shall be damned, useth diligently all means whereby he shall be saved. Here is the strongest difficulty of all: to row against the stream, and to hate a man's self, and then to follow Christ fully.

Edward Taylor (1642?–1729)

THE covenant of grace was to many Puritans the most magnificent example of God's divine wisdom working through His providential design for the world. So it appeared to Edward Taylor (*q.v.*, p. 292), who thus described it in one of his *Christographia* sacrament-day sermons in 1702.

TEXT: Norman S. Grabo, ed., *Edward Taylor's Christographia* (New Haven, 1962).

God's Providence in the Covenants

[From a sermon of 1702]

The first dispensation of divine providence put forth upon man when created was an act of confederation, taking man into the covenant of life with God, Gen. 2:16, 17. And this was a work of transcendent wisdom: for hereby Adam was under special duty to improve all his admirable qualifications, and his so much to be admired person in the most advantageous way possible to his present state, for the glory of God, and his own highest preferment his present state was capable of or attains to. This must needs be wisdom. But yet further, this lay as a foundation dispensation for all that wisdom to be brought to light, that hath given forth its glorious shine, which seems to us to be under an absolute impossibility any other way to be discovered. Now that must be an act full of wonderful wisdom that lays down such a foundation as is an occasion to lay open such wonderful wisdom.

Secondly, the after actings of divine providence towards man now circled about by the arms of divine wisdom in the bosom of providence, and these are various, as:

1. Such as respect the introduction of sin. For seeing the decree had divided mankind by election and rejection, mankind must be circumstanced so as that the execution of these decrees may make the righteousness and grace of God herein illustrious and glorious: and in wisdom's ordering the dispensation of providence so as to effect the same thus will be a demonstration of the glory of wisdom too. Hence providence, having all things in her hand, influences all subordinate agents to their operations according to their own proper natures, and to a regular exercising the actings of their own natures. And according to the law of nature, it is most certain that every particular agent is the proper author of its own act, whether the act is regular or irregular. Now the fallen angels, having poisoned their own nature by the fall, could not thereby be exempted from providence influencing their natures to act according to the law of their natures as created. Hence these influences setting their natures awork according to the law of their natures, their actions they put forth are venomed by the poison of their natures. Now these mischievous acts they put forth are properly their own, and not at all to be appropriated to providence, as the influences that providence lays upon them are proper acts of providence and in no way faulty. But now the fallen angel acting in his poison beguiles our first parents, draws them into sin, Gen. 3. And thus the wisdom of divine providence brings about the everlasting

purpose of God touching the introduction of sin in such a way as sin can no way be reflected upon God as its author, or the least ray of divine providence affected with the least stain thereof. And yet further, it gives a permit to Satan in this matter to bring forth his utmost diabolical subtilty into its highest and magnificent exploits to subvert and overturn the glorious work of God in the creation: and to run it all to ruin. Now, then, herein, being only an accomplishment of the all wise decree of God, and a putting mankind into a possibility of having the everlasting decree of God take place upon it as to election and rejection, and yet so as, mauger all the poisonous malice of hell, secures God from being any cause of sin, is unspeakable wisdom. 2. Such acts of divine providence as are carried on upon the introduction of sin. And in these shine forth infinite wisdom. And here I shall cast a glance upon them as they are carried on in the world, [and in the] end of it. First, such dispensations of providence following upon sin's entrance into this lower world, and here I shall be general.

Providence in general towards fallen man: and this is quite contrary to Satan's design. It's rational to think that he concluded he had blocked up the passage of divine favor from mankind, subverted the design of glory to God, stopped the current of all holiness and happiness for man, and had opened the floodgates of the curse for everlasting vengeance to come tumbling down therethrough upon the head of all men to all eternity. But divine wisdom gives all the foil, and evidently makes a fool of this subtle serpent. For this did but put back the window shuts of divine providence, to let forth the glorious beams of the sun of wisdom to shine upon us in a more glorious way of grace, whereby the glory of divine justice is made to eradiate itself through the bright glass of a new covenant, and new covenant administrations. And therefore:

God doth forthwith plight a new covenant with all mankind in Adam, Gen. 3:15. The seed of the woman shall break the serpent's head. Herein God did confound the masterpiece of hellish policy, and translate his dispensations towards man from the first covenant administrations to the new, and this was transcendently better. For the first covenant was by the least failing imaginable broken unto condemnation, unless satisfaction, which was as to man's attainments impossible, be fully made. But the new covenant doth not lie upon such terms, but it allows certain security from the curse of the law, through the redeemer, to all that come up unto it. Hence now the wisdom of God shines forth in a redeemer forthwith on the entrance of sin, and so Satan's eggs are squashed, and a new way of access to God, and of favor, is evidenced.

Increase Mather (1639–1723)

INCREASE, the second generation of the Mather dynasty and son of Richard, was born in Dorchester, Massachusetts. After his graduation from Harvard he studied in Dublin, where he took an M.A. in 1658, and preached in England. He had a pulpit in Devonshire, and was about to be called to a powerful church in Gloucester when the death of Cromwell and the restoration of the Stuarts effectively cut off opportunities for Puritan ministers in England. He returned to Boston in 1661, and a year later married Maria, the daughter of John Cotton. In 1664 he accepted the post of pastor at the Second Church, Boston, soon becoming, like his father, a powerful factor in the affairs of the colony.

Mather was troubled by what seemed to him an increasing laxity in New England's religious beliefs and practices. The great drive of the original Bay Colony Calvinists appeared to him to be losing impetus and direction, and he set himself (and his son Cotton) to the task of returning New England to the proper path of a stricter and purer faith. Battling against the rising tide of political and religious liberalism, he fought within and without the church for piety, rectitude, and rigor. He served as president of Harvard from 1685 to 1701, when he was practically forced to resign because of his conservatism, and, in one of the great defeats of his life, failed to see his son Cotton chosen as his successor. A learned man and an indefatigable writer, Increase Mather published nearly one hundred and fifty books, pamphlets, and sermons, among which were his *Brief History of the War with the Indians in New England* (1676); his *Essay for the Recording of Illustrious Providences* (1684), a somewhat over-credulous account of some of New England's miraculous and mysterious events; and his *Order of the Gospel* (1700), in which he rebukes the present generation for its "innovations" and expresses the hope that "God will ever bless that society" that "does not hanker after new and loose ways."

TEXT: Increase Mather, *An Historical Discourse Concerning the Prevalency of Prayer* (Boston, 1677).

The Power of Prayer

[From *An Historical Discourse,* 1677]

It was a great word (and if rightly understood, a true word) which Luther spake, when he said, *Est quaedam precum omnipotentia,* there is a kind of omnipotency in prayer; and the reason is obvious, viz., in that the Almighty doth suffer Himself to be prevailed upon and overcome by prayer. Had not Jacob in this respect power with God? Yea when he made his supplication, he had power, and prevailed over the angel, even that angel who is the Lord of Hosts, the Lord is his memorial. Where do we find in all the Book of God a more wonderful expression, then that of the Lord to praying Moses, "Now let me alone"? That ever the eternal God should become thus a petitioner to a poor mortal man! *Feriendi licentiam petit a Mose qui fecit Mosen.* Prayer then is like the sword of Saul, or the bow of Jonathan, which never returned empty from the battle. Prayer is stronger than iron gates. At the prayers of the church the iron gates fly open, and the Apostle's fetters fall off. Sometimes the prayers of one man that hath an eminent interest in God, are a means to preserve a whole town, yea a whole land from destruction; well might the ancient say, *Homine probo orante nihil potentius.* How far did Abraham's prayers prevail for Sodom? Did not Elijah's prayers open and shut the windows of heaven? Did they not bring down showers when the gasping earth was ready to die for thirst? When a fiery drought had like to have devoured the land of Israel, and the prophet Amos prayed and cried to the Lord, saying, "O Lord God, cease I beseech thee, by whom shall Jacob arise? for he is small; the Lord repented for this, and said this shall not be."

Wars, when justly undertaken, have been successful through the prevalency of prayer. Moses in the mount praying, is too strong for all the armies in the valley fighting. When the Philistines went up against the children of Israel, Samuel ceased not to cry to the Lord for Israel, and the Lord thundered with a great thunder that day upon the Philistines, and discomfitted them, that they were smitten before Israel. Jehoshaphat, when surrounded by a multitude of heathen enemies, by prayer overcame them. When Zera the Ethiopian came against the Lord's people with an host of a thousand thousand men, Asa by prayer and faith overcame them all. Hezekiah and Isaiah by their prayers brought an angel down from heaven, who slew an hundred and fourscore and five thousand Assyrians, in the host of Sennacherib in one night.

And besides these and many other scriptural examples, in ecclesiastical story, instances to this purpose are frequently observed. The history of the thundring legion is famously known. Thus it was.

The Emperor Marcus Aurelius going to war against the Quads, Vandals, Sarmats, and Germans, who were nine hundred seventy and five thousand fighting men; the imperialists were so cooped up by their numerous enemies, in strait, dry, and hot places, that the soldiers having been destitute of water for five days together, they were all like to have perished for thirst. In this extremity, a legion of Christian soldiers being in the army, withdrew themselves apart from the rest, and falling prostrate on the earth, by ardent prayers prevailed with God, that He immediately sent a most plentiful rain, whereby the army that otherwise had perished, was refreshed, and dreadful lightnings flashed in the faces of their enemies, so as that they were discomfitted and put to flight. The effect of which was, that the persecution which before that the emperor designed against the Christians, was diverted; and that praying legion did afterwards, bear the name of . . . the Lightning Legion.

Constantine the Great, being to join the battle with the heathen tyrant Licinius, singled out a number of godly ministers of Christ, and with them betook himself to earnest prayer and supplication, after which God gave him a notable and glorious victory over his enemies. But Licinius himself escaped at that time, and raised another army, which was pursued by Constantine, who before he would engage with the enemy, caused a tent to be erected, wherein he did spend some time in fasting and prayer, being attended with a company of holy praying men round about him, after which marching against his enemies, he fought them, and obtained a more glorious victory then the former, and the grand rebel Licinius was then taken prisoner.

Theodosius being in no small danger by reason of the potent army of adversaries he had to do with, in his distress cried unto heaven for help, and behold! the Lord sent such a terrible tempest, as the like was not known, whereby the darts of the enemy were driven back upon themselves, to their own confusion. . . .

It is storied concerning the city of Nisibis that being straitly besieged by Sapores, King of Persia, the distressed citizens desired a devout and holy man amongst them (whose name was James) to be earnest with the Lord in their behalf. He was so: and the effect was, God sent an army of gnats and flies amongst the Persians, which so vexed and tormented them, as that they were forced to raise their siege and depart.

Amongst the Waldenses sometimes an inconsiderable number have prevailed over multitudes of their popish adversaries. At one time five hundred of those poor praying saints overthrew two thousand and five hundred of their enemies, who scoffed at them because they would fall upon their knees and pray before they would fight.

In the land of our fathers' sepulchres, when Oswald (who succeeded his father Ethelfride in the Northern Kingdom) was assaulted by Cedwalla and Penda, two heathen kings, that raised a great army, designing the ruin of Oswald and his people, he humbly and earnestly addressed himself to the Lord of Hosts, the great giver of victory, entreating Him to shew His power in saving and protecting His own people from the rage of heathen adversaries: after which, joining battle with his enemies, albeit their army was far greater then his, he obtained a wonderful victory, wherein Cedwalla himself was slain.

When England was invaded by the Danes under the conduct of their King Osrick, who encamped at Ashdon, King Ethelred betook himself to prayer; and marching against the Danish army, put them to flight, and slew the greatest part of them.

Gustavus Adolphus, the King of Sweden, no sooner landed in his enemies' territories, but he addressed himself to heaven for victory, and encouraged his counsellors and commanders by saying, "the greater the army of prayers is, the greater and more assured shall be our victory." Yea it was his manner when the armies were set in battle array, to lift up his eyes to heaven, and say, "Lord prosper the battle of this day, according as thou seest my heart dost aim at thy glory, and the good of thy church." And how successful did God make that excellent prince to be?

But what need we go far to find examples confirming the truth of this assertion, that prayer is of wonderful prevalency, since our own eyes have seen it? New England may now say, if the Lord (even the prayer-hearing God) had not been on our side when men rose up against us, they had swallowed us up; then the proud waters had gone over our soul. And thus hath it been more then once or twice, especially since the late insurrection and rebellion of the heathen nations round about us. We cannot but acknowledge, and posterity must know, that we were in appearance a gone and ruined people, and had been so ere this day, if the Lord had not been a God that heareth prayer.

Thomas Hooker (1586–1647)

FACE TO FACE with his own soul the Puritan had two tasks — first, to detect and root out the sin he found there, and second, to discipline his intellect, will, and affections by serious and steadfast meditation and prayer. Several "examinations of conscience" might be adduced to illustrate the first task, but one writer happily not only elucidates that matter, he also writes the best brief description of the strenuous intellectual discipline called meditation to come out of New England. Thomas Hooker was born in England of middle-class folk. He took a B.A. at Emmanuel College, Cambridge, in 1608, and an M.A. in 1611. He remained as a fellow of the college from 1609 to 1618, became rector of Esher, Surrey, in 1620, and a lecturer and assistant minister in Chelmsford, Essex, in 1626. In 1630 the High Commission arrested him for nonconformity. Friends raised money to post bond for him and so allow him to jump bail and escape to Holland, where he continued ministering to English congregations. In 1633, with John Cotton and Samuel Stone, he made his way to New England, becoming pastor of the church at Cambridge.

In 1635 Hooker requested permission to move his congregation to Connecticut, but the petition was refused. The following year he founded the colony of Hartford, named for the birthplace of his close friend Samuel Stone; there he remained the dominating figure until his death. Eminently respected as a preacher and a political leader, he defined Congregational church discipline and its determining concepts of nature, reason, and law in *A Survey of the Sum of Church Discipline* (1648). But the energy of his prose and the intellectual sinew of his thought are well expressed by the following selection from the expanded version (1659) of *The Application of Redemption* (1656).

TEXT: Thomas Hooker, *The Application of Redemption*, 2d ed. (London, 1659).

Meditation

[From *The Application of Redemption*, 1659]

Meditation is a serious intention of the mind whereby we come to search out the truth, and settle it effectually upon the heart.

An intention of the mind; when one puts forth the strength of their understanding about the work in hand, takes it as an especial task whereabout the heart should be taken up and that which will require the whole man, and that to the bent of the best ability he hath, so the word is used, Jos. 1:8: thou shalt not suffer the Word to "depart out of thy mind, but thou shalt meditate therein day and night," when either the Word would depart away or our corruptions would drive it away, meditation lays hold upon it and will not let it go, but exerciseth the strength of the attention of his thoughts about it, makes a business of it as that about which he might do his best, and yet falls short of what he should do in it. So David when he would discover where the stream and overflowing strength of his affections vented themselves, he points at this practice as that which employs the mind to the full. Psal. 119:97: "O how I love thy law, it is my meditation all the day," love is the great wheel of the soul that sets all on going, and how doth that appear? it is my meditation day and night; the word in the original signifieth to swim, a man spreads the breadth of his understanding about that work, and lays out himself about the service wherein there is both difficulty and worth.

Serious.] Meditation is not a flourishing of a man's wit, but hath a set bout at the search of the truth, beats his brain as we use to say, hammers out a business, as the goldsmith with his metal, he heats it and beats it, turns it on this side and then on that, fashions it on both that he might frame it to his mind; meditation is hammering of a truth or point propounded, that he may carry and conceive the frame and compass in his mind, not salute a truth as we pass by occasionally but solemnly entertain it into our thoughts; not look upon a thing presented as a spectator or passenger that goes by; but lay other things aside, and look at this as the work and employment for the present to take up our minds. It's one thing in our diet to take a snatch and away, another thing to make a meal, and sit at it on purpose until we have seen all set before us and we have taken our fill of all, so we must not cast an eye or glimpse at the truth by some sudden or flighty apprehension, a snatch and away, but we must make a meal of musing. Therefore the Psalmist makes it the main trade that a godly man drives, professedly opposite to the carriage of the wicked, whether in his outward or inward work, in his disposition or expression of himself in his common practice; whereas they walk in the corrupt counsels of their own hearts, stand in the way of sinners, not only devise what is naught, but practice and persevere in what they have devised, and sit in the seat of the scorners; a blessed man his road in which he travels, his set trade, he meditates in the law of God day and night: that is the counsel in which he walks, the way in which he stands, the seat in which he sits. Look at this work as a branch of our Christian calling, not that which is left to our liberty, but which is of necessity to be attended and that in good earnest as a Christian duty, which God requires, not a little available to our spiritual welfare.

The end is doubly expressed in the other part of the description.

1. The searching of the truth.

2. The effectual settling of it upon the heart.

The search of the truth: meditation is a coming in with the truth or any cause that comes to hand, that we may enquire the full state of it before our thoughts part with it, so that we see more of it or more clearly and fully than formerly we did; this is one thing in that of the prophet Hos. 6:3, then shall ye know if you follow on to know, when we track the footsteps of the truth, in all the passages, until we have viewed the whole progress of it, from truth to truth, from point to point. This it is to dig for wisdom, Prov. 2:2. When men have found a mine or a vein of silver, they do not content themselves, to take that which is uppermost and next at hand within sight which offers itself upon the surface of the earth, but they dig further as hoping to find more, because they see somewhat. So meditation rests not in what presents itself to our consideration, but digs deeper, gathers in upon the truth, and gains more of it then did easily appear at the first, and this it doth:

1. When it recalls things formerly past, sets them in a present view before our consideration and judgment. Meditation sends a man's thought afar off, calls over and revives the fresh apprehension of things done long before, marshals them all in rank together, brings to mind such things which were happily quite out of memory, and gone from a man, which might be of great use and special help to discover our condition according to the quality of it; maybe conscience starts the consideration of but one sin, but meditation looks abroad, and brings to hand many of the same, and of the like kind and that many days past and long ago committed. This distemper now sticks upon a man and brings him under the arrest of conscience and the condemnation thereof. But, says meditation, let me mind you of such and such sins at such and such times, in such and such companies, committed and multiplied both more and worse than those that now appear so loathsome and so troublesome to you; meditation is as it were the register and remembrancer, that looks over the records of our daily corruptions, and keeps them upon file, and brings them into court and fresh consideration, Job 13:26: "Thou makest me to possess the sins of my youth." This makes a man to renew the sins of his youth, makes them fresh in our thoughts, as though new done before our eyes. This interpreters make the meaning of that place, Job 14:17: "My transgression is sealed up in a bag, and thou sewest up mine iniquity"; though God do thus, yet He doth it by this means in the way of His providence, i.e., by recounting and recalling our corruptions to mind, by serious meditation we sew them all up together, we look back to the lineage and pedigree of our lusts, and track the abominations of our lives, step by step, until we come to the very nest where they are hatched and bred, even of our original corruption, and body of death, where they had their first breath and being, links all our distempers together from our infancy to our youth, from youth to riper age, from thence to our declining days. So David, from the vileness of his present lusts is led to the wickedness in which he was warmed, Psal. 51:5. This was typed out in the old law by the chewing of the cud; meditation calls over again those things that were past long before, and not within a man's view and consideration.

Meditation takes a special survey of the compass of our present condition, and the nature of those corruptions that come to be considered: it's the traversing of a man's thoughts, the coasting of the mind and imagination into every crevice and corner, pries into every particular, takes a special view of the borders and confines of any corruption or condition that comes to be scanned, Psal. 119:59: "I considered my ways, and turned my feet unto thy testimonies"; he turned them upside down, looked through them as it were; a present apprehension peeps in as it were through the crevice or keyhole, looks in at the window as a man passeth by; but meditation lifts up the latch and goes into each room, pries into every corner of the house, and surveys the composition and making of it, with all the blemishes in it. Look as the searcher at the seaport, or customhouse, or ships, satisfies himself not to overlook carelessly in a sudden view, but unlocks every chest, rummages every corner, takes a light to discover the darkest passages. So is it with meditation, it observes the woof and web of wickedness, the full frame of it, the very utmost selvage and outside of it, takes into consideration all the secret conveyances, cunning contrivements, all bordering circumstances that attend the thing, the consequences of it, the nature of the causes that work it, the several occasions and provocations that lead to it, together with the end and issue that in reason is like to come of it, Dan. 12:4: "Many shall run to and fro, and knowledge shall increase"; meditation goes upon discovery, toucheth at every coast, observes every creek, maps out the daily course of a man's conversation and disposition.

The second end of meditation is, it settles effectually upon the heart. It's not the pashing of the water at a sudden push, but the standing and soaking to the root, that loosens the weeds and thorns, that they may be plucked up easily. It's not the laying of oil upon the benumbed part, but the chafing of it in, that suppleth the joints, and easeth the pain. It is so in the soul: application lays the oil of the Word that is searching and savory, meditation chafeth it in, that it may soften and humble the hard and stony heart; application is like the conduit or channel that brings the stream of the truth upon the soul; but meditation stops it as it were, and makes it soak into the heart, that so our corruptions may be plucked up kindly by the roots.

This settling upon the heart appears in a threefold work.

It affects the heart with the truth attended, and leaves an impression upon the spirit answerable to the nature of the thing which is taken into meditation: II Pet. 2:8, it's said of Lot, "in seeing and hearing, he vexed his righteous soul." Many saw and heard the hideous abominations, and were not touched nor affected therewith. No more had he been, but that he vexed and troubled his own righteous soul, because he was driven to a daily consideration of them which cut him to the quick. The word is observable, it signifies to try by a touchstone, and to examine, and then upon search to bring the soul upon the rack: therefore the same word is used, Matt. 14:24, "The ship was tossed by the waves"; the consideration of the abominations of the place raised a tempest of trouble in Lot's righteous soul. This the wise man calls laying to the heart, Eccles. 7:1, 2: "It's better to go to the house of mourning than to the house of laughter; for this is the end of all men, and the living will lay it to his heart." When the spectacle of misery and mortality is laid in the grave, yet savory meditation lays it to a man's heart, and makes it real there in the work of it. The goldsmith observes that it is not the laying of the fire, but the blowing of it that melts the metal. So with meditation, it breathes upon any truth that is applied, and that makes it really sink and soak into the soul; and this is the reason why in an ordinary and common course of providence, and God's dealing with sinners (leaving His own exceptions to His own good pleasure), that the most men in the time and work of conversion have that scorn cast upon them, that they grow melancholy. And it's true thus far in the course of ordinary appearance; the Lord usually never works upon the soul by the ministry of the Word to make it effectual, but He drives the sinner to sad thoughts of heart, and makes him keep an audit in his own soul by serious meditation, and pondering of his ways; otherwise the Word neither affects thoroughly, nor works kindly upon him.

It keeps the heart under the heat and authority of the truth that it's taken up withal, by constant attendance of his thoughts. Meditation keeps the conscience under an arrest, so that it cannot make an escape from the evidence and authority of the truth, so that there is no way, but either to obey the rule of it, or else be condemned by it. But escape it cannot. Meditation meets and stops all the evasions and sly pretenses the false-hearted person shall counterfeit. If a man should deny his fault, and himself guilty, meditation will evidence it beyond all gainsaying, by many testimonies which meditation will easily call to mind; remember ye not in such and such a place: upon such an occasion, you gave way to your wicked heart to do thus and thus; you know it, and God knows it, and I have recorded it. If the sinner would lessen his fault, meditation aggravates it; or if he seem to slight it, and look at it as a matter of no moment, yet meditation will make it appear, there is greater evil in it, and greater necessity to bestow his thoughts upon it than he is aware of.

Hence it is meditation lays siege unto the soul, and cuts off all carnal pretenses that a wretched self-deceiving hypocrite would relieve himself by; and still lies at the soul, this you did, at that time, in that place, after that manner; so that the soul is held fast prisoner, and cannot make an escape; but as David said, Psal. 51:3: "My sins are ever before me." Consideration keeps them within view, and will not suffer them to go out of sight and thoughts; and therefore it is Paul joins those two together, I Tim. 3:15: "Meditate in these things, and be in them."

It provokes a man (by a kind of overbearing power) to the practice of that with which he is so affected: a settled and serious meditation of anything, is as the setting open of the floodgates, which carries the soul with a kind of force and violence, to the performance of what he so bestows his mind upon; as a mighty stream let out turns the mill. Phil. 4:9: "Think of these things, and do them": thinking men are doing men. Psal. 39:3: "While I was thus musing, the fire brake out, and I spake": the busy stirring of meditation is like the raising of a tempest in the heart, that carries out all the actions of the man by an uncontrollable command. "I considered my ways, and turned my feet unto thy statutes": right consideration, brings in a right reformation with it.

Redskins, Rebels, and Witches

REDSKINS

While God did not frown consistently on the land he had opened for his chosen people, he nonetheless gave Satan great latitude for temptations and torments — at least so it seemed to pious New Englanders, who fell to jarring and wrangling almost from the time they set foot on American soil. From 1628, when Thomas Morton began selling guns and rum to the Indians near Plymouth, trouble seemed to lie at every hand. The year 1636–37 seems to have been an especially trying one for Massachusetts Bay — the heresies of Anne Hutchinson, the intolerable effrontery of Roger Williams, the embarrassment of Thomas Hooker's walk-out to Hartford with a substantial number of followers, the first real Indian war; and so matters continued. In 1642 a wave of inexplicable sinfulness shook the colony, to be followed by church problems whose only solutions were bound to dissatisfy some and thus further fracture the initial homogeneity of the Bay Colonists. Even their friends in England turned on them, first accusing them of running away from the Puritan cause at home, and then tolerating the most odious forms of religious opinion imaginable. To cap things off, God rebuked New Englanders by returning Charles II to the throne in 1660 and by visiting their land with drought, famine, and even earthquake. No wonder that from time to time the host of Satan's plagues thrust the young Americans into dejection or fierce determination. It was indeed, as John Foxe had written, a period of trial and travail.

Without doubt the sharpest of Satan's instruments against the newcomers was the Indian. The first historian of America's early literature looked back from the enlightened nineteenth century to exclaim, "To us, of course, the American Indian is no longer a mysterious or even an interesting personage — he is simply a fierce dull biped standing in our way; and it is only by a strong effort of the imagination that we can in any degree reproduce for ourselves the zest of ineffable curiosity with which, during most of the seventeenth century, he was regarded by the English on both sides of the ocean." At first, perhaps, the Indian was merely a curiosity — especially the Indian maiden, who offers the prototype of the first truly American romantic legend; but, savage and barbaric as he was, the Indian was also the greatest opportunity Englishmen had to propagate Christ's gospel, and this was among their foremost reasons for coming to the wilderness. Moreover, the Indians' being here in the first place required study, and American anthropology and sociology may be said to begin with the seventeenth-century examinations of the native culture. Equally important, the white man's continued conflicts with the Indian provide matter and form for the longest-lived strain in American literature.

George Alsop (1638–?)

Four years in Maryland was long enough for George Alsop (*q.v.*, p. 15) to come to appreciate the savagery that had threatened southern settlers since the complete loss of Roanoke (1586). The dish of Indian atrocities Alsop served up in *A Character of the Province of Maryland* became standard fare in early Indian accounts.

Text: George Alsop, *A Character of the Province of Maryland*, ed. John G. Shea (Baltimore, 1880).

Customs and Absurdities

[From *A Character of the Province of Maryland*, 1666]

Those Indians that I have conversed withal here in this Province of Maryland, and have had any ocular experimental view of either of their customs, manners, religions, and absurdities, are called by the name of Susquehannocks, being a people lookt upon by the Christian inhabitants, as the most noble and heroic nation of Indians that dwell upon the confines of America; also are so allowed and lookt upon by the rest of the Indians, by a submissive and tributary acknowledgment; being a people cast into the mould of a most large and warlike deportment, the men being for the most part seven foot high in latitude, and in magnitude and bulk suitable to so high a pitch; their voice large and hollow, as ascending out of a cave, their gait and behavior straight, stately, and majestic, treading on the earth with as much pride, contempt, and disdain to so sordid a center, as can be imagined from a creature derived from the same mould and earth. . . .

Their government is wrapt up in so various and intricate a labyrinth, that the speculativest artist in the whole world, with his artificial and natural optics, cannot see into the rule or sway of these Indians, to distinguish what name of government to call them by. . . . All that ever I could observe in them as to this matter is, that he that is most cruelly valorous, is accounted the most noble. Here is very seldom any creeping from a country farm, into a courtly gallantry, by a sum of money; nor feeing the heralds to put daggers and pistols into their arms, to make the ignorant believe that they are lineally descended from the house of the wars and conquests; he that fights best carries it here.

When they determine to go upon some design that will and doth require a consideration, some six of them get into a corner, and sit in junto; and if thought fit, their business is made popular, and immediately put into action; if not, they make a full stop to it, and are silently reserved.

The warlike equipage they put themselves in when they prepare for Bellona's march, is with their faces, arms, and breasts confusedly painted, their hair greased with bears' oil, and stuck thick with swans' feathers, with a wreath or diadem of black and white beads upon their heads, a small hatchet, instead of a scimitar, stuck in their girts behind them, and either with guns, or bows and arrows. In this posture and dress they march out from their fort, or dwelling, to the number of forty in a troop, singing (or rather howling out) the decades or warlike exploits of their ancestors, ranging the wide woods until their fury has met with an enemy worthy of their revenge. What prisoners fall into their hands by the destiny of war, they treat them very civilly while they remain with them abroad, but when they once return homewards, they then begin to dress them in the habit for death, putting on their heads and arms wreaths of beads, greasing their hair with fat, some going before, and the rest behind, at equal distance from their prisoners, bellowing in a strange and confused manner, which is a true presage and forerunner of destruction to their then conquered enemy. . . . The common and usual deaths they put their prisoners to, is to bind them to stakes, making a fire some distance from them; then one or other of them, whose genius delights in the art of paganish dissection, with a sharp knife or flint cuts the cutis or outermost skin of the brow so deep, until their nails, or rather talons, can fasten themselves firm and secure in, then (with a most rigid jerk) disrobeth the head of skin and hair at one pull, leaving the skull almost as bare as those monumental skeletons at Chirurgeons' Hall; but for fear they should get cold by leaving so warm and customary a cap off, they immediately apply to the skull a cataplasm of hot embers to keep their pericranium warm. While they are thus acting this cruelty on their heads, several others are preparing pieces of iron, and barrels of old guns, which they make red hot, to sear each part and lineament of their bodies, which they perform and act in a most cruel and barbarous manner. And while they are thus in the midst of their torments and execrable usage, some tearing their skin and hair of their head off by violence, others searing their bodies with hot irons, some are cutting their flesh off, and eating it before their eyes raw while they are alive; yet all this and much more never makes them lower the top-gallant sail of their heroic courage, to beg with a submissive repentance any indulgent favor from their persecuting enemies; but with an undaunted contempt to their cruelty, eye it with so slight and mean a respect, as if it were below them to value what they did, they courageously (while breath doth libertize them) sing the summary of their warlike achievements.

Now after this cruelty has brought their tormented lives to a period, they immediately fall to butchering of them into parts, distributing the several pieces amongst the sons of war, to intomb the ruins of their deceased conquest in no other sepulchre then their unsanctified maws; which they with more appetite and desire do eat and digest, then if the best of foods should court their stomachs to participate of the most restorative banquet. Yet though they now and then feed upon the carcasses of their enemies, this is not a common diet, but only a particular dish for the better sort; for there is not a beast that runs in the woods of America, but if they can by any means come at him, without any scruple of conscience they'll fall to (without saying grace) with a devouring greediness.

As for their religion, together with their rites and ceremonies, they are so absurd and ridiculous, that it's almost a sin to name them. They own no other deity than the Devil (solid or profound), but with a kind of a wild imaginary conjecture, they suppose from their groundless conceits, that the world had a maker, but where he is that made it, or whether he be living to this day, they know not. The Devil, as I said before, is all the god they own or worship; and that more out of a slavish fear then any real reverence to his infernal or diabolical greatness, he forcing them to their obedience by his rough and rigid dealing with them, often appearing visibly among them to their terror, bastinadoing them (with cruel menaces) even unto death, and burning their fields of corn and houses, that the relation thereof makes them tremble themselves when they tell it.

Once in four years they sacrifice a child to him, in an acknowledgment of their firm obedience to all his devilish powers, and hellish commands. The priests to whom they apply themselves in matters of importance and greatest distress, are like those that attended upon the Oracle at Delphos, who by their magic spells could command a *pro* or *con* from the Devil when they pleased. These Indians ofttimes raise great tempests when they have any weighty matter or design in hand, and by blustering storms inquire of their infernal god (the Devil) how matters shall go with them either in public or private.

When any among them depart this life, they give him no other intombment than to set him upright upon his breech in a hole dug in the earth some five foot long, and three foot deep, covered over with the bark of trees archwise, with his face due West, only leaving a hole half a foot square open. They dress him in the same equipage and gallantry that he used to be trimmed in when he was alive, and so bury him (if a soldier) with his bows, arrows, and target, together with all the rest of his implements and weapons of war, with a kettle of broth, and corn standing before him, lest he should meet with bad quarters in his way. His kindred and relations follow him to the grave, sheathed in bear skins for close mourning, with the tail droiling on the ground, in imitation of our English solemners, that think there's nothing like a tail a degree in length, to follow the dead corpse to the grave with. . . .

I never observed all the while I was amongst these naked Indians, that ever the women wore the breeches, or dared either in look or action to predominate over the men. They are very constant to their wives; and let this be spoken to their heathenish praise, that did they not alter their bodies by their dyeings, paintings, and cutting themselves, marring those excellencies that nature bestowed upon them in their original conceptions and birth, there would be as amiable beauties amongst them, as any Alexandria could afford, when Mark Antony and Cleopatra dwelt there together. Their marriages are short and authentic; for after 'tis resolved upon by both parties, the woman sends her intended husband a kettle of boiled venison or bear; and he returns in lieu thereof beaver or otters' skins, and so their nuptial rites are concluded without other ceremony.

Before I bring my heathenish story to a period, I have one thing worthy your observation: for as our grammar rules have it, *non decet quenquam me ire currentem aut mandantem,* it doth not become any man to piss running or eating. These pagan men naturally observe the same rule; for they are so far from running, that like a hare, they squat to the ground as low as they can, while the women stand bolt upright with their arms akimbo, performing the same action, in so confident and obscene a posture, as if they had taken their degrees of entrance at Venice, and commenced Bawds of Art at Legorne.

John Josselyn (*fl.* 1638–1675)

JOSSELYN was born in Kent, of a noble family. He visited New England from 1638 to 1639, and again in 1663, staying that time for eight years. In 1672 he published a remarkable collection of tall tales, recipes, and descriptions of natural oddities under the title *New England's Rarities Discovered,* and in 1674, *An Account of Two Voyages to New England.* His brother Henry was deputy governor of Maine.

TEXT: John Josselyn, *New England's Rarities,* ed. Edward Tuckerman, in *Trans. and Coll. Amer. Antiq. Soc.,* IV (1860), 231–232.

The Indian Girls

[From *New England's Rarities,* 1672]

[Indian] women, many of them, have very good features; seldom without a "Come to me," or *cos amoris,* in their countenance; all of them black-eyed; having even, short teeth, and very white; their hair black, thick, and long; broadbreasted; handsome, straight bodies, and slender, considering their constant loose habit; their limbs cleanly, straight, and of a convenient stature, — generally as plump as partridges; and, saving here and there one, of modest deportment. . . . Their hair they comb backward, and tie it up short with a border, about two handfuls broad, wrought in works as the other, with their beads. But enough of this.

THE POEM.

Whether white or black be best,
Call your senses to the quest;
And your touch shall quickly tell,
The black in softness doth excel,
And in smoothness; but the ear —
What, can that a color hear?
No; but 'tis your black one's wit
That doth catch and captive it.
And, if slut and fair be one,
Sweet and fair there can be none;
Nor can ought so please the taste
As what's brown and lovely drest.
And who'll say that that is best
To please one sense, displease the rest?
Maugre, then, all that can be said
In flattery of white and red:
Those flatterers themselves must say
That darkness was before the day;
And such perfection here appears,
It neither wind nor sunshine fears.

John Eliot (1604–1690)

FEW New England Puritans have captured and retained the sympathy of later Americans as has John Eliot. Born in England, he was educated at Cambridge, and then became a teacher in Thomas Hooker's school at Little Baddow in 1630. His entrance into the ministry nurtured his partiality for teaching, which he continued to his fame for nearly the remainder of his long life. In 1631 he moved to Massachusetts, becoming John Wilson's assistant in Boston's First Church. Shortly after, he assumed his own pastorate at Roxbury, and there began to propagate the gospel among Indians and slaves. Soon he was known as John the Evangelist, the Apostle to the Indians. His work was of interest to Englishmen, especially Richard Baxter, the prominent divine with whom Eliot helped to form the Society for the Propagation of the Gospel (1649). He enjoyed outstanding success among the Indians and by 1651 had founded the first community of Praying Indians; there would be fourteen such communities by 1675. Among his noted works is a translation of the Bible into the Indian tongue (1661–63), another of the *Catechism* (1654), and *The Indian Primer* (1669). His one excursion into political literature is *The Christian Commonwealth* (1659), a delineation of the naked theocracy Eliot hoped would be established throughout the New World.

TEXTS: *Coll. Mass. Hist. Soc.*, 3d ser., IV (1834).

Admonishing the Indians

[From *The Clear Sunshine of the Gospel Breaking Forth upon the Indians,* 1648]

In my exercise among them (as you know) we attend four things, besides prayer unto God, for His presence and blessing upon all we do.

First, I catechise the children and youth; wherein some are very ready and expert; they can readily say all the commandments, so far as I have communicated them, and all other principles about the creation, the fall, the redemption by Christ, etc., wherein also the aged people are pretty expert, by the frequent repetition thereof to the children, and are able to teach it to their children at home, and do so.

Secondly, I preach unto them out of some texts of scripture, wherein I study all plainness, and brevity, unto which many are very attentive.

Thirdly, if there be any occasion, we in the next place go to admonition and censure; unto which they submit themselves reverently, and obediently, and some of them penitently confessing their sins with much plainness, and without shiftings and excuses: I will instance in two or three particulars; this was one case, a man named Wampoowas, being in a passion upon some light occasion did beat his wife, which was a very great offense among them now (though in former times it was very usual) and they had made a law against it, and set a fine upon it; whereupon he was publicly brought forth before the assembly, which was great that day, for our governor and many other English were then present: the man wholly condemned himself without any excuse: and when he was asked what provocation his wife gave him, he did not in the least measure blame her but himself, and when the quality of the sin was opened, that it was cruelty to his own body, and against God's commandment, and that passion was a sin, and much aggravated by such effects, yet God was ready to pardon it in Christ, etc., he turned his face to the wall and wept, though with modest endeavor to hide it; and such was the modest, penitent, and melting behavior of the man, that it much affected all to see it in a barbarian, and all did forgive him, only this remained, that they executed their law notwithstanding his repentance, and required his fine, to which he willingly submitted, and paid it. . . .

Before I leave this point of admonition, if I thought it would not be too tedious to you, I would mention one particular more, where we saw the power of God awing a wicked wretch by this ordinance of admonition. It was George that wicked Indian, who as you know, at our first beginnings sought to cast aspersions upon religion, by laying slanderous accusations against godly men, and who asked that captious question, "Who made sack?" and this fellow having killed a young cow at your town, and sold it at the College instead of moose, covered it with many lies, insomuch as Mr. Dunster was loath he should be directly charged with it when we called him forth, but that we should rather inquire. But when he was called before the assembly, and charged with it, he had not power to deny it, but presently confessed, only he added one thing which we think was an excuse; thus God hath honored this ordinance among them.

Fourthly, the last exercise, you know, we have among them, is their asking us questions, and very many they have asked, which I have forgotten, but some few that come to my present remembrance I will briefly touch.

One was Wabbakoxet's question, who is reputed an old pow-wow; it was to this purpose, seeing the English had been twenty-seven years (some of them) in this land, why did we never teach them to know God till now? "Had you done it sooner," said he, "we might have known much of God by this time, and much sin might have been prevented, but now some of us are grown old in sin," etc. To whom we answered, that we do repent that we did not long ago, as now we do, yet withal we told them, that they were never willing to hear till now, and that seeing God hath bowed their hearts to be willing to hear, we are desirous to take all the pains we can now to teach them.

Another question was, that of Cutshamaquin, to this purpose, "Before I knew God," said he, "I thought I was well, but since I have known God and sin, I find my heart full of sin, and more sinful than ever it was before, and this hath been a great trouble to me; and at this day my heart is but very little better then it was, and I am afraid it will be as bad again as it was before, and therefore I sometime wish I might die before I be so bad again as I have been. Now my question is, whether is this a sin or not?" This question could not be learned from the English, nor did it seem a coined, feigned thing, but a real matter gathered from the experience of his own heart, and from an inward observation of himself. . . .

Scandal in Israel

[From *A Late and Further Manifestation of the Progress of the Gospel amongst the Indians in New England,* 1655]

There fell out a very great discouragement a little before the time, which might have been a scandal unto them, and I doubt not but Satan intended it so; but the Lord improved it to stir up faith and prayer, and so turned it another way. Thus it was. Three of the unsound sort of such as are among them that pray unto God, who are hemmed in by relations, and other means, to do that which their hearts love not, and whose vices Satan improveth to scandalize and reproach the better sort withal; while many, and some good people are too ready to say they are all alike. I say three of them had gotten several quarts of strong water (which sundry out of a greedy desire of a little gain, are too ready to sell unto them, to the offense and grief of the better sort of Indians, and of the godly English too), and with these liquors, did not only make themselves drunk, but got a child of eleven years of age, the son of Toteswamp, whom his father had sent for a little corn and fish to that place near Watertown, where they were. Unto this child they first gave two spoonfuls of strong water, which was more then his head could bear; and another of them put a bottle, or such like vessel to his mouth, and caused him to drink till he was very drunk; and then one of them domineered, and said, "Now we will see whether your father will punish us for drunkenness" (for he is a ruler among them) "seeing you are drunk with us for company"; and in this case lay the child abroad all night. They also fought, and had been several times punished formerly for drunkenness.

When Toteswamp heard of this, it was a great shame and breaking of heart unto him, and he knew not what to do. The rest of the rulers with him considered of the matter, they found a complication of many sins together.

1. The sin of drunkenness, and that after many former punishments for the same.

2. A wilful making of the child drunk, and exposing him to danger also.

3. A degree of reproaching the rulers.

4. Fighting.

Word was brought to me of it, a little before I took horse to go to Natick to keep the sabbath with them, being about ten days before the appointed meeting. The tidings sunk my spirit extremely, I did judge it to be the greatest frown of God that ever I met withal in the work, I could read nothing in it but displeasure, I began to doubt about our intended work: I knew not what to do, the blackness of the sins, and the persons reflected on, made my very heart fail me. For one of the offenders (though least in the offense) was he that hath been my interpreter, whom I have used in translating a good part of the holy scriptures; and in that respect I saw much of Satan's venom, and in God I saw displeasure. For this and some other acts of apostasy at this time, I had thoughts of casting him off from that work, yet now the Lord hath found a way to humble him. But his apostasy at this time was a great trial, and I did lay him by for that day of our examination, I used another in his room. Thus Satan aimed at me in this their miscarrying; and Toteswamp is a principal man in the work, as you shall have occasion to see anon, God willing.

By some occasion our ruling elder and I being together, I opened the case unto him, and the Lord guided him to speak some gracious words of encouragement unto me, by which the Lord did relieve my spirit; and so I committed the matter and issue unto the Lord, to do what pleased Him, and in so doing my soul was quiet in the Lord. I went on my journey being the sixth day of the week; when I came at Natick, the rulers had then a court about it. Soon after I came there, the rulers came to me with a question about this matter; they related the whole business unto me, with much trouble and grief.

Then Toteswamp spake to this purpose, "I am greatly grieved about these things, and now God trieth me whether I love Christ or my child best. They say, they will try me; but I say, God will try me. Christ saith, 'He that loveth father, or mother, or wife, or child, better than me, is not worthy of me.' Christ saith, I must correct my child, if I should refuse to do that, I should not love Christ. God bid Abraham kill his son, Abraham loved God, and therefore he would have done it, had not God withheld him. God saith to me, only punish your child, and how can I love God, if I should refuse to do that?" These things he spake in more words, and much affection, and not with dry eyes. Nor could I refrain from tears to hear him. When it was said, the child was not so guilty of the sin, as those that made him drunk; he said, that he was guilty of sin, in that he feared not sin, and in that he did not believe his counsels that he had often given him, to take heed of evil company; but he had believed Satan and sinners more then him, therefore he needed to be punished. After other such like discourse, the rulers left me, and went unto their business, which they were about before I came, which they did bring unto this conclusion, and judgment. They judged the three men to sit in the stocks a good space of time, and thence to be brought to the whipping-post, and have each of them twenty lashes. The boy to be put in the stocks a little while, and the next day his father was to whip him in the school, before the children there; all which judgment was executed. When they came to be whipt, the constable fetcht them one after another to the tree (which they make use of instead of a post) where they all received their punishments: which done, the rulers spake thus, one of them said, "The punishments for sin are the commandments of God, and the work of God, and His end was, to do them good, and bring them to repentance." And upon that ground he did in more words exhort them to repentance, and amendment of life. When he had done, another spake unto them to this purpose, "You are taught in catechism, that the wages of sin are all miseries and calamities in this life, and also death and eternal damnation in hell. Now you feel some smart as the fruit of your sin, and this is to bring you to repentance, that so you may escape the rest." And in more words he exhorted them to repentance. When he had done, another spake to this purpose, "Hear all ye people" (turning himself to the people who stood round about, I think not less then two hundred, small and great), "this is the commandment of the Lord, that thus it should be done unto sinners; and therefore let all take warning by this, that you commit not such sins, lest you incur these punishments." And with more words he exhorted the people. Others of the rulers spake also, but some things spoken I understood not, and some things slipt from me. But these which I have related remained with me.

When I returned to Roxbury, I related these things to our elder, to whom I had before related the sin, and my grief: who was much affected to hear it, and magnified God. He said also, that their sin was but a transient act, which had no rule, and would vanish. But these judgments were an ordinance of God, and would remain, and do more good every way, then their sin could do hurt, telling me what cause I had to be thankful for such an issue. Which I therefore relate, because the Lord did speak to my heart, in this exigent, by his words.

☙ Daniel Gookin (1612–1687)

John Eliot's close companion in ministering to the Indians was Daniel Gookin, more philosophical and scientifically minded and a greater man of affairs than Eliot. Gookin was born in England, but by 1630 was living on his father's estate in Virginia. In 1642/3 the Governor and Council of Virginia declared that "all nonconformists upon notice . . . shall be compelled to depart the colony with all convenience." Though he was by then a burgess and had sent for his wife and son to join him from England in 1641, the Puritan-minded Gookin moved the year after the edict to Maryland, and thence to Boston. He played an active part in Massachusetts political affairs as deputy to the General Court for thirty-five years and as emissary to England in 1655 and 1657. Although he was appointed major-general of Massachusetts forces (1681), his most congenial office was as superintendent of Indian affairs. The protection of the Praying Indians fell to his lot during the angry reprisals that followed the massacres of King Philip's War, for which his good sense in urging the colonists not to take out their ire on converted Indians as well as savages earned him widespread denunciation and threats to his life. But these he weathered, regaining the colony's high regard by maintaining colonial rights in the face of English political encroachments during the 1680's.

His *Historical Collections of the Indians in New England* (written in 1674) was not published until 1792, and his *Historical Account of the Doings and Sufferings of the Christian Indians in New England* (1677) remained unprinted until 1836. Both show to advantage his liberality, humanity, and historical sense.

Text: *Coll. Mass. Hist. Soc.*, 1st ser., I (1792).

Conjectures of the Savage, His Original

[From *Historical Collections of the Indians in New England* (1674)]

Concerning the original of the savages, or Indians, in New England, there is nothing of certainty to be concluded. But yet, as I conceive, it may rationally be made out, that all the Indians of America, from the Straits of Magellan and its adjacent islands on the south, unto the most northerly part yet discovered, are originally of the same nations or sort of people. . . .

The color of their skins, the form and shape of their bodies, hair, and eyes, demonstrate this. Their skins are of a tawny color, not unlike the tawny Moors in Africa; the proportion of their limbs, well formed; it is rare to see a crooked person among them. Their hair is black and harsh, not curling; their eyes, black and dull; though I have seen, but very rarely, a grey-eyed person among them, with brownish hair. But still the difficulty yet remains, whence all these Americans had their first original, and from which of the sons of Noah they descended, and how they came first into these parts. . . .

There are divers opinions about this matter.

First, some conceive that this people are of the race of the ten tribes of Israel, that Salmanassec carried captive out of their own country, A.M. 3277, of which we read in II Kings 18:9–12; and that God hath, by some means or other, not yet discovered, brought them into America; and herein fulfilled His just threatening against them, of which we may read, II Kings 17: from 6 to the 19 verse; and hath reduced them into such woeful blindness and barbarism, as all those Americans are in; yet hath reserved their posterity there: and in His own best time, will fulfill and accomplish His promise, that those dry bones shall live, of which we read (Ezek. 37:1–24). A reason given for this is taken from the practice of sundry Americans, especially of those inhabitating Peru and Mexico, who were most populous, and had great cities and wealth, and hence are probably apprehended to be the first possessors of America. . . .

Secondly, another apprehension is, that the original of these Americans is from the Tartars, or Scythians, that live in the north-east parts of Asia; which some good geographers conceive is nearly joined unto the north-west parts of America, and possibly are one continent, or at least, separated, but by some narrow gulf; and from this beginning have spread themselves into the several parts of the North and South America; and because the southern parts were more fertile, and free from the cold winters incident to the northern regions, hence the southern parts became first planted, and most populous and rich. This opinion gained more credit than the former, because the people of America are not altogether unlike in color, shape, and manners, unto the Scythian people, and in regard that such a land travel is more feasible and probable, than a voyage by sea so great a distance as is before expressed, from other inhabited places, either in Europe, Asia, or Africa; especially so long since, when we hear of no sailing out of sight of land, before the use of the loadstone and compass was found. But if this people be sprung from the Tartarian or Scythian people, as this notion asserts, then it is to me a question, why they did not attend the known practice of that people; who, in all their removes and plantations, take with them their kine, sheep, horses, and camels, and the like tame beasts; which that people keep in great numbers, and drive with them in all their removes. But of these sorts and kinds of beasts used by the Tartars, none were found in America among the Indians. This question or objection is answered by some thus. First, possibly the first people were banished for some notorious offenses; and so not permitted to take with them of these tame beasts. Or, secondly, possibly, the gulf, or passage, between Asia and America, though narrow, comparatively, is yet too broad to waft over any of those sort of creatures; and yet possibly men and women might pass over it in canoes made of hollow trees, or with barks of trees, wherein, it is known, the Indians will transport themselves, wives and children, over lakes and gulfs, very considerable for breadth. I have known some to pass with like vessels forty miles across an arm of the sea.

But before I pass to another thing, suppose it should be so, that the origination of the Americans came from Asia, by the north-west of America, where the continents are conceived to meet very near, which indeed is an opinion very probable; yet this doth not hinder the truth of the first conjecture, that this people may be of the race of the ten tribes of Israel: for the king of Assyria who led them captive, as we heard before, transported them into Asia, and placed them in several provinces and cities, as in II Kings 17:6. Now possibly, in process of time, this people, or at least some considerable number of them, whose custom and manner it was to keep themselves distinct from the other nations they lived amongst; and did commonly intermarry only with their own people; and also their religion being so different from the heathen, unto whom they were generally an abomination, as they were to the Egyptians; and also partly from God's judgment following them for their sins: I say, it is not impossible but a considerable number of them might withdraw themselves; and so pass gradually into the extreme parts of the continent of Asia; and wherever they came, being disrelished by the heathen, might for their own security, pass further and further, till they found America; which being unpeopled, there they found some rest; and so, in many hundred of years, spread themselves in America in that thin manner, as they were found there, especially in the northern parts of it; which country is able to contain and accommodate millions of mankind more than were found in it. And for their speech, which is not only different among themselves, but from the Hebrew, that might easily be lost by their often removes, or God's judgment.

A third conjecture of the original of these Indians, is, that some of the tawny Moors of Africa, inhabiting upon the sea coasts, in times of war and contention among themselves, have put off to sea, and been transported over, in such small vessels as those times afforded, unto the south part of America, where the two continents of Africa and America are nearest; and they could not have opportunity or advantage to carry with the small vessels of those times any tame beasts, such as were in that country. Some reasons are given for this notion. First, because the Americans are much like the Moors of Africa. Secondly, the seas between the tropics are easy to pass, and safe for small vessels; the winds in those parts blowing from the East to the West, and the current setting the same course. Thirdly, because it is most probable, that the inhabitants of America first came into the south parts; where were found the greatest numbers of people, and the most considerable cities and riches.

But these, or other notions, can amount to no more than rational conjecture; for a certainty of their first extraction cannot be attained: for they being ignorant of letters and records of antiquity, as the Europeans, Africans, and sundry of the Asians, are and have been, hence any true knowledge of their ancestors is utterly lost among them. I have discoursed and questioned about this matter with some of the most judicious of the Indians, but their answers are divers and fabulous. Some of the inland Indians say, that they came from such as inhabit the sea coasts. Others say, that there were two young squaws, or women, being at first either swimming or wading in the water. The froth or foam of the water touched their bodies, from whence they became with child; and one of them brought forth a male; and the other, a female child; and then the two woman died and left the earth. So their son and daughter were their first progenitors. Other fables and figments are among them touching this thing, which are not worthy to be inserted. These only may suffice to give a taste of their great ignorance touching their original; the full determination whereof must be left until the day, wherein all secret and hidden things shall be manifested to the glory of God.

Of the Praying Indians

[From the same]

Here I shall take the liberty, though it be a digression, to relate a story of remark concerning a child at Natick, a youth of about eleven years of age, who was of a sober and grave carriage, and an attentive hearer of the Word, considering his age and capacity, but he had a weak body and was consumptive. This child hearing Mr. Eliot preach upon a time at Natick, when the ordinance of baptism was to be administered unto some children, whose parents had made profession of their faith and were joined to the church; upon which occasion Mr. Eliot said, that baptism was Christ's mark, which he ordered to be set upon his lambs, and that it was a manifest token of Christ's love to the offspring of His people to set this mark upon them; this child taking special notice of this passage, did often solicit his father and mother that one or both of them would endeavor to join to the church, that he might be marked for one of Christ's lambs before he died. The parents who were well inclined, especially the mother, and being also very affectionate to their child, as the Indians generally are, did seriously ponder the child's reiterated entreaties; and not long after, first the mother, and then the father of the child, joined to the church. Soon after the lad was baptized; in which he did greatly rejoice and triumph, that now he was marked for one of Christ's lambs; and now said he to his father and mother, "I am willing to die"; which shortly after came to pass; and I doubt not, but as the child had Christ's name set upon him in baptism and by faith, so his immortal soul is now in glory, rejoicing in communion with Christ.

This relation, which is a most true and certain thing, should methinks be argumentative to persuade the Antipædobaptists of our age to so much affection and humanity unto their offspring, as the poor Indians had to their child, to offer them up to God, that His mark and name in baptism might be set upon them.

There are many Indians that live among those that have subjected to the gospel, that are catechised, do attend public worship, read the scriptures, pray in their family morning and evening; but being not yet come so far, as to be able or willing to profess their faith in Christ, and yield obedience and subjection unto Him in His church, are not admitted to partake in the ordinances of God, proper and peculiar to the church of Christ; which is a garden enclosed, as the scripture saith.

The manner practiced by these Indians in the worship of God, is thus. Upon the Lord's days, fast days, and lecture days, the people assemble together at the sound of a drum, — for bells they yet have not, — twice a day, in the morning and afternoon, on Lord's days, but only once upon lecture days; where one of their teachers, if they have more than one, begins with solemn and affectionate prayer. Then, after a short pause, either himself or some other thereunto appointed readeth a chapter distinctly out of the Old or New Testament. At the conclusion thereof a psalm, or part of a psalm, is appointed, rehearsed, and solemnly sung. Then the minister catechises and prays before his sermon; and so preacheth from some text of scripture. Then concludeth with prayer, and a psalm, and a blessing pronounced. Sometime, instead of reading the chapter, some persons do answer some part of the catechism.

In all these acts of worship, for I have been often present with them, they demean themselves visibly with reverence, attention, modesty, and solemnity; the menkind sitting by themselves and the womenkind by themselves, according to their age, quality, and degree, in a comely manner. And for my own part, I have no doubt, but am fully satisfied, according to the judgment of charity, that divers of them do fear God and are true believers; but yet I will not deny but that there may be some of them hypocrites, that profess religion, and yet are not sound-hearted. But things that are secret belong to God; and things that are revealed, unto us and our children.

Their teachers are generally chosen from among themselves, — except some few English teachers, — of the most pious and able men among them. If these did not supply, they would generally be destitute: for the learned English young men do not hitherto incline or endeavor to fit themselves for that service, by learning the Indian language. Possibly the reasons may be: First, the difficulty to attain that speech. Secondly, little encouragement, while they prepare for it. Thirdly, the difficulty in the practice of such a calling among them, by reason of the poverty and barbarity, which cannot be grappled with, unless the person be very much mortified, self-denying, and of a public spirit, seeking greatly God's glory; and these are rare qualifications in young men. It is but one of an hundred that is so endowed.

Mr. Eliot hath of late years fallen into a practice among the Indians, the better to prepare and furnish them with abilities to explicate and apply the scriptures, by setting up a lecture among them in logic and theology, once every fortnight, all the summer, at Natick; whereat he is present and ready, and reads and explains to them the principles of those arts. And God hath been pleased graciously so to bless these means, that several of them, especially young men of acute parts, have gained much knowledge, and are able to speak methodically and profitably unto any plain text of scripture, yea, as well as you can imagine such little means of learning can advantage them unto. From this church and town of Natick hath issued forth, as from a seminary of virtue and piety, divers teachers that are employed in several new praying towns; of which we shall hear more, God willing, hereafter.

John Smith (1580–1631)

IN THE preface to his *History of the Five Indian Nations* (1727), Cadwallader Colden says he expects to be criticized for "filling up so great part of the work with the adventures of small parties, and sometimes with those of one single man," but he justifies himself, saying, "The history of Indians would be very lame without an account of these private adventures; for their war-like expeditions are almost always carried on by surprising each other, and their whole art of war consists in managing small parties. The whole country being one continued forest, gives great advantages to these skulking parties, and has obliged the Christians to imitate the Indians in this method of making war." The literature of the seventeenth century supports Colden in its abundant accounts of massacres, tortures, ambushes, excruciating treks through the wilderness, and the humiliations of capture as red men and white sought to satisfy their mutual bloodlust.

The selection that follows, tracing Captain John Smith's (*q.v.*, p. 2) capture and release by Powhatan, may be said to begin the formal captivity narrative in American literature. The most famous portion of his *General History of Virginia,* it not only illustrates Smith's skill as a storyteller, but finds its climax, with not a little art, in the romantic tale of Pocahontas' love for the English soldier.

TEXT: Edward Arber, ed., *Travels and Works of Captain John Smith* (Glasgow, 1910), Vol. I.

The Indian Captivity

[From *The General History of Virginia,* 1624]

But our comedies never endured long without a tragedy; some idle exceptions being muttered against Captain Smith, for not discovering the head of Chickahamania River, and taxed by the Council, to be too slow in so worthy an attempt. The next voyage he proceeded so far, that with much labor by cutting of trees in sunder he made his passage; but when his barge could pass no farther, he left her in a broad bay out of danger of shot, commanding none should go ashore till his return. Himself with two English and two salvages went up higher in a canoe; but he was not long absent, but his men went ashore, whose want of government, gave both occasion and opportunity to the salvages to surprise one George Casson, whom they slew, and much failed not to have cut off the boat and all the rest. Smith, little dreaming of that accident, being got to the marshes at the river's head, twenty miles in the desert, had his two men slain (as is supposed) sleeping by the canoe, whilest himself by fowling sought them victual: who finding he was beset with 200 salvages, two of them he slew, still defending himself with the aid of a salvage his guide, whom he bound to his arm with his garters, and used him as a buckler, yet he was shot in his thigh a little and had many arrows that stuck in his clothes but no great hurt, till at last they took him prisoner. When this news came to Jamestown, much was their sorrow for his loss, few expecting what ensued. Six or seven weeks those barbarians kept him prisoner, many strange triumphs and conjurations they made of him, yet he so demeaned himself amongst them, as he not only diverted them from surprising the fort, but procured his own liberty, and got himself and his company such estimation amongst them, that those salvages admired him more than their own Quiyouckosucks. The manner how they used and delivered him is as follows. . . .

He demanding for their captain, they shewed him Opechankanough, King of Pamaunkee, to whom he gave a round ivory double compass dial. Much they marveled at the playing of the fly and needle, which they could see so plainly, and yet not touch it, because of the glass that covered them. But when he demonstrated by that globe-like jewel, the roundness of the earth, and skies, the sphere of the sun, moon, and stars, and how the sun did chase the night round about the world continually; the greatness of the land and sea, the diversity of nations, variety of complections, and how we were to them antipodes, and many other such like matters, they all stood as amazed with admiration. Notwithstanding, within an hour after, they tied him to a tree, and as many as could stand about him prepared to shoot him, but the king holding up the compass in his hand, they all laid down their bows and arrows, and in a triumphant manner led him to Orapaks, where he was after their manner kindly feasted, and well used.

Their order in conducting him was thus; drawing themselves all in file, the king in the middest had all their pieces and swords borne before him. Captain Smith was led after him by three great salvages, holding him fast by each arm: and on each side six went in file with their arrows nocked. But arriving at the town (which was but only thirty or forty hunting houses made of mats, which they remove as they please, as we our tents) all the women and children staring to behold him, the soldiers first all in file performed the form of a bissone so well as could be; and on each flank, officers as sergeants to see them keep their orders. A good time they continued this exercise, and then cast themselves in a ring, dancing in such several postures, and singing and yelling out such hellish notes and screeches; being strangely painted, every one his quiver of arrows, and at his back a club; on his arm a fox or an otter's skin, or some such matter for his vambrace; their heads and shoulders painted red, with oil and pocones mingled together, which scarlet-like color made an exceeding handsome shew; his bow in his hand, and the skin of a bird with her wings abroad dried, tied on his head, a piece of copper, a white shell, a long feather, with a small rattle growing at the tails of their snakes tied to it, or some such like toy. All this while Smith and the king stood in the middest guarded, as before is said, and after three dances they all departed. Smith they conducted to a long house, where thirty or forty tall fellows did guard him; and ere long more bread and venison was brought him then would have served twenty men. I think his stomach at that time was not very good; what he left they put in baskets and tied over his head. About midnight they set the meat again before him, all this time not one of them would eat a bit with him, till the next morning they brought him as much more, and then did they eat all the old, and reserved the new as they had done the other, which made him think they would fat him to eat him. Yet in this desperate estate to defend him from the cold, one Maocassater brought him his gown, in requital of some beads and toys Smith had given him at his first arrival in Virginia.

Two days after, a man would have slain him (but that the guard prevented it) for the death of his son, to whom they conducted him to recover the poor man then breathing his last. Smith told them that at Jamestown he had a water would do it, if they would let him fetch it, but they would not permit that; but made all the preparations they could to assault Jamestown, craving his advice; and for recompense he should have life, liberty, land, and women. In part of a table book he writ his mind to them at the fort, what was intended, how they should follow that direction to affright the messengers, and without fail send him such things as he writ for. And an inventory with them. The difficulty and danger, he told the salvages, of the mines, great guns, and other engines exceedingly affrighted them, yet according to his request they went to Jamestown, in as bitter weather as could be of frost and snow, and within three days returned with an answer.

But when they came to Jamestown, seeing men sally out as he had told them they would, they fled; yet in the night they came again to the same place where he had told them they should receive an answer, and such things as he had promised them, which they found accordingly, and with which they returned with no small expedition, to the wonder of them all that heard it, that he could either divine, or the paper could speak. Then they led him to the Youthtanunds, the Mattapanients, the Payankatanks, the Nantaughtacunds, and Onawmanients upon the rivers of Rapahanock, and Patawomek, over all those rivers, and back again by divers other several nations, to the king's habitation at Pamaunkee, where they entertained him with most strange and fearful conjurations;

As if near led to hell,
Amongst the devils to dwell.

Not long after, early in a morning a great fire was made in a long house, and a mat spread on the one side, as on the other; on the one they caused him to sit, and all the guard went out of the house, and presently came skipping in a great grim fellow, all painted over with coal, mingled with oil; and many snakes and weasels' skins stuffed with moss, and all their tails tied together, so as they met on the crown of his head in a tassel; and round about the tassel was a coronet of feathers, the skins hanging round about his head, back, and shoulders, and in a manner covered his face; with a hellish voice, and a rattle in his hand. With most strange gestures and passions he began his invocation, and environed the fire with a circle of meal; which done, three more such like devils came rushing in with the like antic tricks, painted half black, half red: but all their eyes were painted white, and some red strokes like mutchatos, along their cheeks: round about him those fiends danced a pretty while, and then came in three more as ugly as the rest; with red eyes, and white strokes over their black faces; at last they all sat down right against him; three of them on the one hand of the chief priest, and three on the other. Then all with their rattles began a song, which ended, the chief priest laid down five wheat corns: then straining his arms and hands with such violence that he sweat, and his veins swelled, he began a short oration: at the conclusion they all gave a short groan; and then laid down three grains more. After that, began their song again, and then another oration, ever laying down so many corns as before, till they had twice encircled the fire; that done, they took a bunch of little sticks prepared for that purpose, continuing still their devotion, and at the end of every song and oration, they laid down a stick betwixt the divisions of corn. Till night, neither he nor they did either eat or drink, and then they feasted merrily, with the best provisions they could make. Three days they used this ceremony; the meaning whereof they told him, was to know if he intended them well or no. The circle of meal signified their country, the circles of corn the bounds of the sea, and the sticks his country. They imagined the world to be flat and round, like a trencher, and they in the middest. After this they brought him a bag of gunpowder, which they carefully preserved till the next spring, to plant as they did their corn; because they would be acquainted with the nature of that seed.

Opitchapam the king's brother invited him to his house, where, with as many platters of bread, fowl, and wild beasts, as did environ him, he bid him welcome; but not any of them would eat a bit with him, but put up all the remainder in baskets. At his return to Opechankanough's, all the king's women, and their children, flocked about him for their parts, as a due by custom, to be merry with such fragments.

But his waking mind in hideous dreams did oft see wondrous shapes,
Of bodies strange, and huge in growth, and of stupendious makes.

At last they brought him to Meronocomo, where was Powhatan, their emperor. Here more then two hundred of those grim courtiers stood wondering at him, as he had been a monster; till Powhatan and his train had put themselves in their greatest braveries. Before a fire upon a seat like a bedstead, he sat covered with a great robe, made of rarowcun skins, and all the tails hanging by. On either hand did sit a young wench of sixteen or eighteen years, and along on each side the house, two rows of men, and behind them as many women, with all their heads and shoulders painted red; many of their heads bedecked with the white down of birds; but everyone with something: and a great chain of white beads about their necks. At his entrance before the king, all the people gave a great shout. The Queen of Appamatuck was appointed to bring him water to wash his hands, and another brought him a bunch of feathers, instead of a towel, to dry them. Having feasted him after their best barbarous manner they could, a long consultation was held, but the conclusion was, two great stones were brought before Powhatan: then as many as could laid hands on him, dragged him to them, and thereon laid his head, and being ready with their clubs, to beat out his brains, Pocahontas, the king's dearest daughter, when no entreaty could prevail, got his head in her arms, and laid her own upon his to save him from death: whereat the emperor was contented he should live to make him hatchets, and her bells, beads, and copper; for they thought him as well of all occupations as themselves. For the king himself will make his own robes, shoes, bows, arrows, pots; plant, hunt, or do anything so well as the rest.

They say he bore a pleasant shew,
But sure his heart was sad.
For who can pleasant be, and rest,
That lives in fear and dread:
And having life suspected, doth
It still suspected lead.

Two days after, Powhatan, having disguised himself in the most fearful manner he could, caused Captain Smith to be brought forth to a great house in the woods, and there upon a mat by the fire to be left alone. Not long after, from behind a mat that divided the house, was made the most dolefullest noise he ever heard; then Powhatan, more like a devil then a man, with some two hundred more as black as himself, came unto him and told him now they were friends, and presently he should go to Jamestown, to send him two great guns, and a grindstone, for which he would give him the country of Capahowosick, and forever esteem him as his son Nantaquoud. So to Jamestown with twelve guides Powhatan sent him. That night they quartered in the woods, he still expecting (as he had done all this long time of his imprisonment) every hour to be put to one death or other: for all their feasting. But almighty God (by His divine providence) had mollified the hearts of those stern barbarians with compassion. The next morning betimes they came to the fort, where Smith, having used the salvages with what kindness he could, he shewed Rawhunt, Powhatan's trusty servant, two demi-culverings and a millstone to carry Powhatan: they found them somewhat too heavy; but when they did see him discharge them, being loaded with stones, among the boughs of a great tree loaded with icicles, the ice and branches came so tumbling down, that the poor salvages ran away half dead with fear. But at last we regained some conference with them, and gave them such toys; and sent to Powhatan, his women, and children such presents, as gave them in general full content.

John Mason (1600–1672)

Two major Indian wars troubled the early colonists — the Pequot War (1637) and King Philip's War (1675–76) — besides which all the other Indian fighting was quite incidental. From about 1632, Massachusetts Bay officials had been having trouble with Sassacus, sachem of the Pequots, a warlike tribe of Algonquians in the Connecticut Valley. In 1636 the apparently unprovoked murder of a small number of settlers brought protests from the Bay which Sassacus met with disdainful threats. Fearful that the growing boldness of Indian raids and an alliance of tribes under Sassacus would wipe out the English settlements, the Bay decided to march on the Indians in the spring of 1637. Surprising the Indians in their flimsy Fort Mystic with the help of Mohegans under the leadership of Uncas, Captains Mason, Norton, Stone, and Underhill so decimated the tribe that it never again functioned as a unit; its survivors were absorbed into other tribes. Of the slaughter the usually mild William Bradford wrote with godly righteousness: "Those that scaped the fire were slain with the sword; some hewed to pieces, others run through with their rapiers, so as they were quickly dispatcht, and very few escaped. It was conceived they thus destroyed about 400 at this time. It was a fearful sight to see them thus frying in the fire, and the streams of blood quenching the same, and horrible was the stink and scent thereof. But the victory seemed a sweet sacrifice, and they gave the praise thereof to God, who had wrought so wonderfully for them, thus to enclose their enemies in their hands, and give them so speedy a victory over so proud and insulting an enemy."

The hero of the encounter was Captain John Mason, born in England, and experienced in battle in the Netherlands under the leadership of Sir Thomas Fairfax. Mason had come to New England early (*c.* 1630), and in time became the commander-in-chief of the colony's forces. He wrote his *Brief History of the Pequot War* around 1670 at the request of the Massachusetts General

Court. It was first published by Increase Mather, who erroneously attributed it to John Allyn, in *A Relation of the Troubles Which Have Happened in New England* (Boston, 1677), and was later corrected by Thomas Prince. Captain Underhill published his account in *News from America* (1638), and the Reverend Philip Vincent recited the event in *A True Relation of the Late Battle Fought in New England Between the English and the Pequot Savages* (1638).

TEXT: Major John Mason, *A Brief History of the Pequot War*, ed. Thomas Prince (Boston, 1735).

The Massacre of Fort Mystic

[From *A Brief History of the Pequot War* (*c.* 1670)]

And after we had refreshed ourselves with our mean commons, we marched about three miles, and came to a field which had lately been planted with Indian corn. There we made another halt, and called our council, supposing we drew near to the enemy: and being informed by the Indians that the enemy had two forts almost impregnable; but we were not at all discouraged, but rather animated, insomuch that we were resolved to assault both their forts at once. But understanding that one of them was so remote that we could not come up with it before midnight, though we marched hard; whereat we were much grieved, chiefly because the greatest and bloodiest sachem there resided, whose name was Sassacus; we were then constrained, being exceedingly spent in our march with extreme heat and want of necessaries, to accept of the nearest.

We then marching on in a silent manner, the Indians that remained fell all into the rear, who formerly kept the van (being possessed with great fear); we continued our march till about one hour in the night: and coming to a little swamp between two hills, there we pitched our little camp; much wearied with hard travel, keeping great silence, supposing we were very near the fort, as our Indians informed us; which proved otherwise. The rocks were our pillows; yet rest was pleasant. The night proved comfortable, being clear and moonlight. We appointed our guards and placed our sentinels at some distance; who heard the enemy singing at the fort, who continued that strain until midnight, with great insulting and rejoicing, as we were afterwards informed. They seeing our pinnaces sail by them some days before, concluded we were afraid of them and durst not come near them; the burthen of their song tending to that purpose.

In the morning, we awaking and seeing it very light, supposing it had been day, and so we might have lost our opportunity, having purposed to make our assault before day, roused the men with all expedition, and briefly commended ourselves and design to God, thinking immediately to go to the assault; the Indians shewing us a path, told us that it led directly to the fort. We held on our march about two miles, wondering that we came not to the fort, and fearing we might be deluded. But seeing corn newly planted at the foot of a great hill, supposing the fort was not far off, a champaign country being round about us; then making a stand, gave the word for some of the Indians to come up. At length Uncas and one Wequosh appeared. We demanded of them, "Where was the fort?" They answered, "On the top of that hill." Then we demanded, "Where were the rest of the Indians?" They answered, "Behind, exceedingly afraid." We wished them to tell the rest of their fellows that they should by no means fly, but stand at what distance they pleased, and see whether Englishmen would now fight or not. Then Captain Underhill came up, who marched in the rear; and commending ourselves to God, divided our men; there being two entrances into the fort, intending to enter both at once: Captain Mason leading up to that on the North-East side; who approaching within one rod, heard a dog bark and an Indian crying "Owanux! Owanux!" which is "Englishmen! Englishmen!" We called up our forces with all expedition, gave fire upon them through the palisado; the Indians being in a dead, indeed their last, sleep. Then we wheeling off fell upon the main entrance, which was blocked up with bushes about breast high, over which the captain passed, intending to make good the entrance, encouraging the rest to follow. Lieutenant Seeley endeavored to enter; but being somewhat cumbered, stepped back and pulled out the bushes and so entered, and with him about sixteen men. We had formerly concluded to destroy them by the sword and save the plunder.

Whereupon Captain Mason seeing no Indians, entered a wigwam; where he was beset with many Indians, waiting all opportunities to lay hands on him, but could not prevail. At length William Heydon espying the breach in the wigwam, supposing some English might be there, entered; but in his entrance fell over a dead Indian; but speedily recovering himself, the Indians some fled, others crept under their beds. The captain going out of the wigwam saw many Indians in the lane or street; he making towards them, they fled, were pursued to the end of the lane, where they were met by Edward Pattison, Thomas Barber, with some others; where seven of them were slain, as they said. The captain facing about, marched a slow pace up the lane he came down, perceiving himself very much out of breath; and coming to the other end near the place where he first entered, saw two soldiers standing close to the palisado with their swords pointed to the ground. The captain told them that we should never kill them after that manner. The captain also said, "We must burn them"; and immediately stepping into the wigwam where he had been before, brought out a fire-brand, and putting it into the mats with which they were covered, set the wigwams on fire. Lieutenant Thomas Bull and Nicholas Omsted beholding, came up; and when it was thoroughly kindled, the Indians ran as men most dreadfully amazed.

And indeed such a dreadful terror did the Almighty let fall upon their spirits, that they would fly from us and run into the very flames, where many of them perished. And when the fort was thoroughly fired, command was given, that all should fall off and surround the fort; which was readily attended by all; only one Arthur Smith being so wounded that he could not move out of the place, who was happily espied by Lieutenant Bull, and by him rescued.

The fire was kindled on the North-East side to windward; which did swiftly overrun the fort, to the extreme amazement of the enemy, and great rejoicing of ourselves. Some of them climbing to the top of the palisado; others of them running into the very flames; many of them gathering to windward, lay pelting at us with their arrows; and we repaid them with our small shot. Others of the stoutest issued forth, as we did guess, to the number of forty, who perished by the sword.

What I have formally said, is according to my own knowledge, there being sufficient living testimony to every particular.

But in reference to Captain Underhill and his party's acting in this assault, I can only intimate as we were informed by some of themselves immediately after the fight. Thus they marching up to the entrance on the South-West side, there made some pause; a valiant, resolute gentleman, one Mr. Hedge, stepping towards the gate, saying, "If we may not enter, wherefore came we here?" and immediately endeavored to enter; but was opposed by a sturdy Indian which did impede his entrance; but the Indian being slain by himself and Sergeant Davis, Mr. Hedge entered the fort with some others; but the fort being on fire, the smoke and flames were so violent that they were constrained to desert the fort.

Thus were they now at their wits' end, who not many hours before exalted themselves in their great pride, threatening and resolving the utter ruin and destruction of all the English, exulting and rejoicing with songs and dances. But God was above them, who laughed His enemies and the enemies of His people to scorn, making them as a fiery oven. Thus were the stout hearts spoiled, having slept their last sleep, and none of their men could find their hands. Thus did the Lord judge among the heathen, filling the place with dead bodies!

And here we may see the just judgment of God, in sending even the very night before this assault, one hundred and fifty men from their other fort, to join with them of that place, who were designed as some of themselves reported to go forth against the English, at that very instant when this heavy stroke came upon them, where they perished with their fellows. So that the mischief they intended to us, came upon their own pate. They were taken in their own snare, and we through mercy escaped. And thus in little more than one hour's space was their impregnable fort with themselves utterly destroyed, to the number of six or seven hundred, as some of themselves confessed. There were only seven taken captive, and about seven escaped.

Of the English, there were two slain outright, and about twenty wounded. Some fainted by reason of the sharpness of the weather, it being a cool morning, and the want of such comforts and necessaries as were needful in such a case; especially our chirurgeon was much wanting, whom we left with our barks in Narragansett Bay, who had order there to remain until the night before our intended assault.

And thereupon grew many difficulties: our provision and munition near spent; we in the enemy's country, who did far exceed us in number, being much enraged; all our Indians, except Uncas, deserting us; our pinnaces at a great distance from us, and when they would come we were uncertain.

But as we were consulting what course to take, it pleased God to discover our vessels to us before a fair gale of wind, sailing into Pequot harbor, to our great rejoicing.

Roger Wolcott (1679–1767)

CAPTAIN MASON's conquest of the Pequots appealed to other literary interests than James Fenimore Cooper's. In 1725 there appeared a slim book titled *Poetical Meditations: Some Improvement of Vacant Hours.* Among its slighter pieces was an epic poem grandly called "A Brief Account of the Agency of the Honorable John Winthrop, Esq., in the Court of King Charles the Second, Anno Dom. 1662. When He Obtained for the Colony of Connecticut His Majesty's Gracious Charter." Most of the poem is supposedly spoken by John Winthrop, Jr., to the king, for whose sake he recounts the discovery, the nature, and the settling of Connecticut. In the course of his tale he recites the slaughter of the Pequots in Dryden-like heroics, respectable enough of their kind, and interesting for their "poetic" transmuting of native materials into classically acceptable form.

The author of "A Brief Account" was Roger Wolcott, Connecticut born and raised. A diligent businessman, he turned his attention in time to military and state affairs, acting as commissary for the Connecticut troops in the 1711 "invasion" of Canada. When Louisburg was captured by the English in 1745, Wolcott was a major-general, and from 1751 to 1754 he was governor of Connecticut, as were his son and grandson after him.

For John Bulkley's preface to Wolcott's *Poetical Meditations,* see page 347, below.

TEXT: Roger Wolcott, *Poetical Meditations* (New London, 1725).

Victory at Mystic

[From "A Brief Account . . . ," in *Poetical Meditations,* 1725]

Brave Mason who had in his breast enshrined,
A prudent and invulnerable mind;
Weighing the case and ground whereon they stood,
The enemy how hard to be subdued:
How if the field should by the foe be won,
The English settlements might be undone.
His little army now was left alone,
And all the allies' hopes and hearts were gone.
These and all other things that might dissuade,
From an engagement having fully weighed:
But looking on his cheerful soldiery,
True sons of Mars, bred up in Brittany;
Each firmly bent to glorify his name
By dying bravely in the bed of Fame,
In his new country's just defense, or else
To extirpate these murtherous infidels;
This raised his thoughts, his vital spirits cleared,
So that no enemy on earth he feared.
And now resolved the city to invade;
He to the thoughtful prince this answer made;
"You say, my men han't yet a Pequot seen;
'Tis true, yet they e're now in wars have been,
Where mighty captains and brave men have shed
Their blood, while roaring cannons echoed,
Yet they undaunted, resolute go on
Where dying springs make sanguine rivers run.
Out-braving danger, mount the highest wall,
Yea play with death itself without appall:
Nor turn the back till they have won the day,
And from the mighty torn the spoils away.
And do you think that any Pequot's face
Shall daunt us much, or alter much the case?
The valor of our foes we always prize,
As that which most our triumph glorifies.

Their strength and courage but allurements are,
To make us more ambitious of the war.
Then don't despair, but turn you back again
Encouraged, and confirm your heartless men,
And hinder them in their intended flight;
Only to see how Englishmen will fight.
And let your eyes themselves be judges then
'Twixt us and Pequots, which are better men."
  Down bowed the prince, down bowed this trembling 'squire;
Greatly the general's courage they admire.
Back to the rear, with speedy haste they went,
And call the captains of their regiment;
To whom the prince doth in short terms declare,
English or Pequots must go and hunt white deer.
No counsel can the general's wrath assuage,
Nor calm the fury of his martial rage.
His men are all resolved to go on,
Unto the Pequot's ruin, or their own:
Then we ourselves will stand in sight and see
The last conclusion of this tragedy.

. . . .

  After devotions thus to heaven paid,
Up to the enemy our army's led,
Silent as the Riphean snow doth fall,
Or fishes walk in Neptune's spacious hall.
  Now Lucifer had just put out his head,
To call Aurora from old Tithon's bed.
Whereat the troops of the approaching light,
Began to beat the reg'ments of the night.
  But Morpheus with his unperceived bands,
Had closed the Pequots' eyes and chained their hands.
All slept secure, save one sagacious wretch,
Whose turn it was to stand upon the watch.
His weighty charge with diligence he applies,
And looking round with fierce Lyncean eyes.
At length our avant couriers he espied,
Straining his lungs aloud, "Auwunux!" cried.
  ("Auwunux," said our King, "What doth that mean?"
"It signifies," said Winthrop, "Englishmen.")
  The startling news doth every soldier rouse,
Each arms and hastens to his rendezvous.
Meantime the English did the fort attack,
And in the same had opened a breach.
Through which our brave Aleides entered first,
In after whom his valiant soldiers thrust.
  Before the breach an unappalled band,
Of warlike Pequots with bow and arrows stand.
With cheerful accents these themselves confirm

To die like men or to outface the storm.
Then gallantly the English they assail,
With winged arrows like a shower of hail.
These ours endure; and with like violence,
Sent lead and sulphur back in recompense.
   And now the fight grew more and more intense,
Each violent death enflames the violence.
Charge answered charge, and shout replied to shout;
Both parties like enraged Furies fought.
Till death in all its horrid forms appears,
And dreadful noise keeps clamoring in our ears.
   Now as some spacious rivers in their way,
By which they travel onwards to the sea,
Meet with some mighty precipice from whence,
Enraged, they throw themselves with violence,
Upon the stubborn rocks that lie below,
To make disturbance in the way they go.
Here though the fury of the fray doth make
The near adjacent rocks and mountains quake.
Still the remorseless stream keeps on its course,
Nor will abate a moment of its force,
But rather hastens by impetuous facts
To throw itself into those cataracts.
   And so it happened with our soldiers here,
Whose fortune 'twas to travel in the rear.
The combatings of these within the breaches,
With dreadful noise their listening ears attaches,
And from their foes and from their bretheren,
Loud cries of fighting and of dying men.
   Sense of the danger doth not them affright,
But rather proves a motive to excite
The martial flame in every soldier's breast,
And on they like enraged lions prest.
Determined upon the spot to die,
Or from the foe obtain the victory.
   Now fortune shews to the beholder's sight,
A very dreadful, yet a doubtful fight.
Whilst mighty men, born in far distant land,
Stood foot to foot engaging hand to hand.
   As when some mighty tempest that arise,
Meet with imbattled fury in the skies:
Fireballs of lightnings and loud thunders rend,
And tear the raging parleys that contend,
   So did the fury of these mighty foes,
With which they did each other's force oppose,
Bring on such ruins as might daunt with fears,
The hearts of any men; excepting theirs.
   Never did Pequots fight with greater pride:

Never was English valor better tried.
Never was ground soaked with more gallant blood
Than the Aceldama whereon we stood.
Sometimes one party victory soon expect,
As soon their eager hopes are counterchecked.
And those that seemed as conquered before,
Repel with greater force the conqueror.
Three times the Pequots seemed to be beat:
As many times they made their foes retreat.
And now our hope and help for victory,
Chiefly depended from the arm on high,
  As when Euroclydon the forest rends,
The bigger oaks fall down, the lesser bends;
The beaten limbs and leaves before him scour,
Affrighted and enforced by his power;
To some huge rock whose adamantine brow,
Outbraves the fury of all winds that blow;
There hoping to be hid from the high charge,
Of fierce pursuers by his mighty verge.
The winds in pressing troops demand surrender,
Of the pursued and boisterous storm and thunder:
But he browbeats, and masters all their pride,
And sends them roaring to the larboard side.
  So Mason here most strongly drest in arms,
Re-animates his men, their ranks reforms,
Then leading on through deaths and dangers goes,
And beats the thickest squadrons of the foes.
Prince Mononotto sees his squadrons fly,
And on our general having fixt his eye,
Rage and revenge his spirits quickening,
He set a mortal arrow in the string.
  Then to his god and fathers' ghosts he prayed,
"Hear, O Immortal Powers, hear me," he said;
"And pity Mystic, save the tottering town,
And on our foes hurl dreadful vengeance down.
Will you forsake your altars and abodes,
To those contemners of immortal god's?
Will those pay hecatombs unto your shrine,
Who have denied your powers to be divine?
O favor us; our hopes on you are built,
But if you are mindful of our former guilt,
Determine final ruin on us all;
Yet let us not quite unrevenged fall.
Here I devote this of our enemies
His precious life to you a sacrifice.
Nor shall I covet long to be alive,
If such a mischief I might once survive.
But O Indulgent, hearken to my prayer;

Try us once more; this once the city spare:
And take my gift, let your acceptance be
An omen we shall gain the victory."
  That very instant Mason did advance,
Whereat rage interrupts his utterance;
Nor could he add a word to what was said,
But drew the winged arrow to the head:
And aiming right, discharged it, whereupon
Its fury made the piercing air to groan.
  But wary Mason with his active spear,
Glanced the prince's arrow in the air:
Whereat the Pequots quite discouraged,
Throw down the gauntlet and from battle fled.
  Mason swift as the chased roe on foot,
Outstrips the rest in making the pursuit:
Entring the palace in a hall he found,
A multitude of foes, who gathering round
This mighty man on every side engaged
Like bears bereaved of their whelps enraged.
  On finding such resistance where he came,
His mind, his weapons, and his eyes stroke flame.
Their boldness much his martial sprite provokes,
And round he lays his deep inveterate strokes,
Making his sword at each enforced blow
Send great-souled heroes to the shades below.
  But as when Hercules did undertake,
A doubtful combat with the Lernian snake;
Fondly proposed if he cut off her head,
The monster might with ease be vanquished:
  But when he the experiment did make,
Soon to his hazard found his dear mistake;
And that as often as he cut off one,
Another instantly sprang in its room;
  So here, though Mason laid so many dead,
Their number seemed not diminished;
And Death the umpire of this martial fray,
Stood yet expecting Mason for his prey.
  But Fate that doth the rule of actions know,
Did this unequal combat disallow.
As too severe to force one man alone,
To beat an army, take a garrison:
Or if he failed in the enterprise,
To fall a victim to his enemies;
Sent Heydon in, who with his sure-steeled blade,
Joining the general such a slaughter made,
That soon the Pequots ceased to oppose,
The matchless force of such resistless foes.
  After so many deaths and dangers past,

Mason was thoroughly enflamed at last:
He snatcht a blazing bavin with his hand,
And fired the stately palace with the brand.
And soon the tow'ring and rapacious flame,
All hope of opposition overcame.
Eurus and Notus readily subjoin,
Their best assistance to this great design;
Drive pitchy flames in vast enfoldings down,
And dreadful globes of fire along the town.
And now the English army marched out,
To hem this flaming city round about;
That such as strived to escape the fire,
Might by the fury of their arms expire.
But O what language or what tongue can tell,
This dreadful emblem of the flames of hell?
No fantasy sufficient is to dream,
A faint idea of their woes extreme.
Some like unlucky comets do appear,
Rushing along the streets with flagrant hair:
Some seeking safety clamber up the wall,
Then down again with blazing fingers fall.
In this last hour of extremity,
Friends and relations met in company;
But all in vain; their tender sympathy,
Cannot allay but makes their misery.
The paramour here met his amorous dame,
Whose eyes had often set his heart in flame:
Urged with the motives of her love and fear,
She runs and clasps her arms about her dear:
Where weeping on his bosom as she lies,
And languisheth on him she sets her eyes;
Till those bright lamps do with her life expire,
And leave him weltering in a double fire.
The fair and beauteous bride with all her charms,
This night lay melting in her bridegroom's arms.
This morning in his bosom yields her life,
While he dies sympathizing with his wife.
In love relation and in life the same,
The same in death, both die in the same flame,
Their souls united both at once repair,
Unto their place appointed through the air.
The gracious father here stood looking on,
His little brood with deep affection,
They round about him at each quarter stands,
With piteous looks, each lifts his little hands
To him for shelter, and then nearer throng,
Whilst piercing cries for help flows from each tongue,
Fain would he give their miseries relief;

Though with the forfeiture of his own life:
But finds his power too short to shield off harms,
The torturing flame arrests them in his arms.
The tender mother with like woes opprest,
Beholds her infant frying at her breast;
Crying and looking on her, as it fries;
Till death shuts up its heart-affecting eyes.
  The conquering flame long sorrows doth prevent,
And vanquished life soon breaks imprisonment,
Souls leave their tenements gone to decay,
And fly untouched through the flames away.
Now all with speed to final ruin haste,
And soon this tragic scene is overpast.
The town its wealth, high battlements, and spires,
Now sinketh welt'ring in conjoining fires.
  The general commands the officers with speed,
To see his men drawn up and martialed,
Which being done, they wheel the ranks,
And kneeling down to heaven all gave thanks.

Mary White Rowlandson (1635–1678)

As THE captivity narrative found its beginnings in John Smith's adventures, it found its most popular pattern in the narrative of Mary Rowlandson. Mrs. Rowlandson was born in Lancaster, in the western part of Massachusetts, on the edge of the frontier. She married the Reverend Joseph Rowlandson, had three children, and lived a quiet life until February, 1676, when she and her children were captured in one of the sudden, savage raids of King Philip's War. On the subsequent march into the forest her youngest child died, but Mrs. Rowlandson and her remaining two children were finally ransomed for twenty pounds and released in May, 1676. She then either wrote or dictated the narrative of her captivity, which was apparently published after her death. No copy of the first edition exists, but the second in 1682 was followed by at least thirty more.

Her narrative is titled, significantly, *The Sovereignty and Goodness of God, Together with the Faithfulness of His Promises Displayed; Being a Narrative of the Captivity and Restoration of Mrs. Mary Rowlandson.* Typical of the Puritan accounts, it stresses the victim's psychological reaction to the captivity experience and focuses on external happenings only to illustrate God's providence at work in the affairs of men. The experience is symbolic of the captivity of all mankind, seized by Satan's emissaries, tried and tested by suffering, and finally released with a greater understanding of human fate and God's will. Such stories, though their end was pious, also functioned as the seventeenth-century version of the modern thriller. Increase Mather even published a collection of them before the end of the century, and through the eighteenth century they fell into the hands of hack journalists who rewrote them for others who claimed to have had similar experiences. In these later versions, the captivity is such a sensational mixture of fact and fancy — often designed to maintain colonial hatred (first of the French, later of the British) of Indian allies — that literary interest far outweighs historical worth. These are the first American "true adventure" stories, sentimental, pathetic, and often exciting; in their episodic structure they anticipate later "captivities" like Harriet Beecher Stowe's *Uncle Tom's Cabin* and perhaps even Mark Twain's *Adventures of Huckleberry Finn.*

TEXT: Henry S. Nourse and John E. Thayer, eds., *The Narrative of the Captivity and Restoration of Mrs. Mary Rowlandson* (Lancaster, Mass., 1903).

Captivity and Restoration

[From *The Sovereignty and Goodness of God,* 1682]

On the tenth of February, 1676, came the Indians with great numbers upon Lancaster: their first coming was about sun-rising; hearing the noise of some guns, we looked out; several houses were burning, and the smoke ascending to heaven. There were five persons taken in one house, the father, and the mother and a sucking child, they knockt on the head; the other two they took and carried away alive. There were two others, who being out of their garrison upon some occasion were set upon; one was knockt on the head, the other escaped: another there was who running along was shot and wounded, and fell down; he begged of them his life, promising them money (as they told me) but they would not hearken to him but knockt him in head, and stript him naked, and split open his bowels. Another seeing many of the Indians about his barn, ventured and went out, but was quickly shot down. There were three others belonging to the same garrison who were killed; the Indians getting up upon the roof of the barn, had advantage to shoot down upon them over their fortification. Thus these murtherous wretches went on, burning, and destroying before them.

At length they came and beset our own house, and quickly it was the dolefullest day that ever mine eyes saw. The house stood upon the edge of a hill; some of the Indians got behind the hill, others into the barn, and others behind anything that could shelter them; from all which places they shot against the house, so that the bullets seemed to fly like hail; and quickly they wounded one man among us, then another, and then a third. About two hours (according to my observation, in that amazing time) they had been about the house before they prevailed to fire it (which they did with flax and hemp, which they brought out of the barn, and there being no defense about the house, only two flankers at two opposite corners, and one of them not finished) they fired it once and one ventured out and quenched it, but they quickly fired it again, and that took. Now is the dreadful hour come, that I have often heard of (in time of war, as it was the case of others) but now mine eyes see it. Some in our house were fighting for their lives, others wallowing in their blood, the house on fire over our heads, and the bloody heathen ready to knock us on the head, if we stirred out. Now might we hear mothers and children crying out for themselves, and one another, Lord, What shall we do? Then I took my children (and one of my sisters, hers) to go forth and leave the house: but as soon as we came to the door and appeared, the Indians shot so thick that the bullets rattled against the house, as if one had taken an handful of stones and threw them, so that we were fain to give back. We had six stout dogs belonging to our garrison, but none of them would stir, though another time, if any Indian had come to the door, they were ready to fly upon him and tear him down. The Lord hereby would make us the more to acknowledge His hand, and to see that our help is always in Him. But out we must go, the fire increasing, and coming along behind us, roaring, and the Indians gaping before us with their guns, spears, and hatchets to devour us. No sooner were we out of the house, but my brother-in-law (being before wounded, in defending the house, in or near the throat) fell down dead, wherat the Indians scornfully shouted, and hallowed, and were presently upon him, stripping off his cloaths, the bullets flying thick, one went through my side, and the same (as would seem) through the bowels and hand of my dear child in my arms. One of my elder sister's children, named William, had then his leg broken, which the Indians perceiving, they knockt him on head. Thus were we butchered by those merciless heathen, standing amazed, with the blood running down to our heels. My eldest sister being yet in the house, and seeing those woeful sights, the infidels hauling mothers one way, and children another, and some wallowing in their blood: and her elder son telling her that her son William was dead, and myself was wounded, she said, "and, Lord, let me die with them"; which was no sooner said, but she was struck with a bullet, and fell down dead over the threshold. I hope she is reaping the fruit of her good labors, being faithful to the service of God in her place. In her younger years she lay under much trouble upon spiritual accounts, till it pleased God to make that precious scripture take hold of her heart, 2 Cor. 12:9: "And he said unto me, my grace is sufficient for thee." More then twenty years after I have heard her tell how sweet and comfortable that place was to her. But to return, the Indians laid hold of us, pulling me one way, and the children another, and said, "Come go along with us"; I told them they would kill me: they answered, if I were willing to go along with them, they would not hurt me.

Oh the doleful sight that now was to behold at this house! "Come, behold the works of the Lord, what desolations He has made in the earth." Of thirty-seven persons who were in this one house, none escaped either present death, or a bitter captivity, save only one, who might say as he, Job 1:15, "And I only am escaped alone to tell the news." There were twelve killed, some shot, some stabbed with their spears, some knocked down with their hatchets. When we are in prosperity, Oh the little that we think of such dreadful sights, and to see our dear friends, and relations lie bleeding out their heart-blood upon the ground. There was one who was chopt into the head with a hatchet, and stript naked, and yet was crawling up and down. It is a solemn sight to see so many Christians lying in their blood, some here, and some there, like a company of sheep torn by wolves. All of them stript naked by a company of hell-hounds, roaring, singing, ranting, and insulting, as if they would have torn our very hearts out; yet the Lord by His almighty power preserved a number of us from death, for there were twenty-four of us taken alive and carried captive.

I had often before this said, that if the Indians should come, I should choose rather to be killed by them then taken alive, but when it came to the trial my mind changed; their glittering weapons so daunted my spirit, that I chose rather to go along with those (as I may say) ravenous bears, then that moment to end my days; and that I may the better declare what happened to me during that grievous captivity, I shall particularly speak of the several removes we had up and down the wilderness.

THE FIRST REMOVE

Now away we must go with those barbarous creatures, with our bodies wounded and bleeding, and our hearts no less than our bodies. About a mile we went that night, up upon a hill within sight of the town where they intended to lodge. There was hard by a vacant house (deserted by the English before, for fear of the Indians). I asked them whether I might not lodge in the house that night to which they answered, "What, will you love Englishmen still?" this was the dolefullest night that ever my eyes saw. Oh the roaring, and singing and dancing, and yelling of those black creatures in the night, which made the place a lively resemblance of hell. And as miserable was the waste that was there made of horses, cattle, sheep, swine, calves, lambs, roasting pigs, and fowl (which they had plundered in the town) some roasting, some lying and burning, and some boiling to feed our merciless enemies, who were joyful enough though we were disconsolate. To add to the dolefulness of the former day, and the dismalness of the present night, my thoughts ran upon my losses and sad bereaved condition. All was gone, my husband gone (at least separated from me, he being in the Bay; and to add to my grief, the Indians told me they would kill him as he came homeward), my children gone, my relations and friends gone, our house and home and all our comforts within door and without; all was gone (except my life), and I knew not but the next moment that might go too. There remained nothing to me but one poor wounded babe, and it seemed at present worse than death that it was in such a pitiful condition, bespeaking compassion, and I had no refreshing for it, nor suitable things to revive it. Little do many think what is the savageness and brutishness of this barbarous enemy, aye, even those that seem to profess more than others among them, when the English have fallen into their hands.

Those seven that were killed at Lancaster the summer before upon a sabbath day, and the one that was afterward killed upon a week day, were slain and mangled in a barbarous manner, by One-eyed John, and Marlborough's praying Indians which Capt. Mosely brought to Boston, as the Indians told me.

THE SECOND REMOVE

But now, the next morning, I must turn my back upon the town, and travel with them into the vast and desolate wilderness, I knew not whither. It is not my tongue, or pen can express the sorrows of my heart, and bitterness of my spirit, that I had at this departure: but God was with me, in a wonderful manner, carrying me along, and bearing up my spirit, that it did not quite fail. One of the Indians carried my poor wounded babe upon a horse; it went moaning all along, "I shall die, I shall die." I went on foot after it, with sorrow that cannot be expressed. At length I took it off the horse, and carried it in my arms till my strength failed, and I fell down with it; then they set me upon a horse with my wounded child in my lap, and there being no furniture upon the horse back, as we were going down a steep hill, we both fell over the horse's head, at which they, like inhumane creatures, laughed, and rejoiced to see it, though I thought we should there have ended our days, as overcome with so many difficulties. But the Lord renewed my strength still, and carried me along, that I might see more of His power; yea, so much that I could never have thought of, had I not experienced it.

After this it quickly began to snow, and when night came on, they stopt: and now down I must sit in the snow, by a little fire, and a few boughs behind me, with my sick child in my lap, and calling much for water, being now (through the wound) fallen into a violent fever. My own wound also growing so stiff, that I could scarce sit down or rise up, yet so it must be, that I must sit all this cold winter night upon the cold snowy ground, with my sick child in my arms, looking that every hour would be the last of its life; and having no Christian friend near me, either to comfort or help me. Oh, I may see the wonderful power of God, that my spirit did not utterly sink under my affliction: still the Lord upheld me with his gracious and merciful Spirit, and we were both alive to see the light of the next morning.

THE THIRD REMOVE

The morning being come, they prepared to go on their way. One of the Indians got up upon a horse, and they set me up behind him, with my poor sick babe in my lap. A very wearisome and tedious day I had of it, what with my own wound, and my child's being so exceeding sick, and in a lamentable condition with her wound. It may be easily judged what a poor feeble condition we were in, there being not the least crumb of refreshing that came within either of our mouths, from Wednesday night to Saturday night, except only a little cold water. This day in the afternoon, about an hour by sun, we came to the place where they intended, *viz.*, an Indian town, called Wenimesset, Norward of Quabaug. When we were come, Oh the number of pagans (now merciless enemies) that there came about me, that I may say as David, Psal. 27:13, "I had fainted, unless I had believed," etc. The next day was the sabbath: I then remembered how careless I had been of God's holy time, how many sabbaths I had lost and misspent, and how evilly I had walked in God's sight; which lay so close unto my spirit, that it was easy for me to see how righteous it was with God to cut off the thread of my life, and cast me out of His presence for ever. Yet the Lord still shewed mercy to me, and upheld me; and as He wounded me with one hand, so He healed me with the other. This day there came to me one Robert Pepper (a man belonging to Roxbury) who was taken in Captain Beers his fight, and had been now a considerable time with the Indians; and up with them almost as far as Albany, to see King Philip, as he told me, and was now very lately come into these parts. Hearing, I say, that I was in this Indian town, he obtained leave to come and see me. He told me he himself was wounded in the leg at Captain Beers his fight; and was not able some time to go, but as they carried him, and as he took oaken leaves and laid to his wound, and through the blessing of God he was able to travel again. Then I took oaken leaves and laid to my side, and with the blessing of God it cured me also; yet before the cure was wrought, I may say, as it is in Psal. 38:5, 6. "My wounds stink and are corrupt, I am troubled, I am bowed down greatly, I go mourning all the day long." I sat much alone with a poor wounded child in my lap, which moaned night and day, having nothing to revive the body, or cheer the spirits of her, but instead of that, sometimes one Indian would come and tell me one hour, that your master will knock your child in the head, and then a second, and then a third, your master will quickly knock your child in the head.

This was the comfort I had from them, miserable comforters are ye all, as he said. Thus nine days I sat upon my knees, with my babe in my lap, till my flesh was raw again; my child being even ready to depart this sorrowful world, they bade me carry it out to another wigwam (I suppose because they would not be troubled with such spectacles), whither I went with a very heavy heart, and down I sat with the picture of death in my lap. About two hours in the night, my sweet babe like a lamb departed this life, on Feb. 18, 1676. It being about six years and five months old. It was nine days from the first wounding, in this miserable condition, without any refreshing of one nature or other, except a little cold water. I cannot but take notice, how at another time I could not bear to be in the room where any dead person was, but now the case is changed; I must and could lie down by my dead babe, side by side all the night after. I have thought since of the wonderful goodness of God to me, in preserving me in the use of my reason and senses, in that distressed time, that I did not use wicked and violent means to end my own miserable life. In the morning, when they understood that my child was dead, they sent for me home to my master's wigwam (by my master in this writing, must be understood Quanopin, who was a Sagamore, and married King Philip's wife's sister; not that he first took me, but I was sold to him by another Narragansett Indian, who took me when first I came out of the garrison). I went to take up my dead child in my arms to carry it with me, but they bid me let it alone: there was no resisting, but go I must and leave it. When I had been at my master's wigwam, I took the first opportunity I could get, to go look after my dead child: when I came I asked them what they had done with it? then they told me it was upon the hill; then they went and shewed me where it was, where I saw the ground was newly digged, and there they told me they had buried it. There I left that child in the wilderness, and must commit it, and myself also in this wilderness-condition, to Him who is above all. . . .

THE EIGHTH REMOVE

On the morrow morning we must go over the river, i.e., Connecticut, to meet with King Philip; two canoes full, they had carried over; the next turn I myself was to go; but as my foot was upon the canoe to step in, there was a sudden out-cry among them, and I must step back; and instead of going over the river, I must go four or five miles up the river farther Northward. Some of the Indians ran one way, and some another. The cause of this rout was, as I thought, their espying some English scouts, who were thereabout. In this travel up the river; about noon the company made a stop, and sat down; some to eat, and others to rest them. As I sat amongst them, musing of things past, my son Joseph unexpectedly came to me: we asked of each other's welfare, bemoaning our doleful condition, and the change that had come upon us. We had husband and father, and children, and sisters, and friends, and relations, and house, and home, and many comforts of this life: but now we may say, as Job, "Naked came I out of my mother's womb, and naked shall I return: the Lord gave, and the Lord hath taken away, Blessed be the name of the Lord." I asked him whether he would read; he told me, he earnestly desired it. I gave him my Bible, and he lighted upon that comfortable scripture, Psal. 118:17, 18, "I shall not die, but live, and declare the works of the Lord: the Lord hath chastened me sore, yet He hath not given me over to death." "Look here, mother" (says he), "did you read this?" And here I may take occasion to mention one principal ground of my setting forth these lines: even as the Psalmist says, to "declare the works of the Lord," and His wonderful power in carrying us along, preserving us in the wilderness, while under the enemies' hand, and returning of us in safety again. And His goodness in bringing to my hand so many comfortable and suitable scriptures in my distress. But to return, we traveled on till night; and in the morning, we must go over the river to Philip's crew. When I was in the canoe, I could not but be amazed at the numerous crew of pagans that were on the bank on the other side. When I came ashore, they gathered all about me, I sitting alone in the midst: I observed they asked one another questions, and laughed, and rejoiced over their gains and victories. Then my heart began to fail: and I fell a-weeping, which was the first time to my remembrance, that I wept before them. Although I had met with so much affliction, and my heart was many times ready to break, yet could I not shed one tear in their sight: but rather had been all this while in a maze, and like one astonished: but now I may say, as Psal. 137:1, "By the rivers of Babylon, there we sat down: yea, we wept when we remembered Zion." There one of them asked me, why I wept, I could hardly tell what to say: yet I answered, they would kill me. "No," said he, "none will hurt you." Then came one of them and gave me two spoonfuls of meal to comfort me, and another gave me half a pint of peas; which was more worth than many bushels at another time. Then I went to see King Philip, he bade me come in and sit down, and asked me whether I would smoke it (a usual compliment nowadays amongst saints and sinners) but this no way suited me. For though I had formerly used tobacco, yet I had left it ever since I was first taken. It seems to be a bait the Devil lays to make men lose their precious time. I remember with shame how formerly, when I had taken two or three pipes, I was presently ready for another, such a bewitching thing it is: but I thank God, he has now given me power over it; surely there are many who may be better employed than to lie sucking a stinking tobacco-pipe.

Now the Indians gather their forces to go against Northampton: over-night one went about yelling and hooting to give notice of the design. Whereupon they fell to boiling of ground-nuts, and parching of corn (as many as had it) for their provision: and in the morning away they went. During my abode in this place, Philip spake to me to make a shirt for his boy, which I did, for which he gave me a shilling. I offered the money to my master, but he bade me keep it, and with it I bought a piece of horse flesh. Afterwards he asked me to make a cap for his boy, for which he invited me to dinner. I went, and he gave me a pancake about as big as two fingers; it was made of parched wheat, beaten, and fried in bear's grease, but I thought I never tasted pleasanter meat in my life. There was a squaw who spake to me to make a shirt for her *sannup,* for which she gave me a piece of bear. Another asked me to knit a pair of stockins, for which she gave me a quart of peas: I boiled my peas and bear together, and invited my master and mistress to dinner, but the proud gossip, because I served them both in one dish, would eat nothing, except one bit that he gave her upon the point of his knife. Hearing that my son was come to this place, I went to see him, and found him lying flat upon the ground: I asked him how he could sleep so? he answered me, that he was not asleep, but at prayer; and lay so, that they might not observe what he was doing. I pray God he may remember these things now he is returned in safety. At this place (the sun now getting higher) what with the beams and heat of the sun, and the smoke of the wigwams, I thought I should have been blind. I could scarce discern one wigwam from another. There was here one Mary Thurston of Medfield, who seeing how it was with me, lent me a hat to wear, but as soon as I was gone, the squaw (who owned that Mary Thurston) came running after me, and got it away again. Here was the squaw that gave me one spoonful of meal. I put it in my pocket to keep it safe, yet notwithstanding somebody stole it, but put five Indian corns in the room of it, which corns were the greatest provisions I had in my travel for one day.

The Indians returning from Northampton, brought with them some horses, and sheep, and other things which they had taken: I desired them, that they would carry me to Albany, upon one of those horses, and sell me for powder, for so they had sometimes discoursed. I was utterly hopeless of getting home on foot, the way that I came. I could hardly bear to think of the many weary steps I had taken, to come to this place. . . .

THE TWENTIETH REMOVE

It was their usual manner to remove, when they had done any mischief, lest they should be found out: and so they did at this time. We went about three or four miles, and there they built a great wigwam, big enough to hold an hundred Indians, which they did in preparation to a great day of dancing. They would say now amongst themselves, that the governor would be so angry for his loss at Sudbury, that he would send no more about the captives, which made me grieve and tremble. My sister being not far from the place where we now were: and hearing that I was here, desired her master to let her come and see me, and he was willing to it, and would go with her, but she being ready before him, told him she would go before, and was come within a mile or two of the place; then he overtook her, and began to rant as if he had been mad; and made her go back again in the rain; so that I never saw her till I saw her in Charlestown. But the Lord requited many of their ill doings, for this Indian her master, was hanged afterward at Boston. The Indians now began to come from all quarters, against their merry dancing day. Among some of them came one Goodwife Kettle: I told her my heart was so heavy that it was ready to break. "So is mine too," said she, but yet said, "I hope we shall hear some good news shortly." I could hear how earnestly my sister desired to see me, and I as earnestly desired to see her: and yet neither of us could get an opportunity. My daughter was also now about a mile off, and I had not seen her in nine or ten weeks, as I had not seen my sister since our first taking. I earnestly desired them to let me go and see them: yea, I intreated, begged, and persuaded them, but to let me see my daughter; and yet so hard-hearted were they, that they would not suffer it. They made use of their tyrannical power whilst they had it: but through the Lord's wonderful mercy, their time was now but short.

On a sabbath day, the sun being about an hour high in the afternoon, came Mr. John Hoar (the Council permitting him, and his own forward spirit inclining him) together with the two forementioned Indians, Tom and Peter, with their third letter from the Council. When they came near, I was abroad: though I saw them not, they presently called me in, and bade me sit down and not stir. Then they catched up their guns, and away they ran, as if an enemy had been at hand; and the guns went off apace. I manifested some great trouble, and they asked me what was the matter? I told them, I thought they had killed the Englishman (for they had in the meantime informed me that an Englishman was come); they said, No; they shot over his horse and under, and before his horse; and they pusht him this way and that way, at their pleasure: shewing what they could do. Then they let them come to their wigwams. I begged of them to let me see the Englishman, but they would not. But there was I fain to sit their pleasure. When they had talked their fill with him, they suffered me to go to him. We asked each other of our welfare, and how my husband did, and all my friends? He told me they were all well, and would be glad to see me. Amongst other things which my husband sent me, there came a pound of tobacco: which I sold for nine shillings in money: for many of the Indians, for want of tobacco, smoked hemlock, and ground ivy. It was a great mistake in any, who thought I sent for tobacco: for through the favor of God, that desire was overcome. I now asked them, whether I should go home with Mr. Hoar? They answered "No," one and another of them: and it being night, we lay down with that answer; in the morning, Mr. Hoar invited the Sagamores to dinner; but when we went to get it ready, we found that they had stolen the greatest part of the provision Mr. Hoar had brought, out of his bags, in the night. And we may see the wonderful power of God, in that one passage, in that when there was such a great number of the Indians together, and so greedy of a little good food; and no English there, but Mr. Hoar and myself: that there they did not knock us in the head, and take what we had: there being not only some provision, but also trading-cloth, a part of the twenty pounds agreed upon. But instead of doing us any mischief, they seemed to be ashamed of the fact, and said, it were some *machit* Indian that did it. Oh, that we could believe that there is nothing too hard for God! God shewed His power over the heathen in this, as He did over the hungry lions when Daniel was cast into the den. Mr. Hoar called them betime to dinner, but they ate very little, they being so busy in dressing themselves, and getting ready for their dance: which was carried on by eight of them; four men and four squaws: my master and mistress being two. He was dressed in his Holland shirt, with great laces sewed at the tail of it; he had his silver buttons, his white stockins, his garters were hung round with shillings, and he had girdles of wampum upon his head and shoulders. She had a kersey coat, and covered with girdles of wampum from the loins upward: her arms from her elbows to her hands were covered with bracelets; there were handfuls of necklaces about her neck, and several sorts of jewels in her ears. She had fine red stockins, and white shoes, her hair powdered and face painted red, that was always before black. And all the dancers were after the same manner. There were two other singing and knocking on a kettle for their music. They kept hopping up and down one after another, with a kettle of water in the midst, standing warm upon some embers, to drink of when they were dry. They held on till it was almost night, throwing out wampum to the standers by. At night I asked them again, if I should go home? They all as one said, "No," except my husband should come for me. When we were lain down, my master went out of the wigwam, and by and by sent in an Indian called James the Printer, who told Mr. Hoar, that my master would let me go home tomorrow, if he would let him have one pint of liquors. Then Mr. Hoar called his own two Indians, Tom and Peter, and bid them go and see whether he would promise it before them three: and if he would, he should have it; which he did, and he had it. Then Philip smelling the business called me to him, and asked me what I would give him, to tell me some good news, and speak a good word for me. I told him, I could not tell what to give him; I would anything I had, and asked him what he would have? He said, "Two coats and twenty shillings in money, and half a bushel of seed corn, and some tobacco." I thanked him for his love: but I knew the good news as well as the crafty fox. My master after he had had his drink, quickly came ranting into the wigwam again, and called for Mr. Hoar, drinking to him, and saying, he was a good man: and then again he would say, "Hang him, rogue." Being almost drunk, he would drink to him, and yet presently say he should be hanged. Then he called for me; I trembled to hear him, yet I was fain to go to him, and he drank to me, shewing no incivility. He was the first Indian I saw drunk all the while that I was amongst them. At last his squaw ran out, and he after her, round the wigwam, with his money jingling at his knees; but she escaped him. But having an old squaw he ran to her: and so through the Lord's mercy, we were no more troubled that night. Yet I had not comfortable night's rest: for I think I can say, I did not sleep for three nights together. The night before the letter came from the Council, I could not rest I was so full of fears and troubles, God many times leaving us most in the dark, when deliverance is nearest: yea, at this time I could not rest, night nor day. The next night I was overjoyed, Mr. Hoar being come, and that with such good tidings. The third night I was even swallowed up with the thoughts of things, viz., that I ever should go home again; and that I must go, leaving my children behind me in the wilderness; so that sleep was almost departed from mine eyes.

On Tuesday morning they called their general court (as they call it) to consult and determine, whether I should go home or no. And they all as one man did seemingly consent to it, that I should go home; except Philip, who would not come among them. . . .

But to return again to my going home, where we may see a remarkable change of providence: at first they were all against it, except my husband would come for me; but afterwards they assented to it, and seemed much to rejoice in it; some askt me to send them some bread, others some tobacco, some others shaking me by the hand, offering me a hood and scarf to ride in; not one moving hand or tongue against it. Thus hath the Lord answered my poor desire, and the many earnest requests of others put up unto God for me. In my travels an Indian came to me, and told me, if I were willing, he and his squaw would run away, and go home along with me: I told him "No": I was not willing to run away, but desired to wait God's time, that I might go home quietly, and without fear. And now God hath granted me my desire. O the wonderful power of God that I have seen, and the experience that I have had: I have been in the midst of those roaring lions, and salvage bears, that feared neither God, nor man, nor the Devil, by night and day, alone and in company: sleeping all sorts together, and yet not one of them ever offered me the least abuse of unchastity to me, in word or action. Though some are ready to say, I speak it for my own credit; but I speak it in the presence of God, and to His glory. God's power is as great now, and as sufficient to save, as when He preserved Daniel in the lions' den; or the three children in the fiery furnace. I may well say as his Psal. 107:12, "Oh give thanks unto the Lord, for He is good, for His mercy endureth forever." Let the redeemed of the Lord say so, whom He hath redeemed from the hand of the enemy, especially that I should come away in the midst of so many hundreds of enemies quietly and peaceably, and not a dog moving his tongue. So I took my leave of them, and in coming along my heart melted into tears, more then all the while I was with them, and I was almost swallowed up with the thoughts that ever I should go home again. . . .

I can remember the time, when I used to sleep quietly without workings in my thoughts, whole nights together, but now it is other ways with me. When all are fast about me, and no eye open, but His who ever waketh, my thoughts are upon things past, upon the awful dispensation of the Lord towards us; upon His wonderful power and might, in carrying of us through so many difficulties, in returning us in safety, and suffering none to hurt us. I remember in the night season, how the other day I was in the midst of thousands of enemies, and nothing but death before me: it was then hard work to persuade myself, that ever I should be satisfied with bread again. But now we are fed with the finest of the wheat, and, as I may say, with honey out of the rock. Instead of the husk, we have the fatted calf. The thoughts of these things: in the particulars of them, and of the love and goodness of God towards us, make it true of me, what David said of himself, Psal. 6:5, "I watered my couch with my tears." Oh! the wonderful power of God that mine eyes have seen, affording matter enough for my thoughts to run in, that when others are sleeping mine eyes are weeping.

I have seen the extreme vanity of this world: one hour I have been in health, and wealth, wanting nothing; but the next hour in sickness and wounds, and death, having nothing but sorrow and affliction.

Before I knew what affliction means, I was ready sometimes to wish for it. When I lived in prosperity, having the comforts of the world about me, my relations by me, my heart cheerful: and taking little care for anything; and yet seeing many, whom I preferred before myself, under many trials and afflictions, in sickness, weakness, poverty, losses, crosses, and cares of the world, I should be sometimes jealous lest I should [not] have my portion in this life, and that scripture would come to my mind, Heb. 12:6, "For whom the Lord loveth He chasteneth, and scourgeth every son whom He receiveth." But now I see the Lord had His time to scourge and chasten me. The portion of some is to have their afflictions by drops, now one drop and then another; but the dregs of the cup, the wine of astonishment: like a sweeping rain that leaveth no food, did the Lord prepare to be my portion. Affliction I wanted, and affliction I had, full measure (I thought) pressed down and running over; yet I see, when God calls a person to anything, and through never so many difficulties, yet He is fully able to carry them through and make them see, and say they have been gainers thereby. And I hope I can say in some measure, as David did, "It is good for me that I have been afflicted": the Lord hath shewed me the vanity of these outward things. That they are the vanity of vanities, and vexation of spirit; that they are but a shadow, a blast, a bubble, and things of no continuance. That we must rely on God Himself, and our whole dependence must be upon Him. If trouble from smaller matters begin to arise in me, I have something at hand to check myself with, and say, why am I troubled? It was but the other day that if I had had the world, I would have given it for my freedom, or to have been a servant to a Christian. I have learned to look beyond present and smaller troubles, and to be quieted under them, as Moses said, Exod. 14:13, "Stand still and see the salvation of the Lord."

John Williams (1664–1729)

FRONTIER Indian danger remained high even after the suppression of King Philip. The French and Indian wars over possession of the territory between the Connecticut and Ohio valleys raged intermittently between 1690 and 1760. The second of these — Queen Anne's War (1701–13) — saw French-inspired Indian raids over the same area formerly plagued by King Philip. Captives were frequently hurried to Canada and turned over to the French for exchange. This gave new motives for writing narratives of captivity: first, to transfer hatred from the Indians to the French who employed them (the same trick was turned on the English during the Revolution), and second, to warn against the French attempts to convert good Congregationalists into Roman Catholics. One narrative from the mid-eighteenth century advertises itself as "necessary to be read by all who are going in the expedition, as well as by every British subject. Wherein it fully appears, that the barbarities of the Indians is owing to the French, and chiefly their priests."

Among the most popular of the stories growing out of these wars was *The Redeemed Captive Returned to Zion* (1707), by John Williams. Williams was born in Roxbury, where his father was a deacon in John Eliot's church. He graduated from Harvard in 1683, taught school for a couple of years, and then moved to Deerfield, one of the northernmost settlements in the Connecticut Valley, as minister. Warned of danger in the winter of 1704, the town secured an extra score of soldiers; but, in spite of their precautions, the town fell on February 29 before some 300 French and Indians. After his ransom, Williams returned to minister to a rebuilt Deerfield.

TEXT: John Williams, *The Redeemed Captive,* ed. Thomas Prince (Boston, 1758).

The Capture

[From *The Redeemed Captive,* 1707]

On the twenty-ninth of February, 1703/4, not long after the break of day, the enemy came in like a flood upon us; our watch being unfaithful, an evil, whose awful effects, in a surprisal of our fort, should bespeak all watchmen to avoid, as they would not bring the charge of blood upon themselves. They came to my house in the beginning of the onset, and by their violent endeavors to break open door and windows, with axes and hatchets, awaked me out of sleep; on which I leaped out of bed, and running toward the door, perceived the enemy making their entrance into the house. I called to awaken two soldiers, in the chamber; and returned toward my bedside, for my arms. The enemy immediately brake into the room, I judge to the number of twenty, with painted faces, and hideous acclamations. I reached up my hands to the bed-tester, for my pistol, uttering a short petition to God, for everlasting mercies for me and mine, on the account of the merits of our glorified Redeemer; expecting a present passage through the valley of the shadow of death; saying in myself, as Isaiah 38:10, 11, "I said, in the cutting off of my days, I shall go to the gates of the grave: I am deprived of the residue of my years. I said, I shall not see the Lord, in the land of the living: I shall behold man no more with the inhabitants of the world." Taking down my pistol, I cocked it, and put it to the breast of the first Indian who came up; but my pistol missing fire, I was seized by three Indians, who disarmed me, and bound me naked, as I was in my shirt, and so I stood for near the space of an hour. Binding me, they told me they would carry me to Quebec. My pistol missing fire was an occasion of my life's being preserved; since which I have also found it profitable to be crossed in my own will. The judgment of God did not long slumber against one of the three which took me, who was a captain, for by sun-rising he received a mortal shot from my neighbor's house; who opposed so great a number of French and Indians as three hundred, and yet were no more than seven men in an ungarrisoned house.

I cannot relate the distressing care I had for my dear wife, who had lain-in but a few weeks before, and for my poor children, family, and Christian neighbors. The enemy fell to rifling the house, and entered in great numbers into every room of the house. I begged of God to remember mercy in the midst of judgment; that He would so far restrain their wrath, as to prevent their murdering of us; that we might have grace to glorify His name, whether in life or death; and, as I was able, committed our state to God. The enemies who entered the house were all of them Indians and Maquas, insulted over me a while, holding up hatchets over my head, threatening to burn all I had; but yet God, beyond expectation, made us in a great measure to be pitied; for though some were so cruel and barbarous as to take and carry to the door, two of my children, and murder them, as also a Negro woman; yet they gave me liberty to put on my clothes, keeping me bound with a cord on one arm, till I put on my clothes to the other; and then changing my cord, they let me dress myself, and then pinioned me again: gave liberty to my dear wife to dress herself, and our children. About sun an hour high, we were all carried out of the house, for a march, and saw many of the houses of my neighbors in flames, perceiving the whole fort, one house excepted, to be taken. Who can tell what sorrows pierced our souls, when we saw ourselves carried away from God's sanctuary, to go into a strange land, exposed to so many trials? The journey being at least three hundred miles we were to travel; the snow up to the knees, and we never inured to such hardships and fatigues; the place we were to be carried to, a popish country. Upon my parting from the town, they fired my house and barn. We were carried over the river, to the foot of the mountain, about a mile from my house, where we found a great number of our Christian neighbors, men, women, and children, to the number of an hundred, nineteen of whom were afterwards murdered by the way, and two starved to death, near Cowass, in a time of great scarcity or famine, the savages underwent there. When we came to the foot of the mountain, they took away our shoes, and gave us, in the room of them, Indian shoes, to prepare us for our travel. Whilst we were there, the English beat out a company, that remained in the town, and pursued them to the river, killing and wounding many of them, but the body of the army, being alarmed, they repulsed those few English that pursued them.

I am not able to give you an account of the number of the enemy slain; but I observed after this fight, no great insulting mirth, as I expected; and saw many wounded persons, and for several days together they buried of their party, and one of chief note among the Maquas. The governor of Canada told me, his army had that success with the loss of but eleven men, three Frenchmen, one of whom was the lieutenant of the army, five Maquas, and three Indians. But after my arrival at Quebec, I spake with an Englishman, who was taken the last war, and married there, and of their religion; who told me, they lost above forty, and that many were wounded. I replied, the governor of Canada said they lost but eleven men. He answered, it is true, that there were but eleven killed outright at the taking of the fort, but that many others were wounded, among whom was the ensign of the French; but, said he, they had a fight in the meadow, and that in both engagements they lost more than forty. Some of the soldiers, both French and Indians, then present, told me so (said he), adding, that the French always endeavor to conceal the number of their slain.

After this, we went up the mountain, and saw the smoke of the fires in town, and beheld the awful desolations of Deerfield. And before we marched any farther, they killed a sucking child of the English. There were slain by the enemy, of the inhabitants of our town, to the number of thirty-eight, besides nine of the neighboring towns. We traveled not far the first day; God made the heathen so to pity our children, that though they had several wounded persons of their own to carry upon their shoulders for thirty miles, before they came to the river, yet they carried our children, incapable of traveling, upon their shoulders, and in their arms. When we came to our lodging place, the first night, they dug away the snow, and made some wigwams, cut down some of the small branches of spruce trees to lie down on, and gave the prisoners somewhat to eat; but we had but little appetite. I was pinioned, and bound down that night, and so I was every night whilst I was with the army. Some of the enemy who brought drink with them from the town, fell to drinking, and in their drunken fit they killed my Negro man, the only dead person I either saw at the town, or in the way. In the night an Englishman made his escape. In the morning I was called for, and ordered by the general to tell the English, that if any more made their escape, they would burn the rest of the prisoners. He that took me was unwilling to let me speak with any of the prisoners, as we marched; but on the morning of the second day, he being appointed to guard the rear, I was put into the hands of my other master, who permitted me to speak to my wife, when I overtook her, and to walk with her, to help her in her journey. On the way we discoursed of the happiness of those who had a right to an house not made with hands, eternal in the heavens; and God for a father, and friend; as also, that it was our reasonable duty, quietly to submit to the will of God, and to say, the will of the Lord be done. My wife told me her strength of body began to fail, and that I must expect to part with her; saying, she hoped God would preserve my life, and the life of some, if not all of our children, with us; and commended to me, under God, the care of them. She never spake any discontented word as to what had befallen us, but with suitable expressions justified God in what had befallen us. We soon made an halt, in which time my chief surviving master came up, upon which I was put upon marching with the foremost, and so made to take my last farewell of my dear wife, the desire of my eyes, and companion in many mercies and afflictions. Upon our separation from each other, we asked for each other, grace sufficient for what God should call us to. After our being parted from one another, she spent the few remaining minutes of her stay in reading the holy scriptures; which she was wont personally every day to delight her soul in reading, praying, meditating of, and over, by herself, in her closet, over and above what she heard out of them in our family worship. I was made to wade over a small river, and so were all the English, the water above knee-deep, the stream very swift; and after that, to travel up a small mountain; my strength was almost spent, before I came to the top of it. No sooner had I overcome the difficulty of that ascent, but I was permitted to sit down, and be unburthened of my pack. I sat pitying those who were behind, and entreated my master to let me go down, and help up my wife; but he refused, and would not let me stir from him. I asked each of the prisoners (as they passed by me) after her, and heard that in passing through the abovesaid river, she fell down, and was plunged over head and ears in the water; after which she traveled not far; for at the foot of this mountain, the cruel and bloodthirsty savage, who took her, slew her with his hatchet, at one stroke; the tidings of which were very awful; and yet such was the hard-heartedness of the adversary, that my tears were reckoned to me as a reproach. My loss, and the loss of my children, was great; our hearts were so filled with sorrow, that nothing but the comfortable hopes of her being taken away in mercy to herself, from the evils we were to see, feel, and suffer under (and joined to the assembly of the spirits of just men made perfect, to rest in peace, and joy unspeakable, and full of glory, and the good pleasure of God thus to exercise us), could have kept us from sinking under, at that time. That scripture, Job 1:21, "Naked came I out of my mother's womb, and naked shall I return thither; the Lord gave, and the Lord hath taken away, blessed be the name of the Lord," was brought to my mind, and from it, that an afflicting God was to be glorified; with some other places of scripture, to persuade to a patient bearing my afflictions. . . .

At Chamblee (Quebec)

[From the same]

The next morning the bell rang for mass: my master bid me go to church: I refused: he threatened me, and went away in a rage. At noon, the Jesuits sent for me to dine with them; for I eat at their table all the time I was at the fort. And after dinner, they told me, the Indians would not allow of any of their captives staying in their wigwams, whilst they were at church; and were resolved by force and violence to bring us all to church, if we would not go without. I told them it was highly unreasonable so to impose upon those who were of a contrary religion; and to force us to be present at such service, as we abhorred, was nothing becoming Christianity. They replied, they were savages, and would not hearken to reason, but would have their wills; said also, if they were in New England themselves, they would go into their churches, to see their ways of worship. I answered, the case was far different, for there was nothing (themselves being judges) as to matter or manner of worship, but what was according to the Word of God, in our churches; and therefore it could not be an offense to any man's conscience. But among them, there were idolatrous superstitions in worship. They said, come and see, and offer us conviction of what is superstitious in worship. To which I answered, that I was not to do evil that good might come on it; and that forcing in matters of religion was hateful. They answered, the Indians were resolved to have it so, and they could not pacify them without my coming; and they would engage they should offer no force or violence to cause any compliance with their ceremonies.

The next mass, my master bid me go to church: I objected; he arose, and forcibly pulled me by my head and shoulders out of the wigwam to the church, which was near the door. So I went in, and sat down behind the door; and there saw a great confusion, instead of any gospel order; for one of the Jesuits was at the altar, saying mass in a tongue unknown to the savages; and the other, between the altar and the door, saying and singing prayers among the Indians at the same time; and many others were at the same time saying over their pater nosters, and Ave Mary, by tale from their chapelit, or beads on a string. At our going out, we smiled at their devotion so managed; which was offensive to them; for they said we made a derision of their worship. When I was here, a certain savagess died; one of the Jesuits told me she was a very holy woman, who had not committed one sin in twelve years. After a day or two, the Jesuits asked me what I thought of their way, now I saw it? I told them, I thought Christ said of it, as Mark 7:7, 8, 9, "Howbeit, in vain do they worship me, teaching for doctrines the commandments of men. For laying aside the commandment of God, ye hold the tradition of men, as the washing of pots and cups; and many other such like things ye do. And he said unto them, full well ye reject the commandment of God, that ye may keep your own tradition." They told me, they were not the commandments of men, but apostolical traditions, of equal authority with the holy scriptures: and that after my death, I should bewail my not praying to the Virgin Mary; and that I should find the want of her intercession for me with her Son; judging me to hell for asserting the scriptures to be a perfect rule of faith: and said, I abounded in my own sense, entertaining explications contrary to the sense of the Pope, regularly sitting with a general council, explaining scripture, and making articles of faith. I told them, it was my comfort that Christ was to be my Judge, and not they, at the great day; and as for their censuring and judging me, I was not moved with it.

One day, a certain savagess, taken prisoner in Philip's War, who had lived at Mr. Buckley's at Weathersfield, called Ruth, who could speak English very well, who had been often at my house, but was now proselyted to the Romish faith, came into the wigwam, and with her an English maid, who was taken the last war, who was dressed up in Indian apparel, unable to speak one word of English, who said she could neither tell her own name, or the name of the place from whence she was taken. These two talked in the Indian dialect with my master a long time; after which, my master bade me cross myself; I told him I would not; he commanded me several times, and I as often refused. Ruth said, "Mr. Williams, you know the scripture, and therefore act against your own light; for you know the scripture saith, 'servants, obey your masters'; he is your master, and you his servant." I told her she was ignorant, and knew not the meaning of the scriptures, telling her, I was not so to disobey the great God to obey any master, and that I was ready to suffer for God, if called thereto: on which she talked to my master; I suppose she interpreted what I said. My master took hold of my hand to force me to cross myself; but I struggled with him, and would not suffer him to guide my hand; upon this, he pulled off a crucifix from his own neck, and bade me kiss it; but I refused once and again; he told me he would dash out my brains with his hatchet if I refused. I told him I should sooner choose death than to sin against God. Then he ran and catched up his hatchet, and acted as though he would have dashed out my brains. Seeing I was not moved, he threw down his hatchet, saying he would first bite off all my nails if I still refused. I gave him my hand, and told him I was ready to suffer; he set his teeth in my thumb nail, and gave a gripe with his teeth, and then said, "no good minister, no love God, as bad as the Devil"; and so left off. I have reason to bless God, who strengthened me to withstand. By this he was so discouraged as never more to meddle with me about my religion. I asked leave of the Jesuits to pray with those English of our town who were with me; but they absolutely refused to give us any permission to pray one with another, and did what they could to prevent our having any discourse together.

REBELS

Not content to menace destruction at the hands of the Indians, Satan nurtured malcontents, all up and down the Atlantic coast, among the settlers themselves. Each represented in his own way an affront to the sometimes self-appointed guardians of morals, faith, and law, and to the concept of the God-ordered universe inherited from the Renaissance, wherein local disorders were seen to have dire cosmic implications. The directness and often the harshness with which dissidents were treated bespeaks not only puritanic righteousness but the understandable defensiveness of the dreadfully weak societies so affronted; for by 1700 there were no more than 200,000 colonists in New England, Maryland, and Virginia combined, and only about 17,000 people in New England during the troubles of the 1630's. The need to maintain authority and public security at the expense of private rights and privileges, when the only alternative seemed chaos, troubled many Americans until well into the National period, as General Washington's regret at the execution of Major André seems to bear out. It may well be that even the earliest colonists felt some compunctions on this score, but by and large they seem to have wasted little sympathy on heretics and other troublemakers.

Thomas Morton (1575–1646)

THOMAS MORTON, who always signed himself "of Clifford's Inn, Gent.," was a lawyer who apparently made the first of four trips to America in 1622. On his second, in 1625, he helped to establish a settlement at Mount Wollaston (or Merry Mount) where he and his companions enjoyed a life quite different from that at nearby Plymouth. His constant ridicule of the Pilgrims and his "frolics" with the Indians were serious enough, but his success at trading with the Indians threatened the economy of the Plymouth colony. Furthermore, there is evidence that Morton traded guns and liquor to the Indians for furs, and taught them how to use both. In 1627, celebrating the traditional English folk-festivities of spring, Morton set up a Maypole, after which Captain Miles Standish and the militia pursued and arrested him. He was sent back to England, where he immediately allied himself with the High Church party which hoped to have the colonial charters revoked. In 1630 he returned to Massachusetts, was arrested, and once more deported. On his fourth visit, in 1643, he was jailed for nearly a year before he was released for lack of evidence of wrongdoing. He retired to Maine, and died there in 1646.

The two following accounts of the Merry Mount affair are delightfully at odds. The first is from William Bradford's *Of Plymouth Plantation* (*q.v.*, p. 25); the second from Morton's *New English Canaan,* written in 1634–35 and published in Holland in 1637, clearly intended to justify his own actions and to make trouble for the Massachusetts Puritans with the King and Parliament. Confused and repetitious, the chief interest of Morton's book lies in its sprightly reflection of Morton's own picturesque character.

TEXTS: William Bradford, *History of Plymouth Plantation,* ed. Worthington C. Ford (Boston, 1912), Vol. II; and Thomas Morton, *New English Canaan,* in Peter Force, *Tracts,* II (New York, 1838, 1947).

William Bradford
Morton of Merrymount

[From *Of Plymouth Plantation*]

Hitherto the Indians of these parts had no pieces nor other arms but their bows and arrows, nor of many years after; neither durst they scarce handle a gun, so much were they afraid of them; and the very sight of one (though out of kilter) was a terror unto them. But those Indians to the east parts, which had commerce with the French, got pieces of them, and they in the end made a common trade of it; and in time our English fishermen, led with the like covetousness, followed their example for their own gain; but upon complaint against them, it pleased the King's Majesty to prohibit the same by a strict proclamation, commanding that no sort of arms or munition should by any of his subjects be traded with them.

About some three or four years before this time, there came over one Captain Wollaston (a man of pretty parts), and with him three or four more of some eminency, who brought with them a great many servants with provisions and other implements for to begin a plantation; and pitched themselves in a place within the Massachusetts, which they called, after their captain's name, Mount Wollaston. Amongst whom was one Mr. Morton, who, it should seem, had some small adventure (of his own or other men's) amongst them, but had little respect amongst them, and was slighted by the meanest servants. Having continued there some time, and not finding things to answer their expectations, nor profit to arise as they looked for, Captain Wollaston takes a great part of the servants, and transports them to Virginia, where he puts them off at good rates, selling their time to other men; and writes back to one Mr. Rasdall, one of his chief partners, and accounted their merchant, to bring another part of them to Virginia likewise, intending to put them off there as he had done the rest. And he, with the consent of the said Rasdall, appointed one Fitcher to be his lieutenant and govern the remains of the plantation till he or Rasdall returned to take further order thereabout. But this Morton abovesaid, having more craft then honesty (who had been a kind of pettifogger of Furnival's Inn), in the others' absence watches an opportunity (and commons being but hard amongst them) and got some strong drink and other junkets, and made them a feast; and after they were merry, he began to tell them he would give them good counsel. "You see," saith he, "that many of your fellows are carried to Virginia; and if you stay till this Rasdall return, you will also be carried away and sold for slaves with the rest. Therefore I would advise you to thrust out this Lieutenant Fitcher; and I, having a part in the plantation, will receive you as my partners and consociates; so may you be free from service; and we will converse, trade, plant, and live together as equals, and support and protect one another," or to like effect. This counsel was easily received; so they took opportunity and thrust Lieutenant Fitcher out o' doors and would suffer him to come no more amongst them, but forced him to seek bread to eat and other relief from his neighbors till he could get passages for England.

After this they fell to great licentiousness and led a dissolute life, pouring out themselves into all profaneness. And Morton became lord of misrule and maintained (as it were) a school of atheism. And after they had got some goods into their hands, and got much by trading with the Indians, they spent it as vainly, in quaffing and drinking, both wine and strong waters in great excess and (as some reported) ten pounds' worth in a morning. They also set up a Maypole, drinking and dancing about it many days together, inviting the Indian women for their consorts, dancing and frisking together like so many fairies (or furies rather), and worse practices, as if they had anew revived and celebrated the feasts of the Roman goddess Flora, or the beastly practices of the mad Bacchanalians. Morton likewise (to shew his poetry) composed sundry rhymes and verses, some tending to lasciviousness, and others to the detraction and scandal of some persons, which he affixed to this idle or idol Maypole. They changed also the name of their place; and instead of calling it Mount Wollaston, they call it Merry Mount, as if this jollity would have lasted ever. But this continued not long, for after Morton was sent for England (as follows to be declared), shortly after came over that worthy gentleman, Mr. John Endecott, who brought over a patent under the broad seal for the government of the Massachusetts, who, visiting those parts, caused that Maypole to be cut down and rebuked them for their profaneness and admonished them to look there should be better walking; so they now, or others, changed the name of their place again and called it Mount Dagon.

Now to maintain this riotous prodigality and profuse excess, Morton, thinking himself lawless, and hearing what gain the French and fishermen made by trading of pieces, powder, and shot to the Indians, he, as the head of this consortship, began the practice of the same in these parts. And first he taught them how to use them, to charge and discharge, and what proportion of powder to give the piece, according to the size or bigness of the same; and what shot to use for fowl and what for deer. And having thus instructed them, he employed some of them to hunt and fowl for him, so as they became far more active in that employment then any of the English, by reason of their swiftness of foot and nimbleness of body, being also quick-sighted, and by continual exercise well knowing the haunts of all sorts of game. So as when they saw the execution that a piece would do, and the benefit that might come by the same, they became mad, as it were, after them, and would not stick to give any price they could attain to for them; accounting their bows and arrows but baubles in comparison of them.

And here I may take occasion to bewail the mischief that this wicked man began in these parts, and which since, base covetousness prevailing in men that should know better, has now at length got the upper hand and made this thing common, notwithstanding any laws to the contrary; so as the Indians are full of pieces all over, both fowling pieces, muskets, pistols, etc. They have also their moulds to make shot of all sorts, as musket bullets, pistol bullets, swan and goose shot, and of smaller sorts. Yes, some have seen them have their screw-plates to make screw-pins themselves, when they want them, with sundry other implements, wherewith they are ordinarily better fitted and furnished then the English themselves. Yea, it is well known that they will have powder and shot when the English want it, nor cannot get it; and that in a time of war or danger, as experience hath manifested, that when lead hath been scarce and men for their own defense would gladly have given a groat a pound, which is dear enough, yet hath it been bought up and sent to other places and sold to such as trade it with the Indians at twelve pence the pound; and it is like they give three or four shillings the pound, for they will have it at any rate. And these things have been done in the same times when some of their neighbors and friends are daily killed by the Indians, or are in danger thereof and live but at the Indians' mercy. Yea, some (as they have acquainted them with all other things) have told them how gunpowder is made, and all the materials in it, and that they are to be had in their own land; and I am confident, could they attain to make saltpeter, they would teach them to make powder. O the horribleness of this villainy! How many both Dutch and English have been lately slain by those Indians, thus furnished, and no remedy provided; nay, the evil more increased, and the blood of their brethren sold for gain, as is to be feared; and in what danger all these colonies are in is too well known. O, that princes and parliaments would take some timely order to prevent this mischief, and at length to suppress it, by some exemplary punishment upon some of these gain-thirsty murderers (for they deserve no better title) before their colonies in these parts be overthrown by these barbarous savages thus armed with their own weapons, by these evil instruments and traitors to their neighbors and country! But I have forgotten myself and have been too long in this digression; but now to return.

This Morton having thus taught them the use of pieces, he sold them all he could spare; and he and his consorts determined to send for many out of England, and had by some of the ships sent for above a score. The which being known, and his neighbors meeting the Indians in the woods armed with guns in this sort, it was a terror unto them who lived stragglingly and were of no strength in any place. And other places (though more remote) saw this mischief would quickly spread over all, if not prevented. Besides, they saw they should keep no servants, for Morton would entertain any, how vile soever, and all the scum of the country or any discontents would flock to him from all places, if this nest was not broken; and they should stand in more fear of their lives and goods in short time from this wicked and debased crew than from the savages themselves.

So sundry of the chief of the straggling plantations, meeting together, agreed by mutual consent to solicit those of Plymouth (who were then of more strength then them all) to join with them to prevent the further growth of this mischief, and suppress Morton and his consorts before they grew to further head and strength. Those that joined in this action (and after contributed to the charge of sending him for England) were from Pascataway, Namkeake, Winisimett, Weesagascusett, Natasco, and other places where any English were seated. Those of Plymouth, being thus sought too by their messengers and letters, and weighing both their reasons and the common danger, were willing to afford them their help, though themselves had least cause of fear or hurt. So, to be short, they first resolved jointly to write to him, and in a friendly and neighborly way to admonish him to forbear those courses, and sent a messenger with their letters to bring his answer. But he was so high as he scorned all advice and asked who had to do with him; he had and would trade pieces with the Indians in despite of all, with many other scurrilous terms full of disdain. They sent to him a second time and bade him be better advised and more temperate in his terms, for the country could not bear the injury he did; it was against their common safety and against the King's proclamation. He answered in high terms as before, and that the King's proclamation was no law, demanding what penalty was upon it. It was answered, more than he could bear, His Majesty's displeasure. But insolently he persisted and said the King was dead and his displeasure with him, and many the like things, and threatened withal that if any came to molest him, let them look to themselves, for he would prepare for them. Upon which they saw there was no way but to take him by force; and having so far proceeded, now to give over would make him far more haughty and insolent. So they mutually resolved to proceed, and obtained of the Governor of Plymouth to send Captain Standish and some other aid with him, to take

Morton by force. The which accordingly was done. But they found him to stand stiffly in his defense, having made fast his doors, armed his consorts, set divers dishes of powder and bullets ready on the table; and if they had not been over-armed with drink, more hurt might have been done. They summoned him to yield, but he kept his house, and they could get nothing but scoffs and scorns from him. But at length, fearing they would do some violence to the house, he and some of his crew came out, but not to yield but to shoot; but they were so steeled with drink as their pieces were too heavy for them; himself with a carbine (overcharged and almost half filled with powder and shot, as was after found) had thought to have shot Captain Standish; but he stepped to him and put by his piece and took him. Neither was there any hurt done to any of either side, save that one was so drunk that he ran his own nose upon the point of a sword that one held before him, as he entered the house; but he lost but a little of his hot blood. Morton they brought away to Plymouth, where he was kept till a ship went from the Isle of Shoals for England, with which he was sent to the Council of New England; and letters written to give them information of his course and carriage; and also one was sent at their common charge to inform their Honors more particularly, and to prosecute against him. But he fooled of the messenger, after he was gone from hence, and though he went for England, yet nothing was done to him, not so much as rebuked, for aught was heard; but returned the next year. Some of the worst of the company were dispersed, and some of the more modest kept the house till he should be heard from. But I have been too long about so unworthy a person, and bad a cause.

Thomas Morton

Of the Revels of New Canaan

[From *New English Canaan,* 1637]

The inhabitants of Pasonagessit (having translated the name of their habitation from that ancient salvage name to Ma-re Mount, and being resolved to have the new name confirmed for a memorial to after ages), did devise amongst themselves to have it performed in a solemn manner, with revels, and merriment after the old English custom, prepared to set up a Maypole upon the festival day of Philip and Jacob; and therefore brewed a barrel of excellent beer, and provided a case of bottles to be spent, with other good cheer, for all comers of that day. And because they would have it in a complete form, they had prepared a song fitting to the time and present occasion. And upon Mayday they brought the Maypole to the place appointed, with drums, guns, pistols, and other fitting instruments, for that purpose; and there erected it with the help of salvages, that came thither of purpose to see the manner of our revels. A goodly pine tree of 80 foot long was reared up, with a pair of buckshorns nailed on, somewhat near unto the top of it, where it stood as a fair sea mark for directions; how to find out the way to mine host of Ma-re Mount. . . .

There was likewise a merry song made, which (to make their revels more fashionable), was sung with a chorus, every man bearing his part; which they performed in a dance, hand in hand about the Maypole, whiles one of the company sung, and filled out the good liquor, like Ganymede and Jupiter.

THE SONG.

Drink and be merry, merry, merry boys,
Let all your delight be in the Hymen's joys,
Iô to Hymen, now the day is come,
About the merry Maypole take a room.

Make green garlands, bring bottles out;
And fill sweet nectar, freely about.
Uncover thy head, and fear no harm,
For here's good liquor to keep it warm.
Then drink and be merry, &c.
Iô to Hymen, &c.

Nectar is a thing assigned,
By the Deity's own mind,
To cure the heart opprest with grief,
And of good liquors is the chief,
Then drink, &c.
Iô to Hymen, &c.

Give to the melancholy man,
A cup or two of't now and than;
This physic will soon revive his blood,
And make him be of a merrier mood.
Then drink, &c.
Iô to Hymen, &c.

Give to the nymph that's free from scorn,
No Irish stuff nor Scotch overworn.
Lasses in beaver coats, come away,
Ye shall be welcome to us night and day.
To drink and be merry, &c.
Iô to Hymen, &c.

This harmless mirth made by young men (that lived in hope to have wives bought over to them, that would save them a labor to make a voyage to fetch any over) was much distasted, of the precise Separatists, that keep much ado about the tithe of mint and cummin, troubling their brains more then reason would require about things that are indifferent: and from that time sought occasion against my honest host of Ma-re Mount, to overthrow his undertakings, and to destroy his plantation quite and clean. . . .

Of a Great Monster Supposed to be at Ma-re Mount

[From the same]

The Separatists, envying the prosperity, and hope of the plantation at Ma-re Mount (which they perceived began to come forward, and to be in a good way for gain in the beaver trade), conspired together against mine host especially (who was the owner of that plantation), and made up a party against him; and mustered up what aid they could, accounting of him, as of a great monster.

Many threatening speeches were given out both against his person, and his habitation, which they divulged should be consumed with fire: and taking advantage of the time when his company (which seemed little to regard their threats) were gone up into the inlands to trade with the salvages for beaver, they set upon my honest host at a place, called Wessaguscus, where (by accident) they found him. The inhabitants there were in good hope of the subversion of the plantation at Ma-re Mount (which they principally aimed at); and the rather because mine host was a man that endeavored to advance the dignity of the Church of England; which they (on the contrary part) would labor to vilify with uncivil terms: enveighing against the sacred book of common prayer, and mine host that used it in a laudable manner amongst his family, as a practice of piety.

There he would be a means to bring sacks to their mill (such is the thirst after beaver), and helped the conspirators to surprise mine host (who was there all alone); and they charged him (because they would seem to have some reasonable cause against him, to set a gloss upon their malice) with criminal things which indeed had been done by such a person, but was of their conspiracy; mine host demanded of the conspirators who it was that was author of that information, that seemed to be their ground for what they now intended. And because they answered they would not tell him, he as peremptorily replied, that he would not stay, whether he had, or he had not done as they had been informed.

The answer made no matter (as it seemed), whether it had been negatively, or affirmatively made; for they had resolved what he should suffer, because (as they boasted) they were now become the greater number: they had shaked off their shackles of servitude, and were become masters, and masterless people.

It appears they were like bears' whelps in former time, when mine host's plantation was of as much strength as theirs, but now (theirs being stronger), they (like overgrown bears) seemed monstrous. In brief, mine host must endure to be their prisoner, until they could contrive it so, that they might send him for England (as they said), there to suffer according to the merit of the fact, which they intended to father upon him; supposing (belike) it would prove a heinous crime.

Much rejoicing was made that they had gotten their capital enemy (as they concluded him), whom they purposed to hamper in such sort, that he should not be able to uphold his plantation at Ma-re Mount.

The conspirators sported themselves at my honest host, that meant them no hurt; and were so jocund that they feasted their bodies, and fell to tippling, as if they had obtained a great prize; like the Trojans when they had the custody of Hippeus' pinetree horse.

Mine host feigned grief, and could not be persuaded either to eat, or drink, because he knew emptiness would be a means to make him as watchful as the geese kept in the Roman Capital: where, on the contrary part, the conspirators would be so drowsy, that he might have an opportunity to give them a slip, instead of a tester. Six persons of the conspiracy were set to watch him at Wessaguscus: but he kept waking; and in the dead of night (one lying on the bed for further surety), up gets mine host and got to the second door that he was to pass, which (notwithstanding the lock) he got open; and shut it after him with such violence, that it affrighted some of the conspirators.

The word, which was given with an alarm, was, "O he's gone, he's gone; what shall we do, he's gone!" The rest (half asleep) start up in a maze, and like rams, ran their heads one at another full butt in the dark.

Their grand leader, Captain Shrimp, took on most furiously and tore his clothes for anger, to see the empty nest, and their bird gone.

The rest were eager to have torn their hair from their heads; but it was so short, that it would give them no hold. Now Captain Shrimp thought in the loss of this prize (which he accoumpted his masterpiece), all his honor would be lost forever.

In the meantime mine host was got home to Ma-re Mount through the woods, eight miles round about the head of the river Monatoquit that parted the two plantations; finding his way by the help of the lightning (for it thundered as he went terribly), and there he prepared powther, three pounds dried, for his present employment, and four good guns for him and the two assistants left at his house, with bullets of several sizes, three hundred or thereabouts; to be used if the conspirators should pursue him thither: and these two persons promised their aids in the quarrel, and confirmed that promise with health in good rosa solis.

Now Captain Shrimp, the first captain in the land (as he supposed), must do some new act to repair this loss, and to vindicate his reputation, who had sustained blemish by this oversight, begins now to study, how to repair or survive his honor: in this manner, calling of council, they conclude.

He takes eight persons more to him, and (like the nine Worthies of New Canaan) they embark with this preparation against Ma-re Mount, where this monster of a man (as their phrase was) had his den; the whole number (had the rest not been from home, being but seven) would have given Captain Shrimp (a quondam drummer) such a welcome as would have made him wish for a drum as big as Diogenes' tub, that he might have crept into it out of sight.

Now the nine Worthies are approached; and mine host prepared: having intelligence by a salvage, that hastened in love from Wessaguscus, to give him notice of their intent.

One of mine host's men proved a craven: the other had proved his wits to purchase a little valor, before mine host had observed his posture.

The nine Worthies coming before the den of this supposed monster (this seven-headed Hydra, as they termed him), and began, like Don Quixote against the windmill, to beat a parley, and to offer quarter (if mine host would yield), for they resolved to send him for England; and bade him lay by his arms.

But he (who was the son of a soldier), having taken up arms in his just defense, replied that he would not lay by those arms, because they were so needful at sea, if he should be sent over. Yet, to save the effusion of so much worthy blood, as would have issued out of the veins of these nine Worthies of New Canaan, if mine host should have played upon them out at his portholes (for they came within danger like a flock of wild geese, as if they had been tailed one to another, as colts to be sold at a fair), mine host was content to yield upon quarter; and did capitulate with them. In what manner it should be, for more certainty, because he knew what Captain Shrimp was, he expressed that no violence should be offered to his person, none to his goods, nor any of his household: but that he should have his arms, and what else was requisite for the voyage: which their herald returns, it was agreed upon, and should be performed.

But mine host no sooner had set open the door, and issued out, but instantly Captain Shrimp and the rest of the Worthies stepped to him, laid hold of his arms, and had him down; and so eagerly was every man bent against him (not regarding any agreement made with such a carnal man), that they fell upon him as if they would have eaten him: some of them were so violent that they would have a slice with scabbert, and all for haste; until an old soldier (of the Queen's, as the proverb is) that was there by accident, clapt his gun under the weapons, and sharply rebuked these Worthies for their unworthy practices. So the matter was taken into more deliberate consideration.

Captain Shrimp, and the rest of the nine Worthies, made themselves (by this outrageous riot) masters of mine host of Ma-re Mount, and disposed of what he had at his plantation.

This they knew (in the eye of the salvages) would add to their glory, and diminish the reputation of mine honest host; whom they practiced to be rid of, upon any terms, as willingly as if he had been the very Hydra of the time.

Edward Johnson (1598–1672)

JOHNSON'S *Wonder-Working Providence* (*q.v.*, p. 32) gives a sprightly account of the spiritual giddiness that seemed to erupt between 1636 and 1638. The trouble centered in the teaching of Anne Hutchinson (1591–1643), wife to William Hutchinson, a merchant, and mother to fourteen children. In England she had been a close follower of John Cotton's preaching when he was vicar of St. Botolph's in Boston, Lincolnshire. Taking Cotton's emphasis on the covenant of grace to heart, she followed him to New England in 1634. There she first praised Cotton's preaching, then held meetings at her home in which she reviewed Cotton's sermons, and soon turned to outspoken criticism of other New England ministers for emphasizing the external, legal, and social aspects of the gospel. She inferred from Cotton's teaching that the Holy Ghost dwelt in the souls of the truly converted, and so gave them an immediate and unquestionable access to the divine will regarding their spiritual state, a position very close to the Inner Light preaching of the Quakers. The theological distinctions involved were complex and subtle, but their implications were appallingly clear to Cotton and the other Boston ministers, since they could only result in complete disregard for the ministry, for education, and in New England for civil law; Cotton denounced his disciple quickly. But other prominent persons defended her, among them the twenty-six-year-old Governor Henry Vane, and so the theological dispute became a political one, dividing families, towns, and for a time the entire colony.

For her "Antinomian" tenets Mrs. Hutchinson was excommunicated by John Cotton himself; and for her civil disorders she was banished from the colony in 1638. Moving first to Rhode Island, she lived there until 1642, when she moved to New York. In August of the following year she was killed by Indians. To Johnson she was merely another of Satan's attempts to subvert God's providence in America; he is careful not to mention her name, referring to her archly as the "Erronist," but he goes beyond other accounts by setting the episode meaningfully within the historical destiny of the Bay Colony.

TEXT: Edward Johnson, *The Wonder-Working Providence,* ed. William F. Poole (Andover, Mass., 1867).

The Erronist and Mr. Shepard

[From *The Wonder-Working Providence,* 1653]

And verily Satan's policy here (as in all places where the Lord Christ is acknowledged) was to keep men from that one right way, by the which He applies Himself to the soul; no marvel then if so many errors arise, like those feigned heads of Hydra, as fast as one is cut off two stand up in the room, and chiefly about the uniting of a soul to Christ by faith. Their errors at this point they reported to be the judgment of the reverend and judicious Mr. John Cotton. But he having spoken for himself . . . , I forbear; only this by the way, take notice of these subtle projectors, the Erronist, I mean, who perceiving this holy man of God Mr. Cotton was and yet is in great esteem with the people of God, for the great grace Christ hath bestowed upon him in his deep discerning the mysteries of godliness, as also discerning some little difference between him and the other elders about this point, comment upon it, and enlarge at their pleasure, and then in daily venting their deceivable doctrines, like subtle logicians, bring in this as their strongest argument in the last place: "I'll tell you, friend, neighbor, brother, if you will forbear to speak of it till you hear farther, this is the judgment of Mr. Cotton," when he, it may be, had never heard of it, or at least wise, when they brought this their bastardly brat to him, they put another vizard on the face of it: but that you may understand their way of broaching their abominable errors, it was in dividing those things the Lord hath united in his work of conversion continued, carrying on a soul to heaven in these four particulars. . . .

The third dividing tenet, by which these persons prosecuted their errors at this time, was between the Word of God, and the Spirit of God, and here these sectaries had many pretty knacks to delude withal, and especially to please the female sex, they told of rare revelations of things to come from the Spirit (as they say); it was only devised to weaken the Word of the Lord in the mouth of His ministers, and withal to put both ignorant and unlettered men and women in a posture of preaching to a multitude, that they might be praised for their able tongue. "Come along with me," says one of them, "I'll bring you to a woman that preaches better gospel then any of your black-coats that have been at the Ninnyversity, a woman of another kind of spirit, who hath had many revelations of things to come, and for my part," saith he, "I had rather hear such a one that speaks from the mere motion of the Spirit, without any study at all, then any of your learned scholars, although they may be fuller of scripture; aye, and admit they may speak by the help of the Spirit, yet the other goes beyond them." Gentle Reader, think not these things feigned, because I name not the parties, or that here is no witness to prove them, should I do so: neither of both is the cause, I assure you, but being somewhat acquainted with my own weakness, should the Lord withdraw the light of His Word, and also I verily believe some of them are truly turned again to the truth, the which I wish to all, yet by relating the story all men may see what a spirit of giddiness they were given up to, and some of them to strong delusions, even to most horrid and damnable blasphemies, having itching ears, or rather proud desires to become teachers of others, when they grossly erred in the first principles of religion themselves. There was a man in one of the farthest towns of the Massachusetts government, where they had no ministers for the present, he being much desirous to shew himself somebody in talking to as many as he could get to hear him on the sabbath day, missing some of his auditors, he meets with one of them some few days after, they passing over the water together. "Where were you," quoth he, "on the sabbath day that you were not at the meeting? We had a notable piece of prophecy." Quoth the man that was missing, "Who was it that preached?" The other replying not, his wife being in presence answered, "It was my husband." "Nay, wife," quoth he, "thou shouldst not have told him. Teach him to stay at home another time." . . . .

The fogs of error increasing, the bright beams of the glorious gospel of our Lord Christ in the mouth of His ministers could not be discerned through this thick mist by many, and that sweet refreshing warmth that was formerly felt from the Spirit's influence was now turned (in these Erronists) to a hot inflammation of their own conceited revelations, ulcerating and bringing little less than frenzy or madness to the patient. The congregation of the people of God began to be forsaken, and the weaker sex prevailed so far, that they set up a priest of their own profession and sex, who was much thronged after, abominably wresting the scriptures to their own destruction. This masterpiece of women's wit drew many disciples after her, and to that end boldly insinuated herself into the favor of none of the meanest, being also backed with the sorcery of a second, who had much converse with the Devil, by her own confession, and did, to the admiration of those that heard her, utter many speeches in the Latin tongue, as it were in a trance. This woman was wonted to give drinks to other women to cause them to conceive; how they wrought I know not, but sure there were monsters born not long after. . . .

But to end this year of sixteen hundred thirty six, take here the sorrowful complaint of a poor soul in miss of its expectation at landing, who being encountered with some of these Erronists at his first landing, when he saw that good old way of Christ rejected by them, and he could not skill in that new light which was the common theme of every man's discourse, he betook him to a narrow Indian path, in which his serious meditations soon led him, where none but senseless trees and echoing rocks made answer to his heart-easing moan. "Oh," quoth he, "where am I become? Is this the place where those reverend preachers are fled, that Christ was pleased to make use of to rouse up His rich graces in many a drooping soul? Here I have met with some that tell me I must take a naked Christ. Oh, woe is me; if Christ be naked to me, wherewith shall I be clothed? But methinks I most wonder they tell me of casting off all godly sorrow for sin as unbeseeming a soul that is united to Christ by faith. And there was a little nimble-tongued woman among them, who said she could bring me acquainted with one of her own sex that would shew me a way, if I could attain it, even revelations, full of such ravishing joy that I should never have cause to be sorry for sin, so long as I live, and as for her part she had attained it already. 'A company of legal professors,' quoth she, 'lie poring on the law which Christ hath abolished, and when you break it then you break your joy, and now no way will serve your turn, but a deep sorrow.' These and divers other expressions intimate unto me, that here I shall find little increase in the graces of Christ, through the hearing of His Word preached, and other of His blessed ordinances. O cunning devil, the Lord rebuke thee, that under pretense of a free and ample gospel shuts out the soul from partaking with the divine nature of Christ, in that mystical union of His blessed Spirit, creating and continuing His graces in the soul. . . .

"But here they tell me of a naked Christ. What is the whole life of a Christian upon this earth, but through the power of Christ to die to sin, and live to holiness and righteousness, and for that end to be diligent in the use of means?" At the uttering of this word he starts up from the green bed of his complaint with resolution to hear some one of these able ministers preach (whom report had so valued) before his will should make choice of any one principle, though of crossing the broad seas back again; then turning his face to the sun, he steered his course toward the next town, and after some small travel he came to a large plain. No sooner was he entered thereon, but hearing the sound of a drum he was directed toward it by a broad beaten way. Following this road he demands of the next man he met what the signal of the drum meant. The reply was made they had as yet no bell to call men to meeting, and therefore made use of a drum. "Who is it," quoth he, "lectures at this town?" The other replies, "I see you are a stranger, new come over, seeing you know not the man; it is one Mr. Shepard." "Verily," quoth the other, "you hit the right. I am new come over indeed, and have been told since I came most of your ministers are legal preachers, only if I mistake not, they told me this man preached a finer covenant of works then the other; but however I shall make what haste I can to hear him. Fare you well." Then hasting thither he crowded through the thickest, where having stayed while the glass was turned up twice, the man was metamorphosed, and was fain to hang down the head often, lest his watery eyes should blab abroad the secret conjunction of his affections, his heart crying loud to the Lord's echoing answer to His blessed Spirit that caused the speech of a poor, weak, pale-complectioned man to take such impression in his soul at present, by applying the Word so aptly, as if he had been his privy counsellor, clearing Christ's work of grace in the soul from all those false doctrines, which the erroneous party had affrighted him withal, and he now resolves (the Lord willing) to live and die with the ministers of New England; whom he now saw the Lord had not only made zealous to stand for the truth of his discipline, but also of the doctrine, and not to give ground one inch.

Thomas Welde (1590?–1662)

JOHN WINTHROP succeeded Henry Vane in the governorship of Massachusetts Bay, and wrote a report of the Hutchinson controversy, *A Short Story of the Rise, Reign, and Ruin of the Antinomians,* which he sent to England in 1638. The work was not published until 1644, when the manuscript came to the hands of Thomas Welde. Welde had graduated from Cambridge in England in 1613, taking up a ministry in Essex. His Puritan opinions led him to emigrate to Massachusetts in 1632, where he was installed as minister of the First Church in Roxbury. He had played a conspicuous part in the prosecution of Anne Hutchinson, and with John Eliot, Richard Mather, and John Cotton in the preparation of the famous *Bay Psalm Book.* Sent to England as colonial agent in 1641, he became involved in an argument with the colonists at home, and was dismissed from his post in 1646. Before his dismissal, however, and in an attempt to appeal to the interests of the newly gathered Westminster Assembly, he wrote a preface to John Winthrop's report, and secured its publication. His lucid description of the theological and social aspects of the Hutchinson controversy was used by the Scottish members of the Assembly as an argument against religious toleration.

TEXT: John Winthrop, *A Short Story of the Rise, Reign, and Ruin of the Antinomians* (London, 1644).

The Heresies of Anne Hutchinson and Her Followers

[From Preface to John Winthrop's *A Short Story of the . . . Antinomians*, 1644]

After we had escaped the cruel hands of persecuting prelates, and the dangers at sea, and had prettily well outgrown our wilderness troubles in our first plantings in New England; and when our commonwealth began to be founded, and our churches sweetly settled in peace (God abounding to us in more happy enjoyments than we could have expected), lest we should now grow secure, our wise God (who seldom suffers His own, in this their wearisome pilgrimage, to be long without trouble) sent a new storm after us, which proved the sorest trial that ever befell us since we left our native soil.

Which was this, that some going thither from hence full fraught with many unsound and loose opinions, after a time, began to open their packs, and freely vent their wares to any that would be their customers. Multitudes of men and women, church members and others, having tasted of their commodities, were eager after them, and were straight infected before they were aware, and some being tainted conveyed the infection to others; and thus that plague first began amongst us, that, had not the wisdom and faithfulness of Him, that watcheth over His vineyard night and day, by the beams of His light and grace cleared and purged the air, certainly we had not been able to have breathed there comfortably much longer. . . .

The opinions (some of them) were such as these; I say, some of them, to give but a taste, for afterwards you shall see a litter of fourscore and eleven of their brats hung up against the sun, besides many new ones of Mistress Hutchinson's; all which they hatched and dandled, as:

That the law, and the preaching of it, is of no use at all to drive a man to Christ.

That a man is united to Christ, and justified without faith; yea, from eternity.

That faith is not a receiving of Christ, but a man's discerning that he hath received Him already.

That a man is united to Christ only by the work of the Spirit upon him, without any act of his.

That a man is never effectually Christ's, till he hath assurance.

This assurance is only from the witness of the Spirit.

This witness of the Spirit is merely immediate, without any respect to [the] Word, or any concurrence with it.

When a man hath once this witness he never doubts more.

To question my assurance, though I fall into murther or adultery, proves that I never had true assurance.

Sanctification can be no evidence of a man's good estate.

No comfort can be had from any conditional promise.

Poverty in spirit (to which Christ pronounceth blessedness, Matt. 5:3) is only this, to see I have no grace at all.

To see I have no grace in me, will give me comfort; but to take comfort from sight of grace, is legal.

An hypocrite may have Adam's graces that he had in innocency.

The graces of saints and hypocrites differ not.

All graces are in Christ, as in the subject, and none in us, so that Christ believes, Christ loves, etc.

Christ is the new creature.

God loves a man never the better for any holiness in him, and never the less, be he never so unholy.

Sin in a child of God must never trouble him.

Trouble in conscience for sins of commission, or for neglect of duties, shews a man to be under a covenant of works.

All covenants to God expressed in works are legal works.

A Christian is not bound to the law as a rule of his conversation.

A Christian is not bound to pray except the Spirit moves him.

A minister that hath not this (new) light, is not able to edify others that have it.

The whole letter of the scripture is a covenant of works.

No Christian must be prest to duties of holiness.

No Christian must be exhorted to faith, love, and prayer, etc., except we know he hath the Spirit.

A man may have all graces, and yet want Christ.

All a believer's activity is only to act sin. . . .

Consider their sleights they used in fomenting their opinions, some of which I will set down, as:

They labored much to acquaint themselves with as many, as possibly they could, that so they might have the better opportunity to communicate their new light unto them.

Being once acquainted with them, they would strangely labor to insinuate themselves into their affections, by loving salutes, humble carriage, kind invitements, friendly visits, and so they would win upon men, and steal into their bosoms before they were aware. Yea, as soon as any new-comers (especially men of note, worth, and activity, fit instruments to advance their design) were landed, they would be sure to welcome them, shew them all courtesy, and offer them room in their own houses, or of some of their own sect, and so having gotten them into their web, they could easily poison them by degrees. It was rare for any man thus hooked in, to escape their leaven. . . .

They commonly labored to work first upon women, being (as they conceived) the weaker to resist; the more flexible, tender, and ready to yield; and if once they could wind in them, they hoped by them, as by an Eve, to catch their husbands also, which indeed often proved too true amongst us there.

As soon as they had thus wrought in themselves, and a good conceit of their opinions, by all these ways of subtlety, into the hearts of people; nextly, they strongly endeavored with all the craft they could, to undermine the good opinion of their ministers, and their doctrine, and to work them clean out of their affections, telling them they were sorry that their teachers had so misled them, and trained them up under a covenant of works, and that themselves never having been taught of God, it is no wonder they did no better teach them the truth, and how they may sit till doomsday under their legal sermons, and never see light; and withal sometimes casting aspersions on their persons, and practice, as well as their doctrine, to bring them quite out of esteem with them. And this they did so effectually, that many declined the hearing of them, though they were members of their churches, and others that did hear, were so filled with prejudice that they profited not, but studied how to object against them, and censure their doctrine, which (while they stood right) were wont to make their hearts to melt and tremble. . . .

But the last and worst of all, which most suddenly diffused the venom of these opinions into the very veins and vitals of the people in the country, was Mistress Hutchinson's double weekly-lecture, which she kept under a pretense of repeating sermons, to which resorted sundry of Boston, and other towns about, to the number of fifty, sixty, or eighty at once; where, after she had repeated the sermon, she would make her comment upon it, vent her mischievous opinions as she pleased, and wreathed the scriptures to her own purpose; where the custom was for her scholars to propound questions, and she (gravely sitting in the chair) did make answers thereunto. The great respect she had at first in the hearts of all, and her profitable and sober carriage of matters, for a time, made this her practice less suspected by the godly magistrates, and elders of the church there, so that it was winked at, for a time (though afterward reproved by the assembly, and called into court); but it held so long, until she had spread her leaven so far, that had not providence prevented, it had proved the canker of our peace, and ruin of our comforts.

By all these means and cunning sleights they used, it came about that those errors were so soon conveyed, before we were aware, not only into the Church of Boston, where most of these seducers lived, but also into almost all the parts of the country round about.

These opinions being thus spread, and grown to their full ripeness and latitude, through the nimbleness and activity of their fomenters, began now to lift up their heads full high, to stare us in the face, and to comfort all that opposed them.

And that which added vigor and boldness to them was this, that now by this time they had some of all sorts, and quality, in all places to defend and patronize them; some of the magistrates, some gentlemen, some scholars, and men of learning, some burgesses of our general court, some of our captains and soldiers, some chief men in towns, and some men eminent for religion, parts, and wit. So that wheresoever the case of the opinions came in agitation, there wanted not patrons to stand up to plead for them; and if any of the opinionists were complained of in the courts for their misdemeanors, or brought before the churches for conviction or censure, still, some or other of that party would not only suspend giving their vote against them, but would labor to justify them, side with them and protest against any sentence that should pass upon them, and so be ready, not only to harden the delinquent against all means of conviction, but to raise a mutiny, if the major part should carry it against them. So in town-meetings, military-trainings and all other societies, yea, almost in every family, it was hard, if that some or other were not ready to rise up in defense of them, even as of the apple of their own eye.

Now, oh their boldness, pride, insolency, alienations from their old and dearest friends, the disturbances, divisions, contentions they raised amongst us, both in church and state, and in families, setting division betwixt husband and wife!

Oh the sore censures against all sorts that opposed them, and the contempt they cast upon our godly magistrates, churches, ministers, and all that were set over them, when they stood in their way!

Now the faithful ministers of Christ must have dung cast on their faces, and be no better than legal preachers, Baal's priests, popish factors, scribes, Pharisees, and opposers of Christ Himself. . . .

Another of them you might have seen so audaciously insolent, and high-flown in spirit and speech, that she bade the court of magistrates (when they were about to censure her for her pernicious carriages) take heed what they did to her, for she knew by an infallible revelation, that for this act which they were about to pass against her, God would ruin them, their posterity, and that whole commonwealth.

By a little taste of a few passages instead of multitudes here presented, you may see what an height they were grown unto, in a short time; and what a spirit of pride, insolency, contempt of authority, division, sedition they were acted by. It was a wonder of mercy that they had not set our commonwealth and churches on a fire, and consumed us all therein.

They being mounted to this height, and carried with such a strong hand (as you have heard), and seeing a spirit of pride, subtlety, malice, and contempt of all men, that were not of their minds, breathing in them (our hearts sadded, and our spirits tired), we sighed and groaned to heaven, we humbled our souls by prayer and fasting, that the Lord would find out and bless some means and ways for the cure of this sore, and deliver His truth and ourselves from this heavy bondage. Which (when His own time was come) He hearkened unto, and in infinite mercy looked upon our sorrows, and did, in a wonderful manner, beyond all expectation, free us by these means following:

He stirred up all the ministers' spirits in the country to preach against those errors, and practices, that so much pestered the country, to inform, to confute, to rebuke, etc., thereby to cure those that were diseased already, and to give antidotes to the rest, to preserve them from infection, and though this ordinance went not without its appointed effect in the latter respect, yet we found it not so effectual for the driving away of this infection, as we desired, for they (most of them) hardened their faces, and bent their wits how to oppose and confirm themselves in their way. . . .

Then we had an assembly of all the ministers and learned men in the whole country, which held for three weeks together, at Cambridge (then called New-Town), Mr. Hooker, and Mr. Bulkley (alias Buckley) being chosen moderators, or prolocutors, the magistrates sitting present all that time, as hearers, and speakers also, when they saw fit. A liberty also was given to any of the country to come in and hear (it being appointed, in great part, for the satisfaction of the people) and a place was appointed for all the opinionists to come in, and take liberty of speech (only due order observed) as much as any of ourselves had, and as freely.

The first week we spent in confuting the loose opinions that we gathered up in the country. . . . The other fortnight we spent in a plain syllogistical dispute (*ad vulgus* as much as might be), gathered up nine of the chiefest points (on which the rest depended) and disputed of them all in order, *pro* and *con.* In the forenoons we framed our arguments, and in the afternoons produced them in public, and next day the adversary gave in their answers, and produced also their arguments on the same questions; then we answered them and replied also upon them the next day. . . . God was much present with his servants, truth began to get ground, and the adverse party to be at a stand; but after discourse amongst themselves, still they hardened one another. Yet the work of the assembly (through God's blessing) gained much on the hearers, that were indifferent, to strengthen them, and on many wavering, to settle them; the error of the opinions and wilfulness of their maintainers laid stark naked.

Then after this mean was tried, and the magistrates saw that neither our preaching, conference, nor yet our assembly meeting did effect the cure, but that still, after conference had together, the leaders put such life into the rest, that they all went on in their former course, not only to disturb the churches, but miserably interrupt the civil peace, and that they threw contempt both upon courts and churches, and began now to raise sedition amongst us, to the endangering the commonwealth. Hereupon for these grounds named (and not for their opinions, as themselves falsely reported, and as our godly magistrates have been much traduced here in England), for these reasons (I say) being civil disturbances, the magistrate convents them, . . . and censures them; some were disfranchised, others fined, the incurable amongst them banished.

Nathaniel Ward (1578–1652)

ALONG with John Winthrop, Nathaniel Ward was one of the few lawyers in the New England colonies. After graduating from Cambridge, he practiced law in England, traveled in Europe, and was finally ordained a minister in Germany. During the troubles with Archbishop Laud and the Ecclesiastical Court in 1634, he left for America to serve as pastor at Ipswich, Massachusetts (then known as Aggawam), until ill health forced him to resign in 1636. In 1637 he drew up a legal code for Massachusetts, which the General Court adopted in 1641 as "The Massachusetts Body of Liberties" in preference to John Cotton's proposed code. He stayed in New England until 1647, when he returned to England and published *The Simple Cobbler of Aggawam in America. Willing to Help Mend His Native Country, Lamentably Tattered, Both in the Upper Leather and Sole, with All the Honest Stitches He Can Take,* under the pseudonym of Theodore de la Guard. This work was a plea for compromise among the contesting religious factions, and for King and Church to come together once more in mutual confidence and respect.

Fed by reports of the troubles in the colonies, many Englishmen naturally assumed that America was a seedbed for wild and radical ideas, and so expressed themselves in books and pamphlets. To allay their fears, the simple cobbler made himself the herald of New England's religious and social orthodoxy. In contrast to Penn, Williams, and others like them, Ward voiced what was more probably the common view of the dangers of liberalism and toleration. His little book went through four editions in the first year of its publication.

TEXT: Nathaniel Ward, *The Simple Cobbler of Aggawam in America* (London, 1647).

Toleration

[From *The Simple Cobbler of Aggawam*, 1647]

Either I am in an apoplexy, or that man is in a lethargy who does not now sensibly feel God shaking the heavens over his head, and the earth under his feet: the heavens so, as the sun begins to turn into darkness, the moon into blood, the stars to fall down to the ground; so that little light of comfort or counsel is left to the sons of men; the earth so, as the foundations are failing, the righteous scarce know where to find rest, the inhabitants stagger like drunken men: it is in a manner dissolved both in religions and relations. And no marvel; for they have defiled it by transgressing the laws, changing the ordinances, and breaking the everlasting covenant. The truths of God are the pillars of the world, whereon states and churches may stand quiet if they will; if they will not, He can easily shake them off into delusions, and distractions enough.

Sathan is now in his passions, he feels his passion approaching; he loves to fish in roiled waters. Though that dragon cannot sting the vitals of the elect mortally, yet that Beelzebub can fly-blow their intellectuals miserably. The finer religion grows, the finer he spins his cobwebs; he will hold pace with Christ so long as his wits will serve him. He sees himself beaten out of gross idolatries, heresies, ceremonies, where the light breaks forth with power; he will, therefore, bestir him to prevaricate evangelical truths, and ordinances, that if they will needs be walking, yet they shall *laborare varicibus,* and not keep their path: he will put them out of time and place, assassinating for his engineers, men of Paracelsian parts, well complectioned for honesty; for such are fittest to mountebank his chemistry into sick churches and weak judgments.

Nor shall he need to stretch his strength overmuch in this work. Too many men, having not laid their foundations sure, nor ballasted their spirits deep with humility and fear, are prest enough of themselves to evaporate their own apprehensions. Those that are acquainted with [hi]story know, it hath ever been so in new editions of churches: such as are least able are most busy to pudder in the rubbish, and to raise dust in the eyes of more steady repairers. Civil commotions make room for uncivil practices: religious mutations, for irreligious opinions: change of air discovers corrupt bodies: reformation of religion, unsound minds. He that hath any well-faced fancy in his crown, and doth not vent it now, fears the pride of his own heart will dub him dunce forever. Such a one will trouble the whole Israel of God with his most untimely births, though he makes the bones of his vanity stick up, to the view and grief of all that are godly wise. The devil desires no better sport then to see light heads handle their heels, and fetch their careers in a time, when the roof of liberty stands open.

The next perplexed question, with pious and ponderous men, will be: "What should be done for the healing of these comfortless exulcerations?" I am the unablest adviser of a thousand, the unworthiest of ten thousand; yet I hope I may presume to assert what follows without just offense.

First, such as have given or taken any unfriendly reports of us New English, should do well to recollect themselves. We have been reputed a colluvies of wild opinionists, swarmed into a remote wilderness to find elbow room for our fanatic doctrines and practices: I trust our diligence past, and constant sedulity against such persons and courses, will plead better things for us. I dare take upon me, to be the herald of New England so far, as to proclaim to the world, in the name of our colony, that all Familists, Antinomians, Anabaptists, and other enthusiasts shall have free liberty to keep away from us, and such as will come to be gone as fast as they can, the sooner the better.

Secondly, I dare aver that God doth nowhere in His Word tolerate Christian states, to give toleration to such adversaries of His truth, if they have power in their hands to suppress them.

Here is lately brought us an extract of a Magna Charta, so called, compiled between the sub-planters of a West Indian island, whereof the first article of constipulation firmly provides free stableroom and litter for all kind of consciences, be they never so dirty or jadish; making it actionable, yea, treasonable, to disturb any man in his religion, or to discommend it, whatever it be. We are very sorrow to see such professed profaneness in English professors, as industriously to lay their religious foundations on the ruin of true religion; which strictly binds every conscience to contend earnestly for the truth; to preserve unity of spirit, faith, and ordinances; to be all like minded, of one accord;

every man to take his brother into his Christian care; to stand fast with one spirit, with one mind, striving together for the faith of the gospel; and by no means to permit heresies or erroneous opinions. But God, abhorring such loathsome beverages, has in His righteous judgment blasted that enterprise, which might otherwise have prospered well, for aught I know; I presume their case is generally known ere this.

If the Devil might have his free opinion, I believe he would ask nothing else, but liberty to enfranchise all other religions, and to embondage the true; nor should he need. It is much to be feared, that lax tolerations upon state pretenses and planting necessities, will be the next subtle stratagem he will spread, to distaste the truth of God and supplant the peace of the churches. Tolerations in things tolerable, exquisitely drawn out by the lines of the scripture, and pencil of the Spirit, are the sacred favors of truth, the due latitudes of love, the fair compartiments of Christian fraternity: but irregular dispensations, dealt forth by the facilities of men, are the frontiers of error, the redoubts of schism, the perilous irritaments of carnal and spiritual enmity.

My heart has naturally destested four things: the standing of the apocrypha in the Bible; foreigners dwelling in my country, to crowd out native subjects into the corners of the earth; alchemized coins; tolerations of divers religions, or of one religion in segregant shapes. He that willingly assents to the last, if he examines his heart by daylight, his conscience will tell him, he is either an atheist, or an heretic, or an hypocrite, or at best a captive to some lust. Poly-piety is the greatest impiety in the world. True religion is *ignis probationis,* which doth *congregare homogenea et segregare heterogenea.*

Not to tolerate things merely indifferent to weak consciences, argues a conscience too strong: pressed uniformity in these, causes much disunity. To tolerate more then indifferents is not to deal indifferently with God; he that doth it, takes His scepter out of His hand, and bids Him stand by. The power of all religion and ordinances, lies in their purity; their purity in their simplicity; then are mixtures pernicious. I lived in a city, where a Papist preached in one church, a Lutheran in another, a Calvinist in a third; a Lutheran one part of the day, a Calvinist the other, in the same pulpit: the religion of that place was but motley and meager, their affections leopard-like.

If the whole creature should conspire to do the Creator a mischief, or offer Him an insolency, it would be in nothing more, then in erecting untruths against His truth, or by sophisticating His truths with human medleys. The removing of some one iota in scripture may draw out all the life, and traverse all the truth of the whole Bible: but to authorize an untruth, by a toleration of state, is to build a sconce against the walls of heaven, to batter God out of His chair. To tell a practical lie, is a great sin, but yet transient; but to set up a theoretical untruth, is to warrant every lie that lies from its root to the top of every branch it hath.

I would willingly hope that no member of the Parliament hath skillfully ingratiated himself into the hearts of the House, that he might watch a time to midwife out some ungracious toleration for his own turn, and for the sake of that, some others. I would also hope that a word of general caution should not be particularly misapplied. Yet, good gentlemen, look well about you, and remember how Tiberius played the fox with the senate of Rome, and how Fabius Maximus cropt his ears for his cunning.

Roger Williams (1603–1683)

ROGER WILLIAMS was born in 1603 in London, the son of a tailor. Little is known of his youth, except that by his skill in shorthand he obtained a post as court stenographer to Sir Edward Coke, the great English justice and exponent of the common law. He later went to Cambridge, graduated in 1627, and remained two more years to study theology. A confirmed dissenter, he took a post as private chaplain to a Puritan noble, and in 1631 decided to emigrate to Massachusetts, where he finally settled in Plymouth.

Godly and kindly, Williams was nevertheless a man of strong personal ideas with no hesitation about expressing them. He raised a number of questions about Massachusetts land tenure and ownership, and others about the relationship between civil magistrates and the clergy. From 1633 to 1635, Williams was constantly in trouble with church and court for "diverse new and dangerous opinions," as Governor Winthrop wrote in his journal, "adjudged by all, magistrates and ministers, to be erroneous and very dangerous." In 1635 he was sentenced by the court "to depart out of our jurisdiction within six weeks," which he did, to Rhode Island in the dead of a cold New England winter to live among the Indians. Eventually, after several trips to London, Williams succeeded in obtaining a charter from Charles II, and Rhode Island became a colony. Williams, three terms its president, made it a haven for dissident sects and refugees from Calvinist orthodoxy, although he himself carried on a violent feud with George Fox and the Quakers.

John Cotton had published a letter proclaiming Williams' banishment, which Williams answered in 1644 in *Mr. Cotton's Letter Lately Printed, Examined and Answered.* Later that year he continued his argument with Cotton in a long dialogue between Peace and Truth titled *The Bloody Tenent [Tenet] of Persecution for Cause of Conscience,* to which Cotton replied in *The Bloody Tenent Washed and Made White in the Blood of the Lamb* (1647). Williams responded immediately with *The Bloody Tenent Yet More Bloody by Mr. Cotton's Endeavor to Wash it White in the Blood of the Lamb,* which was not published until 1652.

There were a number of complex political and theological questions involved in Williams' dispute with Massachusetts authorities, but two were crucial: first, his contention that a state cannot punish errors in religion; and second, his belief that because "the sovereign, original, and foundation of all civil power lies in the people . . . a people may erect and establish what form of government seems to them most meet for their civil condition." Thus, although Williams advocated liberty only within the peace of a society, both of these propositions struck at the very base of the Puritan theocratic commonwealth.

TEXTS: Roger Williams, *The Bloody Tenent of Persecution* (n.p., 1644); and "A Letter to the Town of Providence," January, 1655.

Twelve Theses on Toleration

[From *The Bloody Tenent,* 1644]

First, that the blood of so many hundred thousand souls of Protestants and Papists, spilt in the wars of present and former ages, for their respective consciences, is not required nor accepted by Jesus Christ the Prince of Peace.

Secondly, pregnant scriptures and arguments are throughout the work proposed against the doctrine of persecution for cause of conscience.

Thirdly, satisfactory answers are given to scriptures, and objections produced by Mr. Calvin, Beza, Mr. Cotton, and the ministers of the New English churches and others former and later, tending to prove the doctrine of persecution for cause of conscience.

Fourthly, the doctrine of persecution for cause of conscience, is proved guilty of all the blood of the souls crying for vengeance under the altar.

Fifthly, all civil states with the officers of justice in their respective constitutions and administrations are proved essentially civil, and therefore not judges, governors, or defenders of the spiritual or Christian state and worship.

Sixtly, it is the will and command of God, that (since the coming of His Son the Lord Jesus) a permission of the most paganish, Jewish, Turkish, or antichristian consciences and worships, be granted to all men in all nations and countries: and they are only to be fought against with that sword which is only (in soul matters) able to conquer, to wit, the sword of God's Spirit, the Word of God.

Seventhly, the state of the land of Israel, the kings and people thereof in peace and war, is proved figurative and ceremonial, and no pattern nor precedent for any kingdom or civil state in the world to follow.

Eightly, God requireth not an uniformity of religion to be enacted and enforced in any civil state; which enforced uniformity (sooner or later) is the greatest occasion of civil war, ravishing of conscience, persecution of Christ Jesus in His servants, and of the hypocrisy and destruction of millions of souls.

Ninthly, in holding an enforced uniformity of religion in a civil state, we must necessarily disclaim our desires and hopes of the Jews' conversion to Christ.

Tenthly, an enforced uniformity of religion throughout a nation or civil state, confounds the civil and religious, denies the principles of Christianity and civility, and that Jesus Christ is come in the flesh.

Eleventhly, the permission of other consciences and worships then a state professeth, only can (according to God) procure a firm and lasting peace (good assurance being taken according to the wisdom of the civil state for uniformity of civil obedience from all sorts).

Twelfthly, lastly, true civility and Christianity may both flourish in a state or kingdom, notwithstanding the permission of divers and contrary consciences, either of Jew or Gentile.

Liberty and the Common Peace

[From a Letter to the Town of Providence, 1655]

That ever I should speak or write a tittle that tends to such an infinite liberty of conscience, is a mistake, and which I have ever disclaimed and abhorred. To prevent such mistakes, I shall at present only propose this case: There goes many a ship to sea, with many hundred souls in one ship, whose weal and woe is common, and it's a true picture of a commonwealth, or a human combination or society. It hath fallen out sometimes, that both Papists and Protestants, Jews and Turks, may be embarged in one ship; upon which supposal I affirm, that all the liberty of conscience, that ever I pleaded for, turns upon these two hinges — that none of the Papists, Protestants, Jews, or Turks, be forced to come to the ship's prayers or worship, nor compelled from their own particular prayers or worship, if they practice any. I further add, that I never denied, that, notwithstanding this liberty, the commander of this ship ought to command the ship's course, yea, and also command that justice, peace, and sobriety, be kept and practiced, both among the seamen and all the passengers. If any of the seamen refuse to perform their services, or passengers to pay their freight; if any refuse to help, in person or purse, towards the common charges or defense; if any refuse to obey the common laws and orders of the ship, concerning their common peace or preservation; if any shall mutiny and rise up against their commanders and officers; if any should preach or write that there ought to be no commanders or officers, because all are equal in Christ, therefore no masters nor officers, no laws nor orders, nor corrections nor punishments — I say, I never denied, but in such cases, whatever is pretended, the commander or commanders may judge, resist, compel and punish such transgressors, according to their deserts and merits. This if seriously and honestly minded, may, if it so please the Father of lights, let in some light to such as willingly shut not their eyes.

I remain studious of your common peace and liberty.

Roger Williams

The Quaker Petition

No sect felt the brunt of New England intolerance as directly and consistently as those associates and followers of George Fox commonly called Children of Light or Quakers. Like Anne Hutchinson, they preached a personal spiritualism, but they were even more outspoken in their denunciation of all outward forms of worship and ecclesiastical order, and, in the early seventeenth century, even of the Bible. They first arrived in New England in 1656, and, putting themselves outside all formal authority — civil, ecclesiastical, and theological — by their often eccentric habits and notions, they embraced torture, mutilation, banishment, and even death so willingly that some historians have supposed them to have suffered from a martyr complex. But that they sought both legal and moral redress for their persecutions Samuel Shattuck's *The Quaker Petition* of 1661 shows clearly, as does William Penn's *The Great Case of Liberty of Conscience.*

Text: Joseph Besse, ed., *A Collection of the Sufferings of the People Called Quakers* (London, 1753), Vol. I.

The Quaker Petition

A declaration of some part of the sufferings of the people of God in scorn called Quakers, from the professors in New England, only for the exercise of their consciences to the Lord, and obeying and confessing to the truth, as in His light He had discovered it to them:

1. Two honest and innocent women stripped stark naked, and searched after such an inhuman manner, as modesty will not permit particularly to mention.

2. Twelve strangers in that country, but freeborn of this nation, received twenty-three whippings, the most of them being with a whip of three cords with knots at the ends, and laid on with as much strength as could be by the arm of their executioner, the stripes amounting to three hundred and seventy.

3. Eighteen inhabitants of the country, being freeborn English, received twenty-three whippings, the stripes amounting to two hundred and fifty.

4. Sixty-four imprisonments of the Lord's people, for their obedience to His will, amounting to five hundred and nineteen weeks, much of it being very cold weather; and the inhabitants kept in prison in harvest time, which was very much to their loss; besides many more imprisoned, of which time we cannot give a just account.

5. Two beaten with pitched ropes, the blows amounting to an hundred and thirty-nine, by which one of them was brought near unto death, much of his body being beaten like unto a jelly, and one of their doctors, a member of their church, who saw him, said, it would be a miracle if ever he recovered, he expecting the flesh should rot off the bones, who afterwards was banished upon pain of death. There are many witnesses of this there.

6. Also an innocent man, an inhabitant of Boston, they banished from his wife and children, and put to seek an habitation in the winter, and in case he returned again, he was to be kept prisoner during his life, and for returning again he was put in prison, and hath been now a prisoner above a year.

7. Twenty-five banishments upon the penalties of being whipt, or having their ears cut, or branded in the hand, if they returned.

8. Fines laid upon the inhabitants for meeting together, and edifying one another, as the saints ever did; and for refusing to swear, it being contrary to Christ's command, amounting to about a thousand pounds, beside what they have done since that we have not heard of. Many families, in which there are many children, are almost ruined by their unmerciful proceedings.

9. Five kept fifteen days in all, without food, and fifty-eight days shut up close by the gaoler, and had none that he knew of; and from some of them he stopt up the windows, hindring them from convenient air.

10. One laid neck and heels in irons for sixteen hours.

11. One very deeply burnt in the right hand with the letter "H" after he had been whipt with above thirty stripes.

12. One chained to a log of wood the most part of twenty days, in an open prison, in the winter time.

13. Five appeals to England denied at Boston.

14. Three had their right ears cut by the hangman in the prison, the door being barred, and not a friend suffered to be present while it was doing, though some much desired it.

15. One of the inhabitants of Salem, who since is banished upon pain of death, had one half of his house and land seized on while he was in prison, a month before he knew of it.

16. At a General Court in Boston they made an order, that those who had not wherewithal to answer the fines that were laid upon them for their consciences, should be sold for bondmen and bondwomen to Barbados, Virginia, or any of the English plantations.

17. Eighteen of the people of God were at several times banished upon pain of death; six of them were their own inhabitants, two of which being very aged people, and well known among their neighbors to be of honest conversation, being banished from their houses and families, and put upon traveling and other hardships, soon ended their days, whose death we can do no less than charge upon the rulers of Boston, they being the occasion of it.

18. Also three of the servants of the Lord they put to death, all of them for obedience to the truth, in the testimony of it, against the wicked rulers and laws at Boston.

19. And since they have banished four more upon pain of death, and twenty-four of the inhabitants of Salem were presented, and more fines called for, and their goods seized on to the value of forty pounds for meeting together in the fear of God, and some for refusing to swear.

These things, O King! from time to time have we patiently suffered, and not for the transgression of any just or righteous law, either pertaining to the worship of God, or the civil government of England, but simply and barely for our consciences to God, of which we can more at large give thee, or whom thou mayst order, a full account (if thou will let us have admission to thee, who are banished upon pain of death, and have had our ears cut, who are some of us in England attending upon thee) both of the causes of our sufferings, and the manner of their disorderly and illegal proceedings against us; they began with immodesty, went on in inhumanity and cruelty, and were not satisfied until they had the blood of three of the martyrs of Jesus: revenge for all which we do not seek, but lay them before thee, considering thou hast been well acquainted with sufferings, and so mayst the better consider them that suffer, and mayst for the future restrain the violence of these rulers of New England, having power in thy hands, they being but the children of the family of which thou art chief ruler, who have in divers their proceedings forfeited their patent, as upon strict inquiry in many particulars will appear.

And this, O King! we are assured of, that in time to come it will not repent thee, if by a close rebuke thou stoppest the bloody proceedings of these bloody persecutors, for in so doing thou wilt engage the hearts of many honest people unto thee both there and here, and for such works of mercy the blessing is obtained; and shewing it is the way to prosper.

William Penn (1644–1718)

WILLIAM PENN (*q.v.*, p. 37), like other colonial proprietors, regarded Pennsylvania as investment property to be run for profit, but he was more interested in making it a "holy experiment" in government wherein men might live together in peace, toleration, charity, brotherhood, and liberty. "No man, nor number of men, upon earth," he once wrote, "hath power or authority to rule over men's consciences. . . ." In such a spirit he planned the building of Philadelphia (which swiftly grew to a major colonial city), ordered the first public grammar school in Philadelphia, passed laws granting religious freedom to the persecuted and oppressed, made just treaties with the Indians, and granted liberal government to the colony in the Pennsylvania Charter of Liberties (1701) which served it until the Revolution. The temper of the man, his colony, and its Quaker inhabitants glows through his *The Great Case of Liberty of Conscience.*

TEXT: *A Collection of the Works of William Penn* (London, 1726), Vol. I.

Liberty of Conscience

[From *The Great Case of Liberty of Conscience,* 1670]

The terms explained, and the question stated

First, by liberty of conscience, we understand not only a mere liberty of the mind, in believing or disbelieving this or that principle or doctrine; but "the exercise of ourselves in a visible way of worship, upon our believing it to be indispensably required at our hands, that if we neglect it for fear or favor of any mortal man, we sin, and incur divine wrath." Yet we would be so understood to extend and justify the lawfulness of our so meeting to worship God, as not to contrive, or abet any contrivance destructive of the government and laws of the land, tending to matters of an external nature, directly or indirectly; but so far only, as it may refer to religious matters, and a life to come, and consequently wholly independent of the secular affairs of this, wherein we are supposed to transgress.

Secondly, by imposition, restraint, and persecution, we don't only mean the strict requiring of us to believe this to be true, or that to be false; and upon refusal, to incur the penalties enacted in such cases; but by those terms we mean thus much, "any coercive let or hindrance to us, from meeting together to perform those religious exercises which are according to our faith and persuasion."

The question stated

For proof of the aforesaid terms thus given, we singly state the question thus;

Whether imposition, restraint, and persecution, upon persons for exercising such a liberty of conscience, as is before expressed, and so circumstantiated, be not to impeach the honor of God, the meekness of the Christian religion, the authority of scripture, the privilege of nature, the principles of common reason, the well being of government, and apprehensions of the greatest personages of former and latter ages. . . .

. . . We also prove them [imposition, restraint, and persecution] destructive of the noble principle of reason, and that in these [seven] particulars:

1. In that those who impose, or restrain, are uncertain of the truth, and justifiableness of their actions. In either of these, their own discourses and confessions are pregnant instances, where they tell us, that they do not pretend to be infallible, only they humbly conceive 'tis thus, or is not. Since then they are uncertain and fallible, how

can they impose upon, or restrain others, whom they are so far from assuring, that they are not able to do so much for themselves? What is this, but to impose an uncertain faith, upon certain penalties?

2. As he that acts doubtfully is damned, so faith in all acts of religion is necessary; now in order to believe, we must first will; to will, we must judge; to judge anything, we must first understand; if we cannot be said to understand anything against our understanding, no more can we judge, will, or believe against our understanding; and if the doubter be damned, what must he be that conforms directly against his judgment and belief, and they likewise that require it from him? In short, that man cannot be said to have any religion, that takes it by another man's choice, not his own.

3. Where men are limited in matters of religion, there the rewards which are entailed on the free acts of men, are quite overthrown; and such as supersede that grand charter of liberty of conscience, frustrate all hopes of recompense, by rendering the actions of men unavoidable. But those think, perhaps, they do not destroy all freedom, because they use so much of their own.

4. They subvert all true religion; for where men believe, not because it is true, but because they are required to do so, there they will unbelieve, not because 'tis false, but so commanded by their superiors, whose authority their interest and security oblige them rather to obey, than dispute.

5. They delude, or rather compel people out of their eternal rewards; for where men are commanded to act in reference to religion, and can neither be secured of their religion, nor yet saved harmless from punishment, that so acting and believing, disprivileges them for ever of that recompense which is provided for the faithful.

6. Men have their liberty and choice in external matters; they are not compelled to marry this person, to converse with that, to buy here, to eat there, nor to sleep yonder; yet if men had power to impose or restrain in anything, one would think it should be in such exterior matters: but that this liberty should be unquestioned, and that of the mind destroyed, issues here, "That it does not unbrute us, but unman us: for take away understanding, reason, judgment, and faith, and like Nebuchadnezzer, let us go graze with the beasts of the field."

Seventh and lastly, That which most of all blackens the business, is persecution: for though it is very unreasonable to require faith, where men cannot choose but doubt, yet, after all, to punish them for disobedience, is cruelty in the abstract: for we demand, "Shall men suffer for not doing what they cannot do?" must they be persecuted here if they do not go against their consciences, and punished hereafter if they do? But neither is this all; for that part that is yet most unreasonable, and that gives the clearest sight of persecution, is still behind, namely, "The monstrous arguments they have to convince an heretic with": not those of old, as spiritual as the Christian religion, which were, "to admonish, warn, and finally to reject"; but such as were employed by the persecuting Jews and heathens against the great example of the world, and such as followed him, and by the inhuman Papists against our first reformers, as clubs, staves, stocks, pillories, prisons, dungeons, exiles, etc. In a word, ruin to whole families; as if it were not so much their design to convince the soul, as to destroy the body.

To conclude: There ought to be an adequation and resemblance betwixt all ends, and the means to them; but in this case there can be none imaginable: the end is the conformity of our judgments and understandings to the acts of such as require it; the means are fines and imprisonment (and bloody knocks to boot).

Now, what proportion or assimulation these bear, let the sober judge: the understanding can never be convinced, nor properly submit, but by such arguments as are rational, persuasive, and suitable to its own nature; something that can resolve its doubts, answer its objections, enervate its propositions. But to imagine those barbarous Newgate instruments of clubs, fines, prisons, etc., with that whole troop of external and dumb materials of force, should be fit arguments to convince the understanding, scatter its scruples, and finally convert it to their religion, is altogether irrational, cruel, and impossible. Force may make an hypocrite; "'tis faith grounded upon knowledge, and consent, that makes a Christian." And to conclude, as we can never betray the honor of our conformity (only due to truth) by a base and timorous hypocrisy to any external violence under heaven; so must we needs say, unreasonable are those imposers, who secure not the imposed or restrained from what may occur to them, upon their account; and most inhuman are those persecutors that punish men for not obeying them, though to their utter ruin.

Peter Folger (1617–1690)

Peter Folger was described by his famous grandson Benjamin Franklin as one of the first settlers in New England. In 1675 Folger, sometime surveyor, schoolmaster, and assistant to Thomas Mayhew, an Indian missionary, saw from Nantucket a direct connection between the colony's Indian troubles and its rigid intolerance of those whose religious views were different. He penned his views in what Moses Coit Tyler called "one long jet of manly, ungrammatical, valiant doggerel"—a crude ballad called *A*

Looking-Glass for the Times; or, The Former Spirit of New England revived in this Generation (1676). Franklin's comments in the *Autobiography* on his grandfather's jeremiad constitute an excellent introduction: "I have heard that he wrote several small occasional pieces, but only one of them was printed, which I saw many years since. It was written in 1675, in familiar verse according to the taste of the time and people, and addressed to those then concerned in the government there. It asserts the liberty of conscience, and in behalf of the Anabaptists, Quakers, and other sectaries that had been persecuted. He attributes to this persecution the Indian Wars and other calamities that had befallen the country, regarding them as so many judgments of God to punish so heinous an offense, and exhorting a repeal of those laws, so contrary to charity. This piece appeared to me as written with manly freedom and a pleasing simplicity." No copy of the alleged 1676 edition is known to exist; the following selections are from a reprint of the first known edition, 1763.

TEXT: *Rhode Island Historical Tracts,* no. 16 (Providence, 1883).

A Plea for Toleration

[From *A Looking-Glass for the Times,* 1763]

Let all that read these verses know,
That I intend something to show
About our war, how it hath been,
And also what is the chief sin,
That God doth so with us contend,
And when these wars are like to end.
Read them in love; do not despise
What here is set before thine eyes.

New England for these many years
  Hath had both rest and peace,
But now the case is otherwise;
  Our trouble doth increase.

The plague of war is now begun
  In some great colonies,
And many towns as desolate
  We may see with our eyes.

The loss of many goodly men
  We may lament also,
Who in the war have lost their lives,
  And fallen by our foe.

Our women also they have took,
  And children very small;
Great cruelty they have used
  To some, though not to all.

The enemy that hath done this,
  Are very foolish men,
Yet God doth make of them a rod
  To punish us for sin.

If we then truly turn to God,
  He will remove His ire,
And will forthwith take this His rod,
  And cast it into fire.

Let us then search, what is the sin
  That God doth punish for;
And when found out, cast it away,
  And ever it abhor.

Sure 'tis not chiefly for those sins
  That magistrates do name,
And make good laws for to suppress,
  And execute the same.

But 'tis for that same crying sin,
  That rulers will not own,
And that whereby much cruelty
  To brethren hath been shown:

The sin of persecution
  Such laws established;
By which laws they have gone so far,
  As blood hath touched blood.

It is now forty years ago,
  Since some of those were made,
Which was the ground and rise of all
  The persecuting trade.

Then many worthy persons were
  Banished to the woods,
Where they among the natives did
  Lose their most precious bloods.

And since that, many godly men,
  Have been to prison sent;
They have been fined, and whipped also,
  And suffered banishment.

The cause of this their suffering
  Was not for any sin,
But for the witness that they bare
  Against babes' sprinkling.

Of later time there hath been some
  Men come into this land,
To warn the rulers of their sins,
  As I do understand.

They called on all, both great and small,
  To fear God and repent;
And for their testimonies thus
  They suffered punishment.

Yea, some of them they did affirm,
  That they were sent of God,
To testify to great and small,
  That God would send His rod

Against those colonies, because
  They did make laws not good;
And if those laws were not repealed,
  The end would be in blood.

And though that these were harmless men,
  And did no hurt to any,
But lived well like honest men,
  As testified by many;

Yet did these laws entrap them so,
  That they were put to death,
And could not have the liberty
  To speak near their last breath.

But these men were, as I have heard,
  Against our college men;
And this was, out of doubt to me,
  That which was most their sin.

They did reprove all hirelings,
  With a most sharp reproof,
Because they knew not how to preach,
  Till sure of means enough.

. . . .

Let magistrates and ministers
  Consider what they do;
Let them repeal those evil laws,
  And break those bands in two,

Which have been made as traps and snares
   To catch the innocents,
And whereby it has gone so far
   To acts of violence.

I see you write yourselves in print,
   The balm of Gilead;
Then do not act as if you were
   Like men that are half mad.

If you can heal the land, what is
   The cause things are so bad?
I think instead of that, you make
   The hearts of people sad.

Is this a time for you to press,
   To draw the blood of those
That are your neighbors and your friends?
   As if you had no foes.

. . . .

I would not have you for to think,
   Though I have wrote so much,
That I hereby do throw a stone
   At magistrates *as such.*

The rulers in the country, I
   Do own them in the Lord;
And such as are for government,
   With them I do accord.

But that which I intend hereby,
   Is that they would keep bound,
And meddle not with God's worship,
   For which they have no ground.

And I am not alone herein,
   There's many hundreds more,
That have for many years ago
   Spake much upon that score.

Indeed I really believe
   It's not your business
To meddle with the church of Christ
   In matters more or less.

There's work enough to do besides,
   To judge in *mine* and *thine:*
To succor poor and fatherless,
   That is the work in fine.

And I do think that now you find
  Enough of that to do;
Much more at such a time as this,
  As there is war also.

Indeed I count it very low,
  For people in these days,
To ask the rulers for their leave
  To serve God in His ways.

I count it worse in magistrates
  To use the iron sword,
To do that work which Christ alone
  Will do by His own Word.

The church may now go stay at home,
  There's nothing for to do;
Their work is all cut out by law,
  And almost made up too.

Now, reader, least you should mistake,
  In what I said before
Concerning ministers, I think
  To write a few words more.

I would not have you for to think
  That I am such a fool,
To write against learning, as such,
  Or to cry down a school.

But 'tis that Popish college way,
  That I intend hereby,
Where men are mewed up in a cage;
  Fit for all villainy.

. . . .

Now for the length of time, how long
  These wars are like to be,
I may speak something unto that,
  If men will reason see.

The scripture doth point out the time,
  And 't is as we do choose,
For to obey the voice of God,
  Or else for to refuse.

The prophet Jeremy doth say,
  When war was threatened sore,
That if men do repent and turn,
  God will afflict no more.

But such a turning unto God,
   As is but verbally,
When men refuse for to reform,
   It is not worth a fly.

'Tis hard for you, as I do hear,
   Though you be under rod,
To say to Israel, "Go, you,
   And serve the Lord your God."

Though you do many prayers make,
   And add fasting thereto,
Yet if your hands be full of blood,
   All this will never do.

The end that God doth send His sword,
   Is that we might amend;
Then, if that we reform aright,
   The war will shortly end.

. . . .

If we could love our brethren,
   And do to them, I say,
As we would they should do to us,
   We should be quite straightway.

But if that we a smiting go,
   Of fellow-servants so,
No marvel if our wars increase,
   And things so heavy go.

'Tis like that some may think and say,
   Our war would not remain,
If so be that a thousand more
   Of natives were but slain.

Alas! these are but foolish thoughts,
   God can make more arise,
And if that there were none at all,
   He can make war with flies.

It is the presence of the Lord,
   Must make our foes to shake,
Or else it's like He will ere long
   Know how to make us quake.

Let us lie low before the Lord,
   In all humility,
And then we shall with Asa see
   Our enemies to fly.

But if that we do leave the Lord,
And trust in fleshly arm,
Then 't is no wonder if that we
Do hear more news of harm.

Let's have our faith and hope in God,
And trust in Him alone,
And then no doubt this storm of war
It quickly will be gone.

Thus, reader, I, in love to all,
Leave these few lines with thee,
Hoping that in the substance we
Shall very well agree.

If that you do mislike the verse,
For its uncomely dress,
I tell thee true, I never thought
That it would pass the press.

If any at the matter kick,
It's like he's galled at heart,
And that's the reason why he kicks,
Because he finds it smart.

I am for peace, and not for war,
And that's the reason why
I write more plain than some men do,
That use to daub and lie.

But I shall cease and set my name
To what I here insert,
Because to be a libeller,
I hate it with my heart.

From Sherbon town, where now I dwell,
My name I do put here,
Without offense your real friend,
It is PETER FOLGER.

Nathaniel Bacon and Sir William Berkeley

Dissent and trouble were not limited to New England. Even before their ship had anchored, the seven members of the ruling council of Jamestown were quarreling among themselves; nonconforming evangelists from Massachusetts descended upon the South to undermine established Anglican forms of worship, and invaded New York to unsettle the placid Dutch ways of life there; and Indians were, on the whole, no friendlier elsewhere than they were in New England. Moreover, from almost the moment of their inception, colonial governments faced a conflict, sometimes open and sometimes covert, between haves and have-nots, franchised and unenfranchised, debtor and creditor, backcountry farmer and urban capitalist or coastal planter. Since the machinery of government was usually in the hands of the moneyed class, the merchants and the planters, their alliance with the clergy and the royal governor gave them virtual control of colonial affairs. The seventeenth century was dotted with clashes between these social and economic groups and their interests, but the two most important confrontations occurred in Virginia and New York.

Nathaniel Bacon (1647–1676) came to Virginia from England in 1673 to settle along the James River. Incensed at what he believed to be the shameful lack of protection given to outlying farms against Indian depredations, Bacon and others appealed to Governor William Berkeley (1610?–1677) for more soldiers. This grievance, however, was but one of several held against the Jamestown government by the small farmers. They were being inequitably taxed, they claimed, were denied proper representation in the Assembly, and were being ruined financially by the competition of the large plantations and cheap slave labor. When Berkeley refused to send military aid, Bacon led a volunteer force in 1676 against the Indians and won a notable victory. Since Bacon's expedition was unauthorized, the Governor denied him a military commission; and when Bacon refused to disband his volunteer army, Berkeley declared him a rebel and set a price on his head. Bacon thereupon marched on Jamestown, forced Berkeley to sign his military commission, and coerced the Assembly into passing a number of reform measures. When he marched out once more after Indians, the Governor organized a force against him and again declared him a rebel. Bacon returned, defeated Berkeley, burned Jamestown, and took charge of the government, styling himself "General by consent of the people." In a short time, however, he died of a fever and his leaderless army collapsed. The Governor captured and hanged thirty-seven of Bacon's followers, but the farmers gained two points: the negotiation of a treaty with the Indians and the recall of Berkeley, who died a broken and discredited man a year later.

Thirteen years later, in New York, an alliance of farmers, tradesmen, and workmen, led by Jacob Leisler, took over the government of that colony for two years in protest against what they considered arbitrary aristocratic rule. Leisler surrendered power to the new royal governor appointed by William and Mary — and was promptly hanged for treason on the governor's arrival in 1691.

TEXTS: "Aspinwall Papers," *Coll. Mass. Hist. Soc.*, 4th ser., IX (1871); and *The History of Bacon's and Ingram's Rebellion,* in the "Burwell Papers," *Proc. Mass. Hist. Soc.*, IX (1866).

Declaration against the Proceedings of Nathaniel Bacon

[From the "Aspinwall Papers"]

The declaration and remonstrance of Sir William Berkeley, his most sacred Majesty's Governor and Captain-General of Virginia,

Sheweth: that about the year 1660, Col. Mathews the then Governor died, and then in consideration of the service I had done the country, in defending them from, and destroying great numbers of the Indians, without the loss of three men, in all the time that war lasted, and in contemplation of the equal and uncorrupt justice I had distributed to all men, not only the Assembly, but the unanimous votes of all the country, concurred to make me Governor in a time when, if the rebels in England had prevailed, I had certainly died for accepting it. 'Twas, Gentlemen, an unfortunate love shewed to me, for, to shew myself grateful for this, I was willing to accept of this government again, when by my gracious king's favor I might have had other places much more profitable and less toilsome then this hath been. Since that time that I returned into the country, I call the great God, judge of all things in heaven and earth to witness, that I do not know of anything relative to this country, wherein I have acted unjustly, corruptly, or negligently, in distributing equal justice to all men, and taking all possible care to preserve their proprieties, and defend them from their barbarous enemies.

But, for all this, perhaps I have erred in things I know not of. If I have, I am so conscious of human frailty, and my own defects, that I will not only acknowledge them, but repent of, and amend them, and not, like the rebel Bacon, persist in an error, only because I have committed it; and tells me in divers of his letters that it is not for his honor to confess a fault, but I am of opinion that it is only for divels to be incorrigible, and men of principles like the worst of divels; and these he hath, if truth be reported to me, of divers of his expressions of atheism, tending to take away all religion and laws.

And now I will state the question betwixt me as a governor and Mr. Bacon, and say that if any enemies should invade England, any counsellor, justice of peace, or other inferior officer, might raise what forces they could to protect his Majesty's subjects. But I say again, if, after the king's knowledge of this invasion, any the greatest peer of England should raise forces against the king's prohibition, this would be now — and ever was in all ages and nations — accompted treason. Nay, I will go further, that though this peer was truly zealous for the preservation of his king, and subjects, and had better and greater abilities then all the rest of his fellow subjects, to do his king and country service, yet if the king (though by false information) should suspect the contrary, it were treason in this noble peer to proceed after the king's prohibition: and for the truth of this I appeal to all the laws of England, and the laws and constitutions of all other nations in the world. And yet further, it is declared by this Parliament that the taking up arms for the king and Parliament is treason; for the event shewed that whatever the pretense was to seduce ignorant and well-affected people, yet the end was ruinous both to king and people — as this will be if not prevented. I do therefore again declare that Bacon, proceeding against all laws of all nations, modern and ancient, is rebel to his sacred Majesty and this country; nor will I insist upon the swearing of men to live and die together, which is treason by the very words of the law.

Now, my friends, I have lived thirty-four years amongst you, as uncorrupt and diligent as ever Governor was; Bacon is a man of two years amongst you, his person and qualities unknown to most of you, and to all men else, by any virtuous action that ever I heard of. And that very action which he boasts of was sickly and foolishly, and, as I am informed, treacherously carried to the dishonor of the English nation; yet in it he lost more men then I did in three years' war; and by the grace of God will put myself to the same dangers and troubles again when I have brought Bacon to acknowledge the laws are above him, and I doubt not but by God's assistance to have better success then Bacon hath had. The reason of my hopes are, that I will take counsel of wiser men then myself; but Mr. Bacon hath none about him but the lowest of the people.

Yet I must further enlarge, that I cannot without your help, do anything in this but die in defence of my king, his laws, and subjects, which I will cheerfully do, though alone I do it; and considering my poor fortunes, I cannot leave my poor wife and friends a better legacy then by dying for my king and you: for his sacred Majesty will easily distinguish between Mr. Bacon's actions and mine, and kings have long arms, either to reward or punish.

Now, after all this, if Mr. Bacon can shew one precedent or example where such actings in any nation whatever was approved of, I will meditate with the King and you for a pardon, and excuse for him; but I can shew him an hundred examples where brave and great men have been put to death for gaining victories against the command of their superiors.

Lastly, my most assured friends, I would have preserved those Indians that I knew were hourly at our mercy, to have been our spies and intelligence, to find out our bloody enemies; but as soon as I had the least intelligence that they also were treacherous enemies, I gave out commissions to destroy them all, as the commissions themselves will speak it.

To conclude, I have done what was possible both to friend and enemy; have granted Mr. Bacon three pardons, which he hath scornfully rejected, supposing himself stronger to subvert then I and you to maintain the laws, by which only, and God's assisting grace and mercy, all men must hope for peace and safety. I will add no more, though much more is still remaining to justify me and condemn Mr. Bacon, but to desire that this declaration may be read in every county court in the country, and that a court be presently called to do it before the Assembly meet, that your approbation or dissatisfaction of this declaration may be known to all the country, and the King's Council, to whose most revered judgments it is submitted.

Given the 29th day of May, a happy day in the 28th year of his most sacred Majesty's reign, Charles the Second, who God grant long and prosperously to reign, and let all his good subjects say Amen.

WILLIAM BERKELEY

Declaration in the Name of the People of Virginia July 30th, 1676

[From the "Aspinwall Papers"]

First. For having upon specious pretenses of public works raised great unjust taxes upon the commonality for the advancement of private favorites and other sinister ends, but no visible effects in any measure adequate. For not having, during this long time of his government, in any measure advanced this hopeful colony, either by fortifications, towns, or trade.

Second. For having abused and rendered contemptible the magistrates of justice, by advancing to places of judicature scandalous and ignorant favorites.

Third. For having wronged his Majesty's prerogative and interest by assuming monopoly of the beaver trade, and for having in that unjust gain betrayed and sold his Majesty's country and the lives of his loyal subjects to the barbarous heathen.

Fourth. For having protected, favored, and emboldened the Indians against his Majesty's loyal subjects; never contriving, requiring, or appointing any due or proper means of satisfaction for their many invasions, robberies, and murthers committed upon us.

Fifth. For having, when the army of English was just upon the track of those Indians, who now in all places burn, spoil, murther, and when we might with ease have destroyed them who then were in open hostility, for then having expressly countermanded and sent back our army, by passing his word for the peaceable demeanor of the said Indians, who immediately prosecuted their evil intentions, committing horrid murthers and robberies in all places, being protected by the said engagement and word past of him the said Sir William Berkeley; having ruined and laid desolate a great part of his Majesty's country, and have now drawn themselves into such obscure and remote places, and are by their success so emboldened and confirmed, by their confederacy so strengthened, that the cries of blood are in all places, and the terror and consternation of the people so great, are now become, not only a difficult, but a very formidable enemy, who might at first with ease have been destroyed.

Sixth. And lately, when upon the loud outcries of blood the Assembly had with all care raised and framed an army for the preventing of further mischief and safeguard of this his Majesty's colony:

Seventh. For having, with only the privacy of some few favorites, without acquainting the people, only by the alteration of a figure, forged a commission, by we know not what hand, not only without, but even against the consent of the people, for the raising and effecting civil war and destruction; which being happily and without bloodshed prevented, for having the second time attempted the same, thereby calling down our forces from the defense of the frontiers and most weakly exposed places.

Eighth. For the prevention of civil mischief and ruin amongst ourselves, whilst the barbarous enemy in all places did invade, murther and spoil us, his Majesty's most faithful subjects.

Of this and the aforesaid articles we accuse Sir William Berkeley as guilty of each and every one of the same, and as one who hath traitorously attempted, violated and injured his Majesty's interest here, by a loss of a great part of this his colony, and many of his faithful, loyal subjects, by him betrayed and in a barbarous and shameful manner exposed to the incursions and murther of the heathen. And we do further declare these, the ensuing persons in this list, to have been his wicked and pernicious counsellors, confederates, aiders, and assisters against the commonality in these our civil commotions. . . .

And we do further demand that the said Sir William Berkeley with all the persons in this list be forthwith delivered up or surrender themselves within four days after the notice hereof; or otherwise we declare as followeth:

That in whatsoever place, house, or ship, any of the said persons shall reside, be hid, or protected, we declare the owners, masters, or inhabitants of the said places, to be confederates and traitors to the people, and the estates of them, as also of all the aforesaid persons, to be confiscated; and this we the Commons of Virginia do declare, desiring a firm union amongst ourselves that we may jointly and with one accord defend ourselves against the common enemy: and let not the faults of the guilty be the reproach of the innocent, or the faults or crimes of the oppressors divide and separate us who have suffered by their oppressions.

These are therefore in his Majesty's name to command you forthwith to seize the persons above mentioned as traitors to the King and Country, and them to bring to Middle Plantation, and there to secure them until further order; and in case of opposition, if you want any further assistance, you are forthwith to demand it in the name of the people in all the counties of Virginia.

NATH. BACON,
General by consent of the People.

John Cotton of Queen's Creek (?)

❰ The "Burwell Papers," contemporary accounts of Bacon's Rebellion, were published in full for the first time in 1814, and were subsequently corrected and reprinted by the Massachusetts Historical Society in 1866. One of the papers, "The History of Bacon's and Ingram's Rebellion," existing in an anonymous manuscript, may have been the work of a Virginia planter, John Cotton. It contains two poems on Bacon, one of which was an epitaph presumably written by "the man that waited upon his person, as it is said." Whoever he was, the writer of the epitaph was a man who knew the English metaphysical poets and who himself had a real poetic talent. ❱

Bacon's Epitaph, Made by His Man

Death, why so cruel? What! no other way
To manifest thy spleen, but thus to slay
Our hopes of safety, liberty, our all,
Which, through thy tyranny, with him must fall
To its late chaos? Had thy rigid force
Been dealt by retail, and not thus in gross,

Grief had been silent. Now we must complain
Since thou, in him, hast more than thousand slain,
Whose lives and safeties did so much depend
On him their life, with him their lives must end.

If't be a sin to think Death bribed can be,
We must be guilty; say 'twas bribery
Guided the fatal shaft. Virginia's foes,
To whom for secret crimes just vengeance owes
Deserved plagues, dreading their just desert,
Corrupted Death by Paracelsian art
Him to destroy whose well-tried courage such,
Their heartless hearts, nor arms, nor strength could touch.

Who now must heal those wounds or stop that blood
The heathen made, and drew into a flood?
Who is't must plead our cause? nor trump, nor drum,
Nor deputations; these, alas! are dumb
And cannot speak. Our arms (though ne'er so strong)
Will want the aid of his commanding tongue,
Which conquered more than Caesar. He o'erthrew
Only the outward frame; this could subdue
The rugged words of nature. Souls replete
With dull chilled cold, he'd animate with heat
Drawn forth of reason's 'lembic. In a word,
Mars and Minerva both in him concurred
For arts, for arms, whose pen and sword alike,
As Cato's did, may admiration strike
Into his foes; while they confess withal
It was their guilt styled him a criminal.
Only this difference doth from truth proceed:
They in the guilt, he in the name must bleed,
While none shall dare his obsequies to sing
In deserved measures, until time shall bring
Truth crowned with freedom, and from danger free,
To sound his praises to posterity.

Here let him rest; while we this truth report:
He's gone from hence unto a higher court
To plead his cause, where he by this doth know
Whether to Caesar he was friend or foe.

WITCHES

A belief in the devil and in witches was universal in all classes of seventeenth-century American and European society. It was assumed that Satan really existed, and that he possessed an army of emissaries, some in human form, who harassed God's designs at every turn. Certain people, it was believed, by entering into "covenants" with him, were enabled to perform acts completely against reason, morals, and natural law; such witches should be prosecuted for offenses against God, state, and nature. Since New Englanders were (in their view, at least) God's chosen people, they made a choice target for Satan. In the late seventeenth century many colonists believed themselves hard put upon by the devil, who actively promoted Indian attacks, repressive royal government decrees, "backsliding" religion, paganism and irreverence, and wrangles within church and clergy. Between 1647 and 1662, fourteen people were executed for witchcraft in Massachusetts and Connecticut, but the fear then subsided until the 1680's, when the devil reappeared in Massachusetts. Books by Increase Mather and a number of other divines, recounting certain "memorable providences" and strange occurrences, strained an already tense situation. Finally at Salem, in 1691, a few little girls touched off an explosive witch-hunt by showing unmistakable signs of bewitchment and by scattering accusations right and left. From June to September, 1692, a court of seven judges held a series of trials that rocked the colony.

When the trials ended, twenty men and women and two dogs had been executed for witchcraft, fifty-five had confessed, one hundred and fifty were still imprisoned, and accusations had been leveled at two hundred more. A similar wave of panic had gripped other colonies, but only in Massachusetts were the convicted executed. But it must also be recognized that the Massachusetts authorities made every attempt to keep the trials within proper channels, that the events at Salem were but one part of a worldwide witchcraft scare, and that there were far more convictions and executions in the Old World than in the New.

It is still difficult to establish the blame. Quite unreasonably, posterity has centered responsibility for the Salem trials on Increase and Cotton Mather, as if two men, albeit powerful ones, could have dominated the courts and public opinion of the entire colony. During the trials both Mathers counseled caution, and Increase Mather stated that "it were better that ten suspected witches should escape, than that one innocent person should be condemned." At the same time it is clear that the court, chosen by Governor Phips and composed of honest and upright citizens, handled all the cases under established rules of English law with scrupulous regard for legal procedures. One can only conclude that the leaders of both church and state in Massachusetts succumbed for a time to mass hysteria, then regained their equilibrium and revised their ecclesiastical and legal procedures to prevent a recurrence. There were no more witchcraft incidents.

Roger Clap (1609–1691)

THAT Satan did indeed exist, and that he was responsible for all New England's troubles, both from within and from without, is neatly illustrated in the *Memoirs* (*c.* 1676) of Roger Clap, even before the witchcraft hysteria broke in the last decade of the century. Born in Devonshire, Clap emigrated to Massachusetts in 1630 and settled in Dorchester. He held a number of responsible posts in local government, served as a captain in the Pequot Indian Wars, and was the town's representative to General Court for several years. His memoirs, which were never intended to be anything but a private and personal record for his children (among whom were numbered Experience, Waitstill, Preserved, Hopestill, Wait, Thanks, Desire, Unite, and Supply) are an excellent example of the Puritan's overriding religious awareness and of the tone and temper of Puritan journal-writing.

TEXT: Roger Clap, *Memoirs,* ed. Thomas Prince (Boston, 1731).

Satan's Work in New England

[From *Memoirs* (*c.* 1676)]

I will now return unto what I began to hint unto you before; namely, that Satan and his instruments did malign us, and oppose our godly preachers, saying they were legal preachers, but themselves were for free grace and for the teachings of the Spirit; and they prevailed so by their flatteries and fair speeches, that they led away not only "silly women, laden with their lusts," but many men also, and some of strong parts too, who were not ashamed to give out that our ministers were but legal preachers, and so endeavored to bring up an evil report upon our faithful preachers, that they themselves might be in high esteem; and many of them would presume to preach in private houses, both men and women, much like the Quakers. They would talk of the Spirit, and of revelations by the Spirit, without the Word, as the Quakers do talk of the light within them, rejecting the holy scriptures. But God, by His servants assembled in a Synod at Cambridge, in 1637, did discover His truth most plainly, to the establishment of His people, and the changing of some, and to the recovery of not a few, which had been drawn away with their dissimulations. Thus God delivered His people out of the snare of the Devil at that time. Let us, and do you in your generations, bless the holy name of the Lord. "The snare is broken, and we and ours are delivered." There were some that not only stood out obstinate against the truth, but continually reviled both our godly ministers and magistrates, and greatly troubled our Israel. But, by order of the General Court, they were banished out of this jurisdiction; and then had the churches rest, and were multiplied.

Many years after this, Satan made another assault upon God's poor people here, by stirring up the Quakers to come amongst us, both men and women; who pretended holiness and perfection, saying they spake and acted by the Spirit and light within, which (as they say) is their guide; and most blasphemously said, that the light within is the Christ, the Saviour; and deceived many to their persuasion. But, blessed be God, the government and churches both did bear witness against them, and their loathsome and pernicious doctrine; for which they were banished out of this jurisdiction, not to return without license, upon pain of death. The reason of that law was, because God's people here, could not worship the true and living God, as He hath appointed us in our public assemblies, without being disturbed by them; and other weighty reasons, as the dangerousness of their opinions, etc. Some of them presumed to return, to the loss of their lives for breaking that law, which was made for our peace and safety. . . .

Now as Satan has been a lying spirit to deceive and ensnare the mind, to draw us from God by error, so hath he stirred up evil men to seek the hurt of this country. But God hath delivered His poor people here from time to time; sometimes by putting courage into our magistrates to punish those that did rebel; and sometimes God hath wrought for us by His providence other ways. Here was one Ratcliff spake boldly and wickedly against the government and governors here, using such words, as some judged deserved death. He was for his wickedness whipt, and had both his ears cut off in Boston, A.D. 1631; I saw it done. There was one Morton, that was a pestilent fellow, a troubler of the country, who did not only seek our hurt here, but went to

England, and did his utmost there, by false reports against our Governor; but God wrought for us, and saved us, and caused all his designs to be of none effect. There arose up against us one Bull, who went to the Eastward a trading, and turned pirate, and took a vessel or two, and plundered some planters thereabouts, and intended to return into the Bay, and do mischief to our magistrates here, in Dorchester and other places. But, as they were weighing anchor, one of Mr. Short's men shot from the shore, and struck the principal actor dead, and the rest were filled with fear and horror. They having taken one Anthony Dicks, a master of a vessel, did endeavor to persuade him to pilot them into Virginia; but he would not. They told him that they were filled with such fear and horror, that they were afraid of the very rattling of the ropes; this, Mr. Dicks told me with his own mouth. These men fled Eastward, and Bull himself got into England; but God destroyed this wretched man. . . .

About that time, or not long after, God permitted Satan to stir up the Pequot Indians to kill divers Englishmen, as Mr. Oldham, Mr. Tilly, and others; and when the murderers were demanded, instead of delivering them, they proceeded to destroy more of our English about Connecticut; which put us upon sending out soldiers, once and again, whom God prospered in their enterprises, until the Pequot people were destroyed.

Increase Mather (1639–1723)

INCREASE MATHER (*q.v.*, p. 104), in his attitude towards witchcraft, exemplifies the dangers of bringing high intellectual speculation and immense academic learning into the life-and-death arena of practical affairs. In 1681 he recalled a plan that had been in the air twenty-five years before — a plan for the systematic recording of "illustrious providences," showing the dramatic struggle between Satan and the Lord in the New World. He presented the plan to several ministers, who in May, 1681, determined to present to the world a collection of "such divine judgments, tempests, floods, earthquakes, thunders as are unusual, strange apparitions, or whatever else shall happen that is prodigious, witchcrafts, diabolical possessions, remarkable judgments upon noted sinners, eminent deliverances, and answers of prayer. . . ." No one was better suited to the work than Increase Mather, who brought out the first fruits of that project under the title *An Essay for the Recording of Illustrious Providences* (1684). He had read widely in all the ancient and contemporary authors on witchcraft, demons, and preternatural experience; was fully aware that many non-atheists who were also men of learning denied the existence of witches; and could even write, "It must, moreover, be sadly confessed, that many innocent persons have been put to death under the notion of witchcraft, whereby much innocent blood hath been shed. . . . Superstitious and magical ways of trying witches have been a bloody cause of those murders." Yet he collected and printed as fact stories like that of Ann Cole which follows. His book went through three editions the first year, preparing the way for the outbreaks of 1692.

TEXT: Increase Mather, *An Essay for the Recording of Illustrious Providences* (Boston, 1684).

A Remarkable Relation

[From *Illustrious Providences,* 1684]

Inasmuch as things which are preternatural, and not accomplished without diabolical operation, do more rarely happen, it is pity but that they should be observed. Several accidents of that kind have happened in New England, which I shall here faithfully relate, so far as I have been able to come unto the knowledge of them.

Very remarkable was that providence wherein Ann Cole of Hartford in New England was concerned. She was, and is accounted, a person of real piety and integrity; nevertheless, in the year 1662, then living in her father's house (who has likewise been esteemed a godly man), she was taken with very strange fits, wherein her tongue was improved by a demon to express things which she herself knew nothing of; sometimes the discourse would hold for a considerable time; the general purpose of which was, that such and such persons (who were named in the discourse which passed from her) were consulting how they might carry on mischievous designs against her and several others, mentioning sundry ways they should take for that end, particularly that they would afflict her body, spoil her name, etc. The general answer made amongst the demons was, "she runs to the rock." This having continued some hours, the demons said, "Let us confound her language, that she may tell no more tales." She uttered matters unintelligible. And then the discourse passed into a Dutch tone (a Dutch family then lived in the town), and therein an account was given of some afflictions that had befallen diverse; amongst others, what had befallen a woman that lived next neighbor to the Dutch family, whose arms had been strangely pinched in the night, declaring by whom and for what cause that course had been taken with her. The Reverend Mr. Stone (then teacher of the church in Hartford) being by, when the discourse happened, declared that he thought it impossible for one not familiarly acquainted with the Dutch (which Ann Cole had not in the least been) should so exactly imitate the Dutch tone in the pronunciation of English. Several worthy persons (viz., Mr. John Whiting, Mr. Samuel Hooker, and Mr. Joseph Haines) wrote the intelligible sayings expressed by Ann Cole, whilest she was thus amazingly handled. The event was, that one of the persons (whose name was Greensmith, being a lewd and ignorant woman, and then in prison on suspicion for witchcraft) mentioned in the discourse as an active in the mischief done and designed, was by the magistrate sent for; Mr. Whiting and Mr. Haines read what they had written, and the woman being astonished thereat, confessed those things to be true, and that she and other persons named in this preternatural discourse, had had familiarity with the devil. Being asked whether she had made an express covenant with him, she answered, she had not, only as she promised to go with him when he called, which accordingly she had sundry times done, and that the Devil told her at Christmas they would have a merry meeting, and then the covenant between them should be subscribed. The next day she was more particularly inquired of concerning her guilt respecting the crime she was accused with. She then acknowledged, that though when Mr. Haines began to read what he had taken down in writing, her rage was such that she could have torn him in pieces, and was as resolved as might be to deny her guilt (as she had done before), yet after he had read awhile, she was (to use her own expression) as if her flesh had been pulled from her bones, and so could not deny any longer: she likewise declared, that the Devil first appeared to her in the form of a deer or fawn, skipping about her, wherewith she was not much affrighted, and that by degrees he became very familiar, and at last would talk with her; moreover, she said that the Devil had frequently the carnal knowledge of her body; and that the witches had meetings at a place not far from her house; and that some appeared in one shape, and others in another; and one came flying amongst them in the shape of a crow. Upon this confession, with other concurrent evidence, the woman was executed; so likewise was her husband, though he did not acknowledge himself guilty. Other persons accused in the discourse made their escape. Thus doth the Devil use to serve his clients. After the suspected witches were either executed or fled, Ann Cole was restored to health, and has continued well for many years, approving herself a serious Christian.

There were some that had a mind to try whether the stories of witches not being able to sink under water were true; and accordingly a man and woman, mentioned in Ann Cole's Dutch-toned discourse, had their hands and feet tied, and so were cast into the water, and they both apparently swam after the manner of a buoy, part under, part above the water. A by-stander, imagining that any person bound in that posture would be so borne up, offered himself for trial; but being in the like manner gently laid on the water, he immediately sunk right down. This was no legal evidence against the suspected persons, nor were they proceeded against on any such account; however, doubting that an halter would choke them, though the waters would not, they very fairly took their flight, not having been seen in that part of the world since.

Cotton Mather (1663–1728)

COTTON MATHER was the grandson of John Cotton and Richard Mather, and the son of Increase Mather. Born thus into what was virtually a royal dynasty of Puritan theologians, great things were expected of him. He entered Harvard at twelve, took his B.A. at fifteen, his M.A. at eighteen, and was ordained at twenty-two. For a number of years associated with his father in the pastorate of the Second Church, Boston, young Mather soon became the acknowledged leader in late seventeenth-century New England theology, politics, and letters. A man of tremendous erudition, he wrote nearly five hundred books and pamphlets, mastered a dozen or more languages, interested himself in science, medicine, philanthropical works, politics, and literature, was elected a member of the Royal Society of London, and corresponded with scholars all over the world. Intensely religious and amazingly learned, Mather was conservative but not narrow; his reputation has suffered, not always fairly, from his involvement in the witchcraft controversy.

Five years after his father's *Illustrious Providences,* Cotton Mather continued the good work with a publication called *Memorable Providences Relating to Witchcraft and Possessions* (1689), which included a number of his personal observations. When the children of a family in his congregation showed signs of suffering from witchcraft, Mather took one of the girls into his own house so that he could study the problem carefully and closely, with scientific detachment. Through his counsel and help (which might be called psychiatric treatment today), the child recovered completely. After several "witches" had been tried and executed at Salem in 1692, Mather supported the trials by writing reviews of several typical cases, which he joined with a long and vehement sermon on witchcraft and sent to London, where they were published as *The Wonders of the Invisible World* (1692). His description of the trial of George Burroughs is typical.

TEXT: Cotton Mather, *The Wonders of the Invisible World* (London, 1692).

The Trial of George Burroughs

[From *The Wonders of the Invisible World,* 1692]

Glad should I have been, if I had never known the name of this man; or never had this occasion to mention so much as the first letters of his name. But the government requiring some account of his trial to be inserted in this book, it becomes me with all obedience to submit unto the order.

I. This G. B. was indicted for witchcrafts, and in the prosecution of the charge against him, he was accused by five or six of the bewitched, as the author of their miseries; he was accused by eight of the confessing witches, as being an head actor at some of their hellish rendezvous, and one who had the promise of being a king in Satan's kingdom, now going to be erected: he was accused by nine persons for extraordinary lifting, and such feats of strength, as could not be done without a diabolical assistance. And for other such things he was accused, until about thirty testimonies were brought in against him; nor were these judged the half of what might have been considered for his conviction: however they were enough to fix the character of a witch upon him, according to the rules of reasoning, by the judicious Gaule, in that case directed.

II. The court being sensible, that the testimonies of the parties bewitched use to have a room among the suspicions or presumptions, brought in against one indicted for witchcraft, there were now heard the testimonies of several persons, who were most notoriously bewitched, and every day tortured by invisible hands, and these now all charged the spectres of G. B. to have a share in their torments. At the examination of this G. B. the bewitched people were grievously harassed with preternatural mischiefs, which could not possibly be dissembled; and they still ascribed it unto the endeavors of G. B. to kill them. And now upon his trial, one of the bewitched persons testified, that in her agonies, a little black-haired man came to her, saying his name was B. and bidding her set her hand unto a book which he showed unto her; and bragging that he was a conjurer, above the ordinary rank of witches; that he often persecuted her with the offer of that book, saying, she should be well, and need fear nobody, if she would but sign it; but he inflicted cruel pains and hurts upon her, because of her denying so to do. The testimonies of the other sufferers concurred with these; and it was remarkable, that whereas biting was one of the ways which the witches used for the vexing of the sufferers, when they cried out of G. B. biting them, the print of the teeth would be seen on the flesh of the complainers, and just such a set of teeth as

G. B.'s would then appear upon them, which could be distinguished from those of some other men's. Others of them testified, that in their torments, G. B. tempted them to go unto a sacrament, unto which they perceived him with a sound of trumpet summoning of other witches, who quickly after the sound would come from all quarters unto the rendezvous. One of them falling into a kind of trance, afterwards affirmed, that G. B. had carried her into a very high mountain, where he showed her mighty and glorious kingdoms, and said, he would give them all to her, if she would write in his book; but she told him, they were none of his to give; and refused the motions, enduring of much misery for that refusal.

It cost the court a wonderful deal of trouble, to hear the testimonies of the sufferers; for when they were going to give in their depositions, they would for a long time be taken with fits, that made them uncapable of saying anything. The chief judge asked the prisoner, who he thought hindered these witnesses from giving their testimonies? and he answered, he supposed it was the Divel. That honorable person then replied, "How comes the Divel so loath to have any testimony borne against you?" which cast him into very great confusion.

III. It has been a frequent thing for the bewitched people to be entertained with apparitions of ghosts of murdered people, at the same time that the spectres of the witches trouble them. These ghosts do always affright the beholders more than all the other spectral representations; and when they exhibit themselves, they cry out, of being murdered by the witchcrafts or other violences of the persons who are then in spectre present. It is further considerable, that once or twice, these apparitions have been seen by others at the very same time that they have shewn themselves to the bewitched; and seldom have there been these apparitions but when something unusual and suspected had attended the death of the party thus appearing. Some that have been accused by these apparitions, accosting of the bewitched people, who had never heard a word of any such persons ever being in the world, have upon a fair examination freely and fully confessed the murders of those very persons, although these also did not know how the apparitions had complained of them. Accordingly several of the bewitched had given in their testimony, that they had been troubled with the apparitions of two women, who said that they were G. B.'s two wives, and that he had been the death of them; and that the magistrates must be told of it, before whom if B. upon his trial denied it, they did not know but that they should appear again in the court. Now, G. B. had been infamous for the barbarous usage of his two successive wives, all the country over. Moreover, it was testified, the spectre of G. B. threatening of the sufferers told them, he had killed (besides others) Mrs. Lawson and her daughter Ann. And it was noted, that these were the virtuous wife and daughter of one at whom this G. B. might have a prejudice for his being serviceable at Salem Village, from whence himself had in ill terms removed some years before: and that when they died, which was long since, there were some odd circumstances about them, which made some of the attendants there suspect something of witchcraft, though none imagined from what quarter it should come.

Well, G. B. being now upon his trial, one of the bewitched persons was cast into horror at the ghosts of B.'s two deceased wives then appearing before him, and crying for vengeance against him. Hereupon several of the bewitched persons were successively called in, who all not knowing what the former had seen and said, concurred in their horror of the apparition, which they affirmed that he had before him. But he, though much appalled, utterly denied that he discerned anything of it; nor was it any part of his conviction.

IV. Judicious writers have assigned it a great place in the conviction of witches, when persons are impeached by other notorious witches, to be as ill as themselves; especially, if the persons have been much noted for neglecting the worship of God. Now, as there might have been testimonies enough of G. B.'s antipathy to prayer and the other ordinances of God, though by his profession singularly obliged thereunto; so, there now came in against the prisoner the testimonies of several persons, who confessed their own having been horrible witches, and ever since their confessions had been themselves terribly tortured by the divels and other witches, even like the other sufferers; and therein undergone the pains of many deaths for their confessions.

These now testified, that G. B. had been at witch meetings with them; and that he was the person who had seduced and compelled them into the snares of witchcraft: that he promised them fine clothes, for doing it; that he brought puppets to them, and thorns to stick into those puppets, for the afflicting of other people; and that he exhorted them, with the rest of the crew, to bewitch all Salem Village, but be sure to do it gradually, if they would prevail in what they did.

When the Lancashire witches were condemned, I don't remember that there was any considerable further evidence, than that of the bewitched, and then that of some that confessed. We see so much already against G. B. But this being indeed not enough, there were other things to render what had already been produced credible.

V. A famous divine recites this among the convictions of a witch; the testimony of the party bewitched, whether pining or dying; together with the joint oaths of sufficient persons that have seen certain prodigious pranks or feats wrought by the party accused. Now God had been pleased so to leave this G. B. that he had ensnared himself by several instances, which he had formerly given of a preternatural strength, and which were now produced against him. He was a very puny man; yet he had often done things beyond the strength of a giant. A gun of about seven foot barrel, and so heavy that strong men could not steadily hold it out with both hands; there were several testimonies, given in by persons of credit and honor, that he made nothing of taking up such a gun behind the lock, with but one hand, and holding it out like a pistol, at arm's end. G. B. in his vindication was so foolish as to say, that an Indian was there, and held it out at the same time: whereas, none of the spectators ever saw any such Indian; but they supposed the Black Man (as the witches call the Divel; and they generally say he resembles an Indian) might give him that assistance. There was evidence likewise brought in, that he made nothing of taking up whole barrels filled with molasses or cider, in very disadvantageous postures, and carrying of them through the difficultest places out of a canoe to the shore.

Yea, there were two testimonies that G. B. with only putting the forefinger of his right hand into the muzzle of an heavy gun, a fowling-piece of about six or seven foot barrel, did lift up the gun, and hold it out at arm's end; a gun which the deponents though strong men could not with both hands lift up, and hold out at the butt end, as is usual. Indeed, one of these witnesses was over persuaded by some persons to be out of the way upon G. B.'s trial; but he came afterwards with sorrow for his withdraw, and gave in his testimony: nor were either of these witnesses made use of as evidences in the trial.

VI. There came in several testimonies relating to the domestic affairs of G. B. which had a very hard aspect upon him; and not only proved him a very ill man; but also confirmed the belief of the character, which had been already fastened on him.

'Twas testified, that keeping his two successive wives in a strange kind of slavery, he would when he came home from abroad pretend to tell the talk which any had with them; that he has brought them to the point of death, by his harsh dealings with his wives, and then made the people about him to promise that in case death should happen, they would say nothing of it; that he used all means to make his wives write, sign, seal, and swear a covenant, never to reveal any of his secrets; that his wives had privately complained unto the neighbors about frightful apparitions of evil spirits, with which their house was sometimes infested; and that many such things have been whispered among the neighborhood. There were also some other testimonies, relating to the death of people, whereby the consciences of an impartial jury were convinced that G. B. had bewitched the persons mentioned in the complaints. But I am forced to omit several passages, in this, as well as in all the succeeding trials, because the scribes who took notice of them, have not supplied me.

VII. One Mr. Ruck, brother-in-law to this G. B., testified, that G. B. and he himself, and his sister, who was G. B.'s wife, going out for two or three miles to gather strawberries, Ruck with his sister the wife of G. B. rode home very softly, with G. B. on foot in their company. G. B. stepped aside a little into the bushes; whereupon they halted and hallooed for him. He not answering, they went away homewards, with a quickened pace, without any expectation of seeing him in a considerable while; and yet when they were got near home, to their astonishment they found him on foot with them, having a basket of strawberries. G. B. immediately then fell to chiding his wife, on the account of what she had been speaking to her brother, of him, on the road: which when they wondered at, he said, he knew their thoughts. Ruck being startled at that, made some reply, intimating that the Divel himself did not know so far; but G. B. answered, "My God makes known your thoughts unto me." The prisoner now at the bar had nothing to answer, unto what was thus witnessed against him, that was worth considering. Only he said, Ruck and his wife left a man with him, when they left him. Which Ruck now affirmed to be false; and when the court asked G. B. what the man's name was? his countenance was much altered; nor could he say, who 'twas. But the court began to think, that he then stepped aside, only that by the assistance of the Black Man, he might put on his invisibility, and in that fascinating mist, gratify his own jealous humour, to hear what they said of him. Which trick of rend'ring themselves invisible, our witches do in their confessions pretend that they sometimes are masters of; and it is the more credible, because there is demonstration that they often render many other things utterly invisible.

VIII. Falt'ring, faulty, unconstant, and contrary answers upon judicial and deliberate examination, are counted some unlucky symptoms of guilt, in all crimes, especially in witchcrafts. Now there never was a prisoner more eminent for them, than G. B. both at his examination and on his trial. His tergiversations, contradictions, and falsehoods, were very sensible: he had little to say, but that he had heard some things that he could not prove, reflecting upon the reputation of some of the witnesses. Only he gave in a paper to the jury; wherein, although he had many times before granted, not only that there are witches, but also that the present sufferings of the country are the effect of horrible witchcrafts, yet he now goes to evince it, that there neither are, nor ever were witches, that having made a compact with the Divel, can send a divel to torment other people at a distance. This paper was transcribed out of Ady; which the court presently knew, as soon as they heard it. But he said, he had taken none of it out of any book; for which, his evasion afterwards was, that a gentleman gave him the discourse in a manuscript, from whence he transcribed it.

IX. The jury brought him in guilty. But when he came to die, he utterly denied the fact, whereof he had been thus convicted.

Robert Calef (1648–1719)

WHILE Increase and Cotton Mather busily documented the evidence against the "witches," Robert Calef, a Boston merchant, carefully recorded the events of the trials and the testimonies, petitions, and pleas of the accused. He waited until 1697 when both judges and jurors expressed remorse and contrition for the parts they played in the trials, and then sent his assembled materials to London for publication. There they appeared in 1700 under the sarcastic title *More Wonders of the Invisible World.* Not denying that witches really exist, Calef argued that the Bible provided no clear evidence for establishing whether or not a person actually was a witch and that therefore the trials were unjustifiable and ministers like Increase and Cotton Mather were responsible for murder by going beyond Biblical evidence. Calef's bitterness is heightened by the cool restraint with which he recounts the events and presents his evidence, even, for example, Sarah Good's "curse" of one of the ministers: "God will give you blood to drink!" which Nathaniel Hawthorne later used as a basic element of *The House of the Seven Gables.* When *More Wonders* appeared, Cotton Mather angrily supervised the publication of *Some Few Remarks upon a Scandalous Book* (1701), a slashing attack on Calef that devotes only ten or twelve of its seventy-one pages to the embarrassing subject of witchcraft.

TEXT: Robert Calef, *More Wonders of the Invisible World* (London, 1700).

A Warning

To the Ministers in and Near Boston, January 12, 1696

[From *More Wonders of the Invisible World,* Part II, 1700]

Christianity had been but a short time in the world, when there was raised against it, not only open professed enemies, but secret and inbred underminers, who sought thereby to effect that which open force had been so often baffled in. And notwithstanding that primitive purity and sincerity, which in some good measure was still retained; yet the cunning deceivers and apostate heretics found opportunity to beguile the unwary, and this in fundamentals.

Among others which then sprung up, with but too much advantage in the third century, the Manichee did spread his pestiferous sentiments, and taught the existence of two beings, or causes of all things, viz., a good and a bad: but these were soon silenced by the more orthodox doctors, and anathematized by general councils. And at this day the American Indians, another sort of Manichee, entertaining (thus far) the same belief, hold it their prudence and interest to please that evil being, as well by perpetrating other murders, as by their bloody sacrifices, that so he may not harm them. The iron teeth of time have now almost devoured the name of the former; and as to the latter, it is to be hoped that as Christianity prevails among them, they will abhor such abominable belief.

And as those primitive times were not privileged against the spreading of dangerous heresy, so neither can any now pretend to any such immunity, though professing the enjoyment of a primitive purity.

Might a judgment be made from the books of the modern learned divines, or from the practice of courts, or from the faith of many, who call themselves Christians, it might be modestly, though sadly concluded, that the doctrine of the Manichee, at least great part of it, is so far from being forgotten that 'tis almost everywhere professed. We in these ends of the earth need not seek far for instances, in each respect to demonstrate this. The books here printed, and recommended, not only by the respective authors, but by many of their brethren, do set forth that the devil inflicts plagues, wars, diseases, tempests, and can render the most solid things invisible, and can do things above and against the course of nature, and all natural causes.

Are these the expressions of orthodox believers? or are they not rather expressions becoming a Manichee, or a heathen, as agreeing far better with these than with the sacred oracles, our only rule? the whole current whereof is so diametrically opposite thereto, that it were almost endless to mention all the divine cautions against such abominable belief. . . .

These places, with a multitude more, do abundantly testify that the asserters of such power to be in the evil being, do speak in a dialect different from the scriptures (laying a firm foundation for the Indians' adorations, which agrees well with what A. Ross sets forth, in his *Mistagogus Poeticus,* p. 116, that their ancients did worship the furies and their god *Averinci,* that they might forbear to hurt them).

And have not the courts in some parts of the world, by their practice, testified their concurrence with such belief; prosecuting to death many people upon that notion, of their improving such power of the evil one, to the raising of storms; afflicting and killing of others, though at great distance from them; doing things in their own persons above human strength; destroying of cattle, flying in the air, turning themselves into cats or dogs, etc., which by the way must needs imply something of goodness to be in that evil being, who, though he has such power, would not exert it, were it not for this people, or else that they can some way add to this mighty power.

And are the people a whit behind in their beliefs? Is there anything (above mentioned) their strong faith looks upon to be too hard for this evil being to effect?

Here it will be answered, God permits it. Which answer is so far an owning the doctrine, that the Devil has in his nature a power to do all these things, and can exert this power, except when he is restrained, which is in effect to say that God has made nature to fight against itself. That he has made a creature, who has it in the power of his nature to overthrow nature, and to act above and against it. Which he that can believe may as well believe the greatest contradiction. That being which can do this in the smallest thing, can do it in the greatest. If Moses, with a bare permission, might stretch forth his rod, yet he was not able to bring plagues upon the Egyptians, or to divide the waters, without a commission from the Most High; so neither can that evil being perform any of this without a commission from the same power. The scripture recites more miracles wrought by men than by angels good and bad. Though this doctrine be so dishonorable to the only Almighty Being, as to ascribe such attributes to the evil one, as are the incommunicable prerogative of Him, who is the alone Sovereign Being, yet here is not all: but as he that steers by a false compass, the further he sails the more he is out of his way; so though there is in some things a variation from, there is in others a further progression in, or building upon the said doctrine of the Manichee.

Men in this age are not content barely to believe such an exorbitant power to be in the nature of this evil being; but have imagined that he prevails with many to sign a book, or make a contract with him, whereby they are enabled to perform all the things above mentioned. Another account is given hereof, viz., that by virtue of such a covenant they attain power to commissionate him. And though the two parties are not agreed which to put it upon, whether the devil impowers the witch, or the witch commissionates him; yet both parties are agreed in this, that one way or other the mischief is effected, and so the criminal becomes culpable of death. In the search after such a sort of criminals, how many countries have fallen into such convulsions, that the devastations made by a conquering enemy, nor the plague itself, has not been so formidable.

That not only good persons have thus been blemished in their reputations, but much innocent blood hath been shed, is testified even by those very books: *Cases of Conscience,* p. 33. *Remarkable Provid.* p. 179. *Memor. Provid.* p. 28.

And (to add) what less can be expected, when men, having taken up such a belief, of a covenanting, afflicting, and killing witch, and, comparing it with the scripture, finding no footsteps therein of such a sort of witch, have thereupon desperately concluded; that, though the scripture is full in it, that a witch should not live, yet that it has not at all described the crime, nor means whereby the culpable might be detected?

And hence they are fallen so far as to reckon it necessary to make use of those diabolical and bloody ways, always heretofore practiced, for their discovery. As finding that the rules, given to detect other crimes, are wholly useless for the discovery of such.

This is that which has produced that deluge of blood mentioned, and must certainly do so again, the same belief remaining.

And who can wonder, if Christians that are so easily prevailed with to lay aside their swords as useless, and so have lost their strength (as with Samson), they are led blindfold into an idol temple, to make sport for enemies and infidels, and to do abominable actions, not only not Christian, but against even the light of nature and reason? And now, reverend fathers, you who are appointed as guides to the people, and whose lips should preserve knowledge; who are set as shepherds, and as watchmen; this matter appertains to you. I did write to you formerly upon this head, and acquainted you with my sentiments, requesting that, if I erred, you would be pleased to shew it me by scripture; but from your silence, I gather that you approve thereof. For I may reasonably presume, that you would have seen it your duty to have informed me better, if you had been sensible of any error. But if in this matter you have acquitted yourselves becoming the titles you are dignified with, you have cause of rejoicing in the midst of the calamities that afflict a sinning world.

Particularly, if you have taught the people to fear God, and trust in Him, and not to fear a witch or a devil; that the Devil has no power to afflict any with diseases, or loss of cattle, etc., without a commission from the Most High; that he is so filled with malice, that whatever commission he may have against any, he will not fail to execute it; that no mortal ever was, or can be able to commissionate him, or to lengthen his chain in the least, and that he who can commissionate him is God; and that the scriptures of truth not only assign the punishment of a witch, but give sufficient rules to detect them by; and that (according to Mr. Gaul's fourth head) a witch is one that hates and opposes the Word, work, and worship of God, and seeks by a sign to seduce therefrom; that they who are guilty according to that head, are guilty of witchcraft, and by the law given by Moses, were to be put to death. If you have taught the people the necessity of charity, and the evil of entertaining so much as a jealousy against their neighbors for such crimes, upon the Devil's suggestions to a person pretending to a spectral (or diabolical) sight; who utter their oracles from malice, frenzy, or a Satanical delusion; that to be inquisitive of such, whose spectres they see, or who it is that afflicts, in order to put the accused person's life in question, is a wickedness beyond what Saul was guilty of in going to the witch. That to consult with the dead, by the help of such as pretend to this spectral sight, and so to get information against the life of any person, is the worst sort of necromancy; that the pretending to drive away spectres, i.e., devils, with the hand, or by striking these to wound a person at a distance, cannot be without witchcraft, as pretending to a sign in order to deceive in matters of so high a nature; that 'tis ridiculous to think, by making laws against feeding, employing, or rewarding of evil spirits, thereby to get rid of them; that their natures require not sucking to support it.

That it is a horrid injury and barbarity to search those parts, which even nature itself commands the concealing of, to find some excrescence to be called a teat for those to suck; which yet is said sometimes to appear as a fleabite. Finally if you have taught the people what to believe and practice, as to the probation of the accused, by their saying or not saying the Lord's prayer; and as to praying that the afflicted may be able to accuse; and have not shunned in these matters to declare the whole mind of God; you have then well acquitted yourselves (in time of general defection) as faithful watchmen. But if instead of this, you have, some by word and writing propagated, others recommended, such writings, and abetted the false notions, which are so prevalent in this apostate age, it is high time to consider it. If when authority found themselves almost nonplussed in such prosecutions, and sent to you for your advice what they ought to do, and you have then thanked them for what they had already done (and thereby encouraged them to proceed in those very by-paths already fallen into) it so much the [more] nearly concerns you.

To conclude, this whole people are invited and commanded to humble their souls before God, as for other causes, so for the errors that may have been fallen into in these prosecutions on either hand, and to pray that God would teach us what we know not, and help us wherein we have done amiss, that we may do so no more.

This more immediately concerns yourselves, for 'tis not supposed to be intended, that God would shew us these things by inspiration, but that such who are called to it, should shew the mind of God in these things on both hands; i.e., whether there has been any error in excess or deficiency, or neither in the one nor the other. And if you do not thus far serve the public, you need not complain of great sufferings and unrighteous discouragements, if people do not applaud your conduct, as you might otherways have expected. But if you altogether hold your peace at such a time as this is, your silence, at least seemingly, will speak this language; that you are not concerned, though men ascribe the power and province of the Almighty to the worst of His creatures. That if other ages or countries improve the doctrines and examples given them, either to the taking away of the life or reputations of innocents, you are well satisfied. Which that there may be no shadow of a reason to believe but that your conduct herein may remove all such jealousies, and that God be with you in declaring His whole mind to the people, is the earnest desire and prayer of, reverend sirs, yours to my utmost,

R. C.

[From Part V, "An Impartial Account of the Most Memorable Matters of Fact"]

The 30th of June, the court according to adjournment again sat; five more were tried, viz., Sarah Good and Rebecca Nurse of Salem Village, Susanna Martin of Amsbury, Elizabeth How of Ipswich, and Sarah Wildes of Topsfield; these were all condemned that sessions, and were all executed on the 19th of July.

At the trial of Sarah Good, one of the afflicted fell in a fit, and after coming out of it, she cried out of the prisoner, for stabbing her in the breast with a knife, and that she had broken the knife in stabbing of her; accordingly a piece of the blade of a knife was found about her. Immediately information being given to the court, a young man was called, who produced a haft and part of the blade, which the court having viewed and compared, saw it to be the same. And upon inquiry the young man affirmed, that yesterday he happened to break that knife, and that he cast away the upper part, this afflicted person being then present. The young man was dismissed, and she was bidden by the court not to tell lies; and was improved (after as she had been before) to give evidence against the prisoners.

At execution, Mr. Noyes urged Sarah Good to confess, and told her she was a witch, and she knew she was a witch, to which she replied, "You are a liar; I am no more a witch than you are a wizard, and if you take away my life, God will give you blood to drink." . . .

August 5. The court again sitting, six more were tried on the same account, viz., Mr. George Burroughs, sometime minister of Wells, John Proctor, and Elizabeth Proctor his wife, with John Willard of Salem Village, George Jacobs, Senior, of Salem, and Martha Carrier of Andover; these were all brought in guilty, and condemned; and were all executed, August 19, except Proctor's wife, who pleaded pregnancy.

Mr. Burroughs was carried in a cart with the others, through the streets of Salem to execution; when he was upon the ladder, he made a speech for the clearing of his innocency, with such solemn and serious expressions, as were to the admiration of all present; his prayer (which he concluded by repeating the Lord's prayer) was so well worded, and uttered with such composedness, and such (at least seeming) fervency of spirit, as was very affecting, and drew tears from many (so that it seemed to some that the spectators would hinder the execution). The accusers said the Black Man stood and dictated to him; as soon as he was turned off, Mr. Cotton Mather, being mounted upon a horse, addressed himself to the people, partly to declare that he was no ordained minister, and partly to possess the people of his guilt; saying, that the Devil has often been transformed into an angel of light; and this did somewhat appease the people, and the executions went on; when he was cut down, he was dragged by the halter to a hole, or grave, between the rocks, about two foot deep, his shirt and breeches being pulled off, and an old pair of trowsers of one executed, put on his lower parts, he was so put in, together with Willard and Carrier, one of his hands and his chin, and a foot of one of them being left uncovered. . . .

And now nineteen persons having been hanged, and one prest to death, and eight more condemned, in all twenty and eight, of which above a third part were members of some of the churches in New England, and more than half of them of a good conversation in general, and not one cleared; about fifty having confessed themselves to be witches, of which not one executed; above an hundred and fifty in prison, and above two hundred more accused; the special commission of oyer and terminer comes to a period, which has no other foundation than the governor's commission; and had proceeded in the manner of swearing witnesses, viz., by holding up the hand (and by receiving evidences in writing), according to the ancient usage of this country; as also having their indictments in English. In the trials, when any were indicted for afflicting, pining, and wasting the bodies of particular persons by witchcraft, it was usual to hear evidence of matter foreign, and of perhaps twenty or thirty years standing, about oversetting carts, the death of cattle, unkindness to relations, or unexpected accidents befalling after some quarrel. Whether this was admitted by the law of England, or by what other law, wants to be determined; the executions seemed mixed, in pressing to death for not pleading, which most agrees with the laws of England, and sentencing women to be hanged for witchcraft, according to the former practice of this country, and not by burning, as is said to have been the law of England. And though the confessing witches were many, yet not one of them that confessed their own guilt, and abode by their confession, were put to death. . . .

Samuel Sewall (1652–1730)

BEFORE citing the confession of error written by the jurors, Robert Calef wrote in *More Wonders of the Invisible World,* "Upon the day of the fast, in the full assembly at the south meeting house in Boston, one of the honorable judges, who had sat in judicature in Salem, delivered in a paper, and while it was in reading, stood up; but the copy being not to be obtained at present, it can only be reported by memory to this effect, viz., it was to desire the prayers of God's people for him and his; and that God having visited his family, etc., he was apprehensive that he might have fallen into some errors in the matters at Salem, and pray that the guilt of such miscarriages may not be imputed either to the country in general, or to him or his family in particular." The "paper" to which Calef refers is contained in a *Diary* entry of Samuel Sewall (*q.v.*, p. 83), one of the Salem judges. Dated January 14, 1697, it follows a series of entries that reveal both the Judge's increasing sense of guilt and a number of personal trials, among them the death and sickness of his children.

TEXT: *Coll. Mass. Hist. Soc.*, 5th ser., V (1878), 445.

The Judge's Confession

[From *Diary* (1697)]

Copy of the bill I put up on the fast day; giving it to Mr. Willard as he passed by, and standing up at the reading of it, and bowing when finished; in the afternoon.

Samuel Sewall, sensible of the reiterated strokes of God upon himself and family; and being sensible, that as to the guilt contracted upon the opening of the late commission of oyer and terminer at Salem (to which the order for this day relates) he is, upon many accounts, more concerned than any that he knows of, desires to take the blame and shame of it, asking pardon of men, and especially desiring prayers that God, who has an unlimited authority, would pardon that sin and all other his sins; personal and relative: and according to His infinite benignity, and sovereignty, not visit the sin of him, or of any other, upon himself or any of his, nor upon the land: but that He would powerfully defend him against all temptations to sin, for the future; and vouchsafe him the efficacious, saving conduct of His Word and Spirit.

Parsley Wreaths and Bays

In her "Prologue" to *The Tenth Muse Lately Sprung Up in America,* Anne Bradstreet pleaded,

> And O ye high-flown quills that soar the skies,
> And ever with your prey still catch your praise,
> If e'er you deign these lowly lines your eyes,
> Give thyme or parsley wreath; I ask no bays.
> This mean and unrefined ore of mine
> Will make your glistering gold but more to shine.

In a way her plea stands for all of colonial verse — modest in attempt, but making no claims beyond its ability to perform; provincial, but not ignorant of English literary accomplishment at home; seeking favor, yet realistically self-critical. Grotesquely metaphysical in its mixture of supernatural and commonplace, often mundane and even journalistic in its details and occasions, minding the moment with one eye on eternity, meditative and formal rather than sensuous and imagistic, and focused on meaning rather than event, it nonetheless rises occasionally to snatch a grace beyond the fantastic puns and bookish mythology that distinguish its art. Colonial poetry is in fact a limited poetry — but, in its persistent concern with human character and human values, limited in a way that deserves our attention as it shaped the writers' achievement.

The Bay Psalm Book (1640)

ONE of the most important innovations of the Reformation was the singing of psalms by the whole congregation rather than by a choir alone. A number of metrical versions of the Psalms were made the better to adapt them to group singing; the version most widely used by the English Puritans was the Sternhold-Hopkins translation of the mid-sixteenth century. There were, however, objections to this translation; furthermore, the American Puritans wanted their own. Certain "chief divines" of Massachusetts Bay undertook a new "plain and familiar translation" published at Cambridge, Massachusetts, in 1640. Titled *The Whole Booke of Psalms Faithfully Translated into English Metre,* but better known as "The Bay Psalm Book," this has the distinction of being the first book in English printed in North America. The editors, none of whom claimed to be poets, faced a threefold problem in their translation: it had to be an accurate literal rendering of the Biblical meaning; it had to be in a form suitable for church singing; and it had to be simple, dignified, and unadorned in style, lest the meaning be obscured by embellishment. Working within this mandate, the translators, carefully watched by the Hebrew and Greek experts Richard Mather, Thomas Welde, and John Eliot, succeeded quite well in their purpose, and not without a little art. The Bay Psalm Book remained in common use for more than a century and a half in New England, until replaced by Watts's hymns. The preface, long attributed to Richard Mather, was written by John Cotton, who almost certainly also translated the Twenty-third Psalm.

TEXT: *The Whole Book of Psalms* (Cambridge, 1640).

Preface

. . . As for the scruple that some take at the translation of the book of psalms into meter, because David's psalms were sung in his own words without meter: we answer — First. There are many verses together in several psalms of David which run in rhythms (as those that know the Hebrew and as Buxtorf shews *Thesau.*, p. 629), which shews at least the lawfulness of singing psalms in English rhythms.

Secondly. The psalms are penned in such verses as are suitable to the poetry of the Hebrew language, and not in the common style of such other books of the Old Testament as are not poetical. Now no Protestant doubteth but that all the books of the scripture should by God's ordinance be extant in the mother tongue of each nation, that they may be understood of all; hence the psalms are to be translated into our English tongue. And if in our English tongue we are to sing them, then as all our English songs (according to the course of our English poetry) do run in meter, so ought David's psalms to be translated into meter, that so we may sing the Lord's songs, as in our English tongue so in such verses as are familiar to an English ear — which are commonly metrical: and as it can be no just offense to any good conscience to sing David's Hebrew songs in English words, so neither to sing his poetical verses in English poetical meter: men might as well stumble at singing the Hebrew psalms in our English tunes (and not in the Hebrew tunes) as at singing them in English meter (which are our verses) and not in such verses as are generally used by David according to the poetry of the Hebrew language: but the truth is, as the Lord hath hid from us the Hebrew tunes, lest we should think ourselves bound to imitate them; so also the course and frame (for the most part) of their Hebrew poetry, that we might not think ourselves bound to imitate that, but that every nation without scruple might follow as the graver sort of tunes of their own country songs, so the graver sort of verses of their own country poetry.

Neither let any think, that for the meter sake we have taken liberty or poetical license to depart from the true and proper sense of David's words in the Hebrew verses. No, but it hath been one part of our religious care and faithful endeavor, to keep close to the original text. . . .

If therefore the verses are not always so smooth and elegant as some may desire or expect; let them consider that God's altar needs not our polishings: . . . for we have respected rather a plain translation, then to smooth our verses with the sweetness of any paraphrase, and so have attended conscience rather then elegance, fidelity rather then poetry, in translating the Hebrew words into English language, and David's poetry into English meter; that so we may sing in Sion the Lord's songs of praise according to His own will; until He take us from hence, and wipe away all our tears, and bid us enter into our Master's joy to sing eternal halleluiahs.

Psalm 19

To the Chief Musician a Psalm of David

The heavens do declare
  The majesty of God:
Also the firmament shews forth
  His handy-work abroad.

Day speaks to day, knowledge
  Night hath to night declared.
There neither speech nor language is,
  Where their voice is not heard.
Through all the earth their line
  Is gone forth, and unto
The utmost end of all the world,
  Their speeches reach also:
A tabernacle He
  In them pitcht for the Sun.
Who bridegroom like from's chamber goes
  Glad giants' race to run.
From heaven's utmost end,
  His course and compassing;
To ends of it, and from the heat
  Thereof is hid nothing.

Psalm 23, A Psalm of David

The Lord to me a shepherd is,
  Want therefore shall not I.
He in the folds of tender-grass,
  Doth cause me down to lie:
To waters calm me gently leads
  Restore my soul doth He:
He doth in paths of righteousness:
  For His name's sake lead me.
Yea though in valley of death's shade
  I walk, none ill I'll fear:
Because Thou art with me, Thy rod,
  And staff my comfort are.
For me a table Thou hast spread,
  In presence of my foes:
Thou dost anoint my head with oil,
  My cup it overflows.
Goodness and mercy surely shall
  All my days follow me:
And in the Lord's house I shall dwell
  So long as days shall be.

Anne Bradstreet (1612–1672)

ANNE BRADSTREET was the daughter of one governor of Massachusetts Bay, Thomas Dudley, and the wife of Simon Bradstreet, another. Born in Lincoln, England, she married at sixteen and came to Massachusetts with her husband in 1630 to settle a lonely frontier farm on the Merrimac River. In time stolen from her duties as mother of eight children and wife of a prominent public official, she wrote poetry of such merit that her brother-in-law took some of her manuscripts to England, without her knowledge, for publication. They appeared in 1650 as *The Tenth Muse Lately Sprung Up in America. Or Several Poems, Compiled with Great Variety of Wit and Learning, etc.*, a pretentious title not of her choosing. The bulk of this volume was made up of "quaternions," semi-dramatic pieces dealing with the four elements, the four humours, the four ages of man, the four seasons, and the four monarchies, often didactic and dull, but occasionally marked with the author's own warmth and personality. Until around 1666 she worked at revising the poems, and added others, but the second edition, *Several Poems Compiled with Great Variety of Wit and Learning, Full of Delight,* was not published until after her death. In 1867 John Harvard Ellis' fine edition of Mistress Bradstreet's *Works* brought into print, for the first time, still other poems, including "As Weary Pilgrim" and "To My Dear and Loving Husband."

The Tenth Muse was the first significant volume of American verse. True, much of Mistress Bradstreet's work was derivative, influenced by Spenser, Quarles, and especially by Joshua Sylvester's translations of the French religious poet Du Bartas. But despite occasional lapses into the prosaic and the didactic, Anne Bradstreet's verse displays a skill with language, a sensitivity to nature, art, and daily experience, and a genuine poetic feeling unusual among Puritans. Certainly no English female contemporary was her equal, and even so crabbed a critic as Nathaniel Ward admitted her charm.

TEXTS: Anne Bradstreet, *Several Poems* (Boston, 1678); "Before the Birth of One of Her Children," "As Weary Pilgrim," and "To My Dear and Loving Husband" are from John Harvard Ellis, ed., *The Works of Anne Bradstreet in Prose and Verse* (Charlestown, 1867).

The Four Seasons of the Year

[From *The Tenth Muse,* 1650]

SPRING

Another four I've left yet to bring on,
Of four times four the last quaternion,
The winter, summer, autumn, and the spring,
In season all these seasons I shall bring:
Sweet Spring like man in his minority,
At present claimed, and had priority.
With smiling face and garments somewhat green,
She trimmed her locks, which late had frosted been,
Nor hot nor cold, she spake, but with a breath,
Fit to revive, the numbed earth from death.
Three months (quoth she) are 'lotted to my share
March, April, May of all the rest most fair.
Tenth of the first, Sol into Aries enters,
And bids defiance to all tedious winters,
Crosseth the line, and equals night and day,
(Still adds to th' last till after pleasant May)
And now makes glad the darkned Northern wights
Who for some months have seen but starry lights.
Now goes the plowman to his merry toil,
He might unloose his winter locked soil:
The seedsman too, doth lavish out his grain,
In hope the more he casts, the more to gain:
The gard'ner now superfluous branches lops,
And poles erects for his young clambring hops.
Now digs, then sows his herbs, his flowers, and roots
And carefully manures his trees of fruits.
The Pleiades their influence now give,
And all that seemed as dead afresh doth live.
The croaking frogs, whom nipping winter killed
Like birds now chirp, and hop about the field,
The nightingale, the black-bird, and the thrush
Now tune their lays, on sprays of every bush.
The wanton frisking kid, and soft-fleeced lambs
Do jump and play before their feeding dams,
The tender tops of budding grass they crop,
They joy in what they have, but more in hope:
For though the frost hath lost his binding power,
Yet many a fleece of snow and stormy shower
Doth darken Sol's bright eye, makes us remember
The pinching Northwest wind of cold December.

My second month is April, green and fair,
Of longer days, and a more temperate air:
The sun in Taurus keeps his residence,
And with his warmer beams glanceth from thence.
This is the month whose fruitful showers produces
All set and sown for all delights and uses:
The pear, the plum, and apple tree now flourish,
The grass grows long the hungry beast to nourish.
The primrose pale, and azure violet
Among the virduous grass hath nature set,
That when the sun on's love (the earth) doth shine
These might as lace set out her garment fine.
The fearful bird his little house now builds
In trees and walls, in cities and in fields.
The outside strong, the inside warm and neat;
A natural artificer complete.
The clocking hen her chirping chickens leads,
With wings and beak defends them from the gleads.
My next and last is fruitful pleasant May,
Wherein the earth is clad in rich array,
The sun now enters loving Gemini,
And heats us with the glances of his eye,
Our thicker raiment makes us lay aside,
Lest by his favor we be torrified.
All flowers the sun now with his beams discloses,
Except the double pinks and matchless roses.
Now swarms the busy, witty, honey-bee,
Whose praise deserves a page from more then me;
The cleanly huswife's dairy's now in th' prime,
Her shelves and firkins filled for winter time.
The meads with cowslips, honeysuckles dight,
One hangs his head, the other stands upright:
But both rejoice at th' heaven's clear smiling face,
More at her showers, which water them a space.
For fruits my season yields the early cherry,
The hasty peas, and wholesome cool strawberry.
More solid fruits require a longer time,
Each season hath his fruit, so hath each clime:
Each man his own peculiar excellence,
But none in all that hath preheminence.
Sweet fragrant Spring, with thy short pittance fly,
Let some describe thee better then can I.
Yet above all this privilege is thine,
Thy days still lengthen without least decline.

SUMMER

When Spring had done, the Summer did begin,
With melted tawny face, and garments thin,
Resembling fire, choler, and middle age,
As Spring did air, blood, youth in's equipage.
Wiping the sweat from off her face that ran,
With hair all wet she puffing thus began;
Bright June, July, and August hot are mine,
In th' first Sol doth in crabbed Cancer shine.
His progress to the North now's fully done,
Then retrograde must be my burning sun,
Who to his Southward tropic still is bent,
Yet doth his parching heat but more augment
Though he decline, because his flames so fair,
Have thoroughly dried the earth, and heat the air,
Like as an oven that long time hath been heat,
Whose vehemency at length doth grow so great,
That if you do withdraw her burning store,
'Tis for a time as fervent as before.
Now go those frolic swains, the shepherd lads,
To wash the thick-clothed flocks with pipes full glad
In the cool streams they labor with delight,
Rubbing their dirty coats till they look white:
Whose fleece when finely spun and deeply dyed
With robes thereof kings have been dignified.
Blest rustic swains, your pleasant quiet life,
Hath envy bred in kings that were at strife,
Careless of worldly wealth you sing and pipe,
Whilst they're imbroiled in wars and troubles rife:
Which made great Bajazet cry out in's woes,
"Oh happy shepherd which hath naught to lose,
Orthobulus, nor yet Sebastia great,
But whist'leth to thy flock in cold and heat."
Viewing the sun by day, the moon by night,
Endymion's, Dianae's dear delight,
Upon the grass resting your healthy limbs,
By purling brooks looking how fishes swims.
If pride within your lowly cells ere haunt,
Of him that was shepherd, then King go vaunt.
This month the roses are distilled in glasses,
Whose fragrant smell all made perfumes surpasses.
The cherry, gooseberry are now in th' prime,
And for all sorts of peas, this is the time.
July my next, the hott'st in all the year,
The sun through Leo now takes his career,

Whose flaming breath doth melt us from afar,
Increased by the star Canicular.
This month from Julius Caesar took its name,
By Romans celebrated to his fame.
Now go the mowers to their slashing toil,
The meadows of their riches to despoil,
With weary strokes, they take all in their way,
Bearing the burning heat of the long day.
The forks and rakes do follow them amain,
Which makes the aged fields look young again.
The groaning carts do bear away this prize,
To stacks and barns where it for fodder lies.
My next and last is August, fiery hot
(For much, the Southward sun abateth not)
This month he keeps with Virgo for a space,
The dried earth is parched with his face.
August of great Augustus took its name,
Rome's second emperor of lasting fame;
With sickles now the bending reapers go
The rustling tress of terra down to mow;
And bundles up in sheaves, the weighty wheat,
Which after manchet makes for kings to eat:
The barley, rye, and peas should first had place,
Although their bread have not so white a face.
The carter leads all home with whistling voice,
He plowed with pain, but reaping doth rejoice;
His sweat, his toil, his careful, wakeful nights,
His fruitful crop abundantly requites.
Now's ripe the pear, pear-plumb, and apricock,
The prince of plums, whose stone's as hard as rock.
The Summer seems but short, the Autumn hastes
To shake his fruits, of most delicious tastes,
Like good old age, whose younger juicy roots
Hath still ascended, to bear goodly fruits.
Until his head be gray, and strength be gone.
Yet then appears the worthy deeds he'th done:
To feed his boughs exhausted hath his sap,
Then drops his fruits into the eater's lap.

AUTUMN

Of Autumn months September is the prime,
Now day and night are equal in each clime,
The twelfth of this Sol riseth in the line,
And doth in poising Libra this month shine.
The vintage now is ripe, the grapes are prest,
Whose lively liquor oft is cursed and blest:

For nought so good, but it may be abused,
But it's a precious juice when well it's used.
The raisins now in clusters dried be,
The orange, lemon dangle on the tree:
The pomegranate, the fig are ripe also,
And apples now their yellow sides do show.
Of almonds, quinces, wardens, and of peach,
The season's now at hand of all and each.
Sure at this time, time first of all began,
And in this month was made apostate man:
For then in Eden was not only seen,
Boughs full of leaves, or fruits unripe or green,
Or withered stocks, which were all dry and dead,
But trees with goodly fruits replenished;
Which shews nor Summer, Winter, nor the Spring
Our grandsire was of Paradise made king:
Nor could that temp'rate clime such difference make,
If sited as the most judicious take.
October is my next, we hear in this
The Northern winter blasts begin to hiss.
In Scorpio resideth now the sun,
And his declining heat is almost done.
The fruitless trees all withered now do stand,
Whose sapless yellow leaves, by winds are fanned,
Which notes when youth and strength have passed their prime,
Decrepit age must also have its time.
The sap doth slyly creep towards the earth;
There rests, until the sun give it a birth.
So doth old age still tend unto his grave,
Where also he his winter time must have;
But when the sun of righteousness draws nigh,
His dead old stock, shall mount again on high.
November is my last, for time doth haste,
We now of Winter's sharpness 'gin to taste.
This month the sun's in Sagittarius,
So far remote, his glances warm not us.
Almost at shortest is the shortened day,
The Northern pole beholdeth not one ray.
Now Greenland, Groanland, Finland, Lapland, see
No sun, to lighten their obscurity:
Poor wretches that in total darkness lie,
With minds more dark then is the darkned sky.
Beef, brawn, and pork are now in great request,
And solid meats our stomachs can digest.
This time warm clothes, full diet, and good fires,
Our pinched flesh, and hungry maws requires:
Old, cold, dry age and earth Autumn resembles,

And melancholy which most of all dissembles.
I must be short, and short's the shortned day,
What Winter hath to tell, now let him say.

WINTER

Cold, moist, young phlegmy Winter now doth lie
In swaddling clouts, like newborn infancy,
Bound up with frosts, and furred with hail and snows,
And like an infant, still it taller grows;
December is my first, and now the sun
To th' Southward tropic, his swift race doth run:
This month he's housed in horned Capricorn,
From thence he 'gins to length the shortned morn,
Through Christendom with great festivity,
Now's held (but guest), for blest Nativity.
Cold frozen January next comes in,
Chilling the blood and shrinking up the skin;
In Aquarius now keeps the long wisht sun,
And Northward his unwearied course doth run:
The day much longer then it was before,
The cold not lessened, but augmented more.
Now toes and ears, and fingers often freeze,
And travelers their noses sometimes leese.
Moist snowy February is my last,
I care not how the winter time doth haste.
In Pisces now the golden sun doth shine,
And Northward still approaches to the line,
The rivers 'gin to ope, the snows to melt,
And some warm glances from his face are felt;
Which is increased by the lengthened day,
Until by's heat, he drive all cold away,
And thus the year in circle runneth round:
Where first it did begin, in th' end it's found.

Contemplations

[From *Several Poems,* 1678]

1

Some time now past in the autumnal tide,
When Phoebus wanted but one hour to bed,
The trees all richly clad, yet void of pride,
Were gilded o'er by his rich golden head.
Their leaves and fruits seemed painted, but was true,
Of green, of red, of yellow, mixed hue;
Rapt were my senses at this delectable view.

2

I wist not what to wish, "Yet sure," thought I,
"If so much excellence abide below,
How excellent is He that dwells on high,
Whose power and beauty by His works we know?
Sure He is goodness, wisdom, glory, light,
That hath this under world so richly dight:
More heaven than earth was here, no winter and no night."

3

Then on a stately oak I cast mine eye,
Whose ruffling top the clouds seemed to aspire;
How long since thou wast in thine infancy?
Thy strength and stature, more thy years admire.
Hath hundred winters passed since thou wast born.
Or thousand since thou brak'st thy shell of horn?
If so, all these as nought eternity doth scorn.

4

Then higher on the glistering sun I gazed,
Whose beams was shaded by the leafy tree;
The more I looked the more I grew amazed,
And softly said, "What glory's like to thee?
Soul of this world, this universe's eye,
No wonder some made thee a deity;
Had I not better known, alas, the same had I.

5

"Thou as a bridegroom from thy chamber rushes
And as a strong man, joys to run a race,
The morn doth usher thee with smiles and blushes,
The earth reflects her glances in thy face.
Birds, insects, animals, with vegetive,
Thy heart from death and dullness doth revive:
And in the darksome womb of fruitful nature dive.

6

"Thy swift annual and diurnal course,
Thy daily straight and yearly oblique path,
Thy pleasing fervor and thy scorching force,
All mortals here the feeling knowledge hath.
Thy presence makes it day, thy absence night,
Quaternal seasons caused by thy might:
Hail, creature full of sweetness, beauty, and delight!

7

"Art thou so full of glory that no eye
Hath strength thy shining rays once to behold?
And is thy splendid throne erect so high
As to approach it can no earthly mould?
How full of glory then must thy Creator be,
Who gave this bright light luster unto thee:
Admired, adored forever, be that majesty!"

8

Silent, alone, where none or saw or heard,
In pathless paths I led my wand'ring feet,
My humble eyes to lofty skies I reared,
To sing some song my mazed Muse thought meet.
My great Creator I would magnify,
That nature had thus decked liberally:
But ah, and ah, again, my imbecility!

9

I heard the merry grasshopper then sing,
The black-clad cricket bear a second part;
They kept one tune and played on the same string,
Seeming to glory in their little art.
Shall creatures abject thus their voices raise,
And in their kind resound their Maker's praise,
Whilst I, as mute, can warble forth no higher lays?

10

When present times look back to ages past,
And men in being fancy those are dead,
It makes things gone perpetually to last
And calls back months and years that long since fled;
It makes a man more aged in conceit
Than was Methuselah or 's grandsire great
While of their persons and their acts his mind doth treat.

11

Sometimes in Eden fair he seems to be,
Sees glorious Adam there made lord of all,
Fancies the apple dangle on the tree
That turned his sovereign to a naked thrall.
Who like a miscreant's driven from that place
To get his bread with pain and sweat of face:
A penalty imposed on his backsliding race.

12

Here sits our grandame in retired place,
And in her lap her bloody Cain new-born;
The weeping imp oft looks her in the face,
Bewails his unknown hap and fate forlorn;
His mother sighs to think of paradise,
And how she lost her bliss to be more wise,
Believing him that was, and is, father of lies.

13

Here Cain and Abel came to sacrifice;
Fruits of the earth and fatlings each do bring;
On Abel's gift the fire descends from skies,
But no such sign on false Cain's offering;
With sullen hateful looks he goes his ways,
Hath thousand thoughts to end his brother's days,
Upon whose blood his future good he hopes to raise.

14

There Abel keeps his sheep, no ill he thinks,
His brother comes, then acts his fratricide,
The virgin earth of blood her first draught drinks,
But since that time she often hath been cloyed.
The wretch with ghastly face and dreadful mind
Thinks each he sees will serve him in his kind,
Though none on earth but kindred near then could he find.

15

Who fancies not his looks now at the bar,
His face like death, his heart with horror fraught?
Nor malefactor ever felt like war
When deep despair with wish of life hath fought.
Branded with guilt and crushed with treble woes,
A vagabond to land of Nod he goes;
A city builds, that walls might him secure from foes.

16

Who thinks not oft upon the fathers' ages?
Their long descent, how nephews sons they saw,
The starry observations of those sages,
And how their precepts to their sons were law,
How Adam sighed to see his progeny
Clothed all in his black sinful livery,
Who neither guilt nor yet the punishment could fly.

17

Our life compare we with their length of days;
Who to the tenth of theirs doth now arrive?
And though thus short we shorten many ways,
Living so little while we are alive,
In eating, drinking, sleeping, vain delight.
So unawares comes on perpetual night
And puts all pleasures vain unto eternal flight.

18

When I behold the heavens as in their prime,
And then the earth, though old, still clad in green,
The stones and trees insensible of time,
Nor age nor wrinkle on their front are seen;
If winter come, and greenness then do fade,
A spring returns, and they more youthful made.
But man grows old, lies down, remains where once he's laid.

19

By birth more noble than those creatures all,
Yet seems by nature and by custom cursed;
No sooner born but grief and care makes fall
That state obliterate he had at first:
Nor youth nor strength nor wisdom spring again,
Nor habitations long their names retain,
But in oblivion to the final day remain.

20

Shall I then praise the heavens, the trees, the earth,
Because their beauty and their strength last longer?
Shall I wish there or never to had birth,
Because they're bigger and their bodies stronger?
Nay, they shall darken, perish, fade, and die,
And when unmade so ever shall they lie,
But man was made for endless immortality.

21

Under the cooling shadow of a stately elm
Close sat I by a goodly river's side,
Where gliding streams the rocks did overwhelm;
A lonely place, with pleasures dignified.
I once that loved the shady woods so well,
Now thought the rivers did the trees excel,
And if the sun would ever shine, there would I dwell.

22

While on the stealing stream I fixed mine eye,
Which to the longed-for ocean held its course,
I marked, nor crooks nor rubs that there did lie
Could hinder aught, but still augment its force:
"O happy flood," quoth I, "that holds thy race
Till thou arrive at thy beloved place,
Nor is it rocks or shoals that can obstruct thy pace!

23

"Nor is't enough that thou alone may'st slide,
But hundred brooks in thy clear waves do meet;
So hand in hand along with thee they glide
To Thetis' house, where all embrace and greet:
Thou emblem true of what I count the best,
O could I lead my rivulets to rest,
So may we press to that vast mansion ever blest.

24

"Ye fish which in this liquid region bide,
That for each season have your habitation,
Now salt, now fresh, where you think best to glide,
To unknown coasts to give a visitation,
In lakes and ponds you leave your numerous fry,
So nature taught, and yet you know not why,
You wat'ry folk that know not your felicity.

25

"Look how the wantons frisk to taste the air,
Then to the colder bottom straight they dive;
Elftsoon to Neptune's glassy hall repair
To see what trade they great ones there do drive,
Who forage o'er the spacious sea-green field,
And take the trembling prey before it yield,
Whose armor is their scales, their spreading fins their shield."

26

While musing thus with contemplation fed,
And thousand fancies buzzing in my brain,
The sweet-tongued Philomel perched o'er my head,
And chanted forth a most melodious strain,
Which rapt me so with wonder and delight,
I judged my hearing better than my sight,
And wished me wings with her a while to take my flight.

27

"O merry bird," said I, "that fears no snares,
That neither toils nor hoards up in thy barn,
Feels no sad thoughts, nor cruciating cares
To gain more good or shun what might thee harm;
Thy clothes ne'er wear, thy meat is everywhere,
Thy bed a bough, thy drink the water clear;
Reminds not what is past, nor what's to come doth fear.

28

"The dawning morn with songs thou dost prevent,
Sets hundred notes unto thy feathered crew,
So each one tunes his pretty instrument
And warbling out the old, begin anew.
And thus they pass their youth in summer season,
Then follow thee into a better region,
Where winter's never felt by that sweet airy legion."

29

Man at the best a creature frail and vain,
In knowledge ignorant, in strength but weak,
Subject to sorrows, losses, sickness, pain,
Each storm his state, his mind, his body break;
From some of these he never finds cessation,
But day or night, within, without, vexation,
Troubles from foes, from friends, from dearest, near'st relation.

30

And yet this sinful creature, frail and vain,
This lump of wretchedness, of sin and sorrow,
This weather-beaten vessel wracked with pain,
Joys not in hope of an eternal morrow;
Nor all his losses, crosses, and vexation,
In weight, in frequency and long duration,
Can make him deeply groan for that divine translation.

31

The mariner that on smooth waves doth glide
Sings merrily and steers his bark with ease,
As if he had command of wind and tide,
And now become great master of the seas;
But suddenly a storm spoils all the sport,
And makes him long for a more quiet port,
Which 'gainst all adverse winds may serve for fort.

32

So he that faileth in this world of pleasure,
Feeding on sweets, that never bit of th' sour,
That's full of friends, of honor, and of treasure,
Fond fool, he takes this earth ev'n for heaven's bower.
But sad affliction comes and makes him see
Here's neither honor, wealth, nor safety;
Only above is found all with security.

33

O Time, the fatal wrack of mortal things,
That draws oblivion's curtains over kings,
Their sumptuous monuments, men know them not,
Their names without a record are forgot,
Their parts, their ports, their pomp's all laid in th' dust,
Nor wit nor gold nor buildings 'scape time's rust;
But he whose name is graved in the white stone
Shall last and shine when all of these are gone.

Before the Birth of One of Her Children

[From *Works,* 1867]

All things within this fading world hath end,
Adversity doth still our joys attend;
No ties so strong, no friends so dear and sweet,
But with death's parting blow is sure to meet.
The sentence past is most irrevocable,
A common thing, yet oh inevitable;
How soon, my dear, death may my steps attend,
How soon't may be, thy lot to lose thy friend,
We both are ignorant, yet love bids me
These farewell lines to recommend to thee,
That when that knot's untied that made us one,
I may seem thine, who in effect am none.
And if I see not half my days that's due,
What nature would, God grant to yours and you;
The many faults that well you know I have,
Let be interred in my oblivion's grave;
If any worth or virtue were in me,
Let that live freshly in thy memory,
And when thou feel'st no grief, as I no harms,
Yet love thy dead, who long lay in thine arms:
And when thy loss shall be repaid with gains
Look to my little babes, my dear remains.
And if thou love thyself, or lovest me,
These O protect from stepdame's injury.

And if chance to thine eyes shall bring this verse,
With some sad sighs honor my absent hearse;
And kiss this paper for thy love's dear sake,
Who with salt tears this last farewell did take.

As Weary Pilgrim

[From *Works,* 1867]

As weary pilgrim, now at rest,
Hugs with delight his silent nest,
His wasted limbs, now lie full soft,
That miry steps, have trodden oft;
Blesses himself, to think upon
His dangers past, and travails done:
The burning sun no more shall heat,
Nor stormy rains, on him shall beat.
The briars and thorns no more shall scratch,
Nor hungry wolves at him shall catch;
He erring paths no more shall tread,
Nor wild fruits eat, instead of bread;
For waters cold he doth not long,
For thirst no more shall parch his tongue;
No rugged stones his feet shall gall,
Nor stumps nor rocks cause him to fall;
All cares and fears, he bids farewell
And means in safety now to dwell.
A pilgrim I, on earth, perplext,
With sins, with cares and sorrows vext,
By age and pains brought to decay
And my clay house mould'ring away.
Oh, how I long to be at rest
And soar on high among the blest.
This body shall in silence sleep;
Mine eyes no more shall ever weep;
No fainting fits shall me assail
Nor grinding pains; my body frail
With cares and fears ne'er cumbered be,
Nor losses know, nor sorrows see.
What though my flesh shall there consume?
It is the bed Christ did perfume;
And when a few years shall be gone,
This mortal shall be clothed upon.
A corrupt carcass down it lies,
A glorious body it shall rise.
In weakness and dishonor sown,
In power 'tis raised by Christ alone.

Then soul and body shall unite
  And of their maker have the sight;
Such lasting joys shall there behold
  As ear ne'er heard nor tongue e'er told.
Lord make me ready for that day,
  Then come, Dear Bridegroom, come away.

To my Dear and Loving Husband

[From *Works,* 1867]

If ever two were one, then surely we.
If ever man were loved by wife, then thee;
If ever wife was happy in a man,
Compare with me, ye women, if you can.
I prize thy love more then whole mines of gold,
Or all the riches that the East doth hold.
My love is such that rivers cannot quench,
Nor ought but love from thee give recompense.
Thy love is such I can no way repay;
The heavens reward thee manifold, I pray.
Then while we live, in love let's so persevere,
That when we live no more, we may live ever.

The Author to Her Book

[From *Several Poems,* 1678]

Thou ill-formed offspring of my feeble brain,
Who after birth did'st by my side remain,
Till snatcht from thence by friends, less wise then true,
Who thee abroad, exposed to public view,
Made thee in rags, halting to th' press to trudge,
Where errors were not lessened (all may judge)
At thy return my blushing was not small,
My rambling brat (in print) should "Mother" call,
I cast thee by as one unfit for light,
Thy visage was so irksome in my sight;
Yet being mine own, at length affection would
Thy blemishes amend, if so I could:
I washed thy face, but more defects I saw,
And rubbing off a spot, still made a flaw.
I stretcht thy joints to make thee even feet,
Yet still thou run'st more hobbling then is meet;
In better dress to trim thee was my mind,

But nought save homespun cloth i' th' house I find.
In this array, 'mongst vulgars mayst thou roam,
In critics' hands, beware thou doth not come;
And take thy way where yet thou art not known,
If for thy father askt, say thou hast none:
And for thy mother, she alas is poor,
Which caused her thus to send thee out of door.

John Rogers (1631–1684)

THAT Anne Bradstreet's poems were read and enjoyed by her countrymen is attested by the following tribute, which in its classical eloquence nearly outdoes its subject.

John Rogers, who graduated from Harvard in 1649, was pastor, physician, and experimenter in arts and sciences at Ipswich, Massachusetts. In 1683, after the death of Urian Oakes, Rogers became president of Harvard College, and died in that office the following year, to be heralded as one of New England's most eminent divines by Cotton Mather in the *Magnalia Christi Americana.*

TEXT: Anne Bradstreet, *Several Poems Compiled with Great Variety of Wit and Learning* (Boston, 1678).

Upon Mrs. Anne Bradstreet Her Poems

[From Anne Bradstreet, *Several Poems,* 1678]

1

Madame, twice through the Muses' grove I walkt,
Under your blissful bowers, I shrouding there,
It seemed with nymphs of Helicon I talkt:
For there those sweet-lip'd Sisters sporting were,
Apollo with his sacred lute sate by,
On high they made their heavenly sonnets fly,
Posies around they strowed, of sweetest poesy.

2

Twice have I drunk the nectar of your lines,
Which high sublimed my mean born phantasy,
Flusht with these streams of your Maronean wines
Above myself rapt to an ecstasy:
Methought I was upon Mount Hybla's top,
There where I might those fragrant flowers lop,
Whence did sweet odors flow, and honey spangles drop.

3

To Venus' shrine no altars raised are,
Nor venomed shafts from painted quiver fly,
Nor wanton doves of Aphrodite's car,
Or fluttering there, nor here forlornly lie,
Lorn paramours, not chatting birds tell news
How sage Apollo, Daphne hot pursues,
Or stately Jove himself is wont to haunt the stews.

4

Nor barking satyrs' breath, nor dreary clouds
Exhaled from Styx, their dismal drops distil
Within these fairy, flowery fields, nor shrouds
The screeching night raven, with his shady quill:
But lyric strings here Orpheus nimbly hits,
Orion on his saddled dolphin sits,
Chanting as every humour, age, and season fits.

5

Here silver swans, with nightingales set spells,
Which sweetly charm the traveler, and raise
Earth's earthed monarchs, from their hidden cells,
And to appearance summons lapsed days,
There heav'nly air, becalms the swelling frays,
And fury fell of elements allays,
By paying everyone due tribute of his praise.

6

This seemed the site of all those verdant vales,
And purled springs, whereat the nymphs do play,
With lofty hills, where poets rear their tales,
To heavenly vaults, which heav'nly sound repay
By echo's sweet rebound, here ladies kiss,
Circling nor songs, nor dances circle miss;
But whilst those sirens sung, I sunk in sea of bliss.

7

Thus weltring in delight, my virgin mind
Admits a rape; truth still lies undescried,
It's singular, that plural seemed, I find,
'Twas Fancy's glass alone that multiplied;
Nature with art so closely did combine,
I thought I saw the Muses treble trine,
Which proved your lonely Muse, superior to the nine.

8

Your only hand those poesies did compose,
Your head the source, whence all those springs did flow,
Your voice, whence changes sweetest notes arose,
Your feet that kept the dance alone, I trow:
Then veil your bonnets, poetasters all,
Strike, lower amain, and at these humbly fall,
And deem yourselves advanced to be her pedestal.

9

Should all with lowly congies laurels bring,
Waste Flora's magazine to find a wreath;
Or Pineus' banks 'twere too mean offering,
Your Muse a fairer garland doth bequeath
To guard your fairer front; here 'tis your name
Shall stand immarbled; this your little frame
Shall great Colossus be, to your eternal fame.

Nathaniel Ward (1578–1652)

THE simple cobbler of Aggawam (*q.v.*, p. 192) larded his work with a curious hodgepodge of comments, poems, puns, epigrams, and tirades on a multitude of subjects, ranging from theology to fashions and politics, on both British and American themes. Decrying all newfangledness, in wigs and French clothing as well as in religious opinions, and deeply prejudiced against anything new or liberal, he was at his best when writing invective. But he was also capable of witty and pungent verse, as his prefatory poem to the first volume of Anne Bradstreet's poems clearly shows.

TEXTS: Anne Bradstreet, *The Tenth Muse Lately Sprung Up in America* (London, 1650); and Nathaniel Ward, *The Simple Cobbler of Aggawam in America* (London, 1647).

In Praise of Mistress Bradstreet

[From Anne Bradstreet, *The Tenth Muse*, 1650]

Mercury shewed Apollo, Bartas' book,
Minerva this, and wisht him well to look,
And tell uprightly, which did which excel:
He viewed and viewed, and vowed he could not tell.
They bid him hemisphere his mouldy nose,
With cracked leering glasses, for it would pose
The best brains he had in's old pudding-pan,
Sex weighed, which best, the woman or the man?
He peered and pored, and glared, and said for wore,
"I'm even as wise now, as I was before."
They both 'gan laugh, and said, it was no mar'l
The auth'ress was a right Du Bartas girl.
"Good sooth," quoth the old Don, "tell ye me so,
I muse whither at length these girls will go.
It half revives my chill frost-bitten blood,
To see a woman do aught that's good;
And chode by Chaucer's boots, and Homer's furs,
Let men look to 't, lest women wear the spurs."

Some Remarks on Women's Fashions

[From *The Simple Cobbler*, 1647]

It is known more then enough, that I am neither niggard, nor cynic, to the due bravery of the true gentry: if any man mislikes a bullymong drassock more then I, let him take her, for all me: I honor the woman that can honor herself with her attire: a good text always deserves a fair margent: I am not much offended, if I see a trim, far trimmer than she that wears it: in a word, whatever Christianity or civility will allow, I can afford with London measure: but when I hear a nugiperous gentledame inquire, what dress the Queen is in this week; what the nudiustertian fashion of the court; I mean the very newest: with egg to be in it in all haste, whatever it be; I look at her as the very gizzard of a trifle, the product of a quarter of a cipher, the epitome of nothing, fitter to be kickt, if she were of a kickable substance, than either honored or humored.

To speak moderately, I truly confess, it is beyond the ken of my understanding to conceive, how those women should have any true grace, or valuable virtue, that have so little wit, as to disfigure themselves with such exotic garbs, as not only dismantles their native lovely luster, but transclouts them into gant bar-geese, ill-shapen shotten shellfish, Egyptian hieroglyphics, or at the best into French flirts of the pastry, which a proper Englishwoman should scorn with her heels: it is no marvel they wear drails on the hinder part of their heads, having nothing as it seems in the forepart, but a few squirrels' brains, to help them frisk from one ill-favored fashion to another. . . .

I can make myself sick at any time, with comparing the dazzling splendor wherewith our gentlewomen were embellished in some former habits, with the gut-foundered goosedom, wherewith they are now surcingled and debauched. We have about five or six of them in our colony: if I see any of them accidentally, I cannot cleanse my fancy of them for a moneth after. I have been a solitary widower almost twelve years, purposed lately to make a step over to my native country for a yoke-fellow: but when I consider how women there have tripe-wifed themselves with their cladments, I have no heart to the voyage, lest their nauseous shapes and the sea should work too sorely upon my stomach. I speak sadly; methinks it should break the hearts of Englishmen, to see so many goodly Englishwomen imprisoned in French cages, peering out of their hood-holes for some men of mercy to help them with a little wit, and nobody relieves them.

It is a more common then convenient saying, that nine tailors make a man: it were well if nineteen could make a woman to her mind: if tailors were men indeed, well furnished but with mere moral principles, they would disdain to be led about like apes, by such mimic marmosets. It is a most unworthy thing, for men that have bones in them, to spend their lives in making fiddle-cases for futilous women's fancies; which are the very pettitoes of infirmity, the giblets of perquisquilian toys. I am so charitable to think, that most of that mystery, would work the cheerfuller while they live, if they might be well discharged of the trying slavery of mis-tiring women: it is no little labor to be continually putting up Englishwomen into outlandish casks; who if they be not shifted anew, once in a few moneths, grow too sour for their husbands. What this trade will answer for themselves when God shall take measure of tailors' consciences is beyond my skill to imagine. . . .

It is beyond all account, how many gentlemen's and citizens' estates are deplumed by their feather-headed wives; what useful supplies the pannage of England would afford other countries, what rich returns to itself, if it were not sliced out into male and female fripperies: and what a multitude of mis-employed hands, might be better improved in some more manly manufactures for the public weal. It is not easily credible, what may be said of the preterpluralities of tailors in London: I have heard an honest man say that not long since there were numbered between Temple Bar and Charingcross, eight thousand of that trade: let it be conjectured by that proportion how many there are in and about London, and in all England, they will appear to be very numerous. If the Parliament would please to mend women, which their husbands dare not do, there need not so many men to make and 'mend as there are. I hope the present doleful estate of the realm will persuade more strongly to some considerate course herein, then *I* now can.

Michael Wigglesworth (1631–1705)

THE author of the most popular poem in American colonial literature was born in England and came to New England with his parents at the age of seven. Unfit to help his crippled father in the fields, the youngster was trained for college by the famous Ezekiel Cheever. Always at the head of his class, Wigglesworth graduated from Harvard in 1651, and remained there as tutor for five more years. During his tutorship he kept a diary in which his troubled conscience worried about his relationships with his pupils, his religious doubts, his strong sexual urges, his growing physical illness, and his continual struggle with his parents, especially his father. Ten days after learning of his father's death, he records a marvelous dream of the Day of Judgment, God on His throne separating the sheep from the goats. This dream became the inspiration for *The Day of Doom; or A Poetical Description of the Great and Last Judgment,* a poem of 224 stanzas describing in some detail the punishments and rewards to be passed out on the Judgment Day, and the reasons for the distribution. The eighteen hundred copies of the first edition (1662) were sold out within the year, making the work a runaway bestseller by contemporary standards; and it continued to be reissued in various editions for the next two hundred years.

It is easy to misunderstand the intent of the *Day of Doom,* and to condemn both Wigglesworth and his New England public for a morbid, joyless view of life. Intended to impress upon the reader an awareness of human sinfulness and of God's justice and majesty, *The Day of Doom* contains no more hellfire and brimstone than many twentieth-century evangelistic sermons. Wigglesworth was not here attempting to write artistic poetry, but rather a rhymed explication of Calvinist doctrine in easily-grasped and easily-memorized form. Wigglesworth's literary sense is better revealed in his college oration "Of Elòquence" (*q.v.*, p. 335), and in several of the poems he wrote during the thirty years that his illness incapacitated him for his pastoral duties at Malden. Chief among these is *God's Controversy with New England,* written in 1662 but not published during his lifetime, and the long *Meat Out of the Eater: Meditations Concerning the Necessity, End, and Usefulness of Afflictions unto God's Children. All Tending to Prepare them For, and Comfort them Under the Cross;* the latter, published in 1670, went through four editions in less than twenty years. From 1680 on, his health and vigor returned; a close friend of Samuel Sewall, he became active in public affairs and was even offered the presidency of Harvard on the death of John Rogers. He died in 1705, the most popular poet in America.

TEXTS: Michael Wigglesworth, *The Day of Doom,* ed. Kenneth B. Murdock (New York, 1929); and "God's Controversy with New England," *Proc. Mass. Hist. Soc.,* 2d ser., XII (1873).

The Call to Judgment

[From *The Day of Doom,* 1662]

1

Still was the night, serene and bright,
  When all men sleeping lay;
Calm was the season, and carnal reason
  Thought so 'twould last for aye.
Soul take thine ease, let sorrow cease,
  Much good thou hast in store:
This was their song, their cups among,
  The evening before.

2

Wallowing in all kind of sin,
  Vile wretches lay secure:
The best of men had scarcely then
  Their lamps kept in good ure.
Virgins unwise, who through disguise
  Amongst the best were numbered,
Had closed their eyes; yea, and the wise
  Through sloth and frailty slumbered.

3

Like as of old, when men grow bold
  God's threatnings to contemn,
Who stopt their ear, and would not hear,
  When mercy warned them:
But took their course, without remorse,
  Till God began to pour
Destruction the world upon
  In a tempestuous shower.

4

They put away the evil day,
  And drowned their care and fears,
Till drowned were they, and swept away
  By vengeance unawares:
So at the last, whilst men sleep fast
  In their security,
Surprised they are in such a snare
  As cometh suddenly.

5

For at midnight brake forth a light,
  Which turned the night to day,
And speedily an hideous cry
  Did all the world dismay.
Sinners awake, their hearts do ache,
  Trembling their loins surpriseth;
Amazed with fear, by what they hear,
  Each one of them ariseth.

6

They rush from beds with giddy heads,
  And to their windows run,
Viewing this light, which shines more bright
  Then doth the noonday sun.
Straightway appears (they see't with tears)
  The Son of God most dread;
Who with His train comes on amain
  To judge both quick and dead.

7

Before His face the heav'ns gave place,
  And skies are rent asunder,
With mighty voice, and hideous noise,
  More terrible than thunder.
His brightness damps heav'n's glorious lamps
  And makes them hide their heads,
As if afraid and quite dismayed,
  They quit their wonted steads.

8

Ye sons of men that durst contemn
  The threatnings of God's Word,
How cheer you now? your hearts, I trow,
  Are thrilled as with a sword.
Now atheist blind, whose brutish mind
  A God could never see,
Dost thou perceive, dost now believe,
  That Christ thy Judge shall be?

9

Stout courages (whose hardiness
  Could death and hell outface),
Are you as bold now you behold
  Your Judge draw near apace?
They cry, "No, no! Alas! and woe!
  Our courage all is gone:
Our hardiness (fool hardiness)
  Hath us undone, undone."

10

No heart so bold, but now grows cold
  And almost dead with fear:
No eye so dry, but now can cry,
  And pour out many a tear.
Earth's potentates and pow'rful states,
  Captains and men of might
Are quite abasht, their courage dasht
  At this most dreadful sight.

11

Mean men lament, great men do rent
  Their robes, and tear their hair:
They do not spare their flesh to tear
  Through horrible despair.
All kindreds wail: all hearts do fail:
  Horror the world doth fill
With weeping eyes, and loud outcries,
  Yet knows not how to kill.

12

Some hide themselves in caves and delves,
  In places underground:
Some rashly leap into the deep,
  To 'scape by being drowned:
Some to the rocks (O senseless blocks!)
  And woody mountains run,
That there they might this fearful sight,
  And dreaded Presence shun.

13

In vain do they to mountains say,
  "Fall on us, and us hide
From Judge's ire, more hot than fire,
  For who may it abide?"
No hiding place can from His face,
  Sinners at all conceal,
Whose flaming eyes hid things doth 'spy,
  And darkest things reveal.

14

The Judge draws nigh, exalted high
  Upon a lofty throne,
Amidst the throng of angels strong,
  Lo, Israel's Holy One!
The excellence of whose presence
  And awful majesty,
Amazeth nature, and every creature,
  Doth more than terrify.

15

The mountains smoke, the hills are shook,
  The earth is rent and torn,
As if she should be clean dissolved,
  Or from the center borne.
The sea doth roar, forsakes the shore,
  And shrinks away for fear;
The wild beasts flee into the sea,
  So soon as He draws near.

16

Whose glory bright, whose wondrous might,
  Whose power imperial,
So far surpass whatever was
  In realms terrestrial;
That tongues of men (nor angels' pen)
  Cannot the same express,
And therefore I must pass it by,
  Lest speaking should transgress.

17

Before His throne a trump is blown,
  Proclaiming th' Day of Doom:
Forthwith He cries, "Ye dead arise,
  And unto judgment come."
No sooner said, but 'tis obeyed;
  Sepulchers opened are:
Dead bodies all rise at His call,
  And's mighty power declare.

18

Both sea and land, at His command,
  Their dead at once surrender:
The fire and air constrained are
  Also their dead to tender.
The mighty word of this great Lord
  Links body and soul together
Both of the just, and the unjust,
  To part no more forever.

19

The same translates, from mortal states
  To immortality,
All that survive, and be alive,
  I' th' twinkling of an eye:
That so they may abide for aye
  To endless weal or woe;
Both the renate and reprobate
  Are made to die no more.

20

His winged hosts fly through all coasts,
  Together gathering
Both good and bad, both quick and dead,
  And all to judgment bring.
Out of their holes those creeping moles,
  That hid themselves for fear,
By force they take, and quickly make
  Before the Judge appear.

21

Thus everyone before the throne
  Of Christ the Judge is brought,
Both righteous and impious
  That good or ill had wrought.
A separation, and diff'ring station
  By Christ appointed is
(To sinners sad) 'twixt good and bad,
  'Twixt heirs of woe and bliss.

The Disposition of Heathens and Infants

[From the same]

156

. . . .

Then were brought near with trembling fear,
A number numberless
Of blind heathen, and brutish men,
That did God's laws transgress.

157

Whose wicked ways Christ open lays,
And makes their sins appear,
They making pleas their case to ease,
If not themselves to clear.
"Thy written Word" (say they) "good Lord,
We never did enjoy:
We nor refused, nor it abused;
Oh, do not us destroy!"

158

"You ne'er abused, nor yet refused
My written Word, you plead,
That's true" (quoth He) "therefore shall ye
The less be punished.
You shall not smart for any part
Of other men's offense,
But for your own transgression
Receive due recompense."

159

"But we were blind," say they, "in mind,
Too dim was nature's light,
Our only guide, as hath been tried
To bring us to the sight
Of our estate degenerate,
And curst by Adam's fall;
How we were born and lay forlorn
In bondage and in thrall.

160

"We did not know a Christ till now,
Nor how faln man be saved,
Else would we not, right well we wot,
Have so ourselves behaved.
We should have mourned, we should have turned
From sin at thy reproof,
And been more wise through thy advice,
For our own souls' behoof.

161

But nature's light shined not so bright
  To teach us the right way:
We might have loved it, and well improved
  And yet have gone astray."
The Judge most high makes this reply,
  "You ignorance pretend,
Dimness of sight, and want of light
  Your course heav'nward to bend.

162

"How came your mind to be so blind?
  I once you knowledge gave,
Clearness of sight, and judgment right;
  Who did the same deprave?
If to your cost you have it lost,
  And quite defaced the same;
Your own desert hath caused the smart,
  You ought not me to blame.

163

"Yourselves into a pit of woe,
  Your own transgression led:
If I to none my grace had shown,
  Who had been injured?
If to a few, and not to you,
  I shewed a way of life,
My grace so free, you clearly see,
  Gives you no ground of strife.

164

" 'Tis vain to tell, you wot full well,
  If you in time had known
Your misery and remedy,
  Your actions had it shown.
You, sinful crew, have not been true
  Unto the light of nature,
Nor done the good you understood,
  Nor owned your Creator.

165

"He that the light, because 'tis light,
  Hath used to despise,
Would not the light shining more bright,
  Be likely for to prize.
If you had loved, and well improved
  Your knowledge and dim sight,
Herein your pain had not been vain,
  Your plagues had been more light."

166

Then to the bar, all they drew near
  Who died in infancy,
And never had nor good or bad
  Effected pers'nally,
But from the womb unto the tomb
  Were straightway carried,
(Or at the last ere they transgrest)
  Who thus began to plead:

167

"If for our own transgression,
  Or disobedience,
We here did stand at thy left hand,
  Just were the recompense:
But Adam's guilt our souls hath spilt,
  His fault is charged on us;
And that alone hath overthrown,
  And utterly undone us.

168

"Not we, but he, ate of the tree,
  Whose fruit was interdicted:
Yet on us all of his sad fall,
  The punishment's inflicted.
How could we sin that had not been,
  Or how is his sin our,
Without consent, which to prevent,
  We never had a pow'r?

169

"O great Creator, why was our nature
  Depraved and forlorn?
Why so defiled, and made so vild
  Whilst we were yet unborn?
If it be just, and needs we must
  Transgressors reck'ned be,
Thy mercy, Lord, to us afford,
  Which sinners hath set free.

170

"Behold we see Adam set free,
  And saved from his trespass,
Whose sinful fall hath split us all,
  And brought us to this pass.
Canst thou deny us once to try,
  Or grace to us to tender,
When he finds grace before thy face,
  That was the chief offender?"

171

Then answered the Judge most dread,
"God doth such doom forbid,
That men should die eternally
For what they never did.
But what you call old Adam's fall,
And only his trespass,
You call amiss to call it his,
Both his and yours it was.

172

"He was designed of all mankind
To be a public head,
A common root, whence all should shoot,
And stood in all their stead.
He stood and fell, did ill or well,
Not for himself alone,
But for you all, who now his fall,
And trespass would disown.

173

"If he had stood, then all his brood
Had been established
In God's true love, never to move,
Nor once awry to tread:
Then all his race, my Father's grace,
Should have enjoyed forever,
And wicked sprites by subtle sleights
Could them have harmed never.

174

"Would you have grieved to have received
Through Adam so much good,
As had been your for evermore,
If he at first had stood?
Would you have said, 'we ne'er obeyed,
Nor did thy laws regard;
It ill befits with benefits,
Us, Lord, so to reward'?

175

"Since then to share in his welfare,
You could have been content,
You may with reason share in his treason,
And in the punishment.
Hence you were born in state forlorn,
With natures so depraved:
Death was your due, because that you
Had thus yourselves behaved.

176

"You think, 'if we had been as he,
  Whom God did so betrust,
We to our cost would ne'er have lost
  All for a paltry lust.'
Had you been made in Adam's stead,
  You would like things have wrought,
And so into the self-same woe,
  Yourselves and yours have brought.

177

"I may deny you once to try,
  Or grace to you to tender,
Though he finds grace before my face,
  Who was the chief offender:
Else should my grace cease to be grace;
  For it should not be free,
If to release whom I should please,
  I have no liberty.

178

"If upon one what's due to none
  I frankly shall bestow,
And on the rest shall not think best,
  Compassions' skirts to throw,
Whom injure I? will you envy,
  And grudge at others' weal?
Or me accuse, who do refuse
  Yourselves to help and heal?

179

"Am I alone of what's my own,
  No Master or no Lord?
Or if I am, how can you claim
  What I to some afford?
Will you demand grace at my hand,
  And challenge what is mine?
Will you teach me whom to set free,
  And thus my grace confine?

180

"You sinners are, and such a share
  As sinners may expect,
Such you shall have; for I do save
  None but mine own elect.
Yet to compare your sin with their,
  Who lived a longer time,
I do confess yours is much less,
  Though every sin's a crime.

181

"A crime it is, therefore in bliss
You may not hope to dwell;
But unto you I shall allow
The easiest room in hell."
The glorious King thus answering,
They cease, and plead no longer:
Their consciences must needs confess
His reasons are the stronger.

God's Controversy with New England

(1662)

Our temp'ral blessings did abound,
But spiritual good things
Much more abounded, to the praise
Of that great King of kings.
God's throne was here set up, here was
His tabernacle pight;
This was the place and these the folk
In whom He took delight.

Our morning stars shone all day long
Their beams gave forth such light
As did the noonday sun abash
And's glory dazzle quite.
Our day continued many years
And had no night at all;
Yea, many thought the light would last
And be perpetual.

Such, O New England, was thy first,
Such was thy best estate;
But, lo! a strange and sudden change
My courage did amate.
The brightest of our morning stars
Did wholly disappear;
And those that tarried behind
With sackcloth covered were.

Moreover, I beheld and saw
Our welkin overcast,
And dismal clouds for sunshine late
O'erspread from east and west.

The air became tempestuous;
  The wilderness 'gan quake;
And from above with awful voice
  Th' Almighty thund'ring spake:

"Are these the men that erst at My command
  Forsook their ancient seats and native soil,
To follow Me into a desert land,
  Contemning all the travel and the toil,
Whose love was such to purest ordinances
  As made them set at nought their fair inheritances?

Are these the men that prized liberty
  To walk with God according to their light,
To be as good as He would have them be,
  To serve and worship Him with all their might,
Before the pleasures which a fruitful field,
  And country flowing-full of all good things, could yield?

Are these the folk whom from the British Isles,
  Through the stern billows of the wat'ry main,
I safely led so many thousand miles,
  As if their journey had been through a plain,
Whom having from all enemies protected,
  And through so many deaths and dangers well directed,

I brought and planted on the western shore,
  Where nought but brutes and savage wights did swarm
(Untaught, untrained, untamed by virtue's lore)
  That sought their blood, yet could not do them harm;
My fury's flail them threshed, My fatal broom
  Did sweep them hence, to make My people elbow-room.

Are these the men whose gates with peace I crowned,
  To whom for bulwarks I salvation gave,
Whilst all things else with rattling tumults sound,
  And mortal frays send thousands to the grave?
Whilst their own brethren bloody hands embrewed
  In brothers' blood, and fields with carcasses bestrewed?

Is this the people blest with bounteous store,
  By land and sea full richly clad and fed,
Whom plenty's self stands waiting still before,
  And poureth out their cups well tempered?
For whose dear sake an howling wilderness
  I lately turned into a fruitful paradise?

Are these the people in whose hemisphere
  Such bright-beamed, glistering sun-like stars I placed,

As by their influence did all things cheer,
As by their light blind ignorance defaced,
As errors into lurking holes did fray,
As turned the late dark into a lightsome day?

Are these the folk to whom I milked out
And sweetness streamed from consolation's breast;
Whose souls I fed and strengthened throughout
With finest spiritual food most finely dressed?
On whom I rained living bread from heaven,
Withouten error's bane, or superstition's leaven?

With whom I made a covenant of peace,
And unto whom I did most firmly plight
My faithfulness, if whilst I live I cease
To be their guide, their God, their full delight;
Since them with cords of love to Me I drew,
Enwrapping in My grace such as should them ensue?

Are these the men, that now Mine eyes behold,
Concerning whom I thought, and whilom spake,
First heaven shall pass away together scrolled,
Ere they My laws and righteous ways forsake,
Or that they slack to run their heavenly race?
Are these the same? or are some others come in place?

If these be they, how is it that I find
Instead of holiness, carnality;
Instead of heavenly frames, an earthly mind;
For burning zeal, luke warm indifferency;
For flaming love, key-cold dead heartedness;
For temperance (in meat, and drink, and clothes), excess?

Whence cometh it that pride, and luxury,
Debate, deceit, contention, and strife,
False-dealing, covetousness, hypocrisy,
(With such like crimes) amongst them are so rife,
That one of them doth over-reach another?
And that an honest man can hardly trust his brother?

How is it that security and sloth
Amongst the best are common to be found?
That grosser sins, instead of grace's growth,
Amongst the many more and more abound?
I hate dissembling shows of holiness,
Or practice as you talk, or never more profess.

Judge not, vain world, that all are hypocrites
That do profess more holiness than thou;

All foster not dissembling, guileful sprites,
  Nor love their lusts, though very many do.
Some sin through want of care and constant watch;
  Some with the sick converse till they the sickness catch.

Some, that maintain a real root of grace,
  Are overgrown with many noisome weeds,
Whose heart, that those no longer may take place,
  The benefit of due correction needs.
And such as these, however gone astray,
  I shall by stripes reduce into a better way.

Moreover some there be that still retain
  Their ancient vigor and sincerity;
Whom both their own and others' sins constrain
  To sigh, and mourn, and weep, and wail, and cry;
And for their sakes I have forborne to pour
  My wrath upon revolters to this present hour.

To praying saints I always have respect,
  And tender love, and pitiful regard;
Nor will I now in any wise neglect
  Their love and faithful service to reward;
Although I deal with others for their folly,
  And turn their mirth to tears that have been too jolly.

For think not, O backsliders, in your heart,
  That I shall still your evil manners bear;
Your sins Me press as sheaves do load a cart,
  And therefore I will plague you for this gear.
Except you seriously, and soon, repent,
  I'll not delay your pain and heavy punishment.

And who be those themselves that yonder shew?
  The seed of such as name My dreadful Name!
On whom while'er compassion's skirt I threw
  Whilst in their blood they were, to hide their shame!
Whom My preventing love did ne'er Me take!
  Whom for Mine own I marked, lest they should me forsake!

I looked that such as these to virtue's lore
  (Though none but they) would have inclined their ear;
That they at least Mine image should have bore,
  And sanctified My name with awful fear.
Let pagan's brats pursue their lusts, whose meed
  Is death. For Christian's children are an holy seed.

But hear, O heavens! Let earth amazed stand!
  Ye mountains melt, and hills come flowing down!

Let horror seize upon both sea and land!
  Let nature's self be cast into a stone!
I children nourished, nurtured, and upheld;
  But they against a tender Father have rebelled.

What could have been by me performed more?
  Or wherein fell I short of your desire?
Had you but asked, I would have oped My store,
  And given what lawful wishes could require.
For all this bounteous cost I looked to see
  Heaven-reaching hearts and thoughts, meekness, humility." . . .

Ah dear New England! dearest land to me!
  Which unto God has hitherto been dear —
And may'st be still more dear than formerly
  If to His voice thou wilt decline thine ear.

Consider well and wisely what the rod,
  Wherewith thou art from year to year chastised,
Instructeth thee: repent and turn to God,
  Who will not have His nurture be despised.

Thou still hast in thee many praying saints,
  Of great account and precious with the Lord,
Who daily pour out unto Him their plaints,
  And strive to please Him both in deed and word.

Cheer on, sweet souls, my heart is with you all,
  And shall be with you, maugre Satan's might.
And whereso'er this body be a thrall,
  Still in New England shall be my delight.

Philip Pain (?–1666/7)

PHILIP PAIN is a "lost poet" insofar as all that is known about him is that he was young, and that he drowned in a shipwreck in 1666 or 1667. His *Daily Meditations: or, Quotidian Preparations for, and Considerations of Death and Eternity,* in sixty-four stanzas of morose contemplation, was published at Cambridge in 1668. From the evidence of his verse, it is apparent that Pain was well acquainted with contemporary British poetry, especially the work of George Herbert and Francis Quarles. Pain's honest expressions of doubt break through the intellectual restraints of dogma and join his poetry to a personal and emotional intensity more fully realized only by Edward Taylor among colonial poets.

TEXT: Philip Pain, *Daily Meditations* (Cambridge, 1668).

From
Daily Meditations

THE PORCH

To live's a gift, to die's a debt that we
Each of us owe unto mortality.
What though the dead do ghastly look, and we
Like children frighted are even but to be
Spectators of a dying man or woman?
Yet nothing's to be feared that is so common.
It is not death that we in them do see;
It's but the mask wherewith 'twill veiled be.
Yet where's the man or woman that can look
Death in the face, as in some pleasing book?
Can we contented be to view our face
In such a dreadful, doleful looking-glass?
O where's the man or woman who can cry,
Behold I come, Death I desire to die?
O where's the man or woman that can say,
Lord, I desire my dissolution day?
And what's the reason 'tis so hard to die,
To leave this world so full of vanity?
What makes it terrible? Nought but the sense
Of guilt and sin: break down this potent fence,
And then be sure for aye you shall enjoy
Joys everlasting, everlasting joy.

MEDITATION 4

This world a sea of trouble is, and man
Is swimming through this vast wide ocean.
The billows beat, the waves are angry, and
'Tis seldom that he spies a helping hand
  To buoy his head up. O Great God, let me
  Be kept from sinking into misery.

MEDITATION 10

Alas, what is the world? A sea of glass.
Alas, what's earth? It's but an hourglass.
The sea dissolves; the glass is quickly run:
Behold, with speed man's life is quickly done.
  Let me so swim in this sea, that I may
  With thee live happy in another day.

MEDITATION 25

Alas, poor Death, where does thy great strength lie?
'Tis true, I'm mortal, yet I cannot die.
I tell thee, if I die in Christ, it is
The way thou shew'st me to eternal bliss.
By death I live, if that I live to Christ,
And then thou'lt say the mark I have not missed.

Benjamin Tompson (1642–1714)

LIKE Michael Wigglesworth, Benjamin Tompson, long and erroneously known as America's first native-born poet, studied with Ezekiel Cheever at the Boston Latin School and proceeded to graduate from Harvard (1662). But unlike Wigglesworth, Tompson's interests were predominantly secular. In 1667 he began teaching at the Boston Latin School, and from time to time turned out a kind of society or occasional verse often funereal in subject and tone. *The Grammarian's Funeral,* printed broadside in 1708, will remind readers of Robert Browning's "A Grammarian's Funeral," and is a good example of the kind of verbal wit New Englanders enjoyed. More interesting is his first publication, *New England's Crisis* (1676), which versifies the sacking of New England towns during King Philip's War. The poem is episodic, too long, and often dull, but reflects New England's sense of a golden past in some charming lines at the beginning, and concentrates on typically American frontier experience for its subject matter.

TEXTS: Howard Judson Hall, ed., *Benjamin Tompson His Poems* (Boston, 1924).

Prologue

[From *New England's Crisis,* 1676]

The times wherein old Pompion was a saint,
When men fared hardly yet without complaint,
On vilest cates; the dainty Indian maize
Was eat with clamp-shells out of wooden trays,
Under thatched huts without the cry of rent,
And the best sauce to every dish, content.
When flesh was food and hairy skins made coats,
And men as well as birds had chirping notes.

When cimnels were accounted noble blood;
Among the tribes of common herbage food.
Of Ceres' bounty formed was many a knack.
Enough to fill poor Robin's almanac.
These golden times (too fortunate to hold)
Were quickly sinned away for love of gold.
'Twas then among the bushes, not the street,
If one in place did an inferior meet,
"Good morrow, brother, is there aught you want?
Take freely of me, what I have you ha'nt."
Plain Tom and Dick would pass as current now,
As ever since, "Your Servant, Sir," and bow.
Deep-skirted doublets, puritanic capes,
Which now would render men like upright apes,
Was comelier wear, our wiser fathers thought,
Than the cast fashions from all Europe brought.
'Twas in those days an honest grace would hold
Till an hot puddin grew at heart a-cold.
And men had better stomachs to religion
Than I to capon, turkey-cock, or pigeon.
When honest sisters met to pray not prate
About their own and not their neighbor's state.
During *Plain Dealing*'s reign, that worthy stud
Of th' ancient planters' race before the flood.
These times were good, merchants cared not a rush
For other fare than Jonakin and mush.
Although men fared and lodged very hard,
Yet innocence was better than a guard.
'Twas long before spiders and worms had drawn
Their dungy webs or hid with cheating lawn
New England's beauties, which still seemed to me
Illustrious in their own simplicity.
'Twas ere the neighboring Virgin land had broke
The hogsheads of her worse than hellish smoke.
'Twas ere the islands sent their presents in,
Which but to use was counted next to sin.
'Twas ere a barge had made so rich a freight
As chocolate, dust-gold, and bits of eight.
Ere wines from France and Muscovado too
Without the which the drink will scarcely do,
From western isles, ere fruits and delicacies,
Did rot maids' teeth and spoil their handsome faces.
Or ere these times did chance the noise of war
Was from our towns and hearts removed far.
No bugbear comets in the crystal air
To drive our Christian planters to despair.
No sooner pagan malice peeped forth
But valor snibbed it: then were men of worth

Who by their prayers slew thousands angel-like,
Their weapons are unseen with which they strike.
Then had the churches rest, as yet the coals
Were covered up in most contentious souls.
Freeness in judgment, union in affection,
Dear love, sound truth, they were our grand protection.
These were the twins which in our council sate,
These gave prognostics of our future fate,
If these be longer lived our hopes increase,
These wars will usher in a longer peace:
But if New England's love die in its youth
The grave will open next for blessed truth.
This theme is out of date, the peaceful hours
When castles needed not but pleasant bowers.
Not ink, but blood and tears now serve the turn
To draw the figure of New England's urn.
New England's hour of passion is at hand,
No power except divine can it withstand;
Scarce hath her glass of fifty years run out,
But her old prosperous steeds turn heads about,
Tracking themselves back to their poor beginnings,
To fear and fare upon their fruits of sinnings:
So that the mirror of the Christian world
Lies burnt to heaps in part, her streamers furled;
Grief reigns, joys flee, and dismal fears surprise,
Not dastard spirits only but the wise.
Thus have the fairest hopes deceived the eye
Of the big swoln expectant standing by.
Thus the proud ship after a little turn
Sinks into Neptune's arms to find its urn.
Thus hath the heir to many thousands born
Been in an instant from the mother torn.
Ev'n thus thine infant cheeks begin to pale,
And thy supporters through great losses fail.
This is the prologue to thy future woe,
The epilogue no mortal yet can know.

The Crisis

[From the same]

In seventy-five the critic of our years
Commenced our war with Philip and his peers.
Whether the sun in Leo had inspired
A fev'rish heat, and pagan spirits fired?
Whether some Romish agent hatcht the plot?
Or whether they themselves? appeareth not.

Whether our infant thrivings did invite?
Or whether to our lands pretended right?
Is hard to say; but Indian spirits need
No grounds but lust to make a Christian bleed.

And here methinks I see this greasy lout
With all his pagan slaves coiled round about,
Assuming all the majesty his throne
Of rotten stump, or of the rugged stone
Could yield; casting some bacon-rind-like looks,
Enough to fright a student from his books,
Thus treat his peers, and next to them his commons,
Kenneled together all without a summons.
"My friends, our fathers were not half so wise
As we ourselves who see with younger eyes.
They sell our land to Englishmen who teach
Our nation all so fast to pray and preach:
Of all our country they enjoy the best,
And quickly they intend to have the rest.
This no wunnegin, so big matchit law,
Which our old fathers' fathers never saw.
These English make and we must keep them too,
Which is too hard for them or us to do,
We drink we so big whipt, but English they
Go sneep, no more, or else a little pay.
Me meddle squaw me hanged, our fathers kept
What squaws they would whether they waked or slept.
Now if you'll fight I'll get you English coats,
And wine to drink out of their captains' throats.
The richest merchants' houses shall be ours,
We'll lie no more on mats or dwell in bowers;
We'll have their silken wives, take they our squaws,
They shall be whipt by virtue of our laws.
If ere we strike 'tis now before they swell
To greater swarms then we know how to quell.
This my resolve, let neighboring sachems know,
And everyone that hath club, gun, or bow."
This was assented to, and for a close
He stroked his smutty beard and cursed his foes.
This counsel lightning like their tribes invade,
And something like a muster's quickly made,
A ragged regiment, a naked swarm,
Whom hopes of booty doth with courage arm,
Set forth with bloody hearts, the first they meet
Of men or beasts they butcher at their feet.
They round our skirts, they pare, they fleece, they kill,
And to our bordering towns do what they will.
Poor hovels (better far then Caesar's court

In the experience of the meaner sort)
Receive from them their doom next execution,
By flames reduced to horror and confusion:
Here might be seen the smoking funeral piles
Of wildered towns pitcht distant many miles.
Here might be seen the infant from the breast
Snatcht by a pagan hand to lasting rest:
The mother Rachel-like shrieks out, "My child!"
She wrings her hands and raves as she were wild.
The brutish wolves suppress her anxious moan
By cruelties more deadly of her own.
Will she or nill the chastest turtle must
Taste of the pangs of their unbridled lust.
From farms to farms, from towns to towns they post,
They strip, they bind, they ravish, flea and roast.
The beasts which wont their master's crib to know,
Over the ashes of their shelters low.
What the inexorable flames do spare
More cruel heathen lug away for fare.
These tidings ebbing from the outward parts
Makes tradesmen cast aside their wonted arts
And study arms: the craving merchants plot
Not to augment but keep what they have got.
And every soul which hath but common sense
Thinks it the time to make a just defense.
Alarums everywhere resound in streets,
From West sad tidings with the Eastern meets.
Our common fathers in their councils close
A martial treaty with the pagan foes,
All answers center here that fire and sword
Must make their sachem universal lord.
This arms the English with a resolution
To give the vaporing scab a retribution.
Heav'ns they consult by prayer, the best design
A furious foe to quell or undermine.
Resolved, that from the Massachusetts bands
Be prest on service some Herculean hands,
And certainly he well deserved a jerk
That slipt the collar from so good a work.
Some volunteers, some by compulsion go
To range the hideous forest for a foe.
The tender mother now's all bowels grown,
Clings to her son as if they'd melt in one.
Wives clasp about their husbands as the vine
Hugs the fair elm, while tears burst out like wine.
The new-sprung love in many a virgin heart
Swells to a mountain when the lovers part.
Nephews and kindred turn all springs of tears,

Their hearts are so surprised with panic fears.
But doleful shrieks of captives summon forth
Our walking castles, men of noted worth,
Made all of life, each captain was a Mars,
His name too strong to stand on waterish verse:
Due praise I leave to some poetic hand
Whose pen and wits are better at command.
Methinks I see the Trojan horse burst ope,
And such rush forth as might with giants cope:
These first the natives' treachery felt, too fierce
For any but eye-witness to rehearse.
Yet sundry times in places where they came
Upon the Indian skins they carved their name.
The trees stood sentinels and bullets flew
From every bush (a shelter for their crew)
Hence came our wounds and deaths from every side
While skulking enemies squat undescried,
That every stump shot like a musketeer,
And bows with arrows every tree did bear;
The swamps were courts of guard, thither retired
The straggling blue-coats when their guns were fired,
In dark meanders, and these winding groves,
Where bears and panthers with their monarch moves
These far more cruel slyly hidden lay,
Expecting Englishmen to move that way.
One party lets them up, the other greets
Them with the next thing to their winding-sheets;
Most fall, the rest thus startled back return,
And from their by-passed foes receive an urn.
Here fell a captain, to be named with tears,
Who for his courage left not many peers,
With many more who scarce a number left
To tell how treacherously they were bereft.
This flushed the pagan courage, now they think
The victory theirs, not lacking meat or drink.
The ranging wolves find here and there a prey,
And having filled their paunch they run away
By their hosts' light, the thanks which they return
Is to lead captives and their taverns burn.
Many whose thrift had stored for after use
Sustain their wicked plunder and abuse.
Poor people spying an unwonted light,
Fearing a martyrdom, in sudden fright
Leap to the door to fly, but all in vain,
They are surrounded with a pagan train;
Their first salute is death, which if they shun
Some are condemned the gauntelet to run;
Death would a mercy prove to such as those

Who feel the rigor of such hellish foes.
Posts daily on their Pegasean steeds
Bring sad reports of worse than Nero's deeds,
Such brutish murthers as would paper stain
Not to be heard in a Domitian's reign.
The field which nature hid is common laid,
And mothers' bodies ript for lack of aid.
The secret cabinets which nature meant
To hide her masterpiece is open rent,
The half-formed infant there receives a death
Before it sees the light or draws its breath,
Many hot welcomes from the natives' arms
Hid in their skulking holes, many alarms
Our brethren had, and weary, weary trants,
Sometimes in melting tears and pinching wants:
Sometimes the clouds with sympathizing tears
Ready to burst discharged about their ears:
Sometimes on craggy hills, anon in bogs
And miry swamps better befitting hogs,
And after tedious marches little boast
Is to be heard of stewed or baked or roast;
Their beds are hurdles, open house they keep;
Through shady boughs the stars upon them peep,
Their crystal drink drawn from the mother's breast
Disposes not to mirth but sleep and rest.
Thus many days and weeks, some months run out
To find and quell the vagabonding rout,
Who like enchanted castles fair appear,
But all is vanisht if you come but near,
Just so we might the pagan archers track
With towns and merchandise upon their back;
And thousands in the South who settled down
To all the points and winds are quickly blown.
At many meetings of their fleeting crew,
From whom like hail arrows and bullets flew:
The English courage with whole swarms dispute,
Hundreds they hack in pieces in pursuit.
Sed haud impunè, English sides do feel
As well as tawny skins the lead and steel
And some such gallant sparks by bullets fell,
As might have curst the powder back to hell:
Had only swords these skirmishes decided
All pagan skulls had been long since divided.
The ling'ring war outlives the summer sun,
Who hence departs hoping it might be done,
Ere his return at spring but ah, he'll find
The sword still drawn, men of unchanged mind.
Cold winter now nibbles at hands and toes

And shrewdly pinches both our friends and foes.
Fierce Boreas whips the pagan tribe together
Advising them to fit for foes and weather:
The axe which late had tasted Christian blood
Now sets its steely teeth to feast on wood.
The forests suffer now, by weight constrained
To kiss the earth with soldiers lately brained.
The lofty oaks and ash do wag the head
To see so many of their neighbors dead;
Their fallen carcasses are carried thence
To stand our enemies in their defense.
Their myrmidons inclosed with clefts of trees
Are busy like the ants or nimble bees:
And first they limber poles fix in the ground,
In figure of the heavens convex: all round
They draw their arras-mats and skins of beasts,
And under these the elves do make their nests.
Rome took more time to grow than twice six hours,
But half that time will serve for Indian bowers.
A city shall be reared in one day's space
As shall an hundred Englishmen outface.
Canonicus precincts there swarms unite,
Rather to keep a winter guard then fight.
A dark and dismal swamp some scout had found
Whose bosom was a spot of rising ground
Hedged up with mighty oaks, maples, and ashes,
Nurst up with springs, quick bogs, and miry plashes,
A place which nature coined on very nonce
For tigers not for men to be a sconce.
'Twas here these monsters shaped and faced like men
Took up their rendezvous and brumal den,
Deeming the depth of snow, hail, frost, and ice
Would make our infantry more tame and wise
Then by forsaking beds and loving wives,
Merely for Indian skins to hazard lives:
These hopes had something calmed the boiling passion
Of this incorrigible warlike nation.
During this short parenthesis of peace
Our forces found, but left him not at ease.
Here English valor most illustrious shone,
Finding their numbers ten times ten to one.
A shower of leaden hail our captains feel
Which made the bravest blades among us reel.
Like to some ant-hill newly spurned abroad,
Where each takes heels and bears away his load:
Instead of plate and jewels, Indian trays
With baskets up they snatch and run their ways.
Sundry the flames arrest and some the blade,

By bullets heaps on heaps of Indians laid.
The flames like lightning in their narrow streets
Dart in the face of everyone it meets.
Here might be heard an hideous Indian cry,
Of wounded ones, who in the wigwams fry.
Had we been cannibals here might we feast
On brave Westphalia gammons ready drest.
The tawny hue is Ethiopic made
Of such on whom Vulcan his clutches laid.
There fate was sudden, our advantage great
To give them once for all a grand defeat;
But tedious travel had so crampt our toes
It was too hard a task to chase the foes.
Distinctness in the numbers of the slain,
Or the account of pagans which remain
Are both uncertain, losses of our own
Are too too sadly felt, too sadly known.
War digs a common grave for friends and foes,
Captains in with the common soldier throws.
Six of our leaders in the first assault
Crave readmission to their Mother's vault,
Who had they fell in ancient Homer's days
Had been enrolled with hecatombs of praise.
As clouds disperst, the natives' troops divide,
And like the streams along the thickets glide.
Some breathing time we had, and short, God knows,
But new alarums from recruited foes
Bounce at our ears, the mounting clouds of smoke
From martyred towns the heav'ns for aid invoke:
Churches, barns, houses with most ponderous things
Made volatile fly o'er the land with wings.
Hundreds of cattle now they sacrifice
For airy spirits up to gormandize;
And to the Molech of their hellish guts,
Which craves the flesh in gross, their ale in butts.
Lancaster, Medfield, Mendon, wildered Groton,
With many villages by me not thought on
Die in their youth by fire, that useful foe,
Which this grand cheat the world will overflow.
The wand'ring priest to everyone he meets
Preaches his church's funeral in the streets.
Sheep from their fold are frighted, keepers too
Put to their trumps not knowing what to do.
This monster war hath hatcht a beauteous dove
In dogged hearts, of most unfeigned love,
Fraternal love, the livery of a saint,
Being come in fashion though by sad constraint,
Which if it thrive and prosper with us long

Will make New England forty thousand strong.
But off the table hand, let this suffice
As the abridgment of our miseries.
If mildew, famine, sword, and fired towns,
If slaughter, captivating, deaths and wounds,
If daily whippings once reform our ways,
These all will issue in our fathers' praise;
If otherwise, the sword must never rest
Till all New England's glory it divest.

The Grammarian's Funeral,

or,

An Elegy Composed upon the Death of Mr. John Woodmancy, formerly a Schoolmaster in Boston: but Now Published upon the Death of the Venerable Mr. Ezekiel Cheever, the Late and Famous Schoolmaster of Boston in New England; Who Departed this Life the Twenty-First of August, 1708. Early in the Morning. In the Ninety-Fourth Year of His Age.

[From *The Grammarian's Funeral,* 1708]

Eight parts of speech this day wear mourning gowns:
Declined verbs, pronouns, participles, nouns.
And not declined, adverbs and conjunctions,
In Lyly's porch they stand to do their functions,
With preposition; but the most affection
Was still observed in the interjection.
The substantive seeming the limbed best,
Would set an hand to bear him to his rest.
The adjective with very grief did say,
"Hold me by strength, or I shall faint away."
The clouds of tears did overcast their faces,
Yea all were in most lamentable cases.
The five declensions did the work decline,
And told the pronoun *Tu,* "the work is thine":
But in this case those have no call to go
That want the vocative, and can't say "O!"
The pronouns said that if the nouns were there,
There was no need of them, they might them spare:
But for the sake of emphasis they would,
In their discretion do whate'er they could.
Great honor was conferred on conjugations,
They were to follow next to the relations.
Amo did love him best, and *Doceo* might

Allege he was his glory and delight.
But *Lego* said, "By me he got his skill,
And therefore next the hearse I follow will."
Audio said little, hearing them so hot,
Yet knew by him much learning he had got.
O verbs the active were, or passive sure,
Sum to be neuter could not well endure.
But this was common to them all to moan
Their load of grief they could not soon *depone.*
A doleful day for verbs, they look so moody,
They drove spectators to a mournful study.
The verbs irregular, 'twas thought by some,
Would break no rule, if they were pleased to come.
Gaudeo could not be found; fearing disgrace,
He had withdrawn, sent *Maereo* in his place.
Possum did to the utmost he was able,
And bore as stout as if he'd been a table.
Volo was willing, *Nolo* somewhat stout,
But *Malo* rather chose, not to stand out.
Possum and *Volo* wished all might afford
Their help, but had not an imperative word.
Edo from service would by no means swerve.
Rather than fail, he thought the cakes to serve.
Fio was taken in a fit, and said,
By him a mournful poem should be made.
Fero was willing for to bear a part,
Although he did it with an aching heart.
Feror excused, with grief he was so torn,
He could not bear, he needed to be borne.
Such nouns and verbs as we defective find,
No grammar rule did their attendance bind.
They were excepted, and exempted hence,
But supines all did blame for negligence.
Verbs' offspring, participles hand-in-hand,
Follow, and by the same direction stand:
The rest promiscuously did crowd and cumber,
Such multitudes of each, they wanted number.
Next to the corpse to make th' attendance even,
Jove, Mercury, Apollo came from heaven.
And Virgil, Cato, gods, men, rivers, winds,
With elegies, tears, sighs, came in their kinds.
Ovid from Pontus hastes appareled thus,
In exile weeds bringing *De tristibus*:
And Homer sure had been among the rout,
But that the stories say his eyes were out.
Queens, cities, countries, islands come,
All trees, birds, fishes, and each word in *um.*
What syntax here can you expect to find?

Where each one bears such discomposed mind.
Figures of diction and construction,
Do little: yet stand sadly looking on.
That such a train may in their motion chord,
Prosodia gives the measure word for word.

Edward Taylor (1642?–1729)

THE greatest poet of the American seventeenth century remained unknown for more than two hundred years. Edward Taylor was born in Leicestershire, England, but his early life remains obscure. Welcomed to Boston in 1668 by Increase Mather, Charles Chauncy (the president of Harvard), and John Hull (the wealthy mint-master who later became Samuel Sewall's father-in-law), Taylor immediately entered Harvard and encouraged young Sewall to join him there. The two became close friends and correspondents. When Taylor graduated in 1671 he intended to return as Scholar of the House, but was induced to take a position as minister to the frontier village of Westfield, Massachusetts, where he served for the remainder of his life.

Taylor was a man of vigorous intellect. Though isolated physically from the center of New England intellectual activity, he nonetheless managed to continue his interest in church history, medicine, metallurgy, natural curiosities, church politics, and theology, becoming a remarkably learned man. His learning spilled into several volumes of sermons and translations, and finally distilled into a versified *Metrical History of Christianity,* a number of elegies commemorating the deaths of New England notables and personal friends, a long and complex poem titled *God's Determinations Touching His Elect: and the Elect's Combat in their Conversion, and Coming up to God in Christ together with the Comfortable Effects thereof,* several miscellaneous poems, and 217 very striking poems called *Preparatory Meditations* (1682–1725). Most of these are closely related to his sermons, and this is particularly true of the *Meditations,* which actually accompanied sermons delivered in Westfield on those days when Talyor "prepared" to administer the sacrament of the Lord's Supper, the dominant subject of his poems.

Well acquainted with the meditative tradition of English devotional poetry, Taylor often echoes the work of Donne, Herbert, and Quarles, but his style is strongly his own, individualized, direct, personal. Most evident, of course, is the shock of his imagery—homely, exotic, sometimes quite rude, drawn from household tasks, the law courts, gardening, music, or wherever he finds striking outward analogies of his inward experience of mystical union with

Christ. An intellectually exciting poet, he has in his verse an energy and tension that pulls the reader into the vortex of religious ecstasy with him, perhaps the only New England Puritan to realize artistically the orthodoxy to which he fully subscribed.

TEXTS: Edward Taylor's "Treatise Concerning the Lord's Supper" is edited from manuscript by courtesy of the Trustees of the Boston Public Library; it is part of the Prince Library, deposited in the Boston Public Library by the Deacons of the Old South Church. The poetry is based on the texts in Donald E. Stanford, ed., *The Poems of Edward Taylor* (New Haven, 1960).

Holy Robes for Glory

[From *Treatise Concerning the Lord's Supper* (1694)]

Matt. 22:12. "And he said unto him, 'Friend! How comest thou in hither, not having a wedden garment?' And he was speechless."

Doctrine: *That there is a gospel wedden garment required as absolutely necessary in all those that do approach unto the gospel wedden feast.* This is clear: the king, coming in to view the guests, saw there one that had not on the wedden garment. And he was so greatly displeased with him on this account as did exceed all warrant, if the wedden garment had not been a matter absolutely necessary to the celebration of the solemnity. In speaking to this doctrine, I shall direct my pen to these enquiries, in answering: what this wedden garment is? what this necessity of it is? why is this so necessary to this marriage? And then the use.

What is this wedden garment?

Solution: . . .

1. To describe it. I say it is the robe of evangelical righteousness constituting the soul complete in the sight of God. This is that which I take to be the wedden garment.

1. There is an evangelical righteousness, Matt. 6:33; Rom. 3:6; 14:17. This is styled "fine linen, pure and white," Rev. 19:14, and is promised as white to walk in, Rev. 3:4, 5, and we are all called to Christ to gain it, Rev. 3:18, and that white raiment is "the righteousness of the saints" and the wedden garment also, Rev. 19:8.

2. Now this evangelical righteousness consists in

1. Imputed righteousness, that is, the righteousness of Christ's active and passive obedience made ours by God's imputation and our own [faith in Him], called the righteousness of God by faith, Rom. 10:3; Phil. 3:9, God of His grace accepting of Christ in our stead for the fulfilling the law and also for the satisfying the law broken by us, which reckon Christ's keeping the law and His satisfying of it for us to

be ours. And the soul by faith receiving the same becomes hereby acquitted from the guilt of his sin and stands righteous before God. Hence Christ is made of God unto us righteousness, 1 Cor. 1, and He is become our righteousness by faith, Rom. 10:4.

2. Implanted righteousness. The sanctifying graces of the spirit communicated to the soul. These are the garment of the saints that are washed and made white, or whitened in the blood of the Lamb, Rev. 7:14, and these are to be considered as to their { essence. exercise. }

1. As to their essence or habit in the soul. Though simply and in an abstract sense they cannot be said to be washt in the blood of the Lamb, but to be purchased by it, yet as habits seated in the soul, and taken concretely, they are washed in the blood of the Lamb. . . .

2. As to their exercise. Now the exercise of these graces stands in need of the blood of the Lamb to whiten it in that it is faulty. For they never being exercised by the exercise of their subject, which is as yet the *subjectum inhesionis* of sin, their exercise is imperfect, and that as to its { proficiency. efficiency. }

1. As to the proficiency of grace. This is the internal and natural act of grace whereby it grows and is perfected. And in this respect this garment wants the blood of Christ to whiten it, that is, to put a glory and completeness upon it, for it makes ofttimes a slower proficiency and growth than it should, and often is degraded by a deficiency and decay, which it should not. Hence it needs Christ's blood to its completement and acceptance.

2. As to its efficiency or fruits. All effected in our life and conversation, our works of righteousness, stand in need of the blood of the Lamb to make them beauteous. Otherwise our best righteousness is but as filthy rags, Isa. 64:6, and may not appear in God's presence without Christ's incense, Rev. 8:3. But now being all washed in the blood of the Lamb and made white, we have the righteousness of the saints, which is inherent. And both put together make up this wedden garment in which the soul stands complete before God.

Secondly. To demonstrate this righteousness to be the gospel wedden garment. And for this end I shall give { testimony. arguments. } . . .

Secondly. Arguments. You see the judgment of various learned and godly men touching the wedden garment, that it amounts to this, that it is evangelical righteousness adorning the soul in the sight of God. Now I shall endeavor to fetch light unto it to evidence the same out of such arguments as these following:

1. This wedden garment is such a thing that only some few comparatively do attain unto of those that sit under the call of the gospel.

You see in the parable there were many called and invited, and these neglected the call — husbandmen, merchants, and others; cities and countries regarded it not. Only such as lie in the highways and hedges give acceptance to the call, and of these some do not so regard it as to attain to the wedden garment; here was one without it. Some few of them that came, came without it, and we are not to understand that all in such places were wrought on and brought in, but that those that were brought to the wedden were mostly such as these. Yet if all these be taken, they are comparatively but a few to the multitudes of them that inhabit cities and countries. And hence it appears that they are but a few comparatively that gain this wedden garment. Hence this wedden garment is such a thing that, in this property of it, it's the same with gospel righteousness. For gospel righteousness is the only thing which is tendered to all in general under the gospel, which yet very few attain unto. . . .

2. This wedden garment is such a thing without which the soul may be in a visible state of churchhood, though it ever ought to be where that state is as the reason of it, as you see in our text. For the duties of this state, at least some of them, may not be touched without it, as the celebration of the wedden feast. Now on this argument Haymo rejects baptism and faith from being the wedden garment, in that the soul may not be in this state without them. He must be baptized before he can be in a complete visible church state. So he must have a historical faith professed, or else he cannot enter into this state. But he may enter without evangelical righteousness. This the person without the wedden garment was without when entered. Haymo saith he may enter without charity. By charity he understands saving grace, and that and evangelical righteousness is all one. Though he ought to have this, yet he may be without it, and that to his own smart.

3. The wedden garment is an effect of the highest nature wrought by the gospel ministry — hence, evangelical righteousness. The reason runs thus: that effect of the gospel ministry which is of the highest and most excellent [nature] is evangelical righteousness. None can deny this. It's the very end of the gospel, yea, the highest end of it, as it is said of the times, Dan. 9:24, seventy weeks are determined to bring about everlasting righteousness. So I say the gospel is determined to bring about evangelical righteousness. And this being its highest special end, it cannot produce a more noble effect upon the soul than this is. It's the highest thing in God's determination laid out upon it for it to effect, for this is their conformity to the image of his son, Rom. 8:29. But now the wedden garment is the effect of the most excellent and highest nature wrought by the gospel ministry. The parable that our text belongs to holds it out. You see the servants that went out upon this of bringing the invited to the wedden labor no

further in their ministry than to bring souls adorned to the wedden. Those that came were prevailed with by the ministry of the gospel to come, and they came dressed up in the wedden garment. One, indeed, did delude, and had not on the wedden garment, but doubtless he appeared to have on the same, so that further than this the ministry labored not. It labored to bring them furnished to the wedden feast, and this being the highest service and most honorable that the gospel called them to and employed them in, it labored to bring them answerably accomplished thereto. Now the wedden garment doth fully accomplish thereto, and therefore it is an effect of the highest and most excellent nature that is wrought by the gospel ministry, and hence it appears to be evangelical righteousness.

4. The wedden garment is the highest accomplishment the soul attains unto in its attendance upon the gospel call. The gospel requires no higher accomplishment; it's that which fits completely for the most noble attendance it calls the soul unto. For that attendance which is set forth by the celebration of the wedden feast of the king's son is the highest and most noble that the gospel calls the soul unto, and the wedden garment completely accomplisheth the soul thereunto; there is nothing further required to accomplish the soul for this gospel wedden feast than the wedden garment. Hence this wedden garment is the highest accomplishment the gospel calls for. For it accomplisheth to keep the wedden feast of the king's son, and it's well known that when persons go as invited guests to weddens, they adorn themselves in their best apparel. Nay, if the wedden of a king's son, then in the best they can attain unto. And hence this wedden garment must needs be the best accomplishments that the gospel shops afford. But now evangelical righteousness is the best accomplishment the gospel calls us unto and supplieth us withal. This is such accomplishment that can be had no way else. It's such a rich web that only the gospel markets afford; it's such a web that is only wove in the looms of the gospel, nay, and a richer web and better huswifry it gets not up. Hence it calls for no higher accomplishments. It's the wealthy attire of glorified saints, Rev. 3:4, 5, and is therefore accomplishments fit for eternal glory. Now seeing the wedden garment is the highest accomplishment the gospel affords, and seeing evangelical righteousness is the highest gospel accomplishment, it follows that gospel righteousness and this wedden garment are one and the same.

5. The wedden garment is that whereby a person is evangelically prepared for fellowship with God in all gospel ordinances. For the proof of this I need not budge from the text. You see these in the wedden garment are accepted without objection; the king only takes him to do that had not on the wedden garment; therefore the rest were welcome guests. But now nothing besides evangelical righteous-

ness doth prepare the soul for communion with God in all gospel ordinances. This doth it so that God hath no objection against such. But he that is not such is objected against. The man without the wedden garment is objected against. God objects against every sinner in his sin, will have no fellowship with such, Psalm 94:20; Psalm 50:16, 17, 18. God will not hold fellowship with a person in his sin. Evangelical righteousness only prepares the soul for communion with God, Isai. 1:16, 17, 18; Psalm 15: *per totum;* and hence this wedden garment is evangelical righteousness.

6. This wedden garment is such as all those and only those that are adorned therein are received into singular favor, honor, familiarity, and pleasantness with God. All this is clear in our text. For it was a feast full of joyous matters, and the authors of feasts deal familiarly with their guests, confer the honor of the feast upon them, the pleasantness, the joy of the feast upon them. Now the king here imports God the father, and his acts the acts of God towards His guests, and hence it appears that such as are welcome guests at this feast do enjoy His favor. He deals familiarly with them, confers great honors on them, and entertains them with all the pleasantness and joy of the feast; and these guests, you see, are such and only such as have on the wedden garment. But now all those and only those that are adorned with evangelical righteousness are received into favor, honor, familiarity, and pleasantness with God. God will rejoice over such with joy, and joy over them with singing, Isai. 69:5; Zeph. 37:7, and this implies all the rest. But He will not thus deal with any that are not evangelically righteous, for so to do would argue evangelical righteousness a thing not necessary to this favor, honor, and pleasantness; and so it would argue against Christ and the gospel itself. Hence evangelical righteousness is that which gives acceptance thus into God's favor, honor, familiarity, and pleasure, and so appeareth to be the same with the wedden garment.

7. The wedden garment is such a thing that the soul in want of it at the wedden feast is under the displeasure and wrath of the Almighty. This is plain in the text. The king would never have called him so strictly to an account and have dealt so severely with him for the want of it that had it not, if his being at the wedden feast without it had not greatly displeased him. But evangelical righteousness is the only thing the want whereof in the guests at the wedden is displeasing and provokes the Lord to anger. I would know what else it is that the want of lays the soul under the anger of God. God was angry on this account with those, Rev. 3:16, 17, and therefore He counsels to get it, v. 18; the want of it shut the foolish virgins out of door, Matt. 25:10, 12. Hence evangelical righteousness and the wedden garment appear to be the same.

8. The wedden garment is such a thing the want whereof in the wedden guests is a damning sin. This you see here: the person that had it not is cast into utter darkness, v. 13; it is an affront unto the wedden; it is an unworthy eating and drinking at the feast. It is an indignity put upon the highest honor conferred; the highest dainties prepared; the highest nobility in nature; the highest ornaments obtainable; the highest wedden celebrated; the noblest bridesgroom that ever was wedded; and the highest king that ever reigned. And hence to approach slovenly, to come without the wedden garment, is a damnable sin. But evangelical righteousness is such a thing that the want thereof in the wedden guests is damning. The want of this is damning. Such as are without it are naked, Rev. 3:17, and these are threatened to be spewed out of God's mouth. Those that are naked are in a damnable state; to be naked, therefore, is a damning sin. The shame of spiritual nakedness is damning, and this attends the want of evangelical righteousness. Whosoever is without this righteousness, the best that he hath is but as dog's meat, Phil. 3:8. Well then nothing of good can belong to such an one, and therefore his state is damnable. Now there is nothing but evangelical righteousness is of such concern to man as the want thereof is damning, and hence this is the wedden garment. And thus we see the matter made out, that the wedden garment is evangelical righteousness. And so I have done with this second inquiry.

3. Query is after the reasons of the truth, wherefore this wedden garment is absolutely necessary to the celebration of the wedden supper. Now the reasons I add are these:

1. From the nature of the ordinance. It's styled a wedden feast. For although we render the word in the parable of our text "wedden," or "marriage," and rightly, yet the intent of it is the marriage feast, as is clear from the provision made, v. 4. Now if it be no wedden feast, why is it so styled but because it implieth the marriage of Christ and the soul to be made before? For it is not such a celebration of another's espousals as doth exclude the souls that celebrate it. Hence then the celebration of it declares the souls to be espoused unto Christ, and if the formal reason of its name is to be found in the nature of the thing, then the nature of the ordinance stands out upon the soul's espousal to Christ. But if the soul be espoused unto Christ, it hath the wedden garment. For none espoused to Him are without it. Further, the nature of the ordinance being the celebration of a spiritual wedden feast, it requires all that celebrate it to be suitably adorned and fitted for it. The civil customs of all the world celebrating their weddens in apparel suitable to the solemnity commends this unto us, to attend weddens in wedden dress. . . . Something of this nature you have in Abraham's servant adorning Rebecca, Gen. 24:53. But this wedden in

our parable being spiritual, the ornaments and robes for the celebration of it must be spiritual, as being the robe alone suitable to the nature of the ordinance. And thus you see the nature of the ordinance being a wedden feast requires the wedden garment in all the guests.

2. From the honor on all hands requisite in this case. Hence the reason runs thus. The honor of the wedden makes it necessary that the guests carry it honorably. Here is the most honorable wedden that ever was celebrated; the most honorable provision that ever was made; the most honorable guests that ever were entertained; the most honorable entertainment that ever was given; and the greatest honor in the invitation that ever any invitation did administer. Hence it's absolutely necessary that the guests carry it honorably. For if they do not, they carry it unsuitably to the honorableness of the feast. They dishonor the wedden, they dishonor the bridesgroom, they dishonor the king that makes the feast and invited them, they dishonor all the guests and act mostly to their own shame and dishonor. But now only such guests as are attired with the wedden garment carry it honorably. Others cannot; they have no honorable attire nor honorable qualifications. Hence either such as have the wedden garment carry it honorably or else none do. But some do carry it honorably. For it makes not to the honor of any to feast such that never any of them carry it honorably. Hence such as have the wedden garment are the persons that carry it or can carry it honorably, and thus we see an absolute necessity of the wedden garment to the wedden feast.

3. From the favor of the king that makes the wedden for his son it appears that the wedden garment is necessary to the wedden feast. The reason runs thus: it's necessary that all the guests at the gospel wedden should so attend it as that they may enjoy the favor of the king that makes it. For it proceeds from love, and therefore the guests ought so to carry it as may lodge them more in the love of him that makes it. When the wise man saith that a feast is made for laughter, Eccl. 10:19, he intends thus much, that it's made to increase favor, friendship, and familiarity. Hence the guests ought so to appear and carry it as may conduce to this favor and friendship. That the guests at this feast ought so to carry as may be to the favor of the king that makes it is clear also hence, because his favor is so great and of so great concern that Christ himself came to procure it for them. Hence they ought to carry it so as that they may abide in it. But the gospel wedden garment is absolutely necessary in all the guests at the gospel wedden feast to lodge them in the favor of the king. The want of it is a dishonor of his son's wedden, and this is highly provoking. He saith, "Surely they will reverence my son," Matt. 21:37. Hence He is highly provoked when His son is dishonored. But when the guests appear in the gospel wedden garment, the case is contrary; now

His favor is upon them. He only was angry at him that had not on the wedden garment. Hence the wedden garment is absolutely necessary to the wedden supper.

4. From the benefit of the wedden garment, it is absolutely necessary to the wedden supper. The reason runs thus: that is absolutely necessary to the wedden supper without which there is no benefit come by the wedden supper. This is evident, for the wedden supper is ordained for the benefit of the guests. God hath not ordained things for destruction but for benefit, 1 Cor. 12:7; 2 Cor. 10:8; 13:10. But the wedden garment is absolutely necessary to the guests celebrating the wedden feast in order to the benefit of the same. They cannot approach without and not sin; they cannot approach without it but under the displeasure of the king; they cannot partake of the dainties of the feast without it; they have no appetite thereto; they cannot receive the things of the spirit of God, 1 Cor. 2:14; they cannot partake of spiritual things without; this feast is to nourish the new man, but where the wedden garment is not, there is nothing of the new man. Hence no benefit is attained without it. But where the wedden garment is, there the benefit of the feast is conveyed. On them the king smiles; before them the dainties are placed; to them the king saith, "Eat, O friends! Drink, yea, drink abundantly, O beloved!" Cant. 5:1. On them the benefits of the feast is bestowed. So that on this account we see the wedden garment absolutely necessary unto the wedden supper of the gospel in all that approach thereunto.

Thus we have seen some reasons confirming the truth; and now I come to improve the same in these uses following:

USE 1. By way of information. Is the gospel wedden feast such, as the gospel wedden garment is absolutely necessary unto the same in all that approach thereunto? Then this truth sets before us such conclusions as these:

1. That the gospel wedden feast is a most honorable ordinance. It's the property of other ordinances to put upon the soul the wedden garment, but the wedden garment is the necessary appurtenance to the celebration of the wedden supper. Now the wedden garment is one of the richest effects of the other ordinances, being the absolutely necessary ornament unto the wedden supper, must needs so far advance the honorableness of this ordinance that the most honorable effects produced by other ordinances do not accomplish the soul to be a welcome guest unto this. Hence this is a most honorable ordinance, and these demonstrations shew it.

1. Other ordinances are erected to prepare and fit the soul for this. . . . The preaching of the Word is ordained for the converting of the soul to Christ, and so for the adorning of it with the wedden garment. The web of grace is wrought in the soul by the shuttles of the Word, Rom. 1:16; Ch. 10:17; 1 Cor. 1:21. This then prepares for this feast.

Take baptism, and it initiates the soul into its visible covenant state and right to covenant privileges as the initiatory seal thereof, and so is a preparation in order to this wedden feast. Take a church state, and this is another preparatory step to the wedden supper without which there is no entrance into the feast. Accordingly I might say prayer, meditation, and self-examination are of special use to prepare the soul for this feast. Hence this feast is most honorable. Now as that person's honor is very shining that is attended by honorable persons, Esth. 6:9, 10, 11; Can. 3:7, 8, so that ordinance must needs be most honorable that is attended upon by other ordinances as fitting for it.

2. The honorableness of other ordinances in some sense gives place to this. For there is no wedden garment required as absolutely necessary to all that attend thereupon. For all are bound to attend on them that they may attain the wedden garment, in that they are ordained the means for the attainment thereof. Now the wedden garment being the most honorable ornament that the gospel confers, it must of necessity be that that ordinance is most honorable unto which the wedden garment is necessary, and that the other ordinances give up of their honorableness unto it, in that the wedden garment necessarily required in such as do attend upon it is their preparation made by them.

2. Hence it appears that the gospel wedden feast or the Lord's Supper is no converting ordinance; it's not a grace begetting ordinance; that it never was ordained of God to give the first grace, but that it is only a grace strengthening ordinance. For if the wedden garment (which, as you have heard, is evangelical righteousness) be absolutely necessary to the celebration of the wedden feast, then everyone that comes unto it must have it before he comes. For if he comes without it, he comes without what is necessary unto its celebration. But if he must have it before he comes to the wedden, it cannot be an effect produced and conferred upon the guests by the wedden feast. This it cannot be, for then the wedden should produce the wedden garment before its own essence is produced, which is as absurd as to say the son is before the father. *Operatio sequitur esse.* For actions are the blossoms that essences in their beings and existences produce. Hence if the wedden garment be absolutely necessary unto the wedden supper, it must be before it, and not produced by it; and therefore the feast is no grace begetting, but only a grace strengthening ordinance. . . .

USE 2. By way of trial. Is it thus, that the gospel wedden garment is absolutely necessary to the gospel wedden feast? Then this should put us all to try ourselves whether we have this wedden garment or not. We are under the call to the wedden supper. For us not to come will be dangerous. For us to come without the wedden garment will be alike dangerous in that we come without an absolutely necessary accomplishment. Hence it behooves us, as we would secure ourselves from the peril of our souls, to try our souls whether they be arrayed in this wedden garment: that if we have the same we may have the comfort thereof, and if we have not the same, we might see our nakedness and seek for the wedden garment to be arrayed therewith. And for rules attend these few things following:

1. In general, by the properties of those that have this wedden garment on. For if the wedden garment is yours, the same properties are in you as are special unto the welcome guests. The like properties are in all that are trimmed up in this wedden garment. These are not persons under the regency of contrary dispositions, but they are homogeneous members of the body of Christ, *ejusdem nominis et naturae;* therefore try yourselves whether you are persons of the like frames and dispositions; of the like lives and conversations; of the like spirits and properties. For if your properties differ from theirs, if you be birds of a different feather unto theirs, you have not the wedden garment on. Try therefore thus. But we must know what these properties are, and therefore:

2. In particular. You are to search after these properties in particular; and the particular properties of such as have it are these:

1. An humble frame of spirit. For the soul that hath this wedden garment hath no covering of his own. He is naked without it, and the sense of this doth work poverty of spirit and keep it low and little in its own eyes. For though he is adorned with this stately clothing, yet it's none of his own, but only bestowed on him, and hence he is poor in his own eyes, little in his own account, and sees his own nakedness under it, his own botches and fistulated ulcers running, and his deformed skin under this glorious attire, and this is that which makes him humble. Hence there is a blessing goeth unto the humble, Matt. 5:3. The kingdom of heaven is theirs, and so they are the welcome guests. Hence grace (that constitutes the wedden garment) is given to them, Prov. 3:34; James 4:6; 1 Pet. 5:5. Now then, if thou art humble, thou art the person that hast the property of such as have the wedden garment. But not otherwise.

2. A soul-trembling frame at the Word. . . . For many things strike an awe in such, as the fear lest they should be cheated and account that they have the wedden garment and yet it's not so; they are cheated with a Devonshire kersey instead of a right broadcloth, or, if it be right, yet lest they should defile their garment or be unmannerly and not carry it aright at so honorable a wedden. And so they are trembling and of a trembling spirit. If it be thus with thee, then thou hast another property of one in the wedden garment.

3. An utter enmity against all sin. The soul that hath this wedden garment hates everything that will defile it. . . .

4. An high esteem of the wedden garment. Persons that come hardly by their best robes use to set much by them. So do these that

are arrayed in this royal robe. They hunger and thirst after righteousness, Matt. 5:6. What sayst thou to this? Is it so with thee?

5. A diligent attention and heedfulness to keep this garment clean and undefiled. Oh! how wary are persons that they do not blot or stain, dirty, spartle, or defile their best clothes. So it is with such as have this rich array of the spirit, Rev. 3:4. Hence they keep out of sinful ways; they touch no unclean thing. Now, is it thus with thee? Art thou studious to keep thy garments clean, white, and shining?

6. An holy life and conversation. Such as are adorned in their choicest apparel walk exactly and in clean ways. Such ways as suit this wedden dress are ways of holiness. Holiness becomes God's house forever. Now, if thou dost thus, it's a good note.

7. An high esteem of the bridesgroom and the wedden feast. Here is reason for it. He hath invited them. He hath richly clothed them. He hath provided for them, and His honorableness commands the highest esteem. Hence they cry out, "Whom have we in heaven but thee? And in earth there is none that we desire besides thee," Psalm 73:25. Now, how stands the case with thee in this matter? This will determine whether thou hast a like spirit to such as have this wedden garment. And thus having mentioned some of the properties of those adorned with the wedden garment, I commend them to thee to try thyself by the same. For if thou hast the like properties, the wedden garment is thine; but none of thine if not.

USE 3. By way of exhortation. Is the gospel wedden garment absolutely necessary unto the wedden feast? Then let this truth be spun out into a word or two of exhortation to us all, and that to endeavor to { attain the wedden robe. / attend the wedden feast in it. }

First. To endeavor after this wedden garment. Alas! how many are there that have nothing of it; no, not so much as a thrid of it, and so nothing to cover the shame of their nakedness, and yet sit under the call of the gospel, and that in order unto the wedden supper? Now you that are such are the persons under the present exhortation. Oh! therefore accept of the entertainment this truth prepares for you, and be entreated to make it your great work to get this wedden garment. How should you have it if you seek not for it? Oh! stir up yourselves! Endeavor for it! The urgency of this exhortation comes upon you in these few considerations:

1. You are under a necessity, i.e., an unavoidableness of sin while you abide without this wedden garment. Consider it. For if you abide without what God requires you to have, it's sin in you, it's an opposition to God's command. God commands you to have this garment, Rev. 3:8. God's counseling is commanding. Further, he requires you to come to the wedden feast, for the call of the gospel is such as invites to the wedden feast, Matt. 22:3, 4. Now for you not to come

is sin, for the call makes it your duty to come. And for you to come without the wedden garment is sin, for it is absolutely necessary to the feast. Hence you sin unavoidably if you have not the wedden garment. Endeavor therefore for it.

2. You are under a necessity to attend the wedden, for you are invited. You cannot answer your non-attendance. No plea will be valid in this case, Luke 14:17–24. You are in like necessity to get the wedden robe, for it is necessary to the celebration of the feast. So that, do you what you can, you are exposed to wrath without it. Stay from the feast and wrath comes upon you; step into it and wrath comes upon you. So that this is the only way left you to avoid ruin, viz., to get the wedden garment. Oh! then endeavor after it.

3. The wedden garment will make you a welcome guest at the wedden feast. It's necessary indeed to the right and acceptable carrying on of all other parts of God's worship, though it is not absolutely necessary to the approaching thereunto. But, it being absolutely necessary to the attendance upon the wedden feast, if you have it, you bring your welcome with you, for there is contained in it everything needful to make a right accomplished and welcome guest. And who then would not have this? Oh! then endeavor after it. And having obtained it,

Secondly. Endeavor to attend upon this wedden feast dressed up in it. You have it, and it's the soul's wedden furniture; see then that you attend the wedden. And for this end know:

1. You do not make a right use of it as it is the wedden robe unless you use it in celebrating the wedden feast. For in that it is absolutely necessary for the wedden feast, it is cut out for this as the main design of it under this denomination, wherefore the right use of it is to furnish the soul for and in the celebration of this ordinance. Wherefore now attend upon this ordinance in it; you fail the right use of it otherwise.

2. You will be a glory and an honor to the wedden, and the wedden to you, if you now attend. When guests rightly adorned to celebrate a wedden attend such solemnities, they are the glory of the same. This then will be one of the greatest glories that you can bring to Christ. Therefore see that you honor him thus. And the wedden feast will be one of the greatest glories and honors unto thee. For here is royal entertainment, noble society, and hearty welcome with sweetest familiarity imaginable. Oh! what sweet, what heart-ravishing, and soul-enlivening delight will here be unto thee? Christ will stay thee with flaggons, comfort thee with apples, according to thy prayer, Cant. 2:5, and draw the canopy of love over thee. Therefore attend here the wedden feast, now thou hast this wedden garment, and so thou will honor Christ, and Christ will honor thee.

Huswifery

[From "Poetical Works" (1694?)]

Make me, O Lord, thy spinning wheel complete.
Thy Holy Word my distaff make for me.
Make mine affections thy swift fliers neat,
And make my soul thy holy spool to be.
My conversation make to be thy reel,
And reel the yarn thereon spun of thy wheel.

Make me thy loom then, knit therein this twine:
And make thy Holy Spirit, Lord, wind-quills:
Then weave the web thyself. The yarn is fine.
Thine ordinances make my fulling mills.
Then dye the same in heavenly colors choice,
All pinkt with varnisht flowers of paradise.

Then clothe therewith mine understanding, will,
Affections, judgment, conscience, memory,
My words and actions, that their shine may fill
My ways with glory, and thee glorify.
Then mine apparel shall display before ye
That I am clothed in holy robes for glory.

From

PREPARATORY MEDITATIONS

Awakening

[Meditation 8, First Series (1684)]

John 6:51. "I am the living bread."

I kenning through astronomy divine
The world's bright battlement, wherein I spy
A golden path my pencil cannot line
From that bright throne unto my threshold lie.
And while my puzzled thoughts about it pore,
I find the Bread of Life in't at my door.

When that this Bird of Paradise put in
This wicker cage (my corpse) to tweedle praise
Had peckt the fruit forbad: and so did fling

Away its food; and lost its golden days;
It fell into celestial famine sore:
And never could attain a morsel more.

Alas! alas! poor bird, what wilt thou do?
The creature's field no food for souls e'er gave.
And if thou knock at angels' doors they show
An empty barrel: they no soul bread have.
Alas! poor bird, the world's white loaf is done,
And cannot yield thee here the smallest crumb.

In this sad state God's tender bowels run
Out streams of grace. And He to end all strife
The purest wheat in heaven, His dear-dear Son
Grinds, and kneads up into this Bread of Life.
Which Bread of Life from heaven down came and stands
Disht on thy table up by angels' hands.

Did God mould up this bread in heaven, and bake,
Which from His table came, and to thine goeth?
Doth He bespeak thee thus, "This soul bread take.
Come eat thy fill of this thy God's white loaf?
It's food too fine for angels, yet come, take
And eat thy fill. It's heaven's sugar cake."

What grace is this knead in this loaf? This thing
Souls are but petty things it to admire.
Ye angels, help! This fill would to the brim
Heav'ns whelm'd-down crystal meal bowl, yea and higher.
This Bread of Life dropt in thy mouth doth cry,
"Eat, eat me, Soul, and thou shalt never die."

Purgation

[Meditation 40, First Series (1690)]

I John 2:2. "He is a propitiation for our sin."

Still I complain; I am complaining still.
Oh! woe is me! Was ever heart like mine?
A sty of filth, a trough of washing-swill,
A dunghill pit, a puddle of mere slime,
A nest of vipers, hive of hornets' stings,
A bag of poison, civit-box of sins.

Was ever heart like mine? So bad? black? vile?
Is any divel blacker? Or can hell
Produce its match? It is the very soil

Where Satan reads his charms, and sets his spell;
His bowling alley, where he shears his fleece
At Ninepins, Nine Holes, Morrice, Fox and Geese.

His palace garden where his courtiers walk,
His jewel's cabinet. Here his cabal
Do sham it, and truss up their privy talk
In fardels of consults and bundles all.
His shambles, and his butcher's stall's herein.
It is the fuddling school of every sin.

Was ever heart like mine? Pride, passion, fell
Ath'ism, blasphemy, pot, pipe it, dance,
Play Barleybreaks, and at last couple in hell;
At cudgels, Kit-Cat, cards and dice here prance,
At Noddy, Ruff-and-trumpt, Jing, Post-and-Pare,
Put, One-and-Thirty, and such other ware.

Grace shuffled is away; patience oft sticks
Too soon, or draws itself out, and's out put.
Faith's over-trumpt, and oft doth lose her tricks.
Repentance's chalkt up Noddy, and out shut.
They Post and Pare off grace thus, and its shine.
Alas! alas! was ever heart like mine?

Sometimes methinks the serpent's head I mall;
Now all is still: my spirits do recruit.
But ere my harp can tune sweet praise, they fall
On me afresh, and tear me at my root.
They bite like badgers now, nay worse, although
I took them toothless skulls, rot long ago.

My reason now's more than my sense, I feel
I have more sight than sense. Which seems to be
A rod of sunbeams t'whip me for my steel.
My spirit's spiritless, and dull in me
For my dead prayerless prayers; the spirit's wind
Scarce blows my mill about. I little grind.

Was ever heart like mine? My Lord, declare.
I know not what to do. What shall I do?
I wonder split I don't upon despair.
It's grace's wonder that I wrack not so.
I faintly shun't, although I see this case
Would say, my sin is greater than thy grace.

Hope's day-peep dawns hence through this chink. Christ's name
Propitiation is for sins. Lord, take
It so for mine. Thus quench thy burning flame

In that clear stream that from His side forth brake.
I can no comfort take while thus I see
Hell's cursed imps thus jetting strut in me.

Lord, take thy sword, these anakims destroy,
Then soak my soul in Zion's bucking tub
With holy soap, and nitre, and rich lye.
From all defilement me cleanse, wash and rub.
Then wrince, and wring me out till th' water fall
As pure as in the well, not foul at all.

And let thy sun shine on my head out clear.
And bathe my heart within its radiant beams;
Thy Christ make my propitiation dear.
Thy praise shall from my heart break forth in streams.
This reeching virtue of Christ's blood will quench
Thy wrath, slay sin, and in thy love me bench.

Discipline

[Meditation 138, Second Series (1717)]

Canticles 6:6. "Thy teeth are like a flock of sheep that come up from washing, whereof every one bears twins."

My blessed blessing Lord, I fain would try
To heave thy glory 'bove the heavens above,
But find my lisping tongue can never pry
It up an inch above this dirt, nor move
Thy brightsome glory o'er this dirty slough
We puddle in below and wallow now.

But though I can but stut and blur what I
Do go about and so indeed much mar
Do thy bright shine, I fain would slick up high,
Although I foul it by my pen's harsh jar.
Pardon my faults: they're all against my will.
I would do well but have too little skill.

What golden words drop from thy gracious lips,
Adorning of thy speech with holy paint,
Making thy spouse's teeth like lambs that skip,
Oh flock of sheep that come from washing quaint,
Each bearing twins, a pleasant sight to spy,
Whose little lambs have leaping play and joy.

. . . .

What are these teeth? Pray show. Some do suppose
  They are the spouse's military arms,
The arguments that do destroy her foes,
  And do defend the gospel truths from harms;
  But teeth in sheep are not their weapon though
  The lion's teeth and cur dog's teeth are so.

And others do say they note Christ's ministers,
  That dress the spouse's food. Yet such seem cooks.
When these are 'ployed like teeth 'bout meat as its dresser.
  Yet still this seems a lesson not in books.
  Methinks Christ's ministers may rather bear
  The name of cooks, than teeth that eat the fare.

Hence methinks they the righter judge, that hold
  These teeth import true faith in Christ alone
And meditation on the gospel should
  Be signified thereby to everyone.
  Teeth are for the eating of the food made good,
  And meditation chawing is the cud.

The proper use of teeth gives the first stroke
  Unto the meat and food we feed upon,
And fits it for the stomach there to soak
  In its concoction for nutrition.

And meditation when 'tis concocted there,
  Takes its rich liquor having nourishment,
And distributes the same choice spiritual cheer
  Through all the new man by its instrument,
  And hence that means of grace doth as I think,
  Give nourishment hereby as meat and drink.

This faith and meditation a pair appears,
  As two like to the two brave rows of teeth;
The upper and the nether, well set clear,
  Exactly meet to chew the food, belief.
  Both eat by biting; meditation
  By chewing spiritually the cud thereon.

. . . .

They pair each other too, in whiteness clear,
  As those like Olivant, these sparkling show
With glorious shine in a most brightsome gear
  Of spiritual whiteness that exceeds pure snow,
  Christ's milk-white righteousness and splendent grace
  Faith doth and meditation ever trace.

Vision

[Meditation 12, First Series (1685)]

Isaiah 63:1. "Glorious in his apparel"

This quest rapt at my ears' broad golden doors,
Who's this that comes from Edom in this shine,
In dyed robes from Bozrah? This more o'er
All glorious in's apparel, all divine?
Then through that wicket rusht this buzz there gave,
"It's I that right do speak, mighty to save."

I threw through Zion's lattice then an eye,
Which spied one like a lump of glory pure,
Nay, clothes of gold, buttoned with pearls do lie
Like rags, or shoeclouts unto His He wore.
Heaven's curtains blancht with sun, and stars of light
Are black as sackcloth to His garments bright.

One shining sun gilding the skies with light
Benights all candles with their flaming blaze;
So doth the glory of this robe benight
Ten thousand suns at once ten thousand ways.
For e'ry thrid therein's dyed with the shine
Of all, and each the attributes divine.

The sweetest breath, the sweetest violet,
Rose, or carnation ever did gust out
Is but a foist to that perfume beset
In thy apparel steaming round about.
But is this so? My puling soul, then pine
In love until this lovely one be thine.

Pluck back the curtains, back the window shuts:
Through Zion's agate window take a view;
How Christ in pinkted robes from Bozrah puts,
Comes glorious in's apparel forth to woo.
Oh! if His glory ever kiss thine eye,
Thy love will soon enchanted be thereby.

Then grieve, my soul, thy vessel is so small,
And holds no more for such a lovely He.
That strength's so little, love scarce acts at all.
That sight's so dim, doth scarce Him lovely see.
Grieve, grieve, my soul, thou shouldst so pimping be,
Now such a price is here presented thee.

All sight's too little sight enough to make,
All strength's too little love enough to rear,
All vessels are too small to hold or take

Enough love up for such a lovely dear.
How little to this little's then thy all,
For Him whose beauty saith all love's too small?

My lovely one, I fain would love thee much,
But all my love is none at all I see,
Oh! let thy beauty give a glorious touch
Upon my heart, and melt to love all me.
Lord, melt me all up into love for thee,
Whose loveliness excels what love can be.

The Experience

(1682?)

Oh! that I always breathed in such an air,
As I suckt in, feeding on sweet content!
Disht up unto my soul ev'n in that prayer
Poured out to God over last sacrament.
What beam of light wrapt up my sight to find
Me nearer God than e'er came in my mind?

Most strange it was! But yet more strange that shine
Which filled my soul then to the brim to spy
My nature with thy nature all divine
Together joined in Him that's thou, and I.
Flesh of my flesh, bone of my bone. There's run
Thy Godhead, and my manhood in thy Son.

Oh! that that flame which thou didst on me cast
Might me enflame, and lighten e'ry where.
Then heaven to me would be less at last,
So much of heaven I should have while here.
Oh! sweet, though short! I'll not forget the same.
My nearness, Lord, to thee did me enflame.

I'll claim my right: give place, ye angels bright!
Ye further from the Godhead stand than I.
My nature is your Lord, and doth unite
Better than yours unto the deity.
God's throne is first and mine is next; to you
Only the place of waiting-men is due.

Oh! that my heart, thy golden harp might be,
Well tuned by glorious grace, that e'ry string
Screwed to the highest pitch, might unto thee
All praises wrapt in sweetest music bring.
I praise thee, Lord, and better praise thee would,
If what I had, my heart might ever hold.

John Saffin (1632–1710)

JOHN SAFFIN is another colonial poet who, like Edward Taylor, remained unpublished until the twentieth century. Samuel Eliot Morison suggests that, on the basis of the examples thus set by Saffin and Taylor, "we may infer that much lyrical poetry was written in the English colonies that never reached the printed page." This might be especially true of the writers of love lyrics, of whom Saffin is colonial New England's most notable example. He was born in Devonshire, England; came to New England when he was twelve; and was raised in the house of Edward Winslow, governor of the Plymouth colony. Some time around 1653 he began courting Martha Willet of Plymouth, daughter of a well-to-do fur trader and government official. Martha's father helped arrange a business trip to Virginia for John, who spent four years in the South before returning to claim his bride. The trip was successful, and John and Martha married in 1658. They moved to Boston, where Saffin became a wealthy merchant and in time a judge. An occasional dealer in slaves, Saffin rented a farm to one Adam, agreeing to give him his freedom if he worked well for seven years. At the end of six years Adam was removed from the farm as unsatisfactory, and so was not freed. He complained to the courts, and finally won his freedom from Saffin largely through the efforts of the presiding officer, Judge Samuel Sewall.

In 1665 Saffin began to collect his thoughts and his readings into a commonplace book titled "A Collection of Various Matters of Divinity, Law, and State Affairs, Epitomized Both in Verse and Prose." In it he states that "He that would write well in verse must observe these rules: to consider the true worth and nature of the subject he treats upon, and accordingly frame his style that it be elegant, emphatical, metaphorical, and historical, running in a fluent and smooth channel." Included in the book are the following two poems from the period of his courtship under the general title "Several amorous and youthful poems." The first was written from Virginia in 1654 and was apparently sent as a letter; the second was written in 1658 and is a paraphrase of Quarles's *Argalus and Parthenia.*

TEXT: Caroline Hazard, ed., *John Saffin His Book* (New York, 1928).

"Sweetly (My Dearest) I Left Thee Asleep"

(1654)

Sweetly (my Dearest) I left thee asleep,
Which silent parting made my heart to weep,
Fain would I wake her, but Love did reply,
O wake her not, so sweetly let her lie.
But must I go, O must I leave her so,
So ill at ease, involved in slumbering woe;
Must I go hence, and thus my love desert
Unknown to her, O must I now depart;
Thus was I hurried with such thoughts as these,
Yet loath to rob thee of thy present ease,
Or rather senseless pain, farewell, thought I,
My joy, my dear in whom I live or die;
Farewell content, farewell fair beauty's light,
And the most pleasing object of my sight;
I must be gone, adieu, my Dear, adieu!
Heavens grant good tidings I next hear from you.
Thus in sad silence I alone and mute,
My lips bade thee farewell, with a salute;
And so went from thee. Turning back again,
I thought one kiss too little, then stole twain,
And then another; but no more of this!
Count with yourself how many of them you miss.
And now, my Love, soon let me from thee hear
Of thy good health, that may my spirits cheer.
Acquaint me with such passages as may
Present themselves since I am come away;
And above all things let me thee request
To be both cheerful, quiet, and at rest
In thine own spirit, and let nothing move
Thee unto discontent, my Joy, my Love.
Hoping that all things shall at last conduce
Unto our comfort and a blessed use;
Considering that those things hardly gained
Are most delightful when they are attained.
Gold crowns are heavy; Idalian burns,
And lovers' days are good, and bad by turns;
But yet the consummation will repay
The debt that's due many a happy day.
Which that it may so be, I'll heaven implore
To grant the same henceforth forever more.
And so farewell, farewell, fair beauty's light,
Ten thousand times adieu, my Dear Delight.
Your ever loving friend whilest he
Desolved is, or cease to be.

J. S.

To Her Coming Home

(1658)

Sail, gentle pinnace, Zepherus doth not fail
With prosperous gales; sail, gentle pinnace, sail!
Proud Neptune stoops, and freely condescends
For's former roughness, now to make amends;
Thetis with her green mantle sweetly glides
With smiling dimples singing by our sides.
Sail, gentle pinnace! Zepherus does not fail
With prosperous gales; sail, gentle pinnace, sail!

MICROCOSMOGRAPHY

Human nature was a perennial interest of New Englanders. Perhaps because of their emphasis upon the personal nature of the God they worshipped, a God personally concerned with the most trivial of their activities and thoughts because he valued each of them, they turned regularly in their writing to consider these objects of divine benevolence. In doing so they cultivated a distinctive kind of New England writing — the formal character sketch. Historically the formal "character" derives from the thirty pithy sketches of ethical types composed by Theophrastus (373–284 B.C.). Popularized in England by Joseph Hall's *Characters of Virtues and Vices* (1608), Sir Thomas Overbury's *The Characters* (1614), and John Earle's *Microcosmographie* (1628), the form was widely practiced as a school exercise in rhetoric, emphasizing brevity and point, and calling for the careful selection of telling detail to delineate the essential characteristics of social and ethical types or of particular persons.

Perhaps the form appealed to the New England proclivity to didacticism, for it found its way into almost all New England publications in the seventeenth century. Sometimes it was autobiographical and reflective rather than analytical, as in the personal "relations" of conversions. Sometimes it attempted to set up ideals of Christian behavior or of public duty in sermons. In this manner the character found its way into even the most elevated of theological dissertations. At times it presents strictly typical characters — the good Christian, the truly humble man, the public ruler — while at other times it seeks to penetrate the public notables of the period as individual human beings, and so becomes a biographical element in formal histories. But its most common appearance was in the guise of the funeral elegy.

The funeral elegy is the most interesting form produced in colonial literature. An offshoot of the funeral sermon, it was written by anagram- and acrostic-mad Puritans from all levels of society, either carefully penned and nailed to the hearse of the deceased, or printed and distributed as broadsides. Highly conventional, the elegy usually began by pointing to its subject's early religious vocation, his saintly conduct, his glorious attainments, and concluded by admonishing readers either to emulate the example set before them or to bewail

God's frowns upon what once was a glorious land; but always in the most tortured verbal tricks and puns imaginable. The following selections illustrate typical approaches to the character and the range of styles from Puritan plainness to Classical ornateness.

John Wilson (1591?–1667)

JOHN WILSON, Congregationalist minister who came to New England in 1630, is best known today for his fictitious discourse on sin preached for Hester Prynne in Hawthorne's *The Scarlet Letter.* But in his own day the stern preacher was equally known as an incorrigible versifier, rarely missing a chance to "memorize" the departed in a few lines. The following lines were sent to William Tompson, father of the poet Benjamin, in 1643 when he was waiting out a nasty winter in Virginia's woods. Tompson had been banished to the hinterlands by Governor Berkeley for preaching Nonconformist doctrines, and this was apparently the first word he received of the death of his wife Abigail. Using a typical New England innovation, Wilson has the dead Abigail speak directly to her "former" bridegroom.

TEXT: Kenneth B. Murdock, ed., *Handkerchiefs from Paul* (Cambridge, Mass., 1927).

Anagram upon the Death of Mrs. Abigaill Tompson

(1643)

i am gon to al blis

The blessed news I send to thee is this:
That I am gone from thee unto all bliss,
Such as the saints and angels do enjoy,
Whom neither Devil, world, nor flesh annoy.
To bliss of blisses I am gone: to Him
Who as a bride did for Himself me trim.
Thy bride I was, a most unworthy one,
But to a better bridegroom I am gone,
Who doth account me worthy of Himself,
Though I was never such a worthless elf.
He hath me clad with His own righteousness,
And for the sake of it He doth me bless.
Thou didst thy part to wash me, but His grace

Hath left no spot nor wrinkle on my face.
Thou little thinkst, or canst at all conceive,
What is the bliss that I do now receive.
When oft I heard thee preach and pray and sing,
I thought that heaven was a glorious thing,
And I believed, if any knew, 'twas thou
That knewest what a thing it was; but now
I see thou sawest but a glimpse, and hast
No more of heaven but a little taste,
Compared with that which here we see and have,
Nor canst have more till thou art past the grave.
Thou never toldst me of the tithe, nor yet
The hundred-thousand-thousand part of it.
Alas, Dear Soul, how short is all the fame
Of the third heavens, where I translated am!
O, if thou ever lovest me at all,
Whom thou didst by such loving titles call,
Yea, if thou lovest Christ (as who doth more?)
Then do not thou my death too much deplore.
Wring not thy hand, nor sigh, nor mourn, nor weep,
Although thine Abigaill be faln asleep.
'Tis but her body — that shall rise again;
In Christ's sweet bosom doth her soul remain.
Mourn not as if thou hadst no hope of me;
'Tis I, 'tis I have cause to pity thee.
O turn thy sighings into songs of praise
Unto the Name of God! let all thy days
Be spent in blessing of His name for this:
That He hath brought me to this place of bliss.
It was a blessed, a thrice blessed, snow
Which to the meeting I then waded through,
When pierced I was upon my naked skin
Up to the middle, the deep snow within.
There never was more happy way I trod,
That brought me home so soon unto my God
Instead of Braintree Church; conducting me
Into a better church, where now I see,
Not sinful men, but Christ and those that are
Fully exempt from every spot and scar
Of sinful guilt, where I no longer need
Or Word or seal my feeble soul to feed,
But face to face I do behold the Lamb,
Who down from heaven for my salvation came,
And thither is ascended up again,
Me to prepare a place wherein to reign,
Where we do always halleluyahs sing,
Where I do hope for thee to come ere long
To sing thy part in this most glorious song.

E. B. (Edward Bulkeley?)

TEXT: Nathaniel Morton, *New England's Memorial* (Cambridge, Mass., 1669).

A Threnodia

Upon Our Church's Second Dark Eclipse, Happening July 20, 1663, by Death's Interposition Between Us and that Great Light and Divine Plant, Mr. Samuel Stone, of Hartford

. . . .

A stone more then the Ebenezer famed;
Stone splendent diamond, right orient named;
A cordial stone, that often cheered hearts
With pleasant wit, with gospel rich imparts;
Whetstone, that edgified th' obtusest mind;
Loadstone, that drew the iron heart unkind;
A ponderous stone, that would the bottom sound
Of scripture depths, and bring out arcans found;
A stone for kingly David's use so fit,
As would not fail Goliah's front to hit;
A stone, an antidote, that brake the course
Of gangrene error, by convincing force;
A stone acute, fit to divide and square;
A squared stone became Christ's building rare.
A Peter's living, lively stone (so reared)
As 'live, was Hartford's life; dead, death is feared.
In Hartford old, Stone first drew infant breath,
In New, effused his last: O there beneath
His corpse are laid, near to his darling brother,
Of whom dead oft he sighed, "Not such another."
"Heaven is the more desirable" (said he),
"For Hooker, Shepard, and Haynes's company."

Urian Oakes (1631?–1681)

BORN in England, Urian Oakes was raised in Massachusetts, but after his graduation from Harvard (1649) returned to England to preferment in the clergy under Cromwell's Protectorate. In 1671 he returned to a pastorate at Cambridge, Massachusetts, and in

1675 acted as president of Harvard during a troublous time. An urbane man who thought of his Harvard graduates as "gentlemen, educated like gentlemen," rather than as prospects for the ministry, he enjoyed in his time a reputation for elegance, art, and grace in his prose. Moses Coit Tyler calls his, "perhaps, the richest prose style, — it furnishes the most brilliant examples of originality, breadth, and force of thought, set aglow by flame of passion, by flame of imagination, to be met with in our sermon-literature from the settlement of the country down to the Revolution." Much of this elegance and urbanity is evident in Oakes's fine elegy published just after the death of his close friend Thomas Shepard, Jr., in 1677.

TEXT: Perry Miller and Thomas H. Johnson, eds., *The Puritans* (New York, 1938, 1963).

An Elegy upon the Death of the Reverend Mr. Thomas Shepard

Oh! that I were a poet now in grain!
How would I invocate the Muses all
To deign their presence, lend their flowing vein,
And help to grace dear Shepard's funeral!
  How would I paint our griefs, and succours borrow
  From art and fancy, to limn out our sorrow!

Now could I wish (if wishing would obtain)
The sprightliest efforts of poetic rage,
To vent my griefs, make others feel my pain,
For this loss of the glory of our age.
  Here is a subject for the loftiest verse
  That ever waited on the bravest hearse.

And could my pen ingeniously distill
The purest spirits of a sparkling wit
In rare conceits, the quintessence of skill
In elegiac strains; none like to it:
  I should think all too little to condole
  The fatal loss (to us) of such a soul.

Could I take highest flights of fancy, soar
Aloft; if wit's monopoly were mine:
All would be much too low, too light, too poor,
To pay due tribute to this great divine.
  Ah! wit avails not, when th' heart's like to break,
  Great griefs are tongue-tied, when the lesser speak.

Away loose reined careers of poetry,
The celebrated Sisters may be gone;
We need no mourning women's elegy,
No forced, affected, artificial tone.
  Great and good Shepard's dead! Ah! this alone
  Will set our eyes abroach, dissolve a stone.

Poetic raptures are of no esteem,
Daring hyperboles have here no place,
Luxuriant wits on such a copious theme,
Would shame themselves, and blush to shew their face.
  Here's worth enough to overmatch the skill
  Of the most stately poet laureate's quill.

Exub'rant fancies useless here I deem,
Transcendent virtue scorns feigned elegies:
He that gives Shepard half his due, may seem,
If strangers hear it, to hyperbolize.
  Let him that can, tell what his virtues were,
  And say, this star moved in no common sphere.

Here need no spices, odors, curious arts,
No skill of Egypt, to embalm the name
Of such a worthy: let men speak their hearts,
They'll say, he merits an immortal fame.
  When Shepard is forgot, all must conclude,
  This is prodigious ingratitude.

But live he shall in many a grateful breast,
Where he hath reared himself a monument,
A monument more stately than the best,
On which immensest treasures have been spent.
  Could you but into th' hearts of thousands peep,
  There would you read his name engraven deep.

Oh, that my head were waters, and mine eyes
A flowing spring of tears, still issuing forth
In streams of bitterness, to solemnize
The obits of this man of matchless worth!
  Next to the tears our sins do need and crave,
  I would bestow my tears on Shepard's grave.

Not that he needs our tears: for he hath dropt
His measure full; not one tear more shall fall
Into God's bottle from his eyes; Death stopt
That water-course, his sorrows ending all.
  He fears, he cares, he sighs, he weeps no more:
  He's past all storms, arrived at th' wished shore.

Dear Shepard, could we reach so high a strain
Of pure seraphic love, as to divest
Our selves, and love, of self-respects, thy gain
Would joy us, though it cross our interest.
  Then would we silence all complaints with this,
  Our dearest friend is doubtless gone to bliss.

Ah! but the lesson's hard, thus to deny
Our own dear selves, to part with such a loan
Of heaven (in time of such necessity)
And love thy comforts better than our own.
  Then let us moan our loss, adjourn our glee,
  Till we come thither to rejoice with thee.

As when some formidable comets blaze,
As when portentous prodigies appear,
Poor mortals with amazement stand and gaze,
With hearts affrighted, and with trembling fear:
  So are we all amazed at this blow,
  Sadly portending some approaching woe.

We shall not summon bold astrologers,
To tell us what the stars say in the case,
(Those cousin-germans to black conjurers)
We have a sacred oracle that says,
  When th' righteous perish, men of mercy go,
  It is a sure presage of coming woe.

He was (ah woeful word! to say he was)
Our wrestling Israel, second unto none,
The man that stood i' th' gap, to keep the pass,
To stop the troops of judgments rushing on.
  This man the honor had to hold the hand
  Of an incensed God against our land.

When such a pillar's faln (Oh such an one!)
When such a glorious, shining light's put out,
When chariot and horsemen thus are gone;
Well may we fear some downfall, darkness, rout.
  When such a bank's broke down, there's sad occasion
  To wail, and dread some grievous inundation.

What! must we with our God, and glory part?
Lord! is thy treaty with New England come
Thus to an end? And is war in thy heart?
That this ambassador is called home.
  So earthly gods (kings) when they war intend,
  Call home their ministers, and treaties end.

Oh for the raptures, transports, inspirations
Of Israel's singers when his Jonathan's fall
So tuned his mourning harp! what lamentations
Then would I make for Shepard's funeral.
  How truly can I say, as well as he?
  "My dearest brother, I'm distressed for thee."

How lovely, worthy, peerless, in my view?
How precious, pleasant hast thou been to me?
How learned, prudent, pious, grave and true?
And what a faithful friend? who like to thee?
  Mine eye's desire is vanished: who can tell
  Where lives my dearest Shepard's parallel?

'Tis strange to think: but we may well believe,
That not a few of different persuasions
From this great worthy, do now truly grieve
I' th' mourning crowd, and join their lamentations.
  Such powers magnetic had he to draw to him
  The very hearts, and souls, of all that knew him!

Art, nature, grace, in him, were all combined
To shew the world a matchless paragon:
In whom of radiant virtues no less shined,
Than a whole constellation: but he's gone!
  He's gone, alas! down in the dust must lie
  As much of this rare person as could die.

If to have solid judgment, pregnant parts,
A piercing wit, and comprehensive brain;
If to have gone the round of all the arts,
Immunity from Death's arrest would gain,
  Shepard would have been death-proof, and secure
  From that all-conquering hand, I'm very sure.

If holy life, and deeds of charity,
If grace illustrious, and virtue tried,
If modest carriage, rare humility,
Could have bribed Death, good Shepard had not died.
  Oh! but inexorable Death attacks
  The best men, and promiscuous havoc makes.

Come tell me, critics, have you ever known
Such zeal, so tempered well with moderation?
Such prudence, and such innocence met in one?
Such parts, so little pride and ostentation?
  Let Momus carp, and Envy do her worst,
  And swell with spleen and rancor till she burst.

To be descended well, doth *that* commend?
Can sons their fathers' glory call their own?
Our Shepard justly might to this pretend,
(His blessed father was of high renown,
Both Englands speak him great, admire his name)
But his own personal worth's a better claim.

Great was the father, once a glorious light
Among us, famous to an high degree:
Great was this son: indeed (to do him right)
As great and good (to say no more) as he.
A double portion of his father's spirit
Did this (his eldest) son, through grace, inherit.

His look commanded reverence and awe,
Though mild and amiable, not austere:
Well humored was he (as I ever saw)
And ruled by love and wisdom, more than fear.
The Muses, and the Graces too, conspired
To set forth this rare piece, to be admired.

He governed well the tongue (that busy thing,
Unruly, lawless, and pragmatical),
Gravely reserved, in speech not lavishing,
Neither too sparing, nor too liberal.
His words were few, well seasoned, wisely weighed,
And in his tongue the law of kindness swayed.

Learned he was beyond the common size,
Befriended much by nature in his wit,
And temper (sweet, sedate, ingenious, wise),
And (which crowned all) he was heaven's favorite:
On whom the God of all grace did command,
And shower down blessings with a liberal hand.

Wise he, not wily, was; grave, not morose;
Not stiff, but steady; serious, but not sour;
Concerned for all, as if he had no foes;
(Strange if he had!) and would not waste an hour.
Thoughtful and active for the common good:
And yet his own place wisely understood.

Nothing could make him stray from duty; Death
Was not so frightful to him, as omission
Of ministerial work; he feared no breath
Infectious, i' th' discharge of his commission.
Rather than run from's work, he chose to die,
Boldly to run on Death, than duty fly.

(Cruel disease! that didst (like highwaymen)
Assault the honest traveler in his way,
And rob dear Shepard of his life (Ah!) then,
When he was on the road, where duty lay.
  Forbear, bold pen! 'twas God that took him thus,
  To give him great reward, and punish us.)

Zealous in God's cause, but meek in his own;
Modest of nature, bold as any lion,
Where conscience was concerned: and there were none
More constant mourners for afflicted Sion:
  So general was his care for th' churches all,
  His spirit seemed apostolical.

Large was his heart, to spend without regret,
Rejoicing to do good: not like those moles
That root i' th' earth, or roam abroad, to get
All for themselves (those sorry, narrow souls!),
  But he, like th' sun (i' th' center, as some say)
  Diffused his rays of goodness every way.

He breathed love, and pursued peace in his day,
As if his soul were made of harmony:
Scarce ever more of goodness crowded lay
In such a piece of frail mortality.
  Sure Father Wilson's genuine son was he,
  New England's Paul had such a Timothy.

No slave to th' world's grand idols; but he flew
At fairer quarries, without stooping down
To sublunary prey: his great soul knew
Ambition none, but of the heavenly crown.
  Now he hath won it, and shall wear't with honor,
  Adoring grace, and God in Christ, the donor.

A friend to truth, a constant foe to error,
Powerful i' th' pulpit, and sweet in converse,
To weak ones gentle, to th' profane a terror.
Who can his virtues, and good works rehearse?
  The scripture-bishop's-character read o'er,
  Say this was Shepard's: what need I say more?

I say no more: let them that can declare
His rich and rare endowments, paint this sun,
With all its dazzling rays: but I despair,
Hopeless by any hand to see it done.
  They that can Shepard's goodness well display,
  Must be as good as he: but who are they?

See where our sister Charlestown sits and moans!
Poor widowed Charlestown! all in dust, in tears!
Mark how she wrings her hands! hear how she groans!
See how she weeps! what sorrow like to hers!
  Charlestown, that might for joy compare of late
  With all about her, now looks desolate.

As you have seen some pale, wan, ghastly look,
When grisly Death, that will not be said nay,
Hath seized all for itself, possession took,
And turned the soul out of its house of clay.
  So visaged is poor Charlestown at this day;
  Shepard, her very soul, is torn away.

Cambridge groans under this so heavy cross,
And sympathizes with her sister dear;
Renews her griefs afresh for her old loss
Of her own Shepard, and drops many a tear.
  Cambridge and Charlestown now joint mourners are,
  And this tremendous loss between them share.

Must learning's friend (Ah! worth us all) go thus?
That great support to Harvard's nursery!
Our fellow (that no fellow had with us)
Is gone to heaven's great university.
  Ours now indeed's a lifeless corporation,
  The soul is fled, that gave it animation!

Poor Harvard's sons are in their mourning dress:
Their sure friend's gone! their hearts have put on mourning;
Within their wall are sighs, tears, pensiveness;
Their new foundations dread an overturning.
  Harvard! where's such a fast friend left to thee!
  Unless thy great friend, Leverett, it be.

We must not with our greatest Sovereign strive,
Who dare find fault with Him that is most high?
That hath an absolute prerogative,
And doth His pleasure: none may ask Him, why?
  We're clay-lumps, dust-heaps, nothings in His sight:
  The Judge of all the earth doth always right.

Ah! could not prayers and tears prevail with God!
Was there no warding off that dreadful blow!
And was there no averting of that rod!
Must Shepard die! and that good angel go!
  Alas! our heinous sins (more than our hairs)
  It seems, were louder, and more out-cried our prayers.

See what our sins have done! what ruins wrought
And how they have plucked out our very eyes!
Our sins have slain our Shepard! we have bought,
And dearly paid for, our enormities.
  Ah, cursed sins! that strike at God, and kill
  His servants, and the blood of prophets spill.

As you would loathe the sword that's warm and red,
As you would hate the hands that are embrued
I' th' heart's-blood of your dearest friends: so dread,
And hate your sins; Oh! let them be pursued:
  Revenges take on bloody sins: for there's
  No refuge-city for these murtherers.

In vain we build the prophets sepulchers,
In vain bedew their tombs with tears, when dead;
In vain bewail the deaths of ministers,
Whilst prophet-killing sins are harbored.
  Those that these murtherous traitors favor, hide;
  Are with the blood of prophets deeply dyed.

New England! know thy heart-plague: feel this blow;
A blow that sorely wounds both head and heart,
A blow that reaches all, both high and low,
A blow that may be felt in every part.
  Mourn that this great man's faln in Israel:
  Lest it be said, with him New England fell!

Farewell, Dear Shepard! Thou art gone before,
Made free of heaven, where thou shalt sing loud hymns
Of high triumphant praises evermore,
In the sweet choir of saints and seraphims.
  Lord! look on us here, clogged with sin and clay,
  And we, through grace, shall be as happy as they.

My dearest, inmost, bosom friend is gone!
Gone is my sweet companion, soul's delight!
Now in an huddling crowd I'm all alone,
And almost could bid all the world goodnight:
  Blest be my rock! God lives: Oh let Him be,
  As He is, so all in all to me.

John Norton (1651–1716)

GRADUATING from Harvard in the same class with Samuel Sewall and Edward Taylor (1671), John Norton became pastor of the First Church at Hingham, writing occasionally, but producing nothing equal to the following poem which was appended to the second edition of Mrs. Bradstreet's verse.

TEXT: Anne Bradstreet, *Several Poems Compiled with Great Variety of Wit and Learning* (Boston, 1678).

A Funeral Elegy

Upon that Pattern and Patron of Virtue, the Truly
Pious, Peerless, and Matchless Gentlewoman,
Mrs. Anne Bradstreet,
Right *Panaretes,*
Mirror of Her Age, Glory of Her Sex, Whose
Heaven-born Soul, Leaving Its Earthly Shrine,
Chose Its Native Home, and Was Taken to
Its Rest, upon 16th Sept. 1672.

Ask not why hearts turn magazines of passions,
And why that grief is clad in sev'ral fashions;
Why she on progress goes, and doth not borrow
The smallest respite from th' extremes of sorrow.
Here misery is got to such an height
As makes the earth groan to support its weight,
Such storms of woe, so strongly have beset her,
She hath no place for worse, nor hope for better;
Her comfort is, if any for her be,
That none can shew more cause of grief then she.
Ask not why some in mournful black are clad;
The sun is set, there needs must be a shade.
Ask not why every face a sadness shrouds;
The setting sun o'er-cast us hath with clouds.
Ask not why the great glory of the sky,
That gilds the stars with heavenly alchemy,
Which all the world doth lighten with his rays,
The Persian God, the monarch of the days;
Ask not the reason of his ecstasy,
Paleness of late, in midnoon majesty,
Why that the pale-faced empress of the night
Disrobed her brother of his glorious light.

Did not the language of the stars foretell
A mournful scene, when they with tears did swell?
Did not the glorious people of the sky
Seem sensible of future misery?
Did not the lowring heavens seem to express
The world's great loss, and their unhappiness?
Behold how tears flow from the learned hill,
How the bereaved Nine do daily fill
The bosom of the fleeting air with groans,
And woeful accents, which witness their moans.
How do the goddesses of verse, the learned choir
Lament their rival quill, which all admire?
Could Maro's Muse but hear her lively strain,
He would condemn his works to fire again.
Methinks I hear the Patron of the Spring,
The unshorn deity, abruptly sing.
Some do for anguish weep, for anger I
That ignorance should live, and art should die.
Black, fatal, dismal, inauspicious day,
Unblest forever by Sol's precious ray,
Be it the first of miseries to all;
Or last of life, defamed for funeral.
When this day yearly comes, let every one
Cast in their urn, the black and dismal stone.
Succeeding years, as they their circuit go,
Leap o'er this day, as a sad time of woe.
Farewell, my Muse, since thou hast left thy shrine,
I am unblest in one, but blest in nine.
Fair Thespian Ladies, light your torches all,
Attend your glory to its funeral,
To court her ashes with a learned tear,
A briny sacrifice, let not a smile appear.
Grave Matron, whoso seeks to blazon thee,
Needs not make use of wit's false heraldry;
Whoso should give thee all thy worth would swell
So high, as 'twould turn the world infidel.
Had he great Maro's Muse, or Tully's tongue,
Or raping numbers like the Thracian song,
In crowning of her merits he would be
Sumptuously poor, low in hyperbole.
To write is easy; but to write on thee,
Truth would be thought to forfeit modesty.
He'll seem a poet that shall speak but true;
Hyperboles in others, are thy due.
Like a most servile flatterer he will show,
Though he write truth, and make the subject, you.
Virtue ne'er dies, time will a poet raise,
Born under better stars, shall sing thy praise.

Praise her who list, yet he shall be a debtor,
For art ne'er feigned, nor nature framed, a better.
Her virtues were so great, that they do raise
A work to trouble fame, astonish praise,
When as her name doth but salute the ear,
Men think that they perfection's abstract hear.
Her breast was a brave palace, a Broad-street,
Where all heroic ample thoughts did meet,
Where nature such a tenement had ta'en,
That others' souls, to hers, dwelt in a lane.
Beneath her feet, pale envy bites her chain,
And poison malice whets her sting in vain.
Let every laurel, every myrtle bough
Be stript for leaves t'adorn and load her brow,
Victorious wreaths, which, 'cause they never fade,
Wise elder times for kings and poets made.
Let not her happy memory e'er lack
Its worth in fame's eternal almanac,
Which none shall read, but straight their loss deplore,
And blame their fates they were not born before.
Do not old men rejoice their fates did last,
And infants too, that theirs did make such haste,
In such a welcome time to bring them forth,
That they might be a witness to her worth?
Who undertakes this subject to commend
Shall nothing find so hard as how to end.

Cotton Mather (1663–1728)

MATHER's most important and ambitious work was his *Magnalia Christi Americana; or, The Ecclesiastical History of New England from Its First Planting,* designed to reinvigorate religious zeal by glorifying the golden past and eminent men of the colony. In separate parts Mather treats the history of New England's settlement, the lives of governors and magistrates, the lives of sixty eminent divines, the development of Harvard College, the faith and order of the churches, illustrious providences affecting the country, and the "Wars of the Lord." So large it had to be sent to London for publication in 1702, the *Magnalia* reveals Mather's real skill as a prose writer, and many of the sketches of prominent lives are classic examples of the "character" as a forerunner of the essay and the biography.

TEXT: Cotton Mather, *Magnalia Christi Americana,* ed. Thomas Robbins, Vol. I (Hartford, 1853).

William Bradford

[From *Magnalia Christi Americana,* 1702]

The leader of a people in a wilderness had need been a Moses; and if a Moses had not led the people of Plymouth Colony, when this worthy person was their governor, the people had never with so much unanimity and importunity still called him to lead them. Among many instances thereof, let this one piece of self-denial be told for a memorial of him, wheresoever this *History* shall be considered. The patent of the Colony was taken in his name, running in these terms: "To William Bradford, his heirs, associates, and assigns." But when the number of the Freemen was much increased, and many new townships erected, the General Court there desired of Mr. Bradford, that he would make a surrender of the same into their hands, which he willingly and presently assented unto, and confirmed it according to their desire by his hand and seal, reserving no more for himself than was his proportion, with others, by agreement. But as he found the providence of heaven many ways recompensing his many acts of self-denial, so he gave this testimony to the faithfulness of the divine promises: that he had forsaken friends, houses, and lands for the sake of the gospel, and the Lord gave them him again. Here he prospered in his estate; and besides a worthy son which he had by a former wife, he had also two sons and a daughter by another, whom he married in this land.

He was a person for study as well as action; and hence, notwithstanding the difficulties through which he passed in his youth, he attained unto a notable skill in languages: the Dutch tongue was become almost as vernacular to him as the English; the French tongue he could also manage; the Latin and the Greek he had mastered; but the Hebrew he most of all studied, because, he said, he would see with his own eyes the ancient oracles of God in their native beauty. He was also well skilled in history, in antiquity, and in philosophy; and for theology, he became so versed in it, that he was an irrefragable disputant against the errors, especially those of Anabaptism, which with trouble he saw rising in his colony; wherefore he wrote some significant things for the confutation of those errors. But the crown of all was his holy, prayerful, watchful, and fruitful walk with God, wherein he was very exemplary.

At length he fell into an indisposition of body, which rendered him unhealthy for a whole winter; and as the spring advanced, his health yet more declined; yet he felt himself not what he counted sick, till one day; in the night after which the God of heaven so filled his mind with ineffable consolations, that he seemed little short of Paul, rapt up unto the unutterable entertainments of Paradise. The next morning he told his friends, that the good Spirit of God had given him a pledge of his happiness in another world, and the first fruits of his eternal glory; and on the day following, he died, May 9, 1657, in the sixty-ninth year of his age — lamented by all the colonies of New England, as a common blessing and father to them all. . . .

Plato's brief description of a governor, is all that I will now leave as his character, in an

Epitaph.

Men are but flocks: Bradford beheld their need,
And long did them at once both rule and feed.

Character of a True Christian

[From *Magnalia*]

Behold, [said John Eliot,] the ancient and excellent character of a true Christian; 'tis that which Peter calls "holiness in all manner of conversation"; you shall not find a Christian out of the way of godly conversation. For, first, a seventh part of our time is all spent in heaven, when we are duly zealous for, and zealous on the sabbath of God. Besides, God has written on the head of the sabbath, "Remember," which looks both forwards and backwards, and thus a good part of the week will be spent in sabbatizing. Well, but for the rest of our time! Why, we shall have that spent in heaven, ere we have done. For, secondly, we have many days for both fasting and thanksgiving in our pilgrimage; and here are so many sabbaths more. Moreover, thirdly, we have our lectures every week; and pious people won't miss them, if they can help it. Furthermore, fourthly, we have our private meetings, wherein we pray, and sing, and repeat sermons, and confer together about the things of God; and being now come thus far, we are in heaven almost every day. But a little farther, fifthly, we perform family duties every day; we have our morning and evening sacrifices, wherein, having read the scriptures to our families, we call upon the name of God, and ever now and then carefully catechize those that are under our charge. Sixthly, we shall also have our daily devotions in our closets; wherein unto supplication before the Lord, we shall add some serious meditation upon His Word: a David will be at this work no less than thrice a day. Seventhly, we have likewise many scores of ejaculations in a day; and these we have, like Nehemiah, in whatever place we come into. Eighthly, we have our occasional thoughts and our occasional talks upon spiritual matters; and we have our occasional acts of charity, wherein we do like the inhabitants of heaven every day. Ninthly, in our callings, in our civil callings, we keep up heavenly frames; we buy and sell, and toil; yea, we eat and drink, with some eye both to the command and the honor of God in all. Behold, I have not now left an inch of time to be carnal; it is all engrossed for heaven. And yet, lest here should not be enough, lastly, we have our spiritual warfare. We are always encount'ring the enemies of our souls, which continually raises our hearts unto our Helper and Leader in the heavens. Let no man say, " 'Tis impossible to live at this rate"; for we have known some live thus; and others that have written of such a life have but spun a web out of their own blessed experiences. New England has example of this life: though, alas! 'tis to be lamented that the distractions of the world, in too many professors, do becloud the beauty of an heavenly conversation. In fine, our employment lies in heaven. In the morning, if we ask, "Where am I to be today?" our souls must answer, "In heaven." In the evening, if we ask, "Where have I been today?" our souls may answer, "In heaven." If thou art a believer, thou art no stranger to heaven while thou livest; and when thou diest, heaven will be no strange place to thee; no, thou hast been there a thousand times before.

Jonathan Edwards (1703–1758)

NO ONE in colonial New England probed more searchingly into the workings of human nature than did Jonathan Edwards, America's first noted philosopher, in his studies of religious psychology during the Great Awakening. But though he brought to his subject the new science of Locke and Newton, he often expressed his findings in the form of the traditional "character." The "Character of a Truly Virtuous Person" given below was written around 1723; tradition holds that the young lady is Sarah Pierrepont, whom Edwards married in 1727. The "Character of a Truly Humble Man" is an excerpt from his *Treatise Concerning Religious Affections* (1746).

TEXTS: Sereno E. Dwight, *The Life of President Edwards* (New York, 1830); and *A Treatise Concerning Religious Affections,* ed. John E. Smith (New Haven, 1959).

Character of a Truly Virtuous Person

[From Dwight, *Life,* 1830]

They say there is a young lady in ——— who is beloved of that great Being, who made and rules the world, and that there are certain seasons in which this great Being, in some way or other invisible, comes to her and fills her mind with exceeding sweet delight, and that she hardly cares for anything, except to meditate on Him — that she expects after a while to be received up where He is, to be raised up out of the world and caught up into heaven; being assured that He loves her too well to let her remain at a distance from him always. There she is to dwell with Him, and to be ravished with His love and delight forever. Therefore, if you present all the world before her, with the richest of its treasures, she disregards it and cares not for it, and is unmindful of any pain or affliction. She has a strange sweetness in her mind, and singular purity in her affections; is most just and conscientious in all her conduct; and you could not persuade her to do anything wrong or sinful, if you would give her all the world, lest she should offend this great Being. She is of a wonderful sweetness, calmness, and universal benevolence of mind; especially after the great God has manifested Himself to her mind. She will sometimes go about from place to place, singing sweetly; and seems to be always full of joy and pleasure; and no one knows for what. She loves to be alone, walking in the fields and groves, and seems to have someone invisible always conversing with her.

Character of a Truly Humble Man

[From *Treatise Concerning Religious Affections,* 1746]

A truly humble person, having such a mean opinion of his righteousness and holiness, is poor in spirit. For a person to be poor in spirit, is to be in his own sense and apprehension poor, as to what is in him, and to be of an answerable disposition. Therefore a truly humble person, especially one eminently humble, naturally behaves himself in many respects as a poor man. The poor useth entreaties, but the rich answereth roughly. A poor man is not disposed to quick and high resentment when he is among the rich: he is apt to yield to others, for he knows others are above him; he is not stiff and self-willed; he is patient with hard fare; he expects no other than to be despised, and takes it patiently; he don't take it heinously that he is overlooked, and but little regarded; he is prepared to be in low place; he readily honors his superiors; he takes reproofs quietly; he readily honors others as above him; he easily yields to be taught, and don't claim much to his understanding and judgment; he is not overnice or humoursome, and has his spirit subdued to hard things; he is not assuming, nor apt to take much upon him, but 'tis natural for him to be subject to others. Thus it is with the humble Christian.

LITERARY THEORY

American Puritans rarely wrote directly about literary theory. To them the subject was a branch of oratory, and they had rhetorics enough from England and the Continent to serve their needs in the schools. But often they felt the necessity to commend or defend the particular style of themselves or their friends, or to disarm criticism by justifying in a preface what might prove to be a controversial publication. The ministers, of course, were trained in the subtleties of exegetical criticism both of the Bible and of early church histories, and since they regularly used their exegetical skills in preaching, they were fully conscious of literary niceties. Still, such skills were too often reserved to plead some special case, and never produced a systematic or thorough discussion of literary principle.

Michael Wigglesworth (1631–1705)

In his senior year at college (1650) Wigglesworth presented the following thoughts as one of his required orations or declamations before his tutors and fellow students. So theoretical a treatment could only be the product of a school exercise. The oration was one of two Wigglesworth presented at Harvard on the subject of eloquence.

Text: Samuel Eliot Morison, *Harvard College in the Seventeenth Century* (Cambridge, Mass., 1936), Vol. I.

The Praise of Eloquence

How sweetly doth eloquence even enforce truth upon the understanding, and subtly convey knowledge into the mind, be it never so dull of conceiving, and sluggish in yielding its assent. So that let a good orator put forth the utmost of his skill, and you shall hear him so lay open and unfold, so evidence and demonstrate from point to point what he hath in hand, that he will make a very block understand his discourse. Let him be to give a description of something absent or unknown; how strangely doth he realize and make it present to his hearers' apprehensions, framing in their minds as exact an idea of that which they never saw, as they can possibly have of anything that they have been longest and best acquainted with. Or doth he take upon him to personate some others in word or deeds, why he presents his hearers not with a lifeless picture, but with the living persons of those concerning whom he speaks. They see, they hear, they handle them, they walk, they talk with them, and what not? Or is he to speak about such things as are already known? Why should he here discourse after the vulgar manner, and deliver his mind as a cobbler would do: his hearers might then have some ground to say they knew as much as their orator could teach them. But by the power of eloquence old truth receives a new habit. Though its essence be the same, yet its visage is so altered that it may currently pass and be accepted as a novelty. The same verity is again and again perhaps set before the same guests, but drest and disht up after a new manner, and every manner seasoned so well that the intellectual parts may both without nauseating receive, and so oft as it doth receive it, still draw some fresh nourishing virtue from it. So that eloquence gives new luster and beauty, new strength, new vigor, new life unto truth; presenting it with such variety as refresheth, actuating it with such hidden powerful energy, that a few languid sparks are blown up to a shining flame.

And which is yet more: eloquence doth not only revive the things known, but secretly convey life into the hearer's understanding, rousing it out of its former slumber, quick'ning it beyond its natural vigor, elevating it above its ordinary conception. There are not only objects set before it, but eyes (after a sort) given it to see these objects in such wise as it never saw. Yea it is strengthened as to apprehend that which is taught it, so of itself with enlargement to comprehend many things which are not made known unto it. Hence it comes to pass that after the hearing of a well-composed speech lively expressed the understanding of the auditor is so framed in the mold of eloquence, that he could almost go away and compose the like himself either upon the same or another subject. And what's the reason of this? why his mind is transported with a kind of rapture, and inspired with a certain oratoric fury, as if the orator together with his words had breathed his soul and spirit into those that hear him.

These and the like effects hath eloquence upon the understanding. But furthermore 'tis a fit bait to catch the will and affections. For hereby they are not only laid in wait for, but surprised: nor only surprised, but subdued; nor only subdued, but triumphed over. Yet eloquence beguiles with such honesty, subdues with such mildness, triumphs with such sweetness, that here to be surprised is nothing dangerous, here to be subject is the best freedom, this kind of servitude is more desirable then liberty. For whereas our untractable nature refuseth to be drawn, and a stiff will scorns to be compelled: yet by the power of well-composed speech nature is drawn against the stream with delight, and the will after a sort compelled with its own consent. Although for a time it struggle and make resistance, yet at length it suffers itself to be vanquished, and takes a secret contentment in being overcome.

In like manner, for the affections. Look as a mighty river augmented with excessive rains or winter snows swelling above its wonted channel bears down banks and bridges, overflows fields and hedges, sweeps away all before it, that might obstruct its passage: so eloquence overturns, overturns all things that stand in its way, and carries them down with the irresistible stream of its all controlling power. Wonderful it were to speak of the several discoveries of the power in several affections: wonderful but to think in general, how like a blustering tempest it one while drives before it the raging billows of this troubled ocean: how other whiles (as though it had them in fetters) it curbs and calms the fury at a word. And all this without offering violence to the parties so affected; nay with a secret pleasure and delight it stirs men up to the greatest displeasure and distaste. Doth it affect with grief? why to be so grieved is no grievance. Doth it kindle coals, nay flames of fiery indignation? why those flames burn not, but rather cherish. Doth it draw tears from the eyes? why even tears flow with pleasure. For as is well said by one upon this point, *in omni animi motu etiam in dolore est quaedam jucunditas.* So potently, so sweetly doth eloquence command. And of a skilful orator in point of the affections that may be spoken really, which the poet affirmeth fabulously of Aeolus god of the winds. . . .

But I need instance no more. Some of you I hope will by this time assent unto what has been hitherto proved, that eloquence is of such useful concernment and powerful operation. But methinks I hear some still objecting. 'Tis very true eloquence is a desirable thing, but what are we the better for knowing its worth unless we could hope ourselves to attain it? It is indeed a right excellent endowment but 'tis not every capacity, nay scarce one of a hundreth that can reach it. How many men of good parts do we find that yet excel not here? Cicero indeed, a man in whom vast understanding and natural fluent facility of speech conspire together; no marvel if he make judges weep and princes tremble. But to what purpose is it for a man of weak parts and mean abilities to labor after that which he is never like to compass? Had we not as good toss our caps against the wind as weary out ourselves in the pursuit of that which so few can reach to?

Answer: To these I would answer first, the reason why so few attain it is because there [are] few that indeed desire it; hence they run not as if they meant to win, they pursue not as if they hoped to overtake.

But secondly, let me answer them with Turner's words upon this very argument, *Negligentiam nostram arguit, qui cum non possimus, quod debemus, optimus, nolumus quod possimus, benè:* we cannot do what we would, therefore will not do what we may. This savors of a slothful system. Because we cannot keep pace with the horsemen, shall we refuse to accompany the footmen? Because we cannot run, shall we sit down and refuse to go? We cannot reach so far as ourselves desire and as some others it may be attain; shall we not therefore reach as far as our endeavors may carry us? Because we cannot be *oratores optimi,* do we content ourselves to be *oratores pessimi?*

And as for those that have most excelled in this kind, whence had they their excellency? They did not come declaiming into the world: they were not born with orations in their mouths: eloquence did not sit upon their lips whilest they lay in their cradles: neither did they suck it in from their mothers' breasts. But if you examine the matter you shall find that by incredible pains and daily exercise, they even turned the course of nature into another channel, and cut out a way for the gentle stream of eloquence, where natural impediments seemed altogether to deny it passage: thereby effecting as much as another could brag, *viam aut inveniam aut faciam.* Eminent in this respect is the example of the two best orators that fame has brought to our ears. Of Cicero, who when he had naturally a shrill, screaming, ill-tuned voice rising to such a note that it endangered his very life: yet by art and industry he acquired such a commendable habit, as none with ease could speak more sweetly than he. And Demosthenes, though he were naturally of a stammering tongue, crazy-bodied, and broken-winded, and withal had accustomed himself to a jetting uncomely deportment of his body, or some part of it at least: when, to conclude, he had scarce any part of an orator, save only an ardent desire to be an orator, yet by his indefatigable pains he so overcame these natural defects, as that he came to be reputed prince of the Graecian eloquence. Though this was not gotten without some further difficulty and seeming vain attempts, insomuch as he was several times quite discouraged, and once threw all aside, despairing ever to become an orator because the people laughed at his orations. Yet notwithstanding, being heartened to it again by some of his well-willers, he never left striving till he had won the prize.

Go to, therefore, my fellow students (for to you I address my speech, my superiors I attempt not to speak to, desiring rather to learn of them more of this nature, but) to you give me leave to say: let no man hereafter tell me "I despair of excelling in the oratorical faculty, therefore 'tis bootless to endeavor." Who more unlike to make an orator than Demosthenes except it were one who had no tongue in his head? yet Demosthenes became *orator optimus.* Tell me not "I have made trial once and again, but find my labor fruitless." Thou art not the first that hast made an onset, and been repelled; neither canst thou presage what renewed endeavors may produce. Would you then obtain this skill? take Demosthenes his course; gird up your loins, put to your shoulders, and to it again, and again, and again, let nothing discourage you. Know that to be a dunce, to be a stammerer, unable to bring forth three or four sentences hanging well together, this is an easy matter: but to become an able speaker, *hic labor, hoc opus est.* Would you have your orations please, such as need not be laughed at? why follow him in that also. Let them be such as smell of the lamp, as was said of his. Not slovenly, I mean, but elaborate, *diurnam industriam et nocturnis lubricationibus elaboratae,* such as savor, of some pains taken with them. A good oration is not made at the first thought, nor scarce at the first writing over. Nor is true eloquence wont to hurry it out thick and threefold, as if each word were running for a wager: nor yet to mutter or whisper it out of a book after a dreaming manner, with such a voice as the orator can scantly hear himself speak; but to utter it with lively affection, to pronounce it distinctly with audible voice.

But I shall burden your patience no further at the present. Those and the like vices in declaiming that are contrary to eloquence, were the chief motives that drew me first into thoughts of this discourse. But I see I cannot reach at this season to speak of them particularly, wherefore, with your good leave and God's assistance, I shall rather treat of them at another opportunity. . . .

Cotton Mather (1663–1728)

ADVERSE criticism followed the Bay Psalm Book almost from its beginning. It had been revised ten years after its first publication, and in 1718 the redoubtable Cotton Mather sought to correct its errors and take advantage of the seventeenth century's refinements in poetic method by publishing his *Psalterium Americanum. The Book of Psalms, In a Translation Exactly Conformed unto the ORIGINAL; But All in Blank Verse, Fitted Unto the Tunes Commonly Used in Our Churches.* Like John Cotton before him, he sets out to explain his principles of poetry and translation in a preface which he says must "be attentively perused, that so the whole book may have the good and great ends of it the more effectually accomplished." He enlarged his considerations in his handbook for young ministers, *Manuductio ad Ministerium,* in

1726, taking advantage of the occasion to defend his own usually ornate style; ironically, he defends ornateness most plainly.

TEXTS: Cotton Mather, *Psalterium Americanum* (Boston, 1718); and *Manuductio ad Ministerium* (Boston, 1726).

Preface

[From *Psalterium Americanum*, 1718]

Our poetry has attempted many versions of the Psalms, in such numbers and measures, as might render them capable of being sung, in those grave tunes, which have been prepared and received for our Christian psalmody. But of all the more than twice seven versions which I have seen, it must be affirmed, that they leave out a vast heap of those rich things, which the Holy Spirit of God speaks to in the original Hebrew; and that they put in as large an heap of poor things, which are entirely their own. All this has been merely for the sake of preserving the clink of the rhyme; which after all, is of small consequence unto a generous poem; and of none at all unto the melody of singing; but of how little then, in singing unto the Lord? Some famous pieces of poetry, which this refining age has been treated withal, have been offered us in blank verse. And in blank verse we now have the glorious book of Psalms presented unto us. . . .

For the new translation of the Psalms, which is here endeavored, an appeal may be with much assurance made, unto all that are masters of the Hebrew tongue, whether it be not much more agreeable to the original, than the old one, or than any that has yet been offered unto the world. Perhaps there is more liberty taken here in translating the first verse of the psalter, than almost any verse in the whole book beside. It keeps close to the original; and even when a word of supply is introduced, . . . it is really in the intention and emphasis of the original. Yea, the just laws of translation had not been at all violated, if a much greater liberty had been taken, for the beating out of the golden and massy Hebrew into a more extended English. For, it may be observed, if you translate a French book, suppose, into English, you turn it into English phrase, and make not a French English out of it; for *il fait froid*, for instance, you do not say, "it makes cold," but "it is cold." We have tied ourselves to Hebraisms, more scrupulously, than there is real occasion for. . . .

Most certainly, our translation of the Psalms, without the fetters of rhyme upon it, can be justly esteemed no prejudice to the character of poetry in the performance. For indeed, however it is now appropriated, according to the true sense of the term, to rhyme, itself a *similis desinentia,* or, a likeness of sound in the last syllables of the verse, is not essential. Old Bede will give you such a definition of rhyme, and bring other authorities besides Austin's for it, that Scaliger thereupon holds, all verses wherein regard is had unto the number of syllables, to have a claim unto it. Be that as the critics on the term shall please, our translation is all in meter; and really more tied unto measure, than the original appears to have been, by all the examinations that have as yet been employed upon it. . . .

I am therefore strongly of the opinion, that the poesy of the ancient Hebrews, knew no measure, but that of the unknown music, wherein it was to be accommodated. Our Psalms in the Hebrew, are not so much metrical as musical; and hence, the very inscriptions of them sometimes intimate, that there was a sort of melody, unto which they were adapted. It is true, the oriental nations at this day, have their metered poetry; but it is of a late original. However, 'tis very certain, that all the skill in the world, will hardly find the rules of that metered poetry observed with any exactness in the songs of the sacred scriptures. There is little value to be set on the authority, of either Philo, or Josephus, and after them, of Jerome, who quotes Origen and Eusebius for it, when they go to resolve the Hebrew poesy, into I know not what, lyrics and hexameters. And therefore it may be hoped, that our version may be released from the chime of a *similis desinentia,* without being censured for unpoetical. The sublime thought, and the divine flame, alone is enough, to challenge the character of poetry for these holy composures. And if any beauties be wanting, 'tis owing to the lowness of the language, whereinto a strict and close translation, is what we are here tied unto.

Psalm XXIII. A Psalm of David

[From *Psalterium Americanum*]

My Shepherd is th' eternal God,
  I shall not be in [any] want:
In pastures of a tender grass
  He [ever] makes me to lie down:
To waters of tranquillities
  He gently carries me, [along,]
My feeble and my wandring soul
  He [kindly] does fetch back again;
In the plain paths of righteousness
  He does lead [and guide] me along.
Because of the regard He has
  [Ever] unto His glorious Name.

Yea, when I shall walk in the vale
  Of the dark [dismal] shade of death,
I'll of no evil be afraid,
  Because thou [ever] art with me.
Thy rod and thy staff, they are what
  Yield [constant] comfort unto me.

A table thou dost furnish out
  Richly [for me] before my face.
'Tis in view of mine enemies;
  [And then] my head thou dost anoint
With fatning and perfuming oil:
  My cup it [ever] overflows.

Most certainly the thing that is
  Good with [most kind] benignity,
This all the days that I do live
  Shall [still and] ever follow me;
Yea I shall dwell, and sabbatize,
  Even to [unknown] length of days,
Lodged in the house which doth belong
  To [Him who's] the eternal God.

Of Poetry, and of Style

[From *Manuductio ad Ministerium*, 1726]

8. Poetry, whereof we have now even an antediluvian piece in our hands, has from the beginning been in such request, that I must needs recommend unto you some acquaintance with it. Though some have had a soul so unmusical, that they have decried all verse, as being but a mere playing and fiddling upon words; all versifying, as if it were more unnatural than if we should choose dancing instead of walking; and rhyme, as if it were but a sort of Morisco dancing with bells: yet I cannot wish you a soul that shall be wholly unpoetical. And old Horace has left us an *Art of Poetry,* which you may do well to bestow a perusal on. And besides your lyric hours, I wish you may so far understand an epic poem, that the beauties of an Homer and a Virgil may be discerned with you. As to the moral part of Homer, 'tis true, and let me not be counted a Zoilus for saying so, that by first exhibiting their gods as no better than rogues, he set open the floodgates for a prodigious inundation of wickedness to break in upon the nations, and was one of the greatest apostles the Devil ever had in the world. Among the rest that felt the ill impressions of this universal corrupter

(as men of the best sentiments have called him), one was that overgrown robber, of execrable memory, whom we celebrate under the name of Alexander the Great; who by his continual admiring and studying of his *Iliad*, and by following that false model of heroic virtue set before him in his Achilles, became one of the worst of men, and at length inflated with the ridiculous pride of being himself a deity, exposed himself to all the scorn that could belong unto a lunatic. And hence, notwithstanding the veneration which this idol has had, yet Plato banishes him out of a commonwealth, the welfare whereof he was concerned for. Nevertheless, custom or conscience obliges him to bear testimonies unto many points of morality. And it is especially observable, that he commonly propounds prayer to heaven as a most necessary preface unto all important enterprises; and when the action comes on too suddenly for a more extended supplication, he yet will not let it come on without an ejaculation; and he never speaks of any supplication but he brings in a gracious answer to it. I have seen a travesteering highflyer, not much to our dishonor, scoff at Homer for this; as making his actors to be like those whom the English call Dissenters. But then, we are so much led into the knowledge of antiquities, by reading of this poet, and into so many parts of the recondite learning, that notwithstanding some little nods in him, not a few acute pens beside the old Bishop of Thessalonica's, have got a reputation by regaling us with annotations upon him. Yea, though one can't but smile at the fancy of Croese, who tries with much ostentation of erudition, to show, that Homer has all along tendered us in a disguise and fable, the history of the Old Testament, yet many illustrations of the sacred scriptures, I find are to be fetched from him; who indeed had probably read what was extant of them in his days: particularly, our eighteenth Psalm is what he has evidently imitated. Virgil too, who so much lived upon him, as well as after him, is unaccountably mad upon his fate, which he makes to be he knows not what himself, but superior to gods as well as to men, and through his whole composures he so asserts the doctrine of this nonsensical power, as is plainly inconsistent with all virtue. And what fatal mischief did Fascinator do to the Roman Empire, when by deifying one great emperor, he taught the successors to claim the adoration of gods, while they were perpetrating the crimes of devils? I will not be a Carbilius upon him; nor will I say anything, how little the married state owes unto one who writes as if he were a woman hater: nor what his blunders are about his poor-spirited and inconsistent hero, for which many have taxed him. Nevertheless, 'tis observed, that the pagans had no rules of manners, that were more laudable and regular than what are to be found in him. And some have said, it is hardly possible seriously to read his works without being more disposed unto goodness, as well as being agreeably entertained. Be sure, had Virgil writ before Plato, his works had not been any of the books prohibited. But then, this poet also has abundance of rare antiquities for us: and such things, as others besides a Servius, have imagined that they have instructed and obliged mankind, by employing all their days upon. Wherefore if his *Aeneis,* which though it were once near twenty times as big as he has left it, yet he has left it unfinished, may not appear so valuable to you, that you may think twenty-seven verses of the part that is the most finished in it, worth one and twenty hundred pounds and odd money, yet his *Georgics,* which he put his left hand unto, will furnish you with many things far from despicable. But after all, when I said, I was willing that the beauties of these two poets, might become visible to your visive faculty in poetry, I did not mean, that you should judge nothing to be admittable into an epic poem, which is not authorized by their example; but I perfectly concur with one who is inexpressibly more capable to be a judge of such a matter than I can be: that it is a false critic who with a petulant air, will insult reason itself, if it presumes to oppose such authority.

I proceed now to say, that if (under the guidance of a Vida) you try your young wings now and then to see what flights you can make, at least for an epigram, it may a little sharpen your sense, and polish your style, for more important performances; for this purpose you are now even overstocked with patterns, and *poemata passim.* You may, like Nazianzen, all your days, make a little recreation of poetry in the midst of your more painful studies. Nevertheless, I cannot but advise you, withhold thy throat from thirst. Be not so set upon poetry, as to be always poring on the passionate and measured pages. Let not what should be sauce rather than food for you, engross all your application. Beware of a boundless and sickly appetite, for the reading of the poems, which now the rickety nation swarms withal: and let not the Circaean cup intoxicate you. But especially preserve the chastity of your soul from the dangers you may incur, by a conversation with Muses that are no better than harlots: among which are others besides Ovid's epistles, which for their tendency to excite and foment impure flames, and cast coals into your bosom, deserve rather to be thrown into the fire, than to be laid before the eye which a covenant should be made withal. Indeed, not merely for the impurities which they convey, but also on some other accounts, the powers of darkness have a library among us, whereof the poets have been the most numerous as well as the most venomous authors. Most of the modern plays, as well as the romances and novels and fictions, which are a sort of poems, do belong to the catalogue of this cursed library. The plays, I say, in which there are so many passages, that have a tendency to overthrow all piety, that one whose name is Bedford, has extracted near seven thousand instances of them, from the plays chiefly of but five years preceding; and says awfully upon them, "They are national sins, and therefore call for national plagues; and if God should enter into judgment, all the blood in the nation would not be able to atone for them." How much do I wish that such pestilences, and indeed all those worse than Egyptian toads (the spawns of a Butler, and a Brown, and a Ward, and a company whose name is legion!) might never crawl into your chamber! The unclean spirits that come like frogs out of the mouth of the dragon, and of the beast; which go forth unto the young people of the earth, and expose them to be dealt withal as the enemies of God, in the battle of the great day of the Almighty. As for those wretched scribbles of madmen, My Son, touch them not, taste them not, handle them not: thou wilt perish in the using of them. They are, the dragons whose contagious breath peoples the dark retreats of death. To much better purpose will an excellent but an envied Blackmore feast you, than those vile rhapsodies (of that *vinum daemonum*) which you will find always leave a taint upon your mind, and among other ill effects, will sensibly indispose you to converse with the holy oracles of God your Saviour.

But there is, what I may rather call a parenthesis, than a digression, which this may be not altogether an improper place for the introducing of.

(There has been a deal of ado about a style; so much, that I must offer you my sentiments upon it. There is a way of writing, wherein the author endeavors, that the reader may have something to the purpose in every paragraph. There is not only a vigor sensible in every sentence, but the paragraph is embellished with profitable references, even to something beyond what is directly spoken. Formal and painful quotations are not studied; yet all that could be learnt from them is insinuated. The writer pretends not unto reading, yet he could not have writ as he does if he had not read very much in his time; and his composures are not only a cloth of gold, but also struck with as many jewels, as the gown of a Russian ambassador. This way of writing has been decried by many, and is at this day more than ever so, for the same reason, that in the old story, the grapes were decried: that they were not ripe. A lazy, ignorant, conceited set of authors, would persuade the whole tribe, to lay aside that way of writing, for the same reason that one would have persuaded his brethren to part with the encumbrance of their bushy tails. But however fashion and humour may prevail, they must not think that the club at their coffee-house is all the world, but there will always be those, who will in this case be governed by indisputable reason: and who will think, that the real excellency of a book will never lie in saying of little; that the less one has for his money in a book, 'tis really the more valuable for it; and that the less one is instructed in a book, and the more of superfluous margin, and superficial harangue, and the less of substantial matter one has in it, the more 'tis to be accounted of? And if a more massy way of writing be never so much disgusted at this day, a better gust will come on, as will some other thing, *quae jam cecidere*. In the meantime, nothing appears to me more impertinent and ridiculous than the modern way (I cannot say rule; for they have none!) of criticizing. The blades that set up for critics, I know not who constituted or commissioned 'em! — they appear to me, for the most part as contemptible, as they are a supercilious generation. For indeed no two of them have the same style; and they are as intolerably cross-grained and severe in their censures one upon another, as they are upon the rest of mankind. But while each of them, conceitedly enough, sets up for the standard of perfection, we are entirely at a loss which fire to follow. Nor can you easily find any one thing wherein they agree for their style, except perhaps a perpetual care to give us jejune and empty pages, without such touches of erudition (so to speak in the style of an ingenious traveler) as may make the discourses less tedious, and more enriching, to the mind of him that peruses them. There is much talk of a florid style, obtaining among the pens, that are most in vogue; but how often would it puzzle one, even with the best glasses to find the flowers! And if they were to be chastised for it, it would be with as much of justice, as Jerome was, for being a Ciceronian. After all, every man will have his own style, which will distinguish him as much as his gait: and if you can attain to that which I have newly described, but always writing so as to give an easy conveyance unto your ideas, I would not have you by any scourging be driven out of your gait; but if you must confess a fault in it, make a confession like that of the lad unto his father while he was beating him for his versifying.

However, since every man will have his own style, I would pray, that we may learn to treat one another with mutual civilities, and condescensions, and handsomely indulge one another in this, as gentlemen do in other matters.

I wonder what ails people, that they can't let Cicero write in the style of Cicero, and Seneca write in the (much other!) style of Seneca; and own that both may please in their several ways. But I will freely tell you; what has made me consider the humourists that set up for critics upon style, as the most unregardable set of mortals in the world, is this! Far more illustrious critics than any of those to whom I am now bidding defiance, and no less men than your Erasmus's, and your Grotius's, have taxed the Greek style of the New Testament, with I know not what solecisms and barbarisms; and, how many learned folks have obsequiously run away with the notion! Whereas 'tis an ignorant and an insolent whimsy; which they have been guilty of. It may be (and particularly by an ingenious Blackwall, it has been) demonstrated, that the gentlemen are mistaken in every one of their pretended instances; all the unquestionable classics, may be brought in, to convince them of their mistakes. Those glorious oracles are as pure Greek as ever was written in the world; and so correct, so noble, so sublime in their style, that never anything under the cope of heaven, but the Old Testament, has equaled it.)

John Bulkley (1679–1731)

LIKE many another New England minister, John Bulkley was interested in a wide range of intellectual subjects, among them medicine, philosophy, and letters. The sophistication of his comments prefacing Roger Wolcott's *Poetical Meditations* (1725) reveals the turn occurring in American literary consciousness in the beginning of the eighteenth century. For the historical poetry he here introduces, see pp. 143–149.

TEXT: Roger Wolcott, *Poetical Meditations* (New London, 1725).

Preface

[From Roger Wolcott, *Poetical Meditations,* 1725]

The busy and restless soul of man which in all ages has been fruitful in many inventions, as it has been greatly disserviceable to the good and comfort of human life by the discovery of things prejudicial to it; so at the same time may we not say, has made some compensation by the invention of others of a proportionable advantage and benefit. It were easy by a detail of some of the many useful arts found out by man to give evidence of this, but it must suffice at present, to instance in one only, viz., that art of writing or expressing all sounds, and consequently the conceptions of our minds, by a few letters variously disposed or placed, the commodity or profit of which to mankind is so various and extensive as not to be easily accounted for. This art is styled by one,[1] *admirandarum omnium inventionum humanarum signaculum,* i.e., the wonder or masterpiece of all human inventions: and how deservedly is it so, whether we speak with reference to the

[1] Galileo. [Bulkley's note]

strangeness or the benefit of it? How strange is it that by the various disposition of so few letters as our alphabet contains, all sounds should be expressed, and thereby all the conceptions or ideas of our minds! And as for the commodity of it; not to mention others, from hence it comes to pass that we are furnished with so much useful history, which bringing into our view both persons and things most distant from us in time and place, does greatly delight and entertain us, and at the same time instruct or teach and furnish us with a main part of our most useful knowledge.

In the early ages of the world, before this most certain way of communicating the knowledge of things was found out; other mediums were made use of for that end, the principal of which seems to have been representative symbols or hieroglyphics, which way or method of communication everyone knows still obtains among many unlettered nations in the world. But this as it's very uncertain on the account of that great variety of interpretations such symbols are liable to, and as the misconstruction of them, it's reasonable to think, has been none of the least prolific fountains of the heathen mythology, by which the ancient and true tradition of the first ages of the world has been so much corrupted and altered, so is now out of use with such nations, as among whom the use of letters has been introduced. I said above that to this we are debtors for the useful history we are furnished with: and I must observe on this occasion that there are two ways in which those who have obliged us with it, according to their different genius and humours, have improved this noble invention in composing the histories they have put into our hands; that some therein have confined themselves to poetical numbers, and measures; others not so restricting themselves, have written in prose, which last in latter ages has been the more common way. That a considerable part, especially of our more ancient history, is delivered to us in the former of these ways, is known to most that are not strangers to books; a considerable part of the writings both of the Latin and Greek poets, what are they but *poemata historica*? Among the former, Ovid assures us his book *Metamorphoseon,* in part, at least is no other. . . .

. . . It's true he writes in the strain and manner of others of his tribe, who are wont generally to mingle a great deal of mythology with the truth; yet notwithstanding how easy is it for every intelligent reader to trace in him the footsteps of the sacred history, particularly in its accounts of the most early times?

And may we not with equal truth say the same of Virgil's *Aeneids*? which seem to be no other than a mythological history of the affairs of Aeneas, or the various occurrences of his life; to which Homer his *Iliads* with others from the Greeks might be added. It's observed by some learned men, that this was the most ancient way of writing, and that prose is only an imitation of poetry, and that the Grecians in particular at their first delivery from barbarism, had all their philosophy and instruction from the poets, such as Orpheus, Hesiod, Parmenides, Xenophanes, etc. — which seems to have occasioned those lines of Horace, *Cap. de Arte Poetica:*

> ——— *Fuit haec sapientia quondam*
> *Publica privatis sacernere, sacra profanis:*
> *Concubitu prohibere vago; dare jura maritis:*
> *Oppida moliri: leges incidere ligno.*
> *Sic honor et nomen divinis vatibus atque*
> *Carminibus venit.*

The sum of which is this, viz.,

That in old time poets were the lights and instructors of the world, and gave laws to men for their conduct in their several relations and affairs of life.

And finally, to this seems to agree that of Cato in his *Distichs:*

> *Si Deus est animus nobis ut carmina dicunt,*
> If God a Spirit be as poets teach, etc.

I have premised this in way of apology for the manner in which this worthy person has given us the ensuing history, in composing which he has diverted some of his leisure hours. And from hence 'tis evident he has for a precedent some of the most ancient history, and has trod in the steps of many of the most eminent sages, and earliest writers history gives us any knowledge of, who have taken that same way to raise up monuments to, and eternize the names and actions of their admired heroes.

It's undoubtedly true that as the minds of men have a very different cast, disposition, or genius leading to and accomplishing for very differing improvements, so generally speaking, those are the most accomplished to make a judgment on any performance that have by nature a genius leading to and accomplishing for the same. And it being so, and withal there being none among the whole number of mortals less furnished for a performance of this nature than myself, I may well be excused in omitting the part of a censor or judge upon it, further than to say that the intelligent reader will herein discern an uncommon vigor of mind, considerable reading, and see reason to say, that herein we have a specimen what good parts cultivated with a laudable ambition to improve in knowledge will do, though not assisted with those advantages of education which some are favored withal.

Some there are that have remarked, that the accomplished poet and the great man are things seldom meeting together in one person, or that it's rare those powers of mind that make the one, are found united with those that constitute the other. And perhaps it may be a truth which for the main holds true. For whereas what is properly called wit (which is no other than a ready assemblage of ideas, or a putting those together with quickness and variety wherein there can be found any congruity or resemblance; or to speak more plain, an aptness at metaphor and allusion) is what, as I take it, makes the accomplished poet; exactness of judgment, or clearness of reason (which we commonly and truly say makes the great man) on the other hand lies in an ability of mind nicely to distinguish its ideas the one from the other, where there is but the least difference, thereby avoiding being misled by similitude, and by affinity to take one thing from another. And the process of the mind in these two things being so contrary the one to the other, 'tis not strange if they are powers not ever united in the same subject, yet this notwithstanding, all must say, this is not a remark that universally and without exception will hold true; but that how contrary and inconsistent soever the process of the mind in the exercise of these two powers may seem to be, yet there are instances wherein they are united in a wonderful measure: and many men in whom we find a great deal of pleasantry or wit, are notwithstanding very judicious and rational. And though modesty forbids me to say this of the author, yet this I shall venture to say, viz., that whatever may be said in commendation of this performance by the accomplished for a judgment upon it; yet that there will not that honor be done him thereby, as I conceive may with a great deal of truth and justice otherwise.

Benjamin Franklin (1706–1790)

EXASPERATION has often been the midwife of literary criticism, especially in its more bitter forms. One of the best examples of early satiric criticism comes from the pen of the "universal genius" Benjamin Franklin, and is aimed appropriately, and almost symbolically, at the New England funeral elegy, or, as Franklin terms it, the Kitelic genre. Franklin's "Receipt to Make a New England Funeral Elegy" was the most effective of his Dogood Papers, inspiring others to similar attacks.

TEXT: *The New-England Courant,* June 18-25, 1722.

A Receipt to Make a New England Funeral Elegy

[From Dogood Paper no. VII]

To the author of the *New-England Courant.*
Sir,

It has been the complaint of many ingenious foreigners, who have traveled amongst us, that good poetry is not to be expected in New England. I am apt to fancy, the reason is, not because our countrymen are altogether void of a poetical genius, nor yet because we have not those advantages of education which other countries have, but purely because we do not afford that praise and encouragement which is merited, when anything extraordinary of this kind is produced among us: upon which consideration I have determined, when I meet with a good piece of New England poetry, to give it a suitable encomium, and thereby endeavor to discover to the world some of its beauties, in order to encourage the author to go on, and bless the world with more, and more excellent productions.

There has lately appeared among us a most excellent piece of poetry, entitled *An Elegy upon the Much Lamented Death of Mrs. Mehitabel Kitel, Wife of Mr. John Kitel of Salem, etc.* It may justly be said in its praise, without flattery to the author, that it is the most extraordinary piece that ever was wrote in New England. The language is so soft and easy, the expression so moving and pathetic, but above all, the verse and numbers so charming and natural, that it is almost beyond comparison. . . . And for the affecting part, I will leave your readers to judge, if ever they read any lines, that would sooner make them draw their breath and sigh, if not shed tears, than these following.

Come let us mourn, for we have lost a wife, a daughter, and a sister,
Who has lately taken flight, and greatly we have missed her.

In another place,

Some little time before she yielded up her breath,
She said, I ne'er shall hear one sermon more on earth.
She kissed her husband some little time before she expired,
Then leaned her head the pillow on, just out of breath and tired.

But the threefold appellation in the first line

— a wife, a daughter, and a sister,

must not pass unobserved. That line in the celebrated Watts,

Gunston the just, the generous, and the young,

is nothing comparable to it. The latter only mentions three qualifications of one person who was deceased, which therefore could raise grief and compassion but for one. Whereas the former (our most excellent poet) gives his reader a sort of an idea of the death of three persons, viz.,

a wife, a daughter, and a sister,

which is three times as great a loss as the death of one, and consequently must raise three times as much grief and compassion in the reader.

I should be very much straitened for room, if I should attempt to discover even half the excellencies of this elegy which are obvious to me. Yet I cannot omit one observation, which is, that the author has (to his honor) invented a new species of poetry, which wants a name, and was never before known. His Muse scorns to be confined to the old measures and limits, or to observe the dull rules of critics;

Nor Rapin gives her rules to fly, nor Purcell notes to sing. WATTS.

Now 'tis pity that such an excellent piece should not be dignified with a particular name; and seeing it cannot justly be called, either epic, Sapphic, lyric, or Pindaric, nor any other name yet invented, I presume it may (in honor and remembrance of the dead) be called the Kitelic. Thus much in the praise of Kitelic poetry. . . .

For the title of your elegy. Of these you may have enough ready made to your hands; but if you should choose to make it yourself, you must be sure not to omit the words *aetatis suae,* which will beautify it exceedingly.

For the subject of your elegy. Take one of your neighbors who has lately departed this life; it is no great matter at what age the party died, but it will be best if he went away suddenly, being killed, drowned, or froze to death.

Having chose the person, take all his virtues, excellencies, etc., and if he have not enough, you may borrow some to make up a sufficient quantity: to these add his last words, dying expressions, etc., if they are to be had; mix all these together, and be sure you strain them well. Then season all with a handful or two of melancholy expressions, such as *dreadful, deadly, cruel cold death, unhappy fate, weeping eyes,* etc. Have mixed all these ingredients well, put them into the empty skull of some young Harvard (but in case you have ne'er a one at hand, you may use your own); there let them ferment for the space of a fortnight, and by that time they will be incorporated into a body, which take out; and having prepared a sufficient quantity of double rhymes, such as *power, flower; quiver, shiver; grieve us, leave us; tell you, excel you; expeditions, physicians; fatigue him, intrigue him,* etc., you must spread all upon paper, and if you can procure a scrap of Latin to put at the end, it will garnish it mightily; then having affixed your name at the bottom, with a *Moestus composuit,* you will have an excellent elegy.

N.B. This receipt will serve when a female is the subject of your elegy, provided you borrow a greater quantity of virtues, excellencies, etc.

Sir, your servant, Silence Dogood

Man and Nature: The Critical View

THE NATURAL SCIENCE of colonial America often appeared in strange guise. Early travelers credulously recounted their adventures in a world of hitherto unknown, and often bizarre, plants and animals. But after initial extravagances, learned and curious colonists kept abreast of the growing scientific activity generated by London's Royal Society after 1662, and famous English and Continental scientists made use of American observations in astronomy and botany. But the isolation of Americans from the European scientific community, the paucity of tools for experimentation and even observation, and the lack of training in mathematics until well into the eighteenth century all conspired to reduce the quality, timeliness, and significance of American science. In 1683, Increase Mather and other New England intellectuals formed a Philosophical Society for scientific study, but it lasted no more than a decade. Societies of physicians and surgeons in major colonial towns distributed some scientific information, but as late as 1743 Benjamin Franklin bewailed America's want of an inter-colonial scientific and philosophical society.

Nonetheless, amateur scientists — primarily from Boston, Philadelphia, and Charleston — eagerly submitted their observations and speculations to England and Europe for review and publication. By 1750, ten Americans were Fellows of the Royal Society, including John Winthrop, Jr., William Byrd of Westover, and Cotton Mather; eight more were similarly honored by 1795; and others, although not elected, maintained close contact with the spirit of the Enlightenment. Cadwallader Colden, for example, contributed to Linnaeus' work in botany from New York, as did James Logan from Philadelphia through his encouragement of the naturalist John Bartram. Paul

Dudley published excellent critical studies of American deer, whales, bees, and other fauna; the great Isaac Newton acknowledged his use of Thomas Brattle's 1680 astronomical observations in working out the law of gravitation; and Cotton Mather's papers on hybridization and on inoculation as a weapon against smallpox epidemics not only enjoyed notoriety in his day, but are still respectfully treated by historians of science.

For several reasons these talented amateurs could not pursue their observations to the discovery of significant natural laws; two of these reasons are especially important. First, lacking mathematical sophistication (mathematics was not adequately taught in the colonies until Thomas Robie's tutorship at Harvard from 1712 to 1723), the colonists had no sufficient method by which to analyze, evaluate, and relate their observations, and so were limited to the practical tasks of description and classification. Second, especially until around 1730, all scientific investigation was presumed to lead not to radically new principles, but back to God's divine decrees, fully revealed in the Bible, and systematized by generations of theologians. Natural Philosophy was unmistakably Theology's handmaid. For most Americans, therefore, natural law was indistinguishable from divine law; when one knew beforehand the basic principles of the universe, there seemed little necessity to generalize to them from empirical observation. The "natural theology" of England's John Ray set the pattern, best represented perhaps by Cotton Mather's intention in *The Christian Philosopher* (1721) to prove "that philosophy is no enemy, but a mighty and wondrous incentive to religion."

This tendency to moralize from the marvelous new evidence supplied by the microscope and telescope was long-lived; but inevitably the scientific method's fundamental trust in human reason led eighteenth-century experimenters to stop short of inferences incapable of demonstration. Natural philosophers progressively ignored religious and metaphysical questions, concentrating instead on the rigorous, critical scrutiny of observable events. Whether such events were physical, geological, astronomical, sociological, or psychological, early eighteenth-century writers observed them from an increasingly rational, analytical, self-reliant point of view. The skepticism that would later challenge Americans' most traditional assumptions about social and political order had not quite appeared in the early eighteenth century. But violent upheavals in all spheres — from great earthquakes to great awakenings — called forth the critical temper that would come to fruition in the latter half of the Age of Reason.

John Woolman (1720–1772)

JOHN WOOLMAN, born into a New Jersey Quaker family of limited means, was a tailor, shopkeeper, and schoolmaster, but he spent most of his life as an itinerant minister for the Society of Friends. For more than thirty years he traveled up and down the colonies, from New England to the Carolinas, preaching the Quaker faith to city man, farmer, frontiersman, and Indian, and at the same time crusading for temperance, the abolition of slavery, and other reforms. His journal, which John Greenleaf Whittier called "a classic of the inner life," is a revealing record, not only of the faith of the Quakers, but of the life of a good and kindly man who believed in justice, tolerance, human dignity, and Christian idealism.

TEXT: Amelia Gummere, ed., *The Journal and Essays of John Woolman* (New York, 1922).

Youth

[From *The Journal of John Woolman*, 1774]

I have often felt a motion of love to leave some hints of my experience of the goodness of God: and pursuant thereto, in the thirty-sixth year of my age, I begin this work.

I was born in Northampton, in Burlington county, in West Jersey, in the year of our Lord 1720; and before I was seven years old I began to be acquainted with the operations of divine love. Through the care of my parents, I was taught to read near as soon as I was capable of it; and as I went from school one seventh-day, I remember, while my companions went to play by the way, I went forward out of sight, and setting down, I read the twenty-second chapter of the Revelations: "He showed me a pure river of water of life, clear as crystal, proceeding out of the throne of God and of the lamb," etc.; and in the reading of it, my mind was drawn to seek after that pure habitation, which I then believed God had prepared for His servants. The place where I sat, and the sweetness that attended my mind, remain fresh in my memory.

This, and the like gracious visitations, had that effect upon me, that when boys used ill language, it troubled me, and through the continued mercies of God, I was preserved from it. The pious instructions of my parents were often fresh in my mind when I happened to be among wicked children, and were of use to me.

My parents, having a large family of children, used frequently, on first days after meeting, to put us to read in the holy scriptures, or some religious books, one after another, the rest sitting by without much conversation; which I have since often thought was a good practice. From what I had read, I believed there had been in past ages, people who walked in uprightness before God in a degree exceeding any that I knew, or heard of, now living; and the apprehension of there being less steadiness and firmness amongst people in this age than in past ages, often troubled me while I was still young.

I had a dream about the ninth year of my age as follows: I saw the moon rise near the West, and run a regular course Eastward, so swift that in about a quarter of an hour, she reached our meridian, when there descended from her a small cloud on a direct line to the earth, which lighted on a pleasant green about twenty yards from the door of my father's house (in which I thought I stood) and was immediately turned into a beautiful green tree. The moon appeared to run on with equal swiftness, and soon set in the East, at which time the sun arose at the place where it commonly doth in the summer, and shining with full radiance in a serene air, it appeared as pleasant a morning as ever I saw.

All this time I stood still in the door, in an awful frame of mind, and I observed that as heat increased by the rising sun, it wrought so powerfully on the little green tree, that the leaves gradually withered, and before noon it appeared dry and dead. There then appeared a being, small of size, moving swift from the North Southward, called a sun worm.

[Though I was a child, this dream was instructive to me.]

Another thing remarkable in my childhood was, that once, as I went to a neighbor's house, I saw, on the way, a robin sitting on her nest; and as I came near she went off, but having young ones, flew about, and with many cries expressed her concern for them. I stood and threw stones at her, till one striking her, she fell down dead. At first I was pleased with the exploit, but after a few minutes was seized with horror, as having in a sportive way killed an innocent creature while she was careful for her young. I beheld her lying dead, and thought those young ones for which she was so careful must now perish for want of their dam to nourish them; and after some painful considerations on the subject, I climbed up the tree, took all the young birds, and killed them — supposing that better than to leave them to pine away and die miserably: and believed in this case, that scripture proverb was fulfilled, "The tender mercies of the wicked are cruel." I then went on my errand, but, for some hours, could think of little else but [the cruelties I had committed, and was much troubled.]

Thus He, whose tender mercies are over all His works, hath placed that in the human mind, which incites to exercise goodness towards every living creature, and this being singly attended to, people become tender-hearted and sympathizing; but being frequently and totally rejected, the mind shuts itself up in a contrary disposition.

About the twelfth year of my age, my father being abroad, my mother reproved me for some misconduct, to which I made an undutiful reply; and the next first-day, as I was with my father returning from meeting, he told me he understood I had behaved amiss to my mother, and advised me to be more careful in future. I knew myself blamable, and in shame and confusion remained silent. Being thus awakened to a sense of my wickedness, I felt remorse in my mind, and getting home, I retired and prayed to the Lord to forgive me; and I do not remember that I ever, after that, spoke unhandsomely to either of my parents, however foolish in some other things.

Having attained the age of sixteen, I began to love wanton company: and though I was preserved from profane language or scandalous conduct, still I perceived a plant in me which produced much wild grapes. Yet my merciful Father forsook me not utterly, but at times, through His grace, I was brought seriously to consider my ways; and the sight of my backsliding affected me with sorrow: but for want of rightly attending to the reproofs of instruction, vanity was added to vanity, and repentance. Upon the whole, my mind was more and more alienated from the truth, and I hastened towards destruction. While I meditate on the gulf towards which I traveled, and reflect on my youthful disobedience, my heart is affected with sorrow.

Advancing in age, the number of my acquaintance increased, and thereby my way grew more difficult. Though I had heretofore found comfort in reading the holy scriptures, and thinking on heavenly things, I was now estranged therefrom. I knew I was going from the flock of Christ, and had no resolution to return; hence serious reflections were uneasy to me, and youthful vanities and diversions my greatest pleasure. Running in this road I found many like myself; and we associated in that which is reverse to true friendship. But in this swift race it pleased God to visit me with sickness, so that I doubted of recovering: and then did darkness, horror, and amazement, with full force seize me, even when my pain and distress of body was very great. I thought it would have been better for me never to have had a being, than to see the day which I now saw. I was filled with confusion; and in great affliction both of mind and body, I lay and bewailed myself. [I had not confidence to lift up my cries to God, whom I had thus offended; but in a deep sense of my great folly, I was humbled before Him,] and at length, that Word which is as a fire and a hammer, broke and dissolved my rebellious heart, and then my cries were put up in contrition, and in the multitude of His mercies I found inward relief, and felt a close engagement, that if He was pleased to restore my health, I might walk humbly before Him.

After my recovery, this exercise remained with me a considerable time, but, by degrees, giving way to youthful vanities, they gained strength, and getting with wanton young people I lost ground. The Lord had been very gracious, and spoke peace to me in the time of my distress, and I now most ungratefully turned again to folly, on which account, at times, I felt sharp reproof, but did not get low enough to cry for help. I was not so hardy as to commit things scandalous, but to exceed in vanity, and promote mirth, was my chief study. Still I retained a love and esteem for pious people, and their company brought an awe upon me. My dear parents several times admonished me in the fear of the Lord, and their admonition entered into my heart, and had a good effect for a season; but not getting deep enough to pray rightly, the tempter, when he came, found entrance. I remember once, having spent a part of a day in wantonness, as I went to bed at night, there lay in a window near my bed a Bible, which I opened, and first cast my eye on the text, "we lie down in our shame, and our confusion covers us." This I knew to be my case, and meeting with so unexpected a reproof, I was somewhat affected with it, and went to bed under remorse of conscience, which I soon cast off again.

Thus time passed on, my heart was replenished with mirth and wantonness, while pleasing scenes of vanity were presented to my imagination, till I attained the age of eighteen years, near which time I felt the judgments of God in my soul like a consuming fire, and looking over my past life, the prospect was moving. I was often sad, and longed to be delivered from those vanities; then again my heart was strongly inclined to them, and there was in me a sore conflict. At times I turned to folly, and then again sorrow and confusion took hold of me. In a while, I resolved totally to leave off some of my vanities, but there was a secret reserve in my heart, of the more refined part of them, and I was not low enough to find true peace. Thus for some months, I had great troubles and disquiet, there remaining in me an unsubjected will, which rendered my labors fruitless, till at length, through the merciful continuance of heavenly visitations, I was made to bow down in spirit before the Most High. I remember one evening I had spent some time in reading a pious author, and walking out alone, I humbly prayed to the Lord for His help, that I might be delivered from those vanities which so ensnared me. . . . Thus, being brought low, He helped me, and as I learned to bear the cross, I felt refreshment to come from His presence: but not keeping in that strength which gave victory, I lost ground again, the sense of which greatly afflicted me; and I sought deserts and lonely places, and there with tears did confess my sins to God, and humbly craved help of Him. And I may say with reverence, He was near to me in my troubles, and in those times of humiliation opened my ear to discipline.

I was now led to look seriously at the means by which I was drawn from the pure truth, and I learned this: that if I would live in the life which the faithful servants of God lived in, I must not go into company as heretofore, in my own will; but all the cravings of sense must be governed by a divine principle. In times of sorrow and abasement, these instructions were sealed upon me, and I felt the power of Christ prevail over all selfish desires, so that I was preserved in a good degree of steadiness; and being young and believing at that time that a single life was best for me, I was strengthened to keep from such company as had often been a snare to me.

I kept steady to meetings; spent first-days in the afternoon chiefly in reading the scriptures and other good books; and was early convinced in my mind that true religion consisted in an inward life, wherein the heart doth love and reverence God the Creator, and learn to exercise true justice and goodness, not only toward all men, but also toward the brute creatures. That as the mind was moved by an inward principle to love God as an invisible, incomprehensible Being, by the same principle it was moved to love Him in all His manifestations in the visible world. That, as by His breath the flame of life was kindled in all animal and sensible creatures, to say we love God as unseen, and at the same time exercise cruelty toward the least creature moving by His life, or by life derived from Him, was a contradiction in itself.

I found no narrowness respecting sects and opinions; but believe that sincere, upright-hearted people, in every society, who truly love God, were accepted of Him.

As I lived under the cross, and simply followed the openings of truth, my mind from day to day was more enlightened; my former acquaintance were left to judge of me as they would, for I found it safest for me to live in private and keep these things sealed up in my own breast. While I silently ponder on that change which was wrought in me, I find no language equal to it, nor any means to convey to another a clear idea of it. I looked upon the works of God in this visible creation, and an awfulness covered me: my heart was tender and often contrite, and a universal love to my fellow creatures increased in me. This will be understood by such who have trodden in the same path.

Some glances of real beauty is perceivable in their faces, who dwell in true meekness. Some tincture of true harmony in the sound of that voice to which divine love gives utterance, and some appearance of right order in their temper and conduct, whose passions are fully regulated; yet all these do not fully show forth that inward life to such as have not felt it; but this white stone and new name is known rightly to such only who have it. . . .

Business and Conscience

[From *Journal*]

Until the year 1756, I continued to retail goods, besides following my trade as a tailor; about which time I grew uneasy on account of my business growing too cumbersome. I began with selling trimmings for garments, and from thence proceeded to sell cloths and linens, and at length having got a considerable shop of goods, my trade increased every year, and the road to large business appeared open: but I felt a stop in my mind.

Through the mercies of the Almighty I had in good degree learned to be content with a plain way of living. I had but a small family, [my outward affairs had been prosperous,] and, on serious reflection I believed truth did not require me to engage in much cumbering affairs. It had generally been my practice to buy and sell things really useful. Things that served chiefly to please the vain mind in people, I was not easy to trade in; seldom did it, and whenever I did, I found it weaken me as a Christian.

The increase of business became my burthen, for though my natural inclination was towards merchandise, yet I believed truth required me to live more free from outward cumbers. There was now a strife in my mind betwixt the two, and in this exercise my prayers were put up to the Lord, who graciously heard me, and gave me a heart resigned to His holy will; I then lessened my outward business; and as I had opportunity, told my customers of my intention, that they might consider what shop to turn to: and so in a while, wholly laid down merchandise, following my trade as a tailor, myself only, having no prentice. I also had a nursery of apple trees, in which I spent a good deal of time, howing, grafting, trimming, and inoculating.

In merchandise it is the custom, where I lived, to sell chiefly on credit; and poor people often get in debt, and when payment is expected, having not wherewith to pay, and so their creditors often sue for it at law: having often observed occurrences of this kind, I found it good for me to advise poor people to take such as were most useful and not costly.

In the time of trading I had an opportunity of seeing that a too liberal use of spiritous liquors, and the custom of wearing too costly apparel, led some people into great inconveniences: and these two things appear to be often connected one with the other; for by not attending to that use of things which is consistent with universal righteousness, there is a [necessary] increase of labor which extends beyond what our heavenly Father intends for us: and by great labor, and often by much sweating in the heat, there is, even among such who are not drunkards, a craving of some liquor to revive the spirits: that partly by the wanton, luxurious drinking of some, and partly by the drinking of others, led to it through immoderate labor, very great quantities of rum are annually expended in our colonies, of which we should have no need, did we steadily attend to pure wisdom.

Where men take pleasure in feeling their minds elevated with strong drink, and so indulge this appetite as to disorder their understanding, neglect their duty as members in a family or civil society, and cast off all pretense to religion, their case is much to be pitied. And where such whose lives are for the most part regular, and whose examples have a strong influence on the minds of others, adhere to some customs which powerfully draw toward the use of more strong liquor than pure wisdom [directeth the use of,] this also, as it hinders the spreading of the spirit of meekness, and strengthens the hands of the more excessive drinkers, is a case to be lamented.

As [the least] degree of luxury hath some connection with evil, for those who profess to be disciples of Christ, and are looked upon as leaders of the people, to have that mind in them which was also in Him, and so stand separate from every wrong way, is a means of help to the weaker. As I have sometimes been much spent in the heat, and taken spirits to revive me, I have found by experience that the mind is not so calm in such circumstances, nor so fit for divine meditation, as when all such extremes are avoided; and I have felt an increasing care to attend that Holy Spirit which sets right bounds to our desires, and leads those who faithfully follow it to apply all the gifts of divine providence to the purposes for which they were intended. Did such who have the care of great estates attend with singleness of heart to this heavenly instructor, which so opens and enlarges the mind that men love their neighbors as themselves, they would have wisdom given them to manage, without ever finding occasion to employ some people in the luxuries of life, or to make it necessary for others to labor too hard. But for want of regarding steadily this principle of divine love, a selfish spirit takes place in the minds of people, which is attended with darkness and manifold confusions in the world. . . .

Though trading in things useful is an honest employ, yet through the great number of superfluities which are commonly bought and sold, and through the corruptions of the times, they who apply to merchandise for a living, have great need to be well experienced in that precept which the prophet Jeremiah laid down for Baruk, his scribe: "Seekest thou great things for thyself? seek them not."

A Testimony Against Slavery

[From *Journal*]

The monthly-meeting of Philadelphia having been under a concern on account of some Friends who, this summer, A.D. 1758, had bought Negro slaves, the said meeting moved it in their quarterly-meeting, to have the minute reconsidered in the yearly-meeting, which was made last on that subject: and the said quarterly-meeting appointed a committee to consider it and report to their next; which committee having met once and adjourned, and I going to Philadelphia to meet a committee of the yearly-meeting, was in town the evening on which the quarterly-meeting's committee met the second time, and finding an inclination to sit with them, was, with some others, admitted; and Friends had a weighty conference on the subject. And soon after their next quarterly-meeting, I heard that the case was coming to our yearly-meeting, which brought a weighty exercise upon me, and under a sense of my own infirmities and the great danger I felt of turning aside from perfect purity, my mind was often drawn to retire alone and put up my prayers to the Lord, that He would be graciously pleased to so strengthen me, that, setting aside all views of self-interest and the friendship of this world, I might stand fully resigned to His holy will.

In this yearly-meeting several weighty matters were considered; and, toward the last, that in relation to dealing with persons who purchase slaves. During the several sittings of the said meeting, my mind was frequently covered with inward prayer, and I could say with David, that tears were my meat day and night. The case of slave keeping lay heavy upon me, nor did I find any engagement to speak directly to any other matter before the meeting. Now when this case was opened several faithful Friends spake weightily thereto, with which I was comforted; and, feeling a concern to cast in my mite, I said, in substance, as follows:

"In the difficulties attending us in this life, nothing is more precious than the mind of truth inwardly manifested, and it is my earnest desire that in this weighty matter we may be so truly humbled, as to be favored with a clear understanding of the mind of truth, and follow it: this would be of more advantage to the society, than any mediums which are not in the clearness of divine wisdom. The case is difficult to some who have them; but if such set aside all self-interest, and come to be weaned from the desire of getting estates, or even from holding them together when truth requires the contrary, I believe way will open, that they will know how to steer through those difficulties."

Many Friends appeared to be deeply bowed under the weight of the work; and manifested much firmness in their love to the cause of truth and universal righteousness in the earth. And though none did openly justify the practice of slave keeping in general, yet some appeared concerned, lest the meeting should go into such measures as might give uneasiness to many brethren, alleging that if Friends patiently continued under the exercise, the Lord, in time to come, might open a way for the deliverance of these people, and I, finding an engagement to speak, said: "My mind is often led to consider the purity of the divine Being, and the justice of His judgments; and herein my soul is covered with awfulness. I cannot omit to hint of some cases where people have not been treated with the purity of justice, and the event hath been lamentable. Many slaves on this continent are oppressed, and their cries have reached the ears of the Most High! Such are the purity and certainty of His judgments, that He cannot be partial [toward any.] In infinite love and goodness He hath opened our understandings, from time to [time, respecting] our duty toward this people; and it is not a time for delay. Should we now be sensible of what He requires of us, and through a respect to the outward interest of some persons, or through a regard to some friendships which do not stand on the immutable foundation, neglect to do our duty in firmness and constancy, still waiting for some extraordinary means to bring about their freedom, it may be that by terrible things in righteousness God may answer us in this matter."

Many faithful brethren labored with great firmness, and love of truth, in a good degree, prevailed. Several Friends who had Negroes exprest their desire that a rule might be made to deal with such Friends as offenders who might buy slaves in future. To this it was [replied] that the root of this evil would not be removed from amongst us, till a close inquiry was made in [regard to the righteousness of] their motives [who detained Negroes in their service], that impartial justice might be administered throughout. Several Friends exprest a desire that a visit might be made to such Friends who kept slaves: and many Friends said that they believed liberty was the Negroes' right, to which at length no opposition was made publicly. A minute was [at length] made more full on that subject than any heretofore and the names of several Friends entered who were free to join in a visit to such who [kept] slaves.

A Final Appeal

[From *Considerations on Keeping Negroes,* 1762]

If we seriously consider that liberty is the right of innocent men; that the mighty God is a refuge for the oppressed; that in reality we are indebted to them; that they being set free, are still liable to the penalties of our laws, and as likely to have punishment for their crimes as other people: this may answer all our objections. And to retain them in perpetual servitude, without just cause for it, will produce effects, in the event, more grievous than setting them free would do, when a real love to truth and equity was the motive to it.

Our authority over them stands originally in a purchase made from those who, as to the general, obtained theirs by unrighteousness. Whenever we have recourse to such authority, it tends more or less to obstruct the channels through which the perfect plant in us receives nourishment.

There is a principle which is pure, placed in the human mind, which in different places and ages hath had different names; it is, however, pure, and proceeds from God. It is deep, and inward, confined to no forms of religion, nor excluded from any, where the heart stands in perfect sincerity. In whomsoever this takes root and grows, of what nation soever, they become brethren, in the best sense of the expression. Using ourselves to take ways which appear most easy to us, when inconsistent with that purity which is without beginning, we thereby set up a government of our own, and deny obedience to Him whose service is true liberty.

He that hath a servant, made so wrongfully, and knows it to be so, when he treats him otherwise than a free man, when he reaps the benefit of his labor, without paying him such wages as are reasonably due to free men for the like service, clothes excepted; these things, though done in calmness, without any shew of disorder, do yet deprave the mind in like manner, and with as great certainty as prevailing cold congeals water. These steps taken by masters, and their conduct striking the minds of their children, whilst young, leave less room for that which is good to work upon them. The customs of their parents, their neighbors, and the people with whom they converse, working upon their minds; and they, from thence, conceiving ideas of things, and modes of conduct, the entrance into their hearts becomes, in a great measure, shut up against the gentle movings of uncreated purity.

From one age to another, the gloom grows thicker and darker, till error gets established by general opinion: so that whoever attends to perfect goodness, and remains under the melting influence of it, finds a path unknown to many, and sees the necessity to lean upon the arm of divine strength, and dwell alone, or with a few, in the right committing their cause to Him who is a refuge for His people in all their troubles.

Where, through the agreement of a multitude, some channels of justice are stopped, and men may support their characters as just men by being just to a party, there is great danger of contracting an alliance with that spirit which stands in opposition to the God of love, and spreads discord, trouble, and vexation among such who give up to the influence of it.

Negroes are our fellow creatures, and their present condition amongst us requires our serious consideration. We know not the time when those scales in which mountains are weighed may turn. The Parent of mankind is gracious; His care is over His smallest creatures; and a multitude of men escape not His notice. And though many of them are trodden down, and despised, yet He remembers them; He seeth their affliction, and looketh upon the spreading, increasing exaltation of the oppressor. He turns the channels of power, humbles the most haughty people, and gives deliverance to the oppressed, at such periods as are consistent with His infinite justice and goodness. And wherever gain is preferred to equity, and wrong things publicly encouraged, to that degree that wickedness takes root, and spreads wide amongst the inhabitants of a country, there is real cause for sorrow to all such whose love to mankind stands on a true principle, and who wisely consider the end and event of things.

Charles Chauncy (1705–1787)

For nearly sixty years, Charles Chauncy was a pastor of Boston's First Church, the author of fifty books on theology. He was, however, no hidebound conservative. He did not agree wholly with the orthodox Calvinist doctrine of man's depravity, and even wrote a book, *The Benevolence of the Deity* (1784), to disprove it; he also believed strongly in free discussion and liberal church government.

During the Great Awakening of 1740–45, when waves of revivalism swept New England, Chauncy set himself against Edwardsian evangelism, preaching and writing powerfully against it. He did not trust religious "enthusiasm," feeling that it struck at reason and stability, and that it led to emotional excesses and social unrest. Late in life, he joined the Universalists, who were much more convinced than either the orthodox Calvinist or the evangelical revivalist of man's basic goodness and rationality.

TEXTS: Charles Chauncy, *Seasonable Thoughts on the State of Religion in New England,* Part I (Boston, 1743); and *Enthusiasm Described and Cautioned Against* (Boston, 1742).

A Counsel of Caution

[From *Seasonable Thoughts on the State of Religion in New England,* 1743]

The way in which these fears have been excited, in many places, is not, in my opinion, the best evidence in favor of them. People have been too much applied to, as though the preacher rather aimed at putting their passions into a ferment, than filling them with such a reasonable solicitude, as is the effect of a just exhibition of the truths of God to their understandings. I have myself been present, when an air of seriousness reigned visibly through a whole congregation. They were all silence and attention; having their eye fastened on the minister, as though they would catch every word that came from his mouth. And yet, because they did not cry out, or swoon away, they were upbraided with their hardness of heart and ranked among those who were sermon-proof, gospel-glutted; and every topic made use of, with all the voice and action the speaker was master of, to bring forward a general shriek in the assembly. Nay, in order to give the people a plain intimation of what he wanted, this same preacher sometimes told them of the wonderful effects wrought by the sermon he was then preaching; how in such a congregation, they were all melted and dissolved, and in another so overpowered, that they could not help screaming out, or falling down, as though they had been struck dead. Nay, one of the preachers, in this new way, was so open some months ago, as in plain words, to call upon the people to cry out, and plead with them to do so. This he did three several times in one sermon, and had upon it so many loud cries. And 'tis too well known to need much to be said upon it, that the gentlemen, whose preaching has been most remarkably accompanied with these extraordinaries, not only use, in their addresses to the people, all the terrible words they can get together, but in such a manner, as naturally tends to put weaker minds out of possession of themselves. A friend in the country, in a letter to me, upon these matters, expresses himself in these words, "Under the preaching and exhortations of these itinerants and exhorters (the manner of which is frequently very boisterous and shocking, and adapted to the best of their skill to alarm and surprise the imagination and passions), 'tis no unusual thing for persons to be plunged into the utmost anxiety and distress, which is often attended with a trembling of the body, fainting, falling down, etc. The preacher now frequently grows more tempestuous, and dreadful in his manner of address, and seems to endeavor all he can to increase, and spread the rising consternation, and terror of their souls; which, by this means, is sometimes spread over a great part of an assembly, in a few minutes from its first appearance. I have seen the 'struck' (as they are called) and distressed brought together, from the several parts of the assembly, into the square body by themselves, and two or three persons at work upon them at once, smiting, stamping, and crying out to them with a mighty voice, in the most terrible manner and language; the poor creatures fainting, screeching and bitterly crying out under them. You may easily think what terrors of imagination, distraction of passions, and perplexity of thoughts, they endured. I was last summer at an evening lecture, at a neighboring parish, at which one of the most famous preachers in the new method carried on. He had entered but a little way in his sermon (which was delivered in a manner sufficiently terrible) when there began to be some commotion among the young women. This inspired him with new life. He lifted up his voice like a trumpet, plentifully poured down terrors upon them. About half a score of young women were presently thrown into violent hysteric fits. I carefully observed them. When he grew calm and moderate in his manner, though the things delivered were equally awakening, they by degrees grew calm and still; when he again assumed the terrible, and spake like thunder, the like violent strugglings immediately returned upon them, from time to time. Sometimes he put a mighty emphasis upon little unmeaning words, and delivered a sentence of no importance with a mighty energy, yet the sensible effect was as great as when the most awful truth was brought to view." This account may be relied on. For it is given by one capable of making observation, and who bears as unblemished a character as most ministers in the country.

Agreeable whereto is the account we have printed in the *Boston Post-Boy;* in which the writer, speaking of the itinerant preachers, among other things, observes, "Their main design in preaching, seems not so much to inform men's judgments, as to terrify and affright their imagination; by awful words and frightful representations, to set the congregation into hideous shrieks and out-cries. And to this end, in every place where they come, they represent that God is doing extraordinary things in other places, and that they are some of the last hardened wretches that stand out; that this is the last call that ever they are likely to have; that they are now hanging over the pit of destruction, and just ready, this moment, to fall into it; that hell-fire now flashes in their faces; and that the Devil now stands ready to seize upon them, and carry them to hell: and they will oftentimes repeat the awful words, 'damned!' 'damned!' 'damned!' three or four times over."

'Tis well known, no preacher, in the new way has been more noted for his instrumentality in producing these shriekings and faintings and tremblings, than the Rev. Mr. James Davenport of Southhold; and yet, one of the ministers of this town (who has always been a great friend to that which he esteemed, the good work of God going on in the land) having been, one night, a witness to his inexpressible management among the people, and the terrible effects consequent thereupon in their screaming and crying out, and the like, thought himself obliged in conscience to go to him the next day, and declare against such a method of acting. And accordingly went, and told him to his face (as he himself informed me) that in the appearance of the last night, he was persuaded, there was no hand of the Spirit of God; and that it was no other than might have been expected, if a man raving mad from Bedlam, had gone among the people, and behaved as he had done. And one of the charges exhibited and proved against this Mr. Davenport, when brought before the General Assembly of Connecticut, was, "That he endeavored by unwarrantable means to terrify, and affect his hearers. And that,

"(1.) By pretending some extraordinary discovery and assurance of the very near approach of the end of the world; and that though he did not assign the very day, yet that he then lately had it clearly opened to him and strongly inprest upon his mind, that in a very short time all these things would be involved in devouring flames."

N. B. This same impression, he told the people at Boston, he had lately had upon his mind, and was as sure the day of judgment was at the door, as of the things he then saw with his eyes; and made use of this accordingly, as an argument to work upon their passions.

"(2.) By an indecent and affected imitation of the agony and passion of our blessed Saviour; and also by voice and gesture, of the surprise, horror, and amazement, of persons supposed to be sentenced to eternal misery, and,

"(3.) By a too peremptory and unconditioned denouncing damnation against such of his auditory, as he looked upon as opposers; vehemently crying out, that he saw hell-flames flashing in their faces, and they were now! now! dropping down to hell! And also added, Lord thou knowest, that there are many in that gallery, and in these seats, that are now dropping down to hell!"

An account of Mr. Davenport's preaching, not altogether unlike this, a gentleman in Connecticut wrote to one of the ministers in this town, upon his own knowledge, in these words: "At length, he turned his discourse to others, and with the utmost strength of his lungs addrest himself to the congregation, under these and such like expressions, viz.: 'You poor unconverted creatures, in the seats, in the pews, in the galleries, I wonder you don't drop into hell! It would not surprise me, I should not wonder at it, if I should see you drop down now, this minute into hell. You Pharisees, hypocrites, *now, now, now,* you are going right into the bottom of hell. I wonder you don't drop into hell by scores, and hundreds,' etc. And in this terrible manner, he ended the sermon." 'Tis then added, "After a short prayer, he called for all the distrest persons (which were near twenty) into the foremost seats. Then he came out of the pulpit, and stripped off his upper garments, and got up into the seats, and leapt up and down some time, and clapt his hands, and cried out in those words: 'The war goes on, the fight goes on, the Devil goes down, the Devil goes down!' and then betook himself to stamping and screaming most dreadfully."

And what is it more than might be expected, to see people so affrightned as to fall into shrieks and fits, under such methods as these? Especially, when they have first been possest of the notion, that the persons who make use of them, are men of God in an extraordinary sense; as being sent immediately, as it were, to deliver his messages to them. The mind is now prepared to receive almost any impression from this kind of persons; and 'tis no wonder, if, by their terrifying voice and action, people are thrown into agitations and convulsions.

I doubt not, but the divine Spirit often accompanies the preached Word, so as that, by His influence, sinners are awakened to a sense of sin, and filled with deep distress of soul. But the blessed Spirit must not, at random, be made the author of all those surprises, operating in strange effects upon the body, which may be seen among people. They may be produced other ways; yea, I trust, that has been already said, which makes it evident, they have actually been produced, even by the wild and extravagant conduct of some overheated preachers.

The Religious Enthusiast

[From *Enthusiasm Described and Cautioned Against,* 1742]

. . . The enthusiast is one who has a conceit of himself as a person favored with the extraordinary presence of the Deity. He mistakes the workings of his own passions for divine communications, and fancies himself immediately inspired by the Spirit of God, when all the while, he is under no other influence than that of an over-heated imagination.

The cause of this enthusiasm is a bad temperament of the blood and spirits; 'tis properly a disease, a sort of madness; and there are few, perhaps none at all, but are subject to it; though none are so much in danger of it as those in whom melancholy is the prevailing ingredient in their constitution. In these it often reigns; and sometimes to so great a degree, that they are really beside themselves, acting as truly by the blind impetus of a wild fancy, as though they had neither reason nor understanding.

And various are the ways in which their enthusiasm discovers itself.

Sometimes, it may be seen in their countenance. A certain wildness is discernible in their general look and air, especially when their imaginations are moved and fired.

Sometimes, it strangely loosens their tongues, and gives them such an energy, as well as fluency and volubility in speaking, as they themselves, by their utmost efforts, can't so much as imitate, when they are not under the enthusiastic influence.

Sometimes, it affects their bodies, throws them into convulsions and distortions, into quakings and tremblings. This was formerly common among the people called Quakers. I was myself, when a lad, an eyewitness to such violent agitations and foamings, in a boisterous female speaker, as I could not behold but with surprise and wonder.

Sometimes, it will unaccountably mix itself with their conduct, and give it such a tincture of that which is freakish or furious as none can have an idea of, but those who have seen the behavior of a person in a frenzy.

Sometimes, it appears in their imaginary peculiar intimacy with heaven. They are, in their own opinion, the special favorites of God, have more familiar converse with Him than other good men, and receive immediate, extraordinary communications from Him. The thoughts which suddenly rise up in their minds, they take for suggestions of the Spirit; their very fancies are divine illuminations; nor are they strongly inclined to anything, but 'tis an impulse from God, a plain revelation of His will.

And what extravagances, in this temper of mind, are they not capable of, and under the specious pretext, too, of paying obedience to the authority of God? Many have fancied themselves acting by immediate warrant from heaven, while they have been committing the most undoubted wickedness. There is indeed scarce anything so wild, either in speculation or practice, but they have given in to it. They have, in many instances, been blasphemers of God, and open disturbers of the peace of the world.

But in nothing does the enthusiasm of these persons discover itself more, than in the disregard they express to the dictates of reason. They are above the force of argument, beyond conviction from a calm and sober address to their understandings. As for them, they are distinguished persons; God Himself speaks inwardly and immediately to their souls. "They see the light infused into their understandings, and cannot be mistaken; 'tis clear and visible there, like the light of bright sunshine; shews itself and needs no other proof but its own evidence. They feel the hand of God moving them within, and the impulses of His Spirit, and cannot be mistaken in what they feel. Thus they support themselves, and are sure reason hath nothing to do with what they see and feel. What they have a sensible experience of, admits no doubt, needs no probation." And in vain will you endeavor to convince such persons of any mistakes they are fallen into. They are certainly in the right; and know themselves to be so. They have the Spirit opening their understandings and revealing the truth to them. They believe only as He has taught them: and to suspect they are in the wrong is to do dishonor to the Spirit; 'tis to oppose His dictates, to set up their own wisdom in opposition to His, and shut their eyes against that light with which He has shined into their souls. They are not, therefore, capable of being argued with; you had as good reason with the wind.

And as the natural consequence of their being thus sure of everything, they are not only infinitely stiff and tenacious, but impatient of contradiction, censorious, and uncharitable; they encourage a good opinion of none but such as are in their way of thinking and speaking. Those, to be sure, who venture to debate with them about their errors and mistakes, their weaknesses and indiscretions, run the hazard of being stigmatized by them as poor unconverted wretches, without the Spirit, under the government of carnal reason, enemies to God and religion, and in the broad way to hell.

They are likewise positive and dogmatical, vainly fond of their own imaginations, and invincibly set upon propagating them; and in the doing of this, their powers being awakened, and put as it were, upon the stretch, from the strong impressions they are under, that they are authorized by the immediate command of God Himself, they sometimes exert themselves with a sort of ecstatic violence; and 'tis this that gives them the advantage, among the less knowing and judicious, of those who are modest, suspicious of themselves, and not too assuming in matters of conscience and salvation. The extraordinary fervor of their minds, accompanied with uncommon bodily motions, and an excessive confidence and assurance, gains them great reputation among the populace; who speak of them as men of God in distinction from all others, and too commonly hearken to, and revere their dictates, as though they really were, as they pretend, immediately communicated to them from the divine Spirit.

This is the nature of enthusiasm, and this its operation, in a less or greater degree, in all who are under the influence of it. 'Tis a kind of religious frenzy, and evidently discovers itself to be so whenever it rises to any great height.

And much to be pitied are the persons who are seized with it. Our compassion commonly works towards those who, while under distraction, fondly imagine themselves to be kings and emperors; and the like pity is really due to those who, under the power of enthusiasm, fancy themselves to be prophets, inspired of God, and immediately called and commissioned by Him to deliver His messages to the world. And though they should run into disorders, and act in a manner that cannot but be condemned, they should notwithstanding be treated with tenderness and lenity; and the rather, because they don't commonly act so much under the influence of a bad mind, as a deluded imagination. And who more worthy of Christian pity than those who, under the notion of serving God and the interest of religion, are filled with zeal, and exert themselves to the utmost, while all the time they are hurting and wounding the very cause they take so much pains to advance. 'Tis really a pitiable case; and though the honesty of their intentions won't legitimate their bad actions, yet it very much alleviates their guilt. We should think as favorably of them as may be, and be dispos'd to judge with mercy, as we would hope to obtain mercy.

Eliza Lucas Pinckney (1722–1793)

AT THE AGE of eighteen, Eliza Lucas, daughter of the Governor of Antigua, found herself mistress of her father's extensive plantation near Charleston, South Carolina. An amateur lawyer, physician, observer of unusual natural phenomena, and an eminently practical woman, she governed her estate admirably, furthering the southern cultivation of indigo, and filling her letters with charming insights into eighteenth-century life, its occupations, interests, and diversions. Second wife of the prominent Charles Pinckney, she raised two distinguished sons — Charles Cotesworth Pinckney, minister to France (1796) and Federalist presidential candidate in 1804 and 1808; and Thomas, Governor of South Carolina (1787–89), and sometime minister to England and Spain. A sturdy Anglican, she called attention in the following memorandum and letter to the social unrest aroused by the enthusiasms of the Great Awakening.

TEXT: *Journal and Letters of Eliza Lucas* (Wormsloe, Georgia, 1850).

The Deluded Prophet

[From *Letters* (1742)]

Memorandum, March 11th, 1741/2. Wrote a long letter to my father about the indigo and all the plantation affairs and that Mr. H. B. [Hugh Bryan] had been very much deluded by his own fancies and imagined he was assisted by the divine Spirit to prophesy Charles Town and the country as far as Ponpon bridge should be destroyed by fire and sword to be executed by the Negroes before the first day of next month. He came to town 60 mile twice besides sending twice to acquaint the Governor with it. People in general were very uneasy tho' convinced he was no prophet, but they dreaded the consequence of such a thing being put into the head of the slaves and the advantage they might take of us. From thence he went on (as it was natural to expect when he gave himself up entirely to his own whims) from one step to another till he came to working miracles and lived for several days in the woods barefooted and alone and with his pen and ink to write down his prophecies, till at length he went with a wand to divide the waters, and predicted he should die that night. But upon finding both fail, the water continue as it was, and himself a living instance of the fallacy of his own predictions, was convinced that he was not guided by the infallible Spirit, but that of delusion, and sent a letter to the speaker upon it. . . .

Dear Miss Bartlett

I am willing you should participate of the pleasure we enjoyed yesterday by hearing that Mr. B[ryan] is come to his senses and acknowledges with extreme concern he was guided by a spirit of delusion which carried him the lengths he has lately gone under a notion of inspiration. Poor man! with what anguish must he reflect on making the Spirit of God the author of his weaknesses, and of disturbing the whole community, who though they knew him to be no prophet dreaded the consequence of his prophecies coming to the ears of the African Hosts, as he calls them. I hope he will be a warning to all pious minds not to reject reason and revelation and set up in their stead their own wild notions; he fancied indeed he was supported in his opinions by the sacred oracles, and (as a father of our church observes) so did all the broachers of heresy in the primitive church. But why should we not expect to be deluded when we reject that assistance which the bountiful Author of our being has naturally revealed to us, and set up in every man's mind, without which 'tis impossible to understand [what He (?)] supernaturally reveals; for though there may be things in the Christian system above reason, such as the intervention of our Saviour, etc., yet surely they highly dishonor our religion who affirm there is anything in it contrary to reason.

Jonathan Edwards (1703–1758)

BORN in Windsor, Connecticut, in 1703, Jonathan Edwards was educated by his minister father. By 1715, with rare ability to observe minutely and reason tightly, he was revealing his exceptional precocity in essays on natural and supernatural topics. The following year he entered Yale at the age of thirteen, beginning the careful studies that resulted in his "Notes" on the mind and on natural science. He graduated in 1720, but remained at Yale until 1722, when he moved to a New York Scotch Presbyterian church. In 1723 he returned to Yale, took his M.A., and became a tutor. This intellectual experience as an instructor permitted him to form the basic philosophic positions which underlie his later writings before he became his grandfather's assistant in the Northampton church (1726).

At Northampton, Edwards continued his grandfather Stoddard's "harvests" or revivals, preaching with a horrific vividness designed to make religious ideas felt along the senses — so felt, indeed, that in 1735 his uncle, overwhelmed by the preaching, committed suicide. Edwards reported the effects of such revivals, analyzing the psychology at work in them, in *A Faithful Narrative of the Surprising Work of God in . . . Conversion* (1736) and citing romantic case studies like Phebe Bartlet's. He similarly examined his own mystical experiences a few years later in his *Personal Narrative*. From 1740 a wave of revivals known as the Great Awakening swept the Atlantic seaboard and penetrated the New England backcountry. George Whitefield, a fabulous English evangelist, stormed the country, even joining Edwards for a preaching tour, and Edwards' preaching took on new vigor, as his famous Enfield sermon *Sinners in the Hands of an Angry God* (1741) illustrates. By 1745 the Great Awakening had ended, and to counter the writing of Charles Chauncy and others opposed to the excesses of the revival, Edwards published his *Treatise Concerning Religious Affections* (1746), distinguishing between true and false religious emotion and considering at length the function of beauty, imagination, and taste in religious experience.

In 1750, dismissed by his congregation for seeking to return to less relaxed requirements for church admission, Edwards accepted a call to the utopian Indian community at Stockbridge. The next eight years were his most productive, bringing forth his brilliant considerations of *The Freedom of the Will* (1754), *The Nature of True Virtue* (1755–58), and *The Great Doctrine of Original Sin Defended* (1757). In the face of increasing liberalism in American church life, Edwards' defense of stringent Calvinism in both theology and church discipline netted him only a small group of ardent disciples, called "New Light" divines, at Yale. But his use of the most current speculations in science, psychology, and philosophy — the ideas of Locke and Newton and an independently achieved idealism much like Bishop Berkeley's — to support his Calvinism, earned him a respect among Scottish and English theologians and philosophers that has never waned. In 1757 Edwards' son-in-law — then president of the College of New Jersey (Princeton) — died, and Edwards was invited to succeed him. He went to Princeton, but before he could assume his office, died of a smallpox inoculation.

TEXTS: "Notes on the Mind," in Sereno E. Dwight, *The Life of President Edwards* (New York, 1830); "A Faithful Narrative," "Personal Narrative," and "Sinners in the Hands of an Angry God," in *Works*, ed. Samuel Austin (Worcester, 1808–09), Vols. III, I, and II; *A Treatise Concerning Religious Affections*, ed. John E. Smith (New Haven, 1959); and *Freedom of the Will*, ed. Paul Ramsey (New Haven, 1957).

A Note on Reality

[From "Notes on the Mind" (*c.* 1719)]

The whole of what we any way observe, whereby we get the idea of solidity, or solid body, are certain parts of space, from whence we receive the ideas of light and colors; and certain sensations by the sense of feeling; and we observe that the places, whence we receive these sensations, are not constantly the same, but are successively different, and this light and colors are communicated from one part of space to another. And we observe that these parts of space, from whence we receive these sensations, resist and stop other bodies, which we observe communicated successively through the parts of space adjacent; and that those that there were before at rest, or existing constantly in one and the same part of space, after this exist successively in different parts of space, and these observations are according to certain stated rules. I appeal to anyone that takes notice and asks himself; whether this be not all, that ever he experienced in the world, whereby he got these ideas; and that this is all that we have or can have any idea of, in relation to bodies. All that we observe of solidity is, that certain parts of space, from whence we receive the ideas of light and colors, and a few other sensations, do likewise resist anything coming with them. It therefore follows, that if we suppose there be anything else, than what we thus observe, it is but only by way of inference.

I know that it is nothing but the imagination will oppose me in this: I will therefore endeavor to help the imagination thus. Suppose that we received none of the sensible qualities of light, colors, etc., from the resisting parts of space (we will suppose it possible for resistance to be without them), and they were, to appearance, clear and pure; and all that we could possibly observe, was only and merely resistance; we simply observed that motion was resisted and stopped, here and there, in particular parts of infinite space. Should we not then think it less unreasonable to suppose, that such effects should be produced by some agent, present in those parts of space, though invisible? If we, when walking upon the face of the earth, were stopped at certain limits, and could not possibly enter into such a part of space, nor make anybody enter into it; and we could observe no other difference, no way, nor at any time, between that and other parts of clear space; should we not be ready to say, What is it stops us? what is it hinders all entrance into that place?

The reason, why it is so exceedingly natural to men, to suppose that there is some latent substance, or something that is altogether hid, that upholds the properties of bodies, is, because all see at first sight, that the properties of bodies are such as need some cause, that shall every moment have influence to their continuance, as well as a cause of their first existence. All therefore agree, that there is something that is there, and upholds these properties. And it is most true, there undoubtedly is; but men are wont to content themselves in saying merely, that it is something; but that something is He, "by whom all things consist."

The Case of Phebe Bartlet

[From *A Faithful Narrative*, 1736]

But I now proceed to the other instance that I would give an account of, which is of the little child forementioned. Her name is Phebe Bartlet, daughter of William Bartlet. I shall give the account as I took it from the mouths of her parents, whose veracity, none that know them doubt of.

She was born in March, in the year 1731. About the latter end of April, or beginning of May, 1735, she was greatly affected by the talk of her brother, who had been hopefully converted a little before, at about eleven years of age, and then seriously talked to her about the great things of religion. Her parents did not know of it at that time, and were not wont, in the counsels they gave to their children, particularly to direct themselves to her, by reason of her being so young, and, as they supposed not capable of understanding; but after her brother had talked to her, they observed her very earnestly to listen to the advice they gave to the other children, and she was observed, very constantly to retire, several times in a day, as was concluded, for secret prayer, and grew more and more engaged in religion, and was more frequent in her closet, till at last she was wont to visit it five or six times in a day, and was so engaged in it, that nothing would, at any time divert her from her stated closet exercises. Her mother often observed and watched her, when such things occurred, as she thought most likely to divert her, either by putting it out of her thoughts, or otherwise engaging her inclinations, but never could observe her to fail. She mentioned some very remarkable instances.

She once, of her own accord, spake of her unsuccessfulness, in that she could not find God, or to that purpose. But on Thursday, the last day of July, about the middle of the day, the child being in the closet, where it used to retire, its mother heard it speaking aloud, which was unusual, and never had been observed before; and her voice seemed to be as of one exceeding importunate and engaged, but her mother could distinctly hear only these words (spoken in her childish manner, but seemed to be spoken with extraordinary earnestness, and out of distress of soul!), "Pray Blessed Lord give me salvation! I pray, beg pardon all my sins!" When the child had done prayer, she came out of the closet, and came and sat down by her mother, and cried out aloud. Her mother very earnestly asked her several times, what the matter was, before she would make any answer, but she continued exceedingly crying, and wreathing her body to and fro, like one in anguish of spirit. Her mother then asked her whether she was afraid that God would not give her salvation. She then answered, "Yes, I am afraid I shall go to hell!" Her mother then endeavored to quiet her, and told her she would not have her cry . . . she must be a good girl, and pray every day, and she hoped God would give her salvation. But this did not quiet her at all . . . but she continued thus earnestly crying and taking on for some time, till at length she suddenly ceased crying and began to smile, and presently said with a smiling countenance. . . . "Mother, the kingdom of heaven is come to me!" Her mother was surprised at the sudden alteration, and at the speech, and knew not what to make of it, but at first said nothing to her. The child presently spake again, and said, "There is another come to me, and there is another . . . there is three"; and being asked what she meant, she answered . . . "One is, thy will be done, and there is another . . . enjoy Him forever"; by which it seems that when the child said, "There is three come to me," she meant three passages of its catechism that came to her mind.

After the child had said this, she retired again into her closet; and her mother went over to her brother's, who was next neighbor; and when she came back, the child being come out of the closet, meets her mother with this cheerful speech . . . "I can find God now!" Referring to what she had before complained of, that she could not find God. Then the child spoke again, and said . . . "I love God!" Her mother asked her how well she loved God, whether she loved God better than her father and mother, she said, "Yes." Then she asked her whether she loved God better than her little sister Rachel, she answered "Yes, better than anything!" Then her eldest sister, referring to her saying she could find God now, asked her where she could find God; she answered, "In heaven." "Why," said she, "have you been in heaven?" "No," said the child. By this it seems not to have been any imagination of anything seen with bodily eyes that she called God, when she said, "I can find God now." Her mother asked her whether she was afraid of going to hell, and that had made her cry. She answered, "Yes, I was; but now I shall not." Her mother asked her whether she thought that God had given her salvation; she answered "Yes." Her mother asked her, "When?" She answered, "Today." She appeared all that afternoon exceedingly cheerful and joyful. One of the neighbors asked her how she felt herself. She answered, "I feel better than I did." The neighbor asked her what made her feel better; she answered, "God makes me." That evening as she lay abed, she called one of her little cousins to her, that was present in the room, as having something to say to him; and when he came, she told him that heaven was better than earth. The next day being Friday, her mother asking her her catechism, asked her what God made her for; she answered, "To serve Him"; and added, "everybody should serve God, and get an interest in Christ."

The same day the elder children, when they came home from school, seemed much affected with the extraordinary change that seemed to be made in Phebe; and her sister Abigail standing by, her mother took occasion to counsel her, now to improve her time, to prepare for another world; on which Phebe burst out in tears, and cried out, "Poor Nabby!" Her mother told her, she would not have her cry, she hoped that God would give Nabby salvation; but that did not quiet her, but she continued earnestly crying for some time; and when she had in a measure ceased, her sister Eunice being by her, she burst out again, and cried, "Poor Eunice!" and cried exceedingly; and when she had almost done, she went into another room, and there looked upon her sister Naomi, and burst out again, crying, "Poor Amy!" Her mother was greatly affected at such a behavior in the child, and knew not what to say to her. One of the neighbors coming in a little after, asked her what she had cried for. She seemed, at first backward to tell the reason. Her mother told her she might tell that person, for he had given her an apple; upon which she said, she cried because she was afraid they would go to hell.

At night a certain minister, that was occasionally in the town, was at the house, and talked considerably with her of the things of religion; and after he was gone, she sat leaning on the table, with tears running out of her eyes; and being asked what made her cry, she said it was thinking about God. The next day being Saturday, she seemed great part of the day to be in a very affectionate frame, had four turns of crying, and seemed to endeavor to curb herself, and hide her tears, and was very backward to talk of the occasion of it. On the sabbath day she was asked whether she believed in God; she answered, "Yes." And being told that Christ was the Son of God, she made ready answer, and said, "I know it."

From this time there has appeared a very remarkable abiding change in the child. She has been very strict on the sabbath, and seems to long for the sabbath day before it comes, and will often in the week time be inquiring how long it is to the sabbath day, and must have the days particularly counted over that are between, before she will be contented. And she seems to love God's house . . . is very eager to go thither. Her mother once asked her why she had such a mind to go? Whether it was not to see the fine folks? She said no, it was to hear Mr. Edwards preach. When she is in the place of worship, she is far from spending her time there as children at her age usually do, but appears with an attention that is very extraordinary for such a child. She also appears, very desirous at all opportunities, to go to private religious meetings, and is very still and attentive at home, in prayer time, and has appeared affected in time of family prayer. She seems to delight much in hearing religious conversation. When I once was there with some others that were strangers, and talked to her something of religion, she seemed more than ordinarily attentive; and when we were gone, she looked out very wistly after us, and said . . . "I wish they would come again!" Her mother asked her why: said she, "I love to hear them talk!"

She seems to have very much of the fear of God before her eyes, and an extraordinary dread of sin against Him; of which her mother mentioned the following remarkable instance. Some time in August, the last year, she went with some bigger children, to get some plums, in a neighbor's lot, knowing nothing of any harm in what she did; but when she brought some of the plums into the house, her mother mildly reproved her, and told her, that she must not get plums without leave, because it was sin: God had commanded her not to steal. The child seemed greatly surprised, and burst out into tears, and cried out . . . "I will not have these plums!" And turning to her sister Eunice, very earnestly said to her . . . "Why did you ask me to go to that plum tree? I should not have gone if you had not asked me." The other children did not seem to be much affected or concerned; but there was no pacifying Phebe. Her mother told her she might go and ask leave, and then it would not be sin for her to eat them, and sent one of the children to that end; and when she returned, her mother told her that the owner had given leave, now she might eat them, and it would not be stealing. This stilled her a little while, but presently she broke out again into an exceeding fit of crying. Her mother asked her what made her cry again? Why she cried now, since they had asked leave? What was it that troubled her now? And asked her several times very earnestly, before she made any answer; but at last, said it was because . . . because it was sin. She continued a considerable time crying; and said she would not go again if Eunice asked her an hundred times; and she retained her aversion to that fruit for a considerable time, under the remembrance of her former sin.

She, at some times, appears greatly affected and delighted with texts of scripture that come to her mind. Particularly, about the beginning of November, the last year, that text came to her mind, Rev. 3:20, "Behold I stand at the door and knock: If any man hear my voice, and open the door, I will come in, and sup with him and he with me." She spoke of it to those of the family, with a great appearance of joy, a smiling countenance, and elevation of voice, and afterwards she went into another room, where her mother overheard her talking very earnestly to the children about it, and particularly heard her say to them, three or four times over, with an air of exceeding joy and admiration . . . "Why, it is to sup with God." At some time about the middle of winter, very late in the night, when all were in bed, her mother perceived that she was awake, and heard her as though she was weeping. She called to her, and asked her what was the matter. She answered with a low voice, so that her mother could not hear what she said; but thinking it might be occasioned by some spiritual affection, said no more to her; but perceived her to lie awake, and to continue in the same frame for a considerable time. The next morning she asked her whether she did not cry the last night. The child answered, "Yes, I did cry a little, for I was thinking about God and Christ, and they loved me." Her mother asked her, whether to think of God and Christ's loving her made her cry. She answered "Yes, it does sometimes."

She has often manifested a great concern for the good of other souls; and has been wont, many times, affectionately to counsel the other children. Once about the latter end of September, the last year, when she and some others of the children were in a room by themselves ahusking Indian corn, the child, after a while, came out and sat by the fire. Her mother took notice that she appeared with a more than ordinary serious and pensive countenance, but at last she broke silence, and said, "I have been talking to Nabby and Eunice." Her mother asked her what she had said to them. "Why," said she, "I told them they must pray, and prepare to die, that they had but a little while to live in this world, and they must be always ready." When Nabby came out, her mother asked her whether she had said that to them. "Yes," said she, "she said that and a great deal more." At other times the child took her opportunities to talk to the other children about the great concern of their souls; sometimes so much as to affect them, and set them into tears. She was once exceeding importunate with her mother to go with her sister Naomi to pray. Her mother endeavored to put her off, but she pulled her by the sleeve, and seemed as if she would by no means be denied. At last her mother told her, that Amy must go and pray herself; "But," says the child, "she will not go," and persisted earnestly to beg of her mother to go with her.

She has discovered an uncommon degree of a spirit of charity, particularly on the following occasion: a poor man that lives in the woods, had lately lost a cow that the family much depended on, and being at the house, he was relating his misfortune, and telling of the straits and difficulties they were reduced to by it. She took much notice of it, and it wrought exceedingly on her compassions; and after she had attentively heard him a while, she went away to her father, who was in the shop, and entreated him to give that man a cow; and told him that the poor man had no cow! That the hunters or something else had killed his cow! And entreated him to give him one of theirs. Her father told her that they could not spare one. Then she entreated him to let him and his family come and live at his house; and had much talk of the same nature, whereby she manifested bowels of compassion to the poor.

She has manifested great love to her minister; particularly when I returned from my long journey for my health, the last fall, when she heard of it, she appeared very joyful at the news, and told the children of it with an elevated voice, as the most joyful tidings, repeating it over and over, "Mr. Edwards is come home! Mr. Edwards is come home!" She still continues very constant in secret prayer, so far as can be observed (for she seems to have no desire that others should observe her when she retires, but seems to be a child of a reserved temper), and every night before she goes to bed will say her catechism, and will by no means miss of it. She never forgot it but once, and then after she was abed, thought of it and cried out in tears . . . "I have not said my catechism!" And would not be quieted until her mother asked her the catechism as she lay in bed. She sometimes appears to be in doubt about the condition of her soul, and when asked whether she thinks that she is prepared for death, speaks something doubtfully about it. At other times seems to have no doubt, but when asked, replies "Yes," without hesitation.

The Growth of Inward Faith

[From *Personal Narrative* (*c.* 1740)]

I had a variety of concerns and exercises about my soul from my childhood; but had two more remarkable seasons of awakening, before I met with that change, by which I was brought to those new dispositions, and that new sense of things, that I have since had. The first time was when I was a boy, some years before I went to college, at a time of remarkable awakening in my father's congregation. I was then very much affected for many months, and concerned about the things of religion, and my soul's salvation; and was abundant in duties. I used to pray five times a day in secret, and to spend much time in religious talk with other boys; and used to meet with them to pray together. I experienced I know not what kind of delight in religion. My mind was much engaged in it, and had much self-righteous pleasure; and it was my delight to abound in religious duties. I with some of my school-mates joined together, and built a booth in a swamp, in a very retired spot, for a place of prayer. And besides, I had particular secret places of my own in the woods, where I used to retire by myself; and was from time to time much affected. My affections seemed to be lively and easily moved, and I seemed to be in my element when engaged in religious duties. And I am ready to think, many are deceived with such affections, and such a kind of delight as I then had in religion, and mistake it for grace.

But in process of time, my convictions and affections wore off; and I entirely lost all those affections and delights, and left off secret prayer, at least as to any constant performance of it; and returned like a dog to his vomit, and went on in the ways of sin. Indeed I was at times very uneasy, especially towards the latter part of my time at college; when it pleased God, to seize me with a pleurisy; in which he brought me nigh to the grave, and shook me over the pit of hell. And yet, it was not long after my recovery, before I fell again into my old ways of sin. But God would not suffer me to go on with any quietness; I had great and violent inward struggles, till, after many conflicts with wicked inclinations, repeated resolutions, and bonds that I laid myself under by a kind of vows to God, I was brought wholly to break off all former wicked ways and all ways of known outward sin; and to apply myself to seek salvation, and practice many religious duties; but without that kind of affection and delight which I had formerly experienced. My concern now wrought more by inward struggles, and conflicts, and self-reflections. I made seeking my salvation the main business of my life. But yet, it seems to me, I sought after a miserable manner; which has made me sometimes since to question, whether ever it issued in that which was saving; being ready to doubt, whether such miserable seeking ever succeeded. I was indeed brought to seek salvation in a manner that I never was before; I felt a spirit to part with all things in the world, for an interest in Christ. My concern continued and prevailed, with many exercising thoughts and inward struggles; but yet it never seemed to be proper, to express that concern by the name of terror.

From my childhood up, my mind had been full of objections against the doctrine of God's sovereignty, in choosing whom He would to eternal life, and rejecting whom He pleased; leaving them eternally to perish, and be everlastingly tormented in hell. It used to appear like a horrible doctrine to me. But I remember the time very well, when I seemed to be convinced, and fully satisfied, as to this sovereignty of God, and His justice in thus eternally disposing of men, according to His sovereign pleasure. But never could give an account, how, or by what means, I was thus convinced, not in the least imagining at the time, nor a long time after, that there was any extraordinary influence of God's Spirit in it; but only that now I saw further, and my reason apprehended the justice and reasonableness of it. However, my mind rested in it; and it put an end to all those cavils and objections. And there has been a wonderful alteration in my mind, with respect to the doctrine of God's sovereignty, from that day to this; so that I scarce ever have found so much as the rising of an objection against it, in the most absolute sense, in God's shewing mercy to whom He will shew mercy, and hardening whom he will. God's absolute sovereignty and justice, with respect to salvation and damnation, is what my mind seems to rest assured of, as much as of any thing that I see with my eyes; at least it is so at times. But I have often, since that first conviction, had quite another kind of sense of God's sovereignty than I had then. I have often since had not only a conviction, but a delightful conviction. The doctrine has very often appeared exceeding pleasant, bright and sweet. Absolute sovereignty is what I love to ascribe to God. But my first conviction was not so.

The first instance that I remember of that sort of inward, sweet delight in God and divine things that I have lived much in since, was on reading those words, 1 Tim. 1:17; "Now unto the King eternal, immortal, invisible, the only wise God, be honor and glory for ever and ever, Amen." As I read the words, there came into my soul, and was as it were diffused through it, a sense of the glory of the Divine Being; a new sense, quite different from anything I ever experienced before. Never any words of scripture seemed to me as these words did. I thought with myself, how excellent a Being that was, and how happy I should be, if I might enjoy that God, and be rapt up to Him in heaven, and be as it were swallowed up in Him for ever! I kept saying, and as it were singing, over these words of scripture to myself; and went to pray to God that I might enjoy Him, and prayed in a manner quite different from what I used to do; with a new sort of affection. But it never came into my thought, that there was anything spiritual, or of a saving nature in this.

From about that time, I began to have a new kind of apprehensions and ideas of Christ, and the work of redemption and the glorious way of salvation by Him. An inward, sweet sense of these things, at times, came into my heart; and my soul was led away in pleasant views and contemplations of them. And my mind was greatly engaged to spend my time in reading and meditating on Christ, on the beauty and excellency of His person, and the lovely way of salvation by free grace in Him. I found no books so delightful to me, as those that treated of these subjects. Those words Cant. 2:1 used to be abundantly with me, "I am the rose of Sharon, and the lily of the valleys." The words seemed to me, sweetly to represent the loveliness and beauty of Jesus Christ. The whole book of Canticles used to be pleasant to me, and I used to be much in reading it, about that time; and found, from time to time, an inward sweetness, that would carry me away, in my contemplations. This I know not how to express otherwise, than by a calm, sweet abstraction of soul from all the concerns of this world; and sometimes a kind of vision, or fixed ideas and imaginations, of being alone in the mountains, or some solitary wilderness, far from all mankind, sweetly conversing with Christ, and wrapt and swallowed up in God. The sense I had of divine things, would often of a sudden kindle up, as it were, a sweet burning in my heart; an ardor of soul, that I know not how to express.

Not long after I first began to experience these things, I gave an account to my father of some things that had passed in my mind. I was pretty much affected by the discourse we had together; and when the discourse was ended, I walked abroad alone, in a solitary place in my father's pasture, for contemplation. And as I was walking there, and looking upon the sky and clouds, there came into my mind so sweet a sense of the glorious *majesty* and *grace* of God, as I know not how to express. I seemed to see them both in a sweet conjunction; majesty and meekness joined together; it was a sweet, and gentle, and holy majesty; and also a majestic meekness; an awful sweetness; a high, and great, and holy gentleness.

After this my sense of divine things gradually increased, and became more and more lively, and had more of that inward sweetness. The appearance of everything was altered; there seemed to be, as it were, a calm, sweet cast, or appearance of divine glory, in almost everything. God's excellency, His wisdom, His purity and love, seemed to appear in everything; in the sun, moon, and stars; in the clouds, and blue sky; in the grass, flowers, trees; in the water, and all nature; which used greatly to fix my mind. I often used to sit and view the moon for continuance; and in the day, spent much time in viewing the clouds and sky, to behold the sweet glory of God in these things; in the meantime, singing forth, with a low voice, my contemplations of the Creator and Redeemer. And scarce anything, among all the works of nature, was so sweet to me as thunder and lightning; formerly nothing had been so terrible to me. Before, I used to be uncommonly terrified with thunder, and to be struck with terror when I saw a thunder storm rising; but now, on the contrary, it rejoiced me. I felt God, so to speak, at the first appearance of a thunder storm; and used to take the opportunity, at such times, to fix myself in order to view the clouds, and see the lightnings play, and hear the majestic and awful voice of God's thunder, which oftentimes was exceedingly entertaining, leading me to sweet contemplations of my great and glorious God. While thus engaged, it always seemed natural for me to sing, or chant for my meditations; or, to speak my thoughts in soliloquies with a singing voice.

I felt then great satisfaction, as to my good state, but that did not content me. I had vehement longings of soul after God and Christ, and after more holiness, wherewith my heart seemed to be full, and ready to break; which often brought to my mind the words of the Psalmist, Psal. 119:28: "My soul breaketh for the longing it hath." I often felt a mourning and lamenting in my heart, that I had not turned to God sooner, that I might have had more time to grow in grace. My mind was greatly fixed on divine things; almost perpetually in the contemplation of them. I spent most of my time in thinking of divine things, year after year; often walking alone in the woods, and solitary places, for meditation, soliloquy, and prayer, and converse with God; and it was always my manner, at such times, to sing forth my contemplations.

I was almost constantly in ejaculatory prayer, wherever I was. Prayer seemed to be natural to me, as the breath by which the inward burnings of my heart had vent. The delights which I now felt in the things of religion, were of an exceeding different kind from those before mentioned, that I had when a boy; and what I then had no more notion of, than one born blind has of pleasant and beautiful colors. They were of a more inward, pure, soul-animating and refreshing nature. Those former delights never reached the heart; and did not arise from any sight of the divine excellency of the things of God; or any taste of the soul-satisfying and life-giving good there is in them.

My sense of divine things seemed gradually to increase, till I went to preach at New York, which was about a year and a half after they began; and while I was there, I felt them, very sensibly, in a much higher degree than I had done before. My longings after God, and holiness, were much increased. Pure and humble, holy and heavenly Christianity appeared exceeding amiable to me. I felt a burning desire to be, in everything, a complete Christian; and, conformed to the blessed image of Christ; and that I might live, in all things, according to the pure, sweet, and blessed rules of the gospel. I had an eager thirsting after progress in these things; which put me upon pursuing and pressing after them. It was my continual strife day and night, and constant inquiry, how I should *be* more holy and *live* more holily, and more becoming a child of God, and a disciple of Christ. I now sought an increase of grace and holiness, and a holy life, with much more earnestness, than ever I sought grace before I had it. I used to be continually examining myself, and studying and contriving for likely ways and means, how I should live holily, with far greater diligence and earnestness, than ever I pursued anything in my life; but yet with too great a dependence on my own strength; which afterwards proved a great damage to me. My experience had not then taught me, as it has done since, my extreme feebleness and impotence, every manner of way; and the bottomless depths of secret corruption and deceit there was in my heart. However, I went on with my eager pursuit after more holiness, and conformity to Christ.

The heaven I desired was a heaven of holiness; to be with God, and to spend my eternity in divine love and holy communion with Christ. My mind was very much taken up with contemplations on heaven, and the enjoyments there; and living there in perfect holiness, humility, and love: and it used at that time to appear a great part of the happiness of heaven, that there the saints could express their love to Christ. It appeared to me a great clog and burden, that what I felt within, I could not express as I desired. The inward ardor of my soul, seemed to be hindered and pent up, and could not freely flame out as it would. I used often to think, how in heaven this principle should freely and fully vent and express itself. Heaven appeared exceedingly delightful, as a world of love; and that all happiness consisted in living in pure, humble, heavenly, divine love.

I remember the thoughts I used then to have of holiness; and said sometimes to myself, "I do certainly know that I love holiness, such as the gospel prescribes." It appeared to me, that there was nothing in it but what was ravishingly lovely; the highest beauty and amiableness —a *divine* beauty; far purer than anything here upon earth; and that everything else was like mire and defilement, in comparison of it.

Holiness, as I then wrote down some of my contemplations on it, appeared to me to be of a sweet, pleasant, charming, serene, calm nature; which brought an inexpressible purity, brightness, peacefulness and ravishment to the soul. In other words, that it made the soul like a field or garden of God, with all manner of pleasant flowers; all pleasant, delightful, and undisturbed; enjoying a sweet calm, and the gently vivifying beams of the sun. The soul of a true Christian, as I then wrote my meditations, appeared like such a little white flower as we see in the spring of the year; low and humble on the ground, opening its bosom to receive the pleasant beams of the sun's glory; rejoicing as it were in a calm rapture; diffusing around a sweet fragrancy; standing peacefully and lovingly, in the midst of other flowers round about; all in like manner opening their bosoms, to drink in the light of the sun. There was no part of creature-holiness, that I had so great a sense of its loveliness, as humility, brokenness of heart, and poverty of spirit; and there was nothing that I so earnestly longed for. My heart panted after this — to lie low before God, as in the dust; that I might be nothing, and that God, might be ALL, that I might become as a little child.

While at New York, I was sometimes much affected with reflections on my past life, considering how late it was before I began to be truly religious; and how wickedly I had lived till then: and once so as to weep abundantly, and for a considerable time together.

On January 12, 1723, I made a solemn dedication of myself to God, and wrote it down; giving up myself, and all that I had to God; to be for the future in no respect my own; to act as one that had no right to himself, in any respect. And solemnly vowed, to take God for my whole portion and felicity; looking on nothing else as any part of my happiness, nor acting as if it were; and His law for the constant rule of my obedience; engaging to fight with all my might, against the world, the flesh, and the Devil, to the end of my life. But I have reason to be infinitely humbled, when I consider, how much I have failed, of answering my obligation. . . .

Once as I rode out into the woods for my health, in 1737, having alighted from my horse in a retired place, as my manner commonly has been, to walk for divine contemplation and prayer, I had a view that for me was extraordinary, of the glory of the Son of God, as Mediator between God and man, and His wonderful, great, full, pure, and sweet grace and love, and meek and gentle condescension. This grace that appeared so calm and sweet, appeared also great above the heavens. The person of Christ appeared ineffably excellent with an excellency great enough to swallow up all thought and conception — which continued, as near as I can judge, about an hour, which kept me the greater part of the time in a flood of tears, and weeping aloud. I felt an ardency of soul to be, what I know not otherwise how to express, emptied and annihilated; to lie in the dust, and to be full of Christ alone; to love Him with a holy and pure love; to trust in Him; to live upon Him; to serve and follow Him; and to be perfectly sanctified and made pure, with a divine and heavenly purity. I have, several other times, had views very much of the same nature, and which have had the same effects.

I have many times had a sense of the glory of the third person in the Trinity, in His office of Sanctifier, in His holy operations, communicating divine light and life to the soul. God, in the communications of His Holy Spirit, has appeared as an infinite fountain of divine glory and sweetness; being full, and sufficient to fill and satisfy the soul; pouring forth itself in sweet communications; like the sun in its glory, sweetly and pleasantly diffusing light and life. And I have sometimes had an affecting sense of the excellency of the Word of God as a Word of life; as the light of life; a sweet, excellent, life-giving Word; accompanied with a thirsting after that Word, that it might dwell richly in my heart.

Often, since I lived in this town, I have had very affecting views of my own sinfulness and vileness; very frequently to such a degree as to hold me in a kind of loud weeping, sometimes for a considerable time together; so that I have often been forced to shut myself up. I have had a vastly greater sense of my own wickedness, and the badness of my own heart, than ever I had before my conversion. It has often appeared to me, that if God should mark iniquity against me, I should appear the very worst of all mankind; of all that have been, since the beginning of the world to this time; and that I should have by far the lowest place in hell. When others, that have come to talk with me about their soul concerns, have expressed the sense they have had of their own wickedness, by saying that it seemed to them, that they were as bad as the Devil himself; I thought their expressions seemed exceeding faint and feeble, to represent my wickedness.

My wickedness, as I am in myself, has long appeared to me perfectly ineffable, and swallowing up all thought and imagination; like an infinite deluge, or mountains over my head. I know not how to express better what my sins appear to me to be, than by heaping infinite upon infinite, and multiplying infinite by infinite. Very often, for these many years, these expressions are in my mind, and in my mouth, "Infinite upon infinite — Infinite upon infinite!" When I look into my heart, and take a view of my wickedness, it looks like an abyss infinitely deeper than hell. And it appears to me, that were it not for free grace, exalted and raised up to the infinite height of all the fulness and glory of the great Jehovah, and the arm of His power and grace stretched forth in all the majesty of His power, and in all the glory of His sovereignty, I should appear sunk down in my sins below hell itself; far beyond the sight of everything but the eye of sovereign grace, that can pierce even down to such a depth. And yet it seems to me, that my conviction of sin is exceeding small, and faint; it is enough to amaze me, that I have no more sense of my sin. I know certainly, that I have very little sense of my sinfulness. When I have had turns of weeping and crying for my sins, I thought I knew at the time, that my repentance was nothing to my sin.

I have greatly longed of late, for a broken heart, and to lie low before God; and, when I ask for humility, I cannot bear the thoughts of being no more humble than other Christians. It seems to me, that though their degrees of humility may be suitable for them, yet it would be a vile self-exaltation in me, not to be the lowest in humility of all mankind. Others speak of their longing to be "humbled to the dust"; that may be a proper expression for them, but I always think of myself, that I ought, and it is an expression that has long been natural for me to use in prayer, "to lie infinitely low before God." And it is affecting to think, how ignorant I was, when a young Christian, of the bottomless, infinite depths of wickedness, pride, hypocrisy, and deceit, left in my heart.

I have a much greater sense of my universal, exceeding dependence on God's grace and strength, and mere good pleasure, of late, than I used formerly to have; and have experienced more of an abhorrence of my own righteousness. The very thought of any joy arising in me, on any consideration of my own amiableness, performances, or experiences, or any goodness of heart or life, is nauseous and detestable to me. And yet I am greatly afflicted with a proud and self-righteous spirit, much more sensibly than I used to be formerly. I see that serpent rising and putting forth its head continually, everywhere, all around me. Though it seems to me, that, in some respects, I was a far better Christian, for two or three years after my first conversion, than I am now; and lived in a more constant delight and pleasure; yet, of late years, I have had a more full and constant sense of the absolute sovereignty of God, and a delight in that sovereignty; and have had more of a sense of the glory of Christ, as a Mediator revealed in the gospel. On one Saturday night, in particular, I had such a discovery of the excellency of the gospel above all other doctrines, that I could not but say to myself, "This is my chosen light, my chosen doctrine"; and of Christ, "This is my chosen prophet." It appeared sweet, beyond all expression, to follow Christ, and to be taught, and enlightened, and instructed by Him; to learn of Him, and live to Him. Another Saturday night (January, 1739), I had such a sense, how sweet and blessed a thing it was to walk in the way of duty; to do that which was right and meet to be done, and agreeable to the holy mind of God; that it caused me to break forth into a kind of loud weeping, which held me some time, so that I was forced to shut myself up, and fasten the doors. I could not but, as it were, cry out, "How happy are they which do that which is right in the sight of God! They are blessed indeed; they are the happy ones!" I had, at the same time, a very affecting sense, how meet and suitable it was that God should govern the world, and order all things according to His own pleasure; and I rejoiced in it, that God reigned and that His will was done.

Sinners in the Hands of an Angry God

[From a sermon preached at Enfield, Conn., 1741]

Deuteronomy 32:35 — "Their foot shall slide in due time."

In this verse is threatened the vengeance of God on the wicked unbelieving Israelites, that were God's visible people, and lived under means of grace; and that notwithstanding all God's wonderful works that He had wrought towards that people, yet remained, as is expressed verse 28, void of counsel, having no understanding in them; and that, under all the cultivations of heaven, brought forth bitter and poisonous fruit; as in the two verses next preceding the text.

The expression that I have chosen for my text, "their foot shall slide in due time," seems to imply the following things relating to the punishment and destruction that these wicked Israelites were exposed to.

1. That they were always exposed to destruction; as one that stands or walks in slippery places is always exposed to fall. This is implied in the manner of their destruction's coming upon them, being represented by their foot's sliding. The same is expressed, Psalm 73:18: "Surely thou didst set them in slippery places; thou castedst them down into destruction."

2. It implies that they were always exposed to sudden, unexpected destruction. As he that walks in slippery places is every moment liable to fall, he cannot foresee one moment whether he shall stand or fall

the next; and, when he does fall, he falls at once, without warning: which is also expressed in that Psalm 73:18, 19: "Surely thou didst set them in slippery places; thou castedst them down into destruction: how are they brought into desolation as in a moment."

3. Another thing implied is, that they are liable to fall of themselves, without being thrown down by the hand of another; as he that stands or walks on slippery ground needs nothing but his own weight to throw him down.

4. That the reason why they are not fallen already, and do not fall now, is only that God's appointed time is not come. For it is said, that when that due time, or appointed time, comes, "their foot shall slide." Then they shall be left to fall, as they are inclined by their own weight. God will not hold them up in these slippery places any longer, but will let them go; and then, at that very instant, they shall fall into destruction; as he that stands in such slippery declining ground on the edge of a pit that he cannot stand alone, when he is let go he immediately falls and is lost.

The observation from the words that I would now insist upon is this, "There is nothing that keeps wicked men at any one moment out of hell, but the mere pleasure of God."

By the mere pleasure of God, I mean His sovereign pleasure, His arbitrary will, restrained by no obligation, hindered by no manner of difficulty, any more than if nothing else but God's mere will had in the least degree, or in any respect whatsoever, any hand in the preservation of wicked men one moment.

The truth of this observation may appear by the following considerations.

1. There is no want of power in God to cast wicked men into hell at any moment. Men's hands cannot be strong when God rises up. The strongest have no power to resist Him, nor can any deliver out of His hands.

He is not only able to cast wicked men into hell, but He can most easily do it. Sometimes an earthly prince meets with a great deal of difficulty to subdue a rebel, that has found means to fortify himself, and has made himself strong by the numbers of his followers. But it is not so with God. There is no fortress that is any defense from the power of God. Though hand join in hand, and vast multitudes of God's enemies combine and associate themselves, they are easily broken in pieces: they are as great heaps of light chaff before the whirlwind; or large quantities of dry stubble before devouring flames. We find it easy to tread on and crush a worm that we see crawling on the earth; so it is easy for us to cut or singe a slender thread that anything hangs by; thus easy is it for God, when He pleases, to cast His enemies down to hell. What are we, that we should think to stand before Him, at whose rebuke the earth trembles, and before whom the rocks are thrown down!

2. They deserve to be cast into hell; so that divine justice never stands in the way, it makes no objection against God's using His power at any moment to destroy them. Yea, on the contrary, justice calls aloud for an infinite punishment of their sins. Divine justice says of the tree that brings forth such grapes of Sodom, "Cut it down, why cumbereth it the ground?" (Luke 8:7). The sword of divine justice is every moment brandished over their heads, and it is nothing but the hand of arbitrary mercy, and God's mere will, that holds it back.

3. They are already under a sentence of condemnation to hell. They do not only justly deserve to be cast down thither, but the sentence of the law of God, that eternal and immutable rule of righteousness that God has fixed between Him and mankind, is gone out against them, and stands against them; so that they are bound over already to hell, John 3:18, "He that believeth not is condemned already." So that every unconverted man properly belongs to hell; that is his place; from thence he is; John 8:23, "Ye are from beneath": and thither he is bound; it is the place that justice, and God's Word, and the sentence of His unchangeable law, assign to him.

4. They are now the objects of that very same anger and wrath of God, that is expressed in the torments of hell. And the reason why they do not go down to hell at each moment, is not because God, in whose power they are, is not then very angry with them; as angry, as He is with many of those miserable creatures that He is now tormenting in hell, and do there feel and bear the fierceness of His wrath. Yea, God is a great deal more angry with great numbers that are now on earth; yea, doubtless, with many that are now in this congregation, that, it may be, are at ease and quiet, than He is with many of those that are now in the flames of hell.

So that it is not because God is unmindful of their wickedness, and does not resent it, that He does not let loose His hand and cut them off. God is not altogether such an one as themselves, though they may imagine Him to be so. The wrath of God burns against them; their damnation does not slumber; the pit is prepared; the fire is made ready; the furnace is now hot; ready to receive them; the flames do now rage and glow. The glittering sword is whet, and held over them, and the pit hath opened her mouth under them.

5. The Devil stands ready to fall upon them, and seize them as his own, at what moment God shall permit him. They belong to him; he has their souls in his possession, and under his dominion. The scripture represents them as his goods, Luke 11:21. The devils watch them; they are ever by them, at their right hand; they stand waiting for them, like greedy, hungry lions that see their prey, and expect to have it, but

are for the present kept back; if God should withdraw His hand by which they are restrained, they would in one moment fly upon their poor souls. The old serpent is gaping for them; hell opens its mouth wide to receive them; and, if God should permit it, they would be hastily swallowed up and lost.

6. There are in the souls of wicked men those hellish principles reigning, that would presently kindle and flame out into hell-fire, if it were not for God's restraints. There is laid in the very nature of carnal men a foundation for the torments of hell: there are those corrupt principles, in reigning power in them, and in full possession of them, that are the beginnings of hell-fire. These principles are active and powerful, exceeding violent in their nature, and if were not for the restraining hand of God upon them, they would soon break out, they would flame out after the same manner as the same corruptions, the same enmity does in the hearts of damned souls, and would beget the same torments in them as they do in them. . . .

7. It is no security to wicked men for one moment, that there are no visible means of death at hand. It is no security to a natural man, that he is now in health, and that he does not see which way he should now immediately go out of the world by any accident, and that there is no visible danger in any respect in his circumstances. The manifold and continual experience of the world in all ages, shews that this is no evidence that a man is not on the very brink of eternity, and that the next step will not be into another world. The unseen, unthought of ways and means of persons' going suddenly out of the world are innumerable and inconceivable. Unconverted men walk over the pit of hell on a rotten covering, and there are innumerable places in this covering so weak that they will not bear their weight, and these places are not seen. The arrows of death fly unseen at noonday; the sharpest sight cannot discern them. God has so many different, unsearchable ways of taking wicked men out of the world and sending them to hell, that there is nothing to make it appear, that God had need to be at the expense of a miracle, or go out of the ordinary course of His providence, to destroy any wicked man, at any moment. All the means that there are of sinners going out of the world, are so in God's hands, and so absolutely subject to His power and determination, that it does not depend at all less on the mere will of God, whether sinners shall at any moment go to hell, than if means were never made use of, or at all concerned in the case.

8. Natural men's prudence and care to preserve their own lives, or the care of others to preserve them, do not secure them a moment. This, divine providence and universal experience do also bear testimony to. There is this clear evidence that men's own wisdom is no security to them from death; that if it were otherwise we should see

some difference between the wise and politic men of the world, and others, with regard to their liableness to early and unexpected death; but how is it in fact? Eccles. 2:16, "How dieth the wise man? As the fool."

9. All wicked men's pains and contrivance, they use to escape hell, while they continue to reject Christ, and so remain wicked men, do not secure them from hell one moment. Almost every natural man that hears of hell, flatters himself that he shall escape it; he depends upon himself for his own security, he flatters himself in what he has done, in what he is now doing, or what he intends to do; everyone lays out matters in his own mind how he shall avoid damnation, and flatters himself that he contrives well for himself, and that his schemes will not fail. They hear indeed that there are but few saved, and that the bigger part of men that have died heretofore are gone to hell; but each one imagines that he lays out matters better for his own escape than others have done: he does not intend to come to that place of torment; he says within himself, that he intends to take care that shall be effectual, and to order matters so for himself as not to fail.

But the foolish children of men do miserably delude themselves in their own schemes, and, in their confidence in their own strength and wisdom, they trust to nothing but a shadow. The bigger part of those that heretofore have lived under the same means of grace, and are now dead, are undoubtedly gone to hell; and it was not because they were not as wise as those that are now alive; it was not because they did not lay out matters as well for themselves to secure their own escape. If it were so that we could come to speak with them, and could inquire of them, one by one, whether they expected, when alive, and when they used to hear about hell, ever to be subjects of that misery, we, doubtless, should hear one and another reply, "No, I never intended to come here: I had laid out matters otherwise in my mind; I thought I should contrive well for myself: I thought my scheme good: I intended to take effectual care; but it came upon me unexpectedly; I did not look for it at that time, and in that manner; it came as a thief; Death outwitted me: God's wrath was too quick for me: O my cursed foolishness! I was flattering myself and pleasing myself with vain dreams of what I would do hereafter; and when I was saying peace and safety, then sudden destruction came upon me."

10. God has laid himself under no obligation, by any promise, to keep any natural man out of hell one moment: God certainly has made no promises either of eternal life, or of any deliverance or preservation from eternal death, but what are contained in the covenant of grace, the promises that are given in Christ, in whom all the promises are yea and amen. But surely they have no interest in the promises of the

covenant of grace that are not the children of the covenant, and that do not believe in any of the promises of the covenant, and have no interest in the Mediator of the covenant.

So that, whatever some have imagined and pretended about promises made to natural men's earnest seeking and knocking, it is plain and manifest, that whatever pains a natural man takes in religion, whatever prayers he makes, till he believes in Christ, God is under no manner of obligation to keep him a moment from eternal destruction.

So that thus it is, that natural men are held in the hand of God over the pit of hell; they have deserved the fiery pit and are already sentenced to it; and God is dreadfully provoked, His anger is as great towards them as to those that are actually suffering the executions of the fierceness of His wrath in hell, and they have done nothing in the least to appease or abate that anger, neither is God in the least bound by any promise to hold them up one moment; the Devil is waiting for them, hell is gaping for them, the flames gather and flash about them, and would fain lay hold on them and swallow them up; the fire pent up in their own hearts is struggling to break out; and they have no interest in any Mediator, there are no means within reach that can be any security to them. In short, they have no refuge, nothing to take hold of; all that preserves them every moment is the mere arbitrary will, and uncovenanted, unobliged forbearance of an incensed God.

APPLICATION

The use may be of awakening to unconverted persons in this congregation. This that you have heard is the case of every one of you that are out of Christ. That world of misery, that lake of burning brimstone, is extended abroad under you. There is the dreadful pit of the glowing flames of the wrath of God; there is hell's wide gaping mouth open; and you have nothing to stand upon, nor anything to take hold of. There is nothing between you and hell but the air; it is only the power and mere pleasure of God that holds you up.

You probably are not sensible of this; you find you are kept out of hell, but do not see the hand of God in it; but look at other things, as the good state of your bodily constitution, your care of your own life, and the means you use for your own preservation. But indeed these things are nothing; if God should withdraw His hand, they would avail no more to keep you from falling, than the thin air to hold up a person that is suspended in it.

Your wickedness makes you as it were heavy as lead, and to tend downwards with great weight and pressure towards hell; and, if God should let you go, you would immediately sink and swiftly descend and plunge into the bottomless gulf, and your healthy constitution, and your own care and prudence, and best contrivance, and all your righteousness, would have no more influence to uphold you and keep you out of hell, than a spider's web would have to stop a falling rock. Were it not that so is the sovereign pleasure of God, the earth would not bear you one moment; for you are a burden to it; the creation groans with you; the creature is made subject to the bondage of your corruption, not willingly; the sun does not willingly shine upon you to give you light to serve sin and Satan; the earth does not willingly yield her increase to satisfy your lusts; nor is it willingly a stage for your wickedness to be acted upon; the air does not willingly serve you for breath to maintain the flame of life in your vitals, while you spend your life in the service of God's enemies. God's creatures are good, and were made for men to serve God with, and do not willingly subserve to any other purpose, and groan when they are abused to purposes so directly contrary to their nature and end. And the world would spew you out, were it not for the sovereign hand of Him who hath subjected it in hope. There are the black clouds of God's wrath now hanging directly over your heads, full of the dreadful storm, and big with thunder; and were it not for the restraining hand of God, it would immediately burst forth upon you. The sovereign pleasure of God, for the present, stays His rough wind; otherwise it would come with fury, and your destruction would come like a whirlwind, and you would be like the chaff of the summer threshing floor.

The wrath of God is like great waters that are dammed for the present; they increase more and more, and rise higher and higher, till an outlet is given; and, the longer the stream is stopped, the more rapid and mighty is its course, when once it is let loose. It is true, that judgment against your evil work has not been executed hitherto; the floods of God's vengeance have been withheld; but your guilt in the meantime is constantly increasing, and you are every day treasuring up more wrath; the waters are continually rising and waxing more and more mighty; and there is nothing but the mere pleasure of God, that holds the waters back, that are unwilling to be stopped, and press hard to go forward. If God should only withdraw His hand from the floodgate, it would immediately fly open, and the fiery floods of the fierceness and wrath of God, would rush forth with inconceivable fury, and would come upon you with omnipotent power; and if your strength were ten thousand times greater than it is, yea, ten thousand times greater than the strength of the stoutest, sturdiest devil in hell, it would be nothing to withstand or endure it.

The bow of God's wrath is bent, and the arrow made ready on the string, and justice bends the arrow at your heart, and strains the bow, and it is nothing but the mere pleasure of God, and that of an angry God, without any promise or obligation at all, that keeps the arrow one moment from being made drunk with your blood.

Thus are all you that never passed under a great change of heart, by the mighty power of the Spirit of God upon your souls; all that were never born again, and made new creatures, and raised from being dead in sin, to a state of new, and before altogether unexperienced light and life (however you may have reformed your life in many things, and may have had religious affections, and may keep up a form of religion in your families and closets, and in the houses of God, and may be strict in it), you are thus in the hands of an angry God; it is nothing but His mere pleasure that keeps you from being this moment swallowed up in everlasting destruction.

However unconvinced you may now be of the truth of what you hear, by and by you will be fully convinced of it. Those that are gone from being in the like circumstances with you, see that it was so with them; for destruction came suddenly upon most of them; when they expected nothing of it, and while they were saying, Peace and safety: now they see that those things that they depended on for peace and safety were nothing but thin air and empty shadows.

The God that holds you over the pit of hell, much as one holds a spider, or some loathsome insect, over the fire, abhors you, and is dreadfully provoked; His wrath towards you burns like fire; He looks upon you as worthy of nothing else, but to be cast into the fire; He is of purer eyes than to bear to have you in His sight; you are ten thousand times so abominable in His eyes, as the most hateful and venomous serpent is in ours. You have offended him infinitely more than ever a stubborn rebel did his prince. And yet, it is nothing but His hand that holds you from falling into the fire every moment. It is ascribed to nothing else, that you did not go to hell the last night; that you was suffered to awake again in this world, after you closed your eyes to sleep. And there is no other reason to be given why you have not dropped into hell since you arose in the morning, but that God's hand has held you up. There is no other reason to be given why you have not gone to hell, since you have sat here in the house of God, provoking His pure eyes by your sinful wicked manner of attending His solemn worship: yea, there is nothing else that is to be given as a reason why you do not this very moment drop down into hell.

O sinner! consider the fearful danger you are in: it is a great furnace of wrath, a wide and bottomless pit, full of the fire of wrath, that you are held over in the hand of that God, whose wrath is provoked and incensed as much against you, as against many of the damned in hell. You hang by a slender thread, with the flames of divine wrath flashing about it, and ready every moment to singe it, and burn it asunder; and you have no interest in any Mediator, and nothing to lay hold of to save yourself, nothing to keep off the flames of wrath, nothing of your own, nothing that you ever have done, nothing that you can do, to induce God to spare you one moment. . . .

Thus it will be with you that are in an unconverted state, if you continue in it; the infinite might, and majesty, and terribleness, of the omnipotent God shall be magnified upon you, in the ineffable strength of your torments. You shall be tormented in the presence of the holy angels, and in the presence of the Lamb; and when you shall be in this state of suffering, the glorious inhabitants of heaven shall go forth and look on the awful spectacle, that they may see what the wrath and fierceness of the Almighty is; and when they have seen it, they will fall down and adore that great power and majesty. Isa. 66:23, 24, "And it shall come to pass, that from one moon to another, and from one sabbath to another, shall all flesh come to worship before me, saith the Lord. And they shall go forth and look upon the carcasses of the men that have transgressed against me; for their worm shall not die, neither shall their fire be quenched, and they shall be an abhorring unto all flesh."

It is everlasting wrath. It would be dreadful to suffer this fierceness and wrath of Almighty God one moment; but you must suffer it to all eternity. There will be no end to this exquisite, horrible misery: when you look forward, you shall see a long forever, a boundless duration before you, which will swallow up your thoughts, and amaze your soul; and you will absolutely despair of ever having any deliverance, any end, any mitigation, any rest at all; you will know certainly that you must wear out long ages, millions of millions of ages, in wrestling and conflicting with this Almighty merciless vengeance; and then, when you have so done, when so many ages have actually been spent by you in this manner, you will know that all is but a point to what remains. So that your punishment will indeed be infinite. Oh, who can express what the state of a soul in such circumstances is! All that we can possibly say about it, gives but a very feeble, faint representation of it; it is inexpressible and inconceivable: for "who knows the power of God's anger?"

How dreadful is the state of those that are daily and hourly in danger of this great wrath and infinite misery! But this is the dismal case of every soul in this congregation that has not been born again, however moral and strict, sober and religious, they may otherwise be. Oh, that you would consider it, whether you be young or old! There is reason to think, that there are many in this congregation now hearing this discourse, that will actually be the subjects of this very misery to all eternity. We know not who they are, or in what seats they sit, or what thoughts they now have. It may be they are now at ease, and hear all these things without much disturbance, and are now flattering themselves that they are not the persons; promising themselves that they shall escape. If we knew that there was one person, and but one, in the whole congregation, that was to be the subject of this misery, what an awful thing it would be to think of! If we knew who it was, what an awful sight would it be to see such a person! How might all the rest of the congregation lift up a lamentable and bitter cry over him! But alas! Instead of one, how many is it likely will remember this discourse in hell! And it would be a wonder, if some that are now present should not be in hell in a very short time, before this year is out. And it would be no wonder if some persons, that now sit here in some seats of this meeting-house in health, and quiet and secure, should be there before tomorrow morning.

The Taste for Holy Beauty

[From *A Treatise Concerning Religious Affections,* 1746]

Gracious affections do arise from the mind's being enlightened, rightly and spiritually to understand or apprehend divine things.

Holy affections are not heat without light; but evermore arise from some information of the understanding, some spiritual instruction that the mind receives, some light or actual knowledge. The child of God is graciously affected, because he sees and understands something more of divine things than he did before, more of God or Christ and of the glorious things exhibited in the gospel; he has some clearer and better view than he had before, when he was not affected: either he receives some understanding of divine things that is new to him; or has his former knowledge renewed after the view was decayed; "Everyone that loveth . . . knoweth God" (I John 4:7). "I pray that your love may abound more and more, in knowledge and in all judgment" (I Phil. 1:19). . . . Knowledge is the key that first opens the hard heart and enlarges the affections, and so opens the way for men into the kingdom of heaven; "Ye have taken away the key of knowledge" (Luke 11:52).

Now there are many affections which don't arise from any light in the understanding. And when it is thus, it is a sure evidence that these affections are not spiritual, let them be ever so high.[1] Indeed they have

[1] "Many that have had mighty strong affections at first conversion, afterwards become dry, and wither, and consume, and pine, and die away; and now their hypocrisy is manifest; if not to all the world, by open profaneness; yet to the

some new apprehensions which they had not before. Such is the nature of man, that it is impossible his mind should be affected, unless it be by something that he apprehends, or that his mind conceives of. But in many persons those apprehensions or conceptions that they have, wherewith they are affected, have nothing of the nature of knowledge or instruction in them. As for instance; when a person is affected with a lively idea, suddenly excited in his mind, of some shape, or very beautiful pleasant form of countenance, or some shining light, or other glorious outward appearance: here is something apprehended or conceived by the mind; but there is nothing of the nature of instruction in it: persons become never the wiser by such things, or more knowing about God, or a mediator between God and man, or the way of salvation by Christ, or anything contained in any of the doctrines of the gospel. Persons by these external ideas have no further acquaintance with God, as to any of the attributes of perfections of His nature; nor have they any further understanding of His Word, or any of His ways or works. Truly spiritual and gracious affections are not raised after this manner: these arise from the enlightening of the understanding to understand the things that are taught of God and Christ, in a new manner, the coming to a new understanding of the excellent nature of God, and His wonderful perfections, some new view of Christ in His spiritual excellencies and fullness, or things opened to him in a new manner, that appertain to the way of salvation by Christ, whereby he now sees how it is, and understands those divine and spiritual doctrines which once were foolishness to him. Such enlightenings of the understanding as these, are things entirely different in their nature, from strong ideas of shapes and colors, and outward brightness and glory, or sounds and voices. That all gracious affections do arise from some

---

discerning eye of living Christians, by a formal, barren, unsavory, unfruitful heart and course; because they never had light to conviction enough as yet. . . . 'Tis strange to see some people carried with mighty affection against sin and hell, and after Christ. And what is the hell you fear? A dreadful place. What is Christ? They scarce know so much as devils do; but that is all. Oh trust them not! Many have, and these will fall away to some lust, or opinion, or pride, or world; and the reason is, they never had light enough, John 5:35. John was a burning and shining light, and they did joy in him for a season; yet glorious as it was, they saw not Christ by it, especially not with divine light. It's rare to see Christians full both of light and affection. And therefore consider of this; many a man has been well brought up, and is of a sweet loving nature, mild and gentle, and harmless, likes and loves the best things, and his meaning, and mind, and heart is good, and has more in heart than in shew; and so hopes all shall go well with him. I say there may lie greatest hypocrisy under greatest affections; especially if they want light. You shall be hardened in your hypocrisy by them. I never liked violent affections and pangs, but only such as were dropped in by light; because those come from an external principle, and last not, but these do. Men are not affrighted by the light of the sun, though clearer than the lightning." Shepard, *Parable*, Pt. I, p. 146. [Edwards' note]

instruction or enlightening of the understanding, is therefore a further proof, that affections which arise from such impression on the imagination, are not gracious affections, besides the things observed before, which make this evident.

Hence also it appears, that affections arising from texts of scripture coming to the mind are vain, when no instruction received in the understanding from those texts, or anything taught in those texts, is the ground of the affection, but the manner of their coming to the mind. When Christ makes the scripture a means of the heart's burning with gracious affection, 'tis by opening the scriptures to their understandings; "Did not our heart burn within us, while He talked with us by the way, and while He opened to us the scriptures?" (Luke 24:32). It appears also that the affection which is occasioned by the coming of a text of scripture must be vain, when the affection is founded on something that is supposed to be taught by it, which really is not contained in it, nor in any other scripture; because such supposed instruction is not real instruction, but a mistake, and misapprehension of the mind. As for instance, when persons suppose that they are expressly taught by some scripture coming to their minds, that they in particular are beloved of God, or that their sins are forgiven, that God is their Father, and the like: this is a mistake or misapprehension; for the scripture nowhere reveals the individual persons who are beloved, expressly; but only by consequence, by revealing the qualifications of persons that are beloved of God: and therefore this matter is not to be learned from scripture any other way than by consequence, and from these qualifications: for things be not to be learned from the scripture any other way than they are taught in the scripture.

Affections really arise from ignorance, rather than instruction, in these instances which have been mentioned; as likewise in some others that might be mentioned. As some when they find themselves free of speech in prayer, they call it God's being with them; and this affects them more; and so their affections are set agoing and increased: when they look not into the cause of this freedom of speech; which may arise many other ways besides God's spiritual presence. So some are much affected with some apt thoughts that come into their minds about the scripture, and call it the Spirit of God teaching them. So they ascribe many of the workings of their own minds, which they have a high opinion of, and are pleased and taken with, to the special immediate influences of God's Spirit; and so are mightily affected with their privilege. And there are some instances of persons, in whom it seems manifest that the first ground of their affection is some bodily sensation. The animal spirits, by some cause (and probably sometimes by the Devil), are suddenly and unaccountably put into a very agreeable motion, causing persons to feel pleasantly in their bodies; the animal spirits are put into such a motion as is wont to be connected with the exhilaration of the mind; and the soul, by the laws of the union of soul and body, hence feels pleasure. The motion of the animal spirits don't first arise from any affection or apprehension of the mind whatsoever; but the very first thing that is felt, is an exhilaration of the animal spirits, and a pleasant external sensation, it may be in their breasts. Hence, through ignorance, the person being surprised, begins to think, surely this is the Holy Ghost coming into him. And then the mind begins to be affected and raised: there is first great joy; and then many other affections, in a very tumultuous manner, putting all nature, both body and mind, into a mighty ruffle. For though, as I observed before, 'tis the soul only that is the seat of the affections; yet this hinders not but that bodily sensations, may in this manner, be an occasion of affections in the mind.

And if men's religious affections do truly arise from some instruction or light in the understanding; yet the affection is not gracious, unless the light which is the ground of it be spiritual. Affections may be excited by that understanding of things, which they obtain merely by human teaching, with the common improvement of the faculties of the mind. Men may be much affected by knowledge of things of religion that they obtain this way; as some philosophers have been mightily affected, and almost carried beyond themselves, by the discoveries they have made in mathematics and natural philosophy. So men may be much affected from common illuminations of the Spirit of God, in which God assists men's faculties to a greater degree of that kind of understanding of religious matters, which they have in some degree, by only the ordinary exercise and improvement of their own faculties. Such illuminations may much affect the mind; as in many whom we read of in scripture, that were once enlightened: but these affections are not spiritual.

There is such a thing, if the scriptures are of any use to teach us anything, as a spiritual, supernatural understanding of divine things, that is peculiar to the saints, and which those who are not saints have nothing of. 'Tis certainly a kind of understanding, apprehending or discerning of divine things, that natural men have nothing of, which the Apostle speaks of, "But the natural man receiveth not the things of the Spirit of God; for they are foolishness unto him; neither can he know them, because they are spiritually discerned" (I Cor. 2:14). 'Tis certainly a kind of seeing or discerning spiritual things, peculiar to the saints, which is spoken of, "Whosoever sinneth hath not seen Him, neither known Him" (I John 3:6). . . . And innumerable other places there are, all over the Bible, which show the same. And that there is such a thing as an understanding of divine things, which in its nature and kind is wholly different from all knowledge that natural men have, is evident from this, that there is an understanding of divine things, which the scripture calls spiritual understanding; "We do not cease to pray for you, and to desire that you may be filled with the knowledge of His will, in all wisdom, and spiritual understanding" (Col. 1:9). It has been already shown, that that which is spiritual, in the ordinary use of the word in the New Testament, is entirely different in nature and kind, from all which natural men are, or can be the subjects of.

From hence it may be surely inferred, wherein spiritual understanding consists. For if there be in the saints a kind of apprehension or perception, which is in its nature, perfectly diverse from all that natural men have, or that it is possible they should have, till they have a new nature; it must consist in their having a certain kind of ideas or sensations of mind, which are simply diverse from all that is or can be in the minds of natural men. And that is the same thing as to say, that it consists in the sensations of a new spiritual sense, which the souls of natural men have not; as is evident by what has been before, once and again observed. But I have already shown what that new spiritual sense is, which the saints have given them in regeneration, and what is the object of it. I have shown that the immediate object of it is the supreme beauty and excellency of the nature of divine things, as they are in themselves. And this is agreeable to the scripture: the Apostle very plainly teaches that the great thing discovered by spiritual light, and understood by spiritual knowledge, is the glory of divine things, "But if our gospel be hid, it is hid to them that are lost; in whom the God of this world hath blinded the minds of them that believe not, lest the light of the glorious gospel of Christ, who is the image of God, should shine unto them" (II Cor. 4:3–4). . . . And it must needs be so, for as has been before observed, the scripture often teaches that all true religion summarily consists in the love of divine things. And therefore that kind of understanding or knowledge, which is the proper foundation of true religion, must be the knowledge of the loveliness of divine things. For doubtless, that knowledge which is the proper foundation of love, is the knowledge of loveliness. What that beauty or loveliness of divine things is, which is the proper and immediate object of a spiritual sense of mind, was showed under the last head insisted on, viz., that it is the beauty of their moral perfection. Therefore it is in the view or sense of this, that spiritual understanding does more immediately and primarily consist. And indeed it is plain it can be nothing else; for (as has been shown) there is nothing pertaining to divine things besides the beauty of their moral excellency, and those properties and qualities of divine things which this beauty is the foundation of, but what natural men and devils can see and know, and will know fully and clearly to all eternity.

From what has been said, therefore, we come necessarily to this conclusion, concerning that wherein spiritual understanding consists; viz., that it consists in a sense of the heart, of the supreme beauty and sweetness of the holiness or moral perfection of divine things, together with all that discerning and knowledge of things of religion, that depends upon, and flows from such a sense.

Spiritual understanding consists primarily in a sense of heart of that spiritual beauty. I say, a sense of heart; for it is not speculation merely that is concerned in this kind of understanding: nor can there be a clear distinction made between the two faculties of understanding and will, as acting distinctly and separately, in this matter. When the mind is sensible of the sweet beauty and amiableness of a thing, that implies a sensibleness of sweetness and delight in the presence of the idea of it: and this sensibleness of the amiableness or delightfulness of beauty, carries in the very nature of it, the sense of the heart; or an effect and impression the soul is the subject of, as a substance possessed of taste, inclination and will.

There is a distinction to be made between a mere notional understanding, wherein the mind only beholds things in the exercise of a speculative faculty; and the sense of the heart, wherein the mind don't only speculate and behold, but relishes and feels. That sort of knowledge, by which a man has a sensible perception of amiableness and loathsomeness, or of sweetness and nauseousness, is not just the same sort of knowledge with that, by which he knows what a triangle is, and what a square is. The one is mere speculative knowledge; the other sensible knowledge, in which more than the mere intellect is concerned; the heart is the proper subject of it, or the soul as a being that not only beholds, but has inclination, and is pleased or displeased. And yet there is the nature of instruction in it; as he that has perceived the sweet taste of honey, knows much more about it, than he who has only looked upon and felt of it. . . .

Spiritual understanding primarily consists in this sense, or taste of the moral beauty of divine things; so that no knowledge can be called spiritual, any further than it arises from this, and has this in it. But secondarily, it includes all that discerning and knowledge of things of religion, which depends upon, and flows from such a sense.

When the true beauty and amiableness of the holiness or true moral good that is in divine things, is discovered to the soul, it as it were opens a new world to its view. This shows the glory of all the perfections of God, and of everything appertaining to the divine being: for, as was observed before, the beauty of all arises from God's moral perfection. This shows the glory of all God's works, both of creation and providence: for 'tis the special glory of them, that God's holiness, righteousness, faithfulness and goodness are so manifested in them;

and without these moral perfections, there would be no glory in that power and skill with which they are wrought. The glorifying of God's moral perfections, is the special end of all the works of God's hands. By this sense of the moral beauty of divine things, is understood the sufficiency of Christ as a mediator: for 'tis only by the discovery of the beauty of the moral perfection of Christ, that the believer is let into the knowledge of the excellency of His person, so as to know anything more of it than the devils do: and 'tis only by the knowledge of the excellency of Christ's person, that any know His sufficiency as a mediator; for the latter depends upon, and arises from the former. 'Tis by seeing the excellency of Christ's person, that the saints are made sensible of the preciousness of His blood, and its sufficiency to atone for sin: for therein consists the preciousness of Christ's blood, that 'tis the blood of so excellent and amiable a person. And on this depends the meritoriousness of His obedience, and sufficiency and prevalence of His intercession. By this sight of the moral beauty of divine things, is seen the beauty of the way of salvation by Christ: for that consists in the beauty of the moral perfections of God, which wonderfully shines forth in every step of this method of salvation, from beginning to end. By this is seen the fitness and suitableness of this way: for this wholly consists in its tendency to deliver us from sin and hell, and to bring us to the happiness which consists in the possession and enjoyment of moral good, in a way sweetly agreeing with God's moral perfections. And in the way's being contrived so as to attain these ends, consists the excellent wisdom of that way. By this is seen the excellency of the Word of God: take away all the moral beauty and sweetness in the Word, and the Bible is left wholly a dead letter, a dry, lifeless, tasteless thing. By this is seen the true foundation of our duty; the worthiness of God to be so esteemed, honored, loved, submitted to, and served, as He requires of us, and the amiableness of the duties themselves that are required of us. And by this is seen the true evil of sin: for he who sees the beauty of holiness, must necessarily see the hatefulness of sin, its contrary. By this men understand the true glory of heaven, which consists in the beauty and happiness that is in holiness. By this is seen the amiableness and happiness of both saints and angels. He that sees the beauty of holiness, or true moral good, sees the greatest and most important thing in the world, which is the fullness of all things, without which all the world is empty, no better than nothing, yea, worse than nothing. Unless this is seen, nothing is seen, that is worth the seeing: for there is no other true excellency or beauty. Unless this be understood, nothing is understood, that is worthy of the exercise of the noble faculty of understanding. This is the beauty of the Godhead, and the divinity of Divinity (if I may so speak), the good of the infinite fountain of good; without which God Himself (if that were possible to be) would be an infinite evil: without which, we ourselves had better never have been; and without which there had better have been no being. He therefore in effect knows nothing, that knows not this: his knowledge is but the shadow of knowledge, or the form of knowledge, as the Apostle calls it. Well therefore may the scripture represent those who are destitute of that spiritual sense, by which is perceived the beauty of holiness, as totally blind, deaf and senseless, yea dead. And well may regeneration, in which this divine sense is given to the soul by its Creator, be represented as opening the blind eyes, and raising the dead, and bringing a person into a new world. For if what has been said be considered, it will be manifest, that when a person has this sense and knowledge given him, he will view nothing as he did before; though before he knew all things after the flesh, yet henceforth he will know them so no more; and he is become "a new creature, old things are passed away, behold all things are become new"; agreeable to II Cor. 5:16–17.

And besides the things that have been already mentioned, there arises from this sense of spiritual beauty, all true experimental knowledge of religion; which is of itself, as it were a new world of knowledge. He that sees not the beauty of holiness, knows not what one of the graces of God's Spirit is; he is destitute of any idea or conception of all gracious exercises of soul, and all holy comforts and delights, and all effects of the saving influences of the Spirit of God on the heart: and so is ignorant of the greatest works of God, the most important and glorious effects of His power upon the creature: and also is wholly ignorant of the saints as saints; he knows not what they are: and in effect is ignorant of the whole spiritual world.

Things being thus, it plainly appears, that God's implanting that spiritual supernatural sense which has been spoken of, makes a great change in a man. And were it not for the very imperfect degree, in which this sense is commonly given at first, or the small degree of this glorious light that first dawns upon the soul; the change made by this spiritual opening of the eyes in conversion, would be much greater, and more remarkable, every way, than if a man, who had been born blind, and with only the other four senses, should continue so for a long time, and then at once should have the sense of seeing imparted to him, in the midst of the clear light of the sun, discovering a world of visible objects. For though sight be more noble than any of the other external senses; yet this spiritual sense which has been spoken of, is infinitely more noble than that, or any other principle of discerning that a man naturally has, and the object of this sense infinitely greater and more important.

This sort of understanding or knowledge is that knowledge of divine things from whence all truly gracious affections do proceed: by which therefore all affections are to be tried. Those affections that arise wholly from any other kind of knowledge, or do result from any other kind of apprehensions of mind, are vain.[1]

From what has been said may be learned wherein the most essential difference lies between that light or understanding which is given by the common influences of the Spirit of God, on the hearts of natural men, and that saving instruction which is given to the saints. The latter primarily and most essentially lies in beholding the holy beauty that is in divine things; which is the only true moral good, and which the soul of fallen man is by nature totally blind to. The former consists only in a further understanding, through the assistance of natural principles, of those things which men may know, in some measure, by the alone ordinary exercise of their faculties. And this knowledge consists only in the knowledge of those things pertaining to religion, which are natural. Thus for instance, in those awakenings and convictions of conscience, that natural men are often subject to, the Spirit of God gives no knowledge of the true moral beauty which is in divine things; but only assists the mind to a clearer idea of the guilt of sin, or its relation to a punishment, and connection with the evil of suffering (without any sight of its true moral evil, or odiousness as sin) and a clearer idea of the natural perfections of God, wherein consists, not His holy beauty and glory, but His awful and terrible greatness. 'Tis a clear sight of this, that will fully awaken the consciences of wicked men at the Day of Judgment, without any spiritual light. And 'tis a lesser degree of the same, that awakens the consciences of natural men, without spiritual light, in this world. The same discoveries are in some measure given

[1] "Take heed of contenting yourselves with every kind of knowledge. Do not worship every image of your own heads; especially you that fall short of truth, or the knowledge of it. For when you have some, there may be yet that wanting, which may make you sincere. There are many men of great knowledge, able to teach themselves, and others too; and yet their hearts are unsound. How comes this to pass? Is it because they have so much light? No; but because they want much. And therefore content not yourselves with every knowledge. There is some knowledge which men have by the light of nature (which leaves them without excuse), from the book of creation; some by power of education; some by the light of the law, whereby men know their sin and evils; some by the letter of the gospel; and so men may know much, and speak well; and so in seeing, see not; some by the Spirit, and may see much, so as to prophesy in Christ's name, and yet bid depart; Matt. 7. Now there is a light of glory, whereby the elect see things in another manner: to tell you how, they cannot: it's the beginning of light in heaven: and the same Spirit that fills Christ, filling their minds, that they know, by this anointing, all things: which if ever you have, you must become babes and fools in your own eyes. God will never write his law in your minds, till all the scribblings of it are blotted out. Account all your knowledge loss for the gaining of this. 'Tis sad to see many a man pleasing himself in his own dreaming delusions; yet the poor creature in seeing, sees not; which is God's heavy curse upon men under greatest means, and which lays all waste and desolate." Shepard, *Parable*, Pt. I, p. 147. [Edwards' note]

in the conscience of an awakened sinner in this world, which will be given more fully in the consciences of sinners at the Day of Judgment. The same kind of sight or apprehension of God, in a lesser degree, makes awakened sinners in this world, sensible of the dreadful guilt of sin, against so great and terrible a God, and sensible of its amazing punishment, and fills 'em with fearful apprehensions of divine wrath; that will thoroughly convince all wicked men, of the infinitely dreadful nature and guilt of sin, and astonish 'em with apprehensions of wrath, when Christ shall come in the glory of His power and majesty, and every eye shall see Him, and all the kindreds of the earth shall wail because of Him. And in those common illuminations, which are sometimes given to natural men, exciting in them some kind of religious desire, love and joy, the mind is only assisted to a clearer apprehension of the natural good that is in divine things. Thus sometimes, under common illuminations, men are raised with the ideas of the natural good that is in heaven; as its outward glory, its ease, its honor and advancement, a being there the objects of the high favor of God, and the great respect of men and angels, etc. So there are many things exhibited in the gospel, concerning God and Christ, and the way of salvation, that have a natural good in them, which suits the natural principle of self-love. Thus in that great goodness of God to sinners, and the wonderful dying love of Christ, there is a natural good, which all men love, as they love themselves; as well as a spiritual and holy beauty, which is seen only by the regenerate. Therefore there are many things appertaining to the Word of God's grace delivered in the gospel, which may cause natural men, when they hear it, anon with joy to receive it. All that love which natural men have to God, and Christ, and Christian virtues, and good men, is not from any sight of the amiableness of the holiness, or true moral excellency of these things; but only for the sake of the natural good there is in them. All natural men's hatred of sin, is as much from principles of nature, as men's hatred of a tiger for his rapaciousness, or their aversion to a serpent for his poison and hurtfulness: and all their love of Christian virtue, is from no higher principle than their love of a man's good nature, which appears amiable to natural men; but no otherwise than silver and gold appears amiable in the eyes of a merchant, or than the blackness of the soil is beautiful in the eyes of the farmer. . . .

. . . I have shown that spiritual knowledge primarily consists in a taste or relish of the amiableness and beauty of that which is truly good and holy: this holy relish is a thing that discerns and distinguishes between good and evil, between holy and unholy, without being at the trouble of a train of reasoning. As he who has a true relish of external beauty, knows what is beautiful by looking upon it: he stands in no need of a train of reasoning about the proportion of the features, in order to determine whether that which he sees be a beautiful countenance or no: he needs nothing, but only the glance of his eye. He who has a rectified musical ear, knows whether the sound he hears be true harmony: he don't need first to be at the trouble of the reasonings of a mathematician, about the proportion of the notes. He that has a rectified palate, knows what is good food, as soon as he tastes it, without the reasoning of a physician about it. There is a holy beauty and sweetness in words and actions, as well as a natural beauty in countenances and sounds, and sweetness in food; "Doth not the ear try words, and the mouth taste his meat?" (Job 12:11). When a holy and amiable action is suggested to the thoughts of a holy soul; that soul, if in the lively exercise of its spiritual taste, at once sees a beauty in it, and so inclines to it, and closes with it. On the contrary, if an unworthy unholy action be suggested to it, its sanctified eye sees no beauty in it, and is not pleased with it; its sanctified taste relishes no sweetness in it, but on the contrary, it is nauseous to it. Yea its holy taste and appetite leads it to think of that which is truly lovely, and naturally suggests it; as a healthy taste and appetite naturally suggests the idea of its proper object. Thus a holy person is led by the Spirit, as he is instructed and led by his holy taste, and disposition of heart; whereby, in the lively exercise of grace, he easily distinguishes good and evil, and knows at once, what is a suitable amiable behavior towards God, and towards man, in this case and the other; and judges what is right, as it were spontaneously, and of himself, without a particular deduction, by any other arguments than the beauty that is seen, and goodness that is tasted. Thus Christ blames the Pharisees, that they did not, even of their own selves judge what was right, without needing miracles to prove it (Luke 12:57). The Apostle seems plainly to have respect to this way of judging of spiritual beauty, in Rom. 12:2: "Be ye transformed by the renewing of your mind, that ye may prove what is that good, and perfect, and acceptable will of God."

There is such a thing as good taste of natural beauty (which learned men often speak of), that is exercised about temporal things, in judging of them; as about the justness of a speech, the goodness of style, the beauty of a poem, the gracefulness of deportment, etc. A late great philosopher of our nation, writes thus upon it:

> To have a *taste,* is to give things their real value, to be touched with the good, to be shocked with the ill; not to be dazzled with false lusters, but in spite of all colors, and everything that might deceive or amuse, to judge soundly.
>
> *Taste* and *judgment* then, should be the same thing; and yet 'tis easy to discern a difference. The judgment forms its opinions from reflection: the reason on this occasion fetches a kind of circuit, to

> arrive at its end; it supposes principles, it draws consequences, and it judges; but not without a thorough knowledge of the case; so that after it has pronounced, it is ready to render a reason of its decrees. Good taste observes none of these formalities; ere it has time to consult, it has taken its side; as soon as ever the object is presented it, the impression is made, the sentiment formed, ask no more of it. As the ear is wounded with a harsh sound, as the smell is soothed with an agreeable odor, before ever the reason have meddled with those objects to judge of them, so the taste opens itself at once, and prevents all reflection. They may come afterwards to confirm it, and discover the secret reasons of its conduct; but it was not in its power to wait for them. Frequently it happens not to know them at all, and what pains soever it uses, cannot discover what it was determined it to think as it did. This conduct is very different from that the judgment observes in its decisions: unless we choose to say, that good taste is as it were a first motion, or a kind of instinct of right reason, which hurries on with rapidity, and conducts more securely, than all the reasonings she could make: 'tis a first glance of the eye, which discovers to us the nature and relations of things in a moment.[1]

Now as there is such a kind of taste of the mind as this, which philosophers speak of, whereby persons are guided in their judgment of the natural beauty, gracefulness, propriety, nobleness and sublimity of speeches and actions, whereby they judge as it were by the glance of the eye, or by inward sensation, and the first impression of the object; so there is likewise such a thing as a divine taste, given and maintained by the Spirit of God, in the hearts of the saints, whereby they are in like manner led and guided in discerning and distinguishing the true spiritual and holy beauty of actions; and that more easily, readily and accurately, as they have more or less of the Spirit of God dwelling in them. And thus the sons of God are led by the Spirit of God, in their behavior in the world.

A holy disposition and spiritual taste, where grace is strong and lively, will enable a soul to determine what actions are right and becoming Christians, not only more speedily, but far more exactly, than the greatest abilities without it. This may be illustrated by the manner in which some habits of mind, and dispositions of heart, of a nature inferior to true grace, will teach and guide a man in his actions. As for instance, if a man be a very good-natured man, his good nature will teach him better how to act benevolently amongst mankind, and will direct him, on every occasion, to those speeches and actions, which are agreeable to rules of goodness, than the strongest reason will a man of a morose temper. So if a man's heart be under the influence of an entire friendship, and most endeared affection to another; though he

[1] Chambers, *Cyclopedia,* Vol. 2, under the word "Taste." [Edwards' note]

be a man of an indifferent capacity, yet this habit of his mind will direct him, far more readily and exactly, to a speech and deportment, or manner of behavior, which shall in all respects be sweet and kind, and agreeable to a benevolent disposition of heart, than the greatest capacity without it. He has as it were a spirit within him, that guides him: the habit of his mind is attended with a taste, by which he immediately relishes that air and mien which is benevolent, and disrelishes the contrary, and causes him to distinguish between one and the other in a moment, more precisely, than the most accurate reasonings can find out in many hours. As the nature and inward tendency of a stone, or other heavy body, that is let fall from a loft, shows the way to the center of the earth, more exactly in an instant, than the ablest mathematician, without it, could determine, by his most accurate observations, in a whole day. Thus it is that a spiritual disposition and taste teaches and guides a man in his behavior in the world. So an eminently humble, or meek, or charitable disposition, will direct a person of mean capacity to such a behavior, as is agreeable to Christian rules of humility, meekness and charity, far more readily and precisely, than the most diligent study, and elaborate reasonings, of a man of the strongest faculties, who has not a Christian spirit within him. So also will a spirit of love to God, and holy fear and reverence towards God, and filial confidence in God, and an heavenly disposition, teach and guide a man in his behavior. . . .

What has been said of the nature of spiritual understanding, as consisting most essentially in a divine supernatural sense and relish of the heart, not only shows that there is nothing of it in this falsely supposed leading of the Spirit, which has been now spoken of; but also shows the difference between spiritual understanding, and all kinds and forms of enthusiasm, all imaginary sights of God and Christ and heaven, all supposed witnessing of the Spirit, and testimonies of the love of God by immediate inward suggestion; and all impressions of future events, and immediate revelations of any secret facts whatsoever; all enthusiastical impressions and applications of words of scripture, as though they were words now immediately spoken by God to a particular person, in a new meaning, and carrying something more in them, than the words contain as they lie in the Bible; and all interpretations of the mystical meaning of the scripture, by supposed immediate revelation. None of these things consist in a divine sense and relish of the heart, of the holy beauty and excellency of divine things; nor have they anything to do with such a sense; but all consist in impressions in the head; all are to be referred to the head of impressions on the imagination, and consist in the exciting external ideas in the mind, either in ideas of outward shapes and colors, or words spoken, or letters written, or ideas of things external and sensible, belonging to actions done, or events accomplished, or to be accomplished. An enthusiastical supposed manifestation of the love of God, is made by the exciting an idea of a smiling countenance, or some other pleasant outward appearance, or by the idea of pleasant words spoken, or written, excited in the imagination, or some pleasant bodily sensation. So when persons have an imaginary revelation of some secret fact, 'tis by exciting external ideas; either of some words, implying a declaration of that fact, or some visible or sensible circumstances of such a fact. So the supposed leading of the Spirit, to do the will of God, in outward behavior, is either by exciting the idea of words (which are outward things) in their minds, either the words of scripture, or other words, which they look upon as an immediate command of God; or else by exciting and impressing strongly the ideas of the outward actions themselves. So when an interpretation of a scripture type or allegory, is immediately, in an extraordinary way, strongly suggested, it is by suggesting words, as though one secretly whispered, and told the meaning; or by exciting other ideas in the imagination.

Such sort of experiences and discoveries as these commonly raise the affections of such as are deluded by them, to a great height, and make a mighty uproar in both soul and body. And a very great part of the false religion that has been in the world, from one age to another, consists in such discoveries as these, and in the affections that flow from them. In such things consisted the experiences of the ancient Pythagoreans among the heathen, and many others among them, who had strange ecstasies and raptures, and pretended to a divine afflatus, and immediate revelations from heaven. In such things as these seem to have consisted the experiences of the Essenes, an ancient sect among the Jews, at and after the times of the apostles. In such things as these consisted the experiences of many of the ancient Gnostics, and the Montanists, and many other sects of ancient heretics, in the primitive ages of the Christian church. And in such things as these consisted the pretended immediate converse, with God and Christ, and saints and angels of heaven, of the monks, anchorites, and recluses, that formerly abounded in the Church of Rome. In such things consisted the pretended high experiences, and great spirituality of many sects of enthusiasts, that swarmed in the world after the Reformation; such as the Anabaptists, Antinomians, and Familists, the followers of N. Stork, Th. Muncer, Jo. Becold, Henry Pfeifer, David George, Casper Schwenckfeld, Henry Nicolas, Johannes Agricola Eislebius; and the many wild enthusiasts that were in England in the days of Oliver Cromwell; and the followers of Mrs. Hutchinson, in New England; as appears by the particular and large accounts given of all these sects, by that eminently holy man, Mr. Samuel Rutherford in his *Display of the Spiritual Antichrist.* And in such things as these consisted the experiences of the late French prophets, and their followers. And in these things seems to lie the religion of the many kinds of enthusiasts of the present day. 'Tis by such sort of religion as this chiefly, that Satan transforms himself into an angel of light: and it is that which he has ever most successfully made use of to confound hopeful and happy revivals of religion, from the beginning of the Christian church to this day. When the Spirit of God is poured out, to begin a glorious work, then the old serpent, as fast as possible, and by all means introduces this bastard religion, and mingles it with the true; which has from time to time soon brought all things into confusion. The pernicious consequence of it is not easily imagined or conceived of, till we see and are amazed with the awful effects of it, and the dismal desolation it has made. If the revival of true religion be very great in its beginning, yet if this bastard comes in, there is danger of its doing as Gideon's bastard Abimelech did, who never left till he had slain all his threescore and ten true-born sons, excepting one, that was forced to flee. Great and strict therefore should be the watch and guard that ministers maintain against such things, especially at a time of great awakening: for men, especially the common people, are easily bewitched with such things; they having such a glaring and glittering show of high religion; and the Devil hiding his own shape, and appearing as an angel of light, that men may not be afraid of him, but may adore him.

The imagination or phantasy seems to be that wherein are formed all those delusions of Satan, which those are carried away with, who are under the influence of false religion, and counterfeit graces and affections. Here is the Devil's grand lurking place, the very nest of foul and delusive spirits. 'Tis very much to be doubted whether the Devil can come at the soul of man, at all to affect it, or to excite any thought or motion, or produce any affect whatsoever in it, any other way, than by the phantasy; which is that power of the soul, by which it receives, and is the subject of the species, or ideas of outward and sensible things. As to the laws and means which the Creator has established, for the intercourse and communication of unbodied spirits, we know nothing about them; we don't know by what medium they manifest their thoughts to each other, or excite thoughts in each other. But as to spirits that are united to bodies, those bodies God has united 'em to, are their medium of communication: they have no other medium of acting on other creatures, or being acted on by them, than the body. Therefore it is not to be supposed that Satan can excite any thought, or produce any effect in the soul of man, any otherwise, than by some motion of the animal spirits, or by causing some motion or alteration in something which appertains to the body. There is this reason to think that the Devil can't produce thoughts, in the soul immediately, or any other way, than by the medium of the body, viz., that he can't immediately see or know the thoughts of the soul: it is abundantly declared in the scripture to be peculiar to the omniscient God to do that. But it is not likely that the Devil can immediately produce an effect which is out of the reach of his immediate view. It seems unreasonable to suppose that his immediate agency, should be out of his own sight, or that it should be impossible for him to see what he himself immediately does. It is not unreasonable to suppose that any spirit or intelligent agent, should by the act of his will, produce effects, according to his understanding, or agreeable to his own thoughts, and that immediately; and yet the effects produced, be beyond the reach of his understanding, or where he can have no immediate perception or discerning at all. But if this be so, that the Devil can't produce thoughts in the soul immediately, or any other way than by the animal spirits, or by the body; then it follows, that he never brings to pass anything in the soul, but by the imagination or phantasy, or by exciting external ideas. For we know that alterations in the body, do immediately excite no other sort of ideas in the mind, but external ideas, or ideas of the outward senses, or ideas which are of the same outward nature. As to reflection, abstraction, reasoning, etc. and those thoughts and inward motions which are the fruits of these acts of the mind, they are not the next effects of impressions on the body. So that it must be only by the imagination, that Satan has access to the soul, to tempt and delude it, or suggest anything to it.[1] And this seems to be the reason why persons that are under

[1] "The imagination is that room of the soul, wherein the Devil doth often appear. Indeed (to speak exactly) the Devil hath no efficient power over the rational part of a man: he cannot change the will; he cannot alter the heart of a man. So that the utmost he can do, in tempting a man to sin, is by suasion and suggestion only. But then how doth the Devil do this? Even by working upon the imagination. He observeth the temper, and bodily constitution of a man; and thereupon suggests to his fancy, and injects his fiery darts thereinto, by which the mind and will come to be wrought upon. The Devil then, though he hath no imperious efficacy over the will, yet because he can thus stir and move thy imagination, and thou being naturally destitute of grace, canst not withstand these suggestions; hence it is that any sin in thy imagination, though but in the outward works of the soul, yet doth quickly lay hold on all. And indeed, by this means do arise those horrible delusions, that are in many erroneous ways of religion: all is because their imaginations are corrupted. Yea, how often are these diabolical delusions of the imagination, taken for the gracious operations of God's Spirit? . . . It is from hence that many have pretended to enthusiasms; . . . They leave the scriptures, and wholly attend to what they perceive and feel within them." Anthony Burgess, *The Doctrine of Original Sin* (London, 1659), pp. 369–70. [Edwards' note]

The great Turretine, speaking on that question, "What is the power of angels," says, "As to bodies, there is no doubt, but that they can do a great deal upon all

the disease of melancholy, are commonly so visibly and remarkably subject to the suggestions and temptations of Satan: that being a disease which peculiarly affects the animal spirits, and is attended with weakness of that part of the body which is the fountain of the animal spirits, even the brain, which is, as it were, the seat of the phantasy. 'Tis by impressions made on the brain, that any ideas are excited in the mind, by the motion of the animal spirits, or any changes made in the body. The brain being thus weakened and diseased, 'tis less under the command of the higher faculties of the soul, and yields the more easily to extrinsic impressions, and is overpowered by the disordered motions of the animal spirits; and so the Devil has greater advantage to affect the mind, by working on the imagination. And thus Satan, when he casts in those horrid suggestions into the minds of many melancholy persons, in which they have no hand themselves, he does it by exciting imaginary ideas, either of some dreadful words or sentences, or other horrid outward ideas. And when he tempts other persons who are not melancholy, he does it by presenting to the imagination, in a lively and alluring manner, the objects of their lusts, or by exciting ideas of words, and so by them exciting thoughts; or by promoting an imagination of outward actions, events, circumstances, etc. Innumerable are the ways by which the mind might be led on to all kinds of evil thoughts, by exciting external ideas in the imagination.

If persons keep no guard at these avenues of Satan, by which he has access to the soul, to tempt and delude it, they will be likely to have enough of him. And especially, if instead of guarding against him, they lay themselves open to him, and seek and invite him, because he appears as an angel of light, and counterfeits the illuminations and graces of the Spirit of God, by inward whispers, and immediate suggestions of facts and events, pleasant voices, beautiful images, and other impressions on the imagination. There are many who are deluded by such things, and are lifted up with them, and seek after them, that have a continued course of them, and can have 'em almost when they will; and especially when their pride and vainglory has most occasion for 'em, to make a shew of 'em before company. 'Tis with them, something as 'tis with those who are the

---

sorts of elementary and sublunary bodies, to move them locally, and variously to agitate them. 'Tis also certain, that they can act upon the external and internal senses, to excite them, or to bind them. But as to the rational soul itself, they can do nothing immediately upon that; for to God alone, who knows and searches the hearts, and who has them in His hands, does it also appertain to bow and move them whethersoever He will. But angels can act upon the rational soul, only mediately, by imaginations." François Turretine, *Institutio Theologiae Elencticae* (Geneva, 1680), Vol. *1*, Loc. VII, quest. 8, p. 591; (Geneva, 1734), p. 604. [Edwards' note]

professors of the art of telling where lost things are to be found, by impressions made on their imaginations; they laying themselves open to the Devil, he is always at hand to give them the desired impression.

Before I finish what I would say on this head of imaginations, counterfeiting spiritual light, and affections arising from them, I would renewedly (to prevent misunderstanding of what has been said) desire it may be observed, that I am far from determining that no affections are spiritual which are attended with imaginary ideas. Such is the nature of man, that he can scarcely think of any thing intensely, without some kind of outward ideas. They arise and interpose themselves unavoidably, in the course of a man's thoughts; though oftentimes they are very confused, and are not what the mind regards. When the mind is much engaged, and the thoughts intense, oftentimes the imagination is more strong, and the outward idea more lively; especially in persons of some constitutions of body. But there is a great difference between these two things, viz., lively imaginations arising from strong affections, and strong affections arising from lively imaginations. The former may be, and doubtless often is, in case of truly gracious affections. The affections don't arise from the imagination, nor have any dependence upon it; but on the contrary, the imagination is only the accidental effect, or consequent of the affection, through the infirmity of human nature. But when the latter is the case, as it often is, that the affection arises from imagination, and is built upon it as its foundation, instead of a spiritual illumination or discovery; then is the affection, however elevated, worthless and vain. And this is the drift of what has been now said, of impressions on the imagination.

Concerning the Notion of Liberty, and of Moral Agency

[From *Freedom of the Will*, 1754]

The plain and obvious meaning of the words "freedom" and "liberty," in common speech, is power, opportunity, or advantage, that anyone has, to do as he pleases. Or in other words, his being free from hindrance or impediment in the way of doing, or conducting in any respect, as he wills.[1] And the contrary to liberty, whatever name we call that by, is a person's being hindered or unable to conduct as he will, or being necessitated to do otherwise.

[1] I say not only "doing," but "conducting"; because a voluntary forbearing to do, sitting still, keeping silence, etc. are instances of persons' conduct, about which liberty is exercised; though they are not properly called "doing." [Edwards' note]

If this which I have mentioned be the meaning of the word "liberty," in the ordinary use of language; as I trust that none that has ever learned to talk, and is unprejudiced, will deny; then it will follow, that in propriety of speech, neither liberty, nor its contrary, can properly be ascribed to any being or thing, but that which has such a faculty, power or property, as is called "will." For that which is possessed of no such thing as will, can't have any power or opportunity of doing according to its will, nor be necessitated to act contrary to its will, nor be restrained from acting agreeably to it. And therefore to talk of liberty, or the contrary, as belonging to the very will itself, is not to speak good sense; if we judge of sense, and nonsense, by the original and proper signification of words. For the will itself is not an agent that has a will: the power of choosing, itself, has not a power of choosing. That which has the power of volition or choice is the man or the soul, and not the power of volition itself. And he that has the liberty of doing according to his will, is the agent or doer who is possessed of the will; and not the will which he is possessed of. We say with propriety, that a bird let loose has power and liberty to fly; but not that the bird's power of flying has a power and liberty of flying. To be free is the property of an agent, who is possessed of powers and faculties, as much as to be cunning, valiant, bountiful, or zealous. But these qualities are the properties of men or persons; and not the properties of properties.

There are two things that are contrary to this which is called liberty in common speech. One is *constraint;* the same is otherwise called force, compulsion, and coaction; which is a person's being necessitated to do a thing *contrary* to his will. The other is *restraint;* which is his being hindered, and not having power to do *according* to his will. But that which has no will, can't be the subject of these things. — I need say the less on this head, Mr. Locke's having set the same thing forth, with so great clearness, in his *Essay on the Human Understanding.*

But one thing more I would observe concerning what is vulgarly called liberty; namely, that power and opportunity for one to do and conduct as he will, or according to his choice, is all that is meant by it; without taking into the meaning of the word, anything of the cause or original of that choice; or at all considering how the person came to have such a volition; whether it was caused by some external motive, or internal habitual bias; whether it was determined by some internal antecedent volition, or whether it happened without a cause; whether it was necessarily connected with something foregoing, or not connected. Let the person come by his volition or choice how he will, yet, if he is able, and there is nothing in the way to hinder his pursuing and executing his will, the man is fully and perfectly free, according to the primary and common notion of freedom.

What has been said may be sufficient to shew what is meant by liberty, according to the common notions of mankind, and in the usual and primary acceptation of the word: but the word, as used by Arminians, Pelagians and others, who oppose the Calvinists, has an entirely different signification. These several things belong to their notion of liberty: 1. That it consists in a self-determining power in the will, or a certain sovereignty the will has over itself, and its own acts, whereby it determines its own volitions; so as not to be dependent in its determinations, on any cause without itself, nor determined by anything prior to its own acts. 2. Indifference belongs to liberty in their notion of it, or that the mind, previous to the act of volition be, *in equilibrio*. 3. Contingence is another thing that belongs and is essential to it; not in the common acceptation of the word, as that has been already explained, but as opposed to all necessity, or any fixed and certain connection with some previous ground or reason of its existence. They suppose the essence of liberty so much to consist in these things, that unless the will of man be free in this sense, he has no real freedom, how much soever he may be at liberty to act according to his will.

A moral agent is a being that is capable of those actions that have a moral quality, and which can properly be denominated good or evil in a moral sense, virtuous or vicious, commendable or faulty. To moral agency belongs a moral faculty, or sense of moral good and evil, or of such a thing as desert or worthiness of praise or blame, reward or punishment; and a capacity which an agent has of being influenced in his actions by moral inducements or motives, exhibited to the view of understanding and reason, to engage to a conduct agreeable to the moral faculty.

The sun is very excellent and beneficial in its action and influence on the earth, in warming it, and causing it to bring forth its fruits; but it is not a moral agent; its action, though good, is not virtuous or meritorious. Fire that breaks out in a city, and consumes great part of it, is very mischievous in its operation; but is not a moral agent: what is does is not faulty or sinful, or deserving of any punishment. The brute creatures are not moral agents: the actions of some of 'em are very profitable and pleasant; others are very hurtful: yet, seeing they have no moral faculty, or sense of desert, and don't act from choice guided by understanding, or with a capacity of reasoning and reflecting, but only from instinct, and are not capable of being influenced by moral inducements, their actions are not properly sinful or virtuous; nor are they properly the subjects of any such moral treatment for what they do, as moral agents are for their faults or good deeds.

Here it may be noted, that there is a circumstantial difference between the moral agency of a ruler and a subject. I call it circumstantial, because it lies only in the difference of moral inducements they are capable of being influenced by, arising from the difference of circumstances. A ruler acting in that capacity only, is not capable of being influenced by a moral law, and its sanctions of threatenings and promises, rewards and punishments, as the subject is; though both may be influenced by a knowledge of moral good and evil. And therefore the moral agency of the supreme Being, who acts only in the capacity of a ruler towards His creatures, and never as a subject, differs in that respect from the moral agency of created intelligent beings. God's actions, and particularly those which He exerts as a moral governor, have moral qualifications, are morally good in the highest degree. They are most perfectly holy and righteous; and we must conceive of Him as influenced in the highest degree, by that which, above all others, is properly a moral inducement; viz., the moral good which He sees in such and such things: and therefore He is, in the most proper sense, a moral agent, the source of all moral ability and agency, the fountain and rule of all virtue and moral good; though by reason of His being supreme over all, 'tis not possible He should be under the influence of law or command, promises or threatenings, rewards or punishments, counsels or warnings. The essential qualities of a moral agent are in God, in the greatest possible perfection; such as understanding, to perceive the difference between moral good and evil; a capacity of discerning that moral worthiness and demerit, by which some things are praiseworthy, others deserving of blame and punishment; and also a capacity of choice, and choice guided by understanding, and a power of acting according to His choice or pleasure, and being capable of doing those things which are in the highest sense praiseworthy. And herein does very much consist that image of God wherein He made man (which we read of Gen. 1:26, 27 and ch. 9:6), by which God distinguished man from the beasts, viz., in those faculties and principles of nature, whereby he is capable of moral agency. Herein very much consists the natural image of God; as His spiritual and moral image, wherein man was made at first, consisted in that moral excellency, that he was endowed with.

Conclusion

[From *Freedom of the Will*]

'Tis easy to see how the decision of most of the points in controversy, between Calvinists and Arminians, depends on the determination of this grand article concerning the freedom of the will requisite to moral agency; and that by clearing and establishing the Calvinistic doctrine in this point, the chief arguments are obviated, by which Arminian doctrines in general are supported, and the contrary doctrines demonstratively confirmed. Hereby it becomes manifest, that God's moral government over mankind, His treating them as moral agents, making them the objects of His commands, counsels, calls, warnings, expostulations, promises, threatenings, rewards and punishments, is not inconsistent with a determining disposal of all events, of every kind, throughout the universe, in His providence; either by positive efficiency, or permission. Indeed such an universal, determining providence, infers some kind of necessity of all events; such a necessity as implies an infallible previous fixedness of the futurity of the event: but no other necessity of moral events, or volitions of intelligent agents, is needful in order to this, than *moral* necessity; which does as much ascertain the futurity of the event, as any other necessity. But, as has been demonstrated, such a necessity is not at all repugnant to moral agency, and the reasonable use of commands, calls, rewards, punishments, etc. Yea, not only are objections of this kind against the doctrine of an universal determining providence, removed by what has been said; but the truth of such a doctrine is demonstrated. As it has been demonstrated, that the futurity of all future events is established by previous necessity, either natural or moral; so 'tis manifest, that the sovereign Creator and Disposer of the world has ordered this necessity, by ordering His own conduct, either in designedly acting, or forbearing to act. For, as the being of the world is from God, so the circumstances in which it had its being at first, both negative and positive, must be ordered by Him, in one of these ways; and all the necessary consequences of these circumstances, must be ordered by Him. And God's active and positive interpositions, after the world was created, and the consequences of these interpositions; also every instance of His forbearing to interpose, and the sure consequences of this forbearance, must all be determined according to His pleasure. And therefore every event which is the consequence of anything whatsoever, or that is connected with any foregoing thing or circumstance, either positive or negative, as the ground or reason of its existence, must be ordered of God; either by a designed efficiency and interposition, or a designed forbearing to operate or interpose. But, as has been proved, all events whatsoever are necessarily connected with something foregoing, either positive or negative, which is the ground of its existence. It follows therefore, that the whole series of events is thus connected with something in the state of things, either positive or negative, which is original in the series; i.e., something which is connected with nothing preceding that, but God's own immediate conduct, either His acting or forbearing to act. From whence it follows, that as God designedly orders His own conduct, and its connected consequences, it must necessarily be that He designedly orders all things.

Samuel Danforth (1626–1674)

SAMUEL DANFORTH, a Harvard graduate of 1643, served as minister at Roxbury, Massachusetts, for twenty-four years. Like many other New England divines, he was deeply interested in science, especially in astronomy. He wrote four almanacs, in which he included a number of scientific essays as well as his own poetry. Though he was sufficiently familiar with astronomical research to recognize comets as natural phenomena, subject to natural law, Danforth also interpreted them as God's warnings to mankind of change and disaster, mixing folklore, theology, and Copernican science in a manner quite typical of the times.

TEXT: Samuel Danforth, *An Astronomical Description of the Late Comet* (Cambridge, 1665).

The Nature and Meaning of Comets

[From *An Astronomical Description*, 1665]

I. This comet is no sublunary meteor or sulphureous exhalation, but a celestial luminary, moving in the starry heavens.

The truth hereof may be demonstrated, 1. By the vast dimensions of its body. Some comets have been observed by astronomers to be half as big as the moon, some bigger than the moon, yea some bigger than the earth. The exact dimensions of this comet, I may not presume to determine, but it seemeth not to be of the smallest size. Now 'tis not easy to imagine how the earth should afford matter for a meteor of such a huge magnitude, except we grant the greater part of the lower world to be turned into an exhalation. 2. By the smallness of its parallax. The parallax is the distance between the true place of a planet and the apparent. The lower and nearer any planet is to the earth, it hath the greater parallax. The moon's parallax in her perigee, is one degree and six minutes. I could not by my observation discern that this comet had any considerable parallax. 3. By its large circular motion. If it had moved in the upper region of the air, it might have finished the whole visible arc of its circle in a few hours; but we saw it perform its proper motion with great constancy in a very large circle, such as the air is not capable of. 4. By its long duration and continuance. Had it been a sulphureous vapor kindled in the air, it might have been consumed in a short time; as other fiery meteors are: but this continued about three months. 5. By its visibility to all countries and nations. We already hear that this comet was seen at Virginia, Jamaica, St. Martha, Cartagena, and Barbados, and no doubt but it was visible to the whole habitable world. But the highest region of the air is accounted not much above fifty English miles from the earth, and had this comet been no higher, it had been impossible that other countries and nations so far distant, should have beheld it. Whether this comet was created in the beginning of the world together with the rest of the stars, and hath been hidden in the height and profundity of the heavens, and at a certain time descending toward the earth, becomes visible and signal to the world, I leave free to after-disquisition.

II. This comet is not an opaque body, like the moon and other of the planets, but transparent and pellucid, the sun shining through it.

The moon is enlightened on that part only which is next the sun, and like a looking glass she reflects the solar beams, which are cast upon her: but the sun irradiates the comet and shines through it as through a gem and illustrates a long tract in the heavens beyond it. As the moon, being a thick and dark body, casts a dark shadow from the sun, so the comet being a clear and diaphanous body transmits the light and casts a bright and shining stream from the sun; which alters and varies according to the diverse aspect of the sun.

III. The coma or blazing stream that issues from the comet, is no real flame, but the irradiation and resplendence of the sun through the transparent and pellucid body of the comet.

A comet is denominated from its coma or bushy lock, for the stream hath some resemblance of a lock of hair. Now this stream is not the flagrancy of the comet, but the beams of the sun shining through the diaphanous and translucid head of the comet; and may be argued and demonstrated, 1. By its site and position which is always in opposition to the sun. Had it been a natural flame, arising from its flagrant head it would have constantly moved upward, as the flame of a lamp or torch; unless it had broken forth by violence: but this streaming was sometimes upward, sometimes somewhat downward, sometimes Westward, sometimes Northward, sometimes Eastward, according to the position of the sun: neither can I imagine that any violence caused it so to move. 2. By the diverse form and figure of the stream according to the diverse aspect of the sun. One while it was like a beard, another while like a tail. 3. By the diverse dimensions of the stream. It was sometimes longer, sometimes shorter, sometimes broader, sometimes narrower, according as the comet was nearer or further from the earth. 4. By the diverse quality and color of the stream. It was sometimes bright and radiant, at other times obscure, dullish, and faint, according to the apparent radiation of the sun and the comet's distance from us. 5. By its duration. Had it been a real and natural flame, it is difficult to understand how the head of the comet could have supplied it with food and fuel for so many months together. Objection: if the stream be an irradiation of the sun how comes it to be conspicuous and visible to us? The sunbeams passing through the ethereal heavens are not in themselves visible, neither do they terminate our sight. Answer: the only reason thereof (that I can yet learn) is the refraction and reverberation of the sunbeams, as they pass through the comet's condensed body, whereby they are so congregated and so nearly united, as that they terminate the sight and become conspicuous in the heavens. "I have read of a certain semi-transparent gem, called the heliotrope, that if it be put into fair water, opposed to the beams of the sun, it doth change its beams, and by the repercussion of the air, seems to shadow the clearness of its rays, and so induce a sanguineous color in the air, as if the sun by the interposition of the body of the moon did suffer an ecliptic darkness."

. . . .

A Brief Theological Application of this Strange and Notable Appearance in the Heavens.

I. The holy scriptures, which are the authentic and unerring canon of truth, teach us to look at comets, as portentous and signal of great and notable changes.

Joel 2:30, 31. "I will show wonders in the heavens and in the earth, blood and fire, and pillars of smoke. The sun shall be turned into darkness, and the moon into blood before the great and terrible day of the Lord come."

Luke 21:25. "There shall be signs in the sun, and in the moon, and in the stars."

Acts 2:19, 20. "I will show wonders in heaven above, and signs in the earth beneath: blood, and fire, and vapor of smoke. The sun shall be turned into darkness and the moon into blood before the great and notable day of the Lord come."

II. The histories of former ages, do abundantly testify that comets have been many times heralds of wrath to a secure and impenitent world. Take a few instances.

A little before the Achaic War (as Seneca reports) there appeared a comet fiery and ruddy, which cast a clear light, whereby the night was enlightened.

Anno Christi 56. There appeared a comet. The same year Claudius died, and bloody Nero succeeded, who slew his mother, his wife, and his master Seneca, and exercised a great deal of cruelty and wickedness.

Anno 323. There were diverse comets which preceded the pestilent heresy of Arius.

Anno 337. A comet appeared before the death of Constantine the Great, and innumerable evils followed.

Anno 602. A great comet appeared, which preceded, if not presaged the slaughter of Mauritius the Emperor, and the supremacy of the Bishop of Rome.

Anno 675, and 676. There appeared a comet three months, at which time the Saracens greatly afflicted the Roman Empire.

Anno 729. Two comets appeared, and the same year a great plague invaded the world.

Anno 814. A terrible comet appeared before the death of Charles the Great.

Anno 1066. A comet appeared a long time to the whole world: the same year England was many ways afflicted by William, Duke of Normandy, and at length subdued.

Anno 1618. There appeared a great comet: the same year brake forth the bloody wars in Germany. *Anno* 1652. There appeared a comet at the beginning of Mr. Cotton's sickness, and disappeared a few days after his death. The next year strange and notable changes of state happened in England.

'Tis true, some comets have been thought to presage good to the world, as that in the days of Augustus before the birth of Christ. (I intend not that miraculous star, which appeared to the Magi.) Another before the death of Nero. Another before the reformation by Wycliffe. Another before the reformation by Luther: but most commonly they are observed to precede, if not portend great calamities.

Anno 79. Upon a comet followed horrible winds, an earthquake, and pestilence. When some showed Vespasian this comet, fearing it might portend his death, he answered merrily that this prodigy noted not him, but the King of Parthia. For saith he, "He nourisheth his hair, but I am bald." But not long after, Vespasian died.

III. The commination of wrath according to scripture, is to be understood after a conditional manner, i.e., with an implicit reservation for God's altering and revoking His threatened dispensation upon repentance intervening.

Jer. 18:7, 8. "At what instant I shall speak concerning a nation and concerning a kingdom, to pluck up and to pluck down and to destroy it: if that nation against whom I have pronounced, turn from their evil, I will repent of the evil that I thought to do unto them."

Jer. 36:3, 7. "It may be the house of Judah will hear all the evil, which I purpose to do unto them, that they may return every man from his evil way, that I may forgive their iniquity and their sin. It may be they will present their supplication before the Lord, and will return every one from his evil way: for great is the anger and the fury, which the Lord hath pronounced against this people."

Jonah 3:10. "And God saw their works that they turned from their evil way, and God repented of the evil, that He had said that He would do unto them, and He did it not."

IV. This blazing star being in conjunction with diverse other awful providences and tokens of wrath, calls upon us to awake out of security, and to bring forth fruits meet for repentance.

Cotton Mather (1663–1728)

Cotton Mather, who was interested in virtually every branch of knowledge, was especially interested in science. The author of a number of essays on astronomy, medicine, agriculture, and weather, he was judged worthy of election to the Royal Society of London in 1713. Though his scientific information came to him second-hand, from wide reading rather than from observation and experiment, he was familiar with much of the science of his time and perfectly certain that science and true theology reinforced each other.

The natural world, as Mather saw it, was God's providence in action, an exposition of God's world for man to read. In *The Christian Philosopher* (1721), subtitled "A Collection of the Best Discoveries in Nature, with Religious Improvements," he explained how the will of God manifested itself in every portion of the universe, and how a divine purpose lay behind every phenomenon and law of nature. That same year, after the great smallpox epidemic in Boston, Mather was nearly mobbed for his advocacy of inoculation. An irate Bostonian even threw a clumsily made grenade into Mather's bedroom; the grenade failed to explode, allowing Mather to read the note attached to it: "Cotton Mather, you Dog; Damn you: I'll inoculate you with this, with a pox to you."

TEXTS: Cotton Mather, *Magnalia Christi Americana*, ed. Thomas Robbins (Hartford, 1853), Vol. I; and *The Christian Philosopher* (London, 1721).

The Voice of God in the Thunder

[From *Magnalia Christi Americana*, 1702]

First, it is to be premised, as herein implied and confessed, that the thunder is the work of the glorious God. It is true, that the thunder is a natural production, and by the common laws of matter and motion it is produced; there is in it a concourse of divers weighty clouds, clashing and breaking one against another, from whence arises a mighty sound, which grows yet more mighty by its resonancies. The subtle and sulphureous vapors among these clouds take fire in this combustion, and lightnings are thence darted forth; which, when they are somewhat grosser, are fulminated with an irresistible violence upon our territories.

This is the Cartesian account; though that which I rather choose is, that which the vegetable matter protruded by the subterraneous fire, and exhaled also by the force of the sun, in the vapor that makes our shower a mineral matter of nitre and sulphur, does also ascend into the atmosphere, and there it goes off with fierce explosions.

But, still, who is the author of those laws, according whereunto things are thus moved into thunder? yea, who is the first mover of them? Christians, 'tis our glorious God. There is an intimation somewhere ('tis in Psal. 104:7) that there was a most early and wondrous use of the thunder in the first creation of the world: but still the thunder itself, and the tonitruous disposition and generation with which the air is impregnated, was a part of that creation. Well, and whose workmanship is it all? "Ah! Lord, thou hast created all these things; and for thy pleasure they are and were created." It is also true, that angels may be reckoned among the causes of thunders: and for this cause, in the sentence of the Psalms, where they are called "flames of fire," one would have been at a loss whether angels or lightnings were intended, if the apostolical accommodation had not cleared it. But what though angels may have their peculiar influence upon thunders? Is it but the influence of an instrument; they are but instruments directed, ordered, limited by Him who is the "God of thunders" and the "Lord of angels." Hence the thunder is ascribed unto our God all the Bible over; in the scripture of truth, 'tis called the "thunder of

God," oftener than I can presently quote unto you. And hence we find the thunder, even now and then, executing the purpose of God. Whose can it be but the "thunder of God," when the pleasure of God has been continually thereby accomplished? . . .

One voice of the glorious God in the thunder, is, "that He is a glorious God, who makes the thunder." There is the marvellous glory of God seen in it, when He "thunders marvellously." Thus do these inferior and meteorous "heavens declare the glory of God."

The power of God is the glory of God. Now, His thunder does proclaim His power. It is said, "the thunder of his power, who can understand?" — that is, His powerful thunder; the thunder gives us to understand that our God is a most powerful one. There is nothing able to stand before those lightnings, which are styled, "the arrows of God": castles fall, metals melt; all flies, when "hot thunder-bolts" are scattered upon them. The very mountains are torn to pieces. . . . Yea, to speak in the language of the prophets, fulfilled in the thunder storm that routed the Assyrian armies, "the mountains quake, the hills melt, the earth is burnt. Who can stand before His indignation? and who can abide in the fierceness of His anger? His fury is poured out like fire, and the rocks are thrown down by Him." Suetonius, I think 'tis, who tells us that the haughty and profane Emperor Caligula would yet shrink, and shake, and cover his head at the least thunder, and run to hide himself under a bed. This truly is the voice of the thunder: "Let the proudest sinners tremble to rebel any more against a God who can thus discomfit them with shooting out His lightnings upon them; sinners, where can you shew your heads, if the Highest give forth His voice with hailstones and coals of fire." Methinks there is that song of Hannah in the thunder (I Sam. 2:3, 10), "Talk no more so exceeding proudly; let not arrogancy come out of your mouth. For the adversaries of the Lord shall be broken to pieces; out of heaven shall He thunder upon them." The omnipotent God in the thunder speaks to those hardy Typhons, that are found fighting against Him; and says, "Oh, do not harden yourselves against such a God; you are not stronger than He!" Yea, the great God is proposed as an object for our faith, as well as for our fear in His thunder.

If nothing be too hard for the thunder, we may think surely nothing is too hard for the Lord! The arm that can wield thunder-bolts is a very mighty arm.

From hence pass on, and admire the other "glorious attributes" of God, which He doth in his thunder display most gloriously: when it thunders, let us adore the wisdom of that God, who thereby many ways does consult the welfare of the universe. Let us adore the justice of that God, who thereby many times has cut off His adversaries; and let us adore the goodness of that God, who therein preserves us from imminent and impending desolations, and is not so severe as He would be. . . .

A second voice of the glorious God in the thunder, is, "Remember the law of the glorious God that was given in thunder." The people of God were once gathered about a mountain, on which, from His right hand, issued a fiery law for them; or a law given with lightning. At the promulgation of the ten commandments, we are told in Exod. 20: 18, "All people saw the thunderings, and the lightnings, and the mountain smoking." Yea, they were such, that the Apostle tells us, though Moses himself says nothing of it, they made Moses himself "exceedingly to fear and quake." Well, when it thunders, let us call to mind the commandments, which were once thus thundered unto the world; and bear in mind that, with a voice of thunder, the Lord still says unto us, "Thou shalt love the Lord thy God with all thy heart, and all thy soul, and all thy strength; and thou shalt love thy neighbor as thyself." But when the thunder causes us to reflect upon the commandments of our God, let there be a self-examination in that reflection.

Let us now examine ourselves, what is required, and whether we have not omitted it? what is forbidden, and whether we had not committed it? and what provocation we have given unto the God of glory to speak unto us in His wrath and vex us in His displeasure. Blessed the thunder that shall thunder-strike us into the acknowledgments of a convinced and a repenting soul!

A third voice of the glorious God in the thunder, is, "Think on the future coming of the glorious God in the thunder, and in great glory." When the day of judgment shall arrive unto us, then "our God shall come, and shall not keep silence; a fire shall devour before him, and it shall be very tempestuous round about him." The second coming of our Lord will be, as we are advised in II Thes. 1:7, 8, "with His mighty angels in flaming fire"; the clouds will be His chariot, but there will be prodigious thunders breaking forth from those clouds.

The redemption of the church, for which the Lord hath long been cried unto, will then be accomplished; but at what rate? The Lord will come in the thick clouds of the skies: at the brightness that shall be before Him thick clouds will pass, hail-stones and coals of fire; the Lord also will thunder in the heavens.

I say, then, does it thunder? — Let us now realize unto ourselves that great and notable day of the Lord, which will be indeed a great and thundering day! But how far should we now realize it? — realize it so, as to be ready for it? Oh, count yourselves not safe till you get into such a condition of soul, that your hearts would even leap and spring within you, were you sure that in the very next thunders our precious Lord would make His descent unto us. What if the hour were now turned, wherein the Judge of the whole world were going to break in upon us with fierce thunders, and make the mountains to smoke by His coming down upon them, and reign before His ancient people gloriously? Could you gladly say, "Lo, this is the God of my salvation, and I have waited for Him!" I say, let the thunders drive you on to this attainment.

A fourth voice of the glorious God in the thunder, is, "Make your peace with God immediately, lest by the stroke of His thunder He take you away in His wrath." Why is it that persons are usually in such a consternation at the thunder? Indeed, there is a complectional and constitutional weakness in many this way; they have such a disadvantage in a frightful temper, that no considerations can wholly overcome it. But most usually the frights of people at the thunder arise from the terms wherein they may suspect their own souls to stand before an angry God. Their consciences tell 'em that their sins are yet unpardoned, that their hearts are yet unrenewed, that their title to blessedness is yet unsettled, and that if the next thunder-clap should strike them dead, it had been good for them that they had never been born. . . .

Here then is the voice of God in the thunder: "Art thou ready? Soul, art thou ready? Make ready presently, lest I call for thee before thou art aware." There is in thunder a vehement call unto that regeneration, unto that repenting of sin, that believing on Christ, and that consenting unto the demands of the new covenant, without which no man in his wits can comfortably hold up his face before the thunder. I have now in my house a mariner's compass, whereupon a thunder-clap had this odd effect, that the north point was thereby turned clear about unto the south; and so it will veer and stand ever since unto this day, though the thing happened above thirteen years ago.

I would to God that the next thunder-claps would give as effectual a turn unto all the unconverted souls among us! May the thunder awaken you to turn from every vanity to God in Christ without any delay, lest by the thunder itself it come quickly to be too late. It is a vulgar error, that the thunder never kills any who are asleep: Man, what if the thunder should kill thee in the dead sleep of thy unregeneracy? . . .

A seventh voice of the glorious God in the thunder, is, "Hear the voice of my Word, lest I make you fear the voice of my thunder." When the inhabitants of Egypt persisted in their disobedience to the Word of God, it came to that at last, in Exod. 9:23, "The Lord sent thunder, and the fire ran along upon the ground." Thus the eternal God commands men to let go their sins, and go themselves to serve Him: if they are disobedient, they lay themselves open to fiery thunders. This, you may be sure, is the voice of God in the thunder,

"Hear my still voice in my ordinances, lest you put me upon speaking to you with more angry thunder-bolts." I have known it sometimes remarked that very notorious and resolved sleepers at sermons often have some remarkable suddenness in the circumstances of their death. Truly, if you are scandalously given to sleep under the Word of God; and much more, if to sin under it; and most of all, if to scoff under it; it may be, your deaths will be rendered sudden by the other thunders of heaven lighting on you. When it thunders, God saith to all the hearers of His Word ordinarily preached, "Consider this, and forget not God, lest He tear you in pieces, and there be none to deliver you."

Finally, And is there not this voice of the glorious God in thunder after all? "O be thankful to the gracious God, that the thunder does no more mischief to you all."

Whatever the witch-advocates may make of it, it is a scriptural and a rational assertion, that in the thunder there is oftentimes, by the permission of God, the agency of the Devil. The Devil is the prince of the air, and when God gives him leave, he has a vast power in the air, and armies that can make thunders in the air. We are certain that Satan had his efficiency in it, when the fire of God or the lightning fell upon part of Job's estate. How glad would he have been if the good man himself had been in the way, to have been torn in pieces! And perhaps it was the hellish policy of the wicked one, thus to make the good man suspicious that God was become his enemy. Popes that have been conjurors have made fire thus come from heaven, by their confederacies with evil spirits; and we have in our own land known evil spirits, plainly discovering their concurrence in disasters thus occasioned. A great man has therefore noted it, that thunders break oftener on churches than any other houses, because the demons have a peculiar spite at houses that are set apart for the peculiar service of God.

I say, then, live we thus in the midst of thunders and devils too; and yet live we? Oh! let us be thankful to God for our lives. Are we not smitten by the great ordnance of heaven, discharging every now and then on every side of us? Let us be thankful to the great Lord of heaven, who makes even the wrath of hell to praise Him, and the remainder of that wrath does He restrain.

Of the Vegetables

[From *The Christian Philosopher,* 1721]

The contrivance of our most glorious Creator, in the vegetables growing upon this globe, cannot be wisely observed without admiration and astonishment.

We will single out some remarkables, and glorify our God!

First, in what manner is vegetation performed? And how is the growth of plants and the increase of their parts carried on? The excellent and ingenious Dr. John Woodward has, in the way of nice experiment, brought this thing under a close examination. It is evident that water is necessary to vegetation; there is a water which ascends the vessels of the plants, much after the way of a filtration; and the plants take up a larger or lesser quantity of this fluid, according to their dimensions. The much greater part of that fluid mass which is conveyed to the plants, does not abide there, but exhale through them up into the atmosphere. Hence countries that abound with bigger plants are obnoxious to greater damps, and rains, and inconvenient humidities. But there is also a terrestrial matter which is mixed with this water, and ascends up into the plants with the water: something of this matter will attend water in all its motions, and stick by it after all its percolations. Indeed the quantity of this terrestrial matter, which the vapors carry up into the atmosphere, is very fine, and not very much, but it is the truest and the best prepared vegetable matter; for which cause it is that rain water is of such a singular fertility. 'Tis true there is in water a mineral matter also, which is usually too scabrous, and ponderous, and inflexible, to enter the pores of the roots. Be the earth ever so rich, 'tis observed little good will come of it, unless the parts of it be loosened a little, and separated. And this probably is all the use of nitre and other salts to plants, to loosen the earth, and separate the parts of it. It is this terrestrial matter which fills the plants; they are more or less nourished and augmented in proportion, as their water conveys a greater or lesser quantity of proper terrestrial matter to them. Nevertheless 'tis also probable that in this there is a variety; and all plants are not formed and filled from the same sort of corpuscles. Every vegetable seems to require a peculiar and specific matter for its formation and nourishment. If the soil wherein a seed is planted, have not all or most of the ingredients necessary for the vegetable to subsist upon, it will suffer accordingly. Thus wheat sown upon a tract of land well furnished for the supply of that grain, will succeed very well, perhaps for divers years, or, as the husbandman expresses it, as long as the ground is in heart; but anon it will produce no more of that corn; it will of some other, perhaps of barley: and when it will subsist this no more, still oats will thrive there; and perhaps peas after these. When the ground has lain fallow some time, the rain will pour down a fresh stock upon it; and the care of the tiller in manuring of it, lays upon it such things as are most impregnated with a supply for vegetation. It is observed that spring water and rain water contain pretty near an equal charge of the vegetable matter, but river water much more than either of them; and hence the inundations of rivers leave upon their banks the fairest crops in the world. It is now plain that water is not the matter that composes vegetables, but the agent that conveys that matter to them, and introduces it into the several parts of them. Wherefore the plentiful provision of this fluid supplied to all parts of the earth, is by our Woodward justly celebrated with a pious acknowledgment of that natural providence that superintends over the globe which we inhabit. The parts of water being exactly spherical, and subtle beyond all expression, the surfaces perfectly polite, and the intervals being therefore the largest, and so the most fitting to receive a foreign matter into them, it is the most proper instrument imaginable for the service now assigned to it. And yet water would not perform this office and service to the plants, if it be not assisted with a due quantity of heat; heat must concur, or vegetation will not succeed. Hence as the heat of several seasons affords a different face of things, the same does the heat of several climates. The hotter countries usually yield the larger trees, and in a greater variety. And in warmer countries, if there be a remission of the usual heat, the production will in proportion be diminished.

That I may a little contribute my two mites to the illustration of the way wherein vegetation is carried on, I will here communicate a couple of experiments lately made in my neighborhood.

My neighbor planted a row of hills in his field with our Indian corn, but such a grain as was colored red and blue; the rest of the field he planted with corn of the most usual color, which is yellow. To the most windward side this row infected four of the next neighboring rows, and part of the fifth, and some of the sixth, to render them colored like what grew on itself. But on the leeward side no less than seven or eight rows were so colored, and some smaller impressions were made on those that were yet further distant.

The same neighbor having his garden often robbed of the squashes growing in it, planted some gourds among them, which are to appearance very like them, and which he distinguished by certain adjacent marks, that he might not be himself imposed upon; by this means the thieves 'tis true found a very bitter sauce, but then all the squashes were so infected and embittered, that he was not himself able to eat what the thieves had left of them.

That most accurate and experienced botanist Mr. Ray has given us the plants that are more commonly met withal, with certain characteristic notes, wherein he establishes twenty-five genders of them. These plants are to be rather styled herbs.

But then of the trees and shrubs, he distinguishes five classes that have their flower disjoined and remote from the fruit, and as many that have their fruit and flower contiguous.

How unaccountably is the figure of plants preserved? And how unaccountably their growth determined? Our excellent Ray flies to an intelligent plastic nature, which must understand and regulate the whole economy.

Every particular part of the plant has its astonishing uses. The roots give it a stability, and fetch the nourishment into it, which lies in the earth ready for it. The fibers contain and convey the sap which carries up that nourishment. The plant has also larger vessels, which entertain the proper and specific juice of it; and others to carry the air for its necessary respiration. The outer and inner bark defend it from annoyances, and contribute to its augmentation. The leaves embrace and preserve the flower and fruit as they come to their explication. But the principal use of them, as Malpighi, and Perault, and Mariotte, have observed, is, to concoct and prepare the sap for the nourishment of the fruit, and of the whole plant; not only that which ascends from the root, but also what they take in from without, from the dew, and from the rain. For there is a regress of the sap in plants from above downwards; and this descendent juice is that which principally nourishes both fruit and plant, as has been clearly proved by the experiments of Signor Malpighi and Mr. Brotherton.

How agreeable the shade of plants, let every man say that sits under his own vine, and under his own fig tree!

How charming the proportion and pulchritude of the leaves, the flowers, the fruits, he who confesses not, must be, as Dr. More says, "one sunk into a forlorn pitch of degeneracy, and stupid as a beast."

Our Saviour says of the lillies (which some, not without reason, suppose to be tulips) that Solomon in all his glory was not arrayed like one of these. And it is observed by Spigelius, that the art of the most skillful painter cannot so mingle and temper his colors, as exactly to imitate or counterfeit the native ones of the flowers of vegetables.

Mr. Ray thinks it worthy a very particular observation, that wheat, which is the best sort of grain, and affords the wholesomest bread, is in a singular manner patient of both extremes, both heat and cold, and will grow to maturity as well in Scotland, and in Denmark, as in Egypt, and Guinea, and Madagascar. It scarce refuses any climate. And the exceeding fertility of it is by a pagan Pliny acknowledged as an instance of the divine bounty to man; . . . one bushel in a fit soil, he says, yielding one hundred and fifty. A German divine so far plays the philosopher on this occasion, as to propose it for a singularity in bread, that *totum corpus sustentat, adeo, ut in unicâ bucellâ, omnium membrorum totius externi corporis, nutrimentum contineatur, illiusque vis per totum corpus sese diffundat.* A friend of mine had thirty-six ears of rye growing from one grain, and on one stalk.

But of our Indian corn, one grain of corn will produce above a thousand. And of Guinea corn, one grain has been known to produce ten thousand.

The anatomy of plants, as it has been exhibited by the incomparable curiosity of Dr. Grew, what a vast field of wonders does it lead us into!

The most inimitable structure of the parts!

The particular canals, and most adapted ones, for the conveyance of the lymphatic and essential juices!

The air vessels in all their curious coilings!

The coverings which befriend them, a work unspeakably more curious in reality than in appearance!

The strange texture of the leaves, the angular or circular, but always most orderly position of their fibers; the various foldings, with a duplicature, a multiplicature, the fore-roll, the back-roll, the tre-roll; the noble guard of the films interposed!

The flowers, their gaiety and fragrancy; the *perianthium* or empalement of them; their curious foldings in the calyx before their expansion, with a close couch or a concave couch, a single plait or a double plait, or a plait and couch together; and their luxuriant colors after their foliation, and the expanding of their *petala!*

The *stamina,* with their apices; and the stylus (called the "attire" by Dr. Grew), which is found a sort of male sperm, to impregnate and fructify the seed!

At last the whole rudiments and lineaments of the parent vegetable, surprisingly locked up in the little compass of the fruit or seed!

Gentlemen of leisure, consult my illustrious doctor, peruse his *Anatomy of Plants,* ponder his numberless discoveries; but all the while consider that rare person as inviting you to join with him in adoring the God of his father, and the God who has done these excellent things, which ought to be known in all the earth. . . .

The peculiar care which the great God of nature has taken for the safety of the seed and fruit, and so for the conservation of the plant, is by my ingenious Derham considered as a loud invitation to His praises.

They which dare shew their heads all the year, how securely is their seed or fruit locked up in the winter in their gems, and well covered with neat and close tunics there!

Such as dare not expose themselves, how are they preserved under the coverture of the earth, till invited out by the kindly warmth of the spring!

When the vegetable race comes abroad, what strange methods of nature are there to guard them from inconveniences, by making some to lie down prostrate, by making others, which were by the ancients called *aeschynomenae,* to close themselves up at the touch of animals, and by making the most of them to shut up under their guard in the cool of the evening, especially if there be foul weather approaching; which is by Gerhard therefore called, "the countryman's weather-wiser"!

What various ways has nature for the scattering and the sowing of the seed! Some are for this end winged with a light sort of a down, to be carried about with the seed by the wind. Some are laid in springy cases, which when they burst and crack, dart their seed to a distance, performing therein the part of an husbandman. Others by their good qualities invite themselves to be swallowed by the birds, and being fertilized by passing through their bodies, they are by them transferred to places where they fructify. Theophrastus affirms this of the mistletoe; and Tavernier of the nutmeg. Others not thus taken care for, do, by their usefulness to us, oblige us to look after them.

It is a little surprising, that seeds found in the gizzards of wildfowl, have afterwards sprouted in the earth; and seeds left in the dung of the cattle. The seeds of marjoram and strammonium, carelessly kept, have grown after seven years.

How nice the provision of nature for their support in standing and growing, that they may keep their heads above ground, and administer to our intentions! There are some who stand by their own strength; and the ligneous parts of these, though like our bones, yet are not, like them, inflexible, but of an elastic nature, that they may dodge the violence of the winds: and their branches at the top very commodiously have a tendency to an hemispherical dilation, but within such an angle as makes an equilibration there. An ingenious observer upon this one circumstance, cannot forbear this just reflection: "A visible argument that the plastic capacities of matter are governed by an all-wise and infinite Agent, the native strictnesses and regularities of them plainly shewing from whose hand they come." And then such as are too weak to stand of themselves, 'tis wonderful to see how they use the help of their neighbors, address them, embrace them, climb up about them, some twisting themselves with a strange convolving faculty, some catching hold with claspers and tendrils, which are like hands to them; some striking in rooty feet, and some emitting a natural glue, by which they adhere to their supporters.

But, Oh! the glorious goodness of our God in all these things! . . .

The persuasion which mankind has imbibed of tobacco being good for us, has surprisingly prevailed! What incredible millions have sucked in an opinion, that it is an useful as well as a pleasant thing, for them to spend much of their time in drawing through a pipe the smoke of that lighted weed! It was in the year 1585, that one Mr. Lane carried over from Virginia some tobacco, which was the first that had ever been seen in Europe; and within an hundred years the smoking of it grew so much into fashion, that the very customs of it brought four hundred thousand pounds a year into the English treasury.

It is doubtless a plant of many virtues. The ointment made of it is one of the best in the dispensatory. The practice of smoking it, though a great part of them that use it might very truly say, they find neither good nor hurt by it; yet it may be feared it rather does more hurt than good.

"May God preserve me from the indecent, ignoble, criminal slavery, to the mean delight of smoking a weed, which I see so many carried away with. And if ever I should smoke it, let me be so wise as to do it, not only with moderation, but also with such employments of my mind, as I may make that action afford me a leisure for!"

Methinks tobacco is but a poor Nepenthe, though the takers thereof take it for such an one. It is to be feared the caustic salt in the smoke of this plant, conveyed by the salival juice into the blood, and also the vellication which the continual use of it in snuff gives to the nerves, may lay foundations for diseases in millions of unadvised people, which may be commonly and erroneously ascribed to some other original. . . .

The Tarantula

[From *The Christian Philosopher*]

What amazing effects follow on the bite of the tarantula! the patient is taken with an extreme difficulty of breathing, and heavy anguish of heart, a dismal sadness of mind, a voice querulous and sorrowful, and his eyes very much disturbed. When the violent symptoms which appear on the first day are over, a continual melancholy hangs about the person, till by dancing or singing, or change of air, the poisonous impressions are extirpated from the blood, and the fluid of the nerves; but this is a happiness that rarely happens; nay, Baglivi, this wicked spider's countryman, says, there is no expectation of ever being perfectly cured. Many of the poisoned are never well but among the graves, and in solitary places; and they lay themselves along upon a bier as if they themselves were dead: like people in despair, they will throw themselves into a pit; women, otherwise chaste enough, cast away all modesty, and throw themselves into very indecent postures. There are some colors agreeable to them, others offensive, especially black; and if the attendants have their clothes of ungrateful colors, they must retire out of their sight. The music with the dancing which must be employed for their cure, continues three or four days; in this vigorous exercise they sigh, they are full of complaints; like persons in drink, they almost lose the right use of their understanding; they distinguish not their very parents from others in their treating of them, and scarce remember anything that is past. Some during this exercise are much pleased with green boughs of reeds or vines, and wave them with their hands in the air, or dip them in the water, or bind them about their face or neck; others love to handle red cloths or naked swords. And there are those who, upon a little intermission of the dancing, fall a digging of holes in the ground, which they fill with water, and then take a strange satisfaction in rolling there. When they begin to dance, they call for swords, and act like fencers; sometimes they are for a looking-glass, but then they fetch many a deep sigh at beholding themselves. Their fancy sometimes leads them to rich clothes, to necklaces, to fineries and a variety of ornaments; and they are highly courteous to the bystanders that will gratify them with any of these things; they lay them very orderly about the place where the exercise is pursued, and in dancing please themselves with one or other of these things by turns, as their troubled imagination directs them.

How miserable would be the condition of mankind, if these animals were common in every country! But our compassionate God has confined them to one little corner of Italy; they are existing elsewhere, but nowhere thus venomous, except in Apulia. My God, I glorify thy compassion to sinful mankind, in thy restraints upon the poisons of the tarantula!

Nathaniel Ames (1708–1764)

NATHANIEL AMES, born in Massachusetts and apparently trained as a physician, in 1726 published the first number of his annual Boston almanac, eight years before Franklin's *Poor Richard.* Ames's publication was, for the rest of his life, New England's favorite almanac, selling 60,000 copies a year at the height of its popularity.

A devoted amateur scientist, Ames frequently reprinted scientific essays along with extracts from the English poets and home remedies, and his almanac was an influential medium for transmitting scientific knowledge to the layman. The improved microscope of the late seventeenth century, like the telescope, allowed man to look more closely at the secrets of the universe, and to perceive more clearly than ever before the intricacy of God's design in natural order.

TEXT: Samuel Briggs, ed., *The Essays, Humor, and Poems of Nathaniel Ames, . . . Almanacks, 1726–1775* (Cleveland, 1891).

An Essay upon the Microscope

[From *Almanac for 1741*]

Artificer, go make a watch,
In which no seeming imperfection lurks,
Whose wheels with time exact do onward roll,
And one small spring maintains the motion of the whole,
'Tis all an artless homely botch
Compared with the least of Nature's works.
If through an optic glass
You view a spire of grass
That in the road is trod,
With admiration you may gaze
On veins that branch a thousand ways,
In nice proportion wrought,
Which truly to the assisted eyes are brought,
That he who is not void of common sense
Or filled with daring impudence,
Must own its maker truly to be God.
Pray let your brethren, men,
Use but the optic glass again,
Thy rarest piece to scan;

In thy so well contrived machine,
Those boasted beauties that are seen
After thou hast laid the hammer by,
And done thy best to cheat the naked eye,
We view such large unsightly flaws
Not marked by just proportion's laws
Which shows thou wert a clumsy fingered man.
　　Urania's sons who view the sky,
　　Erect long tubes to assist the eye;
May we believe the intelligence they give,
　　They tell us many a star
　　That we behold is bigger far
Than the small world on which we live.
　　These massy globes their maker's skill display,
　　But the minutest creatures do their part,
The grovelling worm that under foot is trod
　　And smallest mite proclaims a God:
And butterflies as well as they,
The feathers on whose painted wings
Outdo the ornaments of kings
　　And all their costly workmanship of art.
Behold! ye whalers who go forth,
Coasting along the icy north
Under the feeble influence of day,
　　Where huge leviathan does play;
'Gainst whose impenetrable sides the billows roar
Foaming and broke as from some rocky shore;
Tell me, brave lads, tell me when you
The unwieldy tumblings of that watery monarch view,
When all your darts, and strength, and numbers fail,
When with the sportive glances of his tail,
　　Keen as a knife he cuts in twain,
　　Or oars, or boats, or men, —
　　Do not your brethren then,
　　When any of their crew are slain,
　　　　Stand off awhile and gaze,
With wonder and with vast amaze?
This optic glass creates a thought in me,
As wonderful as what you see:
Being not deceived, nor mad, nor frantic,
But with my eyes do really view,
　　Crossing their wide Atlantic
Of but a drop of vinegar or two,
Ten thousand little fish, and here and there a whale,
　　　　Whose bulky size
　　　　By far outvies
　　All other tribes that therein sail,

With more perhaps invisible to sight,
Whose numerous species fall below,
What any glass could ever show;
Small as the beams of light.
At this amazed, Oh! wonderful, said I,
Who made the earth, who rules the sky,
When He his own idea first surveyed,
Before his beauteous works were made,
Then formed the wondrous plan,
And took an atom for a space
To minute down the universe.
Both things inert,
Things animate,
Our rolling world, and every lofty sphere,
The unerring hand divine
In characters immensely fine,
Most truly hath delineated there:
There all his works in true proportion stand.

John Winthrop (1714–1779)

JOHN WINTHROP, a descendant of the original John Winthrop who settled Massachusetts Bay, was Boston-born, a Latin School graduate at fourteen, and a Harvard graduate at eighteen. After graduation he spent six years in private scientific study, culminating in his appointment as Hollis Professor of Mathematics and Natural Philosophy at Harvard. A brilliant lecturer and teacher, Winthrop achieved worldwide recognition for his researches in astronomy, mathematics, and electricity. He was a Fellow of the Royal Society of London and a member of the American Philosophical Society, held an honorary degree from the University of Edinburgh, and received the first honorary Doctor of Laws degree granted by Harvard.

The Lisbon earthquake of 1755, which killed fifty thousand people in eight minutes and ravaged portions of Portugal, Spain, and North Africa, caused much speculation and concern among scientists, philosophers, and theologians. How could one fathom God's purpose in allowing such catastrophes as earthquakes, epidemics, tidal waves, volcanic explosions, or hurricanes? What meaning (both scientific and theological) was to be attached to such natural disasters, and where did they fit into the great, universal design of natural and divine law? Thomas Prince had published his pious observations on these questions in *Earthquakes the Works of God and Tokens of His Just Displeasure* (Boston, 1727), sacrificing science to theology. Winthrop sought to correct the balance in the following Harvard lecture, much of it designed to refute Prince's work.

TEXT: John Winthrop, *A Lecture on Earthquakes* (Boston, 1755).

The Laws Governing Earthquakes

[From *A Lecture on Earthquakes,* 1755]

Imagine, then, the earth trembling with a huge thundering noise, or heaving and swelling like a rolling sea: — now gaping in chasms of various sizes, and then immediately closing again; either swallowing up the unhappy persons who chanced to be over them, or crushing them to death by the middle: — from some, spouting up prodigious quantities of water to a vast height, or belching out hot, offensive and suffocating exhalations; while others are streaming with torrents of melted minerals. Some houses moving out of their places; others cracking and tumbling into heaps of rubbish; and others again, not barely by whole streets, but by whole cities at a time, sinking downright to a great depth in the earth, or under water. On the shore, the sea roaring and rising in billows; or else retiring to a great distance from the land, and then violently returning like a flood to overwhelm it; vessels driven from their anchors; some overset and lost, others thrown up on the land. In one place, vast rocks flung down from mountains, and choking up rivers, which, being then forced to find themselves new channels, sweep away such trees, houses, etc., as had escaped the fury of the shock; in another, mountains themselves sinking in a moment, and their places possessed by pools of water. Some people running about, pale with fear, trembling for the event, and ignorant whither to fly for shelter; others thrown with violence down on the ground, not being able to keep on their feet; and others shrieking or groaning in the agonies of death — even the brute creation manifesting all the signs of consternation and astonishment.

Imagine these things to yourselves, and you will then have a view, though but an imperfect one, of some of those images of horror and desolation, which accompany the more violent earthquakes. . . .

Though these explosions, and consequent concussions of the earth, have indeed occasioned most terrible desolations, and in this light may justly be regarded as the tokens of an incensed Deity, yet it can by no means be concluded from hence, that they are not of real and standing advantage to the globe in general. Multitudes, it is true, have at different times suffered by them; multitudes have been destroyed by them; but much greater multitudes may have every day been benefited by them.

The all-wise Creator could not but foresee all the effects of all the powers He implanted in matter; and, as we find in innumerable instances (and the more we know of His works, the more such instances we discover) that He has established such laws for the government of the world, as tend to promote the good of the whole, we may reasonably presume that He has done it in this case as well as others. To me, at least, the argument on this side the question, drawn from the general analogy of nature, appears to have more force, than any that I have seen offered on the other. For there is nothing, however useful, however necessary, but what is capable of producing, and in fact has produced, damage, in single instances. It were endless to particularize here; I shall therefore only mention one or two things by way of specimen.

The power of gravity — a power of such indispensable importance, that without it the system of nature could not subsist a moment, — has yet proved the destruction of multitudes. The wind, so necessary for the purposes of navigation, as well as to purge the air, which would otherwise stagnate and putrefy — how often has it risen to such a pitch, as to overthrow houses, and wreck vessels, by which means thousands have perished!

Even thunder and lightning, which, next to earthquakes, are the most terrible phenomena of nature, are yet universally allowed to be necessary to free the atmosphere from a certain unwholesome sultriness which often infects it. Other instances of the like sort I leave to your own reflections: and would rather observe, that the world is governed by general laws; and general laws must, from the nature of them, be liable sometimes to do hurt.

However, laws of this sort are sufficiently vindicated, not only as wise, but as good, if upon the whole they produce a maximum of good (to borrow an expression from the mathematicians); and this, it is in the highest degree probable, all the laws of nature do. It may be added, that as in the animal body, the evacuations, which are of absolute necessity to maintain life and health, do yet sometimes run to such extremes as to prove mortal; so in like manner, these explosions of subterraneous vapor, whose effects have sometimes been so fatal, may, notwithstanding this, be highly conducive, and even indispensably necessary, to the good of this globe in general. The explosions themselves, as well as the laws in consequence of which they are produced, may be necessary on various accounts; and particularly to the carrying on the more secret and noble works of nature within the entrails of the earth. Let me dilate a little on this matter.

By the incessant action of gravity and other attractive powers, and by the perpetual consumption of fluids, the earth becomes continually more and more hard, compact, and dense. Now an openness or looseness of contexture, to a certain degree, in the earth, is necessary to carry on the operations of nature within it. So that on the supposition that mineral, metalline, and other subterraneous bodies grow within the earth, it should seem that the earth must become gradually less and less fit for the production of them. Since, then, the direct, immediate, and most general effect of earthquakes is, by shaking, to loosen and disunite the parts of the earth, and to open its pores, it seems agreeable to reason to infer, that this is the end primarily aimed at in these concussions.

But you will take notice, that I speak here only of physical or natural ends. For, though I make no doubt that the laws of nature were established, and that the operations of nature are conducted with a view, ultimately, to moral purposes; and that there is the most perfect coincidence, at all times, between God's government of the natural and of the moral world; yet it would be improper for me to enter into these disquisitions at this time, since my province limits me to consider this subject only in the relation which it bears to natural philosophy. It is in the physical sense alone that I say the disjoining the parts of the earth, and opening its pores, may be the end primarily aimed at in earthquakes, as such mutations in the earth may from time to time become necessary to the production of subterraneous bodies; and perhaps this end could not be effectually answered by less forcible methods. This point may receive some light, if not proof, from the operations of agriculture. We find it necessary, by ploughing, digging, etc., to break the clods of the ground, to comminute and even pulverize it, in order to fit it for the purposes of vegetation; and we find it necessary to renew these labors every year.

Now, the use and tendency of these artificial operations may bear some analogy to those of the greater operations of nature, which we are speaking of. And, indeed, it is not in the least degree improbable, that such a loosening of the parts of the earth may promote even the growth of vegetables on its surface, as well as of minerals in its bowels; it being now well known, that all vegetables, the smaller as well as the larger, shoot some fibres of their roots to vastly greater depths, than those to which any of our instruments of tillage ever penetrate. This, it is likely, may be one reason of the wonderful fertility, for which Ætna and Vesuvio have been so generally and so highly celebrated. Again: it may be necessary now and then, to have such subterraneous vapors, as are generated by fermentation, discharged up into the air; as their continuance below, in the caverns of the earth, might be an impediment to those important processes which are there carrying on. But those very vapors, which might obstruct some sorts of natural processes while below the surface of the earth, may as much advance others when above it. We know that in many cases of the fermentation of bodies, especially of such dense ones as salts and minerals, air is plentifully absorbed; and that in many others it is as plentifully generated: so that great part of the exhalations thrown out by earthquakes may be true, permanent air, and designed to recruit what has been absorbed by bodies here on the surface.

And perhaps the grounds on which the great Newton founded his "suspicion, that the finest, the most subtile, and most spirituous parts of our air, and those which are most necessary to maintain the life of all things, come chiefly from the comets," may equally support another suspicion, that some such particles of air may be derived also from subterraneous eruptions. For among the almost infinite variety of particles which are thrown out of the earth in these eruptions, it is most likely that, if some are noxious, others will be salutary. It may also be necessary from time to time to have the subterraneous streams diverted from their former courses into new ones: partly, that different places in the lower regions may be watered by them; and partly, that the waters themselves, by passing through different beds or channels, may alter their properties, and convey new tinctures to different places.

Index of Authors

BCDEFGHIJ—R—73210/6981